Please remember that this is a library book,
and that it belongs only temporarily to each
person who uses it. Be considerate. Do
not write in this, or any, library book.

WITHDRAWN

Educational Psychology

Learning to Be a Problem Solver

John F. Wakefield

University of North Alabama

HOUGHTON MIFFLIN COMPANY   Boston/Toronto
Geneva, Illinois   Palo Alto   Princeton, New Jersey

In memory of R. Stewart Jones
Teacher, scholar, and friend

Senior Sponsoring Editor: Loretta Wolozin
Senior Associate Editor: Janet Edmonds
Senior Project Editor: Janet Young
Editorial Assistant: Elizabeth Emmons
Senior Production/Design Coordinator: Sarah Ambrose
Senior Manufacturing Coordinator: Priscilla Bailey
Marketing Coordinator: Cindy Voytas

Cover Designer: Darci Mehall
Cover Image by Fae Kontje
Part opener photos: p. xxvi: Will McIntyre; p. 110: Rick Friedman/Black Star;
p. 312: Chip Henderson/Tony Stone Images; p. 590: Jeffrey M. Myers/Stock Boston.
Credits appear following Index.

Printed in the U.S.A.

Library of Congress Catalog Card Number 95-76992

ISBN:
Student Copy 0-395-60466-4
Examination Copy 0-395-76573-0

123456789-DC-98 97 96 95

Brief Contents

Contents

Preface

 As a new teacher, you will face many exciting challenges. These challenges—or teaching problems—will occur in such areas as planning instruction, motivating your students, managing your class, and evaluating learning. These types of challenges will define your professional role. The major premise of this book is that if you see yourself as a problem solver, and if you have the tools with which to solve teaching problems, you will be able to meet your professional challenges successfully.

Why are challenges important? As modern societies become more oriented toward problem solving, they are increasingly in need of decision makers who view problems as challenges and who have the knowledge base and skills to think them through. This societal change is coming about for technological and economic reasons. Routine work that is well paid is disappearing from technological cultures. Jobs that call for repetitive actions are being automated, exported, or reclassified at minimum wage. The effects of this massive change are more apparent in education than they are anywhere else. Not only are teachers challenged to become problem solvers, but they are also challenged to teach problem-solving skills to their students. That is one reason I decided to write this book.

There are also other reasons. Early in my career as a college teacher, I became convinced that textbooks could help education students develop their knowledge base as teachers only if such books communicate information in such a way that a novice teacher can *use* it. Because information presented in textbooks often seems encyclopedic and inert, I decided to write a book that would introduce students to problem solving not only as a subject, but as a *process:* something you can actually do. Editors at Houghton Mifflin were searching for such a textbook and were open to my ideas. The result is *Educational Psychology: Learning to Be a Problem Solver.* This textbook, therefore, not only communicates information, but also activates its problem-solving perspective in as many ways as possible.

I hope that through this textbook and the learning environment your instructor creates, you can learn to become a problem solver and learn about teaching problem solving. This text represents a beginning—a foundation for later developments in your career and in the future.

THIS TEXT'S PROBLEM-SOLVING PERSPECTIVE

While some people might call this text's perspective a "decision-making" perspective, making decisions is only *part* of the larger process of problem solving. I have tried to be inclusive and to communicate the whole process rather than just a part of it. As a consequence, this book presents information that occasionally touches on matters of philosophy, curriculum, and pedagogy that are related to educational psychology but historically have not been presented in educational psychology textbooks. I have carefully selected material that is pertinent to the problem-solving process so that you can see the many ways that problem solving applies to teaching. This text, then, goes beyond other educational psychology textbooks to describe how problem solving—rather than the mere application of principles of psychology—is the intellectual activity teachers engage in when they teach well. Chapter 1 introduces you to this problem-solving perspective.

How This Text Demonstrates Problem Solving

In addition to describing the problem-solving process, this text demonstrates it in many ways. Each chapter's organization uses a problem-solving pattern. Chapters begin with a general question or problem that educational psychology addresses, and then they develop answers or solutions in a form that beginning teachers can use *in classrooms.* These solutions are presented in specially highlighted sections called **Strategic Solutions.** Each Solutions section provides practical, how-to information—a general strategy that you can adapt to your own needs as you face challenges in your classroom.

Where do these strategies come from? Each was derived from psychological theory and research. When additional research has been conducted to evaluate the effectiveness of a particular strategy, it is described in a subsection labeled "Evaluation" at the end of the Strategic Solutions section.

Problem Solving in Chapter Pedagogy

This textbook also demonstrates problem solving in its pedagogy. Five features invite you to participate in problem solving in different ways:

Reflection on Practice.   These boxes offer over thirty first-hand accounts of problem-solving dilemmas, written by teachers, parents, coaches, and counselors. These accounts and the Discussion Questions that follow them highlight major issues in the chapter.

Think It Through.   This three-part feature presents a discussion among a novice preservice teacher (who gives a representation of a problem), an experienced teacher (who generates a solution), and me (I evaluate the solution). The purpose of the Think It Throughs is to help you think about teaching problems posed by other preservice teachers, to consider how experienced teachers might solve these problems, and to see how to go about evaluating a solution in terms of the chapter's contents.

Concept Paper.   Concept Papers are writing assignments at the end of every chapter. Their purpose is to help you reflect on the ideas in the chapter and develop higher-order thinking skills.

Learning Journal Assignments.   These suggestions for daily writing will help you develop reflective thinking as you apply the principles of development and learning to events and experiences in your own life.

Deepening Your Knowledge Base. This feature provides in-depth information and analysis on selected topics and, at least once in every chapter, the opportunity to discuss questions in small groups.

UNIQUE CHAPTERS

This book contains two chapters on topics not treated in any other educational psychology text. Chapter 10, "Cognitive Learning Theories, Part 2: Achieving the Goal of Higher-Order Thinking," and Chapter 15, "The Teacher as Researcher," prepare you in very specific ways for today's and tomorrow's classrooms. These are classrooms where it is more important than ever for teachers and students to be able to 1) develop and use problem-solving abilities and 2) address problems with creative, effective solutions.

READING AND STUDY AIDS

In every chapter, you will find reading and study aids to help you approach concepts and ideas in interactive, meaningful ways. These aids include the following:

- Chapter Orientations and Focusing Questions
- Margin Notes
- Chapter Summaries
- Key Terms
- Suggested Readings

HOW THIS TEXT IS GEARED TOWARD NOVICE TEACHERS

The body of this text and all of the features were developed through extensive class testing in an NCATE-accredited teacher education program known for its strengths. Class testing occurred over two years as the manuscript went through revision. Students evaluated each chapter in terms of the chapter's user-friendliness, clarity of concepts and terms, helpfulness of or need for examples and explanations, and adequateness of length.

Class testing also involved administration of the CLEP (College Level Examination Program) test in educational psychology as a final examination one semester to ensure that the content of the text meets the academic needs of educational psychology students.

Perhaps more than any survey or test results, a note from a student who completed her teacher education program at a well-known private college confirmed my hopes about the book's immediate usefulness. She said, "I wanted to write you a note and tell you how much I have used your book, *Educational Psychology*. I have referred to your book many times during my study of elementary education at_____University. I have used the information for projects as well as for background material for my classes. It has been very beneficial." Although the book aspires to meet needs beyond the preservice program, I was also glad to hear that it fulfilled a student's need for accurate and timely information. In my view, no higher compliment can be paid to a textbook than to have it called useful.

ANCILLARIES TO ACCOMPANY THE TEXT

Student Handbook.   The Handbook is designed to improve reading comprehension and to help students transform Strategic Solutions into procedures for use in teaching. The Handbook includes expanded chapter outlines; training in the problem-solution format to analyze text; and exercises to define key terms, to compose procedures, and to self-test learning.

Instructor's Resource Manual.   This manual contains model syllabi, lecture enrichment outlines and activities, research notes, annotated film lists, and other technology support lists for college instructors, as well as examples of student Concept Papers and suggestions for approaches to teaching educational psychology.

Learning Journal Guide.   This guide for educational psychology instructors helps professors integrate learning journals into their course teaching; discusses research support and rationale for using journals; and provides suggestions about how to set up journals, manage them, and integrate them with course teaching and assessment goals. It is available upon adoption of this text.

Assessment Design Kit.   The Assessment Design Kit, a test bank, contains over 1000 test items that include multiple-choice questions at three levels of learning, short-answer questions, and extended essay questions with guidelines for answers. It also includes a special section on authentic assessment keyed to Chapter 14, "Assessment Design."

Computerized Test Generator.   Computerized versions of the test bank are available on adoption of this text.

Overhead Transparencies.   Eighty colorful transparencies, specifically developed to accompany this text, are available on adoption.

ACKNOWLEDGMENTS

I owe much to colleagues for their contributions to this book. Some of these debts are acknowledged in the text, but I would also like to thank Jim Burney, Pam Fernstrom, Felice Green, Denzil Keckley, Tom Pebworth, and Bob Stevenson for their assistance in particular matters. Librarians who helped me with research on this book include Susan DeGregory, Norman Elsner, and Sue Nazworth. My thanks to you all. Thanks also to the many preschool, elementary, and secondary teachers who let me enter their classrooms, who allowed me to write about learning there, and who contributed Reflections on Practice or parts of Think It Throughs. I also want to thank Tim Tubbs, Assistant Principal at Rogers High School, and other administrators who provided me with crucial background information.

I have two particularly large debts to acknowledge. First, I am indebted to my editorial team at Houghton Mifflin. The editorial team included Janet Edmonds, Merryl Maleska Wilbur, and Loretta Wolozin. They helped me develop my ideas into a book. In my view, our field owes a particular debt to Loretta Wolozin, Senior Sponsoring Editor in the College Division, for her vision of what education might become. I would also like to thank Janet Young, the production editor who attended to countless details, and Marcy Kagan, the photo researcher.

The manuscript reviewers also deserve my thanks. They included:

Julius Adams, *SUNY Fredonia*

Jeanne T. Amlund, *Pennsylvania State University*

James M. Applefield, *University of North Carolina*

Marlowe Berg, *San Diego State University*

John R. Bing, *Salisbury State University*

Edward Caropreso, *Clarion University*

Christopher M. Clark, *Michigan State University*

Victor R. Delclos, *University of New Mexico*

Peggy Dettmer, *Kansas State University*

Michael Gardner, *University of Utah*

Christine Givner, *Trinity College*

Helen Harrington, *University of Michigan*

Kathy Hoover-Dempsey, *Vanderbilt University*

Mark Isham, *Eastern New Mexico University*

Martha Jones, *St. Mary's University*

Samuel D. Miller, *University of North Carolina*

Robert Ohlberg, *Northern Illinois University*

Michael O'Loughlin, *Hofstra University*

Ronald Senzig, *Okaloosa-Walton Community College*

Mary R. Sudzina, *University of Dayton*

Their comments and suggestions made substantial contributions to this text, and I am deeply grateful for their assistance.

Lastly, I want to thank my wife and children. Janelle supported this project and encouraged me from beginning to end. I have her to thank more than anyone else for making it possible. Our children have made the aims of the book more practical. Andrew, in preschool when the project began, gave me two dinosaur stickers one evening for working "two" hard. It was time to play. Rachel made her appearance while the manuscript was in progress. Now two years old, she came to me the other day, pencil in hand, while I was proofreading the final text. Excited at the discovery of a new word in her speaking vocabulary, she exclaimed "Write, write!" I confess to having turned over my copy of the proofs to her, but any stray marks or oversights in the copy that I sent to the publisher are mine.

J.F.W.

Florence, Alabama

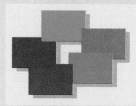

Goal Setting

Part I introduces you to the problem-solving process. It also introduces you to ways that you can become an effective teacher by becoming a problem solver. You will learn about the process of instructional planning and how such planning is a good example of problem solving. You will also learn about educational goals and objectives and how to make sure that your instructional activities address your objectives.

- Chapter 1   Problem Solving and Educational Psychology
- Chapter 2   The Development of Reflective Teaching: Becoming a Better Problem Solver
- Chapter 3   Planning Instruction: Getting Started as a Problem Solver

Problem Solving and Educational Psychology

The goal of this chapter is to introduce you to the activity of problem solving within the context of your classroom. You will discover a positive approach to problem solving; the application of a problem-solving process to your specific teaching challenges; and a detailed description of the ways in which this textbook can help you solve problems. As you read, look for answers to these questions:

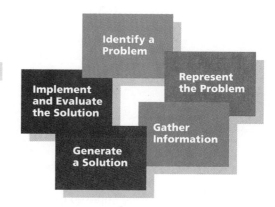

- **What enables a teacher to view a problem as a challenge and not as an obstacle?**

- **What specific types of problems arise in the classroom?**

- **What is the problem-solving process?**

- **Why is becoming a "reflective practitioner" so important?**

- **What are three ways in which this textbook can help you become an effective problem solver?**

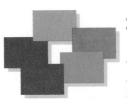

TEACHERS AS PROBLEM SOLVERS

What do you think of when you think of a problem? Perhaps you think of a math problem of the kind that you worked on when you were in school. Or perhaps you think of a problem only in terms of the difficulty that it poses—a car that will not start, or a jacket that you cannot wear because it is torn. When we think of a problem in these ways, we tend to think of it as something that is just "sitting there," an obstacle. Unfortunately, this negative view of problems can itself be an obstacle to understanding the nature of teaching.

There is another way to look at problems. Problems are never just sitting there. The nature of a problem is that it is an unfinished situation that needs a resolution. If you look at problems as dynamic, not static, you will realize that the difficulties they pose are temporary. By seeing yourself as an active participant in problem solving, you will perceive problems as *challenges.* Teachers who perceive problems as challenges are better able to take them on and resolve them. Helping you to become such a teacher is the goal of this book.

> Active participants in problem solving see problems as challenges rather than obstacles.

How do teachers solve problems? Let's begin our inquiry by visiting a high school classroom at the beginning of a normal day. It's 7:58 in the room where Mrs. Clarke teaches American history to students in a general class, as opposed to honors or advanced placement (AP) history, both of which she has also taught. A half-dozen students have arrived early, and you can overhear them chatting with each other. "Do we have anything due today?" "How did you do on the math? I was ending up with kind of big answers." "I finally finished that letter off to Beth. It was eleven o'clock and I had to crash." Does this sound familiar?

> Teachers start solving problems the moment they enter the classroom.

Mrs. Clarke, who has hall duty, enters to ask students if they have picked up a calendar and worksheets, which have been placed on a small table near the door (see Figure 1.1). The calendar indicates that the lesson for Wednesday through Friday will be about the Great Depression. Key questions are "Why did the Great Depression happen?" "What did Hoover and Roosevelt do?" and "What solved the Great Depression?" Students and teacher are clearly thinking about different topics.

The 8:00 bell goes off, the class of twenty-three students begins to settle down, and the teacher takes attendance while two students return to others the written assignment that Mrs. Clarke graded the evening before. "All right, did everybody get the worksheets? Okay, let's make the Great Depression painless." Mrs. Clarke closes the door and begins to review the causes, course, and consequences of World War I, the subject of the written assignment. "Give one cause for the war—Franklin?" "One weapon that was used—Christy?" "What happened after thc war? Chad?" This form of recitation is strategic because it allows Mrs. Clarke to talk about the papers while introducing the new lesson.

Mrs. Clarke: So as a consequence, Germany owed thirty-three billion dollars to France and England. How does a defeated nation pay thirty-three billion dollars? What do you do when you don't have the money to pay someone?

Robin: Get a loan.

Mrs. Clarke: Who has money to loan at the end of the war?

Franklin: The United States.

Without commenting, Mrs. Clarke turns on an overhead projector and begins to outline the cycle of international loan defaults that set off the Great Depression in North America and around the world.

After a few more remarks about the written assignment, she says, "Now let's go into the Great Depression and see what happens." Only at this point—ten minutes into the period—do students pull out their textbooks. She asks questions that lead into the textbook rather than away from it. ("People are paying on time—anyone here buy a car this way? People are doing the same thing with stocks. It's called 'buying on margin.' Robin, read 'Buying on Margin.'") She frames the past in terms that relate to the personal experience of the students. Most importantly, she speaks of past events in the present tense, making them come alive. For the next thirty minutes, it *is* the 1930s.

As Mrs. Clarke questions and occasionally calls on students, she circulates at the front of the room, moving between desks. At one point she moves

Figure 1.1   The Layout of Mrs. Clarke's Classroom

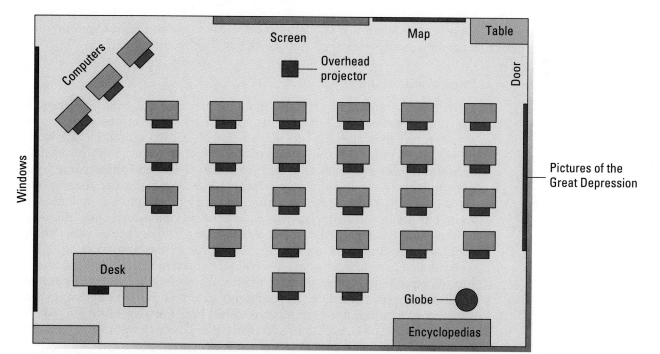

to one side of the room near a whispered conversation, and the whispering ceases. It is now clear that the teacher and most of the students are thinking about the same topic. A sense of collective purpose pervades the classroom. Forty minutes of instruction pass quickly. Seven minutes before the bell rings, Mrs. Clarke tells students to begin their worksheets. She moves quietly among them, leaning over and making personal comments to those who need encouragement or other special attention. Just before the bell rings, she tells the students to finish their worksheets at home and hand them in tomorrow.

Mrs. Clarke as a Problem Solver

You may never teach American history, but chances are that you can remember being in a class like the one taught by Mrs. Clarke. Its events probably sound familiar to you, even if at first it may seem strange to consider Mrs. Clarke as a problem solver. But Mrs. Clarke has made, is making, and will make a series of decisions in relation to this class that will resolve a number of problematic situations. She is a problem solver.

Four Types of Teaching Problems

A **problem** is not an obstacle. It is a goal that someone wants to attain but does not immediately know how to achieve (Bruer, 1993; Newell & Simon, 1972; Voss, 1989). Mrs. Clarke's central problem was to develop student understanding of the Great Depression. The development of understanding is not a problem limited to history, but it extends throughout the academic curriculum and beyond. It will almost certainly be a central problem for you as a teacher, at whatever level and in whatever subject you teach.

Instructional Problems

Instructional problems generally involve selecting and arranging activities to achieve a goal. Mrs. Clarke clearly enjoyed asking questions about history, a preference that probably developed from her own curiosity. Answering questions was the primary activity of students in her class, but the questions served different purposes at different times. At the beginning of the class, questions were used to review the previous lesson. After the review, questions related to the reading were used to develop understanding. Questions took a third form during seatwork, as students answered questions on a worksheet. Teachers tend to select and arrange activities such as questioning to achieve specific goals or purposes during the course of instruction.

Although Mrs. Clarke's goal of developing understanding is clear, it is not her only problem. Other unmet goals make the situation more complex. Take a moment to consider how difficult it must be to interest students in the Great Depression, in contrast to World War I or the Roaring Twenties, which precede the Depression, and World War II, which follows it. Interest is

---

Even deciding where to stand or where to move to is a kind of problem solving.

A problem exists when someone wants to attain a goal but does not know immediately how to do so.

Teachers use activities such as questioning to achieve specific goals or purposes.

These students are obviously interested in what they are talking about. Stimulating interest is a motivational goal for teachers, who might use peer group activities to attain this goal.   *(David Young-Wolff/PhotoEdit)*

a function of motivation, or a willingness to engage in learning. Students will not understand the Great Depression if they are not willing to learn about it.

Motivational Problems

A *motivational problem* involves engaging students in learning. In the early grades, motivational problems are not as pronounced as they are in high school. Stimulating interest in the Great Depression among teenagers is no small task, but Mrs. Clarke accomplished it by using questions that related events during the Depression to events in their lives. ("What do you do when you don't have the money to pay someone?" "People are paying on time—anyone here buy a car that way?") She also used a little trick to make history come alive. She talked as if it were the 1930s.

> Motivational problems are more pronounced in upper grades than in lower grades.

Management Problems

A third type of problem became apparent when Mrs. Clarke moved toward a whispered conversation. A *management problem* involves creating or maintaining a climate conducive to learning. Well-planned instruction and motivation can reduce management problems, but learning may still be interrupted due to lack of responsible participation or respect. The most frequent management problem involves helping students learn to speak in turn—the reason why "raising your hand" is almost a universal practice in schools. What is needed is often not punishment but an environment that channels activity into learning.

> Well-planned instruction and motivation can reduce management problems.

Good management practices involve prevention of misbehavior, positive forms of intervention, and nonpunitive consequences (such as a problem-solving conference with the teacher) before resorting to punishment. By moving in the direction of the whispered conversation, Mrs. Clarke used a positive form of intervention to support self-control. She suppressed the whispering without punishing the students involved.

Assessment Problems

You really did not see Mrs. Clarke address the fourth type of common classroom problem, but an *assessment problem* involves evaluating learning accurately. You are familiar with assessment through tests, but assessment takes many other forms including evaluating homework, collecting feedback during the lesson, and assigning grades to papers, projects, and portfolios. Assessment is a very dynamic topic in education today, but specific strategies are developed by teachers to promote accuracy in making judgments of worth.

It is important for you to realize that in real classroom life, the distinctions between instructional, motivational, management, and assessment problems

> Assessment takes many forms other than tests.

Assessment problems involve evaluating learning accurately. Assessment can involve tests, but it also takes the form of collecting feedback and assigning grades to various work samples.   *(George White Location Photography)*

Planning for younger students often involves integrating learning across subject areas. What academic skill are these students developing as they work on an art project? (Paul S. Conklin/PhotoEdit)

are almost never neat and precise. In your real teaching, these "types" of problems-as-challenges will more often emerge as emphases or focuses rather than as categorical divisions. Because motivational problems, management problems, and assessment problems are so tied in to instructional problems, you will find that this book is about how to solve not only instructional problems but these related problems as well. (See Table 1.1.)

You might want to take a minute to think through how a teacher might deal with a complex situation posing different kinds of problems, then compare your ideas with those of an experienced teacher. Like all beginning and experienced teachers, you will face complex situations every day. If you begin by viewing each situation as dynamic and each problem as a challenge rather than as an obstacle, you will be that much more likely to succeed in finding a satisfactory solution. (See Think It Through, pages 10–12.)

In real teaching there are rarely neat distinctions between types of problems.

Viewing situations as dynamic and problems as challenges increases the likelihood of finding solutions.

Table 1.1   Teaching Problems

Problem Type or Focus	Purpose of Problem Solving
Instructional	Select and arrange activities
Motivational	Engage students in learning
Management	Establish a climate conducive to learning
Assessment	Evaluate learning accurately

think it through

Consider this problem that a novice preservice teacher has **IDENTIFIED** and **REPRESENTED**.

Using the Basal

It is my first week as a first-grade teacher and I'm establishing a reading program in my classroom. I am told by my principal to teach reading strictly from the basal and the supplemental materials provided. I begin to use the basal in my classroom and get a feel for it, but I notice that some children seem lost and others seem bored. I know I have to test the children to see what level they are on, but how do I use the basal to meet the needs of all the children and how do I make using the basal in reading fun and interesting for the children?

Use the basal, do not let it use you! Many modern basals have interesting literary selections. It is possible to do variations of whole language using a basal.

There are many possibilities here. First you need to test for reading levels. Determine if you are going to teach the whole group at the same level or group children according to levels. There is still lots of room for individualization if the students are close enough in level to do whole-group teaching. I would take this option if at all possible.

Unless your principal objects, there is no law that says you must teach the basal page by page, lesson plan by lesson plan. We are going to have fun with it! Let's get the skill planning out of the way first. This approach is more work for you, but more fun for the student. Looking at the scope and sequence of skills taught, you are going to list skills by category, then add under each list page numbers of stories or units where these skills are taught. If you are going to teach the whole class at the same level, you need do this only at that level. If you must group students by level, then you must do this for all levels, lowest to highest. Don't leave out levels between books you are using—get all the work over with now and list all skills by category.

Now the fun begins. Go through the basal and pick out stories that center around a theme. Try to tie the theme in with another subject area. If you are teaching animals in science, go through and pick out all the stories that involve animals. If you are learning to read maps in social studies, go through and choose all the stories that take place in a specific country or city of the world or that mention a lot of specific place names—anything you can locate on a map. If you are planning a field trip, choose stories that could tie in with your trip. You may also group selections by genre—mystery stories, fairy tales, fables, tales of the West. The possibilities are endless! If you are teaching the whole group, your task is a little easier. If you have grouped by levels, find stories at each level to tie in with your theme. Don't worry about sticking to just one level for each group. Most students should be able to handle material from at least one level above or below their targeted level and thus you can choose more stories for your theme unit.

Now look through the stories selected for the unit and match them up with the categories of skills you did earlier. Choose one or two categories of skills to target that seem to match up with a number of your stories—not all have to match up. Don't try to target too many skills. You will constantly refer to the skills categories during the year to ensure you get them all in.

Introduce your theme to the whole group with an activity. Now choose a story (or a story for each group) and plan a regular DRTA (directed reading-thinking activity) lesson. Using the feedback you got from students during the DRTA lesson group, identify those who need more teacher-directed time and those who need extension and enrichment. A writing activity using vocabulary encountered in the story would be excellent here.

This process may take a few days to complete all activities and skills for each story. Take care that the students are spending lots of time on the task at hand—reading and writing. Don't draw the process out to where it becomes boring and cumbersome—just hit the few targeted skills and move on.

Catherine W. Benedict
West Salisbury Elementary School
Salisbury, Maryland
Northwestern Elementary School
Mardela Springs, Maryland

think it through, continued

EVALUATE this problem's possible multiple solutions while you think about the dynamic process of problem solving.

There are two outstanding characteristics of this solution to the problem. First, notice the teacher's attitude. She identifies a *motivational* problem—how to interest the children in reading—and views working under the direction of the principal and within the basal reader as part of the challenge of solving the problem. You might want to reread her response, keeping your eye on her attitude. She has fun designing a way to make learning interesting. She enjoys meeting a challenge and planning as a form of problem solving.

Second, she folds a solution to the motivational problem in with her solution to an instructional problem. The design that she develops to instruct *and* motivate students begins with her own interest in thematic learning activities. These activities integrate learning across subject areas. Planning for this teacher is not limited to the language arts, but it integrates subjects across the curriculum. The purpose of this integration is to weave in motivation with instruction. Let's see how she does it.

The teacher identifies reading skills first. These are found in a "scope and sequence" of skills provided with the basal reader. The scope and sequence indicates which skills are targeted by which reading selections. (*Scope* is an old word for "target.") Considering target skills helps the teacher select readings from the pool that she has generated for her theme. In this manner, final selections of readings are made to match both skills (instruction) and theme (motivation). The consideration of skills and theme allows her to select content relevant to both instructional and motivational goals.

Representing a motivational problem along with the instructional problem does not, however, solve the instructional problem. Remember, a solution to an instructional problem is an *instructional strategy* composed of one or more activities to achieve a goal. The central strategy adopted by the teacher is a "regular DRTA lesson." This type of activity, which is explained in greater detail in courses on the teaching of reading, consists of three steps: predicting, reading, and proving.

For example, a teacher might first use pictures or the title of a selection to ask students to make predictions about the reading selection. ("What do you think the story is going to be about?" "What do you think will happen?") After the group has made a number of predictions, the teacher then has students read one or two pages. After they finish, the teacher asks them to recall their predictions and explain why their predictions proved true (or not). DRTA is a well-respected activity to develop reading comprehension.

While generating her solution to the problem, the teacher makes many interesting suggestions to adapt instruction to learner differences. These are also worth analyzing, but overall, what you should note is (1) her positive attitude toward the problem-as-challenge, and (2) her clever way of folding in the solution to a motivational problem with the solution to an instructional problem. A teacher should always consider motivation along with instruction, and vice versa.

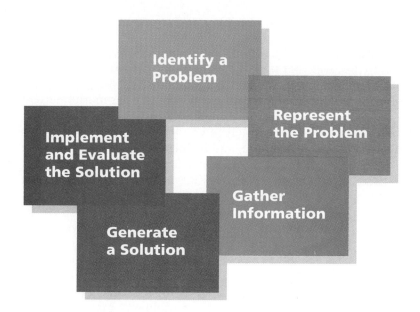

Figure 1.2
The Stages of Problem Solving

THE PROBLEM-SOLVING PROCESS

How does a teacher like Mrs. Clarke solve problems of instruction, motivation, management, and assessment? There is no fixed way, but a frequently described method of solution is the **problem-solving process,** which is a stagelike series of actions to achieve a goal. All models of problem solving have stages or steps, which are really smaller subprocedures within the overall process. Some models have as few as two stages, and others have as many as seven or nine. This text will adopt a five-stage model of problem solving that is similar to most other models (e.g., Bransford & Stein, 1993; Dewey, 1933; Gick, 1986). The stages are represented visually in Figure 1.2.

For purposes of clarity and discussion in this book, the five stages are portrayed independently and sequentially. As parts of a real-life process applied to teaching decisions, though, they are interdependent and overlapping. Although you'll probably use only one of them at a time, remember that you are likely to reuse each during the course of solving problems, and you will probably not use them in exactly the order presented here.

Rather than think of the "problem-solving process" as a unique set of procedures that you must adopt, you should see it as a way to approach teaching problems, turn them into challenges, and make effective everyday decisions. Within that context, we will take a closer look at each of the five stages, but first let's consider the differences between well-defined and ill-defined problems.

> The problem-solving process is a stagelike series of actions used to achieve a goal.

> In real-life situations, the parts of the problem-solving process are interdependent and overlap.

Well-Defined vs. Ill-Defined Problems

When people consider particular problems and the procedures used to solve them, they begin to discover that not all problems and problem-solving procedures are alike. Consider some simple math problems: $3 + 4 = $ _____ , and $7x + 4 = 18$ (solve for x). The problems are clearly presented as mathematical sentences. There are no spare words or symbols, and all of the information necessary to solve the problems is explicit, if you know the rules. The rules are, in the first case, rules of arithmetic, and in the second, rules of algebra. The answer is clearly specified in both cases by rules that leave no room for ambiguity. In other words, these problems are well defined. **Well-defined** problems are highly specified in terms of their circumstances, solution procedures, and goals.

Not all problems are well defined. Deciding which clothes to wear on a given day, planning a meal, and even making out a budget all require you to set either the circumstances, solution procedures, or goal. **Ill-defined** problems are characterized by the lack of specification of the circumstances, the solution procedures, or the goal (Reitman, 1964; Voss & Post, 1988; Wakefield, 1992). All of these characteristics of problems may be almost completely unspecified! For example, in problems that call for creative thinking—such as composing a poem—a person may begin with something that is defined only by very general terms and transform it into something quite specific, but how that transformation should occur and when it is complete cannot be specified beforehand.

If problems were arranged along a line from well defined at one extreme (represented by problems such as $7x + 4 = 18$) to ill defined at the other extreme (represented by problems such as "compose a poem"), most teaching problems would lie somewhere in between the extremes (see Figure 1.3). For example, a set curriculum, a given textbook, or even a given room partially define an instructional problem, but none of these factors will lead automatically to a particular goal and a solution. What you believe as a teacher, how much experience you have, the degree of restriction imposed by your school district or principal, and so on—all more amorphous and open-ended factors—will also play an important role in how you set and achieve a goal.

There is nothing automatic about how solutions flow from teaching problems because these problems so fundamentally involve human beings. The context will always be individual and unique. Ultimately, the dynamics of each context will define the teaching problem.

> Some problems are ill structured or ill defined.

> The context of teaching problems is always individual and unique.

Figure 1.3
Degrees of Definition of Problems

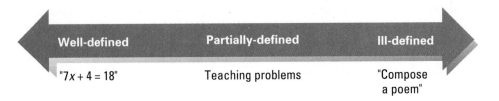

Well-defined	Partially-defined	Ill-defined
"$7x + 4 = 18$"	Teaching problems	"Compose a poem"

Stage 1: Identify a Problem

Problem identification is the recognition of a goal one wishes to attain without having a clear way to achieve it. Another term for identifying a problem is "problem finding." A teaching problem often begins as a dilemma that is felt rather than understood. The most general teaching problem might be "Here is your classroom. Here are your students. Teach them" (Yinger, 1980, pp. 115–116). This problem-as-challenge recurs in some form before most classes that you will teach.

> Teaching problems often begin as dilemmas that are felt rather than understood.

   What are the most common *specific* problems that teachers identify? Take a look at Table 1.2, which presents the results of two recent surveys of classroom problems perceived by beginning teachers who graduated from one school of education (Boccia, 1989, 1991). (Although these lists identify the

Table 1.2   Classroom Concerns of Beginning Teachers

Concern	Rank by Teachers	
	Elementary	Secondary
Lesson and unit planning	1	5
Classroom control, management	2	3
Relevance of subject matter to students	3	1
Dealing with individual differences	4–5	8–9
Handling students with special needs	4–5	10–12
Assessing student learning	6	15
Knowledge of varied teaching techniques	7	10–12
Rapport with students	8	2
Obtaining sufficient supplies, materials	9	16
Own knowledge of curriculum materials	10	6–7
Time spent in preparation, evaluation	11–12	13
Knowledge of student development	11–12	4
Skill in conducting a discussion	13	8–9
Grouping for effective instruction	14	10–12
Knowledge of content area	15	6–7
Class size	16	—
Record keeping, administrative matters	17	18
Standardized testing	18	—
Diagnosis of student capability	—	14
Grading	—	17

Source: Adapted from Boccia, 1989, 1991

concerns of graduates from only one school of education, the results from many other studies are similar [Veeman, 1984].) Among top concerns are instructional planning, classroom control, and relevance of subject matter. Solving instructional problems involves planning; solving management problems involves the issue of control; and solving motivational problems involves choosing relevant subject matter.

Since planning problems are a major concern for beginning teachers, let's reexamine for a moment the problem Mrs. Clarke faced—that of "developing understanding." Typically, a teacher might find this problem-as-challenge as part of a district goal or an objective in a curriculum guide. Presented in this sweeping way and worded so generally, however, the goal of "developing understanding" has few implications for designing instruction. It has been identified, but not clarified. Without further clarification, the problem can have any number of solutions. Two alternatives are:

a. To require students to analyze information in a discussion (a high level of understanding);
b. To use questions to lead students to interpret information (an intermediate level of understanding).

Without going beyond problem identification (stage 1) to problem representation (stage 2), neither of these solutions is more appropriate than the other.

Stage 2: Represent the Problem

Problem representation involves a set of decisions that define a goal in a way that it *can* be achieved. Other terms for problem representation are problem "definition" or problem "framing." Many psychologists believe that careful representation of a problem is the key to effective problem solving. Problem representation is the pivotal stage for solving a problem because it enables you to turn an identified problem into a challenge to be solved. Well-defined problems, for example, are easier to go about solving for the very reason that they *are* well defined: They are presented in an unambiguous form that should not require further reformulation.

> Problem representation is pivotal because it enables you to turn a problem into a problem-as-challenge.

To illustrate how important problem representation or definition is, let's take a simple, well-defined math problem, such as $137 - 68 = $ _____. Take a few seconds to solve it before reading further. (Write in your answer.) Did you mentally rearrange the problem so that the first number was above the second one? The problem was at first represented in a horizontal way that makes it difficult to solve. The problem is easier to solve if the larger number is put above the smaller one (we can then "carry" or "regroup"). The problem is much harder if it is represented in Roman numerals (CXXXVII − LXVIII = _____). Before solving this one, we will most likely have to translate or represent it as Arabic numerals. The way that you represent a problem is critical in determining how successful you will be in solving it.

Representing ill-defined problems such as teaching problems is a two-step procedure. First, you need to *identify the givens in the situation.* Problems are always accompanied by a range of circumstances, or **givens.** It is helpful to picture these givens as occurring along a spectrum. Some of the givens in a particular situation may be very inflexible. This kind of given is often called a "constraint." For a beginning teacher, the constraints may include such factors as curriculum requirements or state laws. Also along the spectrum of givens are other conditions such as the kinds of materials you have available, your students' dispositions or capabilities, and your own beliefs about good teaching. Once you have identified the givens in a particular situation, you will know what you can try to change and what you cannot change.

> The first step in representing a problem is to identify the givens in the situation.

For example, if you faced a problem similar to Mrs. Clarke's of developing understanding, the "understanding" you would be teaching would depend not only on what you determine the term itself to mean (your own beliefs), but on the nature of the curriculum, the students, the instructional setting, and the class resources (such as textbooks, films, and equipment). You cannot develop a "high" level of understanding when critical equipment, such as experimental apparatus in a lab course, is unavailable. You cannot even develop student interpretation of information when a class exceeds a certain size.

You will find that the givens at the constraint end of the spectrum have a genuine impact on the way you represent and ultimately solve a problem. It is important to realize that this does not have to be a negative experience. In fact, constraints help you represent the situation in a realistic manner that points you toward your goal. They help you, for instance, to move along the spectrum to your own beliefs about what "understanding" is and allow you to form judgments about the kind of understanding that *these* students need to develop at *this* point in their work, within the context of their other learning.

As you do this, you will be naturally moving toward articulating a means of solving your problem-as-challenge. In an organic way, you will have moved into the second step of the representation procedure, which is *clarifying the goal*. In other words, once you have examined and explored the givens that are involved, the goal will flow out of the givens. Rather than discard the givens, you will be taking them into consideration as you build and articulate your goal. What you are really striving to achieve will emerge.

> The second step in representing a problem is to clarify the goal.

Stage 3: Gather Information

Information gathering is the collection and analysis of knowledge needed to solve a problem. All types of problems require information gathering to solve. For example, let's say that Mrs. Clarke's general goal is to develop understanding (*problem identification*), and because the students are not trained to think analytically and have difficulty reading the textbook, she has decided as a specific goal to develop interpretations of events described in the textbook (*problem representation*). Such understanding of historical events is not as profound as the result of analysis, but it is not as superficial as knowledge from a lecture. What activities should she use to attain her goal?

> Solving all types of problems requires information gathering.

From where does information about activities come? Mostly it comes from prior knowledge or memory, but it also comes from the teaching situation itself. In particular, four sources are valuable to you as a new teacher: in-

Teachers often face problems other than instructional planning. What type of problem is involved here, and what do you think the goal of the teacher is? *(Wayne Eastep/Tony Stone Images)*

formation from watching your previous teachers, information from your teacher education program, information from your student teaching experience, and information from the current teaching situation.

Consider Information from Your "Teacher Watching"

First, we all spent years as students in classrooms, engaged in activities of one kind or another. We gathered a great deal of information as "teacher watchers" (Barnes, 1989). This fund of background information can supply us models of both how to teach a subject and how not to teach it. This fund of information about activities is limited, however, by your experience as a learner. Other students learning the same subject with other teachers had different experiences. Still, many of your initial ideas about how you should teach have their origins in how you were taught.

Teacher watching is one source of information about activities.

Consider Information from Your Teacher Education Program

Second, your professional education courses, including educational psychology, are a valuable source of information about activities. For example, activities that you will learn about in Chapter 3 include teacher presentations, teacher-student interactions, and student actions (see Figure 1.4). In all like-

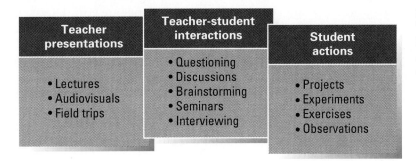

Figure 1.4
Teacher and Student
Participation in Selected
Activities *(Adapted from Henak, 1984)*

lihood, you remember that films and field trips were fun, but since they are teacher presentations, they often involve little more than observation on the part of learners. If your instructional goal is to activate higher levels of learning, you cannot achieve it through films and field trips alone, which are fundamentally motivational. Subsequent chapters will help you identify other activities (such as discussions and projects) that can be used to stimulate higher-level thinking.

Consider Information from Your Own Student Teaching Experience

Cooperating teachers are chosen in part for their abilities to model teaching practices, including how to conduct activities. You will gather some information for class activities from recalling practices of your cooperating teacher. When you begin to teach, your cooperating teacher may become a coach, providing feedback about how to conduct activities (Schön, 1990). This feedback can be valuable information about the effectiveness of activities to achieve certain goals. Despite the value of your cooperating teacher or other teachers as models or mentors, however, you will be working toward limiting your dependence on them for information. You will make an increasing number of your own teaching decisions about effective practices.

> Student teaching experiences also generate information about activities.

Consider Information from the Teaching Situation

Finally, some information can be acquired only in relation to your own situation. Many activities are suggested by the context of a specific class—a rug in a reading corner, bays near a window, blackboards on three walls, or an overhead projector in the room. The physical layout of the room or other location for learning can sometimes suggest ideas for activities. If you are separated from another class by movable walls, for example, you might consider team teaching, particularly when you are contemplating an activity (such as a musical performance by a guest) that could be beneficial to a larger number of students, and might distract them if *not* shared.

You can find more information about activities from teachers' journals, teachers' manuals, or talks with other teachers. Most journals published by professional organizations for teachers in a teaching field keep readers informed of new ideas for the classroom. Teachers' manuals and some curriculum guides also suggest specific activities that are correlated with objectives. Finally, you have other teachers who will exchange ideas about interesting activities, sometimes during formal "in-service" presentations, sometimes during faculty meetings, and sometimes at odd moments—over lunch, or in the faculty lounge. You may very well seek out a more experienced teacher with whom you can talk about such matters, often in the context of general conversation.

Teachers base their decisions on information from many sources. Part of the skill of problem solving is becoming resourceful about ways to gather that information.

> Journals, other teachers, and the physical layout of the classroom are also sources of information about activities.

Stage 4: Generate a Solution

Solution generation is the creation of a means to achieve a goal from the givens. A teacher generates a solution when he or she selects and arranges activities to design a *strategy*. In Mrs. Clarke's history class, for example, the instructional strategy consisted of a single activity—questioning—to develop understanding of the Great Depression.

> Teachers generate solutions when they select and arrange activities to design a strategy.

Questions such as "Why did the Great Depression happen?" "What did Hoover and Roosevelt do?" and "What solved the Great Depression?" structured the class even before it began. Factual questions served the dual purposes of reviewing the written assignment and introducing the topic. Further questioning occurred throughout the remainder of the lesson to help students understand events and their rational progression. The worksheets extended the questioning activity through the rest of the period and into homework. Mrs. Clarke's use of questioning was always strategic—that is, she used questioning to achieve an instructional goal, which was to develop understanding.

Keep in mind that Mrs. Clarke also used questioning as part of a motivational strategy. This observation brings up an important point about your use of activities. Since transitions between activities take time and inevitably disrupt learning, the same activity is often used to meet more than one goal. Within a particular activity as well as across activities, you should consider how many goals can be achieved by students at the same time. Working on a project or discussing a topic in class can lead to the achievement of different kinds of goals, as well as different goals of the same kind.

Stage 5: Try the Solution and Evaluate It

The **implementation** and **evaluation of a solution** begins with trying out a strategy to achieve a goal, and it ends with a judgment of how well the strategy worked. "Trying out" includes a trial, test, or experiment in which the effectiveness of the strategy is judged. We might try out a solution to a simple math problem mentally, but in a problem as complex as developing the understanding of learners, we must try out a solution in experience.

> Trying a solution and judging how well it worked is implementing and evaluating a solution.

One way to think of a strategy is as a hypothesis to try out through informal experimentation. Or you can think of this stage as *verification*, because you attempt to verify whether or not a tentative solution really works. In teaching, the evaluation of strategies occurs partly during the lesson, and partly after the lesson is over. In class, you will monitor students' continuing interests and progress. A puzzled look on several faces might indicate confusion about the way you're presenting the lesson; on one face, it might indicate an individual learner's own lack of background or understanding. An audible sigh or a chin-on-hands might indicate boredom, but then again it might simply mean that the student was up late last night watching an exciting movie on television! From these few examples, you can see that what sometimes *appears* to be one response to your lesson may actually be another. Although none can be taken at (literally) "face" value, each is important as a clue to the effectiveness of both your teaching and your students' learning.

Your evaluation of strategies will continue long after teaching is over. In addition to mulling over your on-the-spot observations, this part of the evaluation may involve listening to students or making mental notes as you read their written assignments or homework papers. An evaluation may also involve feedback to you from a formal assessment of learning. All of these forms of evidence can help you evaluate strategies in terms of your original goals. As problems emerge from the evaluation (and they almost always do), you will find yourself back at the beginning of the problem-solving process. You repeat the cycle, or at least a portion of it, until you achieve your goal.

> Many forms of evidence can help teachers evaluate strategies they use to solve problems.

Applying the Five Stages of the Problem-Solving Process

To see how these five stages of problem solving apply to another real-life situation, take a moment to reflect on the experience of a student teacher who resolved the problem of teaching *Romeo and Juliet* to an unselected group of ninth-grade students in English (see Reflection on Practice: "The Play's the Thing"). The student teacher *identified* the problem in terms of her own feelings, and then *represented* it in terms of givens and goals. She subsequently *gathered information* by thinking about learning activities that could solve the problem. She recalled similarities between *Romeo and Juliet* and *West Side Story*, and thought about the relation between the contemporary setting and the background knowledge of her students. She then *generated a solution* by sequencing two learning activities (audio-visual presentation and discussion) in a strategy or plan to attain her goals. Finally, she *tried out* her solution and *evaluated* it by reflecting on its success.

As you develop as a problem solver, you will *not* be led to perceive the same problems or arrive at the same solutions as other teachers who are equally thoughtful. Teaching situations are generally so ill defined that they allow for the perception of different problems and the success of alternative strategies. For example, if you were an English teacher, you might teach *Romeo and Juliet* quite differently from the teacher we just met. That is only natural. Your goals and knowledge are not exactly the same as hers. What you *will* share with other thoughtful teachers is an ability to observe yourself

> Not all teachers perceive the same problems or try the same solutions.

"The Play's the Thing . . ."

I was teaching ninth-grade English and I had a problem. The school was a small one and I had all the ninth graders in one English class. As I had all levels of students, I feared that many would get lost when we read *Romeo and Juliet.* I wanted to capture the students' attention, motivate them to learn from this play, and also not leave myself open to discipline problems. After much thought about the background knowledge of my students, I decided that showing the movie version of *West Side Story* would be the best tool to accomplish my goal. It took three class days to show the movie, but I feel that it was well worth it.

In order to relate the two, I first spent some time discussing a few of the basic points of similarity. I asked the students to pay attention to the characters of *West Side Story* because we would later relate them to those in *Romeo and Juliet.* I talked after the movie about symbolism, irony, and the climax. I then wanted anyone interested to write a paper for me on the similarities and the differences between the two when we were done. By asking this, I hoped to challenge the better students in the group.

I feel that I was working on the background information of my students so that they would recognize and understand Shakespeare's play. I wanted so much for the story of *Romeo and Juliet* to have meaning for them, and for it not to be another boring story they had to read. When the whole lesson was over, I saw my idea had been worthwhile. My students talked about *West Side Story* and *Romeo and Juliet.* I feel that this is an example of helping students with their background knowledge so that they can process information and learn to the best of their abilities.

LeeAnn DePoyster

Discussion Questions

1. **What types of teaching problems were the focus of this teacher? (Refer back to Table 1.1, page 9, for a list of problem types.)**
2. **What were the "givens" that this teacher identified to define her problem?**
3. **How do we know that the solution was arrived at through careful thought or deliberation?**

consciously and learn from your observations, and the means to put into action a process for viewing teaching problems as challenges and for solving them.

Becoming a Reflective Practitioner

The problem-solving process represents a useful foundation on which to build increasingly more accurate "know how" as you increase in skills as a teacher. Donald Schön (1983) has used the term **reflective practitioner** to describe the role of skilled professionals who solve problems in the course of their work. **Reflection** was defined by the educational philosopher John Dewey (1933) as a process of active, persistent, and careful consideration of any belief or thought in light of its grounds or implications. Practitioners who reflect in the course of their work consider their goals, plan how they will attain them, evaluate their plans as they try them out, and modify their practice to achieve their goals more effectively. Practitioners who are reflective are problem solvers.

As you have just seen in the previous discussion, problems-as-challenges can crop up at any time. Thus, a reflective practitioner will be called on to both reflect *on* action (that is, before and after teaching) and reflect *in* action (that is, during teaching). Becoming a reflective practitioner is important for a third reason, as well—that is, so that you can teach reflection to your students. Let's examine each of these three points below.

Reflecting on action involves solving problems prospectively or retrospectively. Teachers who are reflective practitioners think about teaching problems at all hours—sometimes late at night or early in the morning, even in the shower! Reflecting *on* action is something that you already do in relation to teaching, especially teaching by others. You might wonder why a teacher like Mrs. Clarke reserved a few minutes for seatwork at the end of the lesson, or how you might teach *Romeo and Juliet* differently than the English teacher did. Reflecting on your own actions as a teacher will be more personal, detailed, and involved than reflecting on the actions of others, but it is just an extension of what you are already doing as a prospective teacher.

By way of contrast, reflecting in action involves spontaneously solving teaching problems in the classroom as they arise. It literally and figuratively involves thinking on your feet. Such problem solving is concealed in proficient teaching because it does not call attention to itself. Part of the artistry of a reflective practitioner is to conceal the art. Nevertheless, we can find evidence in Mrs. Clarke's classroom of reflection in action. For example, she suppressed a distracting conversation by moving to the vicinity of the disturbance while she continued to teach. Such moments in which you deal with unexpected behavior or resolve temporary misunderstandings are relatively frequent. Such problems, according to one study, spontaneously arise during teaching on an average of once every two minutes (Clark & Peterson, 1986)! They are solved by reflection in action.

A third reason to become a reflective practitioner is so that you can develop reflective thinking or problem solving in your students. Education in Canada, the United States, and many other countries is beginning to adopt thinking as a goal of instruction. Such instruction may stand alone in a course on thinking skills, or it may be infused throughout the curriculum, or both. Several experimental ways to teach thinking will be reviewed in Chapter 10. Your use of reflection to plan and assess and to "think on your feet" will give you a good foundation for teaching thinking skills to students. You will simply be making your own general thought processes explicit when you describe the general skills that you would like your students to use.

> Reflection is the active, persistent, and careful consideration of any belief or thought in light of its grounds or implications.

> Reflecting on action involves solving problems before or after they occur.

> Reflecting in action involves spontaneously solving teaching problems as they

> By being reflective practitioners, teachers can develop reflective thinking or problem solving in their students.

PROBLEM SOLVING AND THIS BOOK

You have now been introduced to the concept of a teaching-problem-as-challenge; the components of a problem and a description of different problem types; the stages of the problem-solving process; and a concept of the role of the beginning teacher as problem solver or reflective practitioner. The problem-solving process has been applied to several teaching problems, including developing understanding. You may now be wondering: How can the rest of this book help you become a better problem solver?

The Text as Information Source

First, this text supports teachers as problem solvers by supplying a professional **knowledge base**, or a clearly defined body of information and set of values, for teaching as a problem-solving activity (see Table 1.3). Through the consideration of your role as a problem solver, the development of reflective teaching, and goals and objectives (Chapters 1–3), this book can help you identify problems. Through the consideration of student characteristics (Chapters 4–7), it can help you represent problems so you can solve them. Through application of principles of learning (Chapters 8–11), it can help you gather information about learning activities and generate solutions. Through application of principles of motivation and management (Chapters 12 and 13), it can help you solve problems of engaging students in activities and establishing a climate conducive to learning. Through techniques of assessment (Chapter 14), it can help you solve the problems concerning the accurate assessment of learning. Finally, through an introduction to research skills (Chapter 15), it can help you apply the problem-solving process to develop further the knowledge base for teaching. This book, in sum, is dedicated to helping you grow as a professional.

Second, the text serves as an information source about knowledge acquisition and problem solving for your use both as a thinker and as a teacher of thinking. You might want to take a look at Chapter 9 and the sections on

> A professional knowledge base is a clearly defined body of information and set of values.

Table 1.3 Problem Solving and Chapter Contents

Problem-Solving Stage	Chapter Numbers
Identify a problem	1–3
Represent the problem	4–7
Gather information/ Generate a solution	8–13
Try the solution and evaluate it	14–15

Reflection on action involves solving problems before or after teaching. It generally occurs during solitary moments. *(Francisco Rangel)*

mnemonics (memory strategies) and study skills before you start studying this term or take another test. That chapter can help you develop a *learning* strategy for this and other courses. Chapters 9 and 10 also review information that will help you understand the roles of problem solving, decision making, and thinking skills in education. They include descriptions of thinking skills programs and exercises. Even though these exercises and programs will be recommended for your students' benefit, if you have not studied thinking, this information may also benefit you as a learner.

The Text as Model

This text in particular will also provide you with a demonstration of instructional problem solving. The five-part problem-solving process described earlier was the organizational design for developing the contents of this textbook. This design will not be apparent in the same way in each chapter; nevertheless, you might want to look for the process of (1) problem identification, (2) problem representation, (3) information gathering, (4) solution generation, and (5) solution evaluation in the outline of each chapter.

Problem Representation and Strategic Solutions

You'll find that each chapter begins by identifying a problem in the application of psychology to education, then represents the problem in a solvable way. Subsequent parts of each chapter vary as the structures of different prob-

Reflecting in action involves solving problems or managing dilemmas as they occur. How is this kindergarten teacher positioned to deal with a variety of learner needs? *(Paul S. Conklin)*

Each chapter in this book demonstrates the process of solving instructional problems.

lems lead to the discovery of instructional constraints, attainable goals, strategic solutions, and evaluations of strategic solutions. These strategic solutions are highlighted in each chapter to give you specific ideas and applications that you can use in your problem solving as a teacher. Thus, each chapter demonstrates the process of solving instructional problems.

The Text as Problem Poser

You can actively, not just passively, solve problems as you read this textbook. Educational psychology is well suited to the development of higher-order thinking skills such as analysis, synthesis, or evaluation (Martin, 1989). Three types of exercises in this text—*Concept Papers*, *Reflections on Practice*, and *Think It Throughs*—will give you opportunities to develop higher-order thinking skills in the context of solving problems of teaching. A fourth exercise, the *Learning Journal*, is designed to encourage you to develop reflective skills through daily writing.

Concept Papers

Concept Papers use research and writing exercises designed to help develop a higher-order thinking skill.

Each chapter ends with a short writing assignment called a *Concept Paper* designed to help you develop a higher-order thinking skill through a research and writing exercise. Further, the materials required for these assignments—such as articles, homework assignments, or tests in your teaching field—relate to your development as a teacher. Like enrichment exercises in the classes that you will teach, Concept Papers supplement the content of the textbook. You will not be expected to do all of them.

Reflections on Practice

Firsthand accounts of problem solving by a teacher in the classroom or in some closely related activity (such as parenting, coaching, or counseling) are presented throughout the text as *Reflections on Practice.* In each account, a teacher, who may also be a parent or a coach, (1) gives a short description of what led up to a problem, incident, or dilemma; (2) describes what the problem or dilemma was; (3) explains how a principle of learning or development was involved in the solution of the problem or management of the dilemma; and (4) evaluates the outcome, if appropriate. Reflections represent different levels, subject areas, and teaching situations. Often, the writers are much like you or your classmates will be just a few years from now.

Reflections on Practice provide firsthand accounts of problem solving.

These reflections are more than illustrations of text content because they are designed to provoke thought. Not all practices mentioned are "best" practices, and frequently the comments of teachers about specific situations are limited by their perspectives, as all of us are limited by our own points of view. Discussion questions follow each reflection to enhance appreciation of why the teacher solved (or did not solve) a given problem effectively. You might find your interpretation of a situation differs from that of the teacher. Reflections on Practice are tools to develop analytical thinking, not simply to illustrate best practices.

Think It Throughs

As a regular feature of this textbook, you will encounter questions that have been asked by preservice teachers like yourself about problem situations in teaching. Try to think through an answer before reading how an experienced teacher has addressed the problem of what to do. Then read the author's evaluation of the solution. In this way, you will have the opportunity to "try out" some of your own potential solutions to problems related to the subject being discussed in the text.

Think It Throughs help you try out some of your own ideas about how to solve problems.

In addition to these features, the text and course pose interesting problems for you to solve. On your own, you might analyze this text or your educational psychology course for its applications of psychological principles through instructional strategies. Your teacher will be demonstrating some of the techniques described in this text quite consciously as a model teacher. Teaching thinking is not just what is being talked about in the textbook. It is what the course is intended to *do.*

The Learning Journal

Problems are often found in the richness (and confusion!) of experience. A strategy to help you learn to identify and reflect on problematic aspects of your experience is available in the *Learning Journal,* a daily writing experience designed to help you develop reflective habits of thought. More particularly, the

learning journal

Purposes of the assignment

To apply principles of development and learning to events and experiences in life, and to analyze personal experiences in light of principles of development and learning.

Directions for the assignment

1. The assignment calls for *writing* daily for fifteen minutes, Mondays through Thursdays, while you are studying principles of development and learning. You should date each entry.

2. Write to apply or discover principles of learning that can be found in the chapter that you are currently studying. Do not ignore other principles that may apply or be discovered in a given experience, but focus on those of current interest in your textbook.

3. Use a pen, rather than a pencil, because pen is easier to read. Think before you write, but do not bother to recopy. Journal entries are required, but they do not call for polished writing.

4. Each entry should be a narrative, with a beginning, middle, and end. *In each journal entry, describe:*

   - what led up to your experience,
   - the principle(s) of development or learning involved,
   - how the principle(s) applied, and
   - the outcome (if relevant).

   The subject of the entries might one day be something noted in the development of a niece or nephew, or a student of yours. Another day it might be about yourself. The topics of journal entries should be personal, but not private. The journal assignment is designed to be flexible, and your instructor may provide additional topics or readings for your response.

Helpful suggestions

- For the first week or two, you should become familiar with principles of development or learning in the chapter you are studying before you analyze experiences. Applications of principles in your experience that occur to you in class are excellent material for journal entries.

- After a week or two, try to write about something you experienced or observed *today* that manifested at least one of these principles of development or learning. As you begin to analyze experience for principles, your topics should narrow and become more manageable.

- As you learn more principles, and improve in your analytic skills, try to analyze current experiences for *all* relevant principles. Do not keep searching for the same principle, or just one principle, in experience. Usually, developmental or learning experiences involve more than one principle at the same time!

objectives for the assignment are to (1) apply principles of development and learning to events and experiences in your life, and (2) analyze experiences you have had for principles of development or learning.

The Learning Journal is a challenging assignment, but it could be a valuable experience in your preservice teacher education program. Students have reported that it has helped make educational psychology relevant to their lives as well as to their professional development. Some students have elected to keep making entries, even after the assignment is over. The "LJ" can help you become reflective on experience in a way that gives you an enhanced appreciation of the content of the course.

CONCLUSION

As teaching reorients itself from a profession concerned with the transmission of knowledge to one that develops thinking skills in addition to transmitting knowledge, there will be more emphasis on critical examination and evaluation of broad claims of worth that in educational circles are known as "panaceas." No method is a cure-all to teach thinking in the schools, and you should be skeptical of anyone selling a method of problem solving, decision making, or critical thinking who claims to improve these skills without a lot of hard work.

Accordingly, this text cannot develop your problem-solving skills without your carefully aimed effort and the support of your teacher education program. The chapter structure and thinking skills exercises featured in this text exist only as hypotheses—untried solutions—without your active participation and experimentation. They certainly will not succeed without your best effort. Consider the features as "exercise stations" to challenge problem-solving skills. If you take the time and effort to stop and use them, they should help you to develop as a reflective teacher. That is how this text can best serve you.

What will make the task easier for you is your considerable fund of background knowledge about learning in school. You have encountered potential difficulties in learning and teachers who have helped you by anticipating them or resolving them. None of the subjects, case studies, or questions in this text will be completely unfamiliar to you. What you will be asked to develop, however, is a new perspective on familiar events. The new perspective is that of the teacher as problem solver.

concept paper

How I See Myself as a Teacher

Objective of the assignment

To analyze past experiences for core pedagogical values.

(Continued on next page)

(Concept Paper, continued)

Directions for the assignment

1. As a prewriting exercise, describe three *specific* experiences that you believe were *crucial to your decision to become a teacher.* These might be experiences you had as a child or as an adult, as a learner or as a teacher.

   a. Be as specific as possible, but use no more than a page to describe each experience.
   b. Recount each experience as a narrative; that is, it should have a beginning, middle, and an end.
   c. Attach these pages as an appendix to your paper.

2. In a three- to four-page paper, identify *what you value in a teacher* through details of these experiences. Core values will tend to be manifested in all three experiences.

   a. In an introductory paragraph, briefly describe what you essentially value in a teacher.
   b. Identify the sources of the core value(s) in at least three supporting paragraphs, at least one paragraph for each value.
   c. In a conclusion, briefly indicate what you plan to do in the next year that is consistent with these values. Include a specific description of any tactic to attain this goal.

3. Do not forget to attach the descriptions of your three experiences as an appendix to your paper.

SUMMARY

1. A problem should be considered a challenge, not an obstacle, because it is simply an unfinished situation that requires resolution.

2. The major problems-as-challenges that you will face as a teacher have four different but related focuses: instruction, motivation, management, and assessment. Your solutions to these problems will consist of strategies targeted to one or more of these areas.

3. Problem solving happens over a period of time and within several stages. For this reason, it is called a process. The problem-solving model that we will use in this book has five stages: identifying a problem, representing the problem, gathering information, generating a solution, and trying out and evaluating the solution.

4. Using the problem-solving process is particularly important for teachers because teaching problems are *ill-defined*—that is, their solutions are not automatic.

5. Becoming a reflective practitioner is an important goal for a teacher. Reflection involves constantly observing, considering, and evaluating teaching practices in order to solve problems-as-challenges.

6. This book is set up to help you in three specific ways to become an active problem solver in the classroom: as an information source, as a demonstration of the problem-solving process, and as a poser of problems-as-challenges addressed to you.

KEY TERMS

problem p. 6
problem-solving process p. 13
well-defined problems p. 14
ill-defined problems p. 14
problem identification p. 15
problem representation p. 16

SUGGESTED RESOURCES

The following books will help you become oriented to both learning and teaching as problem-solving activities:

Bruer, J. T. 1993. *Schools for Thought.* Cambridge, Mass.: MIT Press. Summarizes very clearly the new synthesis of theory on how students learn. Problem solving in core content areas is featured.

Clark, C. M., and P. L. Peterson. 1986. "Teachers' Thought Processes." In *Handbook of Research on Teaching.* Ed. M. C. Wittrock. 3rd ed., pp. 255–296. New York: Macmillan. Summarizes research on teacher thinking. This chapter has been a common point of departure for many recent studies.

Dewey, J. 1933. *How We Think.* Lexington, Mass.: D. C. Heath. Presents in everyday language some powerful ideas about thinking. At its core is an analysis of reflection as a stagelike, problem-solving process.

Schön, D. 1983. *The Reflective Practitioner.* New York: Basic Books. Applies Dewey's concept of reflection to the way professionals think about complex tasks such as teaching. A touchstone for much discussion by educators in the last decade.

The Development of Reflective Teaching: Becoming a Better Problem Solver

Orientation

The goal of this chapter is to help you build your knowledge of the process of *reflection* and learn how the development of reflective teaching can make you a better problem solver. You will be introduced to two pathways in which your ability as a reflective problem solver can develop—the *deepening* of your capabilities as you grow from a novice to an expert and the *broadening* of the focus of your reflections to include issues larger than those inside your own classroom. As you read, look for answers to these questions:

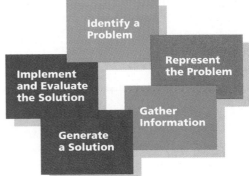

- **Why is it crucial that reflection develop by *both* deepening and broadening?**

- **What are two models for the deepening of reflection and how do their stages compare?**

- **What role do teaching routines play in a teacher's development?**

- **How do the thinking and problem solving of a novice teacher differ from the thinking and problem solving of an expert teacher?**

- **What are the defining features of each of the three arenas of reflection?**

- **What is the most important question that a teacher should keep asking in order to develop into a genuinely reflective teacher?**

CHANGES IN A TEACHER'S THINKING

This chapter is really about *you* and your growth as a teacher. It will focus on your development as a reflective problem solver in the classroom. This chapter will heighten your awareness of *development,* or progressive change, in reflective teaching at the beginning of your career. Perhaps as much as practice itself, awareness of your *potential* for development as a reflective teacher will empower you to become a better problem solver.

This chapter will also continue your introduction to learning to become a problem solver. In Chapter 1, you learned about problem solving and how problem solving can affect teaching. In this chapter, you will focus on your own potential to reflect and grow as a problem solver so that you will be ready to focus on different problems-as-challenges that you will face in your classroom during the course of your career.

Don't let the relative slimness of this chapter fool you. It is a very important chapter because it is about your own journey as a teacher. Taking that journey at the pace it requires and being patient with yourself along the way are the most fundamental steps toward attaining your ultimate goal—helping individual students learn.

Take a minute to think back to your best teachers. What impressed you most about them? Their mastery of subject matter and their skill in teaching it? Their sense of fairness in dealing with a group? Their interest in you as an individual learner? Although such characteristics may have some foundation in personality, research tells us that to a great extent, they can and do develop while one becomes a teacher.

Realize that although you may begin with many concerns, you will not be able to address them all at once. In Greek mythology, Athena, who was goddess of the arts, crafts, and war, sprang forth from the head of Zeus fully prepared for battle. No teacher develops that way! Research tells us that some of your deepest concerns as a beginning teacher are for individual learners, probably because your best teachers treated you as an individual. Most likely, you will have a chance to get to know some individual students well during tutorials or small-group instruction prior to student teaching, but when you actually begin your teaching on a whole-group basis, you will probably need to concentrate on more basic issues such as lesson planning and group management techniques. This will allow you to progress one step at a time toward your long-term goal (Kagan, 1992).

In the following discussion we will explore in more detail just how you can expect to grow as a teacher.

> Teachers need to develop their skills in problem solving.

> Good teachers acquire their skills gradually.

Different Pathways to Growth

Hard work does not lead to better teaching unless there are "shifts" in a teacher's thinking. Consider for a moment how you make a car with a gear shift go faster. By pressing the pedal under your foot, you can make the *engine* go faster, but to make the car go faster, you need to engage in first gear, gain a little speed, then shift to second gear to make the car go faster still. Becoming a teacher who is a better problem solver is a little like shifting the gears of a car. You can become only a little better before you have to "shift gears" to become a lot better.

> Shifting to new ways of thinking can improve problem solving.

What are the shifts that teacher thinking goes through? To consider how teacher thinking develops, we need to reconsider the nature of reflection. In Chapter 1, *reflection* was defined as active, persistent, and careful consideration of any belief or thought in light of its grounds or implications (Dewey, 1933). Reflection is careful thinking.

In Chapter 1 we also discussed a teacher's reflection, or careful thinking, in terms of our five-stage model of problem solving. This model describes reflection as a set of general procedures so that it can be enacted more easily than if it were described in any other way. One of the exciting discoveries we will explore in this chapter is that although reflection using these general problem-solving procedures will certainly help you as a novice teacher to devise and implement your teaching strategies, ultimately its use is *not* limited to the development of such strategies. As we will see, reflection can address a wide variety of pedagogical and even ethical concerns.

> Experience leads to solving some problems without conscious thought.

In fact, as problem solving and reflecting become more and more effective, the conscious process of devising a solution to familiar or typical problems should disappear because you have accumulated experience with similar problems. Their solution becomes a routine way of handling repeated situations, and this in turn frees you up to consider deeper and broader problems-as-challenges. Your thoughts and considerations shift to new problems (problems that increasingly focus reflection on the welfare of the learner) as reflection continues, and thus you grow as a teacher.

Where do these new problems come from and how do they evolve? There seem to be many possible sources (cf. Burden, 1990), but two stand out as major strands or pathways. They are the best known and most frequently studied.

> Teachers should both deepen thinking processes and broaden their ability to reflect critically.

The first pathway to your development as a teacher can best be characterized as the journey from novice to expert; it involves the *deepening* of your thinking as a teacher and the development of **expertise,** which is a high degree of skill or knowledge in a specific domain. The second is the evolution from a teacher concerned with immediate issues of his or her own classroom to a teacher who can ponder that classroom in relation to the larger world; it involves the *broadening* of your thinking as a teacher. This kind of focusing on problems of wider scope does not call for expertise, but for what philosophers call **critical reflection,** or the evaluation of practices in terms of their moral and ethical implications. These pathways will provide you with a road map for career development throughout your life, but first we will use them in this chapter as the primary organizers for our exploration of teacher development.

With practice, routine problems—such as how to motivate students—become easier to solve. Note that this teacher is not having difficulty motivating participation. What are some details that tell you his classroom is an interesting place? *(Mary Kate Denny/ PhotoEdit)*

Before we launch into that exploration, let's look at the reflections of a real-life beginning teacher in order to help you visualize the journey of teacher development more sharply.

Reflections on Beginning Teaching

A first-year, seventh-grade teacher named "Kerrie" recorded her reflections on beginning teaching in a series of interviews (Bullough, 1989). A nontraditional student in college, Kerrie was a twenty-nine-year-old mother of two children. This is how she described her dream of becoming a teacher:

> I always wanted to be a teacher. [As a child, my girlfriend and I] played school all summer long. [I was always the] teacher. We had a nonexistent [class] that we were handing out work to. Sometimes we'd drag in my girlfriend's brothers to be the students. They'd have to be sent to the principal all the time because they were bad. I liked organizing things like my desk. Getting my mom to buy me a roll book. Going around looking through my house at things that I could put on my tv tray which would be my desk. Lining up chairs. Assigning names . . . writing on the chalkboard. (pp. 2–3)

Later, as a preservice teacher, Kerrie's image of what teaching would be like was not so different from her dream. Teaching would involve planning, establishing routines, and maintaining order. Being a mother also influenced how she thought of teaching. She wanted to nurture individual students and their happiness. This idealized image of herself as a teacher represented a response to the typical concerns of beginning teachers—ranging from basic issues of survival to deeper issues of student learning.

Planning must include management issues as well as curriculum.

This image was tested during her first year as a teacher. Although Kerrie had imagined discipline problems and had learned management techniques, she had not developed a strategy to resolve situations that called for management planning (Bullough, 1989, p. 25):

> I don't know [why I didn't think about it]. I think that I thought that if you planned the curriculum really well, the management just falls into place. I really thought that when I was student teaching. If you are not well planned you are *going* to have problems, but planning [instruction] well doesn't solve those problems, you still have [management problems]. At first—I'm changing this idea a lot—I thought more that you could plan your curriculum and [good] behavior would fall into place; you could handle it as it comes. But you really can't. The other half of planning is what you will require at the same time behaviorally and you can plan for that. Now [sixth month], I plan a lot more things, like transition time and walking into the other room [to check on the students].

Kerrie had anticipated the need to plan instruction, but she had not anticipated a parallel need to plan a management strategy (see Chapter 13). As Kerrie discovered, the goal of having a smoothly running classroom is an ambitious one for most beginning teachers.

Confidence about management issues allows focus on other teaching concerns.

By the end of the first year of teaching, however, Kerrie's concern for basic survival issues had largely been resolved. An in-service workshop on management during the first few weeks helped her focus on the relevant problem area, and she began to develop and try out management strategies to cope with situations that would arise daily. As she became a better problem solver in this area, she gained greater confidence. With confidence came renewed interest in mastering teaching (Bullough, 1989, p. 40):

> I went to lunch today and said, "This is the best day I've ever had in my life!" I feel that quite often. Gee, I have really fun things for them [to do]. They're on it, they're on task and they're understanding it . . . and they like school! My morning kids like school!

By the end of her first year, Kerrie was able to shift her focus from basic survival issues to the mastery of teaching. A renewed sense of control had changed the focus of her concerns.

You may well be able to relate to Kerrie's early image of herself as a teacher and to the lack of a management plan that made her first year get off to a rocky start. However, even if you can't relate to these specific details, you have probably envisioned yourself as a teacher dealing with different situations and have formed your own fairly firm image of the teacher you want to be.

Inevitably, this image will be tested in early teaching experiences by the realities of your teaching situation. Throughout these experiences it will be important for you to remember that the meeting of immediate demands is only a foundation for further development. Although relatively little research has been done in this area, exemplary teachers seem to develop a personal philosophy of teaching. This philosophy will be a natural outgrowth of the deepening and broadening your thinking as a teacher undergoes.

The best teachers develop their own philosophy of teaching.

DEEPENING YOUR THINKING AS A TEACHER

With increasing experience and proficiency, your reflection as a teacher will progress to new challenges. In this section we will look at challenges that involve a teacher's increasing *depth* of reflection, or ability to make refinements in how to teach, by looking at two different well-known models. After exploring the models in some detail and then comparing and contrasting them, we will examine them specifically for their interpretation of problem solving. This section will conclude with a brief description of what an expert teacher's thinking and problem solving are really like.

Two Models of a Teacher's Developing Depth

The first of the two models we will explore here is organized around the different levels of concern addressed by teachers as they progress in their careers. The second is a model built on five common stages in the development of expertise. They each have something quite different, but complementary, to say to us about the progress you can make as a teacher as you develop from a brand-new intern to a confident expert.

A Model of Teacher Concerns

How do the concerns that occupy a teacher's attention and thought vary in relation to that teacher's years of experience in the classroom? How do

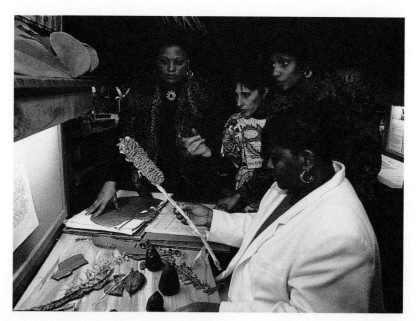

Sometimes an in-service workshop is the best way to focus on a relevant problem area, such as developing plans for instruction, motivation, or management. Here teachers study the wildlife of a rainforest to gather ideas about how to make geography exciting for students. *(Sisse Brimberg/ National Geographic Society Image Collection)*

teachers make the shifts we have been talking about and develop into expert teachers? The first model of teacher concerns (Fuller & Brown, 1975) summarized early theory and research on these questions. This model has three principal levels: a *survival* level, in which the predominant concern is classroom management; a *mastery* level, in which the focus is on improving performance; and a level of *learner needs*, in which concerns cluster around individuals' learning or well-being. The different levels of teaching concern are summarized in Table 2.1.

> Teachers can progress through three levels of concerns: survival, mastery, and learner needs.

Table 2.1   Areas of Concern for Preservice Teachers

Concern	Definition	Example
Survival	Problems of learning climate occupy attention	Need for management planning and development of classroom coping skills
Mastery	Problems arise from expectations of teaching	Preparation of materials, pacing of lessons, workload
Learner needs	Problems of students are the focus	Depth of student understanding, meeting social or emotional needs

Source: Adapted from Fuller & Brown, 1975

Like Kerrie, whom you met earlier in the chapter, and like most preservice teachers, you now probably share all three levels of concern (Guillaume & Rudney, 1993), but you may be able to address them progressively only as your skills as a teacher develop. Let's briefly look at each of these levels below, and look as well at the establishment of *routines* that develop as the levels evolve.

Survival.   Early concerns about *survival*, such as keeping students on task and dealing with unruly behavior, stem from contemplating and going through the first actual teaching experience, which is usually an internship. Survival concerns center on management. A new teacher must find a way to create a climate that is conducive to learning, and develop a smoothly running classroom. Concerns about survival tend to diminish by the time the internship is over.

> Concentration on survival gives way to mastery of teaching.

Mastery.   Concerns about *mastery* of teaching, however, are more likely to focus on the varied demands of teaching different lessons, and the need for methods and materials to meet expectations. Mastery concerns seem to be more persistent than survival concerns. They focus on managing your time and that of your students, and on compiling all sorts of materials and strategies to adapt teaching to different situations. The end result of mastery concerns is generally greater flexibility and increased confidence as a teacher.

By the time a teacher has passed through the survival level and has achieved a mastery level, **routines**—repeated actions that do not require much attention—are typically well in place. In fact, establishing them is a pivotal step along the road to your becoming an expert teacher. These routines—such as taking attendance, reviewing a previous lesson, and even asking "why" questions—play a major role in structuring transitions and activities in a class.

Routines take careful planning and practice to develop, but they allow responses to situations to occur more rapidly and with less attention than before. The net effect of routines is to free attention for other matters. Routines typically begin as solutions to core problems (Scardamalia & Bereiter, 1989) that, once resolved, need no longer occupy a teacher's time or thought. There is more to discover about routines as we explore the second model of a teacher's developing depth and the rest of this chapter.

> Developing routines will free a teacher for other concerns.

Learner Needs.   Last to be addressed are *needs of individual learners*. As you have already discovered, in the early stages of your career you will probably be interested in helping individual learners, but you will spend most of your time preparing lessons and materials, managing the class, establishing a schedule, assigning and distributing work and, in many cases, collecting, marking, and returning work. Your situation and your priorities will probably force you to attend more to what you are doing than to meeting the cognitive, social, and emotional needs of individuals. As you have already seen in the case of Kerrie, that focus on your task is natural. Later, when you have established supportive routines, you will be able to devote much more time and attention to the various needs of individual learners. (See Reflection on Practice: Focus on Learner Needs, page 40.)

> Experienced teachers can give more attention to individual students.

A Model of the Development of Expertise

As we know, beginners certainly do not become experts overnight. The second model of skill development (Dreyfus & Dreyfus, 1986) describes five stages in learning to solve problems in any domain in which problems are not well defined. Teaching is such a domain. In the Dreyfus model, the stages are called *beginner, advanced beginner, competent performer, proficient performer*, and *expert*. Key characteristics of these stages are summarized in Table 2.2, on page 41. Let's briefly look at each stage in turn, beginning with a very general description, then relating it to teaching.

> Teachers develop through five stages from beginner to expert.

Beginner.   A beginner or novice in any domain of learning in which problems are not well defined learns facts and rules and how to apply them. These facts and rules do not seem to arise from a particular context. When applying these rules in the interest of developing a skill, the learner judges performance by how well they are followed.

A beginning teacher acquires knowledge of facts and rules in preservice education courses. Facts might include all types of constructed knowledge in

reflection on practice

Focus on Learner Needs

After teaching for many years, I have had the opportunity to form personal opinions about effective teaching based on sound theory and research. I no longer use teachers' editions as guides to develop lesson plans. Instead, I spend my time and energy creating plans that match the needs of my students and my philosophy. For example, I believe that vocabulary knowledge requires an emphasis on pronunciation, meaning, and application of information. Therefore, I create a variety of context activities, such as having students write meaningful sentences to learn vocabulary words. I utilize my own activities because the philosophy advocated by teachers' editions may be inconsistent with what is needed by my students and what I know to be effective practice.

Sometimes this approach creates a dilemma. Colleagues sometimes will say that I am being too innovative. Parents question if their children aren't doing what children in other classrooms are doing. I can handle these criticisms as long as I know that the strategies I use promote positive, lifelong reading habits. This is a personal and professional goal that I have for every student in my class.

Greg Risner

Discussion Questions

1. **What evidence do you find that this teacher is focused on learner needs, rather than survival or mastery?**

2. **How might his reflection have been different at earlier stages of concern? What evidence do you find that earlier concerns have been resolved?**

3. **Note that concern for learner needs results in some dilemmas. What does a teacher need to manage such dilemmas successfully?**

Beginners concentrate on learning facts and rules.

the areas of history of education, pedagogy or methods, and principles of psychology. The beginner might acquire these facts in any number of ways, but increasingly, observation of and reflection about pupils or teachers will supplement textbook presentations as a source of facts. Rules might include procedures or formats of various kinds, some of which are quite general and others of which are very specific. Like facts, rules can be acquired in different ways, including textbook presentation, observation, and reflection. Because the novice lacks practice in applying facts and rules, however, these tools do not lead directly to the development of teaching routines.

Advanced beginners see facts in context and apply rules flexibly.

Advanced Beginner.   Real situations provide a learner an opportunity to practice a skill until it becomes an acceptable performance. An advanced beginner begins to acquire knowledge on the basis of past experience as well as new experience. This stage of skill learning involves recognizing facts in context and responding to them on the basis of previous experience.

Table 2.2　The Development of Expertise

Stage	Description
Beginner	Focus on learning facts and rules foundational to development of skills
Advanced beginner	Focus on recognizing facts in context and on practicing skills based on experience in applying rules
Competent performer	Focus on using skills flexibly to solve problems
Proficient performer	Focus on recognizing patterns and developing routines
Expert	Focus on using skills intuitively for routine situations

Source: Adapted from Dreyfus & Dreyfus, 1986

A teacher who is an advanced beginner has experienced enough teaching to apply rules but is still developing flexibility in their application. Practical knowledge or "know-how" is beginning to develop. This new form of knowledge primarily involves (1) recognizing facts in context and (2) recognizing when to apply rules. An advanced beginner discovers, for example, that when young children are fussy or easily upset, they are usually tired or hungry. The beginner, on the other hand, might have learned these facts earlier in a psychology course but still interprets fussiness as a problem of order (management) rather than of needs (motivation).

Competent Performer.　The competent performer demonstrates even greater flexibility in the use of a skill. This individual calls on a hierarchy for decision making that allows a learner to use a skill effectively to solve problems of various kinds. Such performance is highly goal directed, and the focus of learning shifts from applying facts or rules to using them in achieving goals.

In teaching, problematic situations frequently overlap. A student may cause a disruption at the other side of the room while a teacher is conducting a reading lesson with a small group. Teachers who are competent performers are able to decide which of several competing problems needs to be addressed first. They are able to set priorities so that multiple goals can be met.

> Competent performers set priorities and achieve goals.

Proficient Performer.　The proficient performer is able to respond to problematic situations without as much deliberation as before. Experience with similar situations has taught this teacher what to look for and how to respond effectively. Routines are now in place that help him or her react efficiently.

A teacher who is a proficient performer recognizes patterns in class situations that are familiar through experience. Such patterns may involve the behavior of groups or individuals. For example, if questions by students before

> Proficient performers recognize patterns and respond routinely.

a test indicate a lack of preparation, the teacher spontaneously elaborates answers to conduct a mini-review before the test. Or if a student's answer to a question indicates difficulty in understanding material, the teacher spontaneously generates clarifying examples until the student understands better than before. In neither case does this teacher's response require much deliberation; it requires knowledge and skills developed through previous successful teaching experience, out of which routines develop.

Expert. Expertise is a knowledge of what to do that is based on mature understanding. In the routine use of their skills, experts intuitively do what works. Because an expert typically does not need to stop what he or she is doing and deliberate, very few interruptions or delays occur. Response to many problematic situations at this level is guided not by rules or procedures but by doing what has worked in the past. However, experts do stop to deliberate when problems are unusual or outcomes are critical.

> Experts can act intuitively in most situations.

An expert teacher has available many routines (sometimes also called *scripts*) that handily resolve most problematic situations (Leinhardt, 1988). As we have already seen, these routines do not require much attention to perform. Normally, a teacher can do something else simultaneously, such as discuss assignments (while distributing them) or address questions to the group (while monitoring the activity of individuals). An expert teacher achieves routine goals spontaneously and engages in active problem solving only to resolve nonroutine or extremely important problems.

A Comparison of the Two Models

To enhance your understanding of these two models and of the underlying process of teacher development, it might be helpful to compare and contrast the two models. Take a moment to study Table 2.3. One of the first things you'll probably notice is that the second model has five stages and the first model has only three. This difference represents only a matter of refinement, however, because the two additional stages in the second model—advanced beginner and proficient performer—are in essence *transitional* stages. You'll

Table 2.3 How the Development of Teacher Concerns Compares with the Development of Expertise

Focus of Teacher Concern	Stage of Expertise
Survival	Beginner
	Advanced beginner
Mastery	Competent performer
	Proficient performer
Learner needs	Expert

deepening your knowledge base

Using the Models Together to Explain the Development of Teaching Routines

Let's use your knowledge of how the stages of the two models mesh. In the following description of how teaching routines develop, notice how the models complement and enhance each other. (Refer to the figure as you read.) Routines for management permit a beginner to shift concerns from survival to mastery, because survival is no longer threatened. The beginner is free to develop competence as a teacher. Similarly, routines for instruction permit a competent performer to shift from mastery to a focus on learner needs, because mastery of teaching is no longer a challenge. The competent performer is free to develop expertise as a teacher. In this way, the beginner develops into a competent performer, and the competent performer into an expert. The figure below shows how teacher concerns and routines change over time.

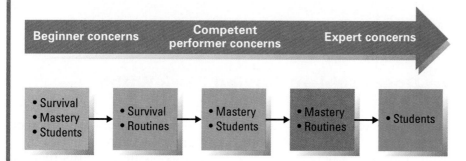

Discussion Questions

1. Why does management tend to take priority over other concerns of a beginning teacher, such as instruction, motivation, and assessment?

2. Think of a minor management problem (such as a child talking out of turn or being out of his or her seat) that you recently saw an experienced teacher resolve. Did the teacher have a routine way of resolving it? How do you know?

3. Do you think that an expert teacher develops routines for meeting learner needs? Explain.

find that the other stages of the models match up fairly well. A teacher who is a beginner focuses on survival; a teacher who is a competent performer focuses on mastery; and a teacher who is an expert focuses on learner needs.

There is one area of significant difference between the two models, and that is the treatment of problem solving. Because this is such an important topic in this book, we will take a longer look in the next section at the way each model handles problem solving and at how that treatment works within our common understanding of the process.

Two models of teacher development are roughly comparable.

Expert teachers often focus on the needs of individual learners. This kindergarten teacher is transcribing a student's words to illustrate her drawings. *(Elizabeth Crews)*

How Does Problem Solving Work Within the Models?

Of the two models, the first—the model of teacher concerns—best matches up with problem solving as described in Chapter 1. As you'll notice by reviewing Table 2.1, page 38, the very definitions of the concerns that face teachers, at each of the three stages, are phrased in terms of problems. Another way to put this is to say that this model acknowledges the presence of problem solving throughout professional development. The complexity and depth of the problems teachers are handling and resolving changes from level to level, but all teachers—beginners through experts—engage in problem solving.

The model of teacher concerns states that all teachers solve problems at some level.

As you know from the discussion of problem solving in Chapter 1, the position taken in this book is similar to that shown in the first model. From their early, preservice days right through their later years, all teachers face problems-as-challenges in their classrooms. What changes is the kinds of problems teachers are able to take on and the capabilities they bring to resolving them. The second model presented here, the development-of-expertise model, differs both from the viewpoint of this text and from that of the model of teacher concerns. Let's define the differences and briefly explore what might account for them.

The developmental model holds that beginners and experts are less involved in solving problems.

According to the developmental model of expertise, problem solving is not a common activity for beginning teachers. They are more concerned with simply learning facts and applying rules. Problem solving slowly increases in importance until the stage of competence, where it peaks. Afterward, as teachers become experts who have already resolved so many routine problems that they have their scripts in place, problem solving declines in importance. If you look back to Table 2.2, you'll notice that the only reference to problem solving occurs in the competent performer stage. Other stages are concerned with other activities. If these changes in the relative importance of problem solving are placed on a graph, they resemble an inverted U (see Figure 2.1).

As you look at this figure, reflect for a moment about the kind of graphic image of problem solving that would be generated by the position of this text or by the position of the model of teacher concerns. The difference is dramatic. How could the model of expertise, which has so much to tell us about teacher development, be so discrepant from another widely held view with respect to problem solving? How could a well-accepted model demonstrate the position that both beginning teachers and expert teachers don't spend much time solving problems, which is often perceived to be such a core activity? There are a number of possible explanations. Let's look at two here. Examining them should help us not only to answer these questions but to deepen our understanding of problem solving as well.

First, the model of expertise is focused on reflection *in* action (Schön, 1983). That is, the type of teacher activity examined by the Dreyfuses was primarily the kind that occurs as a teacher deals with immediate situations in the classroom. This is quite different from reflection *on* action, which involves solving problems prospectively (through planning) and retrospectively (in hindsight). It turns out that if we look only at the kind of problem solving that occurs in the immediate moment (that is, reflection in action), we would indeed find the course of an inverted U. A beginning teacher cannot think in class as quickly and flexibly as a more experienced teacher (Borko & Livingston, 1989). An expert teacher has already had to meet many similar challenges and is able to respond quickly and almost automatically. In between these two ends of the curve, the competent teacher is actively solving problems all the time.

But, as you know, reflection in action is by no means the whole picture. Novice or beginning teachers generally spend more time planning than more experienced teachers do, and their plans are generally more detailed than those of more experienced teachers (Borko & Livingston, 1989). Further, re-

> Beginners solve problems through planning and reflecting.

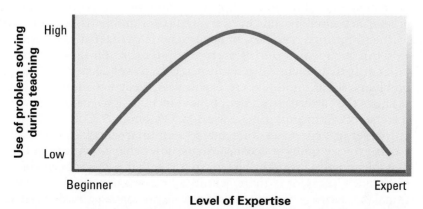

**Figure 2.1
Problem Solving in the Dreyfus Model of Expertise**

flection on action is not limited to planning but often occurs retrospectively (after teaching has occurred) through discussion of cases. Thus, when the full picture is taken into consideration, the position that novice teachers are indeed problem solving from the beginning can coexist with the model of the development of expertise.

What about the other end of the curve, however? How do we explain the model's position that an expert teacher engages in much less problem solving than a less experienced teacher? This seems a troubling conclusion, especially in light of my position in this book that a real goal for your development as a teacher is to become an expert problem solver. Indeed, the image of a *non-reflective* expert would be a portrait of someone with a diminished capacity for self-criticism because he or she claimed privileged knowledge (Welker, 1991). We have all encountered this type of individual, who is extremely competent but who is also unable to develop further through self-criticism—certainly not the kind of teacher I would encourage you to become!

The answer to the troubling questions lies, I believe, in the narrow concept of problem solving and limited definition of problems that the model is based on. That is, the Dreyfuses' model focuses primarily on the kind of problem solving that results in the establishment of *routines* in the classroom. If you think back to our earlier discussions of routines, you will remember that these are essential processes that need to be set in place before teachers feel able to focus on learner needs.

> Expert teachers are free to solve problems of a higher order.

If we cast our view beyond routines and define the activity of problem solving in a way that incorporates problems of self-evaluation as well as the needs of individual learners, we see that expert teachers do indeed solve problems. In fact, we see that they're freed up *by* routines to tackle problems that may be difficult to resolve at the beginning of a career.

Let's continue this discussion of the characteristics of an expert teacher in the discussion of expertise that follows.

Thinking as an Expert Teacher

How does the knowledge of experts differ from the knowledge of novices or beginners? One of the most important differences is that the knowledge of experts is activated by the "deep structure" of problems because experts have learned to ignore "surface" or superficial features (Chi, Feltovich & Glaser, 1981). In other words, during the problem-representation stage, experts reflect differently than novices by rapidly perceiving the "deep structure" of teaching problems. For example, expert teachers can recognize more easily than novice teachers the patterns in student behaviors that signal a management problem (Peterson & Comeaux, 1987; Swanson, O'Connor & Cooney, 1990).

> Expert teachers more easily recognize the essence of a problem.

In a sense, experts do not need to "spin their wheels." They can recognize a pattern very quickly because they know what is typical and what is predictable in a situation (they have what is called a sense of *typicality*). Thus, if a student's behavior is more genuinely a management issue than a motivational one, expert teachers can more easily recognize this deep structure. Furthermore, because they have at their fingertips the teaching routines we have already discussed, they are quickly able to engage appropriate, successful routines whenever a pattern develops that calls for the routine. In addition, as you have seen, the routines free an expert teacher's attention for other matters—usually deeper matters having to do with an individual student's needs and the teacher's own growth and knowledge.

These characteristics and others were described by David Berliner and his research team in a landmark study that used the Dreyfuses' model as a point of departure (Berliner, 1986; Carter, Cushing, Sabers, Stein & Berliner, 1988; Carter, Sabers, Cushing, Pinnegar & Berliner, 1987; Cushing, Sabers & Berliner, 1992). They compared the skills of expert secondary math and science teachers (selected on the basis of at least five years' experience teaching, recommendations by principals, and their own observations) with the skills of beginners and advanced beginners in terms of solving teaching problems. The results of the study are summarized below and in Table 2.4.

First, beginners and advanced beginners relied on information provided about students more than did experts, who relied on their own experience to guide their actions. Experts often either quickly interpreted a situation or adopted a wait and see attitude. Second, evaluative comments made by beginners and advanced beginners while they were observing teaching episodes often focused on control and management. Evaluative comments by experts for the same episodes focused on monitoring students and on how to enhance student learning. Third, beginners and advanced beginners seemed to be interested in getting information about specific students so that they could group the students. By way of contrast, experts possessed a sense of typicality that allowed them to respond almost automatically to a wide range of individuals and situations. More than beginners or advanced beginners, experts knew what to expect.

> Experts use their own experience and focus on learning enhancement.

The phrase "almost automatically" may have a negative ring, but it shouldn't. Keep in mind that there has been no evidence to suggest that expert teachers are any less reflective than other teachers, except with respect to routine problems. One key may be that teachers who develop continue to do so not only in terms of the depth of their concerns but also in terms of the *breadth* of their reflections.

Table 2.4 Differences Found Between Novices and Experts

Novices	Experts
Used provided information to plan	Ignored provided information and relied on past experiences
Focused on control and management	Focused on monitoring student learning
Used information to label or group learners	Used sense of *typicality* to respond to situations
Source: Cushing, Sabers & Berliner, 1992	

think it through

Consider this problem that a novice preservice teacher has IDENTIFIED and REPRESENTED.

Orienting a New Student

I am a beginning second-grade teacher. School has been in session for six weeks. The principal brings a new student into my classroom. The principal informs me that the student is from South America and speaks no English. My question to the master teacher is, How do I handle this situation? Where do I start with the student?

Observe how an experienced practicing teacher GENERATES SOLUTIONS to this problem.

With six weeks of school completed, your students are settled into your daily routine and teaching style. You have also had an opportunity to learn your students' academic and behavioral strengths.

Your first responsibility is to let this student know you are glad to have him or her in your classroom. Facial expressions and hand gestures will communicate that to the student. After settling the student into a desk area, you should find a buddy in the classroom who you feel will be able to help the student with movement through the building to special classes, lunch, and so on, and help him or her in the classroom. If you have Spanish as one of your special-area classes, you might have the Spanish teacher visit your classroom to facilitate translation.

For the daily class activities you will need to assist the student with materials, and so forth. Math should be an area in which language will not be a problem. You will continue to speak to the student and guide his or her activities with language and gestures. At the end of the day, you will want to check for a resource person in the area who will be able to help with tutoring for the student. I am told by friends who have taught Spanish-speaking students that the children are language-mainstreamed into the classes and they do learn to function in English.

Mava Barfield
Morrilton, Arkansas

think it through, continued

EVALUATE this problem's possible multiple solutions while you think about the dynamic process of problem solving.

Did you notice how decisively the teacher addressed the immediate situation, but how she also used available resources to adapt instruction to the needs of the learner? According to Berliner's research, such complex thinking is characteristic of expert teachers.

This teacher expects a student who enters the class after six weeks to lack information about class procedures, so she has a routine for solving this problem. The routine involves making the new student feel welcome and assigning a hand-picked student as a "buddy." The help of a buddy ensures that all kinds of learning will be scaffolded for the new student, and that the new student will have a friend. The advantages of such peer teaching will be discussed further in Chapter 5.

What is *not* routine in this situation is that this particular new student is limited-English-proficient (LEP; a category of student described in Chapter 7). Along with more than half of all teachers in the United States, this teacher has never had an LEP student in class before. Eleven percent of LEP students receive federal assistance through bilingual education programs, but about one out of four LEP students in the United States receives no language assistance at all (McKeon, 1994). This student is fortunate to have a teacher who focuses on the student's communication needs.

The teacher develops a strategy based on available resources. Because the principal brought the student to the teacher, we can assume that there is no bilingual education program in this school. Consequently, the resource person would be more likely to be a counselor than an ESL (English as a second language) teacher. The resource person might arrange for the LEP student to receive assistance under Chapter 1, a federally funded program for disadvantaged learners (see Chapter 7 of this book), and find a volunteer to tutor the LEP student in some specific subjects.

The teacher's openness is characteristic of expert teachers. This openness will provide her with many opportunities to support the child's development of language and academic skills, to bridge instruction with previous learning, and to learn about another culture. Indeed, the whole class might benefit from an enhanced strand of multicultural education throughout the year.

The teacher ends by raising and answering the question of whether or not the LEP student will be able to succeed in an all-English classroom. This question is important and underscores why we need to accommodate learner needs. Without support, the LEP student is at a distinct disadvantage and might not be able to keep up with instruction. Content learning is much more difficult in a second-language environment than in a first-language environment. However, with support from (1) the teacher, (2) a resource person, (3) an aide or a tutor, and (4) a buddy, the LEP student will be at less of a disadvantage and will probably cope successfully with the situation.

We can conclude from Berliner's research that expert teachers tend to deal with *typical* problems in decisive ways. They are also open to experience when they face challenges that are *not* typical. This complex blend of decisiveness and openness to experience is well illustrated by this teacher's response to a difficult challenge.

A beginning teacher relies more on information provided about students than does an expert teacher, who relies more on memory of relevant experiences.
(Janice Rubin/Black Star)

BROADENING YOUR THINKING AS A TEACHER

So far, you have seen how thinking can deepen in the course of developing from a beginner to an expert. Another way that thinking can develop is through acquisition of different *types* of reflection.

As you have seen in the first half of this chapter, *reflection* is often used to describe teachers' consideration of the actual act of teaching, or "what happened, why it happened, and what else they could have done to reach their goals" (Gore, 1987, p. 36). The Dreyfuses' model, for example, largely confines itself to this type of reflection. Other educators, however, have used reflection in a broader way—to include considerations of ethical and moral issues in relation to practice.

If you visualize the developmental path we discussed in the first part of the chapter as steps on a ladder, then in comparison you might envision this form of reflective development as concentric circles that keep widening, something like ripples moving outward from where a pebble has been thrown into a still pool of water. In fact, the different types of reflection we will discuss here have been described as representing concentric "arenas of the problematic" (Tom, 1985). Each arena encompasses problems of different scope. As teachers broaden the focus of their reflections, they move on from considering the more limited concerns of strategy or technique and are ultimately capable of *critical reflection*, which, as you will see, involves quite a different kind of reflecting.

> Teachers can broaden the focus of their reflections.

The first section below will define and examine three commonly accepted arenas of reflection. The next section will explore how the problem-solving process operates within each arena. The last section will look at the development that teachers experience as they progress from one arena to the next.

Arenas of Reflection

Based on the ideas of the German philosopher Jurgen Habermas (1974), three arenas of reflection have been identified (Van Manen, 1977) and are frequently referred to. They are labeled *technical, practical,* and *critical.* **Technical reflection** involves consideration of teaching strategies to achieve goals or objectives. **Practical reflection** involves consideration of the relation between values and teaching practices. **Critical reflection** involves consideration of broad moral and ethical questions related to teaching. These three arenas correspond with different types of teaching concerns that can occur either separately or simultaneously. Technical considerations are the narrowest in scope, and critical considerations are the broadest (see Figure 2.2). Let's examine each type of reflection for what it can tell us about the development of teacher thinking.

Technical Reflection

Novice teachers often use technical reflection in order to develop efficient and effective teaching practices. Here is an example of technical reflection from a student teacher's postlesson journal entry (Gipe & Richards, 1992, p. 55):

> When I used declarative statements, the children didn't respond. It seemed that by giving them a direct statement, they believed that what I said was truth. When I used "wait time," one girl thought I was mad. They are too young and too inexperienced to understand that I wanted them to elaborate. Now I know that I have to guide them through a discussion.

This reflection involved the problem of how to teach thinking to a group of pupils, and the awareness that declarative statements were insufficient to achieve that goal. Here an unmet goal or problem was found (how to teach thinking), and a solution or plan was developed for the future (guiding students through a discussion). The goal did not change, but the student teacher developed a strategy to achieve it. Such considerations are technical because

Figure 2.2
Arenas of Reflection
(Adapted from Tom, 1985)

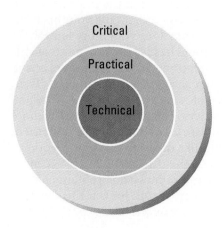

Technical reflection involves achieving given ends, but the strategies teachers use to achieve them can still be quite innovative. What kind of learning activity are these teachers engaging in to develop new ideas for teaching their students about the ocean? *(Lauren Greenfield)*

they are limited to a focus on the strategy to achieve a given goal. The goal itself (teaching thinking) was never questioned.

Let's look at another example of technical reflection by a student teacher, this time in the area of motivation (Gipe & Richards, 1992, p. 56):

> I still don't see why everyone thinks that Sam is such a good teacher. His class seems kind of dull to me. I think visuals in upper levels would help generate interest in the topics and stimulate a desire to learn. Why doesn't he let the students decorate the class with their work?

This reflection concerned the motivational practices of a cooperating teacher, with an implied goal (generating interest) and an explicit strategy for achieving it ("let the students decorate the class with their work"). The focus of the student teacher is on the development of a strategy to attain a goal, not on whether the curriculum goal should be changed. For that kind of reflection, we must look to the second arena of reflection.

> **Technical reflection focuses on the strategy to achieve a given goal.**

Practical Reflection

The second arena of reflection, often described as practical reflection, includes problems of identifying *ends* that are consistent with pedagogical values ("What should I be teaching?"). As its name suggests, practical reflection involves considering the relation of pedagogical values to practice, and vice versa. We could say that technical reflection involves considering how to fulfill the expectations of others (teaching effectively), while practical reflection involves considering how to fulfill one's own expectations (teaching congruently). For example, here is a math teacher's self-assessment of a lesson that

> **Practical reflection considers how to achieve one's own goals in teaching.**

relates curriculum to pedagogical values, not just strategy to goal (Brodkey, 1993, p. 66):

> I would say that I have to contrast the direct variation with inverse variation [two subjects in the math curriculum], and the place to do that is to move this section out of where it is and . . . contrast it with direct variation. So that, I would say, is the big thing, that's the big thing learned. Next year this section should be taught with direct variation about three months earlier in the year. Or [I should] save direct variation for now. It doesn't make sense to split them up; the contrast is lost. That is a big thing to learn, and I hope I remember it.

The "big thing learned" is an indication of a solution to a larger problem than one of technique or strategy. The teacher learned that textbook material or curriculum objectives need to be sequenced differently to bring practice in line with what the teacher perceived to be sound pedagogy.

Or let's take the example of a teacher recently trained to use problem solving to reflect on personal teaching practices (Morris-Curtin, as cited in Sparks-Langer & Colton, 1991). The teacher's goal was to bring practices in line with pedagogical values (p. 42):

> I think the most notable change for me was the ability to start backing away from the need to get an immediate solution to a problem. Instead, by using the problem solving/reflective framing format, I really feel like I'm giving the wealth of knowledge I possess about my profession a chance to come more fully into play. . . . There is something magical and very personal in all of this. Like finally finding just the right word for a poem you've worked on for ages.

The practice that was brought in line was the use of problem solving, which this teacher had previously used only in a technical way. After being trained to conduct inquiry into his or her own practice, the teacher uses problem solving in a more full and personal way, so that it serves the teacher's pedagogical values.

Recall that the result of practical reflection is *congruent* teaching. Can you see how initial practices that do not embody the pedagogical values of the teacher are *incongruent* with them? Practical reflection leads a teacher to alter initial practices until they serve the teacher's values.

Critical Reflection

Critical reflection involves ethical and moral questions about teaching.

The third level of reflection, often described as critical reflection, includes consideration of pedagogical values and practices in relation to wider *ethical* or *moral* questions ("What greater good do I serve?"). If technical reflection involves others' expectations (teaching effectively), and if practical reflection involves your own expectations for teaching (teaching congruently), critical reflection involves discovering expectations of what is good (teaching morally).

In order to reflect critically, a teacher needs to begin by searching for the social roots of personal actions. As a teacher examines personal teaching practices for their social causes, the teacher is in essence ferreting out the social goals that are built into personal pedagogical values and strategies. A teacher who engages in introspection or discussion of personal teaching practices in terms of social values can become aware of hidden assumptions that run counter to widely held moral standards such as equity or compassion. A teacher might become aware of prejudice against certain groups, intolerance of alternative points of view, or aversion to students' independent thinking or collaboration. What leads a teacher to change these teaching practices is an awareness that they do not measure up to widely held moral standards. (To further explore the impact of prejudice on teaching, see Reflection on Practice: Inequity in Teaching Practices, page 56).

In order to discover the social grounds of your practices, you must be willing to conduct a dialogue about these practices with others or to engage in self-critical reflection. Sometimes the incidents that precipitate your dialogue or self-examination will be, on the surface, quite minor or merely puzzling. If you are willing to probe these incidents, you are far more likely to change your practices to *make* them conform to ethical or moral standards than you would be if you did not develop awareness of the social causes of your actions.

> Self-criticism and dialogue with others can contribute to critical reflection.

How Does the Problem-Solving Process Operate Within the Arenas?

The problem-solving process operates somewhat differently within each of the three arenas. We will use this section to explore briefly those operations. First, let's consider problem solving within the technical arena. This is the primary type of problem solving featured in this book. It is built around the model or template for reflection that was introduced in Chapter 1. This kind of problem solving, which focuses on questions such as "How do I teach _____?" or "How do I manage _____?", is often described as technical because it involves establishing *means* or strategies to achieve given ends. That is, the basic, implied question in this arena is: "What works?" These kinds of problems require a fair amount of thought for a novice teacher to solve; thus, they will be the focus of this book and of much of your preservice training.

> Technical problem solving looks for the means to achieve a given end.

Undoubtedly, you will also be dealing with problems within the practical arena. Practical problems are incongruities or inconsistencies between a personal theory of teaching and what is actually done while teaching. Resolving the problem means reducing the incongruity or inconsistency. The problem-solving process can also be a tool for resolving such incongruities between personal theory and practice.

> Practical problem solving seeks out ways to make teaching practices fit one's goals.

The process of solving practical problems differs from that of solving technical problems in that practical problems are generally more difficult to discover than are technical ones. Thus, the process involves actively seeking out problems—problem finding—as well as coming up with a means of resolving apparent problems. Practical problems are often found through

reflection on practice

Inequity in Teaching Practices

The [kindergarten] teacher is not particularly gentle [during rest period time]. She snaps at the ones who squirm around—"Relax!" and "Sleep!"—and forces down their arms and knees. . . .

After 30 minutes pass, the teacher tells the children to sit up. Five of the boys who were most restless suddenly are sound asleep. The others sit up. The teacher tells them, "Folded hands!" They fold their hands. "Wiggle your toes!" They wiggle their toes. "Touch your nose!" They touch their noses.

The teacher questions them about a trip they made the week before. "Where did we go?" The children answer, "Farm!" "What did we see?" The children answer, "Sheep!" "What did we feed them?" A child yells out, "Soup!" The teacher reproves him: "You weren't there. What is the right answer?" The other children answer, "Corn!"

In a somewhat mechanical way, the teacher lifts a picture book of Mother Goose and flips the pages as the children sit before her on the rug.

"Mary had a little lamb, its fleece was white as snow. . . . Old Mother Hubbard went to the cupboard to fetch her poor dog a bone. . . . Jack and Jill went up the hill. . . . This little piggy went to market. . . ."

The children recite the verses with her as she turns the pages of the book. She's not very warm or animated as she does it, but the children are obedient and seem to like the fun of showing that they know the words. The book looks worn and old, as if the teacher's used it many, many years, and it shows no signs of adaptation to the race of the black children in the school. Mary is white. Old Mother Hubbard is white. Jack is white. Jill is white. Little Jack Horner is white. Mother Goose is white. Only Mother Hubbard's dog is black.

"Baa, baa, black sheep," the teacher reads, "have you any wool?" The children answer: "Yessir, yessir, three bags full. One for my master. . . ." The master is white. The sheep are black.

Four little boys are still asleep on the green rug an hour later when I leave the room. I stand at the door and look at the children, most of whom are sitting at a table now to have their milk. Nine years from now, most of these children will go on to Manley High School, an enormous, ugly building just a block away that has a graduation rate of 38 percent.

Jonathan Kozol, 1991, pp. 44–45

Discussion Questions

1. What specific teaching practices illustrate inequity between the teacher and students? How do these practices make the children in this school, most of whom are African American, feel about themselves?

2. Why does Kozol link the inequities that underlie practices in this inner-city kindergarten class with the graduation rate from the local high school? What different types of connection could there be?

3. If you were a substitute teacher assigned indefinitely to this class the next day, what are some short-term goals that you might establish? Specifically, what are some activities that you might use to achieve them?

discussion with other teachers or supervisors, some form of structured or unstructured self-assessment, or research on one's own teaching practices (Griffiths & Tann, 1992; Kent, 1993). For example, a teacher might discover and resolve practical problems in this general way (Whitehead, 1989, p. 43):

- I experience problems when my educational values are negated in my practice.
- I imagine ways of overcoming my problems.
- I act on a chosen solution.
- I evaluate the outcomes of my actions.
- I modify my problems, ideas and actions in light of my evaluations (and the cycle continues) . . . .

In practical reflection, problem finding and solving improve the relation between educational values and teaching practices.

Within the arena of critical reflection, the whole balance shifts. Problem finding now becomes the *primary* problem-solving activity as the focus shifts to the social causes of teaching practices and widely held moral standards. The process of critical reflection may even be limited to a particular type of problem finding called **problematizing** (Freire, 1972) in which questions are asked about the social causes of one's own actions. Problematizing might begin with questions such as these (Smyth, 1992, p. 299):

> Problem finding is the primary activity in critical reflection.

- What do my practices say about my assumptions, values, and beliefs about teaching?
- Where did these ideas come from?
- What social practices are expressed in these ideas?
- What causes me to maintain my theories?
- What views of power do they embody?
- Whose interests seem to be served by my practices?
- What acts to constrain my views of what is possible in teaching?

Through problematizing, a teacher can discover the social causes of his or her own teaching practices. If these grounds fall short of moral and ethical standards for equity or compassion, most teachers will "do the right thing" by changing teaching practices to adhere more closely to the standard.

Table 2.5 on page 58 should provide you with a helpful means of comparing the various focuses of problem solving within the three arenas.

Learning to Become a Versatile Thinker

How do we learn to reflect more broadly on our teaching? Reflection takes a long time to develop fully. It must have a foundation in basic thinking skills (described in Chapter 10) and a supportive environment. It does not develop in isolation or without support. This situation should not discourage you but challenge you to engage in reflective exercises and to value supportive environments, including this class and your teacher education program.

> Skill in reflecting develops over a long time and with outside support.

Table 2.5   Problem Solving Within the Arenas of Reflective Teaching

Arena of Reflection	Type of Teaching	Focus of Problem Solving	Key Question
Technical	Effective	Problem solving	"What works?"
Practical	Congruent	Problem finding and solving	"What should I be teaching?"
Critical	Moral	Problem finding (problematizing)	"What greater good do I serve?"

To a beginning teacher, technical reflection is crucial for developing teaching effectiveness. Novice teachers who practice technical reflection improve their teaching skills more rapidly than those who do not (Gipe & Richards, 1992; McIntyre & Pape, 1993; Simmons & Wild, 1992). The evidence also suggests that technical reflection gradually declines as a priority after the internship (Gipe & Richards, 1992; Guillaume & Rudney, 1993; Pigge & Marso, 1987). Teachers develop routines that permit reflection to focus on concerns other than survival or even the demands of the teaching situation.

There are several pitfalls along the way, however, and unless you actively work at it there are no guarantees that reflective thinking will continue to broaden. For instance, a surprising number of beginning teachers never achieve even a technical level of reflection because they "rely on instinct" or simply "try to fit in." Reliance on instinct usually signals trial-and-error learning, and fitting in usually signals imitation of a cooperative teacher, without much regard for improvement of teaching or learning (Calderhead, 1989). In neither case does thinking develop.

Even a teacher who feels comfortable with technical reflection and has routines in place faces a hurdle. Ironically, the confidence and security offered by successful routines may block further development of reflection. As one teacher commented, "If it works, why fix it?" (Brodkey, 1993, p. 70). The inertia of "what works" can limit the broadening of reflection so that little concern about wider issues develops. Even those beginning teachers who are concerned about wider issues do not necessarily develop the ability to analyze events in terms of sound pedagogical principles (Sparks-Langer, et al., 1990).

What then is the key to being able to broaden one's thinking as a teacher? The answer is that reflective teaching seems to develop most easily in teachers who are disposed all along to ask why questions about their own practices and the practices of others (Goodman, 1988; LaBoskey, 1994). Such questions can prompt reflection, and the more often reflection occurs, the more likely it is to develop. Asking why can lead you to search for what works and to design effective strategies. It can also lead you to search for congruence between your values and practices. Finally, asking why can lead you to search for the moral grounds of your practices, and to affirm or reform them in light of what you find.

> Reflective teaching develops from questioning one's own and others' practices.

Your Own Reflections on the Route to Becoming a Versatile Thinker

There are strong arguments to suggest that as a beginning teacher you should learn to reflect first about "what works." Thus, while other kinds of reflection will be included throughout this book, the problem solving featured is primarily focused on the technical arena. Despite the strong arguments for this position, however, it does not represent the views of all researchers, and there is no real consensus on when the arenas of problem solving should be developed. While many educators argue that the wider arenas should be delayed until you have more technical experience as a teacher, others argue that examination of experience for implicit values and moral implications needs to occur *before* routines are established (Liston & Zeichner, 1987).

The lack of consensus among educators about which route to take to critical reflection can provide you with an intriguing reflection in and of itself. Pair yourself with another student in your class and agree to take one position or the other (that is, either that the focus of reflection should broaden steadily outward from technical to practical to critical or, on the other hand, that values and morals should be the central focus at the very beginning). After each of you has written a defense of your chosen position, compare papers and arguments.

Asking yourself why in different arenas requires a versatility of thinking that is not automatic. It has to be developed. As yet, we know very little about precisely how to develop versatility in thinking as a teacher, but we do know that the surest route to becoming a "set-in-your-ways" kind of teacher is to allow yourself to go along without examining and questioning your experience. Keep observing yourself and your actions as a teacher; continue asking yourself why you made one decision and not another. In these ways you will open the door to self-growth.

CONCLUSION

There is no disagreement about one conclusion: you should not stop thinking as a teacher as long as you are a teacher. The establishment of teaching routines will give you opportunities for professional development well into your career. You need to take advantage of these opportunities to reconsider your practices in light of new learning. In our society, an expert who does not continue to learn soon loses any claim to expertise. An old hand at teaching once told me, "Never stop thinking." Today, as a middle-aged teacher, I consider that pretty good advice for a new teacher. Never stop thinking.

A second conclusion that an increasing number of educators agree on is that depth *and* breadth of thinking are both desirable goals of professional development. Depth of thinking (thinking as an expert) without breadth risks narrowness, or a sort of technical proficiency that does not develop further. Breadth of thinking (versatile use of reflection) without depth risks superficiality, or an inability to find or solve problems of any type competently, let alone proficiently. What is necessary for mature development of teaching skills is both depth and breadth of thinking.

There is much that teacher educators do not yet know about how to achieve this goal, but your knowledge of this goal is significant for its attainment. That is, the more that you expect developments of these types to occur, the more likely it is that they will occur. In itself, awareness is not enough to result in development, but progressive change in thinking will rarely occur without awareness of a goal. People do not wake up one day to find themselves reflective teachers. Reflection is goal directed, effortful thinking, and the more that teachers understand its grounds and ends, the more likely they are to want to engage in it in order to become *better* problem solvers. If you are like me, studying a destination and planning a journey will lead you to want to travel.

concept paper

A Critique of "Reflective Teaching"

Purpose of the assignment

To analyze and evaluate a concept of reflective teaching

Directions for the assignment

1. Reflective teaching means different things to different people. Obtain a copy of an article about reflective teaching that was published within a calendar year of the date that your assignment is due. Consult *Education Index* or the ERIC index under "reflective teaching," or look in recent issues of journals suggested by your teacher.

2. Bring your article to your teacher to verify that the subject is reflective teaching and not some related subject.

3. Analyze the concept of reflective teaching in your article in terms of (1) the development of expertise, and (2) the broadening of the scope of reflection.

   a. How does reflective teaching as discussed in the article compare or contrast with problem solving by beginning, competent, and expert teachers, as discussed in this chapter?

   b. How does reflective teaching as discussed in the article compare or contrast with technical, practical, and critical reflection, as discussed in this chapter?

4. In a three- to four-page paper, critique the author's concept of reflective teaching by reviewing its strengths and weaknesses in light of your analysis. Does the author's concept of reflective teaching take into account

differences among beginning, competent, and expert teachers? Does it include technical, practical, *and* critical reflection?

5. Be sure to attach the copy of the article as an appendix to your paper.

SUMMARY

1. Development is progressive change. Your growth as a teacher will be based on your development as a reflective problem solver.
2. There are two major pathways for growth: a) deepening of your thinking as a teacher and the development of expertise and b) the broadening of your thinking and the development of critical reflection.
3. According to one model, a teacher deepens reflective thinking by moving from concerns of survival to those of mastery of performance to, finally, a genuine focus on his or her students' needs as learners. According to a second model, deepening thinking is defined by five stages: beginner, advanced beginner, competent performer, proficient performer, and expert.
4. An important step toward expertise is the establishment of routines. Once you have routines in place to handle many situations, you will be freed up to focus on the deeper problems-as-challenges your students will present.
5. Expert teachers approach problems differently from novices. By rapidly perceiving the "deep structure" of teaching problems, they can discern what a problem is all about. They can also call upon greater experience with similar situations to solve a problem once it is identified.
6. Broadening your thinking as a teacher, the second pathway to growth, occurs as you widen the scope of the issues and problems that you are able to reflect upon in your teaching. There are three arenas of reflection, each progressively more inclusive: technical, practical, and critical.
7. A versatile thinker is one who can reflect deeply and broadly. There is no one route to achieving this versatility, which is really a lifelong journey, but the key seems to be the ability to ask "why" of oneself and others, all along the way.

KEY TERMS

expertise p. 34

routines p. 39

technical reflection p. 52

practical reflection p. 52

critical reflection p. 52

problematizing p. 57

SUGGESTED RESOURCES

The following readings offer interesting points of departure for further inquiry into teacher development:

Bullough, R. V. 1989. *First-year Teacher: A Case Study.* New York: Teachers College. Describes the transformation of Kerrie into a confident teacher during her first two years of teaching. A good case to study if you want to reflect on some of the problems-as-challenges met by beginning teachers.

Burden, P. R. 1990. "Teacher Development." In *Handbook of Research on Teacher Education* (pp. 311–328). Ed. W. R. Houston. New York: Macmillan. Surveys different models of teacher development. Teacher education programs generally use such models to map out programs of study and learning experiences.

Goodman, J. 1988. "The Political Tactics and Teaching Strategies of Reflective, Active Preservice Teachers." *Elementary School Journal*, 89, 23–41. Describes practical ways student teachers deal with pressures to conform to existing practices in schools. A useful guide for avoiding thoughtless conformity.

Sparks-Langer, G. M., and A. B. Colton. 1991. "Synthesis of Research on Teachers' Reflective Thinking." *Educational Leadership*, 48 (6), 37–44. Summarizes research during the late 1980s on the development of reflective thinking. A highly readable article with a very useful reference list.

Chapter 3

Planning Instruction: Getting Started as a Problem Solver

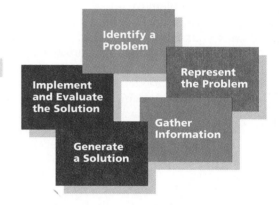

Orientation

The goals of this chapter are to familiarize you with the process of instructional planning and to help you understand why this process is such a good example of the problem-solving cycle. You will learn about educational goals and objectives as they relate to real-life planning, and you will find that thoughtful planning includes selecting instructional activities that genuinely address the objectives you have set yourself. As you read, look for answers to these questions:

- **How does the five-stage problem-solving model match up with a popular three-step problem-solving process for planning?**

- **What are two common planning styles and how do they differ?**

- **Why are objectives categorized into groupings called *taxonomies*?**

- **How can you use these taxonomies to identify *givens* in your teaching situation?**

- **What are two formats for writing objectives and how do they differ?**

- **How does the composition of objectives help you to clarify goals?**

- **How can you be sure that your instructional activities actually address your objectives?**

PROBLEM SOLVING AND INSTRUCTIONAL PLANNING

In Chapter 1, you learned about problem solving and how it applies to teaching. In Chapter 2, you learned about how to deepen and broaden your problem-solving skills as a teacher. In this chapter, which completes your introduction to becoming a problem solver, you will learn how teachers apply problem solving to instructional planning. The planning needs and practices of beginning teachers, however, are somewhat different from the planning needs and practices of more experienced teachers. Because you are at the beginning of your career, the focus of this chapter is on what a beginning teacher needs to learn about instructional planning in order to be successful.

Planning is crucial for successful teaching, but as a student, you almost never saw planning occur. In elementary school, you probably knew that most teachers had a planning book as well as a grade book. Perhaps the planning book was a thin, black, spiral-bound calendar on the teacher's desk, but you probably never saw what was written in it. By high school, you were probably aware that teachers had "planning periods" during which they could be found in their offices reading or grading papers, or in the school office running off copies of worksheets or tests, but still, you never really saw teachers plan. Planning is an important skill for a beginning teacher to master, but because it was hidden from you while you were a student, you never had a chance to learn about it. In this chapter, you will learn about the skill of planning instruction.

A teacher spends a lot of time each week on planning. An elementary teacher often spends between ten and twenty hours per week planning activities. A high school teacher will often have three or more courses to "prep," or prepare, each day. So much time devoted to planning may raise an immediate question in your mind: What can you hope to gain as a teacher from your planning?

I believe that you'll find that the most important and valuable outcome of planning is organization. Reflect once again about your own experiences as a student: at some time, undoubtedly, you have experienced a lesson that was not well organized, and you probably recall that little learning occurred in this situation. The lesson was over your head or covered what you already knew; necessary equipment was missing or in short supply; learning was delayed by procedural matters or a lot time off task; and so on. Such lessons are often the result of insufficient planning by the teacher. You have also undoubtedly experienced many lessons that were well organized: the lesson was at your level; learning began shortly after you arrived and continued until the end of the period; equipment was available; and so forth. Well-organized lessons are an outcome of adequate planning.

> Planning is a necessary part of successful teaching.

> The most valuable result of planning is good organization.

You'll also find that planning reduces anxiety and increases confidence (Clark & Peterson, 1986). Thoughtful planning can harness some of the very natural anxiety that most teachers (especially new teachers) experience as they think about facing a new class, and these feelings can act to motivate preparations. The felt outcome (what you perceive and feel in the situation) of having made these preparations will be a reduction in your anxiety. You are ready to teach.

> Teachers who plan well are less anxious and more confident.

Your anticipated outcomes for your students should also improve your confidence. In planning for your students' learning, you will have created a set of positive expectations for yourself as a teacher. These expectations will boost your confidence. Almost certainly, you will be eager to try out your ideas. Now that you have a clearer sense of the benefits of planning, you may still be wondering about something very fundamental concerning all that time teachers spend in planning: Quite simply, what do teachers actually do when they plan?

A significant amount of planning time is taken up with review of content to be taught. Whether planning for a year or for a single lesson, using unfamiliar or familiar material, teachers review content to transform it into what they will teach (Clark, 1988; Clark & Peterson, 1986). Such transformation becomes easier with experience, but it always takes a significant amount of time, even when you have taught the lesson before. Time spent reviewing content tends to decrease with experience, but even experienced teachers spend hours reviewing content as a part of their planning.

> Part of planning is concerned with course content.

Beyond reviewing content, teachers solve problems as they plan (Borko, Lalik & Tomchin, 1987; Calderhead, 1984, 1993). These problems include the full range of teaching problems—instruction, motivation, management, and assessment. The most common decisions concern activities that will engage learning (Zahorik, 1975). Experienced teachers and reflective beginning teachers also consider what might go wrong in activities and how to prevent or remedy the situation. Because planning involves so much problem solving over and above review of content, many educators consider it a model of problem solving or decision making by teachers. Another way to say this is that we can view the activity of instructional planning in and of itself as representing a full problem-solving cycle.

> Planning is an important way to solve or prevent problems.

Defining Key Planning Terms

Before you can begin to understand the planning process in any depth, there are two key terms that you must grasp—*goals* and *objectives*. These concepts are so important to planning that we'll devote a full section later in the chapter to the exploration of each.

Goals in education come in two formats. In their broadest sense, goals are wide ranging statements of purpose regarding what a community has decided its citizens should learn. These broadest goals are sometimes called *mission statements*. Most school districts and schools have mission statements. Directly derived from mission goals are unit goals, which pertain to a particular unit of study and are more closely linked to instruction in the classroom.

> Goals state a community's broad desires for educating its citizens.

These students in Fairfax, Virginia, are doing a science lab to analyze how much of their school's trash is recyclable (unit goal). What particular ends—or objectives—might they be achieving toward their goal? *(Annie Griffiths Belt/ National Geographic)*

Curriculum guides (which are compilations of goals and objectives) typically contain goal statements that are followed by **student educational objectives** (also known as instructional objectives or simply as objectives). Objectives are particular ends for student learning; they exist for programs, units, and individual lessons. They resemble goals in form and subject, but they are more specific than goals listed in the same documents.

Let's see how goals and objectives are related. One goal for a fifth-grade unit on physical science might be *understanding the practical applications of various concepts in physical science*. It is part of the school's broader mission of intellectual development. This particular unit goal includes understanding practical applications of many concepts of physical science, such as electricity and magnetism; sound, heat, and light; matter and energy; and machines and work. Under machines and work, you might find these instructional objectives:

> Objectives are specific ends that students will achieve in reaching goals.

- define work
- explain the units used to measure work
- calculate work
- demonstrate the principle of conservation of energy

These and other objectives define what is meant by understanding practical applications of work as a concept of physical science (see Table 3.1, page 66).

Table 3.1   Goals and Objectives

Mission goal	Intellectual development
Subject unit goal	Understanding the practical applications of various concepts in physical science
Topic objectives for machines and work	Define work
	Explain the units used to measure work
	Calculate work
	Demonstrate the principle of conservation of energy

Source: Adapted from State of Tennessee, *Science Curriculum Guide, Grade 5* , n.d., p. 1

I want to add a further comment about goals here. You'll recall that we've already discussed goals for problem solving at some length in Chapter 1. As you've probably realized, these kinds of goals and the educational planning goals described above are not identical. However, there is a relationship between planning goals and problem-solving goals; I'll be making this explicit in an upcoming discussion. In the interim, you might reflect on the possible relationships yourself, perhaps even jotting down some ideas.

Planning as a Problem-Solving Cycle

There is a very clear relationship between planning and problem solving. Planning—especially at the beginning of the year, but also at other times—establishes what some educators have called the **problem space,** or the range of choices that a decision maker must evaluate to achieve a goal (Clark & Peterson, 1986). In fact, one very helpful way to conceptualize planning is to say that teachers go through a problem-solving cycle at whatever level they are planning. One model developed by Robert Yinger (1980) includes a three-stage cycle that parallels the five stages of the problem-solving model used in this textbook (see Figure 3.1) Yinger labels his three stages *problem finding; problem formulation/solution;* and *implementation, evaluation,* and *routinization.* As you read the following discussion, which explores his stages, try to connect this new information to knowledge you have already gained about the problem-solving process.

> Planning establishes the choices necessary to achieving a goal.

Problem finding begins with the "general teaching dilemma" to which you were introduced in Chapter 1: "Here is your classroom. Here are your students. Teach them" (Yinger, 1980, pp. 115–116). This general challenge is limited by givens largely beyond the control of the classroom teacher, such as the classroom location, students' characteristics, available resources, and the district curriculum guide with its statement of goals and objectives for learning.

> Problem finding concerns the given conditions under which the teacher works.

Givens that *are* under your control influence the further development of the teaching dilemma as a specific *planning dilemma,* or a need to make preparations that take into consideration your knowledge about the subject

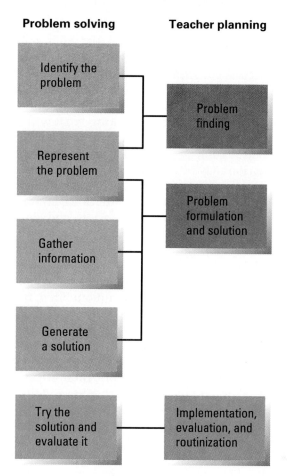

Figure 3.1
Problem Solving and Teacher Planning

Problem solving

- Identify the problem
- Represent the problem
- Gather information
- Generate a solution
- Try the solution and evaluate it

Teacher planning

- Problem finding
- Problem formulation and solution
- Implementation, evaluation, and routinization

matter and how to teach it, your personal teaching goals, and materials. These are the circumstances that are more toward the flexible end of the spectrum of givens. They are things you can change. For example, you can seek additional information about a given subject, alter your personal goals, or generate additional materials. The outcome of the first stage of planning is an initial representation of a problem, with clarified goals for the resolution of the problem; consequently, Yinger's conception of problem finding includes problem representing.

Before exploring Yinger's model further, let's take a moment to consider the relationship between curriculum goals, your personal teaching goals, and goals for resolution of the problem. *Curriculum goals* are typically part of the givens that confront you in a problem-solving situation. Your *personal teaching goals* are also part of the givens, but you exercise greater control over them. Your *problem-solving goal* is the outcome of an interaction between a number of factors, including goals in the curriculum guide (or textbook) and your beliefs about what you should teach (personal teaching goals). Your problem-solving goal, rather than the curriculum guide, determines what you will teach.

Curriculum goals interact with personal teaching goals.

Problem formulation/solution represents a design cycle in which problem representation, information gathering, and solution generation overlap one another. During this cycle, potential learning activities are investigated and analyzed as potential resolutions to the planning dilemma or challenge. A teacher may try out mentally some of the possibilities. Yinger (1980, p. 120) reported that one elementary teacher using this cycle imaginatively projected activities into her classroom, remarking "that will never go," "that might work," or "I can see right now that will never work." Potential activities are analyzed for their feasibility, and ideas that appear workable are elaborated. Further information may be gathered about procedures or the availability of equipment or materials to support the activity. At the end of this cycle, an activity is chosen and integrated into an instructional strategy to resolve the planning dilemma.

Implementation, evaluation, and *routinization* provide information on the usefulness of the activity and may lead to its adoption as a routine, its modification, or its rejection as a solution to the teaching dilemma. The larger scope of this stage of planning, in comparison to problem finding or the design cycle, is due to the need to enact a plan—not just to have one. As the instructional strategy is implemented, it is simultaneously evaluated for its effectiveness. As problems arise, the strategy is modified or "recycled." Notice that this stage is the equivalent of the fifth step in our model, which also includes implementation and evaluation.

Instructional strategies may be tried out for several days or weeks before a final decision is made about their effectiveness (Yinger, 1980). Some of the problems are resolved as students and the teacher become accustomed to the activities. Eventually, the activities either are discarded as unworkable or enter the routines of the students and their teacher.

Yinger's problem-solving model of teacher planning applies to instructional problems, but it can be applied to other aspects of teaching as well. The development of motivational, management, or assessment strategies can follow the same path (Yinger, 1980). Later chapters in this text will explore such applications. Yinger's model of planning is very useful because it is flexible enough to adapt to different areas of concern for beginning teachers, different types of planning, and different subject areas. It can explain how thoughtful planning occurs in virtually every aspect of teaching.

Types of Planning

How large are these planning cycles? The answer depends upon the extent of the learning experience. Planning is often done in relation to the calendar—the year, term, week, day, or even hour. *Annual planning* might include arranging the physical environment, developing or adopting a classroom management system, fitting the curriculum to the learning situation, correlating your plans with those of other teachers, developing a general schedule for each day and week, thinking back on what worked (and did not work) last year, and making arrangements for materials (Borko & Shavelson, 1990;

> Solutions are based on investigating and analyzing possible activities.

> Part of planning is evaluating new activities and modifying them when necessary.

> Planning for the year and for shorter periods will structure the class.

Daily planning often develops according to a general schedule set at the beginning of the year, but it includes last-minute changes and special preparations. Which items in this plan for Friday might appear every Friday? Which appear to be special for this particular day? *(David Young-Wolff)*

Earle, 1992). Annual planning is important because, in many ways, it structures the class.

Within this overall structure established at the beginning of the year is *term planning*, which has not been well researched, but almost certainly focuses on developing an assessment strategy and assigning six-weeks' grades. *Weekly planning* involves organizing around the Monday-through-Friday schedule. *Daily planning* involves last-minute changes in the schedule, or preparations to be made in the morning before school starts or during the day.

There is an additional way that teachers organize their planning—that is, on the basis of the curriculum. This kind of planning includes both unit and lesson planning. *Unit planning* involves the development of well-organized sequences of instructional experiences over several weeks. This type of planning focuses on identifying activities for students, including both learning activities and evaluation. According to surveys of experienced teachers, the most important type of planning within the year is this unit planning, followed by weekly planning and daily planning (Clark & Peterson, 1986).

Of lesser importance to an experienced teacher—but often a handy and even essential focus for a beginning teacher—is *lesson planning*, which concerns everything from the overall curriculum to individual textbook pages, as well as specific activities and the evaluation of learning. As a beginning teacher, you will almost certainly follow a prescribed format for your first lesson plans (including objectives, activities, and evaluation), and these prescribed elements will be the focus of your lesson planning.

As you gain experience, your lesson-plan entries—in planning books, on note cards, or even in the margins of textbooks—will probably become sketchy, because as your experience grows, most planning becomes mental.

> Unit planning develops well-organized sequences of instruction.

If you are like many expert teachers, your lesson plans will probably change into short lists of things to be done—by you, by your students, or by both you and your students. In fact, one way to describe this phenomenon is to say that most lesson plans of experienced teachers resemble short shopping lists (McCutcheon, 1980). The items on the lists—such as page numbers in a text or teachers' guide, or the names of specific activities—are sequenced, but they are only cues to jog memory.

> Experienced teachers can make lesson plans that are less comprehensive.

Now that you understand how planning relates to problem solving, and how planning cycles differ in extent, let's examine more closely the unit- and lesson-planning practices of teachers to see how they represent instructional problems. As you learned in Chapter 1, solving an instructional problem often depends on the way that you represent it. Representing a problem involves *identifying the givens in the situation* and *clarifying goals*. Identifying givens often involves recognizing the constraints or limitations on teaching. Clarifying goals, however, involves specifying what it is that you are trying to achieve. Although we can separate these two steps for analysis (as Yinger did in separating the general from the specific planning dilemma), they actually flow into one another. What occurs is a funneling of the different factors (some that you cannot control, and some that you can) into a representation of a problem as a challenge.

IDENTIFYING GIVENS IN THE CURRICULUM GUIDE

In this section, we want to focus on how you as a teacher can identify the givens in the curriculum guide as you plan. As you learned in the problem-solving model of teacher planning, three givens that are largely beyond your control are the location of the classroom, students' characteristics, and the district curriculum guide. Like other givens in this category, the district curriculum guide often represents an important constraint on instruction. How important is it? That question can be answered in two ways: through case studies of individual teachers, and through research on teachers' planning. First, let's look at case studies.

Case Studies of Teacher Planning: Sarah and Norma

Even if most teachers engage in problem solving as they plan, they still differ greatly in their planning practices. One teacher might use a large planning calendar, while another might use a matrix for each week, drawn on blank paper. One might fit most planning into planning periods, while another might plan in spare moments throughout the day. One might use the objectives in her grade-level curriculum guide as the primary organizers for her unit or lesson plans, while another might use a composite of objectives, themes, and instructional activities to focus and organize her plans.

> Teachers develop their own styles for planning.

While some of the differences among these practices might seem trivial, when taken as a whole these differences characterize an individual teacher's *planning style*. You will elaborate and discover your own planning style during the first few years of your teaching, and it will become one of the hallmarks of your own teaching. Because there is no one right or wrong style, let's look at two case studies—rather than just one—to identify how different teachers use curriculum guides in unit and lesson planning.

Robert Reiser and Edna Mory (1991) studied the planning practices of two fourth-grade teachers, each with over twenty years' teaching experience, who were regarded very highly by their principals. The teachers, who were called Sarah and Norma in the study, were at different schools within the same school district, but because the district used a uniform curriculum guide, they began planning with the same set of goals and objectives.

The researchers studied how the teachers planned a unit on scientific processes. The curriculum guide listed twenty-one objectives for the unit, such as:

- Record data on a chart or table
- Draw inferences from a set of observations
- Predict the outcome of an event based upon previously observed conditions

Further, the curriculum guide described ten activities that could be used to attain these objectives. Activities focused on *change* as a theme: how cities change over time, how putting ice in a soft drink changes both the ice and the soft drink, and so on. Each activity included a short list of objectives (drawn from the master list), a list of materials, a description of the activity, and a description of a related activity that students could do on their own.

Both Sarah and Norma planned units on scientific processes. Sarah used the objectives in the curriculum guide to plan daily lessons for a unit that ran four weeks for about one hour a day (a total of nineteen lessons). Although her planning was initially only mental, she recorded her plans on a weekly planning sheet, which was two full-sized sheets of paper divided into a matrix for the days (rows) and times of each day (columns). She taught science every day, and in the box for science she usually recorded objectives, activities, and a method of evaluation. She generally stated objectives in one or two words, giving them a kind of top billing in her planning box. Activities were not always specified (indicating to us that her written notes were cuing unrecorded mental plans).

In contrast, Norma had two sets of written plans—one a plan for the unit (consisting of four pages of notes) and the other daily lesson plans. The unit plan covered two weeks, about half the time that Sarah spent. The unit plan listed selected objectives from the curriculum guide, twelve vocabulary words, seven films or filmstrips, activities, and the materials needed for those activities. Lesson plans were recorded on a form that Norma had created, in which each day was divided into blocks of time. Although she had referred to the curriculum guide objectives for initial direction, Norma did not include them in her lesson planning block. Instead, in each day's block for

think it through

Consider this problem that a novice preservice teacher has **IDENTIFIED** and **REPRESENTED**.

Coping with the First Day

It is the first day of school and my first teaching job. I am a special education teacher, and I have only a few students in my classroom. The students walk into the classroom and sit down. I get up and introduce myself to them. Now it is time for me to begin teaching, and suddenly I feel completely helpless and unprepared. I don't have the slightest idea where to begin. The students quickly pick up on my insecurities.

What can I do to make sure that on my first day of teaching I do not feel so unprepared and insecure?

Observe how an experienced practicing teacher **GENERATES SOLUTIONS** to this problem.

There is some preparation that you, as a special education teacher, could do to help your first day run smoothly.

First, I feel you should get to know the policies and the procedures of your school district and school in dealing with discipline, homework, violence, and so on. This would involve your duties as a teacher, which are usually given to you by your principal.

Second, I would go to the files of each of my students and I would look in the files for any "flags" that would give me insight into my students. I would also look for possible abuse cases, custody cases, and so on. Along with this, I would talk to the previous teacher(s) of my students to get input into personality, what a student loves to do, and specific habits. It is *imperative*, however, that in this process you not form judgments on your students. You are merely gathering data to help you work with your students.

Third, I would find photographs of each of my students in the school yearbook and I would learn their names before they came into my classroom. In this way, I could greet them by their first name. This sends a message that I care. Also, I would write each student an individual letter telling that student that I am his or her teacher and I am looking forward to working with him or her.

Last, and of critical importance, is the planning of your day. Always overplan. Make sure that the work you are giving your students on the first day is work that is at their independent level and is motivational. Be sure to include activities that touch upon Howard Gardner's seven intelligences. In this way, you can assess strengths and weaknesses in your students. You especially want the first day to be positive so your students leave with a desire to return and a love of learning. Along with this, during the day, observe carefully the actions of all your students. This is your informal assessment of each of your students. It will guide you in preparing for the year. Allow some time during the day to have the students do an independent activity that does not require your supervision. In that time, spend three to five minutes with each student to find out about him or her. An inventory can also be given in writing. The inventory should include what they do in their free time, how they feel about school in general, what they would like to do at school, positive comments about teachers, and negative comments about teachers. Follow this up with a phone call to each parent that night.

In your planning, be sure you have your goals set for the year. What do you hope to accomplish for each student? In doing so, talk to other colleagues.

Be sure to tell your students that it is your first day and you feel nervous. They need to see you as a human also. Be confident in your presentation to them. Believe that you are the best person for them.

Evaluate your day to see what needs to be changed and what can continue. Again, make sure you plan to include activities from the seven intelligences so you can tap into the strengths of your students and teach the students the procedures in your classroom. Take the day slowly and don't push. Make sure everyone leaves knowing you care.

Perry Montoya
Lincoln Elementary School
Mesa, Arizona

think it through, continued

EVALUATE this problem's possible multiple solutions while you think about the dynamic process of problem solving.

Yinger's (1980) model of teacher planning can be used to analyze and to some extent to evaluate this advice. Notice, for example, how early *problem finding* (the first stage of the model) begins in relation to the first day of class. Locating school policies and identifying student characteristics from files is a response to the *general teaching dilemma*. This information about factors that are largely beyond the teacher's control will influence teaching practices in important ways.

The specific *planning dilemma* develops around what the teacher wants to achieve on the first day of class. Factors to consider include personal teaching goals, such as engaging students in activities and providing a range of activities to assess different types of ability. The representation of the problem that emerges focuses on (1) motivating students to learn and (2) assessing abilities.

What is missing in this description of the earliest stage of planning is an indication of the curriculum—either curriculum goals or what the teacher wants the students to achieve during the year. This absence is explained by the original question, which is about a new teacher's anxiety on the first day of teaching. Individualized Education Programs are constructed for all special education students, and they must include long-term goals and short-term objectives (described in Chapter 7), but these programs would have been drawn up by the previous teacher and would not relieve a new teacher's sense of unpreparedness.

The experienced teacher advises the new teacher to focus on motivational and assessment goals. Many of the particular suggestions for achieving these goals represent a *cycle of problem formulation and solution* (the second stage in Yinger's model). To motivate students, the teacher plans to (1) write a letter before the first day, sharing positive expectations with the students, and (2) study yearbook pictures in order to greet each child by name on the first day. Some of the activities (such as independent functioning) are also expected to be motivational.

To assess student abilities, the teacher advises using activities related to Gardner's seven intelligences, a model of intelligence developed by Howard Gardner (1983). Traditional intelligence tests assess linguistic-verbal abilities and logical-mathematical abilities, but Gardner argues that five other areas of intelligence should also be assessed and developed through school activities. These include spatial abilities, musical abilities, bodily-kinesthetic abilities, interpersonal abilities, and intrapersonal abilities (such as ability to know oneself). Opening up assessment and learning to a wider range of abilities affords special education students more opportunities to achieve than a narrowly focused curriculum does.

The advice to "evaluate your day to see what needs to be changed and what can continue" corresponds with the third stage in Yinger's model: *implementation, evaluation,* and *routinization.* A plan for motivation and assessment needs to be evaluated in those terms: Do students feel motivated to learn? Are activities diverse enough to reveal a wider range of student abilities than those revealed by test scores? Did the teacher observe areas of strength as well as weakness? If so, then teaching on the first day will have been successful.

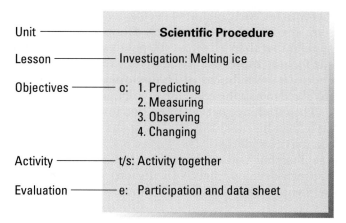

Figure 3.2
Sarah's Lesson Plan
(Adapted from Reiser & Mory, 1991)

science, Norma listed the theme (change), the textbook pages or the experiment used for the lesson and activities. Figure 3.2 is what one of Sarah's written lesson plans looked like. Figure 3.3 shows what one of Norma's lesson plans looked like. Although Norma's notes for activities, like Sarah's, are only cues for mental plans, you can see how much more prominent her activity descriptions are.

Let's examine the two lesson plans for what they reveal about these experienced teachers' different styles of planning. Sarah approached planning in a rational, linear way. For each lesson, she defined a few objectives from those listed in the curriculum guide, considered one or more activities to attain them, and devised a way to evaluate learning. She followed the **rational planning model**, in which (1) objectives are specified, (2) activities are considered, (3) activities are sequenced, and (4) evaluation procedures are designed (Tyler, 1950). The rational planning model is widely taught to beginning teachers, but it does not seem to conform to the planning practices of most experienced teachers (Clark, 1988).

Norma approached planning in a more holistic way. At the beginning she considered the objectives in the curriculum guide, but they were only one

> The rational planning model specifies objectives, then chooses activities to attain them.

Figure 3.3
Norma's Lesson Plan
(Adapted from Reiser & Mory, 1991)

factor in her early planning decisions. Developing a theme and identifying interesting activities were others. Her planning was recursive and resembled a spiral rather than a line. As she progressed in her planning from unit to lesson, she focused more on class activities than on stated objectives. This recursive approach might be called a **holistic planning model**, in which multiple factors involved in solving teaching problems are considered at the same time.

> The holistic planning model considers several factors, including objectives.

The difference between the two forms of planning was largely a matter of style. Sarah's planning was linear and analytical, and Norma's planning was recursive and holistic (see Figure 3.4). What is critical is not which style you use, but that you use planning time to represent teaching problems so that you can develop effective solutions. Curriculum goals and objectives can help you do that within very different styles of planning.

Research on Teachers' Use of Curriculum Guides

You have seen how two elementary teachers use curriculum guides in their planning, but what about other teachers? Do they use curriculum guides to help them represent instructional problems? To answer this question we need to broaden our view to take in research on other teachers' use of curriculum guides.

> Curriculum guides are becoming more influential in teachers' planning.

Thirty years ago, researchers found that teachers largely left curriculum guides on the shelf or in a desk drawer, but by the mid-1980s, this practice was changing. Investigations of influences on teacher planning began to find that at least some teachers were using published curriculum guides extensively to plan instruction (Brown, 1988; Duschl & Wright, 1989). In one study of the unit planning practices of middle school teachers, objectives listed in the district curriculum guide and in state competencies were found to influence planning

**Figure 3.4
Alternative Planning
Styles**

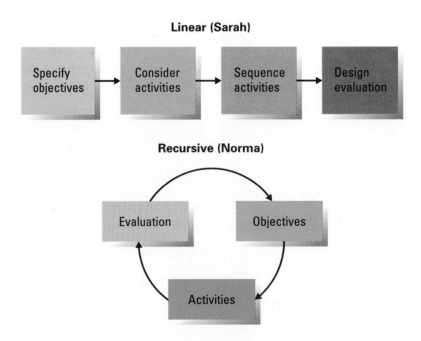

reflection on practice

Drawing a Hamburger

One of the greatest challenges I have as an art teacher is teaching kindergarten students that first lesson. My main objective is that all art students succeed. Anytime I plan a lesson I try to think as a child would think. I can remember how frustrated I would become when I tried to draw something I had visualized in my mind but could not capture that image on paper.

Next I ask myself what I can have them draw that they all are familiar with and they all like. Hamburgers flash into my mind. Next question: How can I get hamburgers into the context of art? Then Andy Warhol's image of a Campbell's Soup can appears. Now I know I will tell the students about a funny white-haired man who painted popular (I would explain that word) items real *big!* And they called it pop art. I have several copies of his work for display, plus a five-foot canvas in the shape of a Polaroid camera. So now my idea is born.

My next step: How do I teach them to draw a hamburger? In order to solve this step, I always draw the object myself, and as I draw, I think of ways I can break this down into small bits so they can draw it. I also mentally talk through the instruction, using words they understand so that I may communicate effectively. Two things result from this process. One, I formulate instructions and try to anticipate problems that may arise; and two, I have a finished product for an example. I have found that the younger the student, the more precise my instructions have to be.

As I draw the hamburger, I realize the first problem will be having the children draw it large enough. Kindergartners have a hard time conceptualizing size. They always draw too large or too small—mostly too small. So as I draw I come up with the following instructions and thoughts:

1. Turn your paper this way (horizontally).
2. Place your hand that you are not using to draw at the edge of the paper like this, so your little finger touches the edge of the paper. Place your pen at your thumb and draw a rainbow that almost goes to the end of the paper.

3. Now we have the top of our hamburger bun. Next draw a line from one side of your rainbow to the end. Great! You've got your top bun.
4. What do you want on your hamburger? As they call out "onions," "tomatoes," and so on, I'll say, Let's start with lettuce. Draw a wavy line like this . . . now connect it on the end with a short wavy line.

5. Let's draw the meat next. Put a letter *C* under the bun (incorporating arts and academics). Now turn it around and put a backward *C* on the other side. Connect the lines and we have meat.

6. Now let's put on the bottom bun. Remember how you made those letter *C*s? Let's make them bigger and do the same thing again.

7. Now let's add mustard, catsup, or mayonnaise by drawing the letter *U*. How will you show which sauce it is? (Color yellow, red, or orange.)

8. Do you want to add onions? Turn your rainbow upside down like this. These could be tomatoes or pickles or onions. How will you know? (Color.) Do you want seeds on your bun? And now their hamburger is complete.

I always break my lessons down into four steps:
a. My introduction (I hope) provides motivation.
b. I ask the children to put their pens down and watch me draw it on the board, giving the above instructions as I go (modeling).
c. Then I draw it again (on the same size of paper the students have), and the students draw with me. After the first step I ask the class to hold up their drawings to see if they have started correctly. I always think of ways to help if they have a problem. For example, if a student has drawn one too small, I'll say we'll make yours one of those fancy buns that have creases.

d. I also always have something else in mind that can be added, on an individual basis, for those who are more advanced and finish first. For this lesson I thought of cola and French fries. I go through the same process, drawing on another paper so the students may follow (modeling).

When I teach this lesson, it is a great success. The children enjoy it, and each goes away proudly thinking he or she is an artist. I really prefer to have less-structured lessons, but the students need to feel secure in trying. By providing them with success at the beginning of the year, I begin to build their self-confidence and skills. As the year progresses, the lessons become less structured.
Doris Welch

Discussion Questions

1. Although this teacher did not follow the rational planning model in detail, some of her planning procedures resembled steps in that model. What were they?

2. The teacher is more comfortable in using "less-structured" lessons. Why did she choose a more structured approach for this lesson? Why might more structure result in more confidence for her students?

3. Do you think the style of planning has an effect on the structure of a lesson? If so, describe some of the effects.

"often" to "very often" (see Table 3.2, page 80). Only students' previous learning and teachers' lesson goal beliefs influenced unit planning more often.

What caused an emphasis on curriculum objectives in teacher planning? Part of the answer can be found in Table 3.2, where state competencies and objectives are prominently featured. By 1990, competency tests were administered to students in most states in the United States, and these tests were geared to "minimum competencies" that were often stated as goals or objectives of instruction. At least some teachers began using curriculum guides to plan instruction so that students would develop required competencies.

A more comprehensive current movement that has roots in competency-based education is **outcome-based education**, or **OBE**, which emphasizes exit outcomes (outcomes measured at the end of schooling) as the source of

Planning in outcome-based education emphasizes reaching minimum competencies.

Table 3.2   Influences on Unit Planning of Twelve Middle School Teachers

Rank	Influence	Mean Rating
1	Student learning	1.17
2	Lesson goal beliefs	1.33
3	**District curriculum guides, objectives**	**1.66**
4	Orderly transition between activities	1.68
5	Student attention	1.75
6	**State competencies**	**1.81**
7	Previous teaching experiences	1.83
8	Avoidance of interruptions during class	1.91
9	**State objectives**	**2.08**
10	Teaching team requirements	2.17
11	**State curriculum guides**	**2.33**
12	Principal's requirements	2.54
13	Standardized tests	2.63
14	Parents	2.75
15	Department chairperson's requirements	2.90
16	Other teachers' suggestions	2.91
17	Professional journals	3.25
18	In-service training	3.33
19	Undergraduate training, textbooks	3.75
20	Teachers' manual	4.08

Note: 1 = very often influences; 2 = often influences; 3 = sometimes influences;
4 = rarely influences; 5 = never influences.

Source: Adapted from Brown, 1988

instructional objectives, multiple learning opportunities, and performance assessment. Currently, forty-two states are involved in some kind of outcome-based reform (Varnon & King, 1993), but most of these reforms incorporate only one or two elements of OBE and go by another name. Among several consequences of "full" OBE is a mandatory focus on objectives in planning, but this systematic approach to instruction is sometimes controversial (see Deepening Your Knowledge Base: Your Own Reflections on Outcome-Based Education, page 82).

Given the importance of students' attainments of competencies or standards, it is important that you consider carefully goals and objectives in curriculum guides. For most beginning teachers, goals and objectives in curriculum guides actually make problem solving easier rather than more difficult. To see how, we need a way to analyze them into categories of activity. Fortunately, such categories already exist.

Most states require schools to administer competency tests to students. These tests assess the achievement of "minimum competencies" that are outlined by the state. *(Bob Daemmrich/ Stock Boston)*

Categories of Objectives

Planning decisions must begin with an understanding of goals and objectives. To understand the goals and objectives in curriculum guides, you need to know more about how and why they exercise limitations on learning activities. A common way to begin is with an analysis of Bloom's Taxonomy, a classification scheme devised in the 1950s to categorize objectives.

A group of educators led by Benjamin Bloom developed a system to classify objectives that would help examiners assess learning of different types. Partly to facilitate their work, they began by classifying learning into three *domains*, or broad categories: cognitive (thinking), affective (having to do with the emotions), and psychomotor (having to do with physical activities). Within each domain, they planned to categorize objectives in a **taxonomy**, which is a set of classifications arranged on the basis of one or more principles (Krathwohl, Bloom & Masia, 1964). Only a taxonomy for the cognitive domain was actually produced by the group. A smaller number of educators from this group later formulated a taxonomy of objectives for the affective domain, and others have argued for a taxonomy of objectives for the psychomotor domain.

Before we continue with our look at categories of objectives, let's take a moment to help you form a better conceptualization of a taxonomy. You are undoubtedly familiar with the taxonomy for arranging books in the library. Books are arranged by the classification of contents because most users want

> Bloom's Taxonomy is a scheme to categorize educational objectives.

---

deepening your knowledge base

Your Own Reflections on Outcome-Based Education

Proponents of OBE describe it as "organizing for results" in the sense that exit outcomes are used to determine goals at the beginning of programs, courses, units, and even specific lessons (Boschee & Baron, 1994; Spady, 1988). The focus on goals is complemented by "mastery learning," a motivational strategy (described in Chapter 12) that provides additional time and enhanced instruction for those students who need it. Achievement of goals is assessed on exams or performance-based exercises (described in Chapter 14) using standards that indicate mastery. Students whose responses do not meet the standards often receive not failing marks but incompletes. Some evidence exists that OBE results in increases in achievement (Evans & King, 1994).

Critics charge that OBE is being sold to administrators and the public without regard to its effects on teachers. More specifically, critics claim that although a few teachers can be involved in planning exit outcomes, most can be involved only in the "technical" capacity of designing strategies to achieve goals that are given to them (Schwarz & Cavener, 1994). OBE, according to these critics, primarily serves the viewpoint that goals for learning should be determined by a centralized authority, which in education is often a bureaucracy. Furthermore, because of its emphasis on mastery learning, which requires the development of supplementary instructional materials and strategies (see Chapter 12), critics claim that OBE requires already-overloaded teachers to work harder without creating any opportunity, let alone any incentive, to do so (Towers, 1992).

The lack of agreement among educators about the benefits of OBE can provide you with an opportunity to reflect on the advantages and disadvantages of others' specifying what teachers should teach and how they should motivate learners. Pair yourself with another student. One of you should develop a list of the advantages, and the other a list of the disadvantages, of specifying what teachers should teach. After each of you is satisfied with your own list, compare your list with that of your partner, and summarize in a much shorter list a few of the fundamental issues that are involved.

---

to know what is in them. Librarians can and do sort books on another basis (such as size, value, or recency of publication), but only a few users need to use these other criteria. A taxonomy, then, is constructed for locating some item in relation to other items according to some purpose. If a single purpose is shared by a large number of users, most users can locate most items relatively quickly in terms of the larger scheme. A user can say that a particular item is "above this," "below that," or "about there."

The taxonomies of objectives were to be similar to a classification system for books because they were to be based on an analysis of contents of objectives, which were *explicit* or *implied actions*. They were to have an additional feature, however, which would reflect development in each domain. We would not expect books higher in the cataloguing scheme of a library to

Bloom's Taxonomy arranges objectives in order of complexity.

further develop the contents of books lower in this scheme, but taxonomies of objectives were to have a *cumulative hierarchical structure*. This feature of the taxonomies of objectives is very important for understanding their use because higher objectives for domains of learning further develop the activities of lower objectives.

Later in this chapter, you will learn exactly what this means for planning decisions. But now, let's take a look at taxonomies for objectives in each of the three domains to understand better their categories of "explicit or implied actions" arranged in "cumulative hierarchical structures." Let's begin with the cognitive domain, because of its relative importance in curriculum guides for all school subjects.

Cognitive Domain

Of the three major categories of objectives, the greatest educational interest has been in the **cognitive domain**, or the area of knowledge, intellectual skills, and intellectual abilities. Tasks in this domain are found at all grade levels in all subjects. Knowledge and intellectual skills and abilities were classified on the basis of complexity of cognitive activities (Bloom, 1956). The categories of cognitive objectives include six major levels of increasing complexity—knowledge, comprehension, application, analysis, synthesis, and evaluation (see Table 3.3).

> Cognitive objectives involve knowledge and intellectual ability.

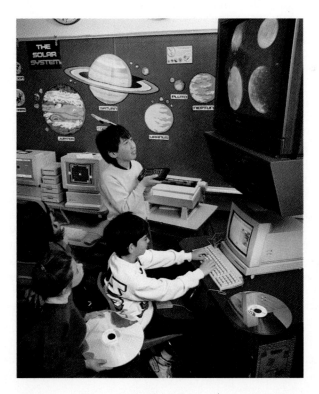

These students are working with computer multimedia to apply knowledge. Notice that the children are not just reading or watching the program, but interacting with it, using what they know. *(James D. Wilson/ The Gamma Liaison Network)*

Table 3.3 Taxonomy for the Cognitive Domain

1.0 Knowledge This category of objective involves recall of specifics and universals; recall of methods and processes; or recall of any pattern, structure, or setting.

1.1 *Knowledge of specifics* The recall of specific bits of information, such as terms or their definitions and the recall of specific facts (for example, dates, events, persons, or places) and given examples.

1.2 *Knowledge of ways and means of dealing with specifics* The recall of ways to organize, study, judge, or criticize something. This subcategory includes knowledge of conventions (rules of punctuation or etiquette), trends and sequences (historical developments), classifications (types of literature), criteria (for assessing the nutritional value of foods), and methodology (the scientific method, methods of coping with emotional stress, bookkeeping procedures).

1.3 *Knowledge of the universals and abstractions in a field* The recall of the schemes and patterns by which a subject field is organized, including principles or generalizations (laws of heredity, basic chemical principles, axioms of geometry) and theories or structures (the theory of evolution, the principle behind the organization of Congress).

2.0 Comprehension This lowest level of intellectual skill requires understanding material (knowledge of what is being "said" in verbal, pictorial, or symbolic form) without necessarily relating it to other information or gaining insight into its full implications.

2.1 *Translation* Care and accuracy in paraphrasing, or rendering the content in one form of communication to another (paraphrasing a speech, translating material from one language to another, plotting points on a graph).

2.2 *Interpretation* Explaining or summarizing a communication. Whereas translation involves a part-to-part correspondence, interpretation involves a reordering, rearrangement, or new approach to information (interpreting graphs, distinguishing accurate from unwarranted or contradicted conclusions, explaining a concept in one's own words).

2.3 *Extrapolation* Extension of what is given to intermediate, past, or future situations; inference with regard to implications, consequences, and corollaries, in accordance with the conditions described in the original communication (estimating or predicting consequences of a described action).

3.0 Application This category of objective includes using abstractions in general situations. The abstractions may be general ideas, rules, methods, principles, or theories to be applied in a particular situation (using trigonometric laws to solve a word problem, applying social-science generalizations to social problems).

4.0 Analysis Breaking down a communication into its constituent parts to detect the relations between the parts or to clarify the organizing principles. Analysis may also be directed at the techniques or means used to communicate an effect (describing a style of writing).

4.1 *Analysis of elements* Detection of elements that permit full comprehension or evaluation (the identification of unstated assumptions or motives, the distinction of facts from hypotheses or premises from conclusions).

4.2 *Analysis of relationships* Determining the relationships among elements or parts of a communication; detecting connections or interactions of parts in the whole (determining consistency of hypotheses with assumptions, distinguishing cause-effect relationships, detecting logical fallacies, comparing and contrasting to identify patterns of similarity or difference).

(Continued on next page)

Table 3.3   Taxonomy for the Cognitive Domain (continued)

4.3 *Analysis of organizational principles* Discovery of purpose, point of view, attitude, or general conception of a work; general form, pattern, structure, or organization of evidence or elements (analysis of a work of art for its organization, inference of an author's point of view, discovery of an author's concept of science, discovery of bias in a historical account).

5.0 Synthesis The putting together of parts so as to form a whole. Arranging or combining elements to constitute a pattern or structure not clearly present before.

5.1 *Production of a unique communication* Developing a communication to convey ideas, feelings, or experiences to others (telling a personal experience, writing a creative story or an essay).

5.2 *Production of a plan or proposed set of operations* Developing a plan or proposal to satisfy requirements of a given or self-set task (development of a plan to solve a problem, test a hypothesis, or teach a unit; the design of a building).

5.3 *Derivation of an abstract set of relations* Developing a set of abstract relations to classify or to explain phenomena; deducing propositions or relations from a basic set of propositions or representations (formulation of a hypothesis or critical theory, discovery of mathematical principles).

6.0 Evaluation Judging the value or worth of material and methods for given purposes. Making quantitative and qualitative judgments about the extent to which something satisfies criteria. Criteria may be determined by the student or given.

6.1 *Judgments based on internal evidence* Judging accuracy from internal criteria such as logical accuracy and consistency (consistent style, logical development, precise wording).

6.2 *Judgments based on external evidence* Evaluating material by criteria appropriate to its type (weighing different courses of action, evaluating health practices, comparing products with works of excellence).

Categories 2–6 include classes of intellectual abilities and skills, as opposed to recall of knowledge only. Objectives in these areas emphasize the processes of organizing and reorganizing supplied or remembered information to achieve a particular purpose.

These categories do not simply represent a list of explicit or implied activities. Except perhaps for the last two (synthesis and evaluation), higher activities depend upon lower ones (Seddon, 1978). Evaluation has not been found to depend upon synthesis, but synthesis and evaluation have been found to depend upon analysis, analysis upon application, application upon comprehension, and comprehension upon ability to recall knowledge (or information). These relationships imply that a learner must know in order to comprehend, comprehend in order to apply, apply in order to analyze, and analyze in order to synthesize or evaluate.

> Higher-level cognitive activities mainly depend on lower ones.

Affective Domain

About ten years after the publication of the taxonomy for the cognitive domain, a taxonomy was published for the **affective domain**, or the area of values, attitudes, and feelings. The organizing principle of this taxonomy was not how complex each activity was, but to what degree an activity involved *internalization of a value* (Krathwohl, Bloom & Masia, 1964). Activities

> The affective objectives involve values and feelings.

deepening your knowledge base

Applying the Taxonomy for the Cognitive Domain

Undoubtedly this taxonomy will seem abstract until you gain experience with cognitive objectives in your teaching field(s). However, there are several steps you can take to get a better grasp of it even before you begin teaching. The first thing you can do is to try to comprehend the taxonomy in your own words. Notice the verbs associated with each major category: To know is to *recognize* or *recall*; to comprehend is to *translate*, to *interpret*, or to *extrapolate*; to apply is to *use*; to analyze is to *break down*; to synthesize is to *formulate*; to evaluate is to *judge*. Try summarizing these six categories in your own "action" words to understand them even better and to help you determine what learning activities they might suggest.

Another step you can take is to analyze given objectives for the level of cognitive activity that each objective requires. Below is a list of cognitive objectives from a variety of fields of study. First, identify the cognitive level of each objective on the list. Second, pick out an objective from this list above the knowledge level, and describe specific *lower* activities it depends upon. Third, pick out an objective below the levels of synthesis or evaluation, and identify a specific activity at a *higher* cognitive level that might be used to attain it.

Assorted objectives in the cognitive domain:

Retell a story

Interpret the feelings of a story character

Use quotation marks when writing conversation

Describe the mental picture created by a short poem

Identify the place value of any digit

Perform conversions between units of time

Find a percentage of a number

Evaluate the nutritional content of popular diets

Explore ways that organisms depend on one another

Describe various cloud formations

Investigate the impact of drug prices on the incomes of consumers

Compare productivity of monopolies with that of competitive firms

Assess the way several items are advertised

Recognize the principles of efficient movement

Plan a personal fitness program

Employ appropriate terminology in art history and appreciation

were classified according to the degree to which they showed that a value had been adopted. In order of least internal to most internal, the five categories of this taxonomy are *receiving, responding, valuing, organization,* and *characterization by a value or value complex.* These categories are described in Table 3.4.

Table 3.4 Taxonomy for the Affective Domain

1.0 Receiving (Attending) Exhibition of *awareness* or consciousness of an affect or value (e.g., awareness of aesthetic factors); *willingness to receive* a communication (listening to others speak); and *controlled or selected attention* given to affects or values (discrimination of mood in music; alertness toward human values recorded in literature).

2.0 Responding Paying active attention or expressing interest through *acquiescence in responding* (obedience or compliance); *willingness to respond* (voluntary participation, acceptance of responsibility); or *satisfaction in response* (enjoyment of self-expression, conversation, or reading).

3.0 Valuing Adoption of consistent behavior that reflects an independent assessment of worth or a characteristic attitude. These objectives include *acceptance of a value* to the point of being identified with it (continuing desire to speak effectively); pursuit of or *preference for a value* (active participation in making arrangements for an art show); and *commitment* or conviction (devotion to ideas of democracy).

4.0 Organization Gradual development toward a system of values in which interrelationships and predominance of particular values are determined. Includes *conceptualization of a value* held (identifies attributes of an admired object, forms judgments as to the responsibilities of society); and *organization of a value system* in which values are in a dynamic equilibrium (weighs alternative policies with the criterion of the public good).

5.0 Characterization by a Value or Value Complex Development of a life outlook characterized by an internally consistent set of values. Includes *generalized set* or selective response at a very high level (readiness or predisposition to revise judgments in light of evidence); and *characterization* by a philosophy of life or view of the universe (development of a code of behavior based on ethical principles consistent with democratic ideals).

Once again, the categories were designed to have a cumulative hierarchical structure; that is, activities in higher categories were assumed to further develop activities in lower ones. Valuing, for example, develops after responding, and responding develops after receiving. Less is known about the relationships between categories in the affective domain, however, than those in the cognitive domain.

> Affective categories are arranged by how much an individual internalizes a value.

Psychomotor Domain

The group of examiners who generated the cognitive taxonomy, and who approved work on the affective taxonomy, did not create a taxonomy for the **psychomotor domain**, or the area of movement, physical skills, and related mental abilities. Partly as a result, several classifications of psychomotor skills were generated to suit different subject fields, but only one classification of the psychomotor domain has been organized according to a developmental principle.

> The psychomotor domain involves movement and physical skills.

Anita Harrow (1972) used the principle of activities related to *physiological development* to identify six categories of objectives—*reflex movements*, *basic-fundamental movements*, *perceptual abilities*, *physical abilities*, *skilled movement*, and *nondiscursive communication*. Note that because the lowest level of activity in this classification scheme (1.0, Reflex Movements) represents a category of behavior not often subject to training,

Applying the Taxonomy for the Affective Domain

Like the taxonomy for the cognitive domain, the taxonomy for the affective domain is difficult to understand until you deal with objectives in your teaching field. Study this sample list from a popular interactive educational computer program. Which are cognitive objectives? What are their levels in the cognitive domain? Which objective is affective? What is its level in the affective domain? Upon what other activities related to the affective domain does its achievement depend?

Objectives for *The Oregon Trail*

1. Understand and discuss the experiences of nineteenth-century American pioneers.
2. Consider alternative solutions to problems and their consequences.
3. Make and justify decisions and act on them.
4. Recognize the legitimacy of values within groups different from their own by studying a community from the past.

Source: Minnesota Educational Computing Corporation, 1986

Harrow's taxonomy for the psychomotor domain effectively has five categories of objectives. (See Table 3.5.)

Like the other taxonomies, this one for the psychomotor domain is helpful primarily in showing how activities are often related. Skilled movements, for example, are dependent upon physical abilities. As you will discover in Chapter 4, you cannot teach a skilled movement such as an overhand serve in volleyball without considering whether or not students possess the arm strength to hit the ball over the net from the end line. About one-third of ninth-grade students do not seem to possess this strength, so they need exercises to develop strength, which is a physical ability, in order to become skilled at the overhand serve.

> Psychomotor objectives are also arranged from lesser to greater development.

Using Taxonomies of Objectives in Planning Decisions

The original use for taxonomies was the categorization of existing objectives in education on the basis of explicit or implied actions. In a recent analysis of the development of the taxonomy for the cognitive domain, Lauren Sosniak (1994) has persuasively argued that the use of the taxonomies for curriculum planning was almost an afterthought. They were primarily designed for test development. Their major function for curriculum planning was and is to remind us of the range of possibilities for activities that we can select while planning.

Table 3.5   Taxonomy for the Psychomotor Domain

2.0 Basic-Fundamental Movements   At this level of objective, the learner develops basic *locomotor* movements (walking, running, jumping, hopping, rolling, climbing), *nonlocomotor* movements (pushing, pulling, swaying, swinging, stooping), and *manipulative* movements (handling, gripping, grasping, manipulating). A typical child enters school with these movements mastered, but objectives may be established for early childhood or special education children.

3.0 Perceptual Abilities   Early childhood educators are interested in the refinement of a child's perceptual abilities, as are teachers of older students. This level of objective includes *auditory* perception (following instructions), *visual* perception (dodging a moving ball), *kinesthetic* perception (adjusting body in a handstand), *tactile* perceptions (determining texture, identifying coins through touch), and *coordinated* perceptions (jumping rope, punting, catching).

4.0 Physical Abilities   The goal of "physical fitness" would generally comprehend this category of objective, which includes *endurance* or strenuous effort (distance running, swimming), *strength* or muscular exertion (weightlifting, wrestling), *flexibility* or axial movements (toe touching, sit-ups, twisting exercises, ballet exercises), and *agility* or quick, precise movements (shuttle run, typing, dodge ball).

5.0 Skilled Movements   A *physical skill* is defined as a "degree of efficiency in performance of a specific, reasonably complex movement behavior" (Harrow, 1972, p. 75). A skill's complexity distinguishes it from basic-fundamental movements. Activities in this classification include skills of sports, dance, recreation, and manipulation in three categories. *Simple adaptive skills* refer to adaptations of basic-fundamental movements (sawing as an adaptation of push-pull, waltzing as an adaptation of walking, piano playing, archery skills, typing and clerical skills, handicrafts, industrial skills). *Compound adaptive skills* require skill in the simultaneous manipulation of a tool or implement in addition to skill in use of the body (racket games). *Complex adaptive skills* require mastering the mechanics of total body involvement (aerial gymnastic stunts, complex dives). Each of the three categories of skilled movements is further subdivided into four levels of proficiency (beginner, intermediate, advanced, highly skilled).

6.0 Nondiscursive Communication   This level of movement involves communication through bodily movements from facial expressions to dance compositions. Its two subcategories are *expressive movement* (posture and carriage, gestures, facial expressions) and *interpretive movement* (art forms of aesthetic and creative movement). Objectives are not typically written for expressive movements, but expressive movements are modified, exaggerated, and utilized in movement interpretations by highly skilled athletes, fine arts students, and even children (the ability to design one's own series of movements in free response activities).

Many educators have noted that curriculum guides, whether developed by the school district, the state, or textbook authors, contain many more lower-level objectives than higher-order ones. The taxonomies serve to remind us that *teachers can use a higher-order activity to meet a lower-order objective.* This rule is crucial for planning decisions. It means that if a curriculum guide lists many lower-order objectives (as many do), you are *not* constrained to teach at a lower level. Instead, you may achieve lower-order objectives in the course of higher-order activities such as analysis in the cognitive domain, valuing in the affective domain, or skilled movement in the psychomotor domain.

A corollary of this rule is that *teachers cannot use a lower-order activity by itself to meet a higher-order objective.* The culture of schools is still

> Higher-order activities can meet lower-order objectives.

These junior high school students in Austin, Texas, are developing psychomotor skills in a physical education class. What is the level of the psychomotor objective that they are working toward? How would you state the objective? *(Robert E. Daemmrich/Tony Stone Worldwide)*

heavily imbued with lower-level activities such as recitation, in which students repeat what they were told or read. Recitation is sufficient to achieve objectives at the knowledge level, but it is insufficient to achieve objectives above the knowledge level, such as comprehension. Students' success in reciting the Gettysburg Address or memorizing the Krebs Cycle, for example, does not mean that students understand the principles that are expressed. In the last section of this chapter, more specific information will be provided about how to "aim high" in our objectives. You will see that higher-order objectives dramatically limit our use of traditional learning activities. They challenge us to use traditional learning activities for new purposes, or to develop altogether new activities.

At this point, it is sufficient to realize that the major function of taxonomies for planning decisions is to encourage teachers to aim high as they plan. As you consider the objectives in curriculum guides or in the margins of your textbooks, realize that you can develop cognitive skills such as analysis, synthesis, or evaluation and still achieve many lower-level objectives along the way. Also, if you should encounter higher-level objectives in curriculum guides or textbooks, realize that many traditional learning activities will not work to attain them. It may once have been true that "all roads lead to Rome," but now we have to pick the route to our destination, after we decide where we want to go.

> Taxonomies help teachers plan activities that can meet objectives.

Evaluation of Taxonomies

If, as you learned about these systems and how to use them for planning, you've questioned the validity and accuracy of the classification of objectives by levels within a taxonomy, you are certainly not alone. Over the years many people have wondered, in particular, about the validity of Bloom's Taxonomy for the cognitive domain, and about whether higher-order thinking skills are actually more complex than lower-order thinking skills. Extensive research in the 1960s and 1970s suggested that they are (Seddon, 1978). Bloom's Taxonomy remains an important framework for understanding cognitive objectives and is in wide and thorough use by curriculum developers today.

However, you should be aware that researchers have found some inconsistencies within Bloom's Taxonomy and have suggested alternative ways to classify objectives that would resolve these inconsistencies. For example, if you read the descriptions of cognitive skills closely, you will notice that inference is classified in Bloom's Taxonomy at two quite different levels. (Can you identify which ones?) Many educational researchers believe that such distinctions are unnecessary, or that inference deserves a category of its own (cf. Quellmalz, 1987).

As a result of these difficulties and even more fundamental questions about adequacy (Furst, 1994), a number of alternative classifications for cognitive objectives have been formulated. One of these (Gagné, 1985) will be described in Chapter 8. It is generally accepted as better than Bloom's Taxonomy for designing sequences of instruction. Another classification scheme (Marzano et al., 1988) has been specifically designed to develop complex process skills such as experimentation. These alternative classification systems remind us that, like the scheme used to classify books in the library, taxonomies of objectives are designed for specific purposes. The closer one's own purpose is to the purpose for which a given classification system was designed, the more useful it appears to be. That is why Bloom's Taxonomy remains useful for categorizing objectives in curriculum guides—that use is close to the one envisioned by its developers.

> Research has developed alternate classsifications for cognitive objectives.

The taxonomies of affective and psychomotor objectives have not been heavily researched. However, during the thirty years of its existence, the taxonomy for the affective domain has had few rivals in teacher planning. Even today, it can be used to categorize most affective objectives in curriculum guides. Harrow's taxonomy for the psychomotor domain has also met with wide acceptance, but a number of alternatives have also been proposed (e.g., Krathwohl, 1994; Simpson, 1966).

CLARIFYING GOALS FOR INSTRUCTION

Classifying the objectives that you are expected to meet can help you identify some of the important givens in your teaching situation, but it cannot give you a much clearer goal. Just what do you want your students to achieve? The answer to this question is much closer to what actually gets taught, or to the curriculum as it is experienced by learners, than to the curriculum guide. To clarify your purpose for instruction, you must clarify your goal for problem solving.

In terms of Yinger's model for planning decisions, clarifying goals involves considering your knowledge about the subject matter and how to teach it, your personal teaching goals, and materials. The outcome of this process should be the representation of a rather specific instructional problem. This problem-solving goal can be expressed in much the same way as the objectives that you find in curriculum guides, *but you must formulate it.*

In order to formulate your own objectives, you need to understand something about how any educational goal or objective is formulated. To this end, educational psychologists have developed explicit procedures for writing objectives. If they are to be meaningful, these procedures must rely on your sense of purpose for instruction. Without an underlying purpose to particularize and clarify, the procedures are not very meaningful.

You will find that two different ways to formulate objectives are useful. Each procedure suits different instructional purposes. In this section we will define each procedure briefly and then explore illustrations and real-life uses of each type.

Specific performance objectives are statements of what a learner will be able to do under certain conditions to a certain degree. They are useful when skills to be learned are relatively simple and highly structured. Vocational education, physical education, and special education often use specific performance objectives, but they can be found in any field.

By way of contrast, **general objectives with specific learning outcomes** are broad statements of what a learner should be able to do, with specific subordinated examples or illustrations. You are most likely to find them useful when skills to be learned are relatively complex or less well structured.

Before we delve into our exploration of these two kinds of objectives, I want to point out an important additional use for objectives in your classroom. You already know that objectives—those that you are given and those that you will formulate—play key roles in planning. However, they also have a very valid role in the lives of your students. In most instructional situations, it is appropriate to share objectives directly with the students themselves. As a result, their learning will be more focused and their retention greater (Melton, 1978). This is true of both kinds of objectives that are described below.

> Teachers clarify goals by considering subject matter, personal goals, and materials.

> Two ways to formulate objectives serve different purposes.

> Students who understand the teacher's objectives will learn better.

Specific Performance Objectives

Objectives can particularize your goals for students in great detail. In the 1950s, an educational psychologist named Robert Mager (1975) popularized the concept of specific performance objectives as (1) what a learner should be able to do (2) under certain conditions (3) to a certain degree. These elements are combined in a single, short sentence. A specific performance objective

1. states a specific performance using an action verb,
2. includes a phrase specifying important conditions under which this performance must occur, and

3. incorporates a criterion or standard for its attainment.

Each performance is specified by beginning with an action verb in the active voice: What the student should be able to do as a result of instruction. Important conditions are established by some phrase or clause specifying the who, what, when, where, or how of the performance. A criterion sets a standard of correctness, such as a minimal degree of accuracy, to help determine whether or not the performance has been achieved.

Fully stated specific performance objectives include conditions and criteria.

In a fully stated performance objective, the performance, conditions, and criterion are all specified in a concise phrase or sentence. The formulation depends on the specific context. For example, one fully stated performance objective for six-year-old students to receive the Presidential Physical Fitness Award is *Complete the shuttle run at six years of age in 12.1 seconds or less*. Completing the shuttle run is a well-defined performance; six years of age is an important condition; and 12.1 seconds is a criterion. As another example, one fully stated performance objective for a sixth grader with a learning disability in spelling might be *Given numerals 1 to 20, spell the numbers with 90 percent accuracy*. Spelling numbers is a well-defined performance; given the numerals is an important condition; and being correct 90 percent of the time is a criterion. An example of a specific performance objective for study skills might be *Given daily class and homework assignments, complete them 90 percent of the time*. Completing an assignment is a well-defined performance; these assignments given by the teacher are an important condition; and 90 percent of the time is the criterion.

Although these three examples are decontextualized, you can see that specific performance objectives are quite particular. In most cases, they specify what the student is to do, the materials or conditions that need to be supplied, and the standard by which you determine when the objective has been met. They often prescribe teaching because in most cases, the learner simply practices the performance under the conditions that you supply until the criterion is met.

Specific performance objectives should be quite particular.

Do teachers really represent instructional problems in such a particular way? The answer is that sometimes they do. If you look ahead in Chapter 7 at the Individualized Education Program for a sixth grader with learning disabilities, you will find an entire page of specific performance objectives. Lists of them can grow out of specific teaching situations, but because of their number, they often require a great deal of effort to write, and they suit some purposes far better than others.

To shorten specific performance objectives, educational psychologists have noted that in many cases, the conditions and criteria of performance can be left out because they are already understood (Dick & Reiser, 1989). For example, a specific performance objective for an eighth grade mathematics lesson on graphs might be *Identify the ordered pair when given a point on the plane*. Identifying an ordered pair (such as [2,3]) is a specific performance; given a point on the Cartesian plane is an important condition; but notice that there is no criterion. None is necessary, because a criterion of 100 percent is implied by the act of identifying. Similarly, *Determine the average of*

Conditions and criteria are sometimes understood and may be omitted.

a set of data is a specific performance, but its condition (given the data) and criterion (the correct average) are only implied. Nevertheless, *Determine the average of a set of data* is a specific performance objective.

Teaching would become fairly routine (and, it could be argued, fairly robotic) if all learning tasks lent themselves to specific performance objectives. Many educators have observed that these objectives are impractical when the task is either complex or not well structured. Such situations call for a more flexible way to write objectives.

General Objectives with Specific Learning Outcomes

Despite the initial popularity of Mager's specific performance objectives, there were many situations in which a complete list of such objectives was simply too long to be practical. In addition, it became clear to a number of educators that specific performance objectives were more suited to lower-order tasks such as factual recall. Furthermore, they were typically too structured to be appropriate for higher-order thinking. Partly in response to these concerns, Norman Gronlund (1995) developed a two-tiered format of general objectives with specific learning outcomes. A general objective with specific learning outcomes

> Higher-order thinking requires more general objectives.

1. states a general objective as a learning outcome, and
2. lists under each objective specific learning outcomes that are representative of the attainment of the objective.

The general objective should begin with a verb (not necessarily an action verb) that describes a category of student behavior. For example, you might choose a verb from among those used for the main categories of the taxonomies (such as *know, comprehend, apply, analyze, formulate,* or *evaluate*), from another source (such as Marzano et al., 1988), or from your own idea for an activity. The specific learning outcomes that are subordinated under the general objective should begin with verbs that are action words and that describe particular student behaviors (such as *interpret, summarize,* and *predict* under "comprehension"). These behaviors all serve to detail what a student would be capable of if he or she had mastered the general objective, but they represent only a sample of specific outcomes.

> General objectives describe a category of student behavior.

> Specific learning outcomes describe examples that fulfill the general objective.

As a teacher formulating general objectives with specific outcomes, you often have greater room for decision making and greater discretion about the kinds of learning activities you will use than you have with specific performance objectives. The general objectives are designed to keep lists of objectives short and to permit complex learning to occur.

Let's look at a general objective with representative outcomes for a complex learning activity such as planning an experiment (adapted from Gronlund, 1995, p. 52):

These visitors to the Bronx Zoo are learning about the life of a prairie dog. What general objective might this experience meet? What are some specific learning outcomes that a teacher might share with students beforehand to structure their experience? *(Michael Nichols/ National Geographic)*

1. Prepares a plan for an experiment.
   1.1 Identifies the problem to be solved.
   1.2 Formulates questions relevant to the problem.
   1.3 Formulates hypotheses in appropriate verbal or mathematical form.
   1.4 Describes controls for variables.
   1.5 Formulates experimental procedures.
   1.6 Formulates observation and measurement procedures.
   1.7 Describes the methods of data analysis.
   1.8 Describes how the results will be presented.

Notice that the general objective is stated as a learning outcome; that is, it begins with a verb (*prepare*) that describes a student performance that is the result of learning. What level of the cognitive domain does the general objective represent? Notice that most of the specific learning outcomes are at the same level, but they are only representative of the outcomes that should be achieved by preparing a plan for an experiment. They are not comprehensive, and some (such as *describes controls for variables*) are below the level of the general objective. Remember that higher-order activities can be used to achieve lower-order objectives. There is no hard and fast rule that says that you cannot include lower-order outcomes among higher-order ones, particularly when they appear in your curriculum guide or otherwise are important.

> Specific learning outcomes need not be comprehensive.

Whatever the differences between them, these two procedures for writing objectives provide you with a means to clarify your goals for teaching. In particular, they have in common a focus on what you want students to achieve. This focus on goals for the student provides you with a framework for representing a problem that is significantly different from the one you might otherwise have. The tendency of most people is to focus on goals for themselves,

> Teachers' goals should focus on what students need to learn.

deepening your knowledge base

Clarifying Teachers' Goals

From your earlier look at planning by Sarah and Norma, you know that experienced teachers do not often write down objectives in either of the formats that we have discussed. Instead, they tend to write down only what they need to jog their memories. Sarah and Norma do, however, briefly express their goals in terms of student actions. These actions can be found in Sarah's list of objectives and in the teaching/learning activities listed by Norma. Your objective for this exercise is *to use the format of general objectives with specific learning outcomes to write statements of their goals.*

Divide up into groups of four. Your group's aim will be to list the goals of each teacher as general objectives with specific learning outcomes. You will find three sources of information: (1) their lesson plans, (2) the discussion of their cases in the text, and (3) the description of a general objective with specific learning outcomes in this part of the chapter. Three members of the group should each be responsible for leading a brief discussion of one of these sources of information, and the fourth person should serve as editor-recorder. Decide among yourselves who is responsible for what.

You might want to begin your analysis and discussion with Sarah's lesson plan, which lists four objectives. Consider these as abbreviated statements of four specific learning outcomes. Ask yourselves how they might be expanded to be fully stated. What general objective can you formulate to encompass them? Write these down in the format of a general objective with specific learning outcomes.

Although Norma's three student activities provide a greater challenge because they integrate teaching and learning activities, you can begin your analysis in the same way. How might each activity in her lesson plan be restated as a specific learning outcome? What general objective might encompass all three outcomes? Again, write these down as a general objective with specific learning outcomes.

Reassemble as a class to compare and contrast your lists.

not someone else. Teaching, however, is an activity that depends upon the activity of other people for its definition. Think about it. Can teaching occur without learning by others? If we talk with students and engage them in activities, but they do not learn, can we say that we teach? In philosophical moments, teachers sometimes debate this question. Whatever your answer, we can probably all agree: The focus of objectives on student learning puts teaching goals squarely where they belong, in the effect of instruction on others.

Evaluation of Objectives

After our extensive discussion of objectives, you may be pondering two real-life concerns about using them in your teaching: (1) Will using objectives really help me plan more effectively, and (2) Will they help students learn?

The answer to the first question is suggested by a recent survey of new teachers from a teacher-education program in which the skill of developing objectives was systematically taught (Earle, 1992). All 100 percent reported that reviewing or developing course goals was crucial or helpful to their planning; 87 percent reported that developing objectives was crucial to their planning. Of the 13 percent who did not, many were probably required to follow objectives or competencies in curriculum guides so closely that developing an independent set of objectives did not seem worthwhile.

Whether others provide objectives for you, you develop them on your own, or both, they will be helpful to your planning decisions. But the question of whether they directly help students learn is more complex. Many studies of this question (summarized in Hamilton, 1985; Klauer, 1984) have involved giving readers some combination of general objectives, specific objectives, or no objectives before they read a passage. The reading exercises have been followed by tests that contained some items keyed to the objectives (*intentional* learning) and some items keyed to information in the passages not mentioned in the objectives (*incidental* learning).

The cumulative results of these studies are displayed in Figures 3.5 and 3.6. In sum, the research indicates that when students learn information,

1. objectives increase *intentional* learning;
2. general objectives increase intentional learning more often than specific performance objectives do;
3. objectives decrease *incidental* learning; and
4. general objectives decrease incidental learning less than specific performance objectives do.

These results might discourage use of specific performance objectives, but remember, these are composite results, and they do not indicate when a set

> Planning with objectives is helpful to most new teachers.

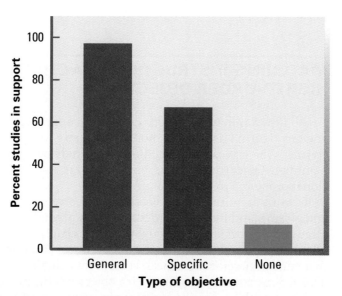

**Figure 3.5
Objectives and
Intentional Learning**
(Klauer, 1984)

**Figure 3.6
Objectives and
Incidental Learning**
(Klauer, 1984)

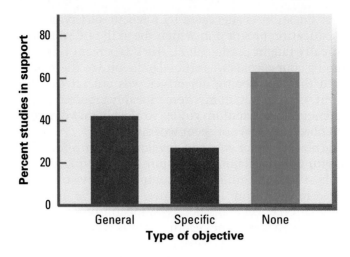

of specific performance objectives might serve your purpose better than a general objective (with or without specific learning outcomes).

When shared with students, objectives clearly increase intentional learning. They function to gain and hold the attention of students (Duchastel & Merrill, 1973; Melton, 1978). Their most effective use for this purpose requires that you

> Intentional learning increases when students know their objectives.

- keep objectives clear and short,
- increase student awareness of and interest in them, and
- tell students the objectives immediately before instruction.

If you use objectives in class this way, you will help students become more attentive, which is an unstated objective from the affective domain for almost every class.

MATCHING INSTRUCTIONAL ACTIVITIES TO HIGHER-ORDER OBJECTIVES

Recall how Sarah used objectives to deduce specific activities for each lesson and how Norma used them more holistically to guide the use of preferred activities. Objectives influenced not only their written plans but their mental planning. Objectives helped both teachers identify and represent instructional problems to be solved.

In working with these objectives, reflective, thinking teachers like Sarah and Norma (and like you someday) have a pivotal responsibility that has been alluded to periodically throughout this chapter. Far more important than whether you work with objectives in a linear or holistic manner is your ultimate underlying focus on the development of higher-order processes and skills. This means not only working with objectives that will encourage such development but also selecting and planning appropriate instructional activities.

"Appropriate" is a key word here. Not all instructional activities are created equal! Teachers have always known that higher-order skills are complex, but how are they related to the range of traditional activities such as lectures, demonstrations, workbook or drill exercises, discussions, and projects? That is a very important question to ask yourself when making planning decisions. As a profession, we cannot hope to encourage thinking and other higher-order skills if for one reason or another we do not engage students in learning activities that actually address these skills and processes.

> Higher-order skills can be developed with appropriate activities.

The real key here is that not all categories of activity address all categories of objective. In general, *higher-order objectives can be attained only through a narrow range of traditional activities*, while *lower-order objectives can be attained through a wide range of traditional activities*. In other words, if you were *not* concerned with addressing higher-order objectives, you could choose any traditional instructional activity for variety or convenience, and count on the fact that you'd be very likely to meet your objective one way or another. However, as soon as you concern yourself with developing processes such as analysis, synthesis, and evaluation, you must plan and select instructional activities very carefully.

> Traditional activities lend themselves more easily to lower-order objectives than to higher-order ones.

Helping you to achieve a high degree of correlation between your objectives and your instructional activities is the purpose of this section. In order to do this, let's reexamine the three categories of instructional activities that were defined in Chapter 1. Once we have explored those in detail, we will see how they match up with higher- and lower-order skills within each of the three domains. This two-step process should help you to make some important planning decisions about which activities you will use to achieve your objectives.

Categories of Traditional Instructional Activities

As introduced in Chapter 1, there are three major categories of activity for teaching and learning: teacher presentations, teacher-student interactions, and student actions (Henak, 1984). This division of activities is based on the degree to which teachers and students participate in a teaching or learning activity. The threefold classification presents a good point of departure for thinking about which activities lead to which kind of learning.

Teacher Presentations

In **teacher presentations**, the instructor is relatively active during the lesson, in contrast to the students. Students are limited to passive participation, including listening and watching. Teacher presentations include these traditional activities:

> Students have a passive role in teacher presentations.

- lectures
- demonstrations
- audio-visual presentations or models
- field trips (without further student involvement)

Although only representative, this list should suffice to illustrate how often learning is expected to develop from situations in which the learner is a relatively inactive or passive participant in the learning process. Think of how many times you as a student have been expected to learn in situations like those listed above.

Teacher-Student Interactions

In **teacher-student interactions**, learners are active participants in the learning process, but the instructor is also an active participant. Teacher-student interactions generally occur in groups no larger than twenty-five or thirty. Most classes are limited to this size to make interaction easier, but if they wish, teachers can also conduct this type of activity in small groups or tutorials. Traditional teacher-student interactions include

- questioning
- discussions
- brainstorming
- seminars
- interviews with specialists
- role-playing
- game-based learning
- committees
- debates

Teacher-student interactions are not limited to this list, but as you can see, all of the activities listed involve students actively learning, and the teacher acting as a participant. The teacher may question the students, or the students may question the teacher, but both participate in the activity. Students may hold a panel discussion or a debate, but even in such cases where student participation outweighs that of the teacher, the teacher actively fills the role of host, moderator, or judge.

Student Actions

There are some situations, however, when students fulfill all of the participatory roles in an activity. In **student actions**, learners are far more active participants than are teachers, who function in a supportive role. Traditional student actions include

- experiments
- exercises
- simulations
- projects

The role of the teacher in student actions is limited to supplying general supervision or technical advice. Teachers do not have to be engaged in a student

> Teacher-student interaction involves both sides actively.

> Teachers support and advise in the student action form of learning.

action for it to proceed, but they often must sponsor, structure, and monitor the activity to resolve any difficulties that might arise.

Matching Instructional Activities to Objectives

These categories are useful because they allow you to address the question, "How do I match traditional activities with objectives in order to make sure the objectives are actually addressed?" The answer involves systematically examining activities for the degree to which they can address different kinds of objectives. In the next few pages, you will see that not all categories are equally flexible. Some traditional activities, in fact, are quite inflexible, and the type of learning that can occur in them is consequently very limited. Your choice of an activity, then, should be made carefully to match with your objectives. That way, you will ensure your objectives can indeed be met through the activity.

> Activities should be chosen carefully to match objectives.

Cognitive Domain

If you consider activities in light of Bloom's Taxonomy for the cognitive domain, you will discover that many activities can be used to meet lower-level objectives, but only a few activities can be used to meet higher-level objectives. The range of activities is steadily constricted as you move from knowledge to evaluation (from left to right in Table 3.6 on page 102). Note that no teacher presentation can directly lead to the development of higher-order thinking skills, and not all student actions lead to higher-order thinking skills.

Only a few traditional activities allow you to achieve higher-order thinking objectives. These activities include *questioning*, *discussions*, *simulations*, *debates*, and *projects*. Each of these five activities has a particular virtue or strength. Questioning (particularly asking "why") can lead students to pursue implications of ideas, deepening their thinking. Discussions can help students formulate and exchange ideas. Simulations, whether they involve structured group situations or computer microworlds, can lead to decision making and evaluation of decisions. Debates, which are pro-and-con discussions, can help students analyze evidence and construct plans. Projects, which often need to be supplemented by prerequisite knowledge, can lead to the development of class presentations or products, including multimedia.

> Only certain activities are conducive to reaching higher-order thinking.

Finally, it is worth noting that even appropriately targeted activities do not *necessarily* lead to higher-order thinking. For instance, just asking questions is not enough. If you ask only factual questions, you will be eliciting and developing only knowledge-level skills. Likewise, if you engage your students in simulations but do so randomly, relying on trial-and-error learning, or if you hold classroom debates in which most of the students wind up watching rather than participating, you are not bringing about higher-order thinking. Instead, set up this way, these activities serve lower-order objectives.

> Appropriate activities must be carried out properly to reach higher-level objectives.

Table 3.6 Traditional Instructional Activities and Cognitive Objectives

Instructional Activity	Knowledge	Comprehension	Application	Analysis	Synthesis	Evaluation
Teacher Presentations						
Lectures	X	X				
Demonstrations	X					
Audio-visual	X	X				
Field trips	X	X				
Teacher-Student Interactions						
Questioning	X	X	X	X	X	X
Discussions	X	X	X	X	X	X
Brainstorming	X	X				
Seminars	X	X				
Interviewing	X	X				
Role-playing	X	X	X			
Games	X	X	X			
Committees	X	X				
Debates	X	X	X	X	X	
Student Actions						
Experiments	X	X	X			
Exercises	X	X	X			
Simulations		X	X	X	X	X
Projects		X	X	X	X	X

Source: Revised from Henak, 1984

Affective Domain

If you consider teacher presentations, teacher-student interactions, and student actions in light of the objectives for the *affective* domain, you will discover a pattern similar to the one for the cognitive domain (see Table 3.7). Many activities can be used to meet lower-order objectives such as *receiving* or *responding*, but only a few activities can be used to meet higher-order objectives such as *valuing*. The choice of activities that can develop a value is very limited.

Look at the affective objectives that run across the top of the table. Notice that any type of activity (with the exception of projects) can develop "receiving" or listening attentively, but that teacher-student interactions and stu-

A limited number of activities will achieve higher-order affective objectives.

Table 3.7   Traditional Instructional Activities and Affective Objectives

Instructional Activity	Receiving	Responding	Valuing	Organizing
Teacher Presentations				
Lectures	X			
Demonstrations	X			
Audio-visual	X			
Field trips	X			
Teacher-Student Interactions				
Questioning	X	X	X	
Discussions	X	X	X	
Brainstorming	X	X		
Seminars	X	X		
Interviewing	X	X		
Role-playing	X	X		
Games	X	X		
Committees	X	X		
Debates	X	X		
Student Actions				
Experiments	X	X		
Exercises	X	X		
Simulations	X	X		
Projects		X	X	

Source: Revised from Henak, 1984

dent actions are necessary to develop the next higher category of the affective domain, which is "responding" or expressing interest. The next higher level, which is "valuing" or making commitments, can be developed only through questioning, discussions, and projects. None of the activities listed can in a single lesson lead to a system of values ("organizing") or to a life outlook ("characterizing"). Development over an extended period is necessary to achieve those levels of affective objectives.

You may wonder why simulations and debates do not lead to the development of values. Participating in simulations and debates frequently entails some interest on the part of a learner (such as desire to learn a skill, or preference for the pro or con side of an issue), but simply participating does not necessarily

Discussions and questioning are best suited to developing values.

change the value that underlies this interest. Also note that projects require some initial orientation and do not develop values as consistently as do questioning and discussions. Discussions and questioning are the only activities listed that can develop values from "receiving" all the way through "valuing."

Psychomotor Domain

The same pattern applies when we analyze activities for their ability to address objectives in the psychomotor domain (see Table 3.8). Any type of activity can develop perceptual abilities, but skilled movements and nondiscursive communication can be developed only by role-playing, game-based learning, simulations, and projects. Questioning and discussions, which are so valuable to develop higher-order thinking and values, do not directly result in improvements in physical abilities or skills. Although questioning

Table 3.8   Instructional Activities and Psychomotor Objectives

Instructional Activity	Perceptual Abilities	Physical Abilities	Skilled Movements	Nondiscursive Communication
Teacher Presentations				
Demonstrations	X			
Audio-visual	X			
Field trips	X			
Teacher-Student Interactions				
Questioning	X			
Discussions	X			
Brainstorming	X			
Seminars	X			
Interviewing	X			
Role-playing	X	X	X	X
Games	X	X	X	X
Committees	X			
Debates	X			
Student Actions				
Experiments	X			
Exercises	X	X		
Simulations	X	X	X	
Projects	X	X	X	X

and discussion may help a student learn what to do, movement is necessary for students to achieve higher-order objectives in the psychomotor domain.

Once again, it is worth noting that activities that can serve higher-order objectives do not always serve them. Simply participating in a game, for example, does not necessarily improve skilled movements. If other players never kick or hit the ball to a player during a game, how can she or he learn to catch it skillfully? Similarly, participating in a play or in a chorus does not necessarily result in performance (nondiscursive communication). If a child learns a role for a play but is not taught to change his or her customary movements and expression how can he or she learn to act? Game-based learning or role-playing must be part of an overall strategy to achieve higher-order objectives. Just participating in the activity is not enough.

> Active participation is necessary to develop higher-order psychomotor skills.

ADDRESSING HIGHER-ORDER OBJECTIVES

As you can see from this analysis, achieving higher-order objectives in all three domains generally requires a relatively high degree of student activity. This activity does not have to be physical, except in the psychomotor domain. Why is a relatively high degree of student activity required to achieve higher-level objectives? The answer to this question lies in the nature of personal knowledge, values, and physical skills, all of which must be constructed or developed by the learner. Student activity during learning is necessary for the processes of construction or development to occur. We will address this question in greater detail in Chapters 4–7, which describe the development of student characteristics.

> Students must be actively involved to develop their own higher-order skills.

Evaluation of Objectives/Activities Matching

If your instructional activities are matched well to your objectives, you are much more likely to meet your objectives than if the activities and objectives are mismatched. How you match them up depends upon how you plan. Remember, there is no one way to plan instruction.

If you begin with objectives (like Sarah), analyze curriculum objectives and your personal teaching goals for the desired degree of emphasis on higher-order skills and then *consider what activities the objectives suggest*. Your teachers' manual, curriculum guide, or list of objectives itself will probably offer some helpful suggestions. If you begin with a theme or a preferred activity in addition to objectives and personal teaching goals (like Norma), *consider how themes, activities, and objectives* relate to one another as well as to an emphasis on higher-order skills. You may find yourself modifying the theme, activity, or objectives to bring them into harmony. There is no one way to solve planning problems, but they require careful representation if you are to arrive at an effective solution.

> There is no single way to plan for teaching.

At present, almost no systematic research exists on the effectiveness of matching activities with objectives. We know that such coordination exists, and that new teachers recently trained in this skill report that it leads to improved planning (Earle, 1992). We do not yet know whether such coordination leads to improved student learning. The research is lacking because the question is still a relatively new one. In the past, with the fairly prevalent emphasis on achieving lower-order skills that could be addressed successfully by a wide range of instructional activities, thoughtfully matching activities to objectives simply wasn't important. However, with increased attention to achieving higher-order thinking, it is likely to be critical. In time, your instructional planning decisions will become part of an even larger design that reflects your voice in all of your teaching decisions. As a consequence, not only will your activities match your objectives but your strategies for instruction, motivation, management, and assessment also will match one another.

CONCLUSION

As the teaching of thinking (described in Chapter 10) becomes more focused and widespread, many teachers will have to aim instruction more carefully in order to hit targeted skills. Virtually any learning activity will do if knowledge or comprehension is your objective, but higher-order thinking skills have more limited routes of access. Frequent use of teacher presentations will be regarded as increasingly inappropriate unless teachers provide thought-provoking activities to supplement them. Lesson planning must involve designs with teacher-student interactions or student actions to address higher-order thinking skills.

Despite this constraint on your planning, you will still have considerable freedom in planning decisions. Your designs for lesson plans during your internship will almost certainly fit a prescribed format, but their contents should reflect the "problem space": your knowledge of student characteristics, the curriculum guide, and the classroom; and your resources, personal teaching goals, and knowledge of content and how to teach it. Your designs should represent *you* in that particular teaching and learning situation. Plans will sometimes be shared among several teachers, but they will still be personal constructs. They will represent your collective design to solve instructional problems.

Although planning is an important and easily overlooked skill, you should not sacrifice flexibility as a result. Your plans should represent significant investments of your time and energy, but when you teach, do not follow them slavishly. If you have prepared well, you will have a mental model or set of expectations for how the class should proceed. That is sufficient. You should have enough confidence to depart from your mental plan to adapt spontaneously to moment-by-moment perceptions that you experience from the time your students enter your class. At its best, teaching is not like following a script. It has a great deal of improvisation in it. Therefore, work flexibility into your design for instruction. Plan to be flexible.

concept paper

Analysis of Objectives

Purpose of the assignment

To analyze two pages of instructional objectives in your teaching field for their potential effects on teaching.

Directions for prewriting

1. Select and copy two pages of instructional objectives (or five to ten objectives) in your teaching field from a state or local curriculum guide. Be sure that you have distinguished objectives from more general goals.

2. Analyze the objectives according to the appropriate domain (cognitive, affective, or psychomotor) and the level within each relevant domain.

   a. Sort your objectives by domain. If you have performance objectives, be careful that you do not assume that performance automatically places an objective in the psychomotor category. Have you found a cognitive, affective, or psychomotor emphasis? If so, why?

   b. Within each domain, sort the objectives by level. If you are uncertain about the level of an objective, or if it seems to overlap two categories, indicate the ambiguity rather than force a categorization.

3. Identify how these objectives limit teaching. Consider limiting effects on the domain of what you teach, the level of activity, and the type of instructional activity.

Directions for the writing assignment

1. In a thesis sentence, characterize how the objectives you have found might affect teaching. What kinds of limitations do they impose? You might want to place your thesis sentence at the end of an introductory paragraph that identifies the source and subject of the objectives.

2. Support your thesis sentence in a three- to four-page paper (typed length) that identifies each limiting effect that you have found. In other words, use your analysis of the domain of objectives, the level of objectives, and the relation of objectives to instructional activities to prove your thesis.

SUMMARY

1. There are two key benefits to instructional planning: significantly improved organization for your lessons and increased confidence for you during teaching.

2. Planning is implemented on two different bases—time periods and segments of instruction. Typical time periods for planning are annual, weekly, and daily. The most important instructional segments are units and lessons.

3. There is a strong relationship between planning and problem solving. Like the stages of the problem-solving process, planning involves confronting an unresolved situation, formulating a solution (the plan), trying it out, and modifying it as necessary.

4. Different teachers have different planning styles. Some start with goals and objectives and base activities on them (the rational planning model). Other teachers focus on activities initially and circle back to goals and objectives (the holistic planning model). Neither style is "right" or "wrong."

5. Educational objectives help to make goals more particular. There are two kinds of objectives: specific performance objectives, which describe very explicitly the new behaviors a learner should be able to demonstrate; and general objectives with representative learning outcomes, which provide a sample checklist of possible behaviors a learner will gain.

6. Objectives can be arranged according to a classification system called a taxonomy. A taxonomy exists for each of three major domains—cognitive, affective, and psychomotor—and describes a hierarchy of key activities that occur within each domain.

7. In planning instruction, you can choose from three primary categories of instructional activities: teacher-directed presentations, teacher-student interactions, and student-based activities.

8. As you match your instructional activities to your objectives, it is important to bear in mind an underlying principle: almost any category of activities can be used to address lower-order objectives, but in order to address higher-order objectives, you must plan and select very carefully.

KEY TERMS

goals p. 64

curriculum guide p. 65

student educational objectives p. 65

problem space p. 66

rational planning model p. 75

holistic planning model p. 76

outcome-based education p. 79

taxonomy p. 81

cognitive domain p. 83

affective domain p. 85

psychomotor domain p. 87

general objectives with specific learning outcomes p. 92

specific performance objectives p. 92

teacher presentations p. 99

student actions p. 100

teacher-student interactions p. 100

SUGGESTED RESOURCES

Anderson, L. W., and L. A. Sosniak. 1994. *Bloom's Taxonomy: A Forty-Year Retrospective.* Chicago, Ill.: National Society for the Study of Education. This volume is Part II of the 1994 Yearbook of the NSSE, and its chapters summarize the educational impact of the taxonomy for the cognitive domain. Also included is a summary of levels in the domain from the 1956 document.

Marzano, R. J., R. S. Brandt, C. S. Hughes, B. F. Jones, B. Z. Presseisen, S. C. Rankin, and C. Suhor. 1988. *Dimensions of Thinking: A Framework for Curriculum and Instruction.* Alexandria, Va.: Association for Curriculum and Development. This proposal for a new framework for analyzing cognitive objectives is thought provoking. A companion volume describing performance assessment using the dimensions framework was published in 1994.

Yinger, R. J. 1980. "A Study of Teacher Planning." *Elementary School Journal,* 80, 107–127. This article outlines the problem-solving model for planning decisions.

Zumwalt, K. K. 1989. "Beginning Professional Teachers: Need for a Curricular Vision of Teaching." In *Knowledge Base for the Beginning Teacher* (pp. 173–184). Ed. M. C. Reynolds. Oxford: Pergamon Press. This chapter makes the case for curriculum as what teachers teach, rather than what is in guides. A useful article for conceptualizing the relationship among various types of goals in teaching.

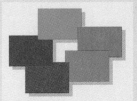

Student Characteristics

The chapters in Part II extend your knowledge of how children's physical, cognitive, and social development occurs. You will learn about the individual differences that will characterize your students. You will also learn why it is important to focus on individual differences as you plan instruction, and how to adapt instruction to these differences.

Physical Development

The goal of this chapter is to provide you with some fundamental information about the process of children's physical development within the framework of the model of problem solving. You will discover how a teacher must respect the maturational givens of *nature* while at the same time setting goals based on the possible influences of *nurture*. As you read, look for answers to these questions:

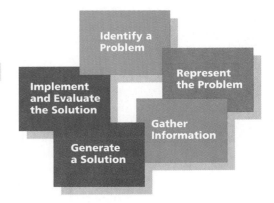

- **In what specific ways does nature provide developmental givens or constraints, while nurture offers goals for further development?**

- **Why are gender differences in motor skills good examples of the interaction of nature and nurture?**

- **What are the three different viewpoints that describe the ways in which motor skills develop?**

- **How can the stages and phases of physical development be folded together?**

- **Why is it important for teachers to respect the maturational givens of physical development?**

- **Why is it important for teachers to promote goals for new learning in physical development?**

- **In what ways can development in the cognitive and social domains be integrated with physical development?**

THE COMPLEMENTARY INFLUENCES OF NATURE AND NURTURE

Your knowledge of your students' characteristics is a key factor in your ability to represent teaching problems as challenges. To begin exploring how these characteristics help define a teaching problem, let's consider children's development. As you have learned, **development** is progressive change. Progressive changes in the body, cognition, and social relations extend throughout life, but they have special significance during childhood and adolescence because they are so rapid during these years.

This chapter will focus on physical and psychomotor development. **Physical development** is progressive change in the body, including its various systems, such as the skeletal system, the nervous system, and the reproductive system. Visible results of physical development include gains in height and weight, changes in the shape of the body, and improvements in coordination. One type of physical development is **psychomotor development**, or progressive change in physical abilities or skills. Examples of psychomotor development are an increased ability to pick up small objects and the coordination of two physical activities, such as kicking a ball while running. Although we will consider the broad topic of physical development in this chapter, we will focus on psychomotor development because of its important role in education. Framing our whole consideration will be the problem-solving process.

The central problem for educators regarding development of any kind is, *How can I build upon and further develop a student's skills within a given capability?* Another way of saying this is that a child's capabilities—physical, intellectual, or social—must be taken into consideration as goals are set for learning. During the developmental period, a child's age is one of the more important factors affecting capabilities. A younger child is almost always less capable than he or she will be as an older child. An extreme example of this is an infant's inability to walk. No matter how elaborate the training he or she might receive, a six-month-old simply does not have the skeletal rigidity and muscle power to walk. The given in this situation—the child's age—places a pivotal constraint or limitation on what can be learned and on goals that can be set.

Not many situations are as clear-cut as this one, however. More typically, the different capabilities that a child of any age brings to a learning situation are affected and enhanced by the experiences designed to develop these capabilities. For instance, a child who is encouraged to ride a tricycle and then a bicycle at an early age will likely become a trike or bike rider well before others of his or her age who have not been encouraged to ride early. In this case, the givens presented by a child's age (determined by nature) generally lead to

Students' physical and psychomotor development affect instructional planning.

A child's current capabilities limit the goals that can be set.

learning journal

Principles of Physical Development

While reading this chapter, write Learning Journal entries about specific experiences in which principles of physical development apply. Tell what led up to the specific experience, name the principles of development involved, and describe how these principles came into play and what relevant outcomes you observed. This chapter contains descriptions of the following principles of physical development:

- nature and nurture
- differentiation through maturation
- proximodistal sequence
- cephalocaudal sequence
- differentiation through learning
- integration or coordination
- gender differences in motor skills
- sex stereotyping
- effects of growth spurt
- effects of early maturation
- stages of motor skills (at least two)
- phases of motor learning (at least two)
- development of feedback
- respecting and promoting readiness
- integrated learning

tricycles and then bicycles, but life and learning experiences (established through nurture) affect how quickly skills at different levels of difficulty become mastered.

While almost all educators acknowledge that both nature and nurture play a role in a child's development, there is a long-standing debate between camps at either end of the spectrum. This debate is commonly known as the nature/nurture controversy.

Different educators emphasize nature and nurture as determining factors in development.

The educators who emphasize the role that nature plays in development tend to see age as a determining factor. That is, in their view, a student's age places real limits on his or her learning capabilities. In terms of our problem-solving model, we could say that these educators emphasize physical development as a series of givens that define instructional problems in relation to the age of a student. For example, such a teacher might wait until age eleven to introduce a child to a sport such as baseball or basketball, because only at that age can a child master the complex movements that most sports require.

At the other end of the spectrum, the educators who focus on the effects of nurture on development define instructional problems purely in relation to the set of prerequisite skills needed, rather than tying these problems to the child's age. Again, in terms of our problem-solving model, we could say that these educators take very little as a limitation or a constraint and instead look straight to the goals that they feel are appropriate to set. For instance, a teacher with these beliefs might introduce a child to a sport as early as six or seven, if that child possessed prerequisite skills and if the sport were made safe for children. For these educators, the representation of instructional problems has less to do with age than with the mastery of prerequisites.

You might be wondering where this book fits within the framework of this nature/nurture controversy. My own belief is that there need be no controversy at all. We will explore, in this chapter, and in subsequent chapters on development, the *complementarity* of nature and nurture. I believe that the resolution of the nature/nurture controversy lies in the realization that both sides are right. As I see it, teachers must constantly address the dual effects of nature and nurture on development as they plan for instruction. And as problem solvers, teachers need to respect the givens *of* development while promoting goals *for* development.

> Nature and nurture can complement each other.

Let's look at a simple example of this complementarity in action within the arena of physical development. Since small children do not generally have the fine-muscle coordination necessary to tie a shoe, "tying a shoe" is not an appropriate goal for most children before grade school. Instead, children younger than six should be encouraged to wear slip-ons or shoes with strip fasteners, and depend on adults to tie the occasional shoelace.

> Children can learn skills when they are developmentally ready.

However, by six or seven, most children should be able to tie a shoelace after appropriate instruction. The skill can be demonstrated in steps, and children can be given feedback as they practice. Adults might see to it that Johnny and Shelley have sneakers that must be tied in order to ensure that they regularly practice tying a shoe. The developmental given (a factor of nature), which blocked the path to a specific goal just a year or two earlier, has changed, setting the stage for instruction (a factor of nurture) and resulting in a successful resolution of the problem.

The next section depicts a classroom scene in which we'll see firsthand how the different aspects of physical development affect instructional problem solving. After we look in on this physical education class for kindergartners, we'll take up each of the topics of nature and nurture and examine them in greater depth. We'll conclude our consideration of the complementarity of nature and nurture by exploring one good example of their interaction—the development of gender differences in commonly measured motor skills.

A Physical Education Teacher Emphasizes Both Nature and Nurture

It's 9:44 in Mr. Ramirez's class, which is held in a gymnasium that doubles as an auditorium when folding chairs are set up. At one end of the gym is a

Children in this physical education class in Washington, DC, are dancing to music, practicing fundamental movement skills such as starting on cue, swinging their arms, and stopping on cue. Movement activities for small children frequently involve exercising fundamental skills in a simple sequence.   *(Paul S. Conklin)*

raised stage. Below the front of the stage, Mr. Ramirez stands with his hand poised on a desk bell. A kindergartner beside him is playing the role of "Mr. Fox." At the other end of the gym are all the other kindergarten students, lined up side by side, facing the stage in anticipation.

At a signal from Mr. Ramirez, all of the children call out, "What time is it, Mr. Fox?" Mr. Fox answers the class with a number—"Six." The other kindergartners take six steps toward Mr. Fox as they count out loud. The teacher punctuates each step with the desk bell. Some of the children have difficulty stopping when they reach a number; others stretch out each stride in order to be the first to reach the other side of the gym. This procedure is repeated until the closest children are clearly only one small number of steps away from Mr. Fox. The child playing Mr. Fox answers their next "What time is it, Mr. Fox?" by calling out "Midnight," and all of the children run delightedly back to the other side of the gym to play again, this time with a new Mr. Fox. The children are exercising both fundamental movement skills and skill at counting.

How does Mr. Ramirez's lesson both respect the givens of physical development and promote goals for new learning in his classroom? First, Mr. Ramirez planned his lesson to account for the fact that five-year-olds are limited in their physical and social capacities. Their games exercise fundamentals such as running, jumping, balancing, and stopping. These skills are developing, not fully developed; consequently, they cannot yet serve as prerequisites for activities such as kick ball, let alone a sport like softball. By the end of their kindergarten year, the children will be playing kick ball, but for now, the givens of physical development limit what can be taught to fundamental skills.

Second, Mr. Ramirez was not just providing the children with an enjoyable exercise or allowing them to practice fundamental skills they already had developed. Instead, he had a specific instructional intent or goal—to develop

Lessons should account for children's development and promote learning goals.

new fundamental movement skills of starting and stopping. Everyone has seen a child hesitate—be unable to start—after kicking a ball, or overrun a base—be unable to stop—after reaching it. In Mr. Ramirez's class, the children were learning *to start and to stop on cue*, whether they were stepping off numbers or running back to their "home" line. The game "What Time Is It, Mr. Fox?" was a strategic solution to the problem set both by the givens and the goal of physical development.

Effects of Nature: Maturational Sequences and Differentiation

As you look at your students' characteristics, you need to be aware of certain well-established givens of physical development. Among the more important trends of physical development are three trends in **maturation**, or the development of full functioning. These trends are differentiation, the proximodistal sequence, and the cephalocaudal sequence (Bukatko & Daehler, 1995; Gallahue & Ozmun, 1995). Each of these represents an important biologically determined pattern of development that begins in the womb and continues to influence development in the school years.

> Differentiation means that development brings increasingly specific functions of body parts.

The first, **differentiation**, or the gross-to-specific trend, refers to the increasing specificity of functions and actions as a result of development. In general, whole-body or limb movements are replaced in time with much more specialized movements of only part of the body, such as a hand or a few fingers. Large-muscle control always precedes fine-muscle control. Have you ever noticed how a young child grips a pencil or a crayon? The whole-hand grasp serves many purposes—to hold on to a bar, to dig, to draw, to paint—but eventually the child will differentiate hand and finger grips specialized to each of these activities. As we will explore in a later discussion in this chapter, differentiation of muscle movements influences the overall activity level of children, which decreases with age.

> Muscles develop according to the proximodistal sequence, beginning nearer the spinal column.

The second well-known trend in development that is biologically determined is the **proximodistal sequence**, or near-to-far trend. This term refers to maturation from the spinal column out to the extremities. Control of muscle groups close to the spinal column (for example, in the neck, arms, or thighs) precedes control of muscles in the hands or feet by virtue of distance from the spinal column. The proximodistal sequence has its greatest effect on the sequence in which physical skills are taught and learned.

> The upper part of the body matures earlier, according to the cephalocaudal sequence.

The third trend is the **cephalocaudal sequence**, or head-to-tail trend; it refers to maturation from the head to the lower part of the trunk. One effect of the cephalocaudal sequence is the relatively early maturation of the head and the eye, both of which approximate adult size and shape in the middle elementary years. Another effect is sexual maturation, which is delayed on average until later elementary or middle school years. This delay has a profound effect on gender differences in motor skills.

The existence in all children of differential, proximodistal, and cephalocaudal trends in growth illustrates the role of nature in physical development. These biologically determined sequences exert a powerful influence over the changes that occur in a child's body and behavior. As a consequence, nature acts as a constraint in the instructional problem-solving process. For example, **fine motor skills** involve proficient use of comparatively small muscles near and in the eyes, hands, and feet. Because fine motor skills are not well developed and differentiated in the preschool and primary years, toys, tools, and clothing fasteners must be oversized. A second example is the effect of the cephalocaudal sequence on contrasts between the sexes, which are relatively small until puberty, when contrasts often require separate physical education classes and athletic competitions for boys and girls.

> Growth sequences influence how children can learn.

Effects of Nurture: Differentiation and Integration

Even though nature may impose profound constraints on instructional problem solving, nurture also plays an important role. Environmental factors such as nutrition, culture, and opportunities for practice with feedback appear to influence strongly certain changes in the body and in behavior. The kinds of experiences parents and teachers structure—for instance, the types of sports activities they organize for their children—affect and promote specific ends of development. In this section we'll look at two effects of nurture in particular: (1) further aspects of differentiation and (2) the process of integration (Bukatko & Daehler, 1995; Gallahue & Ozmun, 1995).

As an illustration of differentiation that occurs through experience, we might contrast childhood competencies in "high food-accumulation cultures" (where many resources are devoted to gathering food) with competencies in "low food-accumulation cultures" (where few resources are devoted to gathering food). In the high food-accumulation cultures typical of the developing world, rudimentary hand movements by one- and two-year-olds, such as reaching and grasping, may later differentiate into activities such as hand digging, planting, or harvesting. In the low food-accumulation cultures typical of the industrialized world, the same rudimentary movements may later differentiate into activities such as building with blocks, cutting with scissors, and writing in cursive letters. The influence of culture on the development and differentiation of physical skills is at least as profound as the influence of nature (Ogbu, 1982).

> Culture affects how children will use their basic physical skills.

The second process of physical development profoundly affected by practice is **integration**, which is the coordination of movements. Hand-eye coordination and foot-eye coordination involve integrated use of the fine motor muscles in the eyes with those in the hands or feet. For instance, simply throwing a ball does not require much integration of muscle movements and thus is quite easy for a child to accomplish and does not need much practice. Catching a ball, on the other hand, is made up of two distinct component movements—visual tracking and grasping—and requires the integration of the two (that is, eye-hand coordination). Both the mastery of these separate movements and the coordination of them can be dramatically assisted by nurture, in the form of practice with feedback.

> Integration of movements is enhanced by practice.

Amount of practice causes great variability in motor skills, often as early as preschool. Some children, aided by strip fasteners for shoes, elastic waistbands, and loose-fitting clothing, will learn to dress themselves in their preschool years, while others will continue to need assistance in first grade. Experience in youth sports will help many children in the elementary grades become proficient at specific sports skills, while other children of the same age who are not involved in youth sports will need carefully guided practice in school to master fundamental motor skills such as catching or dribbling a ball. Individual differences in psychomotor skills are enormous, but improvements can occur in almost all cases if children are given opportunities to practice and to receive feedback.

Examples of the Interaction of Nature and Nurture: Gender Differences in Physical Development

As we have seen, nature and nurture both affect development, each complementing the other in a rich, complex process. This is particularly true in the area of **gender differences,** or contrasts between the sexes. This is where we find some of the most interesting examples of the interaction of nature and nurture in motor skills. The recency of much of the research in this area illustrates the resurgence of interest that motor skill development is receiving in psychology. It also illustrates the need for thoughtfulness on the part of adults.

Natural gender differences in motor skills may be increased by social influences.

Some natural bases for gender differences in motor skills may be found in the relatively high activity level of boys compared to girls and in the average sexual maturation of girls two years before boys (Archer & Lloyd, 1985; Eaton & Enns, 1986). Still, most differences in commonly measured motor skills are small during middle childhood. What natural differences do exist are often exaggerated by the effects of nurture. For example, it is not uncommon to see elementary teachers at recess handing out jump ropes to girls and balls to boys (Thomas & Thomas, 1988). Boys and girls are often the objects of **sex stereotypes**, or rigid conceptions of sex roles, prevalent in our society (Maccoby & Jacklin, 1974). Because of such social influences rather than natural ones, girls and boys at recess often play very different kinds of games (Lever, 1976; Thorne, 1986). Boys tend to play physical and team-oriented games, and girls tend to play more quietly and in smaller groups. As a result, boys tend to be slightly more adept than girls at many sports-related skills in middle childhood (Thomas & French, 1985).

At the onset of adolescence, however, gender differences in motor skills increase dramatically. **Puberty** is the onset of sexual maturation. It is caused by the increased release of sex hormones—*androgen* and *testosterone* in males, and *estrogen* and *progesterone* in females—resulting in relatively rapid maturation of reproductive systems. Puberty generally occurs about a year after the end of the **growth spurt**, or the period of most rapid increase in height and weight. On average, the growth spurt of girls begins at age ten and peaks at eleven (see Figure 4.1). The average age of puberty for girls is twelve.

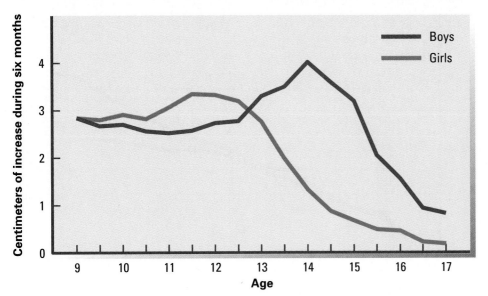

Figure 4.1
Growth Spurts of Boys and Girls
(Baumgartner, Roche & Himes, 1986)

On average, the growth spurt of boys begins at eleven years of age, but it does not peak until thirteen, creating a two-year lag in development. The average age of puberty for boys is fourteen.

The advent of puberty with its accompanying effects of sex-specific hormones means that physical differences between the sexes become tied to gender from about the fourth grade on. While boys and girls are approximately equal in height and weight until about the fourth grade, at that point most girls experience a growth spurt that will last through the end of elementary school. This spurt results in girls being on average slightly taller and heavier than boys during grades 4 through 7 (or ages nine through twelve). Beginning in the seventh grade, the growth spurt of boys, which is longer and more pronounced than that of girls, quickly catches boys up to girls in height, weight, and strength. By fourteen, boys are taller, heavier, and stronger than girls of the same age.

During this time, there are noticeable qualitative changes between the sexes as well. The development of boys' and girls' reproductive systems and primary sexual characteristics is closely followed by the development of **secondary sexual characteristics**, which are sex-related physical changes outside the reproductive system. In the male and to a lesser extent the female, the voice deepens, the texture of the skin changes, and body hair develops. In addition, the male increases in musculature in the neck, chest, and shoulders; the size of the heart and lungs; the ability of the blood to carry oxygen; and the ability of the body to neutralize lactic acid (a waste product of physical exercise). In the female, a higher proportion of fat to muscle is retained, breasts develop and hips broaden. The cumulative effects of these events are greater physical strength and endurance in males than in females, and a corresponding increase in gender differences in motor skills (Archer & Lloyd, 1985).

The picture we have of gender differences in motor skills is one in which small differences *before* puberty seem to be largely the product of nurture (or

> Changes in puberty increase differences in motor skills.

**Figure 4.2a
Gender Differences in
Running**
*(Haubenstricker & Seefeldt,
1986, p. 68)*

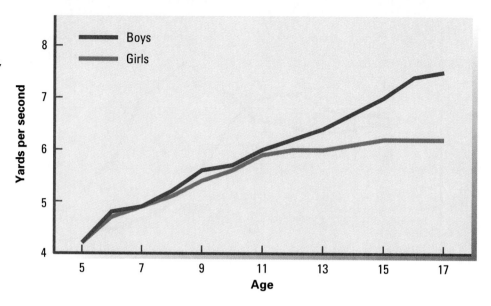

practice), and large differences *after* puberty seem to be the product of nature and nurture combined (Thomas, Thomas & Gallagher, 1993). Until puberty, nurture accounts for most differences in commonly measured motor skills such as running, standing long jump, jump and reach, and even distance throw (see Figures 4.2a to 4.2d). At puberty, nature enters the picture to exaggerate what earlier appear to be relatively small sex differences in many sports-related skills.

At this point in our discussion, it should be clear how gender differences offer us one good example of nature and nurture interacting and comple-

**Figure 4.2b
Gender Differences in
Standing Long Jump**
*(Haubenstricker & Seefeldt,
1986, p. 68)*

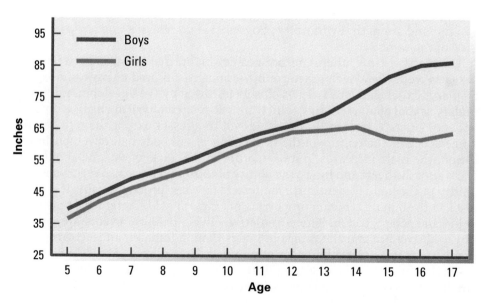

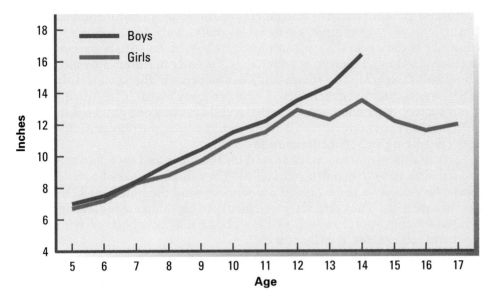

Figure 4.2c
Gender Differences in
Jump and Reach
(Haubenstricker & Seefeldt, 1986, p. 68)

menting one another in the process of physical development. But you are probably also wondering how all of this translates into physical education and your goals and strategies as a teacher. Not surprisingly, there *is* a direct effect on how teachers of either preadolescents or adolescents set up and operate physical education classes and team sports. Mixed competition before puberty often works out well. However, because mixed competition after puberty would take place on a biologically uneven playing field, many games and sports require separate competitions for adolescents. This provides both boys and girls equal opportunities to achieve.

Physical differences affect how teachers plan physical education.

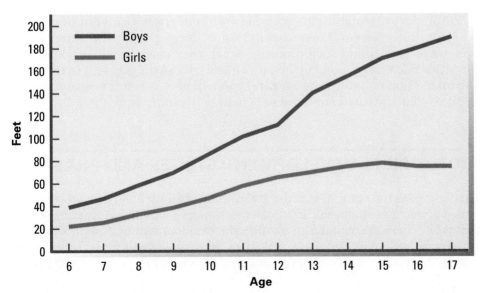

Figure 4.2d
Gender Differences in
Distance Throw
(Haubenstricker & Seefeldt, 1986, p. 68)

More particular problems also emerge as the result of nature and nurture. *Timing effects*, for example, occur when individuals do not mature at the same rate as their peers. Most timing effects have to do with being early, not late (Brooks-Gunn, Petersen & Eichorn, 1985). **Early maturers** are individuals whose bodies develop full functioning before peers of the same sex. It turns out, however, that the experience of being an early maturer is quite different in our society, depending upon whether a child is a boy or a girl. Looking a bit further at this phenomenon will allow us to make some observations about problem solving and educational intervention.

> Early maturation affects boys and girls differently.

Early maturers among males are tall for their age, and they find their size and strength valued by peers and society. They might be asked to try out for sports, be valued for their capacity to work around the house, and feel pressure to date early. They generally find plenty of encouragement and opportunity to develop sports-related skills and social skills, both of which are related to self-esteem (see Chapter 6).

Early maturers among females experience some of the same physical differences in relation to their peers, but often are not as valued for their stature or strength. A sixth-grade girl, for example, may tower over most of the boys in her class and seek to offset her height by leaning or slumping. We know that early maturing girls often suffer a distinctly poorer body image than on-time or late maturing girls (Brooks-Gunn, 1990).

> Early maturation calls for problem solving to set appropriate goals.

What can you do as a teacher dealing with a girl who is day after day feeling this pain of social awkwardness? Merely sympathizing with her or advising her to "wait a few years until things even out" is not enough, for it is not really addressing the girl's problem in a way that resolves it. Instead, providing an early maturing girl encouragement and opportunity to develop sports-related skills may be the best way to dispel her negative body image, influence acceptance by her peers, and improve her self-esteem. In this case, you define a problem as a challenge when you take the givens of lowered self-esteem resulting from early maturation, use them to set teaching goals, and then come up with a developmentally appropriate solution, such as participating in a youth sport.

While early maturation in our society will not always turn out to cause a problem, the more you know about physical development, the more likely you are to understand such problems when they exist, whether you teach physical education or not. Further, if you understand the problem in terms of the interaction of nature and nurture, you will be in a better position to figure out what you can do to assist or benefit your students.

MOTOR SKILL DEVELOPMENT: STAGES AND PHASES

> Development may be considered as stages or phases.

Psychologists who emphasize the givens of development—the effects of nature—divide development into discrete **stages**, which are maturational plateaus. These stages tend to confine the development of a skill to an approximate age range. Other psychologists, who stress goals for learning—the result of nurture—focus on developmental **phases**, which are levels of learn-

These children and their teacher in Walnut Creek, Texas, are about to do leg lifts, a strengthening exercise. Note the individual differences in maturation between children of the same age. From information provided in the text, what age would you say the children are in this class? *(Bob Daemmrich/Stock Boston)*

ing that show relatively continuous change in the direction of increasing proficiency. In a sense, stages and phases represent another form of the nature/nurture controversy.

Three Views of Motor Skill Development

The primary points of contrast between the stage and phase approaches are summarized in Table 4.1. Let's examine that table here so that you can get a firmer grasp of the two viewpoints, which contain some striking differences. After you have a good grasp of these two viewpoints, we'll look at how to combine them to resolve some of the issues that have been raised.

First, the stage approach sees the development of specific skills in relation to age and maturational sequences, while the phase approach is based on learning. Within the phase approach, beginners can develop into intermediates and intermediates into experts at many different ages, depending only on mastery of prerequisite skills. Second, the stage approach provides a sequence of age ranges that are highly predictable in their sequence and duration, but the phases of skill learning are more flexible, lasting different lengths of time for different skills. A given phase may last only a few hours, or it may last years, depending on the skill involved and the amount of practice. Third, the stage approach represents *qualitative* progressions of change, but the phase approach represents *quantitative* progressions of change. That is, the types of skills mastered are key within the stage approach, but within the phase model the focus is on levels of proficiency or increasing speed of performance of a given skill. Fourth, the stage approach emphasizes the givens that characterize the stage, while the phase approach emphasizes goals for learning to be achieved.

Stage theory emphasizes maturation; phase theory, learning.

Table 4.1   Comparison of Stage and Phase Approaches
to Motor Skill Development

Strengths of Stages	Strengths of Phases
Stages are fundamentally maturational (nature)	Phases are fundamentally learning based (nurture)
Stages are relatively constant in sequence and duration	Phases vary greatly in duration depending on skill and practice
Stages represent qualitative progressions (type of skill)	Phases represent quantitative progressions (proficiency, speed of performance)
Stages emphasize givens in problem solving	Phases emphasize goals in problem solving

This analysis of the relative strengths of stages and phases should not only give you a better grasp of each approach to development but also give you a way to discriminate a stage from a phase theory. Theories are sometimes mislabeled—phases may be called stages, or vice versa. You can tell a stage theory from a phase theory through its emphasis on maturation, its invariant sequence of changes related to chronological age, its focus on changes that are qualitative rather than quantitative, and its respect for givens or limitations in problem solving. By the same token, you can tell a phase theory from a stage theory through its emphasis on learning, practice, quantitative changes, and goals in problem solving.

By this point you may well be wondering what model stresses the complementarity of stages and phases, reflecting in a sense the nature/nurture interactive position that I have described in the previous section. Is there a way of folding the two contrasting positions on motor skill development together so that they can coexist and work together in complementary fashion? It turns out that this topic is of interest to psychologists who are searching for ways to combine the two approaches to development in order to devise effective instructional techniques. Thus, while currently there is no consensus in the field of motor development regarding a composite or a mixed theory, there is real speculation and a growing body of research to show that the two viewpoints need not be exclusive.

In the following section, you will encounter a traditional stage theory of motor development. Its large categories represent what many believe to be biological limitations on motor skill development. Afterward, an information-processing theory of motor skill development is described. Its phases of development represent changes in motor skills that occur with increasing proficiency. In the last discussion, I will present some suggestions about the complementarity of the two positions so that you will see the two as potentially working together to help you in solving teaching problems.

> Stage theory and phase theory may be complementary.

The Stage Approach to Motor Skill Development

Although no comprehensive stage model of motor development exists to link development in all types of motor activities, several models that focus on developments relevant to physical education provide a point of departure for analyzing stages of motor development in the school-age child (Gallahue & Ozum, 1995; Haubenstricker & Seefeldt, 1986; Zaichkowsky, Zaichkowsky & Martinek, 1980). Because these models are in close agreement on the four stages through which motor skills progress, only one is presented here. David Gallahue developed this theory, which is widely used to describe progressions in motor development (Gallahue & Ozmun, 1995).

> The stage approach to motor skills identifies four basic stages.

Maturational Stages

The four stages (and associated ages) of this model of motor development are *reflex movement* during infancy (birth to twelve months), *rudimentary movement* during infancy and toddlerhood (birth to two years), *fundamental movement* during early childhood (two to six or seven), and *specialized movement* during middle childhood, adolescence, and adulthood. Each of these four stages of motor development is divided into substages, charted in Table 4.2 and described below.

Reflex Movement.   Reflex movements occur even before a child is born. They include movements such as the grasping reflex, the sucking reflex, and the "startle" reflex (which is a response to a loud noise). Reflexes are supple-

> The first stage of movement is the reflex.

Table 4.2   Stage Theory of Motor Development

0 to 1 Year **Reflex movement**	Reflexes develop (such as grasping, stepping).
0 to 2 Years **Rudimentary movement**	Voluntary movements develop in a sequence determined by maturation (e.g., crawling, creeping, walking).
2 to 6 or 7 Years **Fundamental movement**	Fundamental motor abilities (including running, jumping, throwing, catching, and balancing) develop in *initial*, *elementary*, and *mature* substages.
7 to 14 Years and Up **Specialized movement**	Specialized skills develop from a *transitional* substage (6 or 7 to 10), in which fundamental movements are combined (as in kick ball or jump rope), through an *application* substage (11 to 13), in which a narrowing of interests occurs, into a substage of *lifelong utilization*.

Source: Summarized from Gallahue & Ozmun, 1995

mented by repetitive movements not under voluntary control, which have been labeled "rhythmical stereotypies" (Thelen, 1981). Rhythmical kicking, rocking, and waving are examples of rhythmical stereotypies.

Rudimentary Movement. A second, overlapping stage in motor learning involves the development of rudimentary movements, such as grasping and walking. This stage occupies birth to perhaps the second year of life. Reflexes, such as the grasping reflex, are often replaced by voluntary movements. For example, the child learns to reach and grasp voluntarily, or to wave a rattle to make a noise. Greater precision and control allow the child to manipulate objects, maintain balance or postural control, and move through the environment, in a sequence that culminates in walking at about ten to twelve months.

> The child learns rudimentary, voluntary movements from birth to two years.

Fundamental Movement. The development of fundamental movements is the distinguishing task of early childhood and the first year or two of middle childhood. Fundamental movements include *locomotor, nonlocomotor,* and *projection/reception* skills. Locomotor skills include walking, running, jumping, hopping, galloping, and skipping. Nonlocomotor skills include dynamic or static balancing, and bending/twisting/turning (axial movements). Projection/reception skills include reaching/grasping/releasing, throwing, catching, kicking, and striking. Table 4.3 presents a sample list. These three classes of fundamental movements are subcategories of basic-fundamental move-

> The child learns fundamental movements and skills from age two to seven.

Table 4.3 Sample Fundamental Motor Skills

Locomotor	Nonlocomotor	Projection/Reception
Walk	Swing	Catch
Run	Sway	Throw
Leap	Rock	Kick
Jump	Stretch	Punt
Gallop	Curl	Strike
Slide	Twist	Trap
Hop	Turn	Dribble
Skip	Bend	Roll
Roll	Push	
Stop	Lift	
Start	Pull	
Bounce	Hang	
Fall		
Dodge		

Source: Seefeldt, 1980, p. 317

ment objectives in the psychomotor domain in Chapter 3. From these short lists of fundamental skills, virtually all complex skills can later be derived.

The substages of fundamental movement development (and associated ages) are known as *initial* (two to three years old), *elementary* (four to five years old), and *mature* (six to seven years old). Initially, children develop skills such as running, but movements are not well coordinated or well sequenced. In the elementary substage, children gain better control and rhythmical coordination of movements. In the mature substage, children can perform such fundamental movements in a controlled and efficient way.

According to the stage model, early childhood is the optimal time to develop fundamental motor skills. Teachers encouraging preschoolers to hop to music are not only allowing for fun, but they are also helping their students to exercise a basic skill that will be combined with other skills later on (for instance, with balance and axial movements in hopscotch). Before children can play hopscotch, they need to develop a proficient hop, learning to control its distance and direction.

Vern Seefeldt (1980) hypothesized a *proficiency barrier* between fundamental movements and further motor skill development. He suggested that without proficient performance of fundamental skills, the transitional games of middle childhood cannot be mastered. These games—such as kick ball—combine and modify fundamental movements. If just one of the fundamental movement skills (such as catching) is not mastered, participation in a set of transitional games and later related sports becomes almost impossible. For that reason, the mature substage needs to be achieved in many different fundamental movements before a child can progress to specialized movement activities.

During the application substage of motor skill development (between the ages of eleven and thirteen), many children decide to specialize in a physical activity. This activity might be band or art as easily as it might be a sport. *(Ian Shaw/ Tony Stone Images)*

think it through

Consider this problem that a novice preservice teacher has **IDENTIFIED** and **REPRESENTED.**

The Value of Physical Education

There are quite a few problems that I expect to encounter as a beginning physical education and health teacher. However, the one that really worries me is the fact that a lot of teachers, parents, and students do not understand the importance of physical education and health. It will be difficult to teach a class where half of the students have been told by parents and even other teachers that physical education is useless. Most do not realize that good fitness and health habits that are taught now will last a lifetime. How would you explain to students, parents, and other teachers the importance of physical education and health?

Observe how an experienced practicing teacher **GENERATES SOLUTIONS** to this problem.

You are not alone in this dilemma. Fine arts teachers have the same problem. Education is the key to resolving it, and it must be provided for the parents, students, and other teachers. A good way to do this is to meet with parents and explain your goals for their children. This can be done at a "Parents' Information Night" or an open house. In order for parents to understand the importance of any task, we owe them an explanation. There are plenty of data supporting p.e. and showing the dangers of sedentary lifestyles.

In working with your colleagues I would hope that you might meet with them and ask if there is any way to coordinate your curriculum to enhance what is going on in the general classroom. I work with p.e., art, and music teachers very closely because I teach thematically. I need their help in providing a variety of activities that allow me to meet my educational goals.

Finally, I would caution any preservice teacher to use the most positive of approaches when beginning a school year. Clearly explain your goals for the class and/or the individuals in an exciting way that makes students *want* to participate in your program. Avoid putting the seed of doubt in a student's mind by saying things like, "I know a lot of you don't like . . . " or "Some of you may find what we're going to do of little value. . . ."

Michael Robinson
Center Elementary School
Marion, Indiana

think it through, continued

EVALUATE this problem's possible multiple solutions while you think about the dynamic process of problem solving.

As the experienced teacher suggests, educating parents and students about the value of physical education is one of the responsibilities of a physical education teacher. You can actually write objectives for this goal in the affective domain (development of a value), but to teach others, you need to inform yourself. Let's begin with fitness.

Fitness training often accompanies the development of skills as part of the physical education curriculum. It is appropriate beginning in early childhood for these reasons (Poest et al., 1990):

- The first signs of arteriosclerosis now appear at about age five.
- Most children do not engage in physical activities that are intense enough to increase cardiovascular fitness.
- "Free play," recess, and sports do not improve cardiovascular fitness because movement is not continuous.
- Only half of children ages five to twelve participate in appropriate activities at the minimum frequency and intensity required for cardiovascular health.
- Only 5 percent of elementary children qualify for the Presidential Award for Physical Fitness.
- More children are obese than in the past.

These facts will give those who find physical education "useless" pause to reflect on the value of fitness training to improve the health of children and, later, adolescents (Westcott, 1992).

Now let's go beyond fitness—which was the focus of both the novice and the experienced teacher—to look at some other values for physical education. You have already read how a "proficiency barrier" exists for children who do not master fundamental movement skills by the early grades. We all knew children who could not throw properly, catch consistently, or strike a ball with a bat. The inability to participate in childhood games and sports activities limited their opportunities for further motor development.

To a certain extent, their limited physical skills also limited their opportunities for social development during late childhood, when most children increasingly want to participate in peer group activities, and children are increasingly vulnerable to feeling left out. Physical education can develop aspects of self-esteem that are often difficult to develop through academic subjects.

To give you just one example, I tutor a fifth grader at our lab school who arrived this past fall from another country. He was initially somewhat shy and had few friends. I mentioned to the school counselor one day that the student had enjoyed playing soccer in his first country. The school counselor mentioned this skill to the boy's physical education teacher, who developed a soccer unit. He excelled in this unit, boosting his status in the eyes of his peers and making friends. Our strategy had worked.

As the experienced teacher pointed out, you can also do a lot to integrate physical education with core academic subjects so that teachers and parents perceive it as more useful than they would if it were taught separately. Several general ideas for integrating physical education with moral and cognitive development are presented at the end of this chapter. With a little reading, thinking, and discussion, you can come up with even more strategies to integrate development in different domains.

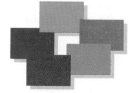

strategic solutions

Activity Level and Motor Development

In this Strategic Solutions section, let's pose two common problems-as-challenges facing teachers of young children: the children's high activity level and their just-developing large-muscle coordination. As you might guess from our earlier discussion of developmental sequences, these two problems-as-challenges are related to each other. Before developing a solution, let's define the problems and examine how they are related.

The **activity level** of any organism refers to its expenditure of energy through movement. Activity level is an indication of muscle use. Since large- (or gross-) **muscle activity**—such as use of arms and legs—expends more energy than does fine motor activity, such as the use of hands or fingers, it results in a high activity level. And since, as we have already discussed in the earlier section on differentiation, large- or gross-muscle activity develops first in children, it is generally true that the younger the child, the higher the activity level. (You probably knew this intuitively anyway!)

In fact, activity level depends not only on age and maturity but to some degree on sex as well, so that younger, less mature, or male children are generally reported to be more active than older, more mature, or female children (e.g., Achenbach & Edelbrock, 1981; Eaton & Yu, 1989; Richman, Stevenson & Graham, 1982; Routh, Schroeder & O'Tuama, 1974). The effects of both a high activity level and a strong degree of early gross motor activity on instruction can be very constraining. Successful instructional strategies for young children must take these limitations into account.

Let's look at activity level first. Figure 4.3 suggests that as far as parents are concerned, three-year-olds are about twice as active as nine-year-olds. As a consequence, preschoolers and kindergartners often appear restless in comparison to school-age children. It is not uncommon to hear adults ask themselves, "Where do they get all their energy?" or "I wish that I could bottle it for myself."

What are some of the instructional ramifications of a high activity level? One important effect is that preschoolers and kindergartners require more frequent rest periods than do older children. Delay of a preschooler's rest period until nighttime will certainly risk irritability and sometimes accident. As a consequence, rest periods during each day should be required for children at this age (Bredekamp, 1987).

In contrast to teachers at higher grade levels, preschool and kindergarten teachers need to set limits on activities (particularly during rest time). They also need to be able to anticipate a relatively great deal of change in activities because high activity level and short attention spans go hand in hand. Planning should generally include a balance of activities: indoor and outdoor,

**Figure 4.3
Activity Levels of
Children 3 to 9**
(Routh, Schroeder &
O'Tuama, 1974)

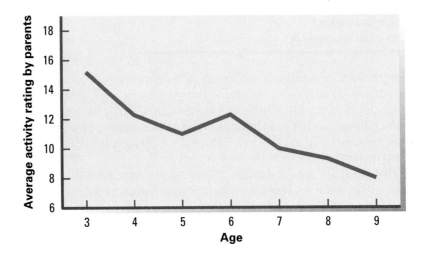

quiet and active, large-muscle and (as becomes appropriate) small-muscle, individual and group, child-initiated and teacher-initiated (Bredekamp, 1987).

A high activity level also brings with it a constant need for a source of energy. Preschoolers get hungry more often than older children do. Healthy snacks not only prevent irritability due to hunger; they also create opportunities to take breaks from more strenuous physical activities, such as outdoor play.

Now, let's examine strategic solutions for teaching a roomful of highly active children who are also just developing gross-muscle skills. First, you should realize that their high activity level does *not* indicate a high skill level. In fact, quite the contrary is true. Since coordination is only developing, plenty of open space, simple play equipment, and constant supervision are necessary.

The large-muscle activities that you choose should focus on development of fundamental movements such as those listed in Table 4.3 (Ignico, 1994). Hopping to music, climbing stairs to a play loft, bouncing or catching an oversized ball, operating a teeter-totter—all of these activities develop fundamental movements. Many preschoolers advance to some simple activities that begin to combine fundamental movements, such as playing freeze tag or steering and pedaling a tricycle, but not until kindergarten do most children learn how to catch a ball while moving, or how to steer and pedal a bicycle. In the meantime, of course, fine motor skills have been developing.

In summary, preschoolers' high activity level and predominant use of large-muscle groups help define instructional problems and strategic solutions. Teachers must accept a comparatively high activity level and a rela-

The high activity level of young children brings with it a need for healthy snacks to supply energy. Snacks also provide a break from more strenuous activities and a chance to exercise fine motor skills. *(Karen Su/ Stock Boston)*

tively primitive level of coordination during the preschool years as a given. The result is that equipment and tasks suitable for older children cannot simply be scaled down for younger children. For example, balls for four- and five-year-olds to throw, catch, or dribble should not be miniaturized but should be larger and softer than balls for older children. Young children must have equipment and activities designed especially for them if you are to solve the instructional problems that are appropriate to their stage of motor development.

Specialized Movement. This stage includes children from ages seven through fourteen. You will be particularly interested in this stage not only because these years coincide with participation in many different organized activities, but because adultlike interests often emerge to set patterns of activity for many years to come.

More sophisticated, specialized movements are the focus at ages seven to fourteen.

For most children, specialized movements begin their development at seven to ten years of age with a *general or transitional movement* substage. During this period, fundamental movements are combined or modified, with or without equipment, to be performed alone or within simple games or activities. The transitional substage is associated with childhood games such as jump rope, hopscotch, kick ball, whiffle ball, and street hockey (see Table

Table 4.4   Some Transitional Games of
Middle Childhood

Kick ball	Tee ball
Jump rope	Whiffle ball
Hopscotch	Foursquare
Freeze tag	Tetherball
Dodge ball	"H-O-R-S-E"
Street hockey	"500"
Field hockey	
Bike riding	
"Red Rover"	
"Marco Polo"	

4.4) as well as with some musical instruments. These games and instruments tend to be played only by the seven-to-ten age group because their function is transitional, facilitating the development of more complex motor performances.

General interest in a variety of sports and activities becomes specialized between eleven and thirteen in an *application* substage, in which the child often decides to specialize in a sport or in an activity such as band or art. The individual makes decisions based on "the extent to which factors within the task, him or herself, and the environment either enhance or inhibit chances for enjoyment and success" (Gallahue & Ozmun, 1995, p. 89). Decisions by fourteen years of age often result in *lifelong utilization*, the last substage of specialized skill development. The individual limits participation to a few movement activities that can be sustained over many years, such as playing a musical instrument, playing tennis, jogging, swimming, or dancing.

Specialized learning influences activity choices in later life.

For many children, transitional games are succeeded rather rapidly by involvement in sports. By far, youth sport is the most common such activity. Few youth sport programs are school-sponsored in the elementary grades, but participation is widespread in North America. Orel Hershiser, pitcher for the Los Angeles Dodgers, for example, participated in Little League (which begins at age nine), a national "throw, hit, and run" contest, and youth hockey, all *before* he became an adolescent. Currently, almost half (45 percent) of children between the ages of six and eighteen participate in non–school-based sports for a variety of reasons that range from fun to friendship (Bigelow, Lewko & Salhani, 1989; Chambers, 1991). Children in later elementary grades seem to rank skill development among the most important reasons for participation in sports, a rationale that appears to be related to emerging competencies (Brodkin & Weiss, 1990; Klint & Weiss, 1987).

Stage theories of motor development like this one help us to identify how maturational trends affect learning both before and during the school years. What they do not provide are specific implications for teaching. Instead, they tend to focus on general goals related to age ranges and indicate what is *not* appropriate at that age. These contributions are very important to understand what to teach and how to teach, but they do not result in many specific instructional strategies.

The Phase Approach to Motor Skill Development

As I described in the introduction to this discussion of approaches, psychologists and educators who favor a phase approach to motor skill development stress learning goals for any individual child. They do not look as much to the limitations end of the spectrum (such as maturational and age considerations) but emphasize instead the flexibility of changes that can take place. One way to put it is that they view development as a series of learning-based changes. Their viewpoint carries with it a different set of instructional implications, which are often highly specific.

> The phase approach to motor skills emphasizes learning goals.

Information Processing and Motor Skill Learning

Phases of motor learning are frequently associated with changes in the way people process information (Schmidt, 1987; Schneider & Shiffrin, 1977; Shiffrin & Schneider, 1977). *Controlled* processing of new information requires attention, but *automatic* processing does not. **Attention**, which is the allocation of short-term memory capacity (described in more detail in Chapter 9), requires that information be processed slowly and a little at a time so that decisions can be made about it—whether to store it or use it; if to store it, how to store it; or if to use it, how to use it, and so on. Consequently, controlled processing is very slow and limited in capacity.

> Learning allows people to process information without giving it so much attention.

Controlled processing occurs in motor skill learning as an individual begins to practice a gymnastics routine, play from sheet music for the first time, or try the steps of a new dance. With consistent practice, however, the processing of information becomes less conscious and much faster, freeing the mind to attend to other aspects of the task, such as form in gymnastics or music, or style in dance. At this point, we might say that processing of routine information has become automatic.

The phases through which learning passes on the way to automatic performance are commonly called (1) "beginning" or "novice," (2) "intermediate" or "proficient," and (3) "advanced" or "expert." These distinctions among skill levels from typing to swimming to piano playing are so common that it might go unnoticed that they suggest a sequence in the development of **automaticity**, or the capacity to respond without attention. Perhaps what automatic processing accounts for best is the ability to pursue some routine motor task such as driving a car, operating a word processor, or playing a musical instrument while simultaneously using higher cognitive processes.

> Automaticity is the ability to respond without paying attention.

Phases of motor learning have different labels, but the beginning or novice phase is frequently described as *cognitive*, the intermediate or proficient phase as *associative*, and the advanced or expert phase as *autonomous* (Fitts & Posner, 1967). These three phases, and associated methods of instruction, are summarized in Table 4.5.

Cognitive Phase

In the cognitive phase of learning, one tries to understand the skill.

In the beginning or *cognitive* phase of motor learning, movements are not smooth but uncoordinated and jerky. The student during this phase is trying to construct a mental plan for the activity and *understand* the skill. The plan consists of a sequence of routines that make up the overall performance, and the student acquires an understanding of the skill by learning which responses must follow each other. Performance in the cognitive phase can be very fatiguing because the student is both exercising muscles and learning to attend to relevant cues in the environment to process information appropriately.

The phases of development can be illustrated with a rather simple motor skill, such as learning to dribble a basketball (Oxendine, 1984). Dribbling is obviously a component skill of the game of basketball. In the beginning or cognitive phase, the child might observe someone else dribbling the ball, then, with encouragement, try it him- or herself. The child might watch the ball for cues for when to strike it, and learn to strike the ball when it is at the top of its bounce. The child also might learn that an open-handed push rather than a sharp strike has the best results. Appropriate demonstrations and feedback from a teacher, coach, or parent provide encouragement and further helpful information that will improve performance.

Associative Phase

Transition to the *associative* or intermediate phase of motor learning is marked by performance in a manner that approximates the final skill. The focus of learning changes from understanding the processes of performance

Table 4.5   Phases of Information Processing in Motor Skill Learning

Skill Phase	Proficiency	Instructional Focus
Cognitive	Beginning/Novice	Modeling and practice of component skills Highlighting of cues
Associative	Intermediate/Proficient	Student practice with developmental feedback
Autonomous	Advanced/Expert	Form, style, strategy, problem solving

Source: Fitts & Posner, 1967

to *practice* of the final performance until it is sequenced and smooth. Many educators believe that cognitive and verbal parts of the learning task drop out during this phase, making learning entirely associative in nature (based on sensory feedback). Learning during this phase generally takes longer than learning during the cognitive phase, includes larger segments of activity, and often involves a practice schedule and either gamelike or realistic conditions.

> In the intermediate, associative phase, one practices and refines the skill.

For example, during the intermediate or associative phase of learning to dribble, practice might involve refinement in control (using fingertips only) and combination of dribbling with running, stopping, and changing directions, all done without looking at the ball. During regular practice sessions with a teacher and sometimes an opponent, the youngster may well learn to identify and correct his or her own mistakes. Regular practice sessions with set drills might be conducted to develop component skills.

Autonomous Phase

Transition to the *autonomous* or advanced phase of motor learning is marked by decreasing attentiveness to routine aspects of the task. Typically, performance in the autonomous phase assumes mastery of component skills to a threshold level, which permits their *automatic* use. Attention of the learner begins to focus on nonroutine aspects of the task, which include form and style. In addition, the mind of the learner is freed to *solve problems* of strategy.

> In the autonomous phase, one can perform automatically and concentrate on style.

During the advanced or autonomous phase, the child might dribble the basketball without conscious control. Feedback often is processed without entering the player's awareness. Rather than think about dribbling, the

These elementary students in Lancaster, Pennsylvania, are learning through computers. Why is automaticity of keyboarding skills a valuable goal for students who will often use computer-based instruction?
(Brian Coats)

player focuses attention on more important matters, such as an opposing player. The player's mind may also be occupied with decision making or problem solving. How will the player get the ball to the goal? The youngster may decide to drive to the goal, or pass off, or pull up for a jump shot, without ever thinking about the skill of dribbling. Automation of routine skills frees the player to make a decision or solve a problem related to the nonroutine elements of the situation.

Automatic performance has been formally studied in the development of several motor skills, from typing (Shaffer, 1975) to playing music (Allport, Antonis & Reynolds, 1972). Benjamin Bloom (1986) has called automaticity "the hands and feet of genius" because of its usefulness at very high skill levels. Automaticity is also a common goal among those who teach physical education, music, and machine operations (such as word processing, sewing, and shop), handwriting, and the use of scientific equipment and calculators. The conditions under which automaticity develops differ depending on the type of skill being practiced.

strategic solutions

Developing Automaticity

The information-processing approach to motor skill development suggests that as learners become experts at a skill, they develop some degree of automaticity. Each phase of learning in the development of automaticity tends to be accompanied by activities and methods designed to enhance learning at that level. The use of these activities and methods in sequence composes an instructional strategy or the solution to an instructional problem. Because certain elements of the sequence are common to the development of many skills, they can be described in general.

In the *cognitive phase* of learning a skill, a student is focused on understanding the skill and attending to learning cues. **Learning cues**, which are words or phrases in which the teacher communicates critical features of movement, should be accurate, critical to the task, limited in number, and appropriate to the age of the learner (Rink, 1993).

Appropriate cues for young children take into account their limited repertoire of motor skills and vocabulary. For young learners, a teacher might rely on demonstration, overemphasizing a skill or freezing an action at critical points. You might freeze the action of throwing a ball at several points, for example, to emphasize keeping the elbow high, stepping with the opposite foot, extending the arm, and snapping the wrist. Learning cues for a young child can also be presented through a picture, diagram, or target. The critical rule to remember when giving cues to young children is "Show, don't tell."

Appropriate cues for older children can take into account their ability to comprehend verbal descriptions. Learning cues for throwing a ball might be "Keep your elbow high and lean forward," "Step to the opposite foot," and "Put your hand out and throw" (Rink, 1993, p. 90). While phrases might be able to call up complex responses in an older child, cues should still be very limited in number.

The *associative phase* of motor skill development primarily involves *practice* and the development of feedback. Rules for effective practice do not seem to generalize easily across many different types of activity. Two types of tasks that recommend different types of practice are closed-movement and open-movement tasks (Gallahue & Ozmun, 1995).

A *closed-movement* task calls for consistent movements under stable conditions. Examples are learning to tie one's shoes, perform music for a recital, or make a basketball free throw. Practice of closed-movement tasks tends to be most effective when it is highly repetitive. An *open-movement* task calls for performance under constantly changing conditions. Tag games, musical improvisation, or dual and group sports are examples of open-movement tasks. Practice of open-movement tasks tends to be most effective under changing conditions.

Some activities are best practiced in their component parts, derived through task analysis, breaking down a procedure into steps. Other activities are best practiced as wholes. Some activities can be mastered in a relatively short time, while others must be learned after intervals of rest or alternative activities. Despite a considerable number of studies in this area of practice effects, psychology has discovered very little about such matters that can be consistently applied to many different skills and situations (Chamberlin & Lee, 1993).

More is known about feedback and its effects on performance. Informational feedback can have many forms, a few of which are summarized in Figure 4.4. *Intrinsic feedback* is information that directly results from an activity. *Extrinsic feedback* is information that is artificially added, or that *in*directly results from the performance of an activity. Feedback may also be described as either *concurrent* or *terminal*, depending on whether it occurs during or after performance. Multiple forms of feedback occur during any practice session, but they may be relatively independent of each other and thus have different characteristics (Schmidt, 1988).

Figure 4.4
Selected Types of
Feedback in Motor Skill
Development

	Extrinsic	Intrinsic
Concurrent	Feedback from verbal or physical guidance Teacher or learning cues guide movement	Feedback from kinesthetic and visual perception; "feel" Self-monitoring of experience
Terminal	Feedback from augmented consequences Teacher says "good"	Feedback from natural consequences Correct performance

For example, guiding a child verbally and physically through a forward roll would be an example of extrinsic and concurrent feedback. The student's sense of what the forward roll "feels like" would be an example of intrinsic and concurrent feedback. Coming upright out of the roll would be an example of intrinsic and terminal feedback. A teacher who says "good" at the conclusion of the roll would be providing extrinsic and terminal feedback. It is possible to receive all four of these forms of feedback when making a forward roll! You might take a moment to use Figure 4.4 to analyze some physical activity in your teaching field for the various types of feedback.

There are some progressions in feedback during the associative phase of skill development. One obvious progression is chronological. Concurrent feedback obviously precedes terminal feedback. A less obvious progression is from extrinsic and concurrent feedback to intrinsic and terminal feedback. Let's examine one example of this below.

If a student is learning to assemble equipment for a chemistry lab experiment, he or she may need a great deal of guidance (extrinsic and concurrent feedback) in early labs. Equipment may be unfamiliar and difficult to assemble, discouraging the student. In later labs, the student may need only the natural consequence of assembling the equipment proficiently (intrinsic and terminal feedback) to continue to improve at this skill. The effect of these progressions is that the attention necessary to monitor routine aspects of a motor skill in early practice sessions decreases over time.

The *autonomous phase* of motor skill development involves *consistent* performance in which attention is freed from the movement itself. Instead of focusing on performance, the learner's attention shifts to problem solving in order for him or her to make last-moment adjustments in form or style or to plan a strategy. In this manner, performance can continue to improve almost indefinitely, as some adjustments become part of new motor patterns that are then automaticized. There is much that we still do not know about automatic performance and how it interacts with cognition, but such research has a promising future in the field of motor learning (Adams, 1987; Lee, Keh & Magill, 1993).

Now that we have looked at strategic solutions to instructional problems from a phase point of view, take a moment to read the Reflection on Practice: Progress in Learning to Bunt. In answering the questions and thinking about the example, you have an opportunity to reflect on the learning *you* are doing.

Evaluation: Developing Automaticity

Preliminary research on the different techniques associated with different phases of learning generally supports the procedures outlined above. For example, researchers have recently summarized sixteen studies of motor skill learning in which instruction was *enhanced* by (1) cues, (2) increased time on task (within a set instructional period), and (3) multiple forms of feedback (Tenenbaum & Goldring, 1989). These enhancements correspond with methods appropriate to the beginning and intermediate levels of motor skill development.

What researchers have found is that in their rate of learning, average students with enhanced instruction outpace three-fourths of students with conventional instruction. Enhanced instruction improves motor skill performance more than conventional instruction does, regardless of motor skill task, year in school, or student gender. These results may not extend to enhanced instruction during the advanced phase of learning, however, when individuals may find extrinsic feedback distracting or unprofitable (Fitts & Posner, 1967).

As yet, researchers know very little about the effect of practice conditions on the development of automaticity in sports-related skills. One research problem lies in the extent of training time required for experimentation on automaticity (Adams, 1987). Another problem lies in the frequent interest of educators in earlier phases of motor learning, where extrinsic feedback seems to have greater value. Nevertheless, increasing interest in very high levels of motor skill performance as early as high school may lead researchers to focus on the effectiveness of instructional strategies in this area in the future.

reflection on practice

Progress in Learning to Bunt

When I coach baseball, I require all my players to achieve to the best of their ability the basic skills of baseball. I had one player, Felipe, who could not bunt the baseball. This is one skill that I really stress the importance of accomplishing. Felipe had the ability, but lacked the proper technique and confidence that he could do it.

We started out in the batting cage working on the proper stance and technique but he still missed the ball. I always found something good to say about his technique. After a few weeks he began bunting the ball in the cage. I knew the biggest step was yet to come and that that would be in a game.

We were ahead one day, and I gave Felipe the bunt sign. He called time out and asked me if I really wanted him to bunt. I told him yes, and that I expected him to be able to do it. He fouled his first two attempts and I had to let him hit away because of the two strikes. While he batted I could see the determination in his eyes. At the time, I did not know that we had just made a big step in confidence to bunt.

Finally, the opportunity arose in another game for Felipe to be successful. It was the seventh inning, 0–0, and one out with a runner on third when I gave Felipe the signal to squeeze bunt. The "squeeze" is when the runner breaks to home plate as the pitcher is throwing to the plate. The batter *must* bunt the ball wherever the pitcher throws it, or the catcher will throw or tag the runner out. Felipe laid down a perfect bunt, and we won the game. Looking back, I can see the steady progress he made to that moment.

Ronald Lewey

Discussion Questions

1. Analyze the progression in bunting in terms of phases of learning. Are all three phases represented here?

2. What changes in coaching technique occurred during the development of this skill? Specifically, how did the coach's feedback to the student change?

3. Why was the coach so concerned about the student's confidence? What did he do to minimize risk during teachable moments?

Complementarity of Stage and Phase Approaches to Motor Skill Development

> Stage and phase models complement each other like nature and nurture.

The third way to approach physical development, and the one that I find most compelling, is to envision the stage model and the phase model as supplements to each other, one emphasizing givens of development to be respected, and the other, goals of development to be attained. On the one hand, the stage view of physical development stresses biological givens and pro-

Development at What Price?

Children whose parents overemphasize tasks that they may be capable of but aren't necessarily maturationally ready for are sometimes called "hurried children." David Elkind (1987) has pointed out that some parents hurry preschoolers into physical and intellectual activities that are appropriate for older children, usually in an effort to develop a competitive edge. Some schools and teachers go along with parental pressures to try to develop skills unusually early. The classic examples of such parents in the sports arena are tennis moms and coach dads who want their children to begin sports in early childhood. If their children do not burn out on a given sport because of the stress (Rotella, Hanson & Coop, 1991) they may develop expertise early, but at considerable expense. Like their parents, they tend to be overly ambitious. As adults, they often have to take time out from successful careers to reconstruct their priorities, putting expertise and winning into a perspective in which other skills and other people are more highly valued.

Mispractices often occur in schools where teachers conform to pressures to develop student expertise rapidly. Perhaps the most well known is "teaching to the test," which can occur at any educational level and in any subject. The test may be a national physical education test, a state band competition, a standardized achievement test, an advanced placement exam, or a rising junior examination. It is worth taking some time to consider the effects of such practices on students and teachers.

Divide up into groups of four to discuss the causes and effects of "hurrying" children, drawing from cases with which you are familiar. Then reassemble as a large group to discuss what you have learned.

Discussion Questions

1. How can you recognize when someone is hurrying a child?
2. What motivates them? (Consider several possibilities.)
3. What is the price of being hurried for students? For the teacher?
4. What ethical or social norm does "teaching to the test" undermine?

vides a broad outline for goals and activities that are maturationally appropriate. Relating this to our original nature/nurture discussion, we might say that in providing this broad outline, nature frames the picture of development, but it does not specify strategies a teacher might use. On the other hand, the phase approach to physical development stresses goals of instructional problem solving and in so doing has a much more direct influence on strategy. We might say that in our picture of development, within the canvas framed by nature, nurture paints the picture.

We may even see the two perspectives of development interacting in the way fundamental motor skills are addressed in the stage theory (see Figure 4.5). Notice that fundamental movements go through three substages—initial, elementary, and mature. Some experts define these changes in terms

Figure 4.5
Phases Within a Stage of
Motor Development

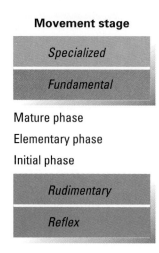

Movement stage

Specialized

Fundamental

Mature phase

Elementary phase

Initial phase

Rudimentary

Reflex

Stage theory and phase
theory may be integrated.

---

of maturation (e.g., Getchell & Roberton, 1989), but others seem to define them in terms of learning (Clark, Phillips & Petersen, 1989). What if we were to consider them the equivalent of beginner, intermediate, and advanced phases of learning a fundamental movement? If so, we could fold phases of learning into the fundamental stage of motor skill development.

Let's look at the evidence that supports folding phases of learning within the fundamental movement stage. Fundamental movements such as throwing, kicking, running, jumping, catching, striking, hopping, and skipping all begin after eighteen months of age and are almost completely developed in most children by age ten (Seefeldt & Haubenstricker, 1982). The period during which most of these skills develop is from age two until seven. During this period, which approximates early childhood, some skills (such as jumping) develop early and progress slowly. Others (such as running) develop early and progress more rapidly. Still others (such as skipping) develop late and progress rapidly. In general, this evidence suggests that progression of any fundamental skill is not influenced as strongly by chronological age as by level of difficulty and amount of practice.

There is no consensus that we can fold phases of learning into each (or any) stage of development, but this conceptualization of development does present a clear and coherent view of progressive change as the product of both nature and nurture. The current trend is to see development as primarily learning-based, just as the trend half a century ago was to see development as primarily maturation-based. Integrating the two views and seeing them as complementary rather than antagonistic can help you to understand children more thoroughly and to construct better instructional strategies.

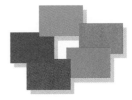

Respecting and Promoting Readiness

In this discussion we will examine an important developmental characteristic that has been dramatically rethought within the last decade or so. The new way of looking at the concept of **readiness** defines it as a set of conditions within both an individual *and* his or her environment that make a task appropriate to master (Gallahue & Ozmun, 1995). As such, readiness gives us an excellent window into the complementary influences of nature and nurture and also into the possible ways in which stage and phase approaches can be folded together.

Thirty years ago, educational psychologists thought of readiness only in terms of physical and mental maturation (nature). As a product of maturation, readiness would have been discussed solely as a limitation or constraint on instructional problem solving (Seefeldt, 1980). Current conceptions of readiness suggest, however, that it is achieved to a great extent through the practice of prerequisite skills. Not only prerequisite learning but also motivation and an enriched environment—including equipment and opportunity to learn—are now considered key factors indicating genuine readiness. In the new view, if a child is "ready," in terms of having a well-developed base for learning, learning can generally occur far more easily and be retained longer than if a child is not ready. Viewed in this manner, readiness is a level of preparedness to learn more complex skills. Just as hopping must be mastered before a child can play hopscotch, or as kicking a ball must be mastered before a child can play kick ball, so a set of fundamentals precedes virtually any sports-related motor skill.

What does this mean in terms of real children and physical development? We find a good example in the changed views of fundamental motor skill development. Whereas active free play in early childhood (that is, letting children do whatever comes naturally) was once thought to develop fundamental motor skills fully, evidence now suggests that even as early as preschool, fundamental motor skills develop better with appropriate guidance than without any guidance at all (Haubenstricker & Seefeldt, 1986). Put another way, there is now some evidence that, despite our maturationally based expectations that children will have typically mastered basic or fundamental motor skills before they enter school, many children have *not* mastered all these skills equally. Failure to master these movements during the preschool years can often be attributed to poor or absent instruction, little or no encouragement, or lack of opportunity to practice them (Gallahue & Ozmun, 1995).

Moreover, significant problems in motor skill development arise by the end of third grade if a child cannot demonstrate mastery of these skills when asked to do so (Reuschlein & Vogel, 1985). At this age, immature skill patterns are likely to interfere with the acquisition of more complex motor skills. As a consequence, some children have increasing difficulty participating in games and team activities and may never progress beyond the stage of fundamental motor movements.

With all this talk of learning and prerequisites for learning, it may seem as if the new view of readiness has merely replaced nature and stages with nurture and phases. However, as we sum up our look at this new definition, we need to stress its duality—the fact that it accommodates not only the newer notion of promoting learning but also the earlier respect for maturational guidelines and prerogatives. Notice how in our example just above, the fundamental skills stage and what that entails was a basic "frame" for the entire discussion.

Let's take a close look now at three teaching strategies that, when taken as a whole, specifically *respect* and *promote* readiness: (1) adapting group activities to individual learners, (2) grouping students by skill level, and (3) peer teaching. With younger children in particular, adaptation of the game, sport, or other activity to the needs of individual students is a commonly recommended strategy (Arbogast & Lavay, 1986). In a game of kick ball, for example, the ball can be pitched at various speeds for kickers with varying degrees of skill. In a more complex game such as soccer, a teacher might first engage the whole class in a "lead-up" activity (such as circle soccer) to practice fundamental movement goals (such as "to kick a ball with accuracy") without boring the more proficient players.

A second strategy is to group students by skill level (Haubenstricker & Seefeldt, 1986). Not all motor skills need to be taught through groups—particularly when everyone in the class is acquiring the skill as a beginner—but grouping may be especially desirable when the class has a wide range of proficiency due to developmental differences, as in junior high school. If you group students by skill level, make sure that learners can progress from group to group, and spend the largest portion of your time with the beginners. Do not try to balance group size, but keep the beginning group as small as possible. As soon as beginners become capable of a complete performance (such as swimming a few strokes in the shallow end of the pool, or hitting the volleyball to the opposite court), move them up to the intermediates, where they will continue to learn from peers, practice, and instructional feedback.

A third way to promote readiness is peer teaching (Rink, 1993). Peer teaching may involve teaching the whole group, but more often it involves students teaching small groups or individuals either the same skill at the same time, or different skills at different "stations." Peer teachers should be selected for their relatively high skill level so that they can teach students in earlier stages or phases of learning. Their strategies should include demonstration and appropriate forms of feedback. You should make sure peer teachers know *what* to demonstrate. Check to verify that they are supplying *positive* feedback. Beginners are particularly in need of modeling and encouragement from peers. Almost all proficient learners will intuitively understand that.

Your strategy will often develop as students become older, from adapting group activities to grouping students by skill level to peer teaching. There are two reasons for this; both are maturationally based, both demonstrate how our respect for the constraints of stages comes into play. First, the variation in levels of a given skill among young children is relatively small and can still be addressed within whole-group activities. This variability increases with age, and it becomes progressively more difficult to address within a single activity. Second, younger children do not always have the social and intellectual maturity to teach each other, whereas older children often do. Older children are likely to have greater patience with other children their age or younger. They also are more likely to recognize how skills develop with practice and feedback. Table 4.6 summarizes the ways in which the sequence of these strategies both respects and promotes readiness.

Table 4.6   *A Sequence of Strategies to Respect and Promote Readiness*

Strategy	Example
Adapt group activities to individual needs	Teacher varies pitch in kick ball
Group students by skill level (beginner, intermediate, advanced)	Use three courts to practice volleyball skills
Use peer teaching	Divide gymnastics class into compatible groups of four, with group leaders who are proficient at movement to be learned

Evaluation: Respecting and Promoting Readiness

Despite many years of research on motor development, the question of what roles maturation and learning play in relation to each other remains unanswered. There is no doubt that both play a role, but the specific roles they play seem to be more a function of research trends than the product of an accumulating body of knowledge. Currently, most research is emphasizing a predominant role for learning. The information-processing approach seems to be ascendant, but maturation clearly plays an important role too. Overall, the knowledge base suggests that changes in skill are related to both age and experience, and that changes are orderly and sequential (Barrett, Williams & Whitall, 1992), but there is no consensus on how these changes occur. The reasons for this lack of consensus are (1) the practical difficulty in separating the effects of nature from nurture, and (2) the increase in individual differences with age.

Many studies of the increasing abilities of children as they grow older suggest that such changes are the product of both maturation and experience, but often it is difficult to separate out one effect from the other. For example, if you look at growth spurts of boys and girls (shown in Figure 4.1), then look at the gender differences in motor skills (in Figure 4.2), you can get an idea of the complementary roles maturation and experience play in these changes. Some of the skill differences between males and females after puberty are the result of changes in underlying abilities such as strength or endurance, but some are also the result of different rates of participation in physical activities, including sports. In trying to untangle the effects of nature from nurture, we run into a chicken-and-egg problem: Which comes first?

A second factor that makes it difficut to analyze changes in motor development is the range of individual differences, which becomes quite large by high school. These differences are the product of (as you might guess by now) nature and nurture. They are illustrated in two studies of the overhand serve in volleyball (French et al., 1991; Rink et al., 1992). Ninth-graders were asked to practice the overhand serve at progressively more difficult skill levels. Students were initially divided into "high," "average," and "low" skill groups from a pretest in which the teacher described and demonstrated the skill to be learned, then asked students to demonstrate the correct movements without a ball.

When students began practice, the initial objective was to stand ten feet from a wall and to hit the ball over an eight-foot-high line using an overhand serve. Students in high and average groups improved with practice and went on to progressively more difficult objectives, but those in the low group did not improve with practice. The researchers commented that the problem in the low groups seemed to be related to lack of force. Force is the application of strength, a physical ability. If you look back in Chapter 3 at the taxonomy for the psychomotor domain, you will notice that physical abilities developmentally precede skilled movements. The least skilled *third* of all participating students needed to develop strength before they could successfully serve overhand.

The range of individual differences in physical skills in these classes was larger than a phase approach would assume. We might say that the beginners (the "low" group) lacked developmental prerequisites. They could not strike a ball overhand with force. Does this mean that their motor development was immature? Probably not at this age (fourteen). It was probably a function of individual differences, which in the practical world are often greater than a single stage would allow.

As a consequence of difficulties in separating the effects of nature and nurture, and of the large role individual differences play in development, you will want to remain skeptical of any formulation of how nature and nurture interact. Nevertheless, you will need a point of departure for thinking about their complementary relationship as you formulate instructional strategies. Folding phases within stages provides a viewpoint with implications for readiness to learn. These implications both respect developmental constraints and promote developmental goals in a manner consistent with your need to solve instructional problems.

HOW PSYCHOMOTOR DEVELOPMENT RELATES TO DEVELOPMENT IN OTHER DOMAINS

When teaching *integrates* learning, it combines objectives from the psychomotor domain with objectives from the cognitive or affective domain. For example, in the description of Mr. Ramirez's kindergarten physical education class, you find evidence that he consciously integrated physical and cognitive learning. Why? For a preschooler, stepping units off makes learning to count easier, and counting makes learning to stop easier. In this section we will take a look at both the givens we need to consider and the goals we are working toward in integrated instruction.

Teaching can integrate physical and cognitive learning in one activity.

Corresponding Developments in Other Domains

Whatever the cause of the correspondences, most children seem to move through similar developmental levels in different domains at about the same time. As a result, teachers need to consider how development in the psychomotor domain may be limited by cognitive and social givens. For example, young children cannot play competitive games without an adult to supervise them. They have little understanding of why they must follow rules; as a consequence, they are liable to ignore the rules to win. Children

Children usually progress through similar levels in different domains at the same time.

Older children adapt rules to the number of players and often require less supervision than younger children, who are more rule-bound. Notice that the older children have begun playing jump rope, while younger children all wait their turn at this or another activity.
(Paul Conklin)

Overspecialization in elementary school can mean making decisions too early in a child's development.

somewhat older will follow rules more diligently, but they will often be so rule-bound that they will not play games without proper equipment or until enough players arrive for full teams. Still older children begin playing spontaneously and adapt rules to the available equipment or numbers of players.

As a teacher, you will have to be alert to any child's tendency toward **overspecialization**—excessive development of a small set of skills—within the motor skills area. To overspecialize during the elementary school years may be unwise because the student's physical, cognitive, and social development may not be equally advanced. For example, unpredictable changes in body size and proportion during adolescence may lead skilled athletes in elementary school to be outperformed in their specialization during secondary school (Clarke, 1968). A boy who wins most races in elementary school because of his size may not become tall enough to compete successfully in track in high school. Thus, although sports participation in elementary school is not detrimental to motor development, early specialization in one sport activity is inappropriate when a few fundamental skills are highly practiced at the expense of others (Gallahue & Ozmun, 1995).

Further, children generally do not possess the cognitive skills necessary to make rational decisions regarding *future* participation in an activity until early adolescence. Deciding on a sport or a specialized activity is often difficult and requires thinking through all the possibilities.

Deciding which movement activities to pursue is based on the individual's consideration of his or her talent, resources, and enjoyment. Consideration of talent requires a knowledge of strengths and weaknesses. Consideration of resources often requires anticipating the availability of organized competition, the affordability of equipment or travel, and accessibility of facilities for practice and performance. Finally, consideration of enjoyment requires awareness of preference for group or individual activities, willingness initially to accept a role in the group that may not be the preferred one, and willingness to practice prerequisite or component skills apart from the actual performance.

If you reflect on all these intertwining factors that need to be part of a well-thought-out decision to specialize in one activity or sport, you will understand how complex a decision this really is, and why motor development and cognitive development are intertwined. These are the principal reasons that schools and, more particularly, physical education and music programs emphasize the development of a broad range of motor skills throughout the elementary years, and respect cognitive, physical, and social limitations on motor skill development (see Deepening Your Knowledge Base: An Interview with Orel Hershiser).

Setting Goals for Integrated Learning

As we have just explored in the previous section, the need to recognize how physical development may be constrained by given cognitive and social developments is important. Now we will look at the other side of the picture—that is, the possibilities for consciously integrating learning. Many physical educators have argued that physical development can itself be used to enhance and expand social and ethical development, especially through participation in supervised group activities, including sports. In this sense, integrating learning can be an instructional strategy in physical education that looks not only toward physical goals but toward social and affective goals as well.

Simply having physical education students participate in a supervised group activity does not lead to integrated instruction, moral reasoning, or even the acquisition of values such as honesty and sportsmanship (Bredemeier & Shields, 1993; Greendorfer, 1987; Weiss & Bredemeier 1990). Recently, however, a more sophisticated approach to integrating physical and moral education has been developed by a number of researchers (e.g., Bredemeier et al., 1986; DeBusk & Hellison, 1989; Romance, Weiss & Bockoven, 1986). They have explored whether or not moral reasoning can be developed through specially structured physical education activities for children in middle childhood.

Early research (Jantz, 1975) discovered that elementary physical education activities—such as basketball—reflected children's developing understanding of rules. This finding set the stage for researchers to ask, Can moral reasoning be developed through physical education activities designed to help students construct their own rules for games? Researchers hypothesized that children could indeed develop a morality that encouraged dialogue and mutual agreement (Haan, 1977) if they participated in discussions of moral dilemmas that occurred during their physical education activities.

In one study (Romance, Weiss & Bockoven, 1986), fifth graders in two physical education classes were given different forms of instruction but similar physical activities to practice. One group received instruction that was supplemented by five discussion strategies to foster moral development (see Table 4.7). The conventionally taught group participated in similar physical educa-

Physical education can be integrated with social and ethical learning.

Table 4.7 Strategies for Moral Development in Physical Education

Strategy	Example
Built-in dilemma/dialogue	Students are asked to substitute themselves out of a game when they feel the need to do so. The success and effects of this self-substitution are discussed.
Built-in dilemma/problem solve	Students are instructed to play the softball lead-up game of "500," in which the first fielder to reach 500 points gets to bat. They may add or change rules to make the game better for all. Discussion of changes then follows.
Create your own game	Students are asked to make up a game in which the object is to hit each other with something safe. The rules of the made-up game are discussed prior to actual play.
Two cultures	The students play whiffle ball with regular strikeout rules and then with rules modified to provide a built-in dilemma (such as a batting tee after two strikes). Discussion of the pros and cons of each way of playing the game follows.
The Listening Bench	Students involved in a spontaneous moral conflict, such as name calling, are to sit on the Listening Bench, turn on a tape recorder, and discuss their dilemma using posted guidelines.

Source: Romance, Weiss & Bockoven, 1986

tion activities but not in dilemma discussions. Dilemmas that naturally arose in the conventional group, such as name calling, were resolved by the teacher.

Results after eight weeks were measured on tests of moral reasoning and physical performance. On the test of moral reasoning, the moral discussion group scored significantly higher than the group that had received conventional instruction. On the tests of physical performance, both groups improved, but in different ways. The moral discussion group had improved more than the conventional group in basketball, a group sport, but less than the conventional group in gymnastics, an individual sport. Overall, the results suggested that physical and moral education can be profitably integrated.

Some interest has recently been expressed in the integration of instruction in psychomotor skills with instruction in thinking skills (Schwager & Labate, 1993), but work in this area is still only theoretical. One theory suggests that

An Interview with Orel Hershiser

Interviewer: Let's start by asking you to tell us about your own experiences in elementary school sports as you were growing up.

Hershiser: My first experience in organized sports was probably my first Little League tryout, where you went out and took three or four swings and then played catch with one of the coaches. Then they had you run the bases, and all the coaches were standing around grading you to see who they were going to pick on their teams through the drafts. I thought that was a lot of fun because, at that age, I excelled in sports. I had been playing baseball with kids in the neighborhood since I was 4 or 5 years old and was excelling, so that was a lot of fun. It was a good experience. I don't know how it would have been for kids who weren't quite as coordinated and as skilled. But my career kind of went downhill from that point because I didn't stay as strong and as big as the rest of the kids in my age group as I grew up. I ended up being one of the slighter-built kids all the way up until my sophomore year in college. However, through the elementary school period I was always one of the better-skilled athletes, so I had a lot of good memories from playing sports at the elementary level. . . .

Interviewer: How many sports did you play as a child?

Hershiser: I just played baseball, and then I played youth hockey when my parents moved to Canada when I was about 12 years old. I played youth hockey in Toronto, Canada, in a house league, not a travel league that was super gung-ho, but it was just like beginner youth hockey. And then, when we moved back to the United States from Canada (we were only there for a year), we moved into Cherry Hill, New Jersey. I picked up hockey again, and I was ahead of the American players because I learned in Canada, so I got to play in some traveling leagues and progressed quite well in hockey in the United States.

Interviewer: So you didn't really specialize in baseball until later?

Hershiser: Baseball was always my specialty. I always had an inkling that I would like to play professionally, because when I was 8 years old, Personna Razor Blades sponsored a contest called "Throw, Hit, and Run." That contest was changed or disbanded later on, so I don't even know if kids nowadays would even think about it or know about it. But I was third in the nation when I was 8 years old. I competed in the Southfield, Michigan, area, and then I won that area, and they compared our scores for the regional. I won the region by comparative scores. And then they flew my father and me from Detroit to Yankee Stadium for the national finals, and I came in third. It was kind of like I had the ability, but I always had to catch up size-wise from then on. Physically, I was always behind. I was a September-born child, and my parents had the opportunity to either put me in school or leave me out. And they put me in, so I was always competing with kids who were a year older than I. I was the last one to drive in my class. I was the last person to

(continued on p. 156)

start shaving. I was always the kid who had a lot of ability but couldn't compete physically.

Interviewer: Do you think that American children tend to specialize in sports too early?

Hershiser: I think that a lot of times parents try to fulfill their frustrated dreams through their kids. And they can really make a mistake in forcing that on their child, especially if the child has a lot of ability. With my own kids, I am just going to expose them to everything, and if they choose to love it and to really want to be dedicated to it, I will support them. I want to teach them dedication, desire, how to compete, about winning, about losing, but I don't want to say, "Do it here." But I do want them to have all those concepts, and if they decide to channel them into one sport, or if they decide to channel them into computers, or whatever, then they've got all those personality qualities.

Source: From "Orel Hershiser," 1991

Discussion Questions

1. What concepts from the chapter do you spot in this interview? Identify *youth sports*, *physical maturity*, *overspecialization*, and *integrated learning*. Refer to specific places in this text that apply to Hershiser's discussion.

2. State in your own words the *values* that should be learned in sports-related activities. Why are they not learned spontaneously?

3. Parents sometimes keep their children out of kindergarten to give them a "competitive edge" in terms of development. What is the fallacy in this practice?

| Cognitive organizing can help a learner analyze problems in psychomotor performance.

through *cognitive organizing*, a student can learn to identify problems in performance and define them in terms of a psychomotor skill rather than as the result of an action (McBride, 1991). In essence, this helps learners turn problems-as-obstacles into problems-as-challenges. Sound familiar? Let's spend a moment examining this theory here not only because it has its own value but also because it can offer you another window into the cognitive problem-solving process that you are now learning and engaging in yourself.

Let's look at the example of an individual who is learning to play golf. Within a cognitive organizing approach, he or she would be encouraged to see a sliced shot in a golf game not as an obstacle but as a symptom of an error in the golf stroke, which turns it into a challenge to be solved. Questions asked by the teacher may further prompt a student to identify a problem in a way that it can be solved. Through *cognitive action* a student can then gather information about how to perform the skill correctly—asking the instructor for feedback or figuring out from other information how errant (or correct) movements occur. The golf student, for example, needs to know about how slices occur and how they should be corrected.

Through *cognitive and psychomotor outcomes*, the student then generates a solution. A cognitive outcome might involve suggesting to the teacher a plan for how to correct the movement. A psychomotor outcome would involve actual performance. Based on the results, the learner might be satisfied with the solution, or modify the plan, attempting to make additional refinements in the motor skill.

Problem solving by students in physical education requires that students learn information about motor skills rather than simply practice skills with feedback. Teachers need to help children define problems in terms they will understand, of course, which is a developmental consideration picked up in the next chapter.

CONCLUSION

Understanding how physical development presents both givens to be respected and goals to be promoted for further learning should help you to define instructional problems in ways that allow you to solve them. After reading this chapter, you should be more likely to consider what is developmentally appropriate for instruction and, within this general frame, how your instructional strategy is influenced by students who are beginners, intermediates, or experts.

You have seen how phases might be folded together within at least one stage of development. They might also be folded together within each other stage. Just as there are children who are beginning to run, so there are children who are beginning to play kick ball, and beginning to play softball or baseball. As a teacher, you will spend most of your time with beginners and intermediates, because they seem to need a teacher more often than do experts. But as experts continue to develop beyond the end of each natural stage, they too need a teacher to encourage them as they enter the next stage of development, becoming a beginner again.

Understanding this overarching pattern of physical development, in which a student becomes an expert only to enter a new stage and become a beginner again, can help you represent and define the problems-as-challenges that you will confront as a teacher. In the next chapter, you will discover how stages and phases can help you define teaching problems related to progressive changes in children's thinking.

c o n c e p t   p a p e r

Psychomotor Skill Development

Purpose of the assignment

To analyze playground activities of school-age children in order to increase awareness of psychomotor skill development.

(Continued on next page)

(Concept Paper, continued)

Directions for the assignment

1. Go to a playground to observe elementary children playing in various ways at recess. Make sure you have approval from the principal and playground supervisor. Your task will be to analyze the various activities for the psychomotor skills involved. You may find the following resources in the textbook helpful:

   a. First, use the *stage* model of motor development presented in this chapter to identify activities at different developmental levels. In particular look for (1) fundamental movement activities, (2) transitional games, and (3) sports skills.

   b. Second, use the *phase* model of motor development, also presented in this chapter, to refine your observations further. Are children who are participating in the activities that you named beginners at them? Intermediates? Experts?

2. Having analyzed the activities for psychomotor development, consider your findings in a wider perspective to develop a thesis that answers the question, How does psychomotor development take place at this playground? What kinds of motor skills are being developed, at what level, and by whom? The big question, of course, is *why*? You might address it in your conclusion.

3. Once you have a thesis that describes how psychomotor development is taking place, organize your discussion of it in a three- to four-page paper, using details from your analysis of psychomotor skills in step 1. Obvious schemes for organization might be chronological (focusing on different ages) or comparison-contrast (focusing on expert/novice or gender differences).

SUMMARY

1. There is a long-standing debate, called the nature/nurture controversy, among educators and psychologists about whether heredity or environment takes precedence in a child's development.

2. Teachers must constantly address the dual effects of both nature and nurture. The central question for educators regarding development is this: How can I build upon and further develop a student's skills within a given capability?

3. In terms of problem solving, nature provides developmental givens or constraints by, for example, setting biological growth sequences when the fine motor skills appear.

4. Nurture offers goals for further development. For example, having children practice catching a ball usually results in dramatic improvement of the integration of movements such as eye-hand coordination.

5. Gender provides an excellent example of the integration of the effects of nature and nurture on physical development. In the early years, differences are minimal and influenced by social factors. After puberty, sex hormones exaggerate the differences, and sports-related skill variations between the sexes become pronounced.

6. The stage approach to physical development emphasizes the effects of nature. Stages, or maturational plateaus, are seen as determining the skills a child should be able to master at a certain age.

7. The phase approach to physical development is based on learning. Phases are flexibly set by how much an individual child has learned and depend only on mastery of prerequisite skills.

8. The complementary approach suggests that within a particular age, a child can be helped to move through phases of learning. This may be the most compelling of the three approaches because it stresses both givens to be respected and goals to be attained.

9. Integrated instruction considers physical development as part of a larger picture that also includes both social development and cognitive development.

KEY TERMS

development p. 114

physical development p. 114

psychomotor development p. 114

maturation p. 118

differentiation p.118

proximodistal sequence p. 118

cephalocaudal sequence p. 118

fine motor skills p. 119

integration p. 119

gender differences p. 120

sex stereotypes p. 120

puberty p. 120

growth spurt p. 120

secondary sexual characteristics p. 121

early maturers p. 124

stages p. 124

phases p. 124

muscle activity p. 133

attention p. 137

automaticity p. 137

activity level p. 133

learning cues p. 140

readiness p. 147

overspecialization p. 152

SUGGESTED RESOURCES

Bloom, B. S. 1986. "Automaticity: The Hands and Feet of Genius." *Educational Leadership*, 43, 70–77. A good survey of the many ways psychomotor automaticity serves higher cognitive functioning.

Council on Physical Education for Children. 1992. *Developmentally Appropriate Physical Education Practices.* Reston, Va.: AAHPERD. This pamphlet published by the American Alliance for Health, Physical Education, Recreation and Dance distinguishes appropriate from inappropriate practices for children's physical development.

Elkind, D. 1987. *Miseducation: Preschoolers at Risk.* New York: Knopf. This book is a highly readable account of how educational programs for elementary-age children are sometimes misappropriated for preschoolers.

Gallahue, D. L., and J. C. Ozmun. 1995. *Understanding Motor Development: Infants, Children, Adolescents, Adults.* 3d ed. Madison, Wis.: WCB Brown & Benchmark. This clearly written text presents Gallahue's stage theory of motor skill development.

Thomas, J. R., and K. T. Thomas. 1988. "Development of Gender Differences in Physical Activity." *Quest,* 40, 219–229. An easily accessible and highly readable summary of gender differences in motor skills.

Cognitive Development:
Contexts for Problem Solving

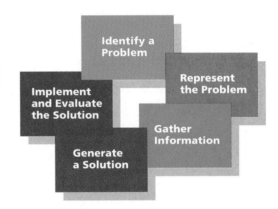

Identify a
Problem

Represent
the Problem

Implement
and Evaluate
the Solution

Gather
Information

Generate
a Solution

Orientation

The goal of this chapter is to provide you with background
information about the ways in which cognitive development occurs as children mature and learn. You will find
that there are several theories of how this development
occurs and that they can coexist and complement one
another within both the nature/nurture spectrum and our
problem-solving framework. As you read, look for answers to these questions:

- **In terms of maturational givens and goals for teaching, what is the
  central problem that this chapter will address?**

- **What are three different viewpoints of how cognitive development occurs?**

- **Which of these approaches most strongly stresses the maturational givens end of the spectrum?**

- **What are the four major stages of Piaget's developmental theory?**

- **What mental activity of the growing child links each stage and
  enables continuing growth?**

- **Within Vygotsky's developmental model, what is the key activity
  that enables cognitive growth?**

- **What is the process of cognitive skill learning called and what are
  its three phases?**

- **How does the complementarity of different models result in a
  "staircase" of development?**

THE GIVENS AND GOALS OF COGNITIVE DEVELOPMENT

By considering the development of children's cognitive abilities and skills, let's continue to study how student characteristics help define instructional problems. **Cognition** is the process of knowing in its broadest sense, including perception, memory, and thinking. *Perception* involves recognizing objects, people, events, processes, and the like. *Memory,* of course, involves recall. *Thinking* involves skills such as those described in Chapter 3: comprehension, application, analysis, synthesis, and evaluation. The last three of these skills are often combined in problem solving. Simply defined, **cognitive development** is progressive change in processes of knowing such as these.

Much as physical development does, cognitive development will present you as a teacher with a broad range of factors to consider. At one end of the spectrum are the more constraining givens—that is, natural constraints on the development of thinking, which you will need to respect as you plan for instruction. With these givens in mind, you will be able to look to the other end of the spectrum—at the great possibilities for enhancement and learning and at the goals for cognitive growth that you will promote.

The cognitive givens that must be respected result from maturational limitations in the brain, which is progressively changing during childhood and adolescence. However, since relatively little is known about the direct influence of neurological development on learning, this chapter will focus on indirect influences such as the effects of maturation on well-defined cognitive abilities like logic or memory. Stage theories of cognitive development, which can be of considerable help to you while solving instructional problems, emphasize age-related givens.

The cognitive goals to be promoted are the improvement of your students' perception, memory, or thought. This intent often underlies the objectives in a curriculum guide, as well as your personal goals for teaching. Cognitive goals are fundamental to academics and include both basic processes (such as reading, writing, and arithmetic) and intellectual skills. Your knowledge of the stages of development, as well as of the social context and the phases that occur during the learning process, will provide you with a solid understanding of development on which to base cognitive goals.

To sum up, when you focus on what is developmentally appropriate for your students, you are considering the givens of cognitive development. When you emphasize how to improve a cognitive skill, you are focusing on the goals of cognitive development. Putting these two emphases together allows you to frame the central instructional problem of this chapter: *How can I develop a student's cognitive skills within a given capability?*

> Perception, memory, and thinking are facets of cognition.

> Age-related givens affect the development of thinking.

> Cognitive goals must be set with developmental stages in mind.

learning journal

Principles of Cognitive Development

While reading about cognitive development, make Learning Journal entries about specific experiences in which principles of cognitive development apply. Tell what led up to the experience, name the principles of development involved, describe how the principles were involved, and describe any relevant outcomes. This chapter contains descriptions of the following principles of cognitive development:

- constructivism
- assimilation and accommodation
- equilibrium and disequilibrium
- variant and invariant functions
- developmental stages (at least two)
- transductive reasoning
- perceptual centration
- development of seriation
- development of classification
- development of causality
- conservation
- the form/content distinction
- developmentally appropriate practices
- the zone of proximal development
- the internalization of thinking
- scaffolded instruction
- phases of cognitive skill learning
- proceduralization
- procedural facilitation
- staircases of development

In a moment, we will look in on one experienced teacher as she accomplishes this in her classroom. First, however, let's rephrase these two ends of the spectrum in terms of the nature/nurture debate that was introduced in the previous chapter. Within the framework of this debate, we might say that nature tells a teacher what cannot be changed greatly in terms of broad developmental sequences, and nurture suggests how to improve skills from this point of departure. (See Deepening Your Knowledge Base: How Do Teachers' Positions on the Nature/Nurture Debate Affect Real-Life Decisions? to explore some ramifications of teachers' positions on this debate.)

deepening your knowledge base

How Do Teachers' Positions on the Nature/Nurture Debate Affect Real-Life Decisions?

Researchers have discovered an intriguing relationship between kindergarten teachers' positions on the nature/nurture controversy and their *retention rates,* or the rates at which they require children to repeat kindergarten (Smith, 1989). In kindergarten, retention rates appear to be less a function of student achievement than of teacher beliefs. In one study, there was a remarkable association between teachers who emphasized the nature end of the spectrum and high rates of retention (above 10 percent). Kindergarten teachers who hold these beliefs assumed that social or cognitive "immaturity" is best addressed by holding students back a year, so they typically retained several students in each class.

On the other hand, teachers who downplayed the importance of nature tended to retain children at lower rates (below 10 percent). They assumed that low achievement is best addressed by adapting instruction to the needs of the learner. They typically retained one or two students at most. In later grades, teachers who emphasized nature-defined givens were also probably more likely than teachers who emphasized nurturant goals to perceive low achievement as a sign of "immaturity" and a signal to retain a student (Peterson, 1989).

Is immaturity a cause for low achievement in the first year of school? The answer in some cases may be yes. Does retaining students for another year in kindergarten, or in a transition class, improve later chances for success? The answer to this question in most cases is no. Researchers agree that on average, after three years formerly retained children are achieving at a level no higher than that of children with similarly low test scores who were promoted anyway (Dennebaum & Kulberg, 1994; Holmes, 1989; Johnson, Merrell & Stover, 1990).

Early retention may actually hurt later achievement. The effect may be direct—in terms of comparatively lower test scores in fourth or fifth grade (Dennebaum & Kulberg, 1994)—or indirect—in terms of comparatively higher risk for dropping out of high school (Grissom & Shepard, 1989). The U.S. Department of Education (1994) recently published data that suggested grade retention is a significant risk factor for dropping out. In short, retention in grade is not only an ineffective way to improve the chances for school success of most low achievers; often, it is counterproductive, hindering later achievement and eventually leading some students who would be capable of passing courses to drop out.

Divide into groups to discuss grade retention, its effects, and its alternatives. After your discussion, reassemble in the larger group to compare and contrast your ideas.

Discussion Questions

1. Are there any cases in which retention in early grades might be justified? Be specific.
2. What are the physical effects in sixth grade of being retained a year in kindergarten? What are the social effects?
3. What would you tell a parent who wanted to "hold back" a child from first grade because the child would be the youngest in the class?
4. Choose a grade level and subject. Three students who failed last year have been passed on to you. How will they affect your annual planning?

The task of balancing maturational givens with goals for improvement might seem difficult at first, but many experienced teachers do it fluently as they plan instruction and as they confront on the spot the problems-as-challenges that arise in the course of teaching. Let's see how.

A Sixth-Grade Teacher Bases Instruction on Both Givens and Goals

Not long ago, I observed a sixth-grade lesson on properties of light. When I walked into the classroom, the twenty-four boys and girls were scattered about, reading independently. Brenda Webb, who was the teacher, used the half hour of independent reading to write directions on the board and set up eight learning stations around the room. She set up a projector in the middle of the U of student desks, aiming it at three words on the board: *opaque, translucent,* and *transparent.* Mrs. Webb then told the children to put away their books and clear their desks. She turned off the overhead lights, turned on the projector, and began her lesson.

Mrs. Webb mentioned that the goal of the day's lesson was to describe light. First, what would happen if she placed different materials, such as waxed paper, construction paper, or a piece of clear plastic, between the projector and the board? After students made predictions for each of these materials, she verified the predictions with demonstrations and introduced the appropriate term from the board. She then asked students to infer some properties of light.

Student 1: Light will not travel through opaque objects.
Student 2: Light will travel through transparent objects.
Teacher: What else?
Student 3: Light travels in a straight line.
Student 4: You can't see light.

The teacher's lesson had clearly anticipated the first two inferences—light will not travel through opaque objects, and light will travel through transparent objects—but the second two inferences were made by students independently. Such opportunities to develop thinking often arise spontaneously if you give them a chance.

Teachers should watch for opportunities to develop thinking.

The lesson became exciting after the teacher confirmed the first three propositions but playfully tested the last one. "Can you see the beam of light? What are you seeing when you see the light beam?" The eyes of the class were riveted on the beam of light that struck the board. One child noticed tiny specks of light in the beam, but other children said that these were only the reflections from dust. A lively discussion then ensued over whether or not light could be seen. It ended only after the teacher called one of the students to the board and asked her if she could see the light. Suddenly, the student caught on, pointed to the projector, and said "There!" The group portion of the lesson ended with the discovery that light is invisible except at its source and on an object that reflects it—something most adults would not realize unless they thought about it.

Now let's examine how Mrs. Webb was making use of both maturational givens and goals for improvement in her lesson. First, the lesson incorporated and built upon the teacher's knowledge of a developmental given of her eleven-year-olds. She knew that starting at age seven or so most children can think about almost anything that they perceive, once their attention is directed to it. (For example, they can make inferences from experience to discern characteristics of people, as in "she is kind," and, in this case, they can make inferences from observations in order to discover some properties of light). By age eleven, many of them are quite skilled at making such inferences from what they perceive. Thus, ability to infer from a perception is a developmental given by the sixth grade.

During this lesson, however, the teacher's goal became to *improve* thinking, not just to exercise students' known cognitive abilities. Did you notice how she did this? The direction of the discussion changed after a student hypothesized that "You can't see light." At this point, the discussion of an *invisible* property called for systematic reasoning, which the children were not yet able to do without support. The teacher began to guide the children toward a goal that might generally be called "thinking systematically." Systematic thinking takes into account all possibilities or, in this case, points of view. It is not something most eleven-year-olds are capable of yet.

> Teachers should guide students toward new cognitive abilities.

By analyzing instructional problems like this one, we can see how good teaching and problem solving respect developmental cognitive givens while promoting goals for cognitive growth. The former broadly constrain teaching strategies to practices appropriate to a given stage of development; the latter include specific practices to improve thinking.

How Cognition Develops: Alternative Viewpoints

There is no one viewpoint about how cognition develops. However, there are several widely accepted theories about this complex topic, each of which helps to shed light on different key elements for us as teachers. First, we will explore the position held by Jean Piaget. It is based upon maturational stages of development and has had tremendous impact on psychologists and educators in this century. Next, we will look at a theory of socially mediated development, introduced earlier in this century by Lev Vygotsky and just now being rediscovered. It emphasizes the role of the social environment in cognitive development. Last, we will look at newer information-processing approaches that stress the phases a learner goes through as he or she progresses.

> Several major theories about cognitive development have been formed.

Throughout all of these theoretical presentations, we'll keep our own context—the classroom and your needs as a new teacher—in mind. This focus will help you relate the varying viewpoints to different situations that arise in classroom life. Toward the end of this chapter, I will offer some thoughts about the complementarity of the different views of cognitive development. A teacher needs to formulate a coherent understanding of cognitive development as a basis for solving problems-as-challenges.

A STAGE THEORY OF COGNITIVE DEVELOPMENT: PIAGET

Jean Piaget (1896–1980) has provided us a remarkably comprehensive stage theory of cognitive development. Piaget received his Ph.D. in natural science from a Swiss university (at the age of twenty-one). By training he was a biologist, but his interest in the thinking of children turned into a career as director of the Jean Jacques Rousseau Institute in Geneva, Switzerland. There he conducted research on how children develop perception, memory, and thought. His life work left a legacy to teachers and researchers that still guides our understanding of children's cognition.

Key Concepts of Piaget's Theory

Before you study Piaget's scheme of cognitive development, you will need to understand some of his central terms and ideas.

Constructivism

The child constructs an understanding of reality, according to Piaget.

Key to Piaget's theory of intellectual development was his belief in **constructivism**. Piaget believed that a child constructs his or her understanding of reality. Knowledge is not an automatic copy of reality but something that must be *built* by each child him- or herself. The construction occurs in different ways at different ages, but it proceeds whenever children have the opportunity to think on their own or in relation to other children. As you read about the rest of these concepts and as we explore the stages themselves, keep the concept of constructivism in mind. It is the "big idea" behind Piaget's whole theory of how children develop thinking (Beilin, 1992).

Adaptation, Assimilation, and Accommodation

Childhood is the time for one to adapt to the environment.

Piaget believed that childhood "is *not* a necessary evil; it is a biologically useful step, the significance of which is that of a progressive *adaptation* to the physical and social environment" (1969, p. 208, emphasis added). **Adaptation** is the process of adjusting to the environment. It was a key term for Piaget because he considered adaptation to be the goal of intellectual development.

Intellectual development occurs when thought *assimilates* or "takes in" an object, event, or idea, and *accommodates* or "adjusts to" whatever it has taken in. For Piaget, intellectual development (or adaptation) was an ongoing process of assimilating and accommodating aspects of the environment. "We can say that thought is adapted to a particular reality when it succeeds at as-

Knowledge is not a copy of reality—it must be constructed by each child for him- or herself. What subject might these upper elementary students be learning about? *(Bob Daemmrich/ Stock Boston)*

similating this reality by its own framework, while accommodating the framework to the new circumstances presented by the reality" (p. 208).

This process may sound complex, but it can be illuminated by the following example. Imagine someone watching a baseball game. If the viewer is somewhat familiar with the rules and practices of the game, the viewer *assimilates* the game—taking in its sights and sounds, virtually all of which are meaningful and easily understood. But if the viewer suddenly notices a signal that is unfamiliar, such as the gesture a shortstop might make behind his glove to the second baseman, he or she will be unable to assimilate it immediately. What did it mean? It might be possible to figure out its meaning by watching the players, by asking someone, or both. In this case, the viewer notices that the signal occurs only when a runner is on first base; it signifies who will cover second base if the runner tries to steal. But until the viewer is able to discover the meaning of the signal and *accommodate* or adjust understanding, confusion will result.

From this brief example, you can appreciate how much accommodation must occur in the understanding of a child for whom not just the shortstop's signal but the whole ball game is often unfamiliar. Imagine what it would be like if you were watching people play a game that was wholly unknown to you (perhaps rugby). You might at first understand almost none of what you were seeing and hearing. Although you would be assimilating sights and sounds, you might quickly become overwhelmed because you would not understand what you perceived. However, if you focused on just one aspect of the game at a time, you could probably determine its significance and begin to develop your understanding of the game.

Accommodation involves adjusting understanding to new information.

Equilibration and Disequilibrium

What regulates the development of understanding, or accommodation? To account fully for accommodation, Piaget needed to explain what started and stopped it. According to Piaget, **equilibration** is the self-regulatory mechanism through which accommodation is activated and terminated. Equilibration acts like a thermostat for accommodation. When a thermostat "senses" that the temperature of a room is too low or high, it activates the heating or cooling system until "equilibrium" is restored, at which time the system cuts off. Intellectual equilibration operates in a similar way. **Disequilibrium,** or discrepancy between what we perceive and what we understand, activates accommodation until equilibrium is restored and we understand what we perceive.

> Equilibration is the process that activates accommodation.

Invariant and Variant Functions

Piaget called processes such as adaptation, assimilation, accommodation, and equilibration *invariant* functions because people possess them at all ages. They are present to some degree at birth and throughout life.

Their form changes, however, as a child grows to maturity. Piaget (1969) pointed out by way of analogy that a tadpole assimilates oxygen with gills, but an adult frog assimilates oxygen with lungs. Both tadpole and adult frog assimilate oxygen, but they use different structures to do it. Similarly, both child and adult assimilate and accommodate experiences, but they do so with different "structures." Consequently, Piaget described the different structures by which people of different ages assimilate and accommodate reality as *variant* functions—ones that change with age. In the following account of developmental stages, note that Piaget named the stages after the structures of understanding that predominate during each stage.

> Variant functions are learning processes that change with age.

The Stages of Cognitive Development

Piaget identified four stages of cognitive development. He named the first stage (birth to two years) the **sensorimotor period** of development because it involved adapting to reality through *sensing and movement.* He called the second stage (two to seven or eight years) the **preoperational period** because it involved processes related to conceptualization *prior* to using logic. Piaget termed the third stage (seven or eight to eleven years) the **concrete operations period** because it involved using *applied reasoning.* The fourth and last stage (eleven to fifteen years and up) was called the **formal operations period** because it involved using *systematic reasoning.* As you read this section, bear in mind the grades that you plan to teach. Which general structure of thought will predominate in your students' understanding or learning?

Be cautious when applying Piaget's stages, however. The age range for each stage is only an average. A given child might be found at one stage on a given task and at another stage on another task. Alternatively, a child who is a rapid learner or a slow learner might be found to differ from the average child on all tasks. Thus, you should become familiar with not just the predominant

> Piaget's research identified four stages of cognitive development.

structure for understanding and learning at the ages or in the grades you will teach, but the structures that predominate in each stage of development. The progress of these variant functions is charted in detail below and in Table 5.1.

Sensorimotor Period (birth to two)

Although a child cannot think logically during the first two years of life, he or she works to understand situations through *sense perceptions* and *motor movements,* the infant's inborn structures for understanding its world. From nine months to a year and a half, a child achieves a milestone in the development of understanding called "object permanence." A sense of **object permanence** is achieved when a child looks for things that are not in view, or makes a movement related to a missing object when remembering it. For example, a child may look over a crib rail for a pacifier that has fallen on the floor, or wave "bye-bye" when remembering someone who has just left. He or she has developed a rudimentary understanding that objects do not cease to exist when they disappear from sight.

The child first learns through sensations and movements.

An infant or toddler is very limited, however, in the knowledge that he or she can construct this way. Knowledge based on the child's own point of view is necessarily **egocentric**, or derived from his or her own experience as a norm for all experience. An infant or a toddler cannot imagine how you see him or her, has no way to comprehend the intentions of others, and indeed has no way to learn apart from his or her own actions and sensations. The egocentrism of an infant or a toddler is *not* a characteristic of selfishness (as Piaget pointed out), but a by-product of using the tools given by nature—the child's own senses and movements—to make sense of the surrounding world.

Young children's knowledge is egocentric, based only on their own experiences.

Preoperational Period (two to seven or eight)

During early childhood, a child is learning "to represent objects or events that are not at the moment perceptible" (Piaget, 1969, p. 48). Construction of

Table 5.1   Piaget's Theory of Cognitive Development

0 to 2 years Sensorimotor period	Learning occurs through the sensorimotor system; object permanence is established.
2 to 7 or 8 years Preoperational period	Learning is based on appearances; concepts are developed in no logical relation to each other.
7 or 8 to 11 years Concrete operations period	Learning is based on figuring out solutions to concrete problems. Operations of mathematics and logic emerge.
11 to 15 years and up Formal operations period	Learning is based on logical form (validity) apart from content (truth value). Reasoning is based on possibilities rather than reality.

Source: Summarized from Piaget, 1969, pp. 46–51

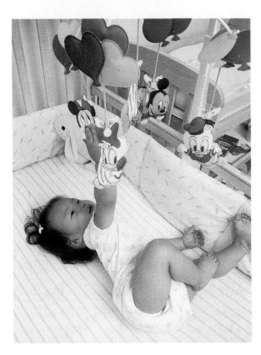

Piaget named the sensorimotor period after the type of learning that occurs during it. What do you think this baby girl is learning as she plays in her crib with her mobile? *(Michael Newman/PhotoEdit)*

Symbols that stand for objects are important concepts learned in early childhood.

knowledge involves acquisition of symbols—such as words and numerals—that stand for objects. This type of learning might be called *conceptualization*, as long as you understand it to be based in perception. For example, children rapidly improve their vocabulary, representational drawing ability, and sense of number during early childhood. New words alone may number half a dozen or more each day! You can appreciate the intellectual energy channeled into this type of learning if you have ever been immersed without a dictionary in a strange culture where you had to learn new words every day from their use and context.

Intellectual capabilities that allow preoperational children to develop concepts include the ability to classify objects (for example, to group differently colored blocks), the ability to match to a sample (given a picture of an object, to select a picture of a similar object from an array), and the ability to seriate (to arrange objects according to size or degree) (Elkind, 1987). The ability to classify or categorize is essential to concept formation, but in general, during this period children cannot use logic to solve problems.

Young children are unlike us because they remain egocentric, a vestige of their earliest form of understanding. As a consequence of their egocentrism, they cannot infer reality from relationships between concepts. Instead, they often make errors that come from drawing conclusions on the basis of only what they have directly experienced. For example, a child may say, "There goes our car!" when a car that looks like the family car passes on the street. This type of error, known as **transductive reasoning**, is caused by reasoning from particular to particular in the child's experience. ("That car is blue; our car is blue; that car must be our car.") Other errors in reasoning spring from the child's intuitive conclusion that properties of things change with changes in appearance. The same amounts of juice in two cups of different size may appear to differ, but only preoperational children will conclude that they *do* differ. Piaget believed that this type of error was a product of **perceptual centration**, in which only a single dimension or perspective of a problem is considered before the viewer generates a solution.

> Children may make errors of reasoning in the early stages of cognitive development.

Piaget focused on errors in the reasoning of young children, but the consequences of many of these errors are not grave. Indeed, we delight in the fact that from one until six, appearance is reality. Magic is real because it appears so. Characters in plays or on television come alive easily because young children easily suspend disbelief. Watch a young child hesitate and then hug a person dressed as Big Bird, Barney, or some other well-known character at the local mall. People not only cherish but foster children's beliefs that are based on appearances.

Furthermore, adults err when they assume that a young child cannot reason at all. Many psychologists have conducted studies that suggest that when given "child-friendly" tasks or placed in natural situations, children can reason or provide logical explanations somewhat earlier than Piaget suggested. Experimenters have found that slight alterations in Piagetian tasks (such as adding emphasis to one word or reducing the number of objects presented) can lead many young children to solve problems in a way that requires logical thinking (Flavell, Green & Flavell, 1987; Gelman & Gallistel, 1978; McGarrigle, Grieve & Hughes, 1978). Such findings generally do not contradict Piaget's results. Rather, they indicate that the emergence of reasoning is continuous.

> The ability to reason develops over time.

Despite the developing capacity of a young child to reason, however, adults must often accommodate explanations to the immature structure of understanding already present in a child. For example, you have almost certainly heard a child ask why something occurred and, after getting an explanation from a well-intentioned adult, ask why again. The child is not asking for a cause for the explanation (as the adult often assumes), but for an explanation to the original question, given in terms that he or she can understand.

How does a young child understand? From Piaget's theory, you know that young children understand through the way things appear to them. "Why does the sun shine?" To make us warm. "Why is it night?" To let us sleep. Such an explanation will generally be accepted as sufficient because it is in terms that focus on the perspective of the child and his or her own experience of the world. Empathy—or sympathetic understanding—is required to communicate explanations to young children (see Reflection on Practice: A Parent's View of Preoperations, page 172).

> Children understand best when explanations are stated on their terms.

Concrete Operations Period (seven or eight to eleven)

The beginning of middle childhood typically marks the slow emergence of a rather complete set of logical operations. Children become capable of figuring out the answers to concrete questions or problems, from specific problems of arithmetic (which are solved through the operations of addition, subtraction, multiplication, or division) to "Why are you using a fork?" ("So that my hands will stay clean"; cause-effect). Children reveal intellectual

> Logical operations begin in middle childhood.

reflection on practice

A Parent's View of Preoperations

My husband and I enjoy taking our children to college basketball games. We almost always sit in the student section, which is on the north side in the lower seating section. But on one particular night we sat with some friends in a different place. We were in the upper seats in the east end section.

When we returned home from that game my daughter, who is five years old, made a comment that the gym had been moved around that night. She thought that the cheerleaders were on a different side of the court than usual and that the pep band sat in a different place.

I tried to explain to her that the gym hadn't been moved and that the cheerleaders and pep band were where they had always been. I told her that everything looked different because we were sitting in different seats and looking at things from a different way. No matter what I told her, she didn't quite seem convinced. To her everything had been changed.

I realize now that the reason she couldn't understand why things looked different was that she was in the preoperational stage of cognitive development as given by Piaget. Logic is generally not yet present because of perceptual centration, which results in focusing on only a single dimension of a problem. Children can consider only one perspective or one dimension at a time.

My daughter was looking at the basketball court from one perspective only. Since she is still in the preoperational stage, when we sat in a different place, she couldn't understand why everything seemed in a different place. And since at this stage "appearance is reality," she was unable to do the logical operations in her mind to figure out that things were in the same place even though they looked different.

Donna Garner

Discussion Questions

1. Use this episode to describe the relationship between *egocentrism* and *perceptual centration*. What, fundamentally, caused the child to think that "they turned the gym around"?

2. Why was the parent's instructional strategy (logical argument) ineffective in convincing the child? Try to formulate your answer in terms of assimilation and accommodation.

3. Suppose that you had been the teacher/parent and that during the ball game, your student/child had told you "they turned the gym around." What instructional strategy could you have adopted to convince the child otherwise?

operations in many situations. In the following Reflection on Practice, for example, a parent reflects on examples of these developments at home, including a thoughtful search for shoes, arrangement of crayons by color and shade, and acceptance of the equivalence of the same amount of juice in different-sized cups.

A Parent's View of Concrete Operations

I have noticed that my seven-year-old daughter is moving from Piaget's pre-operational stage of cognitive development into the concrete operations stage. During the past year she has begun to attack problems in a more logical way.

One example of this is her attempt to find misplaced items. She has acquired the habit of taking her shoes off whenever she is inside. This habit has caused us to spend a lot of time trying to track down lost shoes. I would ask her where she pulled them off, and she could not remember. I would then suggest that she retrace her route through the house. She could not do this until rather recently. She would go to rooms where she had not been, or she would forget which rooms she had been in. Lately, she has been able to retrace her activities in the correct order.

Another example is the way she arranges her crayons. She received a box of seventy-two crayons and a carrying case for her sixth birthday. She took great care in placing the crayons in the case, but there was no order in the way that she arranged them. About three months ago, she brought the crayons to me. She had rearranged them according to color families, from light to dark. She also has started to place her stuffed animals in order according to their size. These arrangements are examples of seriation.

She has also begun to grasp conservation of quantity. She used to be very insistent on receiving the exact amount of milk or juice that her older sister received. If the cups were not identical, she would put up a fuss. Now she has realized that the same amount of milk looks different in different glasses. She tells me to "pour a lot in the little glass."

Shane Conn

Discussion Questions

1. **How does logic enter into finding misplaced shoes? To put the question slightly differently: why couldn't the child find her shoes just a year or so earlier?**

2. **What might be the motivation for arranging crayons or stuffed animals in a series? Why would a child bother? Speculate about the utility of seriation in subjects appropriate to grades 1–3. Generate examples having to do with math, language arts, social studies, science, music, physical education, and art.**

These are not isolated events, but they occur in the homes of many parents. One day, I was startled to find that the pile of shoes at the foot of my son's bed was arranged in order by pairs. It was as if an elf had arranged them in the night. When I asked why he had arranged them, he explained that he had put his "cool" shoes at the end of the rack closest to the foot of the bed. He had arranged his shoes from most favorite to least favorite, and he was able to given a reason for this arrangement. He was in first grade.

Children develop concrete operations to deal with their more complex lives.

Piaget suggested that the slow decline of egocentrism in early childhood eventually permits the development of *concrete operations* (or logical thought structures). *Perceptual decentration,* or the ability to consider more than one perspective, emerges as egocentrism is lost. The immediate cause of the development of concrete operations, however, is probably a need to deal with the complexities of experience with greater efficiency. It is hard to find the crayon of the color you want when you have a bunch that differ but look almost alike. It is also hard to share something with others without identifying equal portions, or to determine what is missing when you have no way to account for what should be there! Everyday problem solving may have as much to do with the emergence of concrete operations as does the decline of egocentrism.

Specifically, what are the logical operations that develop during this period?

- One logical operation is *classification,* which permits deductive reasoning. (If all cars have seat belts, and if this vehicle is a car, then this vehicle must have seat belts.)
- Another common logical operation is *seriation,* the ability to arrange objects or events according to some property (such as length, weight, time). The arrangement of shoes by "coolness" and crayons by color are examples of seriation.
- A third operation is *causality,* an understanding of cause-effect relationships. Understanding why we use a fork to eat, or why people sing around holidays, are examples of understanding cause-effect relationships.

Classification, seriation, and causality develop in middle childhood.

It is important to understand these operations as extensions of what could be done earlier with a few objects, or in simple ways.

In addition to logical operations, mathematical operations emerge. Mathematical operations include addition, subtraction, multiplication, and division. These operations are useful to solve everyday problems related to the need to group objects. For example, if a child knows that he must share a package of cookies among three people for a snack break, how many cookies should each person get? To you and me, this is a "word" problem, but to a child it is real—the child *is* hungry, it *is* snack time, and there really *is* only one package of cookies for herself and two friends. Division may actually develop before multiplication because of its usefulness to resolve the problems of sharing.

Children learn more easily the skills they can use.

As teachers, we have to understand that we do not just teach a curriculum or skills, but we teach children, who must have a specific use for a skill before they should be asked to learn it. A perceptive teacher can discern these real uses of reading, writing, and arithmetic in the life of a child, and a reflective teacher will discover the state of a child's skill before trying to develop an instructional strategy to develop it.

Piaget tried to identify core understandings that unified the many operations emerging throughout the concrete operations period. Perhaps the most central one was **conservation,** an understanding that equivalencies underlie all changes in appearance. For example, the fact that three sets of two cookies are the same as one set of six cookies illustrates conservation of number. Piaget systematically explored children's understanding of conservation of length, number, volume, and weight. He believed that an understanding of conservation underlay the ability of a child to reason out the solution to many concrete problems.

Conservation is a critical understanding for problem solving.

What are the effects of the development of logical and mathematical operations? At school, children not only are able to add and subtract, but also are able to understand relationships between addition and subtraction or multiplication and division. In terms of the sciences, they can develop hypotheses about concrete phenomena (such as effects of materials of different transparency on light), and in discussions, they can construct logical rationales for their positions on issues dealing with topics such as the environment or social relationships. In terms of the arts, writing a story for others about a current theme (such as a ghost story for Halloween) helps them discover the need to sequence descriptions of events; drawing pictures to be viewed by others helps them discover that spatial organization needs to be coherent. Piaget believed that the role of the school is to present opportunities for such developments in thought to occur.

Formal Operations Period (eleven to fifteen and up)

The onset of adolescence usually marks the beginning of formal operational thinking. At this level, thinking begins to focus on *form* rather than on content. In logical argumentation, form refers to the *validity* of an argument. You can separate the validity of an argument from the truth or falsity of its propositions. For example, if you accept that all men are mortal, and if you accept that Jack Sprat is a man, then you must conclude what? That Jack Sprat is mortal. The *form* of this argument is as follows (see Figure 5.1, p. 176):

Adolescents can develop the ability to understand logic apart from experience.

> If the circle is in the square,
> and if the dot is in the circle,
> then the dot must be in the square.

The *conclusion* (the third statement) is implicit in your acceptance of the other two statements, which are called *premises.* The premises may not be true—Jack Sprat is not a real person—but if you accept them as true, then you must also accept the conclusion. The validity of an argument has nothing to do with the truth of its propositions. Formal operations focus on the validity of logic, *not* on the truth of propositions.

During the formal operations period, thinking "no longer bears exclusively on directly perceivable objects and realities, but also on 'hypotheses,' that is to say, on propositions from which it is possible to draw necessary consequences without deciding on their truth or falsity before having examined the result of these implications" (Piaget, 1969, p. 51). Systematic thinking is required in science to work with hypotheses, as Piaget implied, but it is also required in legal argumentation, and in art. Conventions exist in science, law, and art to separate the *validity* of an argument (correct inference or de-

Formal operations involve separating form from content.

**Figure 5.1
Illustration of a Logical
Argument**

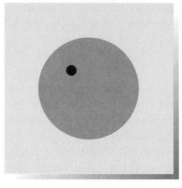

"If the circle is in the square,
and if the dot is in the circle,
then the dot must be in the square."

duction) from *verisimilitude* (appearance of truth or reality). Without such conventions, science, law, and art would not exist as we know them.

As a consequence of the onset of formal operations, an adolescent becomes capable of reasoning about possibilities that may or may not be realistic. Idealistic causes may be defended with logical arguments, but the formal properties of science (such as controlling for alternative hypotheses), art (such as geometric perspective), and justice (such as legal defense of the accused) can be appreciated for the first time. The newly found ability to separate form from content can also be the source of reasoning by analogy or communication through irony, both of which communicate through form rather than through content.

Deepening Your Knowledge Base: The Plant Problem contains a problem about feeding plants that was designed by researchers to test everyday use of formal operations (Kuhn & Ho, 1977). You might like to try it, but remember, formal operations require you to consider all aspects of a problem, not just your personal preference. When researchers gave this problem to fourth graders, sixth graders, eighth graders, and college students, fourth graders and sixth graders tended to use concrete operations to solve it incompletely. No thinking beyond concrete operations entered into solutions until the sixth grade, and even by college, only 65 percent of students used formal operations to reach complete solutions. Typically, the problems used by Piaget were even more difficult, and only about 20 percent of college students have been able to solve them through systematic reasoning (Schwebel, 1975; Siegler, 1981).

What happens if children try to understand a complex phenomenon before they are capable of formal operations? Let's take a look at the law of gravity. Students all hear the story of Newton's apple and understand that gravity was the force that drew the apple to the earth. Their understanding of gravity is constructed in elementary school years, probably long before they can think systematically. Thus, they probably never consider the possibility that grav-

deepening your knowledge base

The Plant Problem

A student has a lot of plants in her room that she has been growing from seedlings, and she has been trying out different types of plant food on them. The plant foods will be referred to as red, green, and blue, as those are the colors of the packets in which they came. There are two different types of plants—leafy and flowery. The student gave some plants all three varieties of plant food; some just two or one. She gave no plant food of any type to a few plants.

Some of the plants have grown much larger than others, and she wants to know which plant food to use. As the foods are expensive, she doesn't want to use any more than is necessary. The table below presents the size of each plant and the type of food used. Results for the leafy and flowery plants are given separately, as it seemed possible that plant foods could affect various types of plants differently.

Growth of Plants by Food Type

Leafy Plants		Flowery Plants	
Plant food	Height	Plant food	Height
green, blue, and red	6"	red	3"
blue and red	6"	red, blue, and green	9"
red	3"	green and red	6"
red and green	6"	blue	6"
green	6"	no plant food	3"
no plant food	3"	red and blue	6"
green and blue	6"	green and blue	9"
blue	6"	green	6"

Discussion Questions

1. For the leafy plants, what plant food should the student use? How did you decide?

2. For the flowery plants, what plant food should the student use? How did you decide?

Source: Adapted from Kuhn & Ho, 1977, courtesy of Rosemary Sutton

Answers to questions: (1) "green or blue," (2) "green and blue." The typical error is to say just "green" or "blue" in response to question 1.

---

ity might have drawn the earth *toward* Newton's apple, even as the apple fell toward earth.

Only through systematically reasoning about what can *and cannot* be perceived can students develop the hypothesis that gravity is a force of *mutual*

> Mature, systematic reasoning provides the most accurate understanding.

attraction, which is actually what Newton hypothesized. The discovery that knowledge developed during elementary school years is probably not very accurate is hardly comforting to us as adults. Although it is usually much easier to go on in life without thinking again about such things until we need to resolve some discrepancy, formal operations have value in helping us understand the world more completely than before. Thinking is always a bit of an adventure.

strategic solutions

Developmentally Appropriate Practices

Developmentally appropriate practices are instructional strategies designed in accordance with Piagetian views of development to match the age and individual needs of the learner. They were originated in the early to mid-1980s because of the efforts of a number of psychologists, educators, and parents who had become concerned about increasingly inappropriate attempts to accelerate the development of children, particularly in the preschool years (Elkind, 1981; Suransky, 1982; Winn, 1983).

These practices all respect the givens of development that are the hallmark of Piaget's stage theory. They have two dimensions (Bredekamp, 1987):

1. *Age appropriateness.* Information on predictable changes for a given age span "provides a framework from which teachers prepare the learning environment and plan appropriate experiences" (1987, p. 2). This framework operates as a given for teachers as they solve instructional problems.

2. *Individual appropriateness.* Information on individual differences in pattern or timing of growth, personality, learning style, and family background needs should be considered in solving instructional problems. This information allows teachers to adapt instruction to individual differences (a goal that we will discuss in greater detail in Chapter 7).

There are two general principles behind these developmentally appropriate practices (Bredekamp, 1987). These principles include

- providing *preschoolers* with opportunities to observe, to interact, and to solve problems to develop their understanding of themselves, others, and the world around them

- providing *primary-grade children* with developmentally appropriate materials to explore and to think about, and with opportunities to interact with other children and adults

Although these principles do not take the form of specific instructional strategies, their effect is primarily to limit instructional strategies to a given range of appropriate practices. Table 5.2 lists some developmentally appropriate practices for preschoolers alongside developmentally *in*appropriate practices (see page 180).

Developmentally appropriate practices in elementary school are often designed to supplement formal instruction rather than to replace it. A teacher in the first three grades is under strong pressures to instruct children in academic skills, such as reading, writing, and arithmetic. Although such instruction may be *in*appropriate for children before six years of age, it is increasingly appropriate as children become less physically active and more purposeful in thought.

Even in later school years, however, developmentally appropriate practices have their place, particularly during stage transitions. A general approach called *discovery learning* was invented by Jerome Bruner and other educators in the 1960s to implement some of Piaget's ideas in science education. These educators generated the **readiness hypothesis**: "any subject can be taught effectively in some intellectually honest form to any child at any stage of development" (Bruner, 1960, p. 33). This hypothesis spurred educators over the next decade to find ways to create a curriculum, particularly in science and mathematics, composed of tasks that emphasized age-appropriate cognitive activities for the learner.

This ambitious project will be discussed in greater detail in the chapter on teaching thinking (Chapter 10). What is important here is that you understand how creating and resolving disequilibrium can develop understanding. Many opportunities arise in the classroom for discovery lessons (Kamii, 1984; Wakefield, 1993). For example, elementary teachers have long taught children how to identify leaves according to tree type (deciduous, coniferous, and so on). Discovery learning might have children collect a variety of leaves on a nature walk or bring them from home and then, as a group, begin to sort them under the teacher's guidance. In what categories do the leaves belong? This question can lead to a lively discussion of appropriate categories (size, shape, color). The group's discovery of a real hierarchy of categories among the leaves exercises concrete logic. Once categories of leaves are understood in relation to each other, categories of trees can be introduced, building on the previous findings. In this manner, knowledge of trees can be constructed so that it is not a fragile or inert product of drill and practice.

Table 5.2 *Some Developmentally Appropriate vs. Inappropriate Practices for 4- and 5-Year-Olds*

Appropriate Practices	*Inappropriate Practices*
Teachers prepare the learning environment to facilitate active exploration and interaction among children and adults, other children, and materials.	Teachers use highly structured, teacher-directed lessons almost exclusively.
Children select many of their own activities from a variety of learning areas the teacher prepares, including dramatic play, blocks, science, math, games and puzzles, books, recordings, art, and music.	The teacher directs all the activity, deciding what children will do and when. The teacher does most of the activity such as cutting shapes or performing steps in an experiment for the children.
Teachers facilitate the development of self-control in children by using positive guidance techniques such as modeling and encouraging expected behavior, redirecting children to a more acceptable activity, and setting clear limits. Teachers' expectations match and respect children's developing capabilities.	Teachers spend a great deal of time enforcing rules, punishing unacceptable behavior, humiliating children who misbehave, making children sit and be quiet, or refereeing disagreements.
Children develop understanding of concepts about themselves, others, and the world around them through observation, interaction with people and real objects, and the exploration of solutions to concrete problems. Learnings about math, science, social studies, health, and other content areas are all integrated through meaningful activities.	Instruction stresses isolated skill development through memorization and rote practice, such as counting, circling an item on a worksheet, memorizing facts, watching demonstrations, drilling with flashcards, or looking at maps. Children's cognitive development is seen as fragmented into content areas.

Source: Excerpts from Bredekamp, 1987, pp. 54–56

An example of teaching math by discovery is described by a teacher in Reflection on Practice: Teaching Division for Understanding, page 182.

One important closing note to this discussion: To conduct this type of lesson you cannot begin with fragile or memorized knowledge. One of the de-

Almost any type of material can be used to develop classification skills. These boys from the Boston area are trading cards and are classifying them by team as well as by individual value. *(Globe Staff Photo/ Mark Wilson)*

mands of developing understanding is that the teacher not only understand the material for the lesson but be a keen judge of students' thinking. If you do not understand the material well, it—rather than the thinking of students— will occupy your attention. For this reason, you might decide to begin such a lesson in a favorite content area and have a backup lesson prepared in case what you hoped would work does not work as expected, creating a disequilibrium in your own understanding that you will have to resolve later.

Evaluation of Developmentally Appropriate Practices

The earliest evidence that developmentally appropriate practices are more effective than developmentally *in*appropriate practices came from Head Start. The Head Start program began in 1965 as a part of the War on Poverty initiated by President Lyndon Johnson. It was and is a *compensatory education* program designed to break the "cycle of poverty" in which children from impoverished backgrounds often drop out of school, have difficulty obtaining employment, and subsequently raise their own children in poverty.

Head Start programs used different approaches. Some early Head Start programs were Piagetian; others were socially oriented; others emphasized academic skills (drill and practice); and still others had emphases different from these. An example of the Piagetian approach was the Montessori program. Working with impoverished children in Rome at the turn of the century, Maria Montessori (1964) developed a cognitively oriented preschool program

strategic solutions, continued

reflection on practice

Teaching Division for Understanding

Teaching division in a third-grade setting can be very difficult and frustrating for all involved. Some teachers I have observed introduce the division task as "the opposite of multiplication." This approach, I found, did not work for me. I realized that I must allow them to *first* discover what division *is*.

The method for the introduction of this concept takes a one-hour class period. First, I pose a problem by placing twelve books in one stack on top of a shelf. I ask them to think about how we could divide that one stack into two the same size, and how many we might have in each stack if we do that. After a short time to think, I ask a volunteer to come up and move the books to represent "dividing by two." Next, I give each child twelve straws and I ask them all to discover as many ways as they can to divide their straws into groups with the same number in each group. They find that there are several ways and begin to apply multiplication sentences to their division.

After this we take out the textbooks, which show pictures of fruit divided into clusters, and the children discuss and solve these problems in many ways. For example, I might hear phrases like "twelve in all," "four in each cluster," "three clusters," and so forth. The final step is a chalkboard demonstration in which we draw pictures and circle groups to represent division, putting the division sentences underneath. After we have worked through several of these problems together, the students are ready to move on to the division sentence without any visuals.

I have used this method for a couple of years and find that the students are able to understand the meaning of division better than they would through the textbook alone. After they have discovered the meaning of division, then and only then can they begin to see it as a reverse process of multiplication.

Beth M. Vinson

Discussion Questions

1. **How does this teacher demonstrate an intuitive grasp of the discovery approach to teaching?**

2. **At what point in her planning does she have to take concrete operations into account to develop a workable strategy? Why?**

that used carefully structured materials to promote inquiry and provide feedback to children. An example of the socially oriented approach was the traditional nursery school, with its emphases on spontaneous play and social development. An example of an academic skills program was DISTAR, an

Traditional nursery schools
emphasize spontaneous play
and social development.
*(Joseph Schuyler/ Stock
Boston)*

acronym for Direct Instruction System for Teaching Arithmetic and Reading
(Bereiter & Engelmann, 1966).

All three types of program were compared for their effectiveness in Head
Start research projects (Royce, Darlington & Murray, 1983; Stallings &
Stipek, 1986). The first phase of research revealed that all three programs had
only minimal effects on boosting intelligence quotients or achievement.
(Academic programs had boosted IQ and achievement scores significantly,
but the effect disappeared by second grade.)

A second phase of research, however, revealed dramatic, long-term benefits of two of the programs—the Piagetian and socially oriented programs. In
comparison to disadvantaged children who had not participated in Head
Start, former students in these two types of program were less frequently retained in a grade and required special educational services less often.
Furthermore, these former Head Start children dropped out less frequently,
graduating from high school at higher rates than the children from similar
backgrounds who had not participated in Head Start. None of these results
pertained to the academic program groups (see Figure 5.2).

What do these results tell us? First, the significant outcomes of Head Start
are probably attitudes toward school and **dispositions to learn** (patterns of behavior directed toward broad goals). They are not IQ gains or achievements in
terms of grades. Second, developmentally appropriate forms of preschool education develop these attitudes and dispositions, whereas developmentally

Figure 5.2
Graduation Outcomes
for Head Starters
(Karnes, Shwedel &
Williams, 1983, p. 159)

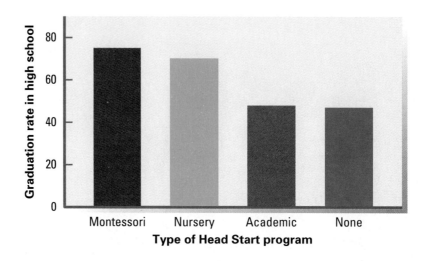

inappropriate forms of preschool education do not. Cognitive-developmental and socially oriented preschool programs are generally appropriate for preschoolers, whereas drill and practice of academic skills is developmentally inappropriate.

Lilian Katz (1992) has gone a step further and hypothesized that developmentally inappropriate practices in preschool actually damage dispositions toward learning. Specifically, curiosity, creativity, independence, and responsibility may be damaged by the cumulative effects of early academic skills training and drill and practice. She points out that few early childhood programs assess attitudinal outcomes, yet as the results of Head Start indicate, the enduring effects of preschool programs may be in dispositions to learn, rather than in IQ or school achievement.

Recently, another source of information on the effects of developmentally appropriate practices has been research comparing developmentally appropriate to developmentally inappropriate practices (such as those in Table 5.2) in existing kindergartens. Along with her colleagues, Diane Burts (1992, 1993) has found developmentally inappropriate practices to be more stressful, and to lead to lower marks in first grade, than more appropriate practices. Furthermore, inappropriate practices in kindergarten lower academic outcomes in first grade in virtually all subject areas, suggesting damage to underlying dispositions, as Katz hypothesized. Because there is a reasonable possibility that stress imposed by premature drill and practice may actually damage children's dispositions to learn, teachers and parents need to resist the temptation to hurry children into academic skills during early childhood.

How effective are practices designed to address the developmental stages of learners at later ages? Educational researchers have not had much success in efforts to *change* the stage of a child's thinking, but it is reasonable to believe that discovery learning can facilitate advancements that are already under way (Nagy & Griffiths, 1982). In terms of the leaf-sorting example above, the cognitive activity required by sorting leaves is only as advanced as what you might expect of children in the first few years of elementary school. But this activity can facilitate the development of classification skills at the same time that it develops understanding of different types of trees.

Discovery learning is an appropriate means of developing logical thinking, but unlike developmentally appropriate practices used during early childhood, developmentally appropriate practices applied during later years do not exclude extensive or intensive practice. Once a skill has emerged, it often needs to be practiced if it is to be further developed. In elementary school, this practice may involve worksheets and recursive exercises of the type that are not appropriate for preschool or kindergarten. We will return to this topic near the end of this chapter when we look at the complementarity of stages of development and phases of learning. For now, it is sufficient to conclude that discovery learning cannot be used to accelerate stages of thinking, but it can facilitate transitions in progress and lay the groundwork for further consolidation of a skill.

Reexamining Piaget

Our study of Piaget would not be complete without a brief look at some recent criticisms of his theory. There is, in fact, a whole group of developmental psychologists called **neo-Piagetians**, who work within the basic stage theory framework of Piaget but who have branched out from his theory in new ways. Although they and others have verified the major elements of Piaget's work, they have criticized Piaget's assumption that the growth of logic is the source of cognitive development. They are by now fairly well agreed that progressive changes in logic are of only intermediate importance.

The challenge for these psychologists has been to define the real source of cognitive development. Recently, they have become interested in **working memory**, which is a memory structure that roughly corresponds to consciousness and increases in capacity throughout childhood. (You will learn much more about it in Chapter 9.) Although working memory capacity may not be strictly a function of maturation or nature, the changes in this structure are easily measured and are likely to result in plateaus or stages of development.

Working memory appears to expand with age.

The developing capacity of working memory has often been measured through a memory task called "digit span" (Flavell, Miller & Miller, 1993). Typically, a person is given a string of random digits to recall (such as 4-1-9-0-7-3-8) without using any grouping strategies. The digits are presented at about one per second, without any rhythm. An adult with an exceptional short-term memory can recall strings of nine digits. An average adult can recall strings of about seven. Before adolescence, children generally can correctly recall only relatively short strings (see Table 5.3). The younger the child, the shorter the string will be—a phenomenon that suggests that this capacity develops with age throughout childhood.

> Neo-Piagetians focus on memory structure as the basis for development.

Neo-Piagetian psychologists such as Robbie Case (1991, 1993) believe that developmental limitations in the capacity of working memory imply that younger children cannot solve problems as complex as those that can be solved by older children. Complex problems require more working memory than simple problems, at least until solution procedures become routine. Neo-Piagetians like Case are thus able to accept many of the fundamental ideas of Piaget regarding stagelike limitations on complexity of thought, while focusing on memory structure, rather than logic, as the source of these limitations.

THE SOCIAL ORIGINS OF THOUGHT: VYGOTSKY

Although Piaget's ideas have been widely applied to explain the development of logic through social studies, science, and mathematics, they have not been widely applied to explain the development of cognitive skills through the language arts. Another constructivist theory, proposed over sixty years ago by Lev Vygotsky (1896–1934), a Byelorussian psychologist, has often been

Table 5.3 Increase in Working Memory Capacity with Age

Age	Digit Span
2.5	2
3.0	3
4.5	4
7.0	5
10.0	6
Adult	7
Superior adult	9

Source: Compiled from data in the 1973 *Stanford-Binet Intelligence Test* scoring manual (Boston: Houghton Mifflin)

What an individual can do if aided by others is often of greater significance for development than what the individual can already do alone.   *(David Young-Wolff/PhotoEdit)*

used to explain how language can affect cognitive development. Vygotsky's theory is not a stage approach, although he acknowledged the effect of maturation on development. Instead of stages, Vygotsky focused on a *zone* of development, and the impact of social influences within this zone at any age.

The Zone of Proximal Development

The **zone of proximal development** is the difference between a child's unaided level of thinking and his or her potential level if aided by a more expert peer or adult. The idea that a zone of greater development exists beyond what an individual can do unaided appears to have originated in observations by Vygotsky about individualized tests that measure what a child or adolescent already knows. These tests are not useful for diagnosing what the individual *could* do, if given help by others. Vygotsky believed that what an individual could do if aided by others was of greater significance for development than what the individual could already do alone (Vygotsky, 1987). Anticipating the role of the teacher, Vygotsky remarked that "the teacher must orient his work not on yesterday's development in the child but on tomorrow's" (1987, p. 211). Accordingly, the teacher needed to understand each student's zone of proximal development to understand his or her potential for development.

What in practice defines the zone of proximal development? Vygotsky (1987) stated that it is not indicated by any biological state of maturation, but by the productivity of instruction for a given child at a particular time. For

The zone of proximal development indicates how much one's thinking can improve with help.

Teaching should be oriented to the student's potential for development.

example, if you have been around first graders, you will probably have witnessed some highly productive interactions that led to the rapid development of literacy. When instruction is within the zone, children learn to read and write independently within a matter of a few months. Instruction outside the zone of proximal development does not have this effect, and the same teaching methods may be ineffective.

Vygotsky did not concern himself with the effects of maturation on this zone, and the absence of a defined role for maturation remains a problem in his theory today (Wertsch & Tulviste, 1992). Nevertheless, the zone of proximal development remains a thought-provoking idea, and the search is on for methods that have the effect Vygotsky described—a sudden increase in proficiency that is attributable to the degree of support or assistance that a teacher or peer provides. (See Reflection on Practice: Tutoring in the Zone of Proximal Development.)

The Internalization of Thinking

In addition to the idea of proximal development, Vygotsky described **internalization**, a process by which social discourse is transformed into thinking. "Every function in the child's cultural development appears twice: first, on the social level, and later, on the individual level; first *between* people . . . and then *inside* the child" (Vygotsky, 1978, p. 57). In short, he theorized that higher-order thinking is an internalization of discourse between people. According to this idea, problem solving in group discussions (on the social level) eventually internalizes to become problem solving by the individual. In Vygotsky's view, all higher-order intellectual skills developed this way through the medium of language. Essentially, thought was internalized discussion and, it might be added, discussion was externalized thought.

> Social discussion is changed into thinking by the process of internalization.

As a prime example of the process of internalization, Vygotsky (1987) chose to analyze "egocentric speech," a phenomenon among young children that Piaget (1969) had also noted. Whereas Piaget explained the self-talk of three- and four-year-olds as a product of their egocentrism, Vygotsky found self-talk to be an intermediate step in the development of self-control. Egocentric speech, he observed, was intermediate between external speech and inner speech. External speech for a young child was often regulatory, such as a mother guiding her child. Egocentric speech often represented the child guiding him- or herself. Inner speech, he concluded, was essentially self-regulatory.

> Egocentric speech is a way to guide oneself.

Whose explanation of egocentric speech is more accurate, Piaget's or Vygotsky's? Many psychologists and educators would now prefer Vygotsky's explanation, if for no other reason than that we can confirm it in our own experiences. When we face difficult or complex tasks, we often revert to speaking to ourselves to guide our actions—as if we were giving ourselves directions. The difficulty or complexity of the task drives us to externalize in words what is normally internal and unspoken. We revert to an earlier stage in the development of thought. When the task becomes easier or simpler, we regulate ourselves through inner speech, or thinking.

Tutoring in the Zone of Proximal Development

This past year I had a student named Philipe in my third-period freshman English class who was repeating the course after failing it the previous year. He told me in broken English after class on the first day that he needed to be in "basic" English and not "grade level" English. I could tell right away that English was not his first language, so I decided to talk to his counselor about the situation. His counselor told me that he should be in grade level because he was definitely smart enough, but that the language barrier caused him to fail last year. We talked extensively about his potential and decided to keep him in the grade level class.

Philipe proved to be a very bright student, but sometimes he was slow at learning a particular concept or finishing his work because English was not his native language. After several weeks, though, I noticed that he needed extra help but was embarrassed to ask me to come to his seat because he didn't want the other kids to know he was a little slower than they. I also did not want to embarrass him by always going to his desk to help him even though I noticed that Philipe's grades were slipping from the C range to the D range. It got to the point that he would pretend to be finished or to understand something just to avoid having me check his work. He was a year older than the other students, and that also contributed to the embarrassment he felt about being slow. I talked with him after class, but Philipe was not very communicative.

After the first six weeks, I tried a new approach that might help Philipe bring his grades up and help him to understand the material better but not draw more attention to him than was necessary. George, a very bright and caring student, had been sitting next to Philipe since the beginning of the year. I asked George if he would mind helping Philipe when it appeared that he was "stumped," but not to be too obvious so as not to embarrass Philipe. George was delighted to help because he usually finished with his work first.

Philipe's grades went from the D range to the B range after only a few weeks. George was very pleased to help another student and his grades stayed the same as they had been prior to tutoring Philipe. I also believe that a special friendship was formed between the two boys in the process.

I believe that peer tutoring was successful in Philipe's case. It demonstrates the zone of proximal development as studied and described by Vygotsky. Vygotsky's conclusion that the higher-achieving student would remain at the same level of learning and the lower-achieving student would be brought up to that level proved to be true in this situation.

Jennifer Lowman

Discussion Questions

1. **How did this teacher establish the student's potential for development? Compare and contrast this method with that described by Vygotsky.**

2. **Why is a peer often better than a teacher for tutoring a fellow student? Use evidence from this case to support your explanation.**

3. **Do you think that Philipe will become dependent on George? What could you do to ensure that Philipe will develop as an independent learner?**

strategic   solutions

Scaffolded Instruction

These ideas have profound implications for education, but for years, they lay suppressed in the Soviet Union and dormant in the West. In the late 1970s, Vygotsky's ideas became ascendant in the West as part of a trend toward socially oriented learning activities. For example, studies began on how parents "scaffold" or structure learning experiences for their children (e.g., Wood, Bruner & Ross, 1976). Teaching that aids the mental work of the student became known as **scaffolded instruction.** In this form of teaching, the student's mental structuring ability is supplemented by the scaffolding influence of more expert peers or adults, just as the scaffolding around a building supports its construction.

Scaffolded instruction is generally considered to consist of three elements in the teaching/learning relationship (Beed, Hawkins & Roller, 1991). First, teacher and student *interact in a collaborative context that honors the intention of the student.* Collaboration may involve activities such as reading a story together, illustrating or analyzing a document, planning a science project, working with tools, or solving a math problem. To honor the intentions of the student, you must follow the intention of the student rather than lead the student to achieve your goals. Second, the teacher and student *operate within the student's zone of proximal development.* This zone is generally just beyond the student's level of competence or independent functioning. The teacher assists the student to the extent that the student requires assistance to achieve a goal. Third, the teacher should *gradually withdraw support as the student develops competence.* Because the level of independent functioning changes during practice, the scaffolding must change. Assistance is phased out as the student internalizes the skill.

Diminishing external support as internalization proceeds may follow a general pattern called *contingent scaffolding* (Beed, Hawkins & Roller, 1991; Wood, Wood & Middleton, 1978). This pattern or sequence of scaffolding moves from a maximum level of support, in which most of the activity is done by the teacher (for instance, modeling a skill), to a minimum level of support, in which nearly all of the activity is done by the student, with the teacher providing general cues. Teachers should approach the pattern (summarized in Table 5.4) from the point of minimum support (E) to identify the level of proficiency that the student has achieved. As student competence develops, the teacher should progressively remove the scaffolding until independent functioning is achieved. Contingent scaffolding is not the only scaffolding strategy, but it can be applied in a wide variety of situations to help students internalize skills. In Chapter 10 we shall examine another common scaffolding strategy called "reciprocal teaching."

Table 5.4   *A General Pattern for Scaffolding Instruction*

Elements in the Pattern	Example
A. Model the skill	"Let's sound out this word by breaking it into smaller parts."
B. Invite student performance	"Can you sound out the letters in this part of the word?"
C. Cue specific elements	"Try to break this word into smaller parts."
D. Cue specific strategies	"Have you tried sounding out the word?"
E. Provide general cues	"What should you do when you don't recognize a word?"

Source: Adapted from Beed, Hawkins & Roller, 1991, p. 650

Evaluation of Scaffolded Instruction

A long-standing debate over how scaffolding should be used is reflected in an article titled, "Scaffolding: Who's Building Whose Building?" (Searle, 1984). As originally described by cognitive psychologists such as Jerome Bruner (1975), the word *scaffolding* referred to responses by parents that supported intentions shared with a child, but *scaffolding* has been adopted by some educators as a metaphor to describe any support or assistance given to students for achieving outcomes, even those that ignore students' intentions. Clearly, the intentions of teachers and students can differ for any number of reasons (Dyson, 1990), and to the extent that they differ, scaffolding is less likely to be effective.

Research on the effectiveness of scaffolding has generally not taken into account whether the strategy respects the intentions of the learner. Research on scaffolding that has not distinguished differences between students, for example, has generally not found scaffolding to lead to improved learning over other strategies of interaction (Day, Cordon & Kerwin, 1989). Research on scaffolding that has accounted for these differences has found it to be a more effective instructional strategy than repeated modeling of a performance (Day & Cordon, 1993), but even this research did not scaffold instruction to support intentions shared with the learner.

Under optimal assessment conditions—which respect the intentions of the learner—scaffolded instruction is likely to be even more effective than existing research tells us. At the end of the next discussion we will turn to the question of the place of this strategy in developing cognition.

PHASES OF LEARNING APPROACH: INFORMATION-PROCESSING THEORISTS

If you reflect on it for a moment, you'll realize that you already know a good deal about this topic from two previous chapters. In Chapter 2, you learned about the journey a reflective teacher makes as he or she grows from a novice thinker to an expert. In this section we will take another look at that journey as it applies to cognitive learning in general.

As we do so, you will also see how much of what you learned about information-processing theory and motor skills learning in Chapter 4 applies to cognitive development as well. The same concept of phases of learning and the same emphasis on automaticity as a goal of learning still apply. In fact, that model of skill development is applied by several influential cognitive psychologists such as John Anderson (1995) and Robert Glazer (1990) to help distinguish novice from expert thinkers. So, as you read through this next section, try to connect it to the learning you have already done and try to build upon the concepts you have already started forming.

It should also be helpful to contrast what you will learn here to the cognitive development approach of Piaget. That theory, as you know, places great emphasis on the maturational givens that define a child's capabilities at a particular age. The information-processing approach, on the other hand, accords a far greater role to environment, stressing the learning that comes with experience.

In the two following sections we will look first at the key distinguishing characteristics that differentiate novice thinkers from expert thinkers and next at the phases of learning that a learner most likely progresses through on the journey from novice to expert.

The Differences Between Novice and Expert Thinkers

Overall, we can describe novice thinkers as having few *routine* thought processes related to particular cognitive tasks, while expert thinkers have many of these routine processes. This is a critical distinction because, as you'll remember from Chapter 2, routine or automated processes free an expert's attention for nonroutine, or deeper, aspects of the task.

When faced with solving a physics problem, for example, novice thinkers tend to focus on *surface features* (obvious but superficial elements such as words used) and to sort problems according to these features. Thus, a key word such as *friction* used in several different problem statements or similar objects used in the problem statement (for instance, a merry-go-round and a rotating disk) are important organizers to a novice. Experts, on the other hand, will sort physics problems according to the *deep structure* or underlying principles of each problem and agree with one another on what constitutes the deep structure of the problem (Chi, Feltovich & Glaser, 1981).

Expert thinkers focus on the deep structure of a problem.

It seems that hypothetical memory structures called **schemata** (plural of *schema*), which contain categories of knowledge, are not only made up of different kinds of knowledge for novices and experts but also organized differently. Novices tend to possess **declarative knowledge**, or information about facts and rules associated with a given type of problem. Experts tend to possess **procedural knowledge**, or "know-how," which includes solution methods. Examples of procedural knowledge include actions that a child might use to add two one-digit numbers, to recognize a word when reading, or to capitalize the first letter of each sentence when writing. It's important to remember that even though you cannot see such cognitive skills, they are no less real than motor skills.

> Experts have procedural knowledge that includes methods for solving problems.

A key to the emergence of higher-order concepts in an expert's thinking seems to be the *clustering* of knowledge (Chi & Cesi, 1987; Chi & Koeske, 1983). On the other hand, the far less systematically organized knowledge of a novice does not permit the same kind of deeper thinking. In Figure 5.3, you'll find an illustration of experts' clustered knowledge, represented by systematic linkages between concepts A and C and concepts B and D.

We can summarize four differences in the knowledge bases of novices and experts (Anderson, 1982; Larkin et al., 1980; Murphy & Wright, 1984; Spilich et al., 1979):

1. Novices at task possess fewer routine cognitive processes related to that task than do experts.
2. The knowledge structures of novices are activated by surface features of a problem, whereas those of experts are activated by the deep structure of the problem.
3. Novices tend to represent their knowledge in declarative form (statements of fact), whereas experts represent their knowledge in a procedural form (methods for solving problems).

Figure 5.3 Idealized Representation of Knowledge of a Novice and an Expert
Think of concepts (circles) as nouns, attributes (triangles) as adjectives, and the links between them (lines) as a network, representing knowledge. *(Chi & Ceci, 1987, p. 117)*

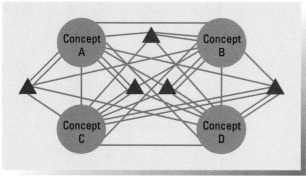

Organization of novice knowledge

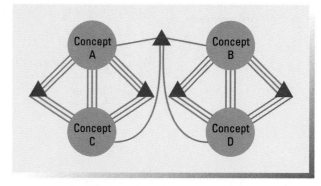

Organization of expert knowledge

Table 5.5   Dimensions of Novice and Expert Knowledge

Dimension	Novice Knowledge	Expert Knowledge
Process	Few routines	Many routines
Activated by	Surface features	Deep structure
Contents	Declarative	Procedural
Organization	Associative	Systematic

4. The knowledge of novices is not as well organized as the knowledge of experts.

These differences between novice and expert knowledge are also summarized in Table 5.5.

The Process of Proceduralization

How is the more superficial, declarative knowledge of a novice transformed into the systematic, procedural knowledge of the expert? Although it is still being researched, **proceduralization** (Anderson, 1995) is the process by which novice knowledge (which is declarative) is transformed through experience into expert knowledge (which is procedural).

Although various labels have been given to phases in the learning sequence (Shuell, 1990), the most commonly used ones are identical to the phases of learning a psychomotor skill that were discussed in Chapter 4: the *cognitive* phase, the *associative* phase, and the *autonomous* phase (Anderson, 1995). The cognitive phase corresponds with novice knowledge, and the autonomous phase corresponds with expert knowledge (see Table 5.6).

> Novice knowledge becomes expert through proceduralization.

Cognitive (Novice) Phase

The novice or cognitive phase of learning a cognitive skill involves the acquisition of facts *about* a skill (declarative knowledge). This type of knowl-

> In the cognitive phase of learning, one acquires facts.

Table 5.6   Phases of Cognitive Skill Learning

Skill Phase	Proficiency	Learning Process
Cognitive	Novice	Rehearse rules or facts; use general procedures
Associative		Construct and combine procedures
Autonomous	Expert	Generalize, discriminate, and strengthen procedures

The young girl in this picture is rehearsing the rules of chess, while her grandfather is absorbed in teaching her. A novice acquires facts and rules about a skill, but an expert uses a skill strategically—he is just one pawn up.   *(David Young-Wolff/ PhotoEdit)*

edge consists of facts or rules for action, often recited by the learner as cues, but it seldom includes the procedures for application of the fact or rule.

Novice knowledge of grammar, for example, might include the statement, "Capitalize the first word in every sentence." This rule is from a popular grammar book for ninth graders. Initial application may involve reciting the relevant rule aloud or to oneself while using procedures for interpreting rules from past experience. Because working memory is very limited, intermediate results are easily forgotten during this phase, and learners have to pay close attention to what they are doing or frequently have to repeat their procedures.

Perhaps you remember this phase of learning a popular board game such as Monopoly. In the cognitive phase, you watched other players and tried to learn from them, but sooner or later you had to learn the rules. Perhaps others explained them to you or you read the instructions; even then you probably forgot the rules or became confused and had to ask other players or consult the written rules quite frequently to resolve questions of how to proceed. Playing the game by the rules was at first laborious and not a whole lot fun, but it was necessary to learn the game.

Associative Phase

Recall of verbatim facts and rules is inefficient because it takes time and requires a large portion of working memory. With practice (and the compilation of knowledge that practice implies), a learner can convert declarative knowledge into procedural knowledge and begin to apply facts and rules without verbal restatement. As learners practice, they construct specialized condition-action statements ("if-then" statements), which allow declarative knowledge to drop out. For example, the grammar rule might be interpreted as follows:

If a word begins a sentence, then find the first letter of the word.

If the first letter of the first word has been found, then capitalize it.

The new statements incorporate the rule to be applied in a form that is a procedure. Another process that increases the efficiency of thought is the combination of condition-action statements ("If a word begins a sentence, then find the first letter and capitalize it.") Combining steps in a sequence makes the procedure more fluent and fast.

> In the associative phase, one develops procedures and gains fluency.

In terms of the board game, you entered the associative phase as you began to apply the rules and procedures spontaneously. You did not have to ask someone else what to do or consult the rules except in unusual circumstances. You simply followed rules whenever appropriate conditions arose. When you landed on some unowned "property," for example, you went ahead and bought it if you had the "money." You developed a sequence of routines, but you did not typically adopt a strategy. You practiced as you played, but you typically did not try to win by any means other than by purchasing property and trusting to luck. A real investor would not stay in business for long that way, and generally you were out of the game fairly early.

Autonomous (Expert) Phase

The expert or autonomous phase of learning a cognitive skill involves *tuning* (Rumelhart & Norman, 1978) or refinement of the skill, and the development of strategy. Refinement occurs through the generalization, discrimination, and strengthening of procedural knowledge.

> In the autonomous phase, one refines thinking skills and develops strategy.

Generalization extends the application of procedures to a wider category of problems ("Capitalize the first letter of the first word in each line of poetry"). *Discrimination* limits the application of procedures to a narrower category of problems ("but not the poetry of e. e. cummings"). *Strengthening* eliminates inefficiencies in the procedures (simply capitalizing the first letter of a sentence as you write is more efficient than finding the first word of the sentence, then capitalizing its first letter). Processes such as generalization, discrimination, and strengthening continue to modify the cognitive skills of the expert, who never stops "fine-tuning" his or her procedural knowledge.

In the procedural phase, a learner can also use procedures *strategically*. For instance, in Monopoly, a strategy might begin with setting the goal implied by the name of the game—driving opposing players out of the game. A strategy might involve acquiring property rapidly until all properties in a "block" are secured, then "mortgaging" or selling properties to the bank to generate enough cash to build rapidly on the block. A player whose attention is focused on a strategy may be only intermittently aware of the rules, such as when a player misses a turn or plays out of turn.

> Some cognitive skills may approach the level of automaticity.

Some question remains over whether a cognitive skill can be as fully automated as a motor skill. Some experts have argued that because of its nature, a cognitive skill never becomes fully automated, but others argue that pattern recognition and the repeated use of a simple cognitive skill bring on the development of automaticity. We learn to recognize patterns in reading words, music, speedometers, and road signs. We also may approach automaticity in the use of simple cognitive skills, such as the ability to add one-digit numbers. The issue of whether cognitive skills (or motor skills, for that matter) can be fully automated has yet to be resolved, but it is probable that no skill can ever become as automatic as a reflex, which is entirely unconscious.

strategic solutions

Procedural Facilitation

One developmental strategy that can be related to the phase theory of skill development is called **procedural facilitation.** In this strategy, procedures themselves are the object of explicit instruction (e.g., Hillocks, Kahn & Johannessen, 1983; Scardamalia & Bereiter, 1986). Procedural facilitation involves (1) clear and specific objectives, (2) materials and problems carefully selected to engage the learner in *how* to do a particular type of writing, and (3) activities that lead to a high level of peer interaction.

The general strategy can be stated this way: *To facilitate the development of expertise, state rules as procedures.* Procedures can be as simple as a series of learning cues or prompts or as complex as a set of directions. For example, if you wanted to teach the skill of summarizing text (Rosenshine & Meister, 1992, p. 27), you might use this series of cues or prompts:

Identify the topic.

Write two or three words that reflect the topic.

Use these words as a prompt to help figure out the main idea of the paragraph.

Select two details that elaborate on the main idea and are important to remember.

Write two or three sentences that best incorporate these important ideas.

Much as an objective does, each of these cues begins with an action verb and is relatively short. Unlike objectives, they are arranged in a specific sequence that defines a procedure. The repeated use of the procedure leads to proceduralization of knowledge, specifically of how to summarize text.

Do procedures need to be stated like a series of objectives? Not necessarily. Procedural facilitation can occur with any sequence of cues or prompts for actions as long as the actions amount to a series of steps that can be repeated. In learning to interrogate a text, for example, students may learn to ask "who, what, where, when, and why." *Ask* is understood to be the action.

To facilitate proceduralization, however, prompts need to be relatively short lists of things to do. Long lists, or lists of prompts unrelated to actions (such as sentences with blanks in them) are unlikely to make proceduralization or the development of know-how, easier.

Evaluation: Procedural Facilitation

Research on procedural facilitation is in its infancy, but procedurally oriented teaching has been found to be more effective than lecture, "natural process," or individualized modes of teaching written composition (Hillocks, 1984, 1986). For example, in one study of advanced high school English classes, two classes were taught in a way that was designed to facilitate proceduralization of knowledge (*how* to write an extended definition), while the third was taught in a conventional way (Hillocks, Kahn & Johannessen, 1983). During the first four days of instruction, the procedurally taught groups were trained in strategies of definition: (1) how to circumscribe a concept, (2) how to compare examples to establish criteria for distinguishing the target concept from related concepts, and (3) how to generate examples to clarify these distinctions. The conventional group was taught in an traditional manner (involving discussion and practice) from a textbook. The last two days of instruction for both procedurally taught and conventional groups consisted of reviewing what had been learned and outlining extended definitions.

Although the conventionally taught group improved significantly at the task of defining a concept, the procedurally instructed groups improved even more, suggesting that training in how to execute the skill facilitated the acquisition of procedural knowledge. A recent case study of student compositions (Smagorinsky, 1991) suggests that instruction in task-specific procedures increases the *purposefulness* of thought during composition.

Although this research extends only to the teaching of writing, it has some interesting implications for all skill learning. If you examine most textbooks in your teaching field, you will find that many rules are *not* expressed as procedures or sequences of action. They are declarative. You will notice, by way of contrast, that rules in some other textbooks (such as this one) are generally expressed as procedures or sequences of action. They are imperative rather than declarative, and are often arranged according to some sequence. Is this difference important? The research on procedural facilitation suggests that it is, if students are expected to apply rules under specific conditions.

Nevertheless, many questions remain. For example, although some procedures may improve compositions on a sentence level, they do not seem to improve them on the thematic level (e.g., Scardamalia & Bereiter, 1983). They are too specific to have an effect on the overall quality of writing. Other procedures (e.g., Hillocks, Kahn & Johannessen, 1983) seem to have more positive results on overall quality of writing, but the results have not been replicated by independent investigators. What we know about how to facilitate the development of composition skills—and cognitive skills in general—will surely grow as more is discovered about the match between procedures and skills (cf. Graham, MacArthur & Schwartz, 1995).

Complementarity of Stages, Zones, and Phases

Thus far, we have explored three different approaches to cognitive development: stages of development, socially mediated development, and phases of learning. Are these different approaches compatible? This is not just an academic question, because teachers require integrated knowledge or a working theory of development on which to act. We cannot act consistently on knowledge that is not integrated or that is not consistent with itself.

As you discovered in the last chapter, however, different theories of development are not necessarily incompatible. In fact, a theoretical integration of findings from the information-processing approach with the constructivist ideas of both Piaget and Vygotsky seems to be occurring, although the integration is not yet complete (Liben, 1987; Resnick, 1987). If we think back to our nature/nurture spectrum, another way to put this is to say that the different emphases accorded nature and nurture by constructivism and information-processing theory reflect views of development that may be compatible, just as nature is compatible with nurture.

Different theories of cognitive development may be compatible.

To understand how they can be integrated, we need to reexamine Piaget's fundamental metaphor for development, which is a building. Stages are floors, and transitions between stages are stairs. Floors are relatively smooth plateaus; transitions between floors (stairs) are relatively uneven (representing disequilibrium). If we look at progress as climbing to the top floor of the building, then the periods of most rapid progress are represented by being on the stairs, or during stage transitions. In Piaget's theory, these "stairs" typically occur around ages two, seven or eight, and eleven to fifteen.

Research supports a staircase (plateau) model of learning.

Say, however, that we view progress as horizontal rather than vertical. Any obstacle that we would have to climb would slow us down. Climbing anything would not represent a period of rapid progress, but of slow and laborious progress. Psychologists who advocate the information-processing approach to cognitive development view progress in a different dimension than did Piaget. Increasing skill proficiency is as different from changing skill quality as horizontal progress is from vertical progress.

The complementarity view would see development as both: a little progress up, then a little progress over, then a little progress up, and so on. We discovered in the last chapter that one convenient way to combine stage and phase approaches is to "fold" phases within stages. This may not be the only way to combine stages and phases, but it serves as a working hypothesis to integrate disparate views of development.

Robbie Case, the neo-Piagetian psychologist whose research on working memory we've already discussed, has been a strong advocate of an integrated model of cognitive development. He combined phases of learning with stages to produce a "staircase" model of development, in which substages (or phases) account for skill development within each stage. In his theory, there are four stages, just as in Piaget's theory, and they roughly correspond with the same ages as found in Piaget's theory. There are also three substages within each stage, corresponding to phases of learning (Case, 1993).

What is fascinating is that the results of research by psychologists who have favored an information-processing approach also support the hypothesis of "staircases" of development (Means & Voss, 1985; Schneider, Korkel & Weinert, 1989). These studies, often originally focused on expert/novice differences, have simultaneously uncovered significant **age effects** or differences in skill levels based on age apart from experience. For example, in a German study of memory and inference in children, researchers divided students in grades 3, 5, and 7 into "experts" and "novices" based on their knowledge of soccer rules (Schneider, Korkel & Weinert, 1989). The researchers played a tape-recorded story about a young soccer player participating in an important match and then used measures of recall and inference to test the students' knowledge. Some of what they found is displayed in Figures 5.4 and 5.5.

Figure 5.4
Memory in Grades 3 and 7 *(Schneider, Korkel & Weinert, 1989)*

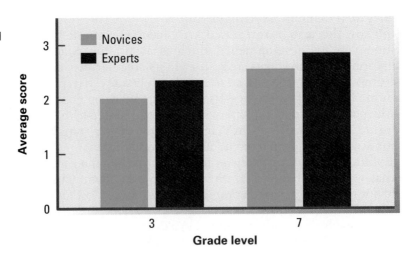

Scaffolding during the intermediate phase of learning should involve progressions in cues and feedback. Note that this teacher is listening carefully to the student to determine what help is needed. *(Andy Sacks/ Tony Stone Worldwide)*

Grade 3 represents concrete operations, and grade 7 represents formal operations. (The results for grade 5 in each graph are omitted because only the average ages in the other two grade levels clearly represent different stages of development.) What is interesting about these results for recall (Figure 5.4) and inference (Figure 5.5) is that—just as Case predicted—they both look like staircases: two steps, then a landing, then two steps. *Novices* at the higher stage seem to outperform *experts* at the lower stage, even through the improvement between stages is small.

Most improvements in proficiency seem to occur *within* a stage of development. These improvements within a stage appear to be largely the effect of practice. During the *intermediate*, or associative, phase of skill learning,

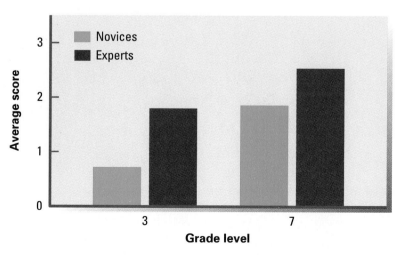

Figure 5.5
Inference in Grades 3 and 7
(Schneider, Korkel & Weinert, 1989)

think it through

Consider this problem that a novice preservice teacher has **IDENTIFIED** and **REPRESENTED**.

Discipline Problems

I believe a challenging situation for me would be handling discipline problems: for example, what to do if young children refuse to do the work you assign them. Getting students to do their homework and classwork and keeping them on task might sometimes be difficult. I have heard of cases where a kindergarten or first-grade student chooses to remain off task rather than do the assigned work.

My question for other teachers would be: What would you do if a young child refuses to do the work and tells you that you cannot make them do the work?

Observe how an experienced practicing teacher GENERATES SOLUTIONS to this problem.

This problem seems to be twofold: a choice to remain off task and a power struggle between a teacher and a student.

In dealing with students in early grades, a choice to remain off task can be dealt with as a choice that evokes consequences. Consequences for poor choices need not be punitive or degrading to a student. It can be stated to a child very simply. "I'm sorry you chose to spend your time not completing the assignment. I hope that you will use the time when the rest of the students are [involved in some reward activity such as free time] to complete your work. When your work is completed, you can join the rest of us in [the reward activity]." Should a child remain off task and not complete work, then free time, free choice, or recess become a nonreality for that student.

Another possibility is to redirect the student to another worthwhile task of the same nature. The task can be modified or an option can be given to complete it in another way or form.

In choosing one of the above-mentioned solutions, it is imperative to find out why the choice was made *not* to complete the assignment. Many times students will react extremely negatively to tasks they believe they cannot do. It is more appealing to appear defiant than to appear ignorant. I would begin by questioning students to be sure they did, in fact, understand the assignment. If they did, I would choose the option that gives them time to complete the task while others per-

form a more pleasurable activity. If they did not, I would explain the task again and then reassign or modify the task and ask for it at a later date.

The power struggle needs to be dealt with in a slightly different manner. If a student is belligerent in nonconformance, first try to find out why. Once again, students will react negatively to tasks they believe they cannot do. When teachers work with young students, this is often the case. If so, can the task be modified? I also hope that we are talking about a worthwhile assignment. Many times the assignments don't make sense to students because they don't lead to any worthwhile learning. That is, they are mindless busywork. I hope a teacher would remove this kind of assignment from the task list by saying something like, "Do the rest of you see this as a dumb thing to do?" If they all do, perhaps they are right!

Students *are* correct in assuming that a teacher *cannot* force them to do an assignment. What you need to explain calmly is that although you can't force the assignment, you *can* remove the student from other more pleasurable activities, you *can* lower grades, you *can* call caregivers, and so on. I hope you can reason with the students. It simply becomes a waiting game. I recommend extreme patience in waiting for the desired behavior.

Michael Robinson
Center Elementary
Marion, Indiana

think it through, continued

EVALUATE this problem's possible multiple solutions while you think about the dynamic process of problem solving.

It is important to recognize how developmentally appropriate this solution is. Developmentally appropriate management practices for grades 1–3 focus on developing self-control, or what Vygotsky might have termed "self-regulation." Techniques to develop self-control that are appropriate during the primary-school years involve the following (Bredekamp, 1987, p. 73): setting clear limits in a positive manner; involving children in establishing rules for social living and for solving misbehavior; redirecting children to an acceptable activity; meeting with an individual child who is having problems or with children and their parents.

These techniques balance control with self-control. Setting limits and redirecting younger children require a degree of control, while involving children in establishing rules and meeting with an individual child and his or her parents encourage the development of self-control.

Does the solution of the experienced teacher meet the criterion of a developmentally appropriate practice? My estimation is that it does. Notice the emphasis in the first part of the solution on positive control techniques. These include setting clear limits and redirecting the student. You will want to refer to the classroom rules as limits, but special measures for coping with misbehavior are also sometimes necessary. Here, the expert teacher models coping by setting up a positive consequence for *appropriate* behavior—"When your work is completed, you can join the rest of us." The experienced teacher would set a goal for the student (finishing the work) and an incentive to achieve it. The teacher also suggests redirecting the student to another task—also developmentally appropriate.

The "power struggle" that the experienced teacher senses is commonly the result of developmentally *in*appropriate practices, which may exist or have existed in other contexts (such as at home or during kindergarten). Developmentally inappropriate practices crop up when "teachers place themselves in an adversarial role with children, emphasizing their [own] power" (Bredekamp, 1987, p. 73). Notice how the experienced teacher would respond to the student's expectation of a power struggle by talking with the student to find out what is wrong. Perhaps the problem is the assignment! If so, you can change that. What emerges from many meetings with children (and their parents) is a collaborative form of problem solving.

Collaborative problem solving is a developmentally appropriate practice that provides you with a wonderful opportunity to scaffold the development of self-control. Ask the student to help you identify the problem ("What's wrong?"); set a goal that is achievable; gather ideas about how to achieve it; generate a strategy; implement and evaluate the strategy.

Chapter 13 will give you some specific techniques for solving problems with students. It will also give you more ideas about how to scaffold self-control as you develop a strategy with a student.

Problem solving with students is developmentally appropriate even in first grade because most students are becoming capable of "figuring things out." The process needs to be scaffolded for most of them to be successful at it, but in the five-step model of problem solving you have a ready-made scaffold to help students develop self-control.

skills should become more fluent, allowing problems to be solved more quickly and easily than before. You'll find that the practice you provide your students is most effective when it focuses on increasing the difficulty level of particular types of problems, not on the introduction of new skills. As a teacher, you will want to take this finding into account when you provide worksheets to individuals or groups in class, schedule time for practice on the computer, or plan homework assignments. Your instructional focus during the intermediate phase of learning should be on scaffolding instruction so that competent performance develops from progressions in cues and feedback (Rosenshine & Meister, 1992).

Any given skill does not improve as rapidly for beginners as it does for intermediates. This insight tells us that teachers should *not* expect learners to improve rapidly in fluency or speed of performance during stage transitions. Rather, stage transitions are periods of relatively slow and laborious change. Just why this is so is not yet clear. Perhaps age effects are due to changes in *quality* of cognition, rather than in *quantity* of cognition (Means & Voss, 1985). As I mentioned earlier in the chapter, differences in stages generally represent changes in quality, while differences in phases represent changes in quantity, resulting from increasing speed or proficiency.

As a teacher you need to adapt your plans and expectations when new skills are being introduced. This entails both lowering expectation of speed and fluency and using teaching strategies and techniques, such as unpressured discovery and scaffolding which respects the intentions of the learner, that are appropriate to novices and new skill learning. Notice, for instance, how Mrs. Webb changed her strategy when a student made a hypothesis that required a new stage of thinking to verify. She did not immediately verify the answer for students as she had done for their "concrete" inferences just a moment earlier. She let her students explore the problem, and indeed, she was probably exploring it with them.

> Practice and help produce more improvement within stages of development.

> Learning is harder during stage transitions.

> Teaching a new skill calls for different expectations and strategies.

CONCLUSION

Educational psychologists have only begun to understand the impact of progressive cognitive changes on how students learn. They have also only begun to explore how teachers need to represent instructional problems in order to solve them. Only in the last decade have educational psychologists really begun to understand how the small pieces of skill development fit into a larger picture that has profound implications for teachers.

In the decade ahead, you can expect the legacy of Piaget to continue to define what is developmentally appropriate. Educators will also explore in greater depth Vygotsky's ideas about the role of social context. They will use information-processing theory more and more to develop specific cognitive skills. You can also expect the slow emergence of theory that integrates different viewpoints into a more coherent whole, both respecting the givens of cognitive development and suggesting cognitive goals.

concept paper

Designing a Developmental Strategy

Purpose of the assignment

To formulate a developmental strategy within the context of a game-based learning activity.

Directions for reflection

1. Identify a game designed to teach a specific cognitive skill or set of cognitive skills within your teaching field. You can often find such games in recent issues of professional magazines or books of teaching techniques.

2. Identify the age group for which the game is intended. Is the game age-appropriate? What developments does it assume? If the game is not age-appropriate, choose another game and begin again.

3. Use the rules of the game to formulate a procedure for students' participation. Follow the description of procedural facilitation in this chapter to write your list of steps; that is, sequence them, keep them short, and limit their number, so that they can serve as learning cues or prompts.

4. How do you plan to be involved in teaching the game? Develop a scaffolding strategy for your participation, leading students to competence or mastery.

Directions for writing

5. Write a three- to four-page paper describing:
   a. the name of the game and where you found it
   b. at least one cognitive skill that the game is intended to teach
   c. what age the players should be
   d. why the game is age-appropriate
   e. the procedure that you have developed for students to learn how to play
   f. a scaffolding strategy for your participation

6. Attach a photocopy of the printed rules of the game as an appendix to your paper.

SUMMARY

1. Cognitive development is progressive change in thinking processes such as perception, memory, and thinking skills. It is affected by both maturational limitations and environmental influences.

2. Jean Piaget's stage theory has had enormous impact on educator's and psychologists' views of cognitive development. It emphasizes age-related stages of intellectual development.

3. Constructivism is the central belief behind Piaget's theory. It defines learning as an active process in which each child constructs his or her own understanding of reality as new events are experienced.

4. The four stages of Piaget's theory are named after the type of learning that occurs during them: sensorimotor (age zero to two); preoperations (two to seven or eight); concrete operations (seven or eight to eleven); and formal operations (eleven to fifteen and up).

5. A teacher respects maturational stages in the classroom by holding developmentally appropriate expectations for behavior and learning when planning instruction. For instance, a teacher would not expect young children to sit and listen quietly for long periods of time.

6. Neo-Piagetians are developmental psychologists who work within Piaget's framework but who believe that the developing capacity of working memory—rather than the growth of logical thought—is most pivotal to cognitive development.

7. A socially oriented theory of cognitive development was proposed early in the century by Lev Vygotsky. According to this theory, cognition develops through the internalization of social interaction, so the mental activity of the student often needs to be supported, or scaffolded, by the structuring of the teacher.

8. A third theory of cognitive development stresses the phases, from novice to expert, that a learner passes through. Phases are not determined by age or biology but by environmental influences and experience, primarily the degree and kind of training in a skill.

9. Studies reveal that phases of learning may exist within stages of development and that scaffolding can assist the novice and the intermediate learner.

KEY TERMS

SUGGESTED RESOURCES

Bredekamp, S. 1987. *Developmentally Appropriate Practice in Early Childhood Programs Serving Children from Birth Through Age 8*. Washington, D.C.: National Association for the Education of Young Children. *The* source for identifying developmentally appropriate practices in early childhood education. Its author has also done an audiotape titled *Developmentally Appropriate Practice* for the Association for Supervision and Curriculum Development.

Piaget, J. 1970. *The Science of Education and the Psychology of the Child*. New York: Orion Press. This translation of two articles that Piaget wrote for the French encyclopedia summarizes his stage theory and many of his other ideas.

Shuell, T. J. 1990. "Phases of Meaningful Learning." *Review of Educational Research*, 60, 531–547. An article that summarizes much of the research on phases of learning. A valuable resource for sorting out differences in terminology among theorists.

Vygotsky, L. S. 1978. *Mind in Society*. Cambridge, Mass.: Harvard University Press. These excerpts from Vygotsky's work still represent the best introduction to his ideas.

Wertsch, J. V., and P. Tulviste. 1992. "L. S. Vygotsky and Contemporary Developmental Psychology." *Developmental Psychology*, 28, 548–557. Originally a speech, this clearly written article summarizes the major influences of Vygotsky on current thinking in human development and education.

Social Development:
Contexts for Problem Solving

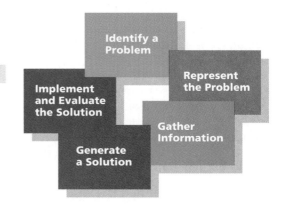

Orientation

The goal of this chapter is to extend your knowledge of children's development as it occurs in the areas of social and emotional development. You will discover how the complementary influences of nature and nurture affect the formation of social skills and personality characteristics. You will learn as well how the processes of psychosocial and moral development relate to your educational goals and expectations in the classroom. As you read, look for answers to these questions:

- **How do nature and nurture interact in the development of empathy?**

- **What are the eight stages or crises of Erikson's psychosocial development theory?**

- **Of these, which is the key crisis and when does it typically occur?**

- **How can teachers increase gender equity, students' social skills, and feelings of competence in the classroom?**

- **How is moral development both different from and related to psychosocial development?**

- **What are three viewpoints about the development of morality in children?**

- **What are some measures teachers can take to foster moral development?**

Principles of Social Development

While reading about social development, you'll need to make Learning Journal entries about specific experiences in which principles of social development apply. Remember to tell what led up to the experience, name the principles of development involved, and describe any relevant outcomes. This chapter contains descriptions of the following principles:

- natural empathy/nurturing empathy
- epigenesis (in psychosocial development)
- crises in psychosocial development
- sex typing
- gender inequity/equity
- peer rejection/acceptance
- social skills training
- social problem solving
- compensatory theory of self-concept
- learning goals vs. performance goals
- identity states
- vocational identity
- stages of moral development (Piaget)
- levels of moral development (Kohlberg)
- morality of caring (Gilligan)
- identification
- role modeling

SOCIAL GIVENS AND GOALS

Your understanding of the givens and goals that define instructional problems would be inc\omplete if you did not consider social development. As a topic of study, **social development** involves progressive change in relationships between an individual and others. It includes some of the most interesting topics in educational psychology, such as friendship, moral development, social competence, and self-concept. **Emotional development**, which is progressive change in attitudes and values, is almost always fostered by social settings. Consequently, emotional development is a subtopic that is inextricably intertwined with social development.

By nature human beings are highly social. Although each of us can spend some time alone, virtually none of us can spend all of our time alone. It is natural for a child to develop in relation both to adults and to other children—to be cared for and to care for others. When this nature is violated, young chil-

By nature, human beings are social. During early and middle adolescence, children often prefer to explore and learn with a small group of peers. *(David Young-Wolff/Tony Stone Worldwide)*

All children need social relationships to develop properly.

dren cannot flourish, and their ability to function later as adults is impaired (Skeels, 1966). One of the great insights in the education field during the late nineteenth and early twentieth centuries was the realization that social activity is natural during childhood and should be structured into learning situations as a given.

Just as there are important social givens, there are also important social goals. Social goals include developing positive attitudes toward work (vocational goals); developing respect, trust, cooperation, care for others, and moral judgment or integrity (civic goals); and both developing a positive self-concept and maintaining emotional adjustment (personal goals). Recall the three domains—cognitive, psychomotor, and affective—that were introduced in Chapter 3. The goals we are concerned with in this chapter are closely related to the affective domain and to the development of values.

These goals may not seem academically important, but when they go unmet, we see obstacles to learning emerge. You might encounter a student who devalues work, disrespects others, fails to cooperate or to care about others, has a negative self-concept, or simply is unhappy. Although behaviors such as these can result in obstacles to learning, they do not mean that the student has a "learning problem." Rather, they probably represent unmet social goals: the child may not have learned yet to value work, respect others, care about others, or value and respect him- or herself. As a teacher confronting these kinds of behaviors, it will be important for you to sort out such social and emotional issues from genuine learning or instructional problems. As a consequence, you will be able to consider ways to meet social and emotional challenges when appropriate.

Problems with social attitudes can interfere with children's academic progress.

Despite an overlap of social givens and goals with formal instruction, most social development occurs outside the classroom. During the elementary years, social and emotional developments take place as children play together on the playground or in small groups after school. During the secondary school years, social and emotional developments occur between classes, after school, or on weekends. Let's take a moment to look at a school setting where social development is obvious—a high school club fair, where the high school administration and teachers are accommodating social givens and setting social goals for this annual May event.

Social Givens and Goals at a High School Club Fair

It is 8:10 A.M., and in the large "commons" of Bradshaw High, juniors and seniors are busy assembling displays for the club fair. The commons is a linoleum space bounded on three sides by doors to the gymnasium, the cafeteria, and the school auditorium. Over by the gymnasium, students are putting up displays of the Spanish, French, German, and Latin clubs. By the cafeteria, students are working on displays for the business, journalism, art, and scholars' clubs. Against the doors to the auditorium, students are clustered around posters for creative writing workshops, drama club, student council, and chorus. By the fourth wall, students are putting up displays for Key club (a service organization), the debating team, science club, and athletics groups. The displays are to impress the guests who will be arriving in a few moments—the eighth graders who will be freshmen next year.

The eighth graders, each with a name tag, file into the adjoining auditorium under the direction of their "old" teachers, who seem a little out of place. After the audience is seated, the senior student council president, who hosts the assembly, quiets the group and extends greetings and an invitation to join one of the clubs they are about to see represented in the commons. The rest of the assembly consists of short speeches by the principal, the athletic director, and the senior class guidance counselor, who will serve the entering class. Members of the drama club, the chorus, and the jazz band provide interludes of entertainment.

After the assembly, the eighth graders file out of the auditorium and into the commons. Many seem uncertain at first and talk among themselves, but small groups drift toward the display tables. Student council representatives, who are out in front of their table, mingle with the eighth graders. Many greet the new students by name. "Welcome to Bradshaw, Dave. Did you like the show?" They may have gone to the same junior high school as the younger students or may know a guest's brother or sister. Connections, not just contacts, are being made.

The eighth graders who venture farther than this large, informal group often know someone at one of the other tables and bring along a friend. Their motivation seems to be a mixture of shared acquaintance and genuine interest. It is generally the older student who reaches out first. "Hey, girl. Saw you last night at the game with your sister. Hi, Monica. My name's Sandra. Do you want to find out about our club?" This is the way that many students get to know each other and sign up for a club.

On this day, social givens and goals seem to predominate the mission of a school, but normally, they are unobtrusive. For example, at the club fair, you find young men and women adopting roles of mentors, taking care of the incoming freshmen. Some of the care is cognitive, as the older students give information to alleviate concern or stimulate interest. Much of the care is affective—expressions of positive feelings and the value they place on the eighth graders. If you were to put the overarching goal of the club fair into words, it would be something like "Use the social leadership of the high school to meet the social and emotional needs of entering freshmen." Objectives could exist for both the social leadership (to apply their social skills) and the entering freshmen (to clarify their values).

> School activities can be arranged to promote children's social goals.

The Nature and Nurture of Social Development

> Sharing another's emotion is an important social characteristic.

Exactly what are the givens of social development? Does nature have anything at all to do with social development, which has often been assumed to be the product of the environment? These questions have recently posed challenges in the study of **empathy**, or sharing the perceived emotion of another person (Eisenberg & Strayer, 1987). Empathy is very important for social development. It is unlike most other emotional characteristics because it is found to differing degrees in different children at very early ages, and these differences are relatively stable. Because of its social importance, and because of its stability, empathy has been the focus of an increasing amount of research into the complementary roles of nature and nurture.

The Nature of Empathy

According to Piaget, empathy develops slowly. An infant cannot at first distinguish itself from others, a fact that Piaget explained by theorizing that a young child was egocentric. To Piaget and many other psychologists, empathy as a form of understanding is part of cognitive development. It is the product of the loss of egocentrism, which brings on the ability to adopt the perspective of another person. Within these psychologists' view, the development of empathy begins in middle childhood.

An increasing number of psychologists disagree with this explanation of the development of empathy. The research of one of the most important of these psychologists, Martin Hoffman (1981), did not actually contradict Piaget's observations, but it did lay the foundation for the investigation of empathy *apart from* cognitive development.

In Hoffman's view, the failure of an infant to distinguish self from others may represent not the absence of empathy but the natural state of empathy at that point in development. Hoffman observed that an infant cries as a reflex response to the cry of another infant, even though he or she does not cry upon hearing another noise of the same volume. The feeling of distress is shared, but the "empathic" infant cannot distinguish its own distress from that of the other. Only at the toddler stage does a child learn to distinguish personal distress from the distress of another, because a toddler has distinguished its self from others.

Hoffman suggested that the capacity to share feelings of others may have an origin in the genetic make-up of human beings. Psychologists now theorize that the ability to share the distress of others evolved in humans because of its survival value. Recent research with infant twins supports this view of empathy.

Developmental psychologists at the University of Colorado, Penn State, Yale, Berkeley, Harvard, and the National Institute of Mental Health have recently cooperated in a study of the origins of the emotional development of infants (Emde et al., 1992). Researchers visited one-year-old twins in their homes and, as one of the procedures to assess emotional development, feigned distress at hurting a finger while closing a box of testing materials, in order to probe the extent to which each twin shared the emotion of the researcher. Thirty minutes later, the researchers had the children's mother feign distress—a hurt knee—for the same purpose. Two weeks later, each set of twins and their mother visited the researchers, where two additional probes to uncover empathy were administered.

What the researchers found were different reactions from *identical* and *fraternal* twins. (As you probably are aware, identical twins share exactly the same genetic material, whereas fraternal twins share no more genetic material than any other two children with the same biological parents.) In response to the feigned distress of adults, identical twins responded more identically than did fraternal twins. These findings suggested that empathy has a genetic origin. Researchers who revisited the homes six months later found that the differences between the responses of identical and fraternal twins persisted (Zahn-Waxler, Robinson & Emde, 1992).

These findings are consistent with Hoffman's ideas about the origin of empathy. They suggest that empathy has a genetic basis. Although natural empathy cannot be distinguished from "learned" empathy after a few years, natural differences may underlie the development of the cognitive ability to understand others later in life. Leaders in play groups, for example, exhibit more concern for others—particularly weaker individuals—than do other members of a group (Eibl-Eibesfeldt, 1989). It is a long way from the natural empathy of an infant to the concern and care of an older adolescent for a younger adolescent at a club fair in high school, but there is likely to be some developmental continuity that links the two events.

> Empathy may have a biological basis.

The Nurture of Empathy

If some natural empathy is present at birth, how is it then affected by life experiences? To a great extent, the answer to this question is not yet known, but developmental psychologists are beginning to formulate an answer. Mothers, for example, can "teach" empathy in face-to-face play, which be-

> Empathy can be increased by teaching and other environmental factors.

gins at about two months of age. A mother both models and imitates expressions of love and joy. Face-to-face play probably accounts for some development of shared feeling on the part of the child (Thompson, 1987).

Other environmental influences on the development of empathy include the reliability of responsiveness of the caretaker to the distress of an infant or a toddler, the presence of other children in the family, and experiences in preschool and in formal education. Shared feeling seems to develop best in an environment that

1. satisfies the emotional needs of a child, enabling perception of the needs of others,
2. encourages identification with and expression of a broad range of feelings, and
3. facilitates interaction with others who are emotionally sensitive and responsive (Barnett, 1987).

> Lack of empathy may result when a child's emotional needs are not met.

When diminished empathy is found in children, the above environmental characteristics are typically found to be lacking; many of the children's emotional needs are unmet. When these environmental factors *are* present, they are very likely the source of empathy development beyond what is genetically programmed (Eisenberg et al., 1991). Later in this chapter we will explore these more highly developed forms of empathy in our discussion of moral development. Even now, however—without knowing how far empathy can develop— you can still appreciate how something like the structured environment at the high school club fair can promote empathy both in the high school leaders and in the eighth graders.

The atmosphere of the club fair represented an environment that was almost ideal for the development of empathy in both older and younger students. Older students were developing care-giving skills while easing the anxieties of younger students over school transition. They were being responsive to emotional needs. Younger students were being cared for and also expanding their awareness of others in the new environment. They were being prepared to be responsive.

Programs that use older students to ease transitions of younger students develop empathy, and they exist at all school levels. Kindergartners may be assigned sixth graders as "big brothers" and "big sisters" for essentially the same purpose. Such arrangements are generally made through the school counselor.

You are now in a position to appreciate more fully the complementary roles of nature and nurture in social development. Although nature may take a back seat to nurture in the social domain, its influence is still significant. We know very little as yet about the interaction between nature and nurture in social development, but we can say with some assurance that cooperative group activities often increase empathy, while competitive activities often decrease it.

> Cooperative activities can increase empathy; competition may not.

Try to keep your new knowledge about social givens and goals in mind as you read and think about the topics in the two major sections of this chapter.

How do social givens and goals complement each other in the course of psychosocial and moral development?

PSYCHOSOCIAL DEVELOPMENT

The theory of psychosocial development, originally proposed by Erik Erikson in 1950 and completed in 1982, is remarkable for its wide-ranging discussion of many social and emotional developments. **Psychosocial development** is a theory of directive change in personality that emphasizes relationships with others. Erikson labeled it "psychosocial" to distinguish it from Sigmund Freud's "psychosexual" theory of personality development. As a young man, Erikson had trained as a psychoanalyst in Vienna with Freud, and his theory owes several debts to Freud's—for instance, the first five stages of his theory parallel the five stages of sexual development proposed by Freud (cf. Hall, 1954).

Erikson was born in Germany in 1902 and immigrated to the United States in 1933. He had himself experienced a deep upheaval over his identity in adolescence. It was this experience that provided him with the impetus to develop his theory of personality development, which, as you will discover in this section, has as its core the formation of identity through various "crises."

In our discussion of Erikson's theory, let's first define and examine the stages themselves. Then we will use the theory as a framework for interpreting events in the social and emotional lives of children. We will look especially at a number of events that have been widely researched—*gender role development, peer acceptance*, and *competence*.

Despite their study by different groups of psychologists, these issues eventually converge on the development of *identity*, which is Erikson's key concept. For this reason, we will conclude our study of psychosocial development with a look at the formation of identity, especially during adolescence, which brings disparate strands of analysis and research together.

> Erikson's theory of personality development stresses identity formation.

Stages of Psychosocial Development

The fundamental concept of psychosocial development is borrowed from a sequence of prenatal developments. In embryology, the science of the early development of organisms, the process by which fetal organs mature from the single fertilized cell is known as "epigenesis." In epigenesis, each organ has a time of origin, known as a *critical period* in its development. "The result of normal development," Erikson noted, "is proper relationship of size and function among all body organs" (1982, p. 27).

After a child is born, "the maturing organism continues to unfold, by growing planfully and by developing a prescribed sequence of physical, cognitive, and social capacities" (1982, p. 28). In Erikson's theory, **epigenesis** is the ordered, stagelike development of capacities before *and after* birth. Development after birth is supported by the surrounding culture and influenced by what other people expect of the child. Nature and nurture interact during a succession of **crises**, which are critical periods in the formation of the personality.

In each crisis, the individual struggles to resolve a conflict between opposing *attitudes* toward others. The outcome of each crisis is an enduring attitude or disposition, such as hope or fidelity, which becomes characteristic of the individual. Erikson calls these outcomes *strengths*. The ultimate outcome of ideal personality development is the acquisition of a number of strengths from successive crises.

Eight stages of psychosocial development reflect what Erikson calls "the life cycle." They cover developments from "womb to tomb," emphasizing early development but also extending into old age. Each stage is labeled by the opposing attitudes that put the individual in crisis or internal conflict.

The stages (with associated ages) are *trust versus mistrust* (birth to one), *autonomy versus shame and doubt* (one to three), *initiative versus guilt* (three to six), *industry versus inferiority* (six to twelve or so), *identity versus identity confusion* (adolescence), *intimacy versus isolation* (early adulthood), *generativity versus self-absorption* (middle adulthood), and *integrity versus despair* (old age). For the growing child and the maturing adult, the polar opposites in each crisis are experienced as the normal product of biological drives, the emergent self, and the social environment. The crises are not only *instructive*, as the individual learns how to experience extremes in life without losing a sense of the self, but they are actually *essential*, since the growth of one's personality emerges only as the result of these crises.

The strength that can emerge from each crisis represents what has been learned from experiencing both elements of the crisis, as long as the positive element predominates. For example, the crisis associated with elementary school years is "industry versus inferiority." Industriousness or hard work tends to result in competence, but competence emerges only after the child has both worked hard and sometimes felt inferior to other children or adults who already possess a given competency. The child who has become competent will have identified his or her areas of strength and weakness and will have learned that areas of weakness require harder work to develop competence than do areas of strength.

Take a moment now to get further acquainted with an overview of the eight stages (listed in Table 6.1) before we move to our descriptions of each stage.

Trust versus Mistrust (the first year of life)

The crisis of the first year of life is created by the extreme dependency of an infant on another person for food, cleanliness, assurance, and love. A child tends to *trust* a responsive caretaker (often the mother) but *distrust* one who does not respond adequately on demand. As long as mistrust does not pre-

The child develops according to prescribed stages, called epigenesis.

Personality is developed by resolving eight separate crises of opposing attitudes.

Successive ages are associated with particular crises.

Table 6.1 Erikson's Theory of Psychosocial Development

0–12 Months Trust vs. mistrust	Infant depends on adult for all needs. Emergence of *hope.*
1–3 Years Autonomy vs. shame and doubt	Child asserts independence from adult. Emergence of *will.*
3–6 Years Initiative vs. guilt	Child undertakes relationships in play. Emergence of *purpose.*
6–12 Years Industry vs. inferiority	Child accomplishes tasks in school. Emergence of *competence.*
Adolescence Identity vs. identity confusion	Adolescent or youth defines sexual and occupational roles. Emergence of *fidelity.*
Young adulthood Intimacy vs. isolation	Young man or woman establishes a shared identity. Emergence of *love.*
Middle adulthood Generativity vs. self-absorption	Middle-aged person invests in the next generation or creative work. Emergence of *care.*
Old age Integrity vs. despair	Elderly person reviews life in the face of death. Emergence of *wisdom.*

Source: Summarized from Erikson, 1982

dominate (due to poor child-rearing practices), conflicting experiences of trust and mistrust are positively resolved through *hope,* which is a confident expectation that needs will be met.

> The infant develops hope by learning trust.

Autonomy versus Shame and Doubt (one to three)

The crisis of what Erikson calls "early childhood" is created by the assertion of self, sometimes resulting in what parents call "the terrible twos." *Autonomy* means independence, which at first can take the form of negation of the will of the parent ("no, I don't want to"). *Shame* results from violating the expectations of parents, and if shame predominates, it can result in self-doubt. The conflicting experiences of autonomy and shame are positively resolved through the emergence of a sense of *will,* which motivates development of a point of view, an opinion, or a particular kind of behavior in response to social conditions.

> The toddler develops a sense of will by learning independence.

Initiative versus Guilt (three to six)

Preschool children develop a sense of purpose.

The crisis that Erikson associated with "the play years" involves children learning to be more cooperative within the family unit. At this stage, children often want to help or to do things on their own. *Initiative* implies "insistence on goal, pleasure of conquest" (1982, p. 37), often in play. *Guilt* is inspired if adults respond by too frequently blocking a child's initiative, and predominant guilt can lead to inhibition. The internal conflict is positively resolved by the child through the development of *purpose* for action.

Industry versus Inferiority (six to twelve or so)

In the elementary grades, children should come to feel competent.

The crisis of the elementary school years involves the exercise of skills to achieve some task. *Industry* means "a love to learn as well as to play," especially "to learn most eagerly those techniques which are in line with the ethos of production" (1982, p. 75). Comparisons with others inevitably produce a sense of inferiority that is in conflict with industry. Excessive comparison may result in a predominant sense of inferiority, but normally, the crisis is resolved through growing *competence* derived through accomplishments.

Identity versus Identity Confusion (adolescence)

As you read this description, notice how many more terms there are for this stage than for others. As the linchpin of Erikson's theory, it is very important. For that reason, we will be devoting several later sections to understanding it. For now, you can use the two terms to become familiar with their overall meaning. You might also compare this characterization with your own experience of adolescence. Outwardly turbulent or not, it is virtually always a memorable time in a person's life cycle.

The adolescent's main crisis leads to a sense of identity.

The "identity crisis" is characteristic of adolescence. Establishing a sexual and vocational *identity* requires construction of answers to the questions of "Who am I?" and "What do I want to be?" The answers come from "selective affirmation and repudiation of childhood identifications" (1982, p. 72) and from the way others identify or recognize each adolescent.

The experience of *identity confusion* is normal and necessary under such circumstances. During this time of weighing alternatives, an adolescent might profit from a *moratorium*, or a period in which commitments are put on hold. If confusion predominates, however, it can lead to rejection of *any* socially acceptable role—or a *negative identity*. A more positive resolution to the crisis is the emergence of *fidelity*, or the ability to sustain chosen commitments.

Later Crises

Three separate crises of adulthood also need to be described for you to complete your understanding of the theory, even though you will probably not teach adults. First is the crisis that occurs in early adulthood—that of *intimacy versus isolation*; it involves the establishment of enduring commitments (as opposed to increasing isolation). Sexual intimacy is not as crucial as psychological intimacy, although the two may well be experienced together, especially in a close and enduring marriage or similar relationship. The strength that can emerge from such friendships is *love*.

Adult stages of development include love, caring, and wisdom.

The next crisis, of *generativity versus self-absorption,* or the "midlife crisis," involves developing a relationship to the next generation (as opposed to increasing selfishness). Although one's own children provide an opportunity to be generative, they are not the only means because the same end can be accomplished through teaching, medicine or nursing, social interest groups (such as the Red Cross, UNESCO, or religious organizations), and even art. The strength that can emerge from such involvement with youth or society is *care.*

Finally, old age brings a review of one's past and moments of both self-acceptance and negativism in a crisis of *integrity versus despair.* Integrity involves not only a sense of honesty in the evaluation of one's life but also an acceptance of death as a part of life (integrity as a sense of wholeness). A detached yet active concern for life in the face of death is what Erikson calls *wisdom.*

With these understandings of each of the eight life-cycle stages in mind, let's now explore three critical social developments in a child's growing sense of self. As you read each, you will likely gain greater insights if you think both of Erikson's framework and of your own experiences as a maturing person.

Gender Role Development

The development of a **gender role**, or a sense of what is appropriate for males or females, begins very early. A gender role develops as a response not so much to body parts as to differential treatment by adults. Long before children are aware of differences in anatomy between males and females, parents accentuate gender differences by dressing babies in sailor suits or frilly dresses, and other adults respond to such cues by remarking "How big he is!" or "How cute she looks!" The process by which children are identified with one gender or the other is called **sex typing**. Societies and parents differ in the extent to which they sex-type their children and, as a result, within a few years their children differ in the extent to which they are sex-typed in their preferences for clothing, toys, and activities (Fagot, Leinbach & O'Boyle, 1992).

Children begin to learn about gender roles early in life.

Biology and the early influences of the home undoubtedly provide a strong foundation for the development of a gender role, but play styles also seem to have an effect (Thorne, 1986). It is no secret that boys tend to prefer more rough-and-tumble play than girls do. Such play may stem from the relatively high activity level of boys (see Chapter 4), or from other biological factors,

Boys' play is more physical; girls' play is more social.

but whatever its source, dominance and physical attempts to influence others are its themes. For example, boys on the playground will try to "top" each other in a race or with tests of strength or physical skill. Sometimes they enjoy tackling, sliding into, or piling on one another, but it is rare to see girls engaged in such activities.

Play by girls tends to be active but quieter than play by boys. Girls often play in groups of two or three near the building during school or in homes after school. Their playground games often involve jumping and tests of physical skill in which turns are taken. Girls can often be seen in games of hopscotch, jump rope, or foursquare. Cooperation, rather than dominance, appears to be the theme of choice, and the way they influence others is often verbal persuasion.

The differences between the play styles and influence techniques of boys and girls may sometimes make their play together stressful or confused. Perhaps as a result, children begin to spend more and more time in same-sex play groups. At four and one-half years of age, children already spend three times as much play with same-sex peers as with opposite-sex peers. By six and one-half years, they spend *eleven* times as much play with same-sex as with opposite-sex children (see the results of Maccoby & Jacklin, 1987, shown in Figure 6.1).

What develops in these same-sex play groups? Your own experience is probably a good guide. If you think back on your years in upper elementary grades, chances are that you will find (1) your small play group was all of the same gender, (2) it was often engaged in a sex-typed play activity, and (3) it enforced rather rigid codes of behavior. In such play groups, gender role consolidation seems to occur. Typical is the experience of one psychologist who as

> Children gravitate to same-sex play groups by the time they reach school age.

Figure 6.1
Gender of Play Partners
(Maccoby & Jacklin, 1987, p. 259)

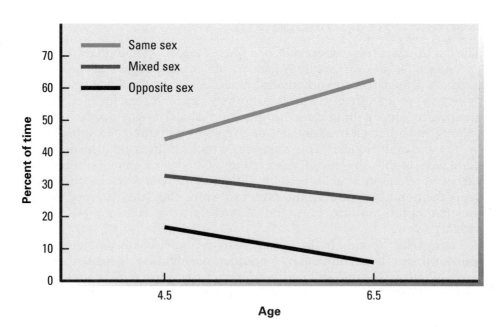

By school age, children tend to spend much more time with same-sex than opposite-sex peers. Gender differences in play styles explain why. What is the play style of this group? *(Paul Conklin)*

a second grader was a charter member of a club called the Penguins with "two major activities[:] acquiring extensive information about penguins and standing outside in the freezing weather without a coat for as long as we could" (Rubin, 1980 p. 96).

Perhaps you were a member of such a club at eight or nine. These groups are short-lived, but they are experiments in social organization that are related to gender role development. Preadolescent friendship groups provide a setting for developing "impression management," a skill in monitoring one's own behavior to keep it within artificially narrow conceptions of a gender role (Fine, 1981).

> Friendship groups steer children toward specific gender role behaviors.

One intriguing hypothesis is that gender roles tend to be adopted only in the social situations where they have been developed (Deux & Major, 1987; Maccoby, 1990). That is, sex-typed gender roles may become temporarily exaggerated whenever the individual is within a same-sex group. That may be why some adolescents behave in an exaggeratedly antagonistic way toward the opposite sex in group situations—at school, in the mall, at the pool, or on the beach. These situations seem to evoke highly sex-typed gender roles. Such sex-typed gender roles may not be as inflexible as was once thought, however, due to the situation-specific manner in which they are scripted and frequently played out.

Whereas at one time narrowly defined gender roles had a major impact on the educational achievements and aspirations of children and adolescents (see Reflection on Practice: The Identity Status of Women), they have much less influence today. Since vocational opportunities have opened up for women in a wider array of careers; since textbooks have achieved greater gender equity in content and illustrations; and since teachers have become

> Gender roles have become less rigid because of recent emphasis on equity.

Figure 6.2a
Gender Differences in Reading
(U.S. Department of Education, 1994, p. 139)

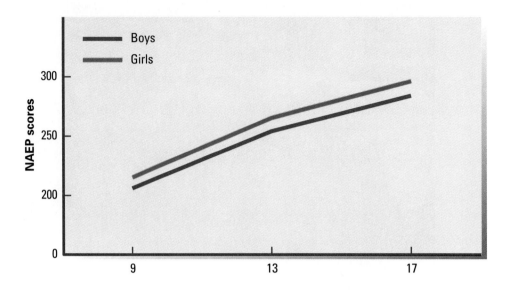

aware of gender inequities in their interactions, gender differences in student test scores have generally decreased (Sadker, Sadker & Klein, 1991). By the early 1990s, differences between boys and girls on many cognitive ability and achievement tests had all but disappeared (Feingold, 1988; Friedman, 1989; Hyde & Linn, 1988; Linn & Hyde, 1991). Significant differences remained in some specific areas of academic achievement, such as writing skills.

Figure 6.2b
Gender Differences in Mathematics
(U.S. Department of Education, 1994, p. 83)

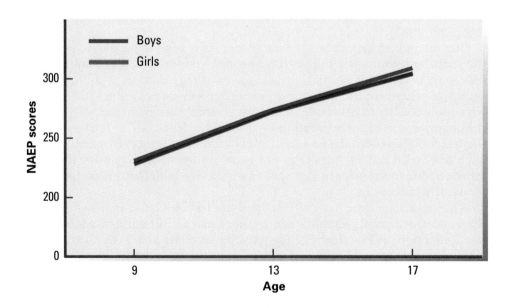

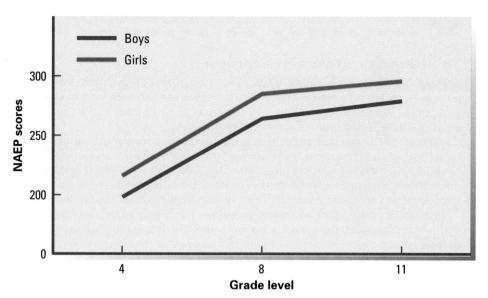

Figure 6.2c
Gender Differences in
Writing Skills
(U.S. Department of
Education, 1994, p. 197)

Figures 6.2a–d, for example, present four gender differences on the U.S. National Assessments of Educational Progress in 1992. Differences in all areas except writing proficiency are relatively small. The big picture is one of insignificant or relatively small gender differences in most areas of academic achievement, and somewhat larger differences in specialized abilities or skills (e.g., Becker, 1990).

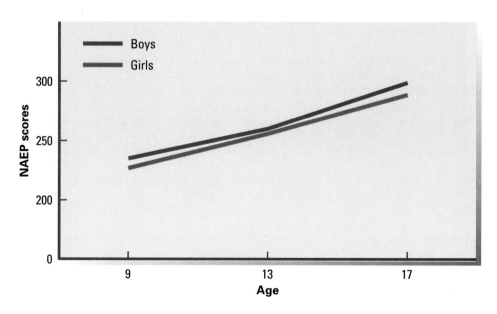

Figure 6.2d
Gender Differences in
Science
(U.S. Department of
Education, 1994, p. 39)

reflection on practice

The Identity Status of Women

Throughout my years in public school until I graduated high school in 1967, girls were taught that their primary role in life would be to care for a husband and family. We were required to take one year of home economics and encouraged to take two more years in addition.

With all of the rapid changes that have occurred, beginning at about the time I got out of high school, there seemed to be a sort of protracted "identity crisis" for many women, if not most. Marriage was difficult to keep together if one had ambitions outside the home. Ambitions outside the home were hard to concentrate on, given a woman's heavy responsibilities for the family.

In short, the education we had received had not prepared us, nor the men with whom we lived, for the lives we were actually living. Many of us floundered and could not establish and maintain any real resolution as to what we would "be when we grew up."

Communities and educational institutions have responded over the years and begun to offer courses that attempt to bridge that gap. For example, my local community college has a course entitled "Choices for Success" for women reentering the job market. Religious groups have also begun to sponsor marriage enrichment courses on weekends to help couples learn to get along and be more supportive of one another in order to survive all of these changed expectations. I can see that Erikson's stages of psychosocial development do have a great deal of merit and should be studied, although I do not think they apply [to women of my age] in any strict sense.

Melanie Holst

Discussion Questions

1. The women's movement raised identity questions for the author *after* adolescence. What are the implications for Erikson's psychosocial theory?

2. What kinds of events can raise identity questions in later life? In other words, in what kinds of life situations is a "moratorium" likely to be more helpful than commitment?

3. Beginning in kindergarten, what are some things teachers should do to reduce the intensity or shorten the duration of identity crises in adolescence or adulthood?

strategic solutions

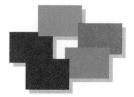

Proportionate Attention and Gender Equity

Gender differences that remain in some important areas of achievement today may be due to disproportionate attention and encouragement. For example, it is well known that boys at all levels tend to receive more than their fair share of attention from teachers. For example, boys in science classes are called on to answer questions and provide demonstrations much more frequently than girls are. This disproportion of attention, which exists in other subject areas and in extracurricular activities, increases with grade level (Bailey, 1993). The effect of disproportionate attention may not have a great effect on test scores, but it may have a significant effect on self-esteem, especially in early grades (Entwisle et al., 1987). For example, a child may decide to take an enriched math class—or to pursue music or a sport—as much on the basis of attention from a caring teacher as on the basis of grades. Such choices, which allow the child to utilize his or her talents more fully, can affect the development of self-esteem.

What teachers need to pursue is equitable treatment of boys and girls in instructional materials, activities, and interactions. To maintain progress toward gender equity, teachers should *distribute attention proportionately among students.* This distribution should extend across all subject matters and extracurricular activities.

Further progress toward gender equity is possible, particularly in areas such as proportionate attention. The impact of your interest on learners who need your attention can be immeasurable in terms of choice of an elective class or a career that best utilizes the learner's talents. Gender equity is a crucial prerequisite for the full use of talent both in and outside the classroom.

Evaluation: Proportionate Attention and Gender Equity

Progress toward gender equity appears to have had some real impact on achievement differences in the past twenty years. Women have achieved higher levels of education more frequently, and they have made highly significant advances in law, medicine, business, and architecture. They have also made significant advances in science, mathematics, and engineering (Meece & Eccles, 1993). For example, women currently represent 40 percent of those enrolled in college calculus courses.

Are the differences that remain innate or natural differences? Scholarly arguments have been advanced on both sides of the issue, but in light of past progress and the size of the imbalances that remain, more weight should be given to the argument that achievement differences are *not* inborn. Areas of imbalance need to be redressed by monitoring progress and developing new strategies to establish gender equity in both academics and extracurricular activities.

Peer Acceptance

What leads children to accept a child into a play group? What leads them to reject someone else? These questions, which interest teachers at all levels, have been studied from preschool through high school (e.g., Dodge, 1983; Ladd & Price, 1987; Parkhurst & Asher, 1992).

The results suggest that as children progress through school, the basis of their friendships will shift from physical proximity to similarity of personality (Epstein, 1989). Physical proximity explains why most friendships between preschool children are between children who are neighbors or between relatives who frequently encounter each other. During elementary school, similarity in age takes precedence over proximity (see Figure 6.3). Boys and

> Friendships are based first on proximity, then age, then personality.

Figure 6.3
The Selection of Friends
(Epstein, 1989, p. 180)

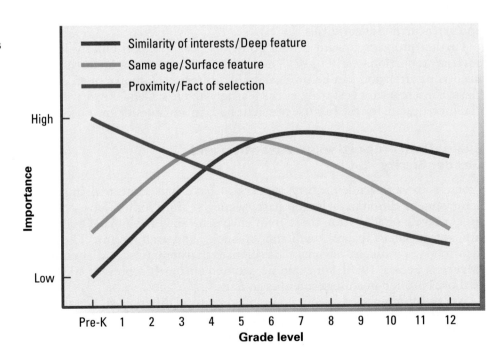

deepening your knowledge base

Developing Strategies to Promote Gender Equity

Most of the research on gender equity has been focused on inequity of opportunities for the achievement of girls, but the imbalances in achievements indicated in Figures 6.2a–d work both ways, sometimes favoring boys and sometimes favoring girls. Note that these differences are mostly small, they begin early, and they persist. What kinds of experiences contribute to such differences?

It is clear that some of these differences originate in the home environment (Eccles, Jacobs & Harold, 1990). Parents may hold expectations for their children which do not match their interests and competencies. The result can affect a child's perception of his or her competence.

It is less clear, but also probable, that some of these differences are influenced by peers. Decisions about achievement-related issues are affected by discussions between close friends, most of whom are the same sex (Berndt, Laychak & Park, 1990). Boys may decide, for example, that grades in English are relatively unimportant, or girls may decide not to do extra-credit work for a science report. Same-sex peers may consequently affect motivation.

Teachers constitute a third source of influence. Divide into groups to discuss gender inequity in achievements, its social causes, and strategies to promote gender equity. After your discussion, reassemble in the larger group to compare and contrast your ideas. (The impact of teachers' expectations on motivation to achieve will be described in greater detail in Chapter 12.)

Discussion Questions

1. What gender-related expectations expressed by parents, peers, or teachers influenced your achievement-related decisions? Make a list. Include at least one experience from each individual in your group.

2. Circle the items on your list that occurred in school. What strategies can you devise for avoiding such situations and promoting gender equity?

---

girls increasingly choose age-mates as friends. By high school, similarity of personality is more important than similarity of age. High school students tend to choose friends who have values similar to their own.

As children develop, they acquire *social skills,* which generally fall into the categories of self-control and altruism. Peer rejection can occur, however, if a child is either aggressive or submissive and at the same time lacks self-control or altruism. Aggressive or submissive children are tolerated as long as they possess social skills, but otherwise an aggressive or submissive child typically suffers rejection by peers.

The evidence of long-term effects on the child is much clearer for cases of aggression than for those of submission. The aggressive child who is rejected often persists in his or her aggressive tendencies. Both aggression and peer re-

Social skills are important to maintaining friendships.

jection appear to carry over from preschool to elementary school and may contribute to later academic and adjustment difficulties as well as to adult criminality (Kupersmidt, Coie & Dodge, 1990; Patterson, DeBaryshe & Ramsey, 1989).

The tendency for the submissive child to withdraw often results in neglect. Submissive children who lack social skills feel lonely and worry about their relations with others more often than do average students (Parker & Asher, 1987). Researchers do not yet know if submissive children who are neglected by their peers suffer from more serious problems, such as chronic depression or risk for suicide, later on.

strategic solutions

Social Skills Training

You might be surprised by the fact that, on average, two or three children in a class report having only one friend there, and at least one in an average class reports having none (Gronlund, 1959). If excessive aggression or submission is the cause, there are many ways to handle the situation, but you might want to focus on development of social skills. Remember, peers will tolerate some aggressive or some submissive behaviors if a child can also be self-controlled and altruistic.

Many specific behaviors associated with self-control and altruism—such as asking questions, leading, or offering supportive statements—can be taught in a process generally called *social skills training* (Bierman & Furman, 1984; Ladd, 1981). Although some training programs focus on the home, others have been developed for use in the schools, where your involvement as a classroom teacher is essential for their success. Many social skills training programs involve a core procedure:

1. identify specific behaviors to be attained
2. structure situations in which the child rehearses the desired behaviors with peers
3. praise appropriate behaviors
4. practice over a series of sessions

To implement this procedure, you might set aside some time to invite a child who has been rejected or neglected by peers into a small-group activity and talk to the children about positive questions that they might ask each other about the activity. (See Deepening Your Knowledge Base: An Illustration of Social Skills Training, page 230.) You might praise appropriate questions, particularly from the child who is often rejected, then request children to ask such questions during the activity.

Another time, you might invite the child into a group and ask each member for useful suggestions or directions they might give each other during an activity or a game. Again, appropriate ideas should be praised and the ideas rehearsed during the activity. If the rejected child is particularly aggressive, you might also discuss a list of rules for the activity (such as no fighting, no arguing, no yelling). Discussion of rules can enhance the effectiveness of social skills training for aggressive children (Bierman, Miller & Stabb, 1987).

Evaluation: Social Skills Training

Social skills training programs have an uneven record of success when desired improvements are measured in terms of ratings by peers rather than ratings by the rejected or neglected child (e.g., Bierman, Miller & Stabb, 1987; Bulkeley & Cramer, 1990). There are several reasons. First, social skills training sometimes fails because peers may have already developed stereotypes of rejected children that are resistant to change, even when the behavior of the rejected child has changed. In these cases, the child must be able to maintain the new social skills through a period of continued rejection or neglect before they can really make a difference. Second, inappropriate behavior is sometimes sustained by a dysfunctional home environment. In such cases, you will want to seek help from specialized school personnel, such as a social worker or the school counselor.

Finally, it may turn out that aggressiveness or submissiveness is not a root problem after all. Certainly, peers sometimes reject children for other reasons. On the one hand, a child's hygiene may be the cause of rejection. In this case, you will want to consult with the school counselor about a sensitive way to intervene. On the other hand, a child's appearance or even a disability may cause peer rejection or neglect. In this case, counseling the peers might be a better solution than intervening with the child.

The limited success of social skills training should not lead you to reject it as a solution to the problem of peer acceptance. Rather, it highlights the importance of accurately defining the problem and developing a strategy to attain your goal. You must also accurately define the audience for your strategy. If the problem belongs to the peers rather than the rejected or neglected child, a strategy that addresses them rather than the child is far more likely to succeed, and vice versa.

An Illustration of Social Skills Training

Instructor: To begin, I'd like to talk with you about an idea that might make a game more fun to play and help you get to know other kids while you are playing. One way you can make a game fun and get to know other kids is to ask questions that are positive. Okay, [child's name], if you were playing a game with some kids, what is a way that you might ask a question that's positive?

Child: How do you play this game?

Instructor: Good, that's a positive question. Now, what do you think another person might say or do if you said that?

Child: Probably tell me the rules . . . give some directions.

Instructor: Yes, something like that might happen. Okay, now, what would be an example of a question that isn't positive?

Child: Ahh . . . can't you do anything right?

Instructor: Yes, that would be a question that isn't positive. What do you think another person might say or do if you said that?

Child: They'd probably get mad . . . maybe tell you to get lost.

Instructor: Yes, I guess something like that could happen . . . [After completing this procedure with each child] . . . Okay, now let's try to play this game together. While we play this game I would like you to try out asking questions that are positive . . . [As children play] How could I find out if [child's name] likes this game? Show me how you'd do it. . . . [Child's name], what is a question you have about this game? . . .

Child: Do you think this is a fun game?

Peer: Yeah, kinda. How 'bout you?

Instructor: Good, [children's names], those are positive questions.

Source: Ladd, 1981, p. 174

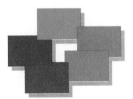

Social Problem Solving

When interpersonal problems arise, social skills training for the child should be augmented with training in social problem solving. This strategy helps children think through the problem so that they can select a socially acceptable solution. Social problem solving usually begins with training in the use of a problem-solving procedure, much like the five-stage process that you have already learned in this book (Coie, Underwood & Lochman, 1991). Problem solving is then applied in real contexts through a process called *dialoguing* (Shure, 1989).

Deepening Your Knowledge Base: An Illustration of Social Problem Solving, page 232, illustrates dialoguing with Robert, a preschooler who has just grabbed some magnets from another four-year-old named Erik. In the dialogue, the teacher helps Robert identify the problem or goal ("You wanted to play with the magnets"), generate alternative solutions, and try them out. You might want to take a moment to match each of the five stages of problem solving with a portion of the discussion to appreciate how dialoguing works.

A critical period in the development of social problem-solving skills appears to occur in the lower elementary grades. The technique of dialoguing scaffolds the use of problem solving for children who might be too young to apply a problem-solving procedure on their own, or who might apply it ineffectively. As you learned in the last chapter, the scaffolding provided by the teacher should be gradually removed as the child internalizes social problem-solving skills and becomes a more proficient social problem solver.

Evaluation: Social Problem Solving

Social problem solving is a promising strategy to develop social skills (Compas, 1987). The advocates of this approach have been able to demonstrate a reasonably strong relationship between social problem-solving skills and social adjustment. What they and others have not been able to demonstrate consistently are which conditions for teaching these skills result in better adjustment. Attempts to develop adjustment through teaching social problem-solving skills have sometimes succeeded but at other times failed (Compas, 1987; Hughes, 1990).

Among the relevant factors that need to be considered are the cognitive and social resources that must be in place to support social problem solving. Learners as young as four or five, for example, are capable of generating alternative solutions to a problem, but the ability to apply a problem-solving procedure independently probably does not develop until about second or third grade. That is why dialoguing is so important to scaffold social problem solving for children. Furthermore, the success of social problem solving is dependent on social, not just cognitive, resources. A supportive climate (including a supportive teacher) can make a big difference. Trying to reason in a climate that encourages reasonableness is much easier than trying to reason in one that does not! Despite its limitations, social problem solving can be a valuable supplement to social skills training.

strategic solutions, continued

---

deepening your knowledge base

An Illustration of Social Problem Solving

Teacher: Robert, what happened when you snatched those magnets from Erik?

Robert: He hit me.

Teacher: How did that make you feel?

Robert: Sad.

Teacher: You wanted to play with magnets, right?

Robert: Right.

Teacher: Snatching it is one way to get him to give them to you. Can you think of a different idea?

Robert: Ask him.

Teacher: [Calls Erik over.] Robert, you thought of asking him for the magnets. Go ahead and ask him.

Robert: [to Erik] Can I hold the magnets?

Erik: No!

Teacher: Oh, Robert, he said no. Can you think of a *different* way?

Robert: [Starts to cry.]

Teacher: I know you're feeling sad now, but I bet if you think real hard, you'll find a different idea. You could ask or . . . ?

Robert: [after several seconds] I'll give 'em back when I'm finished.

Erik: [reluctantly] Okay.

Teacher: Very good, Robert. You thought of another way to get Erik to let you play with those magnets. How do you feel now?

Robert: [Smiles.] Happy.

Teacher: I'm glad, and you thought of that all by yourself.

Source: Spivak & Shure, 1974, p. 62

Still other strategies exist to develop social skills. For example, you can develop social skills by using cooperative learning or peer collaboration techniques. These strategies place less socially skilled children in groups with their more socially skilled peers. In cooperative groups, children develop mutual concern. In collaborative groups, they learn to justify their own opinions and communicate them more clearly (Damon & Phelps, 1989). Cooperative learning strategies, and their effects on interpersonal relationships, will be described in greater detail in the chapter on motivation (Chapter 12).

Competence

Competence, according to Erikson, is the strength that emerges from the crisis of industry versus inferiority during the elementary school years. Indeed, a wealth of research has suggested that competence is an important development in middle childhood, particularly in relation to academic achievement. Competencies are frequently defined in terms of the **self-concept**, which is an individual's assessment of his or her own strengths and weaknesses.

Competence appears to have two sources, one internal and the other external. On the one hand, competence develops from a child's sense of effectiveness. In school tasks, this internal source of competence may derive from mastering the three R's as well as other subjects or skills. On the other hand, competence develops from evaluative feedback from significant others. How parents, friends, or teachers react to perceived success (or failure) influences whether or not a child feels competent.

A competent self-concept comes from success and positive feedback.

Children generally begin school thinking quite highly of their own competence in both academic and nonacademic areas; their feelings of competence decline slowly thereafter. This decline is generally interpreted as an effect of children becoming more realistic about their abilities, particularly in relation to school subjects (Frey & Ruble, 1987).

What appears to happen is that as children become realistic about their competencies, they are also differentiating them, defining areas of strength or weakness (see Figure 6.4, page 234). Thus a child might begin to feel competent in certain academic tasks but not in others. A child high in academic competence is said to have a high *academic* self-concept. Alternatively, the child might begin to feel competent in one or more types of nonacademic activities. Depending on the activity, you would say that this child has a high *social, emotional,* or *physical* self-concept. A global self-concept or self-assessment remains, but it appears to become increasingly differentiated along these or similar lines as a child grows to maturity (Harter, 1982; Marsh, 1989; Marsh, Craven & Debus, 1991; Shavelson, Hubner & Stanton, 1976).

The child develops a different self-concept in various areas.

The impact of different perceptions of competence is that children begin to react to failure in a new way (Fincham, Hokoda & Sanders, 1989; Miller, 1985). To a child younger than nine or ten, failure might be explained by bad luck or a difficult task. Because failure does not imply incompetence, the child continues to work to master the task even after he or she has failed initially.

During later elementary grades, however, failure becomes more specifically tied to what the child perceives to be personal strengths and weaknesses. Thus, if a preadolescent child fails at a specific task, his or her future motivation to perform that task is typically undermined. At this point children preserve a sense of competence by pursuing alternative activities that allow them to develop different aspects of themselves (Nicholls, 1989). This is often called the "compensatory theory" of self-concept. By the time the child reaches high school, self-perceptions of competence stabilize (Marsh, 1989; Nottelmann, 1987).

Failure may undermine motivation and turn children to pursuing alternatives.

Figure 6.4
Areas of Self-Concept

Global self-concept

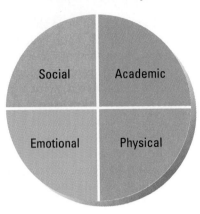

However, there are several possible pitfalls along the way. First, the compensatory abilities that the child has developed are usually *at the expense of other competencies*. This can result in a kind of vicious circle—the strong areas get stronger and the weak weaker. Also, for too many children, the perceived failures result in a frustration that develops into motivational problems and a more permanently lowered sense of competence.

strategic solutions

Learning Goals

There are some important implications in all of this for teachers of children who have failed an achievable task, whether academic or nonacademic. Since the problem is usually a lack of motivation to try again after initial failure, the solution focuses on helping the child restore motivation. This can be accomplished most effectively if you *help the student focus on improvement rather than on goal attainment*. By doing this you are helping your students to focus on their incremental gains and successes along the way rather than setting their sights on a long-term goal that may feel unattainable. Another way to put this is that you are helping your students set **learning goals**, the purpose of which is to increase competence, rather than **performance goals**, the purpose of which is to obtain a favorable judgment of competence (Dweck & Leggett, 1988; Elliott & Dweck, 1988).

Incremental successes and improvements can help to break the vicious circle and will ultimately lead not only to restored motivation but to mastery of the task itself. This process can help to build an enduring sense of competence that will sustain motivation in the future despite occasional setbacks. This outcome is just as true of social, emotional, and physical competencies as it is of academic competencies.

How should you recognize achievement of a learning goal? Children do not always need to be praised or rewarded, particularly if their improvements are obvious to them and give them an internal sense of satisfaction. But at other times, when improvements in skill, coping, or conduct are not obvious or are likely to be overlooked, a teacher needs to draw attention to the improvement with a thoughtful comment. There is no magic in the formula for how to develop competence—just time taken to note subtle improvements in a sincere and attentive way.

Evaluation: Learning Goals

Does focus on improvement actually restore motivation? Although we can say with some certainty that it often does, the strategy does not work for all students. Students with a long history of failure in a school subject or activity are least likely to be responsive. They may not "buy into" a definition of success that emphasizes improvement. They are the first to say that they succeeded not because of their own efforts but because you made the task easier, or they "got lucky." A strategy for dealing with this situation is described in Chapter 12 as "attribution retraining"; it explains how you must help these students to learn to take credit for success. Students who have *not* experienced much failure, or who have experienced some success along with failure, are much more likely to be responsive to a focus on improvement.

Identity Formation

Until adolescence, children temporarily identify with a series of others. During early childhood, they often identify with a parent or relative of the same gender. During middle childhood, they identify with an older brother or sister, a professional athlete, a television star, or what is more likely, all of the above. During early adolescence, they often identify with small groups of peers. These identifications with others do not lead directly to the establishment of a personal identity, which teenagers must integrate or synthesize from their own experience. In other words, achieving an identity requires

think it through

Consider this problem that a novice preservice teacher has **IDENTIFIED** and **REPRESENTED**.

Inadequate Hygiene

I have a child in my second-grade classroom. This child is very sweet and is a good student, academically, and he gives me no discipline problems. But he is not very clean. The children make fun of him because his clothes are dirty and he smells very bad. I need to talk to his mother, but how do I tell her to keep her child clean?

Observe how an experienced practicing teacher GENERATES SOLUTIONS to this problem.

This happens every year and it is the hardest situation you deal with as a teacher. I think we are so kind by nature that we don't confront others easily, and this is a sticky situation. You need to contact the parent immediately. Arrange a conference—face to face—because you need to determine if the cleanliness issue is a "home" issue or a child issue. If it is a home problem, get the school social worker or counselor involved, and the school nurse. Make sure the family has running water and facilities to be clean in. If it is a child issue, make sure you involve the same people to at least talk about any abuse. Once this has been ruled out, you need to tell the child that kids are making fun of him or her and stress how to keep clean. If necessary, set up a daily chart in the nurse's office to check off items such as nails and hair and have a conference with the child's contact person first thing in the morning. Teach the child how to wash clothes, if you have a machine at school, and have the student bring an extra set of clothes daily so he or she can change clothes. Check tennis shoes! Kids do not realize how funky these can get, so talk about spray and have some ready to use. I have had students that I have had to railroad into showering before they could go to class and had kids who had to be cleaned prior to the bus picking them up (these were *severe* behavior problems). The point is that parents send the best they have and then we teach from where the student is. If your student needs to learn grooming techniques, then that is your curriculum. You owe it to the child to deal with the concerns of cleanliness, for that is a lifelong lesson that needs to be taught.

Barbara Peterson
Lincoln, NE

think it through, continued

EVALUATE this problem's possible multiple solutions while you think about the dynamic process of problem solving.

Developing a student's social self-concept sometimes requires you to set goals related to improving a student's hygiene. This can be accomplished in more than one way, but the experienced teacher chose contacting the parent, defining the problem in terms of child or home, and developing a strategy based on that definition. Let's look at problem solving at each stage.

The teacher would contact the parent to assess the situation. You should be in regular contact with parents, so the assessment can be tactful. Confronting the situation does *not* mean confronting the parent. Rather, you can assess the situation during a regularly scheduled parent-teacher conference by asking some tactful (rather than pointed) questions, and by observing the parent. Your purpose is not interrogation but, as the experienced teacher notes, making a determination about whether the problem stems from the home environment or from abuse or neglect of the child.

Both types of problem are common. "Home" problems generally require educating the family about the importance of personal hygiene. A letter or note home to all the parents, for example, can stress reasons for cleanliness and provide some common guidelines. Units on health and hygiene should also be a standard part of the curriculum, and these can be modified to address specific topics. In this manner, no one is singled out or has reason to be embarrassed. If the problem continues, you might ask the school social worker, counselor, or nurse to follow up.

"Child" problems generally require more active intervention of a social worker or counselor. They often stem from child abuse or neglect. The experienced teacher in this case assumed the problem was a home problem because there were no signs of abuse in the background information. These signs would include unusual feelings or ambivalence toward the parent, poorly explained absences, or bruises—all of which might lead you to ask the child some questions. Abuse or neglect can have many different sources. If you suspect child abuse or neglect, the school will often have a procedure for you to follow, which involves alerting the principal, social worker, or counselor.

The solutions described by the experienced teacher are resourceful and practical. There is no substitute for talking with other teachers about what to do, but before becoming extensively involved, talk with the parent too. Volunteering to wash a student's clothes in the machine at school, or to have him or her take a shower before class, should be your last resort. It can provide the model, feedback, and motivation a parent needs.

I would hope that last resorts will not be necessary in such situations, and that you can focus on teaching the child rather than the parent. I agree wholeheartedly with the experienced teacher that when children need to learn about cleanliness, it should be a part of your curriculum. Just as you plan how to solve other instructional problems, you need to plan to solve this one, implement your plan, and evaluate how well it worked, to the end that you either adopt the plan as a routine for such situations or recycle the problem through the problem-solving process.

integration as well as differentiation of strengths and weaknesses. Identity often takes years to develop, and in general, we recognize these years as adolescence.

> Adolescents establish an identity based on their own experiences.

As you read these sections on identity formation, you should realize that educators do not all agree that instructional problems should be designed to help students resolve identity issues. Nonetheless, because such issues are so often confronted by adolescents at some point in their school-age years, your awareness of identity states will help you better understand where your students "are at." This can only help as you aim to develop instructional goals and strategies that are sensitive to the significant social and emotional goals of first, the child, and later, the adolescent.

Peer Conformity and Identity

Erikson believed that early adolescence was a time during which identification with peers was particularly important. The middle school years, for example, are generally acknowledged to be a period during which **peer conformity**, or adoption of the norms of a group with similar attributes, is greatest. Although research supports the idea that early adolescents are more subject to peer pressure than younger or older age groups, the evidence does *not* suggest as great a difference as once was believed (Brown, Clasen & Eicher, 1986).

> Middle school students seem most influenced by peers.

Furthermore, peer conformity does not necessarily imply rejection of adult norms. Although an increasing number of teenagers experiment with illicit drugs during these years (see Figure 6.5), the most common drug is alcohol, which is illicit only as long as the adolescent is underage. In general, rates of teenage drinking reflect rates of adult drinking in the same commu-

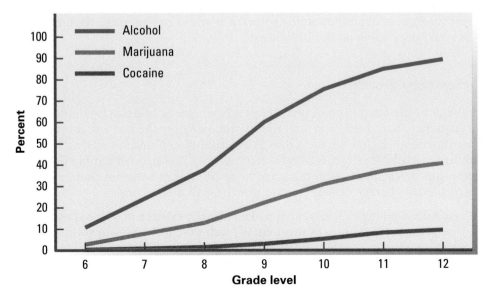

Figure 6.5
Teenagers Having Tried Drugs
(Johnston, O'Malley & Bachman, 1991, p. 92)

Although peer conformity peaks in middle school years, it can and often does continue to influence young people in high school.
(Joe Rodriguez/Black Star)

nity, suggesting that adolescent peer groups are modeling their actions after adult peer group behaviors rather than rejecting adult norms.

Erikson believed that as adolescents progress into high school and beyond, they can attain an optimal sense of **identity** through three developments: "a feeling of being at home in one's body, a sense of 'knowing where one is going,' and an inner assuredness of anticipated recognition from those who count" (1968, p. 165). Identity emerges as a "fit" between one's own needs and talents on the one hand and a developing sexuality and work role on the other. Identity formation often involves discovery of this fit, as the adolescent alternates experiences of exploration and introspection, with more or less risk, depending on the individual.

> Identity merges one's needs and talents with work and sexual roles.

Identity States

How does the formation of identity progress? James Marcia (1980) identified a sequence, based on Erikson's theory, focusing on the factors of crisis and commitment. In his view, a crisis is a period of exploration during which a choice is made among meaningful alternatives. A commitment is a degree of personal investment. According to the relationship between these two factors, identity can be classified in one of these four categories:

> Identity is reached by exploring choices and committing to one.

- An individual who has never entered an identity crisis, and who has made no commitments to values in any domain (such as sexuality, occupation, philosophy, or religion) is said to be in the state of *identity diffusion*. The identity-diffused type is typically a young adolescent whose identity crisis is yet to come.

- An individual who has never entered an identity crisis but who makes commitments unquestioningly to the same values as his or her parents is said to be in the state of *foreclosure*. In everyday life, this adolescent may appear much like someone who has achieved an identity, but his or her key goals and values have been determined by others. (See Reflection on Practice: An Adolescent's Experience of Foreclosure, page 242.)
- An individual who experiences an identity crisis and who defers commitments in light of the need to explore alternatives is said to be in a *moratorium*. This person is often an older adolescent who is, in terms of thoughts or behaviors, in the process of trying out different roles and values.
- Finally, an individual who has resolved an identity crisis through chosen commitments is said to be in a state of *identity achievement*. This older adolescent or young adult possesses a stable self-definition and relatively high self-esteem in comparison with individuals in the other three states.

Figure 6.6 summarizes the development of identity as described by Erikson and Marcia. Notice the three possible pathways. Development typically moves from identity diffusion to foreclosure or, more successfully, from identity diffusion to moratorium to genuine identity achievement. A third possibility may occur if the crises experienced are too stressful; in this case, the individual may do exactly what those around him do not wish or expect and may develop a "negative identity."

The Development of Sexuality

The development of sexuality and a sexual identity has a profound effect on the overall development of identity among adolescents. It involves the further definition of a gender role and the consolidation of sexuality. As part of this process, adolescents do a considerable amount of exploration and introspection about their own sexuality. Statistics in different reports do not al-

Part of developing an identity involves sexuality.

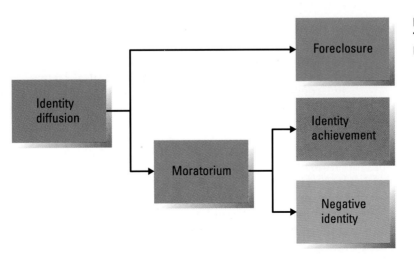

**Figure 6.6
The Development of Identity**

reflection on practice

An Adolescent's Experience of Foreclosure

Both of my parents are involved in education. They have both been school-teachers and are currently involved in the school in some way. Perhaps this is why I have always assumed I would be a teacher. Not only did I want to please my parents, but I wanted to be like them. By the end of elementary school, I knew I would be a teacher. I knew my parents would be pleased.

Throughout high school, I watched many of my friends go through crises while trying to decide who they were and who they were going to be. I really couldn't relate to their dilemmas. I was going to be a teacher. Because I sang frequently, some friends suggested I become a singer, but I quickly dismissed the idea. I had committed myself to a career of teaching without the typical crisis. I guess I had experienced a form of foreclosure.

The summer after my senior year of high school, I traveled with a singing group and loved it. After I began college, I began to doubt my career choice. This sparked a three-year "floating" phase. I fluctuated in my commitment to teaching, counseling, singing, and writing. I was experiencing the crisis that many of my friends had already faced. It was frustrating. I couldn't settle in on a specific goal, but I wanted to be committed to something. I often asked myself, "Am I going into education because I want to, or because my parents would like it?"

My question was answered through several experiences: teaching some private voice lessons, helping with kids' choir, and taking a music methods class in which I went to an elementary school and taught a lesson. The crisis was over. I knew *I* wanted to be a teacher. I fully committed myself, and my grades and performance improved dramatically.

Looking back, I believe I "foreclosed" my options at a young age, desiring to please my parents. In college, I went through the normal crisis associated with determining my identity, and I am very pleased with the decision I made.

Laurie Livingston

Discussion Questions

1. **What was the identity state of the author in college? Justify your response in terms of crisis and commitment.**

2. **Children often have talent in the same area as a parent, and parents are often pleased to have children follow in their footsteps. Why do these two conditions make the establishment of identity more difficult?**

ways agree, but we can patch together the story of adolescent sexual development from several reports (Hofferth, Kahn & Baldwin, 1987; Kahn, Kalsbeek & Hofferth, 1988; Sonenstein, Pleck & Ku, 1991; The Alan Guttmacher Institute, 1994).

By thirteen, most girls and boys have not gone out on a date yet, so their time together is generally limited to semipublic situations such as parties, group outings, or school events. The average age of the first date is about fourteen, but it varies greatly. Dating serves a wide variety of functions for different individuals, from recreation to companionship, from socialization to personality development, from gender role experimentation to fulfillment of needs for love and affection, from opportunity for sexual experimentation to mate selection. Dating may serve one, several, or all of these functions simultaneously or at different times in the life of a teenager.

Average adolescents experience a range of sexual activities. Masturbation and petting are common during these years, but they are not universal, and again, individual experiences vary widely. Figure 6.7, page 244, shows the cumulative percentages of teenagers who have had premarital intercourse. The data for men are from 1988, and those for women are from 1982. Even though they represent different cohorts, these data lead to two generalizations. First, most younger teenagers have not had intercourse, whereas most older teenagers have. Second, gender differences in premarital sexuality are relatively small. Although boys appear to become sexually active somewhat earlier than girls, the differences that are considerable at seventeen are not so great by eighteen—only one year later. By nineteen, the cumulative percentages are about the same. So much for the "double standard," which may exist only in feelings about sexual activity (more girls than boys report guilt feelings).

What the graph does not show are changes over the past decade in sexual activity of both boys and girls, and changes in risk factors. Most people are aware of the "sexual revolution" of the 1970s, but they also assume that the politically conservative mood of the 1980s and the threat of contracting AIDS decreased sexual activity among teens. The proportion of teenagers who became sexually active at younger ages actually increased far into the 1980s (Sonenstein, Pleck & Ku, 1991).

Sexual activity poses problems for many adolescents.

The 1980s' increase in sexual activity at earlier ages among teens of both sexes entailed significantly earlier risks of pregnancy and sexually transmitted diseases. Although these increased risks were to some extent offset by the fact that a total of 77 percent of sexually active teenagers used an effective method of birth control (Mosher & McNally, 1991), birth control is never completely effective, and a sizable minority of sexually active teens (23 percent) reported that they did not use any effective means of birth control.

The consequences of pregnancy risk are apparent in every community. About one out of ten teenage women (fifteen to nineteen) becomes pregnant each year (Henshaw & Vort, 1989). Only about one out of five teens who become pregnant is married. Of the other four, typically one will marry during the pregnancy, two will bear the child out of wedlock, and one will obtain an abortion (Cooksey, 1990).

All of this is important information for anyone who works with adolescents, because most sexually active teenagers have not yet resolved identity issues and thus are not yet developmentally able to sustain psychological intimacy. Attempts to be intimate before one is able to achieve psychological intimacy often result in role confusion with the other person (Erikson, 1968). And without psychological intimacy, marriage is difficult to sustain; thus, it is no surprise that teenage marriages are among those at highest risk for ending in divorce. In addition, the interruption in schooling and the delay in

Confusion can result from sexual activity without a developed sense of identity.

Figure 6.7
Premarital Sexual
Activity of Teens
*(Data for males from
Sonenstein, Pleck & Ku,
1991, p. 163. Data for
females from Hofferth,
Kahn & Baldwin, 1987,
p. 48)*

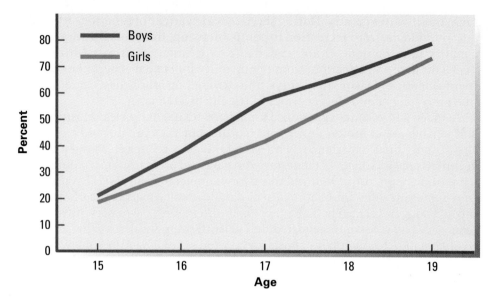

vocational choice that are often the results of teenage pregnancy leave important identity issues unresolved.

Finally, although not directly tied to identity development, no discussion of adolescent sexual activity in today's world would be complete without mentioning the reality facing all teens: unprotected intercourse can be deadly. Acquired immune deficiency syndrome, or AIDS, now kills over 100,000 people in the United States each year. It still has a nearly 100 percent mortality rate, and its only means of prevention are abstinence or effective condom use. Because this disease has a median incubation period of ten years, it is exhibited by very few teenagers. Development of the disease in one's twenties, however, is often the result of exposure in one's teens.

strategic solutions

Sex Education and AIDS Education

Although your role with regard to sex education or AIDS education will probably be strictly limited by local school board policy, you cannot afford to be unaware of these issues. You may be asked to give up a week of your science lessons to a teacher who enters your class to teach about such matters, and at minimum, you should be aware of why these forms of education are necessary.

Ask junior high school students about pregnancy or AIDS, and they will tell you that yes, they are scared. Without sex education or AIDS education, they are also often ignorant of how pregnancy occurs or how sexually transmitted diseases are contracted. Sex education and AIDS education offer a means to reduce mistaken beliefs about these subjects. Such mistaken beliefs can cause pregnancy or the accidental spreading of disease. Researchers point out that teaching how to abstain from sex and how to reduce the risks of sexual activity are as essential as teaching how to drive defensively and how to buckle up to reduce the risk of injury.

Mistaken beliefs are the root of irrational fears that can cause added obstacles for someone who has become pregnant or who has tested positive for exposure to the AIDS virus. If a girl becomes pregnant, she and the young father will almost certainly be frightened and worried. The same will probably be true of a boy or girl who has tested HIV-positive for exposure to the AIDS virus. At that point, what is needed most is for you to *support and accommodate that student.* An accident happened or a mistake was made long ago, and its present consequences need to be gracefully accepted.

Evaluation: Sex Education and AIDS Education

Does sex education work to reduce sexual activity or consequent risks of pregnancy or disease transmission? Resistance skill training (which focuses on abstinence) and AIDS education both are associated with very recent *declines* in sexual activity and pregnancy among unmarried teens, as well as *increases* in condom use (Ku, Sonenstein & Pleck, 1992). Researchers are by no means certain that sex education and AIDS education have caused these changes, but the possibility that they have contributed to them is the subject of continuing investigation.

Vocational Identity

A second major area of identity development is the choice of a vocation. Such choices may be difficult for a number of reasons. First, the most recent *Dictionary of Occupational Titles* lists over 12,000 occupations, many of them future possibilities for most teenagers. Such vast opportunity can create uncertainty and make a decision difficult. Second, the difficulty of making a choice is magnified by a quickly changing job market that sometimes

Vocational choice is a major aspect of identity.

leaves even veteran workers unemployed. Automation, overseas invest-ments, changes in governmental expenditures, and the long-term trend toward a service (rather than an industrial) economy lead to changing oppor-tunities. Third, several popular areas of vocational interest, such as the cre-ative arts, science, and the human services professions, can employ only a fraction of the teenagers who express interest in them. Competition for jobs in these areas is intense and often leads teenagers to take a second look at training demands in light of the chance of finding a job in a given field.

Despite the difficulty of a career choice—or perhaps because of it—many teenagers begin to explore a career as early as junior high school. Several early theorists in the field of career development based their ideas on developmen-tal stage theories. Perhaps the one most closely related to the stage theory of Erikson is the career development theory of Donald Super (1991), which fo-cuses on the growth of self-concept. Stages and substages of this theory are summarized in Table 6.2.

According to Super's theory, the vocational plans of the individual are ini-tially in a *growth stage,* in which the self-concept develops through a series of identifications with others. This stage lasts from birth to puberty. During this period, a maturing child bases vocational preferences first on imagina-tive identifications (often during play), then on interests, and finally on abil-ities.

During the next decade of life, the adolescent or youth is in an *exploration* stage in which a vocational identity develops through self-examination and tryouts of vocational roles. Vocational identity is achieved through tentative, transitional, and trial commitments. Later stages of career development (and their associated ages) are *establishment* (twenty-five to forty-five), *mainte-nance* (forty-five to sixty-five), and *decline* (beginning in the mid-sixties).

> Individuals reach a voca-tional identity through a series of stages.

Table 6.2   Super's Stages of Career Development

Stage	Characteristics
Growth (birth to 12 or 14)	Identification with others; self concept emerges. Fantasy helps develop interests, but awareness of capacities eventually makes interests more realistic.
Exploration (14–25)	Self-examination and career role tryout. Vocational identity emerges through tentative and trial commit-ments as long as career decisions are not foreclosed.
Establishment (25–45)	Attempts to stabilize, consolidate, and advance a career.
Maintenance (45–65)	Focus on preserving one's place in the world of work despite changes and competition.
Decline (mid-60s on)	Deceleration and selective disengagement from the world of work.

Source: Summarized from Super, 1991, pp. 42–45

Key to this and other theories of career development is the emergence of a **vocational identity**, or a clear and stable picture of one's talents, interests, and career goals (Holland, 1985). Recent studies (Munson, 1992) support Super's theory that early vocational identity is typically associated with high self-esteem. Other factors associated with the emergence of vocational identity are normal family functioning, high socioeconomic status, and high grade point average (Penick & Jepsen, 1992). All of these factors seem to facilitate what to many teenagers is a series of very difficult decisions about their future.

strategic solutions

Developing Vocational Identity

The educational implications of vocational development are relatively straightforward. A vocational identity is the result of many trial identifications; consequently, preschool and elementary teachers need to *give pupils in early and middle childhood the means to identify imaginatively with many roles.* The context should be equitable in terms of race, gender, and range of abilities. Erikson believed that play offered children the opportunity for "a vast number of imagined identifications and activities" (1982, p. 77). As an early childhood or primary grade teacher, you can facilitate such imaginative identifications by planning for such activities as guest-speaker visits, field trips, story writing, dramatic performances, and programs using books that describe different careers.

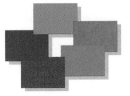

To develop vocational identity further, secondary teachers need to *provide opportunities for secondary students to reflect on their identity and career plans.* Activities focusing on choices among competing interests are particularly helpful (Waterman, 1989). The high school club fair, for example, was such an activity. A teen who joins the debate club, for example, will be challenged to improve his or her public-speaking skills. If successful, the teenager might be led to think of a college major such as English or political science, or perhaps a career in law or government. If unsuccessful, the teenager might choose another activity or club. Social activities based on abilities rather than just interest have the potential to develop tentative commitments.

In the current environment, where a diffused state of identity among adolescents is common (Archer, 1989), secondary teachers should also *treat adolescents as capable of identifying and resolving the major issues in their*

Secondary students need opportunities to reflect on their identity and their career plans. Participating as a student legislator is one way to try out an adult role in government. *(Bob Daemmrich/Stock Boston)*

lives. One of your roles may be to help teenagers formulate identity *questions* by discussing and writing about themes that arise from the literature and history taught in class, or by identifying career opportunities that relate to classroom subjects. These discussions may help teenagers become aware of identity issues and begin to question who they are and what they want to become (Csikszentmihalyi, 1987). Class discussions of identity issues may also help some teenagers to resolve areas of crisis.

Finally, remember that if a crisis is too stressful, an individual may resolve it by developing a negative identity—that is, by becoming exactly what others do not want the individual to be: an intentionally failing student, a gang member, a drug abuser, and so on. If a teenager is heading in a negative direction with his or her identity struggle, your *being supportive rather than punitive* will likely be far more helpful.

Negativism may not be harmful if it is only a temporary role that is tried and rejected. When adults react punitively to negativism, however, their actions confirm exactly what the teen wants to believe about him- or herself— that he or she is no good to anyone. A better way for an adult to respond is to provide a structured environment in which the adolescent can think through choices without having to make major commitments, and thereby allow that student a moratorium. This structured environment may take the form of volunteer work, work-study, a summer program for youth, or an after-school job. As a teacher you will not always be in a position to provide this support, but at the least, you should be aware of opportunities that exist.

Evaluation: Developing Vocational Identity

Although vocational identity plays a strong role in social development, for several reasons it has not been given much attention in relation to education. First, researchers have found that most teenagers in Canada, the United States, and Western Europe today are *not* in a period of crisis with regard to most decisions, including vocational ones. This fact does not contradict Marcia's theory, but highlights another element of it—that the predominant identity state of teenagers changes in response to the surrounding culture. Identity crises similar to those described by Erikson for younger adolescents (Côté & Levine, 1989) now appear to be faced during college years, or even later. Decisions regarding identity, including career decisions, are often delayed in present-day Western societies. The reason is unclear, but it is probably related to the complexity of the decision.

Another reason that so little attention is paid to the role of vocational identity within the schools is the gulf between identity issues as conceived by psychologists and as conceived by guidance counselors. Developmental psychologists generally perceive identity to play a leading role in career development, but in the schools guidance has typically been limited to administering interest and aptitude surveys and calling students in for remedial interventions (Vondracek, 1992). The club fair that you read about at the opening of the chapter represents a welcome departure from this pattern. Ideas for other ways to promote social development will undoubtedly take hold as guidance counseling supplements its remedial function with a developmental one.

MORAL DEVELOPMENT

Discussions among developmental psychologists about morality fall into a gray area somewhere between cognitive development and social development. Moral development really cannot be separated from cognitive development except for pedagogical purposes. As we shall consider it here, moral development is a subtopic of social development that is driven by cognitive changes, such as the increasing ability to take on the perspective of the other in any relationship. It is not that a specified code of behavior is learned, but rather that the capability to reason about rules and understand the perspective of others develops. Thus **moral development** can be considered to be progressive change in a child's reasoning about rules and his or her under-standing of others.

There are several different theories that explain how moral development occurs. They are not necessarily contradictory, but each takes a different angle on the process. In the following sections, we will explore two widely known theories; in the final section, we will look at some newer alternatives. As you study these discussions, reflect on your knowledge of the spectrum of givens and goals that we have been using as part of our problem-solving framework. Where along this spectrum would you place each theory?

> Moral development affects one's reasoning about rules and understanding of people.

Stages of Moral Development

Jean Piaget found a child's understanding of rules to have major implications for his or her sense of morality, because "all morality consists in a system of rules" (1948, p. 1). Piaget engaged in a great deal of research on children's use of rules by studying children playing marbles and by asking them to teach him the game. He also posed to children several "moral dilemmas," in which he told them stories about erring children, asking which of two children was naughtier or how a child should be punished.

> Children at first do not understand rules.

From the results of such studies, Piaget concluded that reasoning about rules develops in three stages: *premoral* (from birth to two), *constraint* (from two to ten), and *cooperation* (ten and after). In the premoral stage, which co-incides with the sensorimotor period, a child really has no sense of rules. Game pieces (such as marbles or tokens) are toys for manipulation or imagi-native play. In the morality of constraint, a child becomes increasingly aware of rules and regards them as sacred or unalterable. During this period, a child adopts rules as moral absolutes.

You can see the morality of constraint operating among children in the pri-mary grades. Recently, I visited a third-grade class where children were work-ing on art projects. Earlier, the teacher had cleaned out the cage of the class hamster, warning those who wanted to help that he was "a little bent out of shape" that day and might bite. The teacher had to leave momentarily to take some of her students to the library, and several children remained behind to work on an art project. During her absence, one boy went over to pick up the hamster. On seeing this, another child said to him, "I can tell—'He picked up the hamster.'" Then the child pointed at me. "Also *he* can tell." I busied my-self in watching something else.

> Rules are later understood as absolute.

In this case, the "tattler" saw the teacher's warning about touching the hamster as a rule that had to be enforced—rather than as warning about the natural consequences of some action. Tattling, which is common during the primary school years, owes its source to the morality of constraint. Rules at this stage are considered to be moral absolutes that are neither subject to interpretation nor related to natural consequences. They are simply to be obeyed, and if they are violated, the trespasser should suffer for the violation, regardless of the natural consequence of his or her action.

At about ten years of age, children understand rules as reasonably and co-operatively established. Piaget labeled this stage a morality of *cooperation*.

Children's understanding of rules—including moral codes—is often reflected in the way that they play games. Piaget began his study of moral reasoning by watching children play marbles. *(Tony Freeman/ PhotoEdit)*

During this stage rules and interpretations are understood to be conventions with a rational basis. They can be changed by mutual consent. Punishment, when deemed appropriate, is logically related to the offense. Intentions and motives are considered, not just the consequences of an act. This mature sense of rules complements intellectual developments occurring at about the same age, but it may never be achieved by some children if the practices of teachers or parents are inappropriate.

Children finally see rules as rational and changeable.

strategic solutions

Moderate Control

Can a teacher's style of instruction affect children's reasoning about rules? Piaget (1969) argued that it could. Many researchers have suggested that you should *be moderately controlling if you want children to reason about rules.* Children need to follow some procedures, but these procedures should be neither highly restrictive nor highly permissive (Maccoby & Martin, 1983; Prawatt & Anderson, 1988). This moderate style of governance is sometimes referred to as *authoritative* rather than authoritarian or permissive

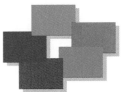

(Baumrind, 1973). Authoritative teachers are firm and controlling, but they are also warm, rational, and receptive to communication with their students. Authoritative teachers establish reasonable rules and explain the consequences for breaking them, which often include a conference with the teacher.

Evaluation: Moderate Control

During the last few decades, some of Piaget's ideas about moral development have been confirmed. Researchers have found that younger pupils provide more *extrinsic* reasons for following rules than do older pupils, who provide more *intrinsic* reasons (those related to natural consequences) (Blumenfeld, Pintrich & Hamilton, 1987). This finding validates Piaget's distinction between moralities of constraint and cooperation.

In the same study, first-grade teachers who made many specific controlling remarks had pupils who provided more extrinsic reasons for following rules than first-grade teachers who made comparatively few controlling remarks. The students of this latter group of teachers tended to give more intrinsic or natural reasons for following rules (see Figure 6.8). Moderate, rather than high, control seemed to encourage a morality of cooperation.

**Figure 6.8
Controlling Remarks
and Pupil Reasoning**
*(Blumenfeld, Pintrich &
Hamilton, 1987)*

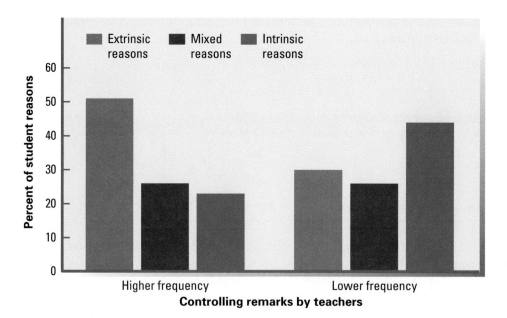

Perspective Taking

Piaget's work on reasoning about rules inspired psychologist Lawrence Kohlberg (1985, 1987) to generate a theory of moral development that focuses on **perspective taking**, or the ability to adopt the viewpoint of another as a prerequisite to a mature sense of right and wrong (Selman, 1980). Perspective taking is not the same as empathy because it requires greater cognitive resources.

Kohlberg's theory of moral development describes reasoning about right and wrong through three successive levels. After you read the definitions of the three levels listed below, you'll find it helpful to study Table 6.3, which summarizes the levels.

> Kohlberg's theory sees moral development as a process of reasoning at higher levels.

- The *preconventional* level refers to reasoning about right and wrong, but only from the perspective of the individual doing the reasoning. It is egocentric.
- The *conventional* level refers to reasoning that upholds the rules and expectations of society. It assumes the individual adopts the perspective of at least one other in making decisions about competing claims of justice.
- The *postconventional* level refers to reasoning with regard to general principles underlying social rules and expectations. Kohlberg believed that these principles exist prior to rules and therefore take precedence.

Kohlberg's levels of moral development do not line up easily with those of Piaget. First, they are more conditional than those of Piaget—that is, Kohlberg did not assume that they would necessarily develop as a child went through developmental stages. He noted, for example, that even as adults, some individuals remain at the lowest level of moral development, never

Table 6.3   Levels (and Sublevels) of Moral Reasoning

Level	Description

1. **Preconventional**   *Reasoning in interest of self only*
   a. Rules are external; reasons for doing right are the power of authority and the desire to avoid punishment
   b. Rules are followed because they are instruments to meet personal needs	

2. **Conventional**   *Reasoning in interest of both self and others*
   a. Rules are followed to fulfill expectations or to maintain trust
   b. Rules are followed to fulfill chosen duties or to maintain social order	

3. **Postconventional**   *Reasoning with regard to general moral principles*
   a. Rules are followed to fulfill implicit contract with society, but individual rights take precedence
   b. Self-chosen universal, ethical principles are followed in place of rules	

Source: Kohlberg, 1987, pp. 284–286

obeying rules for the sake of others and always considering rules as external to the self. Also different from Piaget and others is Kohlberg's belief that moral reasoning can be "postconventional" or exist at a level where a sense of justice is derived apart from rules and conventions. Philosophers have been skeptical about this third level of moral reasoning, however, because it assumes that general principles can exist apart from cultural expectations (Crittenden, 1990).

strategic solutions

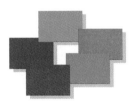

Dilemma Discussions and Just Communities

Kohlberg recommended two procedures for the development of moral reasoning. The first is the discussion of "moral dilemmas." The second, which grew out of dilemma discussions, is the development of a "just community."

Moral dilemmas are essentially scenarios and accompanying questions that call for moral reasoning. Questions such as "Why shouldn't you steal from a store?" can elicit revealing responses. At the preconventional level typical responses might be "Because I might get caught" or "Because I want to stay out of trouble." The reasons given for following rules are clearly self-centered. Responses to the same question at the conventional level might be "Because you might make the store owner mad" or "Because we're not supposed to steal what belongs to other people." The progress from preconventional to conventional moral reasoning is generally from egocentric reasoning to concern for the perspectives of others.

As a teacher you will likely find that the material for such moral dilemmas grows naturally out of the practical dilemmas and questions that arise in the course of daily instruction. A student may find money missing, discover money lying on the floor, find a lunch bag missing, or cheat on a test. Your role as a teacher in such an event may be to use the incident to stimulate a discussion with the individual or group involved. Moral development tends to occur out of the conflicting ideas often proposed as solutions. As a facilitator, your role is not so much to introduce "higher" moral reasoning but to *encourage students to take the viewpoint of one another in dilemma discussions* (Nucci, 1987). For example, if one person has hurt another in some way, it is important that everyone involved be able to take the perspectives of the victim *and* the accused.

As an extension of his original work, Kohlberg began to research the formation of moral communities within the school, which he labeled "just

Moral education often involves the discussion of dilemmas, which provides an opportunity to understand the viewpoint of others. Note the role of the teacher. What is she modeling? *(Paul Howell/Gamma Liaison)*

communities." A just community is a school-based group of up to one hundred students and five teachers that meets weekly to discuss rules and rule violations (Kohlberg, 1985).

Just communities differ from student councils because of their participatory, rather than representative, nature. The components of a just community are an agenda committee, advisory groups (ten to fifteen students and their teacher-advisor), community meetings, and a discipline committee. In the schools where just communities have been initiated, the advisory groups have met weekly to raise issues to be discussed in the upcoming community meeting. At the core of all meetings is the democratic principle of one person, one vote (including teachers). The community establishes its own rules within the general framework of school policy, and the discipline committee determines what is a fair retribution to the community when rules are violated.

Evaluation: Dilemma Discussions and Just Communities

The effectiveness of direct intervention to develop moral thinking—such as discussion of moral dilemmas—is tentatively supported by the research. Summarizing the results of fifty-five studies of moral education programs, researchers found that discussion of moral dilemmas promotes moral development in small but significant ways (Schlaefli, Rest & Thoma, 1985). Such well-structured discussions in any subject area stimulate more development than do literature and social studies classes alone, where moral issues are often embedded in the content but may never precipitate a discussion, or may never be set in practical or personal terms.

Just communities also seem to have a significant impact on moral reasoning. In one just community, moral reasoning of participants improved the equivalent of ten years over the course of three to four years (Power, Higgins & Kohlberg, 1989). The duration of the strategy beyond a year or two did not seem to be as important as the quality of the community experience.

Although moral thinking is not the same as moral doing, there is a discernible relationship between the two (Vitz, 1990). Furthermore, observers of just communities have reported decreases in thefts, fights, and other discipline problems as students develop their moral thinking. Such communities offer a means to intervene on the level of the entire school when individual problems have become deeply embedded in the culture of school. Just communities require considerable administrative support, however, and are as yet only experimental.

Alternative Concepts of Moral Development

In addition to Piaget's and Kohlberg's theories of moral development, there are several other viewpoints and alternative ways of conceiving of moral qualities. Those that we will look at here stress the cultural origins of moral reasoning and the contexts in which moral development occurs.

Since the context within which an individual develops moral reasoning clearly includes one's gender, the fact that Kohlberg first tested his theory only on a sample of boys and men has come under scrutiny, originally by Carol Gilligan (1982). Gilligan and others (Baumrind, 1986; Lyons, 1989) have pointed out that girls and women are less likely than boys and men to focus on principles of justice as core moral values. According to Gilligan, many girls and women appear to adopt a morality of *caring*, which develops from a sensitivity to the needs of others. As a result, the highest moral reasoning women reach is restricted to Kohlberg's conventional level, with its emphasis on awareness of the thoughts and feelings of others.

Males and females tend to focus on different moral principles.

To illustrate, Deepening Your Knowledge Base: An Illustration of Moral Reasoning provides an example of moral reasoning by Henry, an eight-year-old boy, and Nicole, his eleven-year-old sister. The two children were asked,

An Illustration of Moral Reasoning

When children are asked questions such as "Why shouldn't you steal from a store?" they sometimes respond as expected, but not always. As an example, let's take these separate interviews with Henry, a third-grade boy, and Nicole, his sixth-grade sister.

Interviewer:	Henry, why shouldn't you steal from a store?
Henry (age eight):	Because it's wrong.
Interviewer:	Why is it wrong?
Henry:	Because it's against the law.
Interviewer:	Any other reason?
Henry:	Because you might go to jail.

Henry's answer revealed what he believed—that you should not steal because stealing violated the law and "you might go to jail" if you break the law. At this level of moral development (Level 1), laws are obeyed because of an implicit fear of punishment, not because obeying laws serves the welfare of others (Level 2) or because it reflects a commitment to a moral principle (Level 3).

When Nicole, his sixth-grade sister, was asked "Why shouldn't you steal from a store?", she replied:

Nicole (age eleven):	Because you might get into big trouble.
Interviewer:	Any other reason?
Nicole:	Because if you have anybody who looks up to you, they might start doing it too. Like if me and my brother went into a store, and he saw me steal something, he might too.

Nicole's first answer (Level 1) was not much more developmentally advanced than that of her younger brother. It was not in her interest to get into trouble. When pressed for an added reason, however, she responded in a way that revealed some understanding of a perspective other than her own (Level 2). Her perspective taking did not result in reasoning about justice (or invoking the rights of the store owner), but not all moral reasoning appears to focus on the value of justice. Nicole's ability to take the perspective of her young brother resulted in a relatively advanced reply, with a focus on the value of caring for others.

"Why shouldn't you steal from a store?" Henry's response fit Kohlberg's scheme quite well. His response could be classified as an illustration of preconventional morality. Nicole's response also fit the classification scheme quite well. Because it showed concern for another, Nicole's reply could be classified as an illustration of conventional morality. Notice, however, that Nicole did not adopt the perspective of the store owner but that of her own brother. Henry was often her responsibility, and he both literally and figuratively looked up to her. There was a morality of caring that influenced her reply.

Although several reviews of research have failed to corroborate Gilligan's claims of sex bias in Kohlberg's classification, this does not imply that there are no sex differences in moral reasoning. One possible explanation for both the similarities and the dissimilarities between male and female responses focuses on an individual's *motives* for perspective taking. That is, why we take the view of the other is perhaps just as significant as whether or not we take it. Kohlberg's classification scheme, built as it is upon different *levels* of moral reasoning, may not be sensitive to these different *modes* of moral reasoning (Gibbs, Arnold & Burkhart, 1984).

When viewed in an even broader contextual picture, caring and justice themselves may be only two among *several* culturally defined moralities. In addition to moralities of caring and justice, cross-cultural research has found a morality based on the "collective good," common in countries such as China, India, and Israel (Snarey, 1985). Furthermore, while Kohlberg sees these qualities as hierarchical, two or more moralities may overlap in many individuals and societies, and a person or society can simultaneously espouse both caring and justice (Gilligan & Attanucci, 1988).

Both the work of Gilligan and her colleagues and cross-cultural research suggest that moral development is at least partially learned through processes of identification and socialization. In this view, moral reasoning is affected by parental and cultural values. Natural empathy forms a basis for identifications with the same-sex parent, cultural heroes, and peer groups. These successive identifications taken together may play as strong a role as reasoning in moral development (Hoffman, 1987).

Let's look in particular at a recent study that reanalyzed Kohlberg's original data from a social learning perspective (Hart, 1988). Kohlberg had interviewed parents and their sons ages ten, thirteen to fourteen, and seventeen to eighteen. Hart looked at how the moral maturity of sons (as determined by the original research) correlated with the identification of sons with parents, and with parents' involvement in play and activities with the sons.

The pattern of results in the reanalysis was clear. Involvement by the father in play with the son was strongly related to the moral maturity of the son at all ages. Identification of the son with the father was also related to the son's moral maturity, although not as strongly. Identification of the son with the mother and her involvement in play and activities did not appear to have much effect on the moral maturity of the son.

This reanalysis provides some limited evidence in support of alternative concepts of moral development. A father's involvement in play or activities with a boy seems to be strongly related to the moral development of that child. One clear conclusion is that a parent can be a powerful role model in moral development, especially for a child of the same gender.

Different cultures seem to stress different moral values.

Parental involvement can affect the moral development of children.

Role Modeling

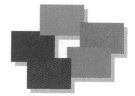

Although less powerful than that between a parent and a child, the relationship between a teacher and a student can nevertheless afford a genuine opportunity for positive role modeling. This is especially true to the extent that you become involved in student activities. As you do, you will almost certainly model how to set rules, play by them, and sometimes change them. You will also model how to take the perspective of others—in demonstrating good sportsmanship, sharing facilities or equipment, or giving special consideration to those with special needs. You will model how to care for individuals and, at times, how to put the interests of the group above individual interests, including your own. In brief, you will be a model of moral maturity.

You can deliberately teach some of these skills by using the techniques of observational learning that are described in Chapter 8. Perhaps the most important strategy is to *create a use for a social skill, then model it.* Creating a use for a skill focuses attention and supplies motivation. Modeling the skill may involve a physical demonstration, a verbal description, or both.

For example, to help students establish rules in student council, you might recommend that council members proceed by an established code of rules of order. This would include their electing a student (a sergeant at arms) to be responsible for adherence to the rules. You can intervene in meetings, but you should do so only to model social skills, such as how to adhere to the rules or how to change them.

Similarly, as a coach or club sponsor, you might encourage good sportsmanship or concern for the good of the group over individual interests, modeling these social skills when called for and appropriate. For instance, students can learn a great deal from you at the end of a spirited game with a heated rival when you shake hands publicly with the rival coach. At such times, social learning occurs, and you can be a powerful role model for your students.

Evaluation: Role Modeling

The research on learning by observation, which will be reviewed in Chapter 8, has not focused on moral development, but it does suggest that the most powerful influence on such learning is the competence of the model (Schunk, 1987). Your gender, race, and age may make you a stronger or weaker role model for one student than for another, but overall, your competence in a skill probably plays the most important role in your effectiveness as a model of that skill. Competence in a skill, not similarity to the learner, is the key to teaching effectively through demonstration.

A teacher needs to be a positive role model, demonstrating both subject-related skills and social skills such as helping others. This resident artist is helping a child make a clay tile.   *(George White Location Photography)*

Even if you demonstrate moral behaviors, however, students may not learn them. Either the student has no use for the skill (and is inattentive or unmotivated) or models of competing behavior are more powerful. The proponents of identification or socialization theories of moral development increasingly acknowledge the value of dilemma discussion to develop moral reasoning (Gibbs & Schnell, 1985; Snarey, 1985; Vitz, 1990). Being a role model and provoking discussions of moral dilemmas are not exclusive strategies. They can serve you compatibly as you strive to foster moral development in your students.

CONCLUSION

In this and the preceding two chapters you have studied physical, cognitive, and social progressions as separate domains of development. Before you turn to the subject of individual differences and exceptionality, take a moment now to examine how developmental changes fit together as a whole. Table 6.4 charts physical, cognitive, psychosocial, and moral developments side by side so that you can see corresponding developments in different domains.

Table 6.4 Summary of Motor, Cognitive, Social, and Moral Developments in the School Years

Ages	Motor	Cognitive	Social	Moral
0–2	reflex/rudimentary	sensorimotor	hope and will	premoral
2–7	fundamental skills	preoperational	will and purpose	moral constraint
7–10 or 11	transition to sports skills	concrete operations	competence	moral constraint to cooperation
10 or 11+	sports skills	formal operations	fidelity	moral cooperation

This summary table should help you to integrate your knowledge of development.

Such integrated knowledge can suggest integrated strategies. For example, cooperative activities can be very useful in elementary school for developing an understanding of the perspectives of others while developing concrete operations. If you teach on the secondary level, you may choose to focus on issues, to stimulate both perspective taking and formal operations. Seeing both sides of an issue and thinking through implications of a point of view are often compatible objectives. At whatever grade level you teach, the interrelationships of different domains of development can suggest strategies to integrate learning.

concept paper

A Moral Dilemma for Teachers

Purpose of the assignment

To formulate a solution to a moral dilemma based on perspective taking.

Directions for the assignment

1. Your task will be to formulate a solution to a moral dilemma based on perspective taking. Consider the following dilemma, which actually occurred.

   The first winter that I was working at X School, it was bitterly cold outside. Inside, I was working with a group of third graders. As I looked around the group, I saw that several of the girls had on sleeveless summer dresses, and one of the boys had on tennis shoes that were split on both sides of the soles from the toes to the arch. The soles flapped up and down as he wiggled his foot.

   We were going to do an exercise called "Walk a Mile in My Shoes." I had collected a whole sack full of shoes from my house to dump on the floor. They were to get some shoes and develop a character: How did they think this person would look and act? They had a great time doing this and were quite creative.

(Continued on next page)

(Concept Paper, continued)

When class was over, one child came up to me. She had an old pair of tennis shoes in her hand that had belonged to one of my children. She asked me if she could have these shoes. I looked at the old, almost worn-out shoes in her hand. As I hesitated, she added, "They're better than mine."

The dilemma of the teacher was, *How should I reply?* Your task is to decide how the teacher should reply, and explain your reasoning.

2. To begin thinking, frame the problem by asking yourself, "Whose perspectives do I need to consider?" Try to come up with at least four.

3. Second, consider alternative replies (solutions to the dilemma) by the teacher. Consider reactions to different replies from each perspective.

4. Third, formulate a solution to the dilemma based on your analysis of the situation. The solution should answer the question "What should the teacher say?" Your advice may go beyond the immediate situation, but it *must* address the immediate situation—the student has just asked if she can have these shoes (in her hand). What should the teacher say?

5. In a three- to four-page position paper, write what you believe the teacher should say, and explain why, giving (a) some other alternatives, (b) potential reactions to alternatives from different perspectives, and (c) anticipated reactions to your advice from different perspectives.

SUMMARY

1. Social development involves progressive change in relationships between an individual and others. Emotional development, which is progressive change in attitudes and values, evolves within a social setting. Thus it is considered a subtopic of social development.

2. Like other kinds of development, social development includes the influences of both nature and nurture. A good example is the development of empathy, the roots of which are present from birth but which must be fostered in social situations in order to flourish.

3. Psychosocial development is a theory of personality development that emphasizes social functioning. It was originally proposed by Erik Erikson. It describes eight stages, or age-related critical periods (called "crises"), through which an individual passes as he or she achieves a sense of identity.

4. Identity formation typically occurs during adolescence but may occur later. It is the linchpin of Erikson's theory. Positively resolving this crisis is essential to the ability to sustain chosen commitments and to maintain a sense of well-being in one's life.

5. Teachers can have impact on children's social development through strategies that, for example, emphasize gender equity or help train social skills like cooperation.

6. Moral development is progressive change in a child's reasoning about rules and his or her understanding of others. It is a subtopic of social development that is driven by cognitive changes such as the ability to take on the perspective of

another person.

7. One view of moral development, offered by Piaget, describes moral reasoning as progressing through three stages: premoral (birth to two years), constraint (two to ten), and cooperation (ten and after).

8. A related view of moral development, generated by Lawrence Kohlberg, focuses on perspective-taking and describes three levels of reasoning about right and wrong: preconventional, conventional, and postconventional. The progression is not tied to age.

9. Recent alternative theories stress the cultural origins of moral reasoning and the social contexts (such as one's gender-related experiences) in which morality develops.

10. Teachers can have impact on children's moral development by using strategies that involve, for example, dilemma discussions or role modeling.

KEY TERMS

social development p. 209

emotional development p. 209

empathy p. 212

psychosocial development p. 215

crises p. 216

epigenesis p. 216

gender roles p. 219

sex typing p. 219

self-concept p. 233

learning goals p. 234

performance goals p. 234

peer conformity p. 239

identity p. 240

vocational identity p. 247

moral development p. 249

perspective taking p. 253

SUGGESTED RESOURCES

Eisenberg, N., and J. Strayer. 1987. *Empathy and Its Development.* New York: Cambridge University Press. This book is one of several available to introduce you to research and thinking on empathy.

Erikson, E. H. 1968. *Identity: Youth and Crisis.* New York: Norton. This book, which emerged in the turbulent sixties, still offers one of the best descriptions of what we have come to know as "the identity crisis."

Gilligan, C. 1982. *In a Different Voice.* Cambridge, Mass.: Harvard University Press. This book widened the study of moral development to be much more inclusive of "a morality of caring." Gilligan's recent work on blended moralities is also interesting.

Nucci, L. P. 1987. "Synthesis of Research on Moral Development." *Educational Leadership,* 44, 86–92. The article presents a summary of research on moral development and points of departure for further inquiry. Particularly valuable for its emphasis on what the teacher can do.

7

Individual Differences: Considering Specific Learners

The goal of this chapter is to provide you with background information about individual differences in achievement that will characterize your students. You will learn how to adapt instruction to these differences, which tend to widen over the school years. You will also learn about groups of students with specific characteristics that put them more at risk than other students or that pose particular problems-as-challenges. All of these students will require your informed attention as you adapt instruction to address their special needs. As you read, look for answers to these questions:

Identify a Problem

Represent the Problem

Implement and Evaluate the Solution

Gather Information

Generate a Solution

■ **Why is it important that you focus on individual differences during your instructional planning?**

■ **Why do individual differences widen as children mature?**

■ **What is the one key element of ability grouping that must be present in order for this strategy to enhance learning effectively?**

■ **What is "people-first language," and why is it important?**

■ **As defined by the law, what are the four most common types of disabilities that your students are likely to have?**

■ **What is your role as a classroom teacher in the referral process?**

■ **Besides high intellectual ability, what are some characteristics that help to identify a gifted learner?**

■ **Why is teacher support important for disadvantaged students?**

■ **How does multicultural education seek to end discrimination?**

■ **What is the overarching goal of bilingual instruction in the U.S.?**

As life progresses, individual differences generally increase. Temporary differences due to different rates of maturation will even out, but other differences will increase as children of the same age progress. *(Elizabeth Crews)*

learning journal

Dimensions of Individual Difference

While reading about individual differences, make Learning Journal entries about specific experiences in which dimensions of individual differences apply. Tell what led up to the experience, name the dimension of individual difference that was involved, describe how the dimension was involved, and describe any relevant outcome. This chapter contains descriptions of the following dimensions of individual difference:

- normal variability in achievement
- specific learning disabilities
- attention deficit hyperactivity disorder
- attention deficit disorder without hyperactivity
- speech or language impairment
- mental retardation
- serious emotional disturbance
- other disabling conditions
- giftedness (any named type)
- educational disadvantage
- minority group
- ethnic minority group
- limited proficiency in English

ADAPTING INSTRUCTION TO THE LEARNER

Development is progressive change, but such change does not occur to students at the same time or in the same way. There is no student who is "average" in every respect. Each student is different, and in general, these differences do not decrease over the school years. If anything, their effects tend to accumulate, resulting in distinctive personalities and different domains and levels of achievement. Our task as teachers is not to reduce the differences between learners but to adapt instruction to individual needs in a group setting.

The physical, cognitive, and social differences among children—usually of minimal significance at first—increase as life progresses. For example, at the beginning of first grade, some children are nonreaders, most can read a few words, and some can read simple sentences. By third grade, some children are still nonreaders, while others have progressed to reading magazines and books. The phenomenon is similar in math, music, and any other teaching field. The problem-as-challenge for you as a teacher is this: *How can I adapt instruction to individual needs in a group setting?* This challenge and its solution are the focus of the present chapter.

The problem of adapting instruction to individuals is not new. It existed even in ancient times (Corno & Snow, 1986), as expressed, for example, in the

Students progress at different rates, and differences tend to increase through the years.

writings of a Chinese philosopher in fourth century B.C., in ancient Hebrew writings, and in a classic handbook of Roman rhetoric.

The problem today would be relatively simple if teachers had only a few pupils or students; but in the modern school, they are expected to teach classes that typically range from fifteen to thirty-five or more students, depending on grade level, annual enrollments, and school policy. In this setting, adapting instruction to individual learners is a major challenge. Teachers often have limited planning time, limited opportunities for one-on-one work with students, little choice of textbooks, and pressures to teach large groups in short periods.

> The pressures on teachers make it difficult to adapt instruction to individuals.

What can help are strategies that have been developed to adapt instruction to individual learners in group settings. As an example, we'll consider the way one teacher responds to the challenge of adapting instruction to individual children in the fifth grade. This example should help you not only to orient to the problem but also to understand why it needs to be solved by planning even *before* you attempt to teach a lesson. Next, we'll look at some definitions of "normal" and at the variability among individuals that you can probably expect to find in your classroom. Then, in the heart of the chapter, we'll examine several important dimensions of individual difference that are crucial to school success, along with various strategies that have been developed to address these dimensions of difference.

Individual Learners with Individual Needs in Mrs. Zajac's Class

In your eyes as a teacher, each child will be special in some way. To adapt instruction to individual learners, then, you will need to address both diverse levels of achievement and the physical, cognitive, and social characteristics that underlie this diversity. To see how a teacher does both, let's look at the class of Chris Zajac, a fifth-grade teacher in Holyoke, Massachusetts, through the eyes of Tracy Kidder (1989), author of *Among Schoolchildren*. Kidder spent twelve months shadowing Mrs. Zajac, taking notes on her planning and activities, even before the school year began.

> Experienced teachers form their own opinions of students, without reading the students' records.

Mrs. Zajac was not tempted to look at the cumulative folders to identify individual characteristics of students in the year ahead. She had found through experience that it was usually better at first to let her own opinions form. Her method conformed to what we now know is the practice of most experienced teachers regarding information that might be prejudicial (Carter et al., 1987). She initially ignored such information, preferring to use her own experience to identify individual differences.

Mrs. Zajac let students choose their own desks on the first day of class, but by the second day, several informal diagnostic exercises had given her a pretty good idea of the needs of individuals. Desks were to be laid out in a U shape, with the open end of the U facing the board and four widely spaced desks in the middle. On the second day, Mrs. Zajac reseated the children to address the needs of learners which she had identified the day before (Kidder, 1989, pp. 14–15):

One boy, Julio, had the beginnings of a mustache. Julio was repeating fifth grade. He wrote in one of his first essays:

> *Yesterday my mother and my father unchul cusint me we all went to springfield to see the brudishduldog and rode piper ricky stemdout ladey is fight for the lult*

She put Julio in one of the middle-person desks. ("He's sort of a special project, and I also know he's got to be pushed. He's very quiet. He doesn't bother anyone. That was the problem last year, I'm told. He didn't bother anyone. He just didn't *do* anything.")

Kimberly, whom Chris had noticed squinting yesterday and who confessed she'd lost her glasses, got a seat on the wing of the perimeter, up near the board.

Chris moved Claude to the wing farthest from her desk. ("Because he seems to be the type who would be up at my desk every minute, and if he's going to drive me crazy, he's going to do it over there.") Claude was a pale boy with elfin ears. He had spent most of the first day picking at his lip and making it bleed. When Chris took the globe out of her closet and carried it up to the front table, Claude piped up, "My uncle got a big globe like that. It cost about, let's see, a hundred and ninety-two dollars. It stood up this high."

"Oh my," said Chris.

Other children were also strategically reseated. In the process, Mrs. Zajac began to address the physical, cognitive, and social differences among them. Kimberly needed to sit close enough to the board to read it without glasses; Julio was an underachiever who lacked motivation to learn; Claude needed personal attention on the teacher's terms rather than on his own; and so on. The strategic arrangement of all the children allowed Mrs. Zajac to address individual differences throughout the year while the class was engaged in whole-group activities.

Seating strategies can help address differences in students.

You may or may not choose to adapt instruction in the way that Mrs. Zajac did; but the problem of *how* to do so is compelling enough that you will need to find a solution. As a beginning teacher, you may want to consider ability-grouping strategies that address different levels of achievement, and you will probably benefit from consultation with other teachers about special needs. As you gain experience, you will become more adept at using different kinds of groupings, identifying individual differences, and adapting the curriculum to meet them, often with little awareness on the part of students.

Planning to Meet Diverse Learner Needs

Adapting instruction to the learner begins with planning. The reason that it must begin *before* instruction is that student diversity is a given of instructional problem solving. As you know, givens are best considered as early as possible in the problem-solving process because they help you represent a problem in a way that leads to its solution. Acknowledging the diversity of physical, cognitive, and social characteristics of specific students before you teach will help you plan goals, strategies, and activities to address diverse

Planning must account for differences in students.

learner needs. Whatever these goals, strategies, and activities for a lesson may be, they must include all learners to be effective.

For example, if you are a third-grade teacher, what would you do in a normal reading lesson to address the needs of Billy, who is a nonreader? Or Sally, who reads as well as any high school student? Or if you are a high school history teacher, or math teacher, or music teacher, how would you address the special needs of Jerry, who learns much more slowly than the average student? Such concerns are very real when you start teaching. If you realize the need to address them during planning—rather than waiting until class time presses them urgently upon you—you will be able to use your resources more effectively.

If you do not address such concerns during planning, you will probably never address them properly. Especially as a beginning teacher, you will most likely find that you simply have too much to do just implementing the instruction that you have planned. As a consequence, several children may become frustrated or bored. If their needs are neglected over a long enough period, they will give up trying, or they will act out, or both. Some, having long been neglected as learners, may come to you with well-established attitudes and patterns of failure. You can help prevent or remove these obstacles to learning by adapting instruction to the needs of individual learners at the beginning of the year, during planning periods, or whenever you consider your goals and strategies. At such times, you will want to make sure that you have included every class member in your plans.

NORMAL VARIABILITY IN THE CLASSROOM

Imagine, if you will, a car race. Cars are lined up in their "pole positions" for the start of the race. They follow the pace car and start the race all bunched together. What happens as the race develops? The combined effects of different cars, different drivers, different support teams, luck, and the turn of events spread the cars out. Statisticians call the "spread" in any characteristic—such as the distance different cars have gone at any moment during the race—its **variability**. At the beginning of the race, the variability or spread of progress is small, but by the end of the race, the difference in progress is quite large.

> Variability describes the differences in progress over time.

Life may or may not be like a race, but children start out life together. Everyone is a novice at everything. What happens after just a few years? The combined effects of different capabilities and experiences "spread out" their progress in any given respect. Motor skills not only improve, but they increase in variability. Reading skills not only improve, but they increase in variability. Social skills not only improve, but they increase in variability. Increases in characteristics or skills are the products of progress, but so are increases in variability. Thus, as the "average" progresses, the extremes of high and low spread out—a little like the increases in distance between the first and last cars during the course of a race.

The Range of What Is "Normal"

The average value of any characteristic or skill is described as its **norm**. Nevertheless, when you hear people discuss what is "normal," they often are talking not about an average but about values *around* the average. There is no set percentage in what is normal, but statisticians include as many as 95 percent of all values in this category. Only a few percent of values, then, are too high to be included in what is normal, and a few percent of values are too low.

These percentages are not completely arbitrary. Rather, they are identified by what statisticians call a **normal curve,** which is a line that describes the random distribution of values around the average. Figure 7.1 portrays a normal curve. The height of any point on the curve represents the frequency of occurrence of any given value along the bottom. As you can see, the curve is highest at its middle (which represents the norm) and lowest at its ends (which represent extremes). Normal curves describe, for example, the distribution of distances that cars have gone at any given point during a race, or the heights and weights of children at any given age, or the scores of an ordinary class of third graders on a reading test.

> A normal curve illustrates the distribution of values around the average.

Normal curves are not all the same shape. They can be steeper or flatter depending on the "spread" of values. Steeper curves represent *lower* variabilities because values are bunched up in the middle. Flatter curves represent *higher* variabilities because values are spread out.

What happens to variability as students progress through grade levels? The next figure (Figure 7.2, p. 273), shows idealized reading achievement at the beginning of grades 3, 5, and 7. To facilitate visual comparison, you see just the line below normal values, not the curves themselves. An X marks each norm or average. What may surprise you is the extent to which test experts believe the range of achievement spreads out in just four years. The distance between more proficient and less proficient readers is expected to increase, much like the distance between faster and slower cars increases during the progress of a race.

> The range of student achievement seems to increase as students become older.

Literacy experts tell us that throughout the elementary and secondary years, the range of reading achievement in an average classroom will be at

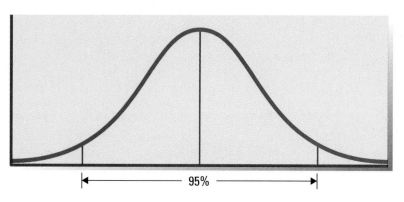

**Figure 7.1
The Normal Curve**

95%

think it through

Consider this problem that a novice preservice teacher has **IDENTIFIED** and **REPRESENTED**.

Meeting Learner Needs with a Variety of Solutions

My philosophy of teaching emphasizes meeting the needs and abilities of each child in my classroom. Through the integration of the whole-language approach and the basal, I feel this can be accomplished. One method of instruction alone is not sufficient in accomplishing this, since my student population will include children of various backgrounds and abilities who will also have different and individual needs.

My concern is how I will respond to parents who expect to see their children's progress through "daily take-home worksheets," depicting what was done in class. Studies show that neither the basal nor the whole-language experience works for every child. Therefore, it is necessary to integrate the two in order to arrive at the best way to help children learn.

Observe how an experienced practicing teacher GENERATES SOLUTIONS to this problem.

Often parents will question their child's progress because they have not seen an adequate amount of paperwork. Communication is key in establishing a positive relationship with parents. This also builds a trust that you are meeting their child's academic needs.

Parent education is essential to their understanding teacher approaches and parent concerns. It is important to remember parents do know their children best. Listen to them. Children also know a lot about their own learning style. They can tell you if asked! Conferences, discussions, and providing material for parents helps to give a common ground for understanding.

There is no one approach that works for everything in life, so why should this be true for reading? Just as parents have a variety of styles, teachers do, too! Use and try them all. Children learn best through a variety of approaches. If one doesn't work another will! A combination of approaches provides children with a menu of strategies to choose from.

I use a "mixed bag" of approaches. I evaluate my success by each child's progress. I keep a portfolio of each child's work and assessments, and I share this with parent and child.

I send home weekly booklets (child-made) of work. I save pieces of work from the week and file them. Children make covers and assemble books at the end of the week. I attach a brief newsletter about what we have covered. A goal for the following week is written on each child's [book] cover. This is for parent and child to share. A "Super Student" award is attached if the child reached his or her goal for the week. This is my way of keeping parent and child informed.

Joyce Yoshizumi
Hanscom Elementary School
Lincoln, Massachusetts

think it through, continued

EVALUATE this problem's possible multiple solutions while you think about the dynamic process of problem solving.

The experienced teacher rightly stresses two-way communication with children and their parents as a means of developing an awareness of different learner needs and styles. What you can do to prepare for encounters with different needs and styles is to develop a variety of techniques and strategies to suit different learners. This variety of techniques and strategies should serve you like a tool kit. The more "tools" you have in your kit, the better prepared you will be to solve different kinds of problems. You will also have more than one "tool" to use for any given problem.

The experienced teacher is also right to point out that children learn better from a variety of approaches than from just one. So often a teacher will find that a given technique works with a given child, then assume that it works with all children. It becomes "the" answer—as if problems in education were that well structured. On the contrary, they are often ill structured, and the "givens" often vary for different teachers and learners.

What you need to develop is flexibility in your approach, which comes only from a willingness to try out different possibilities—even some that you may not prefer at first. The whole-language approach to literacy, for example, is frequently discussed in opposition to the use of basal readers, but the two approaches can be used to complement each other. When you hear people advocate one or the other approach all of the time, consider whether or not they have been led into a false dichotomy based on an intellectual commitment rather than on the evidence of what works.

Most evidence of the effectiveness of strategies is based on group averages. Advocating that a strategy should be used 100 percent of the time because it works 55 percent of the time just doesn't make sense. It is far better to supplement the "55 percent solution" with a "25 percent" one and a "10 percent" one, rather than to use the "55 percent" one all of the time and the others not at all. There will always be situations in which nothing you do for a student seems to work, but another teacher may find a way to reach that student. Don't be too hard on yourself. Your efforts may have laid the foundation for later success.

Finally, the experienced teacher demonstrates that she understands parents' need to know what their children are doing in school and how well they are doing it. Some of this need to know probably springs from curiosity about what their child is up to all day long, but parents also require information that guides them in knowing how best to support your efforts. This information should be provided to parents long before report cards are due. Keep lines of communication open through notes, schedules, returned work, conferences, invitations for special events, and so on.

Parents can effectively support you in many ways. They can help with homework and class activities, especially in the case of younger students. You need to tell them *how* to help with homework (a time to be together) and *when* you need help with class activities. They will also provide you with feedback about your efforts. Most of the feedback will be informational. Accept praise graciously, and reflect on any criticism; but also do what you think is best for each child. Many parents will want to help as they discover that you are working to help their child learn.

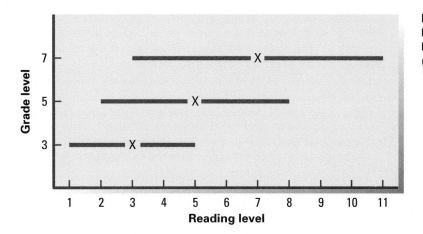

Figure 7.2
Ranges of Reading
Levels
*(Adapted from Hillerich,
1990, p. 48.)*

least the same as the grade of the classroom, plus one year (Harris & Sipay, 1990; Hillerich, 1990). Thus, in an ordinary *third*-grade class at the beginning of the year, you can expect normal reading achievement to range at least *four* years, or from the first- to the fifth-grade level; in an ordinary *seventh*-grade class, you can expect normal reading achievement to range at least *eight* years, or from the third- to the eleventh-grade level; and so on. As you can see, adapting instruction to the normal range of skills in just one area—literacy—becomes quite a challenge as students progress through school. The

The normal range of reading achievement in an average classroom will be at least as many years as the grade level, plus one year. If the children in this class were in fifth grade, what might the normal range of reading be?
(Lawrence Migdale/Tony Stone Images)

Individual Differences in P.E.

Every year in my physical education class we are required to administer a physical fitness test at least twice. Our department usually gives it at the beginning and end of the school year. The test is made up of five parts: the flexed arm hang, sit-ups, shuttle run, U-sit and reach, and the one-mile walk/run. The last is the least favorite and, therefore, the greatest challenge for motivation.

Motivation is very complex because the students are so varied:

- Latoya is an athlete (a cross-country runner, to be exact) and is motivated within herself to beat the stopwatch. She enjoys the competition of running against her earlier times. She is a high achiever.
- Jaime is a low achiever in the one-mile walk/run. She is very obese (300 pounds). She can barely walk one mile, let alone run.
- Helen hates to run. In her earlier years, she was made to run laps as a punishment for talking in p.e. She does not lack ability but fails to put forth the effort.
- Angelina runs because of the health benefits. She is a big girl who has little endurance or athletic ability but is motivated by the thought that running helps keep her weight down.

My whole class is made up of complex personalities, so the issue of motivation is also very complex. Students like Latoya and Angelina are internally motivated, whereas students like Jaime and Helen need to be externally motivated.

Earlene Entrekin

Discussion Questions

1. **How do motivational differences affect achievement in any domain, not just that of physical education? What are the sources of these differences?**
2. **Let's say it is the beginning of the school year and you are the physical education teacher. What kinds of goals might the fitness test help you establish? Be specific.**
3. **What different strategies might you use to achieve these goals with different students? Again, be specific.**

challenge becomes even greater when you consider that many experts now believe the normal range (95 percent) to be even larger. On the reading subtest of the *California Test of Basic Skills,* for example, the normal range for seventh-grade reading achievement is from second to twelfth grade—a span of *ten* years rather than the eight that we calculated by formula (Hillerich, 1990). Further, scores of *at least* one child in every class are not included in the normal range! Similar increases in variability develop in other areas of achievement (see Reflection on Practice: Individual Differences in P.E.).

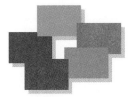

Ability Grouping That Focuses on the Individual

One common solution to the problem of adapting instruction to normal variability is for teachers to group students by skill or ability level, a procedure also called **homogeneous grouping**. (It contrasts with **heterogeneous grouping,** in which learners are classified by age without regard to ability or skill levels.) If carefully used, homogeneous grouping can adapt instruction to the individual learner.

The assumption behind homogeneous groups is that adapting techniques, materials, and pacing to students of similar skill levels is easier and more effective than adapting instruction to students of mixed skill levels. However, similar abilities do not automatically translate into adaptive techniques, materials, or pacing. Therefore, notice that there are *two* aspects to this strategy. In order to be a truly effective strategic solution, ability grouping must include both (1) *the grouping of students by specific skill or ability* and (2) *genuine adaptation of instruction to individual differences in learning.* Let's look in more detail at these two aspects before we go on to define the different kinds of homogeneous groups that exist.

In order to accomplish genuine adaptation to individuals' needs, a teacher must pay attention to each of two factors. First, in setting up ability groups, you need to be sure that you are placing individuals in groups according to strengths or needs in specific areas of achievement or instruction, not simply by general ability. Because individuals learn at different rates, you also need to make your placements flexible and open to change. Second, you should match the level and pace of teaching as closely as possible to the level and pace of learning. If you have two or three groups, you should have two or three different lessons, thereby truly adapting your instruction to the skill level of each group.

With the placement issues and learner needs constantly in mind, a teacher has several different options for homogeneous ability grouping: *within* class, *between* class, or *without* class (as in an ungraded school). *Within-class* ability grouping (sometimes called "intraclass" grouping) divides a classroom of students into two or three homogeneous groups. If there are three groups, typically one is above grade level, one is at grade level, and one is below grade level. Within-class ability grouping is primarily used for reading or math in elementary schools. Reading groups, for example, are very common in the primary grades, but their popularity decreases as grades progress. Within-class ability groupings are not very common in high school, but they can occur whenever separation of novices, intermediates, and experts makes adapting instruction easier.

Between-class ability grouping (sometimes called "interclass" grouping) involves division of students into homogeneous classes at different levels. In some high schools, for example, there are three "tracks" or streams of

strategic solutions, continued

instruction in English: basic, general, and college-bound. Between-class ability groups may exist for some but not all subjects, or for all subjects (as in certain high schools). They may be formed across grade levels or coexist at the same level.

One popular form of between-class grouping for elementary reading instruction is known as the *Joplin Plan.* Named after Joplin, Missouri, where it was first publicized, this approach to teaching reading requires that the reading period be scheduled at the same time by teachers at different grade levels. At the beginning of the year, pupils in grades 4, 5, and 6, for example, might be assessed for their reading level and then rank-ordered from lowest to highest. The top third might be assigned to the sixth-grade teacher, the middle third to the fifth-grade teacher, and the lowest third to the fourth-grade teacher. Variability within each group is not eliminated by this procedure, but it can be markedly reduced. Table 7.1 summarizes grouping practices.

Table 7.1   *Summary of Grouping Practices*

Type	*Description*	*Example*
Heterogeneous	mixed-ability groups	traditional classroom
Homogeneous	sorted-ability groups	
Within class	grouping within classroom	three reading groups in class
Between class	grouping across classrooms	Joplin Plan/tracking in high school

Evaluation: Ability Grouping That Focuses on the Individual

In order to judge the effectiveness of ability grouping, teachers must focus their attention on the second element of the strategy. In other words, they must ask, Is instruction genuinely adapted to the individual learner's needs in the ability group setting? If instruction is *not* adaptive, then it should not be expected to be advantageous in comparison to heterogeneous (mixed-ability) classes.

Recent research suggests that if teachers place students in flexible groups related to specific abilities, and if they adapt the level and pacing of instruction to each group, then ability grouping can be successful in increasing achievement as compared to matched classes *not* grouped by ability (Slavin, 1987, 1990). Specifically, at the elementary school level, the Joplin Plan and some forms of within-class grouping that attend to these factors appear to increase achievement. Otherwise, ability grouping achievement is not greater. There do not appear to be any great advantages or detriments for between-class ability grouping at the secondary level. (Note, however, that less research had been conducted on the effects of ability grouping at this level.)

Between-class ability grouping for all classes is and probably will remain controversial. "Tracking," as it is often called, raises several questions unrelated to achievement gains or losses because it tends to separate the children of heterogeneous local populations along racial or economic lines (Oakes, 1985). The social cost of tracking is difficult to measure, but its unintended effect may be to limit the development of mutual understanding as students progress through secondary school. This effect may itself be a function of how early and consistently students are kept in tracks. Tracking practices persist, however, because of measurable gains in higher-ability groups that do not appear to have occurrred at the expense of achievement of lower-ability groups (Kulik & Kulik, 1991).

DIMENSIONS OF INDIVIDUAL DIFFERENCE

Grouping strategies can deal with the normal range of differences in achievement within your classroom, but they do not address the extremes of achievement you will probably confront. Educators who are concerned about adapting instruction to individual differences are particularly concerned with low achievers and high achievers, whatever the causes of low or high achievement. Generally, the concern has focused on low achievement, its causes, and its remediation, but there has also been growing interest in high achievement with respect to identification of it and accommodation to it.

In the remainder of this chapter, you will be introduced to several groups of children, each with a dimension of individual difference that can account for low or high achievement. These groups of children encompass (1) students with disabilities, (2) students who are gifted, (3) students who are educationally disadvantaged, (4) students in an ethnic or a cultural minority, and (5) students with linguistic differences. With perhaps the exception of giftedness, all of these dimensions are regarded as risk factors; that is, they put students at risk for academic failure or for dropping out of school. There are many other dimensions of individual difference that could be analyzed if space allowed, but none of these has demonstrated a potential impact on achievement equivalent to that of the five areas listed here.

Before proceeding with this discussion, however, I want to point out something important about the language used to refer to these groups of students. Notice that for each group I have referred first to the child and then to the dimension. This I have done deliberately, in accordance with special education standards that are reflected in a 1990 law called the *Individuals with Disabilities Education Act.* These standards call for what is known as "people-first" language.

> Certain characteristics can account for low or high achievement.

Take a moment now to consider the difference that words can really make. Labels depersonalize real people. By thinking of children as "the disabled" or "the disadvantaged," you give more importance to the dimension of difference than to the children themselves. If instead you think of children as individual persons who happen to have particular characteristics or conditions, you will be enabling yourself to see the humanity of those children. At the same time, you will be encouraging yourself to notice the similarities, rather than the differences, that exist between yourself and the children and between them and other children. These attitudes reflect and promote genuine respect for *all* children.

Students with Disabilities

Federal legislation requires specified instruction for students with disabilities.

The law that first mandated the adaptation of instruction for students with disabilities in the United States was the *Education for All Handicapped Children Act*, or *Public Law 94-142*, which was passed in 1975. This federal legislation, together with several companion laws, was renamed in 1990 and is now collectively known as the law mentioned above: the *Individuals with Disabilities Education Act* (or *IDEA*).

Before continuing, notice one other important language difference between the two laws. Not only does the new law use "people-first" language but it also replaces the word *handicapped* with the word *disabilities*. This is a key distinction for you to keep in mind throughout your teaching. As Nancy Hunt and Kathleen Marshall point out, "A disability is a limitation, such as difficulty in learning to read, or the inability to hear, walk, or see. A handicap is not the same as a disability; it is the limitations imposed by the environment and by attitudes toward people with disabilities" (1994, p. 4). This distinction will help you achieve a better understanding of individuals with disabilities and the barriers that they encounter.

These laws originated as civil rights legislation, with key provisions for integrating students with disabilities into the regular classroom. The fundamental purpose of IDEA is "to assure the availability of early intervention services to all infants and toddlers, and a free, appropriate public education to all children and youth with disabilities" (U.S. Department of Education, 1994c, p. i). IDEA mandates special education and related services for children with disabilities from birth through the end of their school years (defined as age twenty-one in most states).

Children with disabilities are a significant portion of all those enrolled in schools.

There is no easy path to the identification of students with disabilities, but the most commonly traveled one has been set by federal legislation and regulations, which have established thirteen categories of disability. All of these categories (except traumatic brain injury) are listed in Table 7.2. Together, these categories account for almost 12 percent of school enrollments, or about one of every eight children. Not all of these children participate in regular classroom learning; but with some assistance, an increasing number do, particularly in elementary schools. The students with disabilities most commonly served under IDEA are those with *specific learning disabilities*,

Table 7.2 Disabilities Served Under IDEA in 1991–1992

Category	Percentage of Enrollment[a]
Specific learning disabilities	5.3
Speech and language impairments	2.4
Mental retardation	1.3
Serious emotional disturbance	1.0
Hearing impairments	.1
Orthopedic impairments	.1
Other health impairments	.1
Visual impairments	.1
Multiple disabilities	.2
Deafness/blindness	<.1
Autism	<.1
Preschool disabled	1.2
All conditions	11.8

Source: U.S. Department of Education, 1994b, p. 65

[a]These percentages are ratios of each disability over total school enrollment. They can be expected to vary between grade levels.

speech and language impairments, mental retardation, or *serious emotional disturbance.* These four categories account for most children classified with disabilities under IDEA and will be the focus of our discussion here.

Students with Specific Learning Disabilities

Specific learning disabilities have been defined by the U.S. Congress as disorders in "one or more of the basic psychological processes involved in understanding or in using language, spoken or written, which may manifest itself in an imperfect ability to listen, think, speak, read, write, spell, or to do mathematical calculations." This definition of specific learning disabilities encompasses perceptual disabilities such as *dyslexia,* the inability to perceive accurately the form, position in space, or serial arrangement of letters. Under the law, the definition excludes potentially overlapping categories of disability and educational disadvantage.

A functional definition of specific learning disabilities is based on three components (Mellard & Deshler, 1992). First, a learning disability results in *a discrepancy between expected and actual achievement.* Expected achievement is often based on normal or above-normal scores on individual intelligence (or school ability) tests (see the section on mental retardation for a description of these tests). When these expectations are not realized in school achievements (such as scores on a standardized achievement test), a learning

> Specific learning disabilities involve failure to achieve as expected.

Table 7.3 Achievement Areas in Which Students Can Demonstrate Significant Discrepancies

basic reading skills

reading comprehension

mathematical calculation

mathematical reasoning

oral expression

listening comprehension

written expression

Source: *Federal Register,* 1977

disability may be the cause. Accordingly, learning disabilities are often identified in relation to one of the seven skill areas listed in Table 7.3.

Second, *the aptitude-achievement discrepancy is not due to some other condition excluded by definition or by law.* This "exclusionary" component refers to other disabling conditions (such as emotional disturbance), as well as to underachievement due to economic limitations, educational limitations, or cultural differences. It is hard to operationalize, however, because it involves ruling out multiple alternatives. Third, *a learning disability entails failure to achieve in the regular classroom.* This component aids in the determination of whatever particular services are needed.

The federal estimate of the frequency of true learning disabilities is 3 percent of school enrollments, but rates of students being served in this category are almost twice that high, for a number of reasons. Perhaps the most important of these is that the functional definition of a learning disability includes everyone of school age who is average or above average in school ability, is a low achiever in a key academic area or areas, and is ineligible for assistance under another category or program.

In addition there are also several disorders associated with this category that are not themselves truly learning disabilities. Two common ones are *attention deficit hyperactivity disorder* (ADHD) and *attention deficit disorder without hyperactivity* (ADD/wH). Students with ADD/wH tend to be distractible and impulsive, and require inordinate supervision. Students with ADHD exhibit such additional symptoms as fidgeting, squirming, talking excessively, and abnormally high activity levels for their age. Often diagnosed by physicians, ADD/wH and ADHD are treated with drugs (primarily Cylert, Dexedrine, or Ritalin) or behavior therapy. Estimates of elementary students with ADD/wH or ADHD run as high as 5 percent of enrollments, but these disabilities currently tend to be overdiagnosed. Although they do not constitute a separate category of disability under the law, a 1991 U.S. Department of Education policy memorandum states that children with these disorders are eligible for special education services and may be classified either in the learning disabilities category or in the categories of emotional disturbance or other health impairments (Lerner & Lerner, 1991).

Attention deficit disorders are associated with specific learning disabilities.

Students with Speech and Language Impairments

Speech and language impairments involve inabilities to formulate, transmit, or receive information through a conventional symbol system (McCormick, 1990; Yoder & Crais, 1992); they are also known as "communication disorders." **Speech impairments** entail distortions of spoken language. Categories of speech impairment include articulation or phonology (such as substitution of the *w* sound for that of *r*), voice (unusual volume or pitch), fluency (stuttering), and resonance (excessive nasality).

Language impairments involve abnormalities in expression or comprehension of ideas through spoken language. Some children with language impairments do not develop spoken language capabilities at a normal pace (*aphasia*); others use words abnormally (for example, in uncontrollable expressions) or echo words spoken to them.

Speech impairments (such as stuttering or articulation disorders) are quite common, particularly during early childhood and the elementary school years, but language impairments are relatively rare. Most speech impairments are remedied easily in comparison to language impairments. The federal estimate of the frequency of speech or language impairments is 3 percent of school enrollments.

> Speech impairments are more common than language impairments.

Students with Mental Retardation

Mental retardation is defined by the American Association on Mental Retardation (AAMR) as "significantly subaverage intellectual functioning, existing concurrently with related limitations in two or more . . . adaptive skill areas" (AAMR, 1992, p. 1). Areas of adaptive skills include communication, self-care, home living, social skills, community use, self-direction, health and safety, functional academics, leisure, and work. The AAMR definition ensures that at least two factors—general intellectual functioning and adaptive skills—are considered in the identification process.

> Mental retardation is marked by subaverage intellectual and adaptive functioning.

Intellectual functioning is typically measured by individual *intelligence tests.* These tests originated during the late nineteenth century as a way to identify students who could not profit from regular classroom instruction. Alfred Binet and Theophile Simon are credited with the invention of the first intelligence test, which was given to schoolchildren in Paris. In the second decade of the twentieth century, Lewis Terman at Stanford University imported the Binet test and adapted it for American schoolchildren. Today, after several further revisions, it is known as the *Stanford-Binet Intelligence Scale* or, more simply, as the Stanford-Binet (Thorndike, Hagen & Sattler, 1986).

The Stanford-Binet is just one of many individual tests of intelligence. Another frequently used in education was invented by David Wechsler at Bellevue Hospital in New York. It is called the *Wechsler Intelligence Scale for Children—Third Edition,* or WISC-III (Wechsler, 1991). The norm for intelligence on the WISC-III is a score of 100. Ninety-five percent of intelligence test scores fall between 70 (low) and 130 (high). The range of scores from 70 to 130 is considered normal intelligence.

> Two popular intelligence tests are the Stanford-Binet and the WISC-III.

Although "significantly subaverage functioning" is defined by an intelligence test score significantly below the norm (that is, a score below 70 to 75), it is important to remember that low test scores, by themselves, are insufficient evidence of mental retardation. Significant deficits in adaptive skill areas must be determined independently. Identification of adaptive skill deficits safeguards against misplacement of children who, for reasons other than retardation, might perform poorly on an individual intelligence test. Consideration of adaptive skills has historically resulted in the *de*classification of many children with low intelligence test scores as retarded. Given the AAMR definition, the frequency of students with this disability is approximately 1 percent of enrollments (Patton & Polloway, 1990).

Students with Serious Emotional Disturbance

Serious emotional disturbance, also known in some states as *behavior disorder*, has been defined by the federal government as encompassing at least one of these five conditions, shown *to a marked degree over a period of time:*

1. an inability to learn that cannot be explained by other disabling conditions
2. an inability to build or maintain satisfactory interpersonal relationships
3. inappropriate behaviors or feelings in normal situations
4. a pervasive mood of unhappiness or depression
5. a tendency to develop physical symptoms or fears from personal or school problems

Serious emotional disturbance is identified by extreme and long-lasting disordered behavior.

Many students fulfill one of these criteria at one point or another, but very few exhibit one or more of the criteria to a marked degree over a period of time. The extremity and duration (but not the type) of disorder distinguishes serious emotional disturbance from normal behavior (Smith, Wood & Grimes, 1987).

Emotional disturbance can be environmental or personal.

Disturbances can be subcategorized into one of two general classes: *environmental conflict* or *personal disturbance* (Epstein & Cullinan, 1992). Children who are experiencing environmental conflict tend to *externalize* their disturbances through aggression, hyperactivity, or social maladjustment. Alternatively, children who are experiencing personal disturbance tend to *internalize* their disturbances, which are manifested as anxiety and depression or social incompetence. Boys with emotional disturbances tend to externalize more than girls, so they are often easier to identify than girls with such disturbances. Students who either externalize or internalize disturbances over a prolonged period have great difficulty maintaining relationships with teachers or peers. Teachers consistently report that students with this disability (estimated at 2 percent of school enrollments) are very difficult to teach.

Identification Procedures

Currently, the majority of states either require or recommend a *prereferral* procedure in which the concerns of a teacher or parent about a student can be brought to a special educator or a school psychologist for consultation and assistance (Carter & Sugai, 1989). Prereferral procedures generally follow the problem-solving process: identify the problem, define it in terms of givens and goals, gather information, design a solution, and implement/evaluate the solution. In this context, the overarching problem to be solved is the need to adapt instruction to the learner (Fuchs et al., 1990; Graden, Casey & Christenson, 1985).

In many cases, the classroom teacher implements the prereferral intervention strategy, which consists of special modifications of instruction, behavior management procedures, or other methods. In an increasing number of cases, a building-based support team or a teacher assistance team (with a special educator included) supplements the teacher's classroom role by providing supportive services. Nevertheless, you, as teacher, will probably play a greater part in the implementation of the strategy than will anyone else.

> Intervention can begin with an informal prereferral strategy.

If you and the team decide that the prereferral intervention has not been successful, you have substantial data on which to base a formal *referral* of a case to a special services committee. This committee appoints a *multidisciplinary team* that is responsible for assessing whether or not a child has a disability that interferes with school learning. Consent must be obtained from the parent(s) before this team can conduct its evaluation. The team itself must include, at a minimum, a licensed evaluator and the child's teacher. One team, for example, might consist of a school psychologist, a counselor, and a teacher to assess whether or not a given child is seriously emotionally disturbed. The purpose of the team is to collect, interpret, and report unbiased information for classification and program planning decisions. Parents must be notified of the results of the assessment.

> A multidisciplinary team will decide whether a referred child needs special services.

If the multidisciplinary team determines that the child is disabled in some way, the special services committee appoints a planning committee to design an *Individualized Education Program*, or *IEP*. This planning committee must include at least one person who has served on the multidisciplinary assessment team. It must also include the child's teacher, a special education supervisor, the child's parent(s), and the child (if appropriate). (See Figure 7.3.) By law, the IEP itself must specify (1) current levels of educational performance, (2) annual goals and objectives, (3) services to be provided to the child, (4) the date such services will be initiated and their likely duration, and (5) criteria and schedules for determining whether objectives have been achieved.

> An Individualized Education Program sets out the child's current performance and what services will be provided.

Figure 7.4 on page 284 shows an IEP for a sixth grader ("Sam") who was assessed as having learning disabilities. A referral was made, and the assessment team found that significant discrepancies existed between this student's average intelligence scores on the WISC-III and his below-average achievement scores in key academic areas. Neither the intelligence test scores nor the calculations of significant discrepancies (using what are called

Figure 7.3   The Referral Process

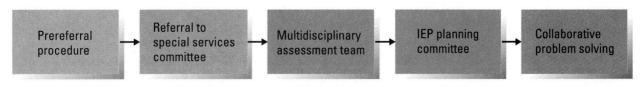

| Prereferral procedure | → | Referral to special services committee | → | Multidisciplinary assessment team | → | IEP planning committee | → | Collaborative problem solving |

Form 1

NAME Sam H.
BIRTHDATE 2/1/83 GRADE 6
SCHOOL YEAR '94-'95
IEP FROM 8/22/94 TO 5/26/95
   FROM _____ TO _____

AREA(S) OF DISABILITY
PRIMARY Learning disability
SECONDARY None
SECONDARY _____
SECONDARY _____

PRESENT LEVEL OF PERFORMANCE SUMMARY

DATE	ASSESSMENT INSTRUMENT & SCORES		STRENGTHS	NEEDS
4/15/94	WIAT	Grade level s-scores		
	Basic Reading	85		3.6
	Math Reasoning	92	4.6	
	Spelling	76		2.9
	Reading Comprehension	83		3.1
	Numerical Operation	89	5.0	
	Listening Comprehension	96	4.9	
	Written Expression	76		K:2

Form 2

STUDENT NAME Sam H. SCHOOL YEAR '94-'95

AREA Reading Comprehension

ANNUAL GOAL Sam's reading comprehension skills will improve to a 4.5 grade level.

OBJECTIVE		Type of Evaluation or Agency Responsible	Projected Check Date or Initiation Date	Date/Degree of Mastery or Completion Date
OBJECTIVE	Given 4.5 reading passage, Sam will answer questions pertaining to it with 80% accuracy.	WRM or GDRT-D	Weekly & 5/95	
OBJECTIVE	Given his choice of pleasure reading books, Sam will read one complete book each week.	Teacher OB	Weekly & 5/95	
OBJECTIVE	Given a 4.0 reading passage, Sam will be able to summarize the sequence of events with 90% accuracy.	TMT	Weekly & 5/95	
OBJECTIVE	Given an incomplete 4.0 reading passage, Sam will draw logical conclusions in 4/5 attempts.	TMT	Weekly & 5/95	
OBJECTIVE				
OBJECTIVE				
OBJECTIVE				

Add additional pages if needed.

Form 3

Name Sam H. School Year '94-'95

REGULAR CLASS PARTICIPATION (27 HOURS PER WEEK)

MODIFICATIONS IN THE REGULAR EDUCATION PROGRAM

If modifications to the regular education program are necessary to ensure the student's participation in that program, those modifications must be described in the student's IEP. Any modification to the regular education program must be indicated by writing the letter(s) of the modification description on the line beside the area.

MODIFICATION	MODIFICATION	MODIFICATION
READING D, E	LANGUAGE ARTS D, E	HOMEROOM _____
ENGLISH D, E	SOCIAL STUDIES D, E	LUNCH _____
SPELLING D, E	VOCATIONAL ED _____	LIBRARY _____
MATH D, E	HEALTH D, E	ART _____
SCIENCE D, E	Typing (Computer) C, D	_____
MUSIC _____	Handwriting D, E, C	_____

MODIFICATION DESCRIPTIONS

A. Modify presentation   D. Modify materials   G. _____
B. Modify environment   E. Use groups and peers   H. _____
C. Modify time demands   F. Use paraprofessionals   I. _____

The following TESTING MODIFICATION(S) is/are made in the special education program.

AREA	MODIFICATION
Science	If necessary, tests will be read aloud.
Social Studies	If necessary, tests will be read aloud.
Language	If necessary, tests will be read aloud.

CHECK ONE OF THE FOLLOWING ITEMS:

_____ This IS NOT a state testing program year for this student.
___✓___ This IS a state testing program year for this student. See attached documentation.

PHYSICAL EDUCATION: Regular _____ Modified _____ Special _____ NA ✓

TRANSPORTATION: Regular _____ Special _____ NA ✓

Form 4

The student will have the opportunity to participate as appropriate in NONACADEMIC and EXTRACURRICULAR activities unless the IEP states otherwise. Reasons for nonparticipation, if appropriate, are as follows:

CHECK APPROPRIATE LEAST RESTRICTIVE ENVIRONMENT

[ ] 01 Regular (less than 6 hours per week)
[✓] 02 Resource (6-21 hours per week) 8
[ ] 03 Separate (over 21 hours per week)
[ ] 04 Public Day School
[ ] 05 Private Day School
[ ] 06 Public Residential
[ ] 07 Private Residential
[ ] 08 Home
[ ] 09 Hospital
[ ] 10 Corrections
[ ] 11 Private School (placed by parents)

JUSTIFICATION FOR THE LEAST RESTRICTIVE ENVIRONMENT IS AS FOLLOWS:

Sam needs small-group instruction on a daily basis in reading and spelling based on declining standard scores on the WIAT. He needs fewer distractions and one-on-one training in memory skills, structuring and organizing thoughts and materials. These needs can best be met in the resource room. Being a part of an inclusion effort last year did not prove to be successful for Sam in these areas.

THE FOLLOWING PERSONS ATTENDED THE IEP MEETING

IEP COMMITTEE MEMBER'S SIGNATURE	DATE	POSITION
Marsha H.	5/12/94	PARENT
Jean M.	5/12/94	LEA REPRESENTATIVE
Daniel R.	5/12/94	TEACHER
		STUDENT
Priscilla C.	5/12/94	LD Teacher

NAME	SOURCES OF ADDITIONAL INPUT	POSITION

"standardized test scores") are directly recorded on the IEP. What is recorded is the identification of one or more learning disabilities.

The IEP describes individualized goals along with strategies for meeting them. The first page of the IEP reports Sam's scores on the *Wechsler Individual Achievement Test (WIAT)*. If Sam had performed as well as the average fifth grader in the ninth month of the school year, he would have achieved a total *grade equivalent score* of 5.9. But he did not score this well on any subtest. On four subtests, his performance was more than two years below grade level, and on two other subtests, it was three or more years below grade level.

Grade equivalent scores form the basis for goals and objectives over the next six pages of the IEP. The areas listed on these pages (not all of which are shown in Figure 7.4) are reading decoding, reading comprehension, written expression, spelling, math reasoning, numerical operations, handwriting, typing (on a computer), and study skills. If the IEP had been written for a student sixteen years of age or older, *transition goals* to support adjustment to the world of work would also have been included.

Note that the objectives for reading comprehension include the conditions and criteria of performance. These objectives are examples of specific performance objectives, which were described in Chapter 3. Also note that evaluation of progress requires the use of either a diagnostic test (the *Woodcock Reading Mastery Tests* or the *Gray Oral Reading Tests—diagnostic*), a teacher-made test (TMT), or teacher observation. Evaluation occurs weekly and at the end of the school year.

Least Restrictive Environment and Inclusion

The last page of the IEP contains indications of placement according to the **least restrictive environment**, which consists of conditions that include the student with disabilities in as many *mainstream* (that is, "normalized" and nonsegregated) activities as possible. The degree of inclusion for a particular child depends on the nature and severity of his or her particular disability. A "cascade" of services flows from least to most restrictive. Not all school districts have the same cascade, but services generally flow (as shown on the IEP) from regular class, to resource room, to separate class, to separate school, to homebound instruction, to hospital or residential facility. As the last page of the IEP indicates, Sam is classified as receiving instruction in a resource room for eight hours per week and in the regular class for twenty-seven hours per week.

Today, more students with disabilities are learning in regular classes because of a current reform movement in special education. Special educators have adopted the term **inclusion** to describe this movement (Fuchs & Fuchs, 1994). Inclusion appears to be having a significant impact on the location of services for students with some of the more common types of learning disability.

Figure 7.5 charts the changes in location of services for all students with disabilities in neighborhood schools from 1984 to 1991. As you can see,

Figure 7.4
An Individualized Education Program (opposite page)
(This program courtesy of Martha Felker)

The IEP is to place the student in the least restrictive environment.

The trend is toward including children with disabilities in the regular classroom.

Figure 7.5
Changes in Location of Services
(Annual reports to Congress, various years)

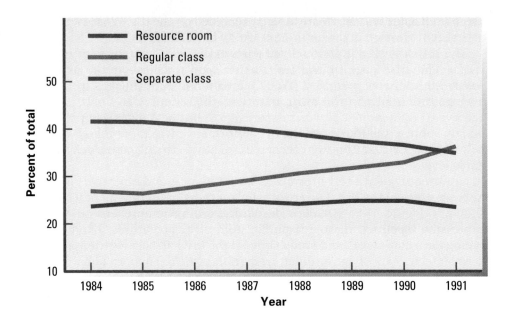

reforms in special education appear to have shifted such services primarily from the resource room to the regular classroom, thus including more children with disabilities in regular classroom instruction. And beginning in 1991, more students with disabilities received services in the regular classroom than in any other location. The statistics do not tell the whole story, however, because they fail to indicate that even though some students—such as Sam—are still classified as receiving services in a resource room, they are also participating more fully in the regular classroom than they would have been only a few years ago. Furthermore, virtually all students with disabilities in high school now take at least one academic course each year (U.S. Department of Education, 1994c). As a teacher in an inclusion classroom, you will increasingly work side by side with specialized teachers and professionals. Indeed, new models for collaboration among all student-support providers are rapidly evolving.

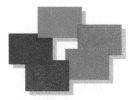

strategic solutions

Inclusion Strategies

Sometimes the implementation of an IEP requires a special educator or other support person to be the primary provider of services, but given the current emphasis on inclusion, you as the classroom teacher will be increasingly expected to interpret and implement provisions in the IEP. Since you will be part of the IEP planning committee, this task should not be difficult, but it

Peer tutoring is becoming a recommended way to address the needs of students with disabilities in the regular classroom. *(George White Location Photography)*

does require collaboration with support personnel.

This collaboration should extend beyond problem identification and definition. It should include gathering information about teaching strategies, generating an *inclusion strategy*, and both implementing and evaluating it; in short, it should involve the full problem-solving procedure (e.g., Graden & Bauer, 1992; Hitzing, 1992). The only difference between this procedure and the one you learned in Chapter 1 is the collaborative nature of the task. To succeed, an inclusion strategy must be developed during a collaborative planning period every few weeks, if not more often.

The first step is to *identify the inclusion problem*. Remember, a problem is a challenge, not an obstacle. With a particular student in mind, ask each other, "How can we adapt instruction to this child's needs in a group setting?" Focus on the goal of inclusion, but remember that you may not be able to include all students in all class learning activities.

Once you have identified the problem, *represent it in terms of givens and goals that will allow you to solve it together.* You will need to consider givens such as the proportion of students with disabilities (as many as a third of enrollments in some areas), specific student characteristics (abilities as well as disabilities), your collective resources (such as time, special materials, or peers able to serve as tutors), and the overall expectations of the school curriculum. You will also be incorporating goal statements and specific objectives on the IEP as you establish the problem-solving goal(s) for this particular child and situation.

Third, *pool information about inclusive learning activities.* One possibility is to use modifications of assignments given to learners who do not have disabilities (Stainback, Stainback & Moravec, 1992). These modifications may involve the type of learning, the difficulty level of individual portions of group assignments, or the substitution of functional (that is, life skills) assignments for academic assignments. For example, **aptitude-treatment-interaction (ATI) research** matches student characteristics with specific instructional strategies based on achievement outcomes. Indeed, ATI research has found that very specifically defined activities are generally more effective for low-achieving groups than are other activities (Gerber, 1987; Gersten, 1985; Kavale, 1990; Lloyd, 1987). Learning activities of this type are described in Chapters 8, 9, and, to some extent, 10. In order to maintain strategies entailing these activities in the regular classroom, you will need the help of the student's peers or a support person trained in these techniques.

Another modification in techniques that you can consider for your strategy involves the use of peers as tutors. **Peer tutoring**, which involves one-on-one teaching between students, is becoming a recommended way to address the needs of students with disabilities in the regular classroom (Fuchs, Fuchs & Fernstrom, 1993; Miller et al., 1993). Tutoring may be *cross-age* or *same-age*, and *classwide* or not, depending on the circumstances. In most cases, the special education teacher will be required to train the tutors to provide specific feedback that is helpful. Note that classwide tutoring is of particular value when a given group consists of a relatively high proportion of students with disabilities.

Fourth, *generate an inclusion strategy.* There is no magic formula for doing so; the objective is simply to adapt instruction to the needs of the learner. The inclusion strategy you choose may involve all or part of the day, identical or parallel learning activities, and educational support personnel or student peers.

Look back for a moment at the inclusion strategy developed for Sam. You'll see that it included both modification of class materials in all subjects and peer tutoring, as well as eight hours of one-on-one instruction in study skills (in the resource room)—specifically because inclusion the previous year did not seem to have helped in this area.

Finally, *implement and evaluate the inclusion strategy.* As the classroom teacher, you may well have primary responsibility for implementing the inclusion strategy. In this capacity, you will monitor the strategy, spontaneously adapt it to changing conditions, and, together with your colleagues who have collaborated in its development, evaluate its success once it has been put in place.

In evaluating the strategy, you will begin by assessing mastery of IEP objectives; but you will also take into account the grading policies at your school. For example, in most secondary schools, students with disabilities who participate in regular classes receive grades according to the same criteria as those applied to the learning of other students. How will these grades affect your student? The interpersonal attitudes and self-concepts both of learners with disabilities and of class members are also important outcomes. How will they be affected? Such questions should be answered collaboratively by those colleagues who have worked on the inclusion problem so that you can all identify new goals.

Evaluation: Inclusion Strategies

There are two ways to look at the effectiveness of strategies for adapting instruction to learners with disabilities. One is to consider the effectiveness of policy; the other is to determine the effectiveness of practice. Another way to put this is to ask two questions about the effectiveness of these strategies: (1) Is the policy of inclusion achievable and, in fact, being achieved? (2) Is inclusion a beneficial practice that helps students learn?

Current policy departs from past practices by more frequently including special education students in regular class activities. It appears to be addressing a problem that was *not* resolved by past mandates such as mainstreaming or the Regular Education Initiative whereby, despite well-meaning intentions, identification of a disability often led to unnecessary segregation from able learners. Occasionally inclusion still leads to inappropriate separation; in such cases, we can say that the policy is not working.

Still, there are rational limits to the adaptiveness of inclusion to individual needs. If *all* students were to be included in *all* regular class activities, some of the adaptive advantages of special education would be lost. Separate activities, classes, and schools are both adaptive *and* appropriate for some learners with some disabilities. What educators are beginning to realize is that inclusion problems need to be addressed on an individual basis, not by category (cf. York et al., 1992). In other words, instruction should be adapted primarily to the learner.

To examine the second concern, the effectiveness of practice, we must consider whether instructional techniques for regular classes are sufficiently flexible to adapt to the needs of individuals with disabilities. The answer is a qualified "yes." For example, the Language Experience Approach (a procedure in which a student reads back his or her own words and stories) has been used successfully with students with learning disabilities (Hollingsworth & Reutzel, 1988). It may also work with some students with mental retardation (see Reflection on Practice: Richie). In addition, peer tutoring has been used successfully with students with learning disabilities and mental retardation (Beirne-Smith, 1991; Vacc & Cannon, 1991). Other activities, such as discovery learning (see Chapter 10), may not work as well. Keep in mind that specifically defined activities have been found to work best for most students with most disabilities.

The most positive outcome of inclusion is that it is likely to lead to the attainment of important goals of social development, such as self-acceptance. What inclusion has *not* demonstrated is significant improvement in

reflection on practice

Richie

Richie, a twenty-year-old student with mental retardation in the tenth grade, fascinates me with his desire to achieve. He currently has a second-grade level of word recognition. Last year, when he returned to school after a two-year absence, he was attempting to read pre-primer words. His family had placed him, through Vocational Rehabilitation, in a work adjustment program following the eighth grade. Richie was not happy with the placement and wanted to return to school.

The special education coordinator felt that it was a move in the wrong direction to serve Richie in the high school setting. His parents felt that, earlier, he had not received appropriate training in reading. They also indicated that at work, he was told he could not learn to read and was assigned menial tasks and odd jobs. IDEA grants all children a free appropriate public education in the least restrictive environment up to age twenty-one, so Richie returned to school.

I was not informed of all the circumstances leading up to Richie's placement in my room. After conducting the necessary assessments so as to develop an Individualized Education Program, I realized that I would need to start at the initial stages to teach him to read. This wasn't going to be easy what with eighteen other students at all different levels.

Richie is motivated by curiosity and eagerness to learn. A reading approach that I have found to capitalize on intrinsic motivation is the Language Experience Approach. The student tells about an event he or she has experienced. The teacher writes the story on a chart or blackboard for the student to copy to notebook paper. The sentences are then put on sentence strips and the strips are cut up so that each word appears on a separate flashcard. The strategy is to move from the whole to parts. One story is reread for several days until the student has mastered all the words shown individually. Richie's topics for this method are, for example, a trip to Texas, a day in p.e., and activities after school.

Richie's success so far has been tremendous. He receives great satisfaction from reading both his own stories and those in basal readers. I cannot predict what level he may reach, but he will be able to read survival sight words in addition to some entertainment reading. Richie and his parents have appreciated the time and effort I have devoted to him. I am thrilled to have been able to aid in his learning and only regret that I could not have contributed earlier.

Paula Reck

Discussion Questions

1. **How does the above illustration reflect adaptation of instruction to the learner? Name several ways in which instruction was adapted in this case.**

2. **The author is a special education teacher. In what ways might the regular classroom setting limit or constrain the use of such methods by the regular classroom teacher?**

academic learning among students with disabilities placed in regular classes as opposed to other locations (Jenkins et al., 1991). However, enabling students with disabilities to achieve self-esteem and social goals, coupled with the absence of a negative impact on achievement, is sufficient reason to include many students with disabilities in most regular class activities.

Students Who Are Gifted

The inception of gifted education can be traced to 1957, when the former Soviet Union astonished Americans by orbiting *Sputnik*, the first artificial earth satellite. In reaction to a widespread perception that the Soviets were superior to the West in science, technology, and foreign languages, the U.S. Congress declared an educational emergency in 1958 and passed laws to allocate funds for developing talent in these domains.

Since that time, American society has developed a "love-hate" relationship with gifted education (Colangelo & Davis, 1991). This ambivalence probably reflects the nation's simultaneous commitment to equality and admiration of excellence. The coexistence of these two values is certainly advantageous to our society, but it has also been a source of frustration for educational policy makers and teachers of the gifted. The frustration often begins with the problem of identifying just *who* is a gifted and talented student (Reis, 1989).

Identification of Students Who Are Gifted

Definitions of **giftedness** vary enormously. The following is one cited in the Jacob K. Javits Gifted and Talented Students Education Act of 1988 (Section 4103[1]):

> The term "gifted and talented students" means children and youth who give evidence of high performance capability in areas such as intellectual, creative, artistic, or leadership capacity, or in specific academic fields, and who require services or activities not ordinarily provided by the school in order to fully develop such capabilities.

By including diverse categories or domains of performance, this definition acknowledges that giftedness is a more inclusive concept than high intelligence. Such an inclusive concept meshes well with recent theories (see Deepening Your Knowledge Base: Alternative Concepts of Intelligence) that broaden the concept of intelligence to cover areas of giftedness other than intellectual ability. This definition, or some variation of it, has been adopted by legislation concerning gifted and talented children in most states.

The initial problem has been to identify accurately those students who qualify as gifted and talented under this definition. Almost all earlier

Giftedness is defined to include talent in any of several areas.

deepening your knowledge base

Alternative Concepts of Intelligence

How many different kinds of intelligence are there? Traditional intelligence tests assume that there is only one (called the general or g factor), but recent theories have challenged this view. Let's look at these alternative concepts of intelligence.

First, consider Robert Sternberg's (1985) "triarchic" theory, which describes three forms of intelligence: *analytic, synthetic,* and *practical.* Analytic intelligence involves being "able to dissect a problem and understand its parts" (Sternberg, 1991, p. 45). People with high analytic skills do well on conventional tests and receive good grades. They have high IQs as measured by traditional intelligence tests. In contrast, synthetic intelligence involves being "insightful, creative, or just relatively adept at coping with novel situations" (Sternberg, 1991, p. 45). People with high synthetic skills see problems in new ways. Although they may not have the highest IQs, they often make original contributions to society. Finally, practical intelligence "involves applying whatever analytic or synthetic ability you may have to everyday, pragmatic situations" (Sternberg, 1991, p. 46). People with high pragmatic skills go into a setting, figure out how to succeed, then do succeed. Their strengths lie in areas such as interpersonal relations and impression management.

Second, there is Howard Gardner's (1983) theory of "multiple intelligences," with seven components. Like Sternberg, Gardner takes account of traditional intelligence—in this case, by locating it within two of the seven components: *linguistic* and *logico-mathematical* intelligences. People with high linguistic skills are very good with words and language. And those with high logical or mathematical skills are good at reasoning, computation, and notation. Both linguistic and logico-mathematical intelligences are more highly valued in schools than are the other five intelligences, summarized as follows. *Spatial* intelligence involves "the capacity to represent and manipulate spatial configurations"; *bodily-kinesthetic* intelligence "refers to the ability to use all or part of one's body (like one's hands or one's mouth) to perform a task or fashion a product"; *musical* intelligence involves both an ability to hear themes and a sensitivity to pitch, rhythm, texture, and timbre; *interpersonal* intelligence involves "the ability to understand other individuals"; and *intrapersonal* intelligence "refers to a person's understanding of self" (Ramos-Ford & Gardner, 1991, pp. 57–58).

Using these two theories and definitions, discuss in your small groups the following actual case, in which only the name has been changed. Then reassemble to discuss your findings.

A highly productive and successful Nashville songwriter at thirty-seven, William is also a high school dropout. By late childhood, he could pick up almost any stringed instrument and, with a little practice, play it. Lyrics would occur to him in the course of his chores, such as mowing the lawn. At thirteen, he was earning $250 per week in part-time jobs as a musician, often performing his own songs. He was a straight-A student in high school, but he found school irrelevant to his talents, so at sixteen, he persuaded his father (a high school teacher) to let him drop out to pursue a career as a songwriter and performer.

Although the current federal definition of giftedness does not include physical ability, a definition of giftedness based on Howard Gardner's theory would include "bodily-kinesthetic" intelligence. *(Jon Riley/ Tony Stone Images)*

Discussion Questions

1. Describe William's gifts as a songwriter from the perspective of the triarchic theory of intelligence. In what respects is the triarchic theory a more appropriate tool than the traditional concept of intelligence?

2. Describe William's gifts as a songwriter from the perspective of multiple intelligences. In what respects is the theory of multiple intelligences a more appropriate tool than the traditional concept of intelligence?

3. Could school have been made more relevant to William's prodigious talents? If so, how?

definitions of intelligence focused only on *intellectual ability* (often interpreted as "school ability"), typically assessed by an individual intelligence test, achievement test scores, or grades. States generally do not specify minimum intelligence test scores to qualify for gifted education but particular programs often set them around 130, which identifies the top 2.5 percent of scores.

However, with the new emphasis on the wider concept of intelligence and broader definitions of giftedness, educators are realizing that numerical limits on IQ scores do not, by themselves, adequately identify all gifted and talented students. For example, highly creative adults are as likely to have intelligence test scores (IQs) below 130 as above. Indeed, one study (MacKinnon, 1978) found that groups of architects, research scientists, and mathematicians nominated as creative by their peers had IQs that *averaged* around 130 (ranging from 118 to 152). No one knows what the average IQs of

IQ scores alone cannot identify all gifted individuals.

creative individuals might be in less educationally oriented careers. Accordingly, high *creative ability,* often included as a separate category of giftedness in gifted education programs, is variously identified through paper-and-pencil tests of creativity (e.g., Torrance, 1984), inventories of creative personality characteristics, assessments of problem-finding ability (cf. Csikszentmihalyi & Getzels, 1988), teacher or peer nominations, and self-reports of creative accomplishments. More will be said about creative thinking in Chapter 11.

Other categories of giftedness include *artistic ability,* often measured through student performance competencies (e.g., Porath & Arlin, in press); *leadership capacity,* often reflected in student activities; and *specific academic abilities,* often measured through scores on a specific achievement scale or aptitude test. Teacher, peer, and even parent nominations are also commonly accepted as evidence of talent in any of these areas.

The federal estimate of the number of individuals included under the earlier definition of *gifted and talented students* is 3 to 5 percent of a school enrollment (Haring & McCormick, 1990), but alternative definitions are more inclusive. A less restrictive concept of giftedness and talent might identify as many as 20 to 25 percent of a school population as an academic "talent pool" (e.g., Renzulli & Reis, 1991). And a more diversified concept of giftedness and talent (e.g., Gagné, 1991) might classify many if not most children as gifted or talented in some way. In practice, however, fewer than 6 percent of students in the United States are enrolled in programs for the gifted and talented (U.S. Department of Education, 1987).

strategic solutions

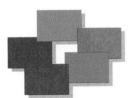

Individualized Learning

Although some states require that IEPs be developed for children identified as gifted or talented, no single, overarching strategy for teaching gifted children has been mandated by law. Rather, broad strategies of intervention can be classified as modifications of the school environment or of the curriculum content and skills to be mastered (Gallagher, 1985). Modifications of the school environment include enrichment in the regular classroom, a consultant teacher (who helps you develop lessons), a resource room (or "pull-out" program), mentoring (often by a professional in the community), independent study (often a special project), special-interest classes (such as creative writing), special classes (such as advanced-placement biology), and special schools (such as a statewide science and math school). Most of these modifications parallel services available for adapting instruction to students with disabilities.

Unlike modifications of the school environment, modifications of content and skills for children who are gifted are often quite different from such mod-

Enrichment programs and special-interest classes are two strategies for individualizing learning. These students and their teacher are hunting for fossils. *(Bob Daemmrich/Stock Boston)*

ifications for students with disabilities. Content modifications for gifted students might include content acceleration (such as early admission, grade skipping or "telescoping" two years into one), content enrichment (materials designed to elaborate on basic concepts in the standard program), content sophistication (more abstract or fundamental considerations of basic concepts), and content novelty (such as units on highly specialized topics). Modifications of skills to be mastered include training in component skills of problem solving (such as problem finding, information gathering, or strategies of solution generation), various forms of problem solving (such as creative, cooperative, or competitive problem solving), and development of creativity.

One comprehensive strategy for individualizing environment, content, and skills for the gifted student is to use a contract that specifies the goal, strategy, and evaluation of learning (see Figure 7.6). A **contract** is an agreement between individuals, such as the learner, the teacher, and (when relevant) others, including the special education teacher or the parent(s). A contract can be specified by the teacher; but particularly with students who are gifted, negotiation should be carried out in such a way that the learner assumes some of the responsibility for the design and implementation of what is essentially an informal IEP.

Contracts are useful because of their flexibility. The contract in Figure 7.6 has room for descriptions of five activities, each corresponding to a stage of problem solving. A problem involves a goal, so it should be stated in terms of

strategic solutions, continued

**Figure 7.6
An Individualized
Learning Contract**

CONTRACT

A. Goal

My goal is to _____
_____.

The duration of this project will be

     from _____

     to _____.

B. Strategy

My strategy for attaining this goal is to accomplish the following.

1. Learning activity #1:
_____

2. Learning activity #2:
_____

3. Learning activity #3:
_____

4. Learning activity #4:
_____

5. Learning activity #5:
_____

C. Evaluation

1. The evaluation will be ongoing. _____
2. The evaluation will occur at completion. _____
     (Check one or both.)
     Method of evaluation: _____

Student's signature: _____

Teacher's signature: _____

Today's date _____

what the student is expected to accomplish or create. The accomplishment may involve learning, understanding, or applying a body of information; but above all it should entail higher-order thinking, such as performing an analysis of a policy or an issue (in social studies), planning and conducting an experiment (in science), or writing a paper or short story (in language arts). The accomplishment or product is the goal, and the five activities should be sequenced to attain it.

Let's say your class is studying ancient Egypt, and, because a learner who is academically gifted already knows about this subject, she would be bored by this unit. Why not suggest a project of some kind? Be open to ideas that use the talents and skills of the learner. For example, you might suggest creating a multimedia "trip" to Egypt, using a script written by the child and slides, artwork, or pictures scanned by computer. Identifying an interesting problem or goal (namely, this project) might be the first activity; defining specific tasks to be accomplished (such as planning the "trip" and selecting archaeological sites to "visit") might be the second; gathering information (obtaining information and collecting visuals) might be the third; developing the solution to the problem within a particular format (assembling and rehearsing the presentation) might be the fourth; and trying out and evaluating the answer (making the presentation and asking for peer feedback) might be the fifth.

Another form of enrichment might involve either teaching a class of younger students or tutoring. Under the category of teaching, you might share an interesting collection or creation that reflects the talents of the learner—either passively, in a display format, or more actively, in an interview. The tutoring, in turn, might entail the preparation of lessons designed to assist one or more learners with disabilities. Contrary to what some people would predict, gifted students generally believe that tutoring of less capable learners is the fairest way for everyone in a class to learn (Thorkildsen, 1993).

Evaluation: Individualized Learning

Gifted education faces comparison with other special education programs which have made progress on all fronts. Progress in gifted education has indeed been slower, perhaps because a national policy toward gifted and talented students has been lacking, along with funding for research on gifted education. However, as recent legislation has established funds for a National Research Center for the Gifted and Talented, leadership training, and demonstration sites (Reis, 1989; Renzulli, 1991), progress toward the resolution of key challenges is likely in the future.

Gifted education does face a number of challenges, but none is insurmountable. These challenges exist in the areas of rationale, identification procedures, and effectiveness research. First, educators sometimes point out that gifted education has failed to create a compelling rationale parallel to that which exists for students with disabilities. Recall that laws mandating special education for students with disabilities originated as civil rights legislation to end segregation of these students. Gifted students already spend most if not all of their day in the regular classroom (Cox, Daniel & Boston, 1985), and a compelling reason for removing them for part or all of the day has yet to be found. Accordingly, attention in gifted education may focus on adapting instruction to the gifted learner in the regular classroom (Parke, 1989), with occasional absences to participate in a specific activity.

Problems of identification also exist. In combination with the rationale problems just noted, they evoke the perception that gifted education is for the privileged few. Table 7.4 presents national survey data on racial representation in gifted and talented programs. When the percentage of students in gifted programs by race is calculated, non-Asian racial minorities (such as Native Americans, African Americans, and Hispanics) are on average found to be underrepresented in gifted and talented programs by a factor of 2. Some educators believe that underrepresentation of these racial groups can be corrected through preparatory programs (e.g., Rito & Moller, 1989), diversified identification procedures (Richert, 1991), and referrals from minority parents (Scott et al., 1992).

strategic solutions, continued

Table 7.4 *Percentage of Students by Race in Gifted Education Programs*

Native American	Asian	African American	Hispanic	White	Total
2.2	9.1	2.7	2.6	7.0	5.5

Source: Developed from data in U.S. Department of Education, 1987, Table 2

A third key challenge is summed up by this question: What genuinely effective modifications are possible in learning environment, content, and skills? Educators and researchers involved in gifted education have not yet examined this question sufficiently. For example, separate classrooms are sometimes created to serve gifted students, but their effectiveness apart from content acceleration (which occurs in many gifted classrooms) has not been demonstrated (Slavin, 1990). Given the controversial nature of tracking practices, educators of the gifted might want to study more closely different possibilities for accelerating content for gifted learners in the regular classroom.

Research tells us that content acceleration does appear to be a relatively successful academic modification for a child who would otherwise be bored (Southern & Jones, 1991). At the same time, early admission and grade skipping, both of which involve content acceleration, do not involve removing gifted students from regular classrooms. As long as children are not socially and emotionally "hurried" by adult pressure to achieve early (Elkind, 1981), the socio-emotional impact of practices such as these appears to be positive (Cornell, Callahan & Loyd, 1991). Gifted education seems to be moving, albeit slowly, toward its rightful place among the many ways to adapt instruction to individual learners.

Students Who Are Educationally Disadvantaged

Students who are **educationally disadvantaged** have insufficient background experience for school success, often due to poverty. Educational disadvantage tends to occur most often when poverty affects the home, the school, *and* the community. At least 20 percent of children in the United States live in homes that are below the poverty line, the minimum income level established by the federal government to define low socioeconomic status. Of these children, four out of five are either black or Hispanic, even though only one out of four children in the United States is identified as such (U.S. Department of Education, 1994a, 1994b).

Poverty can affect school achievement and dropout rates.

Researchers have found that an educational disadvantage tends to show up very early in a child's achievement test scores, and that it contributes significantly to his or her risk of dropping out in secondary school. Only about 70 percent of children from low-income homes graduate from high school, as compared to 86 percent of children from middle-income homes and 97 percent of children from high-income homes. In other words, about a third of children from poor homes drop out. The most frequent reason for dropping out is, of course, low achievement (Natriello, McDill & Pallas, 1990).

Educational disadvantage can also be identified in achievement test scores. Figure 7.7 compares reading test scores at three grade levels for advantaged urban areas, nationally average students, and disadvantaged urban areas (U.S. Department of Education, 1993). Reading score 200 corresponds with partially developed skills and understanding; reading score 300 corresponds with understanding complicated information. In particular, note the early appearance and persistence of the effects of educational disadvantage. By fourth grade, disadvantaged children have not achieved partially developed skills and understanding, whereas advantaged children have. And by twelfth grade, disadvantaged children have not achieved understanding of complicated information—again, in contrast to advantaged children.

The statistical gap in achievement between disadvantaged students and advantaged students seems not to widen over time in Figure 7.7, but this appearance is deceiving inasmuch as the analysis omits school dropouts. The effect of these "lost" students on achievement statistics is to inflate the average scores of disadvantaged students throughout secondary school. In actuality, the achievement gap between disadvantaged and advantaged students grows larger throughout the school years.

> The difference in achievement between advantaged and disadvantaged students grows larger in the upper grades.

Figure 7.7   Reading Scores and Economic Status *(U.S. Department of Education, 1993, p. 110)*

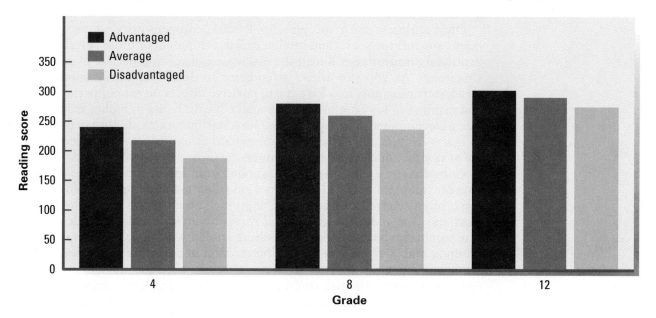

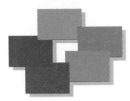

Intervention Programs and Extra Support

Here we consider two different but related kinds of strategic solutions for children who are educationally disadvantaged. The first is a group of intervention programs that exist to help children and families receive better care and prepare for school more successfully. These include both (1) prenatal-care services provided to expectant mothers and (2) **compensatory education programs** designed to reduce educational disadvantages resulting from poverty. You may or may not play a major role as the classroom teacher in these kinds of interventions, but you will definitely have a key role in the second type of strategic solution we will be examining—that of providing extra "teacher support" for educationally disadvantaged students in certain focused ways.

Before continuing, let's take a brief look at some programs with which you will probably have the least involvement but that are nonetheless important for you to know about. Because the nutrition of expectant mothers and infants is essential to normal psychological development (Lozoff, 1989), several intervention programs for disadvantaged children have been designed to provide maternal and child care. Programs such as Medicaid, Aid to Families with Dependent Children (AFDC), and the Supplemental Food Program for Women, Infants, and Children (WIC) all provide nutrition and health care for children who, because of poverty, are at risk for educational disadvantages later in their lives. As adequate shelter is also necessary for normal psychological development (Rafferty & Shinn, 1991), federal, state, and local governments give homeless families with children priority for available and affordable permanent housing.

Once children reach the preschool years, compensatory education programs support the social and intellectual development of those at risk for educational disadvantage. Recall the discussion of age-appropriate practices in Chapter 5. As you saw there, attendance in developmentally appropriate Head Start programs had long-term, positive effects on school performance and resulted in fewer referrals to special education and in higher graduation rates. Developmentally appropriate Head Start programs *create a disposition to learn—that is, a positive attitude toward school tasks*—in students who are at risk for educational disadvantage.

Compensatory education is also funded from kindergarten through grade 8 under Chapter I of the Elementary Consolidation and Improvement Act of 1981, often referred to simply as Chapter I. These funds are used by school districts (1) to reduce teacher/pupil ratios by hiring classroom aides, (2) to hire teachers who specialize in teaching students from disadvantaged backgrounds, and (3) to provide special instruction in cognitive skills. Special instruction is provided in the regular classroom, through pull out programs (often in resource rooms), through add on programs (that is, before or after school), in separate classrooms, or in schoolwide programs. The pull-out mode is most commonly used, but it has not proven to be more effective than the other approaches.

Compensatory education programs have also been designed for high school and beyond. Generally, these programs take the form of summer schools that attempt either to reduce achievement losses during the summer months or to ease the transition to college. The Summer Training and Education Program (STEP), for example, is a demonstration program that employs disadvantaged fourteen- and fifteen-year-olds while instructing them in basic reading and math skills. Upward Bound, on the other hand, is a summer residential program, held on college campuses, for disadvantaged high school juniors and seniors.

In your role as a classroom teacher, your compensatory education tasks may be quite varied. You might find yourself working with a Chapter I aide in your own room, referring students to a trained Chapter I teacher who teaches your students in a resource room, or perhaps picking up in-service training so that you become part of a Chapter I program yourself. Regardless of which task you take on, however, you should be aware that certain instructional strategies have traditionally been found to be more effective than others with educationally disadvantaged students. The most effective strategies include peer teaching (discussed in this chapter), computer-assisted instruction (Chapter 8), cognitive skills instruction (Chapters 9 and 10), mastery learning (Chapter 12), and cooperative learning (Chapter 12). Meanwhile, for a specific application of instructional strategy, see Reflection on Practice: "Math Their Way," which describes a hands-on approach to teaching math.

In addition to being aware of these kinds of instructional strategies, it is very important that as a classroom teacher you provide extra support and encouragement to your students. This objective is so important that it is presented here as a strategic solution on a par with the intervention programs just discussed. In fact, a study of the effects of classroom climate on the achievement of educationally disadvantaged elementary students found that the best environmental predictor of student achievement was teacher support, attention, and encouragement (Haynes & Comer, 1990).

Too often, educationally disadvantaged students feel that they have to go it alone with few resources and at substantial risk (Gore, 1991). Our support and involvement may be what makes the difference. That support will be returned with abundant appreciation, emotionally enriching our lives because we have taken the time to care. Teachers cannot be social workers, but we do need to remain aware that ours is a human services profession.

Evaluation: Intervention Programs and Extra Support

Do compensatory education programs and instructional strategies for educationally disadvantaged students effectively adapt instruction to learner characteristics? From the effectiveness research, we would have to conclude "yes, but." Cognitive and esteem gains from compensatory education tend to be significant during and shortly after the program, but they also fade out after the passage of time (McKey et al., 1985). In general, Chapter I programs have had a small positive impact on chances for academic success (Natriello, McDill & Pallas, 1990), and both teenage programs (STEP and Upward Bound) seem to be moderately successful insofar as they encourage larger percentages of disadvantaged students to continue their education.

What all of these programs have in common is that they promote a relationship to school that leads to the pursuit of further studies. This finding, though explored in only a handful of studies, suggests that the support role played by Head Start and Upward Bound is the most important one of all. Indeed, it corroborates the discovery described earlier—that the single most important predictor of student achievement is teacher support, attention, and encouragement (Haynes & Comer, 1990).

Students Who Are Culturally Different

Many ethnic groups make up the population of the United States.

Population statistics usually classify people in one of five or six racial categories, but ethnically most people are far more diverse. In the United States, for example, there are more than one hundred different **ethnic groups**, which consist of individuals who identify with a differentiated social and cultural heritage passed from one generation to the next. Most U.S. citizens identify with at least one ethnic group. And most (but not all) ethnic groups are identified by national or regional origin.

The ten largest groups in the United States are English, German, Irish, African American, French, Italian, Scottish, Polish, Mexican, and Native American. All of these groups except the African Americans, Mexicans, and Native Americans are from Europe and constitute what is sometimes called the "European emigrant majority." Other non-European groups—both the large groups mentioned here and other, smaller groups—are often referred to as **ethnic minority groups**.

Although the term *ethnic minority group* may seem objective, it is not universally accepted. Especially in a society as heterogeneous and eclectic as ours, some question why their particular group should be known as a "minority." And of course, as defined above, *any* group with unique cultural habits and traditions, and sometimes specific physical characteristics, is indeed an ethnic group. Thus, it could be argued that Swedes or Germans or any other specific European group do indeed constitute an ethnic minority.

In our current society, however, the term *ethnic minority* is usually used for groups that are of non-European background, whereas the term *mainstream* generally refers to the European emigrant majority. Minorities are often treated by members of the mainstream in a negative and prejudicial way; such treatment is known as *discrimination*. Discrimination occurs not

reflection on practice

"Math Their Way"

As a Chapter I aide I am currently involved with the "Math Their Way" program at my school. This program involves teaching math with the use of manipulatives (blocks, cubes that connect, plastic chain links, and so on) —anything that children can get their hands on. Recently, kindergarten teachers have been teaching children the correct way to write numbers. They write the number for the class to see and, while doing so, say a short rhyme about that number. The children then practice tracing the number with their hands, on the floor, and in the air, while repeating the rhyme.

At first I was unsure of how well the children would remember the rhymes. I felt this way until about two days ago, when I noticed one child tracing numbers in the sand. As he wrote the number, he said the rhyme that went along with that number, describing the way it is drawn. For example, "a straight line one is fun," and "around a tree and around a tree—that's three." These rhymes are very helpful to the children in writing their numbers. It gives them a way of relating to the construction of each number.

Jill Wright

Discussion Questions

1. **This teaching program uses what different sensory modes to help children learn numbers?**

2. **How might Piaget analyze this approach to learning? What developmental level(s) does the strategy address?**

3. **How might the technique be particularly suitable for a Chapter I kindergarten class? In other words, how is instruction adapted to the learner?**

just in the United States but in virtually every society throughout the world. In Ukraine, for example, ethnic Russians, Tartars, and Jews are among those who feel the effects of discrimination. In the Moslem republic of Azerbaijan ethnic Armenians (mostly Christians) are among those discriminated against. And in the United States, it is often the groups mentioned above— African Americans, Mexicans, and Native Americans—who suffer discrimination at the hands of the European emigrant majority.

Discrimination takes many forms. In educational materials, it may appear in the form of language, inadequate portrayals of ethnic minorities in textbooks, and culturally biased information. History textbooks in particular often reflect a European bias, which is unconsciously shared by many teachers in the United States—most of whom (87 percent) are of European ancestry themselves. Despite twenty years of progress toward a culture-fair treatment of history and other subjects, vestiges of a Eurocentric bias are still often packaged as truth rather than identified as a construction that is not shared by all people (e.g., Sleeter & Grant, 1991).

For instance, consider a history unit titled "The Westward Movement" in light of these questions: Who was moving west, the European emigrants or

Educational materials can be biased for or against certain ethnic groups.

the Native Americans? What region in the United States was referred to as the West? Why? The point of these questions is to help students understand that "The Westward Movement" is a Eurocentric term, inasmuch as Lakota Sioux were already living in the West and thus were not "moving" (Banks, 1992). Clearly, not just the title but the entire unit could be inherently biased.

What effect does a Eurocentric bias in content and curriculum have on students of non-European ancestry? John Ogbu (1992), an anthropologist, has found that the effect varies, depending on the relationship of the ethnic minority group to its schooling. Those groups whom he calls *immigrant minorities* (such as Chinese, Asian Indian, and Cuban) came to the United States voluntarily. Collectively, their school achievements apparently have *not* been affected adversely by Eurocentric biases. Ogbu theorizes that school has become a place for many immigrant minorities to achieve status; indeed, their graduation rates are often higher than those of the European emigrant majority (Gibson, 1989).

> Ethnic minorities may differ in how they perceive school and how they achieve.

In contrast, the groups whom Ogbu calls *involuntary minorities* (such as African Americans, Mexicans, and Native Americans) were brought into present society through slavery, conquest, or colonization. Their achievements *have* been affected adversely. School has not become a place for involuntary minorities to achieve status because discriminatory biases in schooling have been perceived as an aspect of subjugation. Accordingly, the graduation rates of involuntary minorities are generally lower than those of the European emigrant majority.

strategic solutions

Multicultural Education Strategies

The obvious remedy for this situation is to rid schools of discriminatory practices. **Multicultural education**, which helps individuals become aware of and appreciative of cultural diversity, was fundamentally designed to address the problem of discrimination. There are several different approaches to multicultural education (Sleeter & Grant, 1987); a particularly interesting one is called the *transformative* approach (Banks, 1993).

The fundamental strategy of the transformative approach is to *help students transform their personal knowledge in a way that reduces cultural bias.* As an initial activity, you can ask your students about their personal knowledge of a subject to be studied in the textbook. Continuing with the previous example, you might ask students what comes to mind when they think of "The West." What experiences did their ancestors have in this location? Were they similar to each other, or different? Next, you might discuss how "The West" is portrayed in popular culture by having students view the movie *How the West Was Won.* What are the film's major themes and images? How are different cultures represented? Do the representations seem fair?

Finally, you can present students with one or more contrasting perspectives to help them transform their personal and cultural knowledge into knowledge that represents more than one point of view. For instance, you might have them view the video *How the West Was Won and Lost,* narrated by Marlon Brando, or segments from the movie *Dances with Wolves.* Then, as the final part of the strategy, you can present the textbook unit. Students should be able to identify cultural biases in the textbook presentation, now that they realize the textbook represents constructed knowledge—that is, knowledge presented from a particular point of view. They will be in a better position to evaluate the culture-fairness of this unit and others than if they had begun their study of "The West" with just the textbook.

For maximum effectiveness, you should supplement transformative strategies in your classroom with other strategies. For instance, you might encourage a member of an involuntary minority group who has achieved status in the mainstream culture to return to the neighborhood school to speak to the children (Ogbu, 1992). Children—especially those who are members of involuntary immigrant minorities—need role models. This consideration is even more important in schools where the curriculum or personnel are Eurocentrically biased.

Evaluation: Multicultural Education Strategies

As an approach to multicultural education, the transformation of personal knowledge has the advantage of addressing cultural bias, in which many textbook authors, teachers, and students unconsciously particpate. If vestiges of discrimination were eliminated from the curriculum, however, schools would more likely be perceived by all students as a means to achieve status in society.

Does multicultural education reduce bias and improve the status of involuntary minority groups in school? Very few studies on this important issue have been reported. What does exist is adequate documentation of continued cultural biases in textbooks and among teachers as well as students. Clearly, further studies of the effectiveness of instructional strategies to promote multicultural awareness and appreciation need to be conducted.

Students with Linguistic Differences

Differences in language have long been the heritage of nations expanded by the inclusion of people from different cultures. Some people communicate well in their first language but have limited proficiency in their second.

When their second language is English, they are described as having *limited English proficiency (LEP)*. They are also often referred to as L2 (second-language) students.

L2 students come from many linguistic backgrounds, but the first language of most is Spanish. Dropout rates for Hispanic students in the United States are significantly higher than those for non-Hispanic whites or African Americans. In the twenty- to twenty-four-year-old age bracket, 90 percent of non-Hispanic whites and 83 percent of African Americans have graduated from high school or completed the GED, but only 59 percent of Hispanics have done so (U.S. Department of Education, 1994a). The high dropout rate of Hispanics, particularly in contrast to that of African Americans, is assumed to be the result of limited English proficiency.

> Limited English proficiency can increase dropout rates, especially for Hispanic Americans.

A group of eighth-grade L2 students who had just enough English proficiency to get by in class was recently studied by the U.S. Department of Education (1992). Two-thirds of their teachers were unaware that a language other than English was spoken at home; it was unlikely that instruction was adapted for these students in any way. The LEP status of these students appeared to contribute to relatively low educational aspirations and relatively high rates of failure on a reading achievement test. About one out of five L2 students who planned to attend college failed this test. In sum, the report provides evidence that the limited English proficiency of these students impeded both their educational plans and their academic progress.

strategic solutions

Bilingual Instruction

The overarching strategy for helping students who experience disadvantages in the classroom because of their limited English proficiency is **bilingual instruction**. All bilingual instruction involves (1) instruction in two languages, (2) use of the two languages as mediums for instruction in any or all subjects, and (3) study of the history and culture associated with each language. In the United States, such instruction was first mandated by the Bilingual Education Act of 1968. Subsequently, in 1974, the U.S. Supreme Court ruled on a suit brought on behalf of Chinese-speaking children in San Francisco (*Lau v. Nichols*) that school districts must help those who lack proficiency in English to comprehend their classroom experiences.

Before looking at some of the particular elements of bilingual strategies, we need to examine a fundamental underpinning of bilingual instruction in the United States. Unlike the situation in many other countries—including Canada and the European Community—bilingualism (that is, fluency in two languages) is typically *not* the underlying purpose of bilingual instruction in the United States. Nor has maintenance of the first language been a priority goal of bilingual instruction in this country. Indeed, when provided at all, such education is often controversial (McGroarty, 1992). This may seem a strange set of circumstances, but if you look again at the *Lau* decision just noted and reflect on the problems for students with LEP that were discussed in the previous section, you'll probably see why the compelling rationale for bilingual instruction in the United States has been the need to increase the relatively low achievement of language-minority students and to reduce their relatively high dropout rate.

This is an important factor for you as a classroom teacher because it explains why bilingual instruction in the United States generally focuses on the transition from learning in the first language (Spanish, Chinese, Korean, and so on) to learning in English as the language of the school and the wider culture. Far more often than not, bilingual education programs are used as vehicles to effect this transition. Toward this end, the general strategy of bilingual teachers is to teach in the language to be acquired but to use the first language of the learner when necessary to ensure comprehension (Cook, 1991; Fillmore & Valadez, 1986).

It is also important for you to realize that a certain amount of controversy surrounds this rationale. Indeed, there is a range of opinions, rather than a real consensus, regarding the degree and pacing of instruction that should occur in English, in first languages, and in subject areas. Some programs, known as English as a Second Language (ESL), provide early instruction in English so that students can learn sufficient English to become successful in the regular classroom. Others, which are true **bilingual education** programs, focus on ongoing instruction in the students' first language, usually providing simultaneous instruction in English as well. The differences between the two positions are often not just pedagogical but also may be political in nature.

Here are some additional terms associated with education for L2 students:

- *Maintenance* programs, such as bilingual education, aim to preserve the language-minority students' first language while they acquire a second language.
- *Transitional* programs, such as ESL, aim to facilitate the movement of students into educational programs that use only the second language. Transitional programs tend to last from three years (early exit) to six years (late exit).
- *Structured immersion* programs place students in classrooms where the teacher instructs in the language to be acquired but uses the first language of the students when they are having learning difficulties.

The extent to which the students' first language is used varies a great deal from teacher to teacher and program to program—even within a program. Often, the teachers must decide when it is necessary to communicate in the students' first language (a practice called *codeswitching*). For example,

Bilingual instruction is a general strategy to aid learners with limited English proficiency. What specific type of bilingual instruction is being practiced in this classroom? *(Elizabeth Crews)*

teachers commonly use the students' first language to keep individuals on task. At other times, a student may ask a question in his or her first language, and the teacher must decide whether the problem involves language comprehension—and if it does, whether it is more appropriate to respond in the student's first or second language.

So far we have focused on the various kinds of bilingual programs, involving specially trained bilingual teachers, that may exist in your school system. You need to be aware of these special programs, along with the rationales and strategies associated with them, as you work with L2 students in your own classroom. However, there are also ways in which you as a regular classroom teacher can adapt instruction to the needs of students acquiring a second language. Here are some recommendations (Genishi, 1989; Soto, 1991).

1. *Encourage use of the second language, and be patient.* Second-language learners may be silent at first, out of concern that you will judge them or fear that others may laugh.
2. When students do speak in English, *respond to the substance of their thoughts, modeling acceptance of transitional language.* Do not correct

their grammar. Use of an "interlanguage" is a natural stage in the development of a second language.

3. *Develop ideas about what you can do to help solve any comprehension problems.* Providing extra time or a peer tutor can be helpful.
4. *Support students' relationship to their first culture while helping to strengthen their relationship to their second culture.* Indeed, they have knowledge of their first culture and insights about their second culture that are potentially valuable to the class.

Evaluation: Bilingual Instruction

Bilingual programs ultimately have to be judged on the criteria relevant to the problem that they address, which in the United States has been low achievement and a high dropout rate for students with LEP. Research in this area is only beginning to emerge. One study recently conducted for the U.S. Department of Education (Ramirez, Yuen & Ramey, 1991) suggests that immersion and transitional bilingual programs tend to help language-minority students achieve national norms in reading and mathematics and, more specifically, that late-exit transition programs (continuing through elementary school) may help these students sustain their achievement gains. The researchers noted that parents were more involved in the late-exit programs inasmuch as they were "more likely to help their children with homework" (p. 14). Although the results of this study were not definitive (no comparison group was established, and only Hispanic language-minority students were studied), they do suggest that well-structured immersion and late-exit transitional programs are effective in achieving their goals.

CONCLUSION

In this chapter, you have surveyed a variety of individual differences that should be kept in mind when you plan instruction. No instructional problem can be adequately defined without consideration of the individual student characteristics on this checklist:

- The statistics tell us that you will almost certainly have several students with disabilities in each class. How do you plan to accommodate instruction for them?
- You are likely to have one or two students with exceptional gifts in each class. How do you plan to accommodate them?
- You will certainly have learners from diverse ethnic backgrounds. How can you decrease unintentional bias by increasing awareness and appreciation of cultural differences?

■ Unless you have a very unusual classroom, you will also have a number of students at risk because of educational disadvantage. How will you be prepared to help them?

■ Finally, you are likely to have one or more language-minority students. What special help can you offer a student with limited English proficiency?

These questions address the problem of adapting instruction to individual needs in a group setting. Your answers should be found long before you deliver instruction. Indeed, both the questions and their answers must be considered as you plan, if your goal of adaptive education is ever to be achieved.

concept paper

Development of Individual Differences

Purpose of the assignment

To analyze an autobiography so as to characterize the relationship between the author's individual difference and his or her education.

Directions for the assignment

1. Determine how the writer conceives of his or her identity, and how that conception has been affected by education.

    a. Choose an autobiography by (*not* a biography about) a person whose characteristics as a child would fit a category of individual difference mentioned in this chapter (such as learning disabled, blind/deaf, gifted, educationally disadvantaged, or ethnic minority).

    b. Read the early chapters for relevant passages about the developmental impact of his or her individual difference.

       (1) How did the difference change (or not change) during the developmental years?

       (2) How was the difference seen by significant others?

       (3) How did attitudes and actions of others affect how the author felt about him- or herself?

    c. Skim back over the early chapters, and read the rest of the book for relevant passages about the impact of teachers and school on the author's individual difference.

       (1) How did teachers and school change (or not change) the difference?

       (2) Did teachers or school affect how the individual difference was seen by others? If so, in what way?

       (3) Did teachers or school affect how the author felt about him- or herself? If so, in what ways?

2. You should have enough material at this point to write a four-page paper answering the question, "How did teachers and schooling affect a crucial aspect of the author's self-concept?"

SUMMARY

1. As life progresses, differences among children that are first of minimal significance tend to increase. As a teacher, your task will generally be not to try to reduce these differences but instead to adapt instruction to individual needs in a group setting.

2. The range of what is "normal" spans a large degree of variability. This means, for example, that the normal range of skills in reading in a typical fourth grade classroom can include as many as four or five grade levels.

3. One means teachers often use to meet the challenge inherent in such variation is ability grouping. However, ability grouping is only effective if it genuinely adapts instruction to individual differences.

4. Individual differences also include disabilities. There are four categories of students with disabilities—as defined by law—that you are most likely to encounter in your classroom. These are students with learning disabilities, students with speech and language impairments, students with mental retardation, and students with serious emotional disturbance.

5. As a classroom teacher, you will play an important role in developing strategies to address the needs of learners with disabilities. You will be involved in the design of an educational plan for the child (an Individualized Education Program, or IEP) and probably in its implementation as well.

6. Under the policy of inclusion, students with special needs are educated in regular classrooms as much as possible. The policy of mainstreaming and the policy of the least restrictive environment are two means of achieving inclusion.

7. Other students for whom you will need to adapt instruction are students who are gifted, students who are educationally disadvantaged, and students who are culturally or linguistically different.

8. Multicultural education benefits not only students who are in a cultural minority but those in the majority as well. It can provide an effective means of addressing children's attitudes toward discrimination.

KEY TERMS

variability p. 268

norm p. 269

normal curve p. 269

homogeneous grouping p. 275

heterogeneous grouping p. 275

specific learning disabilities p. 279

speech impairments p. 281

language impairments p. 281

mental retardation p. 281

serious emotional disturbance p. 282

least restrictive environment p. 285

inclusion p. 285

aptitude-treatment-interaction (ATI) research p. 288

peer tutoring p. 288

giftedness p. 291

contract p. 295

educationally disadvantaged p. 298

compensatory education programs p. 300

ethnic groups p. 302

ethnic minority groups p. 302

multicultural education p. 304

bilingual instruction p. 306

bilingual education p. 307

SUGGESTED RESOURCES

Banks, J. A. (1994). Transforming the mainstream curriculum. *Educational Leadership, 51* (8), 4–8. This short article provides you with an excellent introduction to the transformative approach to multicultural education.

Colangelo, N. and G. A. Davis. (1991). *Handbook of Gifted Education.* Boston, Mass.: Allyn and Bacon. A very useful collection of articles that cover a wide range of issues in gifted education.

Fuchs, D. and L. S. Fuchs. (1994). Inclusive Schools Movement and the Radicalization of Special Education Reform. *Exceptional Children, 60,* 294–309. This article puts the inclusive school movement in a historical perspective and advocates rational limitations.

Stainback, S. and W. Stainback. (1992). *Curriculum Considerations in Inclusive Classrooms.* Baltimore, Md.: Paul H. Brookes. This book contains many ideas for implementing inclusion strategies in the classroom.

Approaches to Learning

Part III introduces you to the learning process through which educational goals are achieved. You will also learn about creative thinking and how to identify and solve motivational and management problems.

Behavioral Learning Theories: Achieving the Goal of Behavior Change

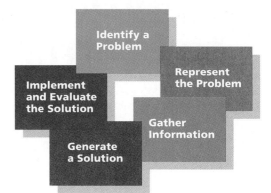

Orientation

The goal of this chapter is to familiarize you with the basic principles of the behavioral approach to learning and their application in your classroom. You will discover how these principles can be used to help you gather information about learning activities, generate a strategy, and implement a solution to achieve the goal of behavior change. Toward the end of the chapter, you will also meet the observational learning approach, which grows out of behavioral principles but includes cognitive aspects of learning. As you read, look for answers to these questions:

- **Why is conducting a learning analysis so important?**

- **What makes the consequences of a behavior so significant?**

- **What are four different behavioral contingencies?**

- **Why is positive reinforcement used so frequently and punishment used far less frequently in education?**

- **Why are natural consequences more effective than contrived consequences?**

- **What is programmed instruction, and how does it use computers?**

- **Which program types best suit the behavioral learning approach?**

- **What role do expectations play in observational or social learning?**

- **What are the four elements of observational learning, and which is the key element?**

- **What is the relationship between cognitive modeling and self-talk?**

learning journal

Principles of Behavior Change

While reading about behavior change, make Learning Journal entries about specific experiences in which principles of behavior change apply. Tell what led up to the experience, name the principles of behavior change involved, describe how the principles were involved, and describe any relevant outcome. This chapter contains descriptions of the following principles or their applications related to behavior change:

- discrimination
- generalization
- learning analysis
- learning hierarchy
- positive reinforcement
- presentation punishment
- removal punishment
- negative reinforcement
- scheduling
- contingency contract

- shaping
- drill-and-practice programs
- tutorial programs
- Hawthorne effect
- functional value of behavior
- modeling
- vicarious reinforcement
- self-reinforcement
- cognitive modeling

SOLVING THE PROBLEM OF BEHAVIOR CHANGE

So far, you have learned how to identify and represent instructional problems. The key to clear representation of an instructional problem is careful consideration of the givens of your situation—including the characteristics of your students—as you set goals for instruction. The next few chapters will focus on ways to attain goals by sequencing activities to develop instructional strategies.

In this chapter we will focus on achieving the goal of behavior change through application of principles of learning derived from behavioral learning theories. Behavioral theories define **learning** as relatively permanent change in behavior due to experience. Because you know what goals are, and how to interpret, analyze, and write behavioral objectives, you already have a firm foundation on which to build new knowledge from this chapter.

The behavioral definition of learning makes possible a systematic approach to instructional problem solving. In brief, the process looks like this:

> Learning is a relatively permanent change in behavior caused by experience.

- A problem is identified and defined in terms of a *behavioral objective.*
- Information is gathered through a *learning analysis* to discover activities that will lead to the achievement of the objective.
- A strategy is generated and implemented through a *behavior analysis* and a *program of instruction.*
- The strategy is evaluated through *error analysis.*

This chapter focuses on several key steps in the middle of the process—learning analysis, behavior analysis, and programs of instruction. We will look at how behavioral learning theories apply to these steps that teachers follow as they design instruction.

How do teachers change students' behavior? To answer that in a practical way, let's visit the classroom of Mrs. Olive, who teaches consumer mathematics. Consumer math is a basic version of secondary math that focuses on applications such as computing pay, buying food and goods, budgeting, and maintaining checking or savings accounts. If you pick up a consumer math textbook, you will notice that the topics have been carefully sequenced in terms of progressions in life and in math skills.

The day I visited Mrs. Olive's class, the objective listed in the textbook was to *estimate quotients of whole numbers using compatible numbers.* The skill being developed was estimation of answers for division problems. This complex skill rested on understanding the concept of compatible numbers, or numbers that divide easily into each other (such as 20 divided by 5). The concept of compatible numbers rested on the ability to calculate simple division problems in one's head, or do "mental math." Students had been working on sharpening their mental math skills in the previous lesson. Now they were turning to the concept of compatible numbers and to the more complex skill of estimating quotients based on them.

Learning in Mrs. Olive's Consumer Math Class

When the students entered the classroom, Mrs. Olive was busy writing problems on the board. After the second bell rang, she said, "While I'm checking homework, copy down the problems on the board, but use *mental* math to solve them." Grade book in hand, Mrs. Olive went down the rows of desks, glancing at the homework papers displayed on each desk to see if the mental math problems left over from the last lesson had written answers. She said something encouraging (such as "good" or "better") to most students. If homework was missing or unattempted, a dot went into her grade book. The dot represented a deduction of 5 points from 100 freely given at the beginning of the term for homework.

After she completed her rounds, Mrs. Olive read the answers to the homework problems, repeated any answer requested, and then asked students if they wanted any problems worked on the board. Review took the form of working selected problems, calling students to the board to explain their solutions to the in-class problems, and discussing the in-class problems, all in the first fifteen minutes. A twenty-minute lesson followed about estimation skills.

She first introduced the concept of compatible numbers, providing both examples (such as 730/10, $420 \div 30$, and $70\overline{)28,000}$) and nonexamples (such as 735/11, $426 \div 28$, and $61\overline{)28,753}$). Next she presented a series of division problems with *in*compatible numbers (such as 896/47). She then queried, "How do we estimate the solution to problems when the numbers are *in*compati-

Consumer math involves applied skills. Skilled shoppers use consumer math every day to make quick and accurate estimates. *(Bob Daemmrich)*

ble?" The task involved using mental math to find compatible numbers and estimate quotients. Some of these problems were simple, and some were more complex. All were worked individually by students in their seats and then by volunteers at the board. Mrs. Olive was careful to accept a variety of answers to any estimation problem, pointing out that estimation did not result in uniquely correct answers.

During the last few minutes of the lesson, Mrs. Olive challenged the class with the question "Why not use rounding to estimate quotients?" Rounding was an estimation skill students had learned the previous week for difficult addition, subtraction, and multiplication problems. She put several division problems to the students, some of which yielded no compatible numbers through rounding the numerator and the denominator. The class discovered a simple procedure for solving estimation problems: when an estimation problem involves addition, subtraction, or multiplication, use rounding; when it involves division, use compatible numbers.

Finally, Mrs. Olive gave a worksheet to students so that they could practice this problem-solving skill for the remainder of the period. During these last few minutes, she circulated to help individuals who were having difficulty. The worksheet presented sixteen math problems that required estimation, some of which were division problems and some of which were not, some of which were word problems and some of which were not. Homework consisted of finishing the worksheet. Students busied themselves with the worksheet, which, along with the in-class problems, would go into their notebooks. As part of an evaluation strategy, students would have a quiz at the end of the week and an open-notebook test before the end of the term.

Achieving the Goal of Behavior Change

Instructional plans can change student behavior.

Significant changes in behavior can occur in the course of a single period, and Mrs. Olive used several practices specifically designed to change behavior. First, she identified and defined the instructional problem as a behavioral objective. She built on the objective in the textbook, which was to estimate quotients of whole numbers using compatible numbers. Mrs. Olive's objective sounded simpler, yet was more difficult to achieve: *to solve all estimation problems with whole numbers.* Her objective went beyond the textbook to include a problem-solving skill that involved higher-order thinking.

Higher-order thinking, an intellectual skill, required mastery of prerequisite skills. The most important prerequisite to problem solving in estimation was knowledge of the rules for estimation. Estimates in addition, subtraction, and multiplication were made by rounding, whereas estimates in division were made by using compatible numbers. The prerequisite for estimating quotients was finding compatible numbers. This skill, in turn, required understanding the concept of compatible numbers and using mental division. Finally, understanding key concepts (such as quotient and whole number) required skills of elementary arithmetic.

Instructional goals may affect the sequence of items to be learned.

Mrs. Olive approached instruction by reversing the order of the skills that were prerequisite to problem solving:

- First, she reviewed skills in mental division.
- Second, she taught students to find compatible numbers, distinguishing them from incompatible numbers.
- Third, she had students apply the higher-order rule for estimating quotients.
- Fourth, she helped students develop a problem-solving procedure that allowed them to solve all whole-number estimation problems.

Mrs. Olive's lesson consisted of achieving four objectives sequenced from simple to complex. The worksheet merely extended practice at problem solving into homework. (See Figure 8.1.)

Mrs. Olive's approach to teaching estimation skills sounds technical, and it is, but consider her subject and her students. Technical skills are involved in making quick and accurate estimates. Skilled shoppers and salespeople use these skills every day. Mrs. Olive's consumer math students were being taught them in a way that was more precise than teaching in most classrooms. Let's take a closer look at this teaching technique.

LEARNING ANALYSIS: GATHERING INFORMATION ABOUT LEARNING ACTIVITIES

Before you can design a sequence of activities to achieve the goal of behavior change, you have to be able to discover what leads to that particular behavior. You can do this very systematically by performing a **learning analysis,** which is a procedure for discovering prerequisites to the achievement of a behavioral objective. A learning analysis permits the construction of a **learning hi-**

Estimation

Objectives (activities):
    1. Use mental math (review)
    2. Use compatible numbers (discussion)
       a. Understand concept
       b. Find compatible numbers
    3. Estimate quotients (discussion)
    4. Solve estimation problems (discussion, homework)

Evaluation:
    Homework, quiz Friday

Figure 8.1
Mrs. Olive's Lesson Plan

erarchy, which is a logically arranged sequence of activities to achieve the goal of behavior change.

Robert Gagné (1985) pioneered the use of a learning analysis by teachers to identify relevant learning activities. Today, this process stands as a model of instructional design in subjects as diverse as math (Carnine, 1993), music (Maclin, 1993), and human environmental sciences (Haass, 1988). Through a learning analysis and a learning hierarchy, a teacher can devise a sequence of activities that leads to a goal broadly defined as behavior change. We will examine this process in some depth in the Strategic Solutions section. Before that, however, you need to understand the concepts on which learning analysis is based—those of behavioral learning theories (Resnick, 1976).

> Learning analysis permits discovery of prerequisites.

Operant Conditioning: Learning Processes

The most important behavioral learning theory in the twentieth century was that of psychologist B. F. Skinner (1938), who proposed a number of behavioral learning principles collectively known as **operant conditioning.** Skinner defined *operants* as behaviors that affect the environment. He distinguished them from *respondents*, which are reflexes. By the 1960s, many psychologists were applying the principles of operant conditioning in institutional settings, including schools, to make learning more efficient.

The basic principles of operant conditioning fall into two categories: *learning processes* and *consequences.* Although these categories overlap, they have led to different applications of learning theory in education. Learning processes led to learning analysis, and consequences led to behavioral analysis. Let's look now at some of the most basic operant conditioning principles that pertain to learning processes and that undergird the process of learning analysis.

Discrimination

Skinner and many other behavioral psychologists investigated two processes that they believed were necessary and sufficient for learning to occur. They

Discrimination refers to the ability to recognize the difference between one thing and another. This young girl is making two discriminations simultaneously to construct a series—what are they?
(Paul Conklin)

Discrimination is the ability to recognize differences.

called these processes *discrimination* and *generalization*. **Discrimination** is the ability to recognize the difference between one thing and another. Discrimination occurs whenever you and I learn, but it is perhaps most evident in the learning of young children.

Gagné (1985) suggested that discriminations are the building blocks of concepts. Often young children are given sorting tasks to help them discriminate colors, shapes, sizes, and textures. Important discriminations are necessary to distinguish letters (such as *B* and *D*), words (such as alligator and elevator), and concepts (such as today and tomorrow).

In Mrs. Olive's class, students had to make discriminations to understand the concept of compatible numbers. Her technique for teaching discriminations was to ask students whether two numbers (that she had invented) were compatible for division and then provide students with feedback. In some cases the numbers were compatible (such as 730 divided by 10), and in some cases they were not (such as 731 divided by 11). The basic procedure used by all teachers to teach discrimination of concepts is to require students to distinguish examples from nonexamples, providing appropriate feedback to students for each response.

Generalization

Generalization is the transfer of learning to other situations.

The process of **generalization** occurs whenever a specific response transfers to features of the environment that have not been responded to before. When a child uses arithmetic learned in elementary school to solve a mental math problem, the child is generalizing a response made in a lower grade. In education, we call generalization the **transfer** of learning.

Generalization of comparatively simple skills to more complex responses is called *vertical* transfer. Arithmetic skills transfer vertically to mental math skills, and mental math skills transfer vertically (or generalize) to the

reflection on practice

Lateral Transfer

In 1989, I was substitute teaching in a high school alternative class called Maryland Tomorrow. This class/program was especially designed for under-achieving, high-risk students who were on the verge of dropping out of school. In this program, students learned about practical things in life, including balancing a checkbook, filling out job applications, budgeting, renting a house or an apartment, buying a house or car, and completing income tax forms. I discovered later how beneficial this program actually was. I ran into three or four of the pupils I had taught in this class later on in the year and the following summer. None of them had dropped out of school. Three of them had graduated or were preparing to graduate from high school and had found jobs, and they had found or were looking for their own apartments (using what they had learned in the program about how to go about these tasks). So the skills that they had learned in the Maryland Tomorrow program had trans-ferred and been applied to living in the "real" world.

Two of these students also told me that had it not been for the program, they would have probably dropped out of school and learned nothing, be-cause they had "had it" with the regular courses and were having too much trouble learning in them. I really feel strongly that this sort of program should exist in all school systems.

Marty Nunnelly

Discussion Questions

1. It is obvious that skills taught in class were transferring to real life. What enabled these students to accomplish a relatively easy transfer of the skills for daily living?

2. Do you think college-bound students or academic achievers should be enrolled in such courses? If such courses or skills were included for all students in the curriculum, what might the consequences be?

3. Discuss this entry in light of your perceived need for skills for daily survival as a new teacher. What are some classroom survival skills that you need? What might be left out, if you were only taught survival skills to prepare you to teach?

finding of compatible numbers. Generalization to different environments (rather than to more complex skills) is called *horizontal* or *lateral* transfer. Word problems require lateral transfer of math skills. Lateral transfer also in-cludes generalization of skills from school to applied settings, such as math skills to buying goods, planning a garden, or anticipating expenses (see Reflection on Practice: Lateral Transfer).

Generalization operated in Mrs. Olive's classroom to permit the transfer of simple skills to more complex ones as the sequence of activities unfolded. It also permitted the transfer of skills from simplified to applied problems. Throughout the lesson, Mrs. Olive facilitated generalization by varying the format and difficulty of division problems. She used different symbolic

Transfer may be vertical or lateral.

representations for division (/, ÷ , ⌐), different problem types, and different degrees of difficulty. The basic procedure used by teachers to facilitate generalization is to vary examples to represent all types of cases.

Behavioral psychologists believe that discrimination and generalization are necessary and sufficient processes for learning to occur. If no one ever made discriminations, nothing would ever be learned. If no one ever generalized, learning would never develop beyond individual instances. Both learning processes have to occur for learning to develop, and in the behavioral view these two processes are sufficient to explain all learning.

> Behaviorists believe discrimination and generalization produce all learning.

strategic solutions

Learning Analysis

Learning analysis is built on the processes of discrimination and generalization and consists of three stages: (1) *classify a learning task*, (2) *construct a learning hierarchy*, and (3) *assess prior knowledge* (Gagné, 1985). Of greatest importance to the development of a solution to an instructional problem is the construction of a learning hierarchy because it results in a set of real activities. Let's look at that step here as well as at the steps on either side of it.

Classify Learning Tasks

The first stage of learning analysis comprises categorizing the task. Gagné believed that any learning task can be classified according to hierarchies similar to the cognitive, affective, and psychomotor taxonomies that you considered in Chapter 3. However, Gagné offered a somewhat different set of categories: *verbal information, intellectual skills, cognitive strategies, attitudes,* and *motor skills.* Among these five categories, intellectual skills are of greatest interest for our purposes because of the relation of these skills to almost all learning tasks.

Intellectual skills involve *making discriminations, learning concepts, using rules, using higher-order rules,* and *using procedures* (see Table 8.1). As you examine this classification of intellectual skills, notice how—although there are few exact correspondences—it runs parallel to the categories in the taxonomy for the cognitive domain.

Making discriminations. You already know that discriminations involve the ability to distinguish one thing from another. They are an intellectual skill in their own right, but they are also useful, in fact a prerequisite, to the formation of concepts.

Learning concepts. A **concept** is a class or collection of things whose members share one or more characteristics. A concept is developed by generalizing from particular examples and discriminating examples from nonexamples. For instance, in Mrs. Olive's lesson students learned what compatible

Table 8.1   *Intellectual Skills and the Cognitive Domain*

Intellectual Skills (Gagné)	Cognitive Domain (Bloom)
Making discriminations	Knowledge
Learning concepts	Comprehension
Using rules	Application
Using higher-order rules	Analysis
Using procedures	Synthesis
	Evaluation

numbers were by determining what characteristic they had in common—namely, the ability to divide easily into each other. Concept learning required tudents to identify examples of compatible numbers (such as 12/4 and 260/10) and then discriminate examples from nonexamples (such as 11/4 and 263/14). Other concepts in the consumer math lesson were estimate, quotient, and whole numbers, all of which had been learned in previous consumer math lessons or through experiences with arithmetic in elementary school.

Using rules.   **Rules** are relatively simple relationships between concepts. For example, finding compatible numbers is a rule that relates compatible numbers to estimation. Students use the rule in enough specific cases to understand how to apply it. For example, the rule for finding compatible numbers required trying out different possibilities and accepting a degree of inaccuracy in relation to the actual problem.

Using higher-order rules.   Rules that are composed of more than one rule are known as **higher-order rules.** To estimate quotients of whole numbers using compatible numbers required finding compatible numbers *before* determining the quotient.

Using procedures.   Multiple rules in a sequence form **procedures.** When Mrs. Olive taught students a procedure for deciding which higher-order estimation rule to apply, she taught problem solving. A procedure was not developed in the textbook lesson in consumer math, but Mrs. Olive modified the lesson to help students develop a problem-solving skill at the end and apply it in the homework.

Construct a Learning Hierarchy

The second stage of a learning analysis is the design of a learning hierarchy. It proceeds by asking, "What knowledge, intellectual skills, attitudes, and psychomotor performances are prerequisite to the accomplishment of this learning task?" Prerequisites to a single task may be found in only one domain or in several. Many psychomotor performances, for example, have attitudinal prerequisites (such as willingness to perform) and intellectual skill prerequisites (such as use of a rule) in addition to motor prerequisites (such as a specific set of fundamental movements).

As you discover each prerequisite, ask yourself, "What are the prerequisites of this task?" The result of repeatedly asking this question is a hierarchy of related tasks, each stated in the form of a behavioral objective. For example, in Mrs. Olive's consumer math lesson the prerequisites of deciding which estimation skill to use (problem solving) were skills at estimation (higher-order rules). The prerequisites of estimating quotients (a higher-order rule) were skills at finding compatible numbers (a rule) and mental division.

Figure 8.2 portrays something like the learning hierarchy that structured the skill of estimation in consumer math. Note the portions of the hierarchy that Mrs. Olive used in just one lesson (green) and how she adapted the hierarchy to include instruction in problem solving (top box). Given the state of most textbook exercises in math and other subject areas, you may need to make similar adaptations of textbook material to include higher-order thinking and problem solving in your lesson plans. Learning hierarchies are not difficult to construct once you have mastered the topic to be taught and are motivated to teach it. Often, however, preservice and novice teachers find these hierarchies difficult because they are introduced with inappropriate examples.

**Figure 8.2
An Incomplete
Hierarchy of Estimation
Skills**

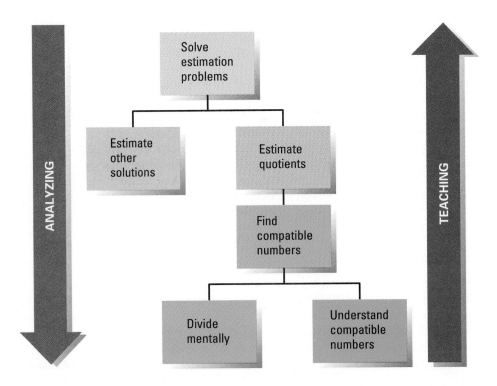

Say, for instance, that you are performing a learning analysis for this objective: compare productivity between monopolistic and competitive firms in a free-enterprise economy. You are far more likely to be interested in analyzing this objective, and to have the structural knowledge to do so, if you are a social science teacher than if you are a math teacher or an elementary teacher. Similarly, an elementary teacher might be more interested in developing a learning hierarchy for beginning reading (see Figure 8.3), his or her own area of expertise, than a high school teacher would be. (If you realize that both interest in teaching a subject and familiarity with it are prerequisites to the skill of conducting a learning analysis, you can use this experience to gain a deeper understanding of the importance of prerequisites to *all* learning, even your own.)

Assess Prior Knowledge

The third stage of a learning analysis involves a preassessment of the knowledge of the learner in order to identify learner needs. For example, students in a consumer math class who are learning to apply the rule for estimating quotients would be able to do elementary mathematics, but not all would have mastered mental math skills. Because estimating quotients requires mental division, some students would need additional exercises in this skill before they could estimate quotients. Mrs. Olive identified "entry-level" students

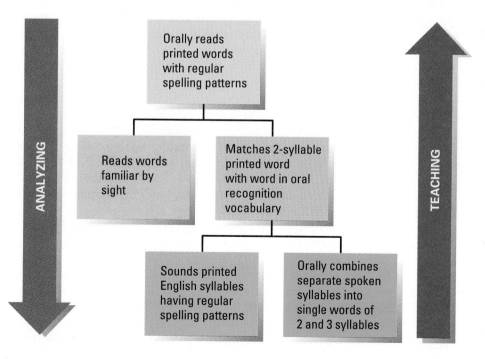

Figure 8.3
An Incomplete Hierarchy of Reading Skills
(Adapted from Gagné, 1991, p. 140)

ANALYZING

TEACHING

Orally reads printed words with regular spelling patterns

Reads words familiar by sight

Matches 2-syllable printed word with word in oral recognition vocabulary

Sounds printed English syllables having regular spelling patterns

Orally combines separate spoken syllables into single words of 2 and 3 syllables

informally during the homework review. These students were the ones she helped at the end of the lesson.

Evaluation: Learning Analysis

Learning analysis results in sequences of activities that are more systematic in their approach to skill development than are intuitive sequences used by many teachers. Is the analytic effort necessary to construct a learning hierarchy justified by the outcome? Learning hierarchies result in measurably improved achievement at least some of the time (Walberg, 1986). The key question is, When are learning hierarchies most useful?

In the 1960s, educational researchers studied the effectiveness of "ascending" sequences of objectives, particularly from "low" to "high" intellectual skills. Collectively, these studies became known as the "scramble" studies because they compared a hypothesized sequence of objectives (and activities) with a scrambled sequence. Many of the researchers were surprised and disappointed to discover that the sequence hypothesized to lead to improved learning sometimes made no difference in achievement when compared to a scrambled sequence (Van Patten, Chao & Reigeluth, 1986). What happened?

One hypothesis, which is widely accepted today (e.g., Carnine, 1993), is that the higher-ability individuals used in many of the studies were able to figure out relationships between skills without the help of a hierarchy. This hypothesis explains why lower-ability individuals did better when they had sequenced materials than scrambled materials and why higher-ability groups experienced no advantage to skills sequencing. It also explains why subjects (such as consumer math) that are taken by lower-ability students are often carefully sequenced by educators and why the students' learning benefits from careful sequencing.

Another hypothesis is that the effectiveness of skill sequences is related to the degree of structure in a subject. Because an agreed-on structure for knowledge and skills exists in fields such as mathematics, the natural sciences, and life sciences, learning analyses are easier to conduct in these subjects than they are in fields in which no consensus exists about structure (Dunn, 1984). Learning hierarchies designed to develop skills in mathematics and science are probably more clearly advantageous for most students than are learning hierarchies in subjects such as history or language arts.

Are learning anlayses unnecessary in less well structured subjects such as language arts? Researchers have compared the achievement of students who have learned to read through the basal approach (skill sequences) with the achievement of those who have learned through approaches based on whole-language beliefs (no preset skill sequences). In general, they have found that skill sequences do not diminish achievement, but they do not always enhance it either (Stahl & Miller, 1989). Skill sequencing in learning to read may benefit children who are slow to acquire literacy skills through ap-

Skill sequencing—often encountered by children learning from basal readers—does not diminish achievement, but it does not always enhance it either. In practice, elementary teachers need to use different approaches for different children. *(Jeffrey W. Myers/ Stock Boston Inc.)*

proaches such as whole-language immersion. In practice, many elementary teachers use different approaches to literacy with different children or different approaches at different times with the same child.

Overall, a learning analysis is a useful procedure to gather information about relevant learning activities and how to sequence them.

BEHAVIORAL ANALYSIS: GENERATING A SOLUTION

Sequencing in and of itself is not a complete or powerful enough strategy to solve an instructional problem because it doesn't automatically lead to discrimination and generalization. To understand what will motivate these types of learning, we must look at another aspect of behavioral theory, behavioral analysis. Let's define it first.

Suppose a child in your class raises his or her hand to ask a question. The question is what psychologists call the **antecedent** of the behavior, or what immediately precedes it. Behavioral psychologists would say that the antecedent of a behavior is relatively unimportant compared with its **consequence,** or what immediately follows it. You smile when you see the hand go up and say the child's name. Your smile, friendly way of responding, and perhaps praise for the question itself are perceived by the child as consequences of raising a hand to ask a question. If these consequences strengthen behavior (lead to more hand raising with questions), a discrimination has occurred.

The correlation of an activity with the stimuli that immediately precede and follow it is called a **behavioral analysis,** or, simply, an *ABC* analysis. *A*

Behavioral analysis concerns the antecedents and consequences of a behavior.

stands for the antecedent (what happens before the behavior), *B* for the behavior or activity, and *C* for the consequence (what happens after the behavior). In Mrs. Olive's class, some of the antecedents for specific behaviors were math problems written in the book or on the board and expectations about homework. The students' behavior involved everything from using math skills, to bringing homework to class, to doing the worksheet. Consequences ranged from a dot in Mrs. Olive's grade book, to praise from her for improvement, to having fewer books to carry home if the worksheet was finished by the end of the period. To explore consequences further, let's examine the applicable principles of operant conditioning and then investigate how these principles come together to form an instructional strategy.

Operant Conditioning: Consequences

The dependent relationship between a behavior and its consequence is known as a **contingency.** Contingencies can always be stated as "if . . . then" relationships between a behavior ("If you finish your worksheet in class,") and a consequence ("then you do not have to take it home with you"). Contingencies can be formulated either to strengthen a behavior or to weaken one. Relationships between behaviors and consequences that strengthen the behaviors are known as **contingencies of reinforcement.**

Four different types of contingencies are summarized in Figure 8.4. They are based on relationships between any given behavior and different possibilities for its consequence (or what follows it). A consequence for any given behavior can be either presented or removed. In addition, it can be either a **reinforcer,** a stimulus that increases the probability of a behavior when it follows that behavior, or an **aversive stimulus,** an undesirable consequence that weakens the probability of a behavior.

> Contingencies of reinforcement involve consequences that strengthen a behavior.

Positive Reinforcement

The presentation of a reinforcer following a behavior is known as **positive reinforcement.** In Mrs. Olive's class, the students were visibly pleased when they learned that their answers to various homework problems were correct. The more correct answers they discovered, the more closely they listened for correct answers.

Correct answers are generally reinforcing because most students want to be right, but the power of a reinforcer lies not in itself but in its effect on the behavior of an individual. That is, what is a reinforcer to one student may not be a reinforcer to another. Praise and grades, for example, are generally assumed to be reinforcers, but they do not affect the behavior of all students in the same way. Some students go out of their way to avoid praise or high grades, which might negatively affect their standing in a peer group.

> What works as positive reinforcement varies from student to student.

Presentation Punishment

The application of an aversive stimulus, which is usually a painful experience, is known as **presentation punishment.** Examples of presentation pun-

	Present	**Remove**
Reinforcer	Positive reinforcement Giving correct answers to reinforce listening	Removal punishment Removing points for not bringing homework
Aversive stimulus	Presentation punishment Making critical comments about grammar errors	Negative reinforcement Removing fear of being incorrect

Figure 8.4
Four Types of Contingencies

ishment include reprimands and critical comments on papers. It was not observed in Mrs. Olive's classroom, and, as we discuss in the next section, it is far less likely to be used in classrooms than some form of reinforcement.

Removal Punishment

Also decreasing the likelihood of a behavior, **removal punishment** involves the removal of a reinforcer rather than the application of an aversive stimulus. A dot placed in Mrs. Olive's grade book was removal punishment (signaling removal of points) for failure to bring homework to class. Removal punishment often translates into the loss of a privilege—in this case, homework points that had been freely awarded at the beginning of the term.

> Punishment can involve applying an aversive stimulus or removing a reinforcer.

Negative Reinforcement

The removal of an aversive stimulus following a behavior is called **negative reinforcement.** In Mrs. Olive's class, negative reinforcement occurred when the teacher demonstrated acceptance of different estimates as solutions to problems. She removed the undesirable consequence of being wrong. As a result, students were offering multiple estimates for quotients by the end of the lesson, whereas they had offered only one or two earlier in the lesson.

> Negative reinforcement removes an aversive stimulus in order to strengthen behavior.

Many people have difficulty distinguishing negative reinforcement from punishment. This difficulty occurs for two reasons. First, the label itself causes confusion. The word *negative* typically implies something undesirable. However, in the case of negative reinforcement, the negative or undesirable element is being *removed.* Think of this as a kind of "double negative"—the overall effect is positive.

Second, many people don't see the difference between negative reinforcement and punishment. For example, negative reinforcement in its common form might sound like this: "I know that you are hungry, but we can't go to lunch until you quiet down." Although this appears to be a punishment, it is not. Unlike punishment, which happens after the fact, the recipient has some control over the situation. He or she can choose to quiet down in order to escape the condition of being hungry. Punishment always involves some sanction, such as loss of five minutes of lunch, or the assignment of clean-up duty. Remember, punishment always tries to *decrease* a particular behavior. In this case, the attempt is to *strengthen* or reinforce the particular behavior (self-control).

> Punishment decreases a behavior, while negative reinforcement strengthens a behavior.

These four principles of operant conditioning form a basic set of consequences on which you can elaborate if you choose to learn more about contingencies. The major distinction to be made is between reinforcement and punishment. Skinner and many other behavioral psychologists believed that educators have underused reinforcement and overused punishment.

Constraints on the Use of Punishment

Punishment is less common in the management of academic behavior than in the management of social behavior in schools (see Chapter 13). Punishment of students for failing to learn may occasionally be necessary for positive incentives to be effective (Pfiffer & O'Leary, 1987), but punishment does not teach students what to learn and can have emotional side effects, such as fear, anger, or resentment, that interfere with learning.

> Punishment for failure to learn may have negative emotional side effects.

Each of these side effects is accompanied by a distinctive behavior (Skinner, 1968). Fear is accompanied by physical or mental withdrawal. A student who receives a failing grade may come late to the next class or be inattentive. Anger is accompanied by counterattack, sometimes just within earshot of the teacher and sometimes on books and schools (vandalism). Resentment is accompanied by refusal to respond—the "you can't make me" glare. Which response a student shows to punishment depends on his or her temperament. No one who feels punished escapes them all. The sad fact is that these side effects must always be dealt with before further learning can occur.

Failing grades are sometimes warranted, but their side effects can dampen enthusiasm for learning—and teaching. Because the rewards of teaching come so much from seeing your students learn and enjoy learning, the ultimate effect of punishing failure in the classroom is almost always a diminished sense of your own success as a teacher.

> A positive attitude can counteract the side effects of punishment.

If punitive interactions develop between you and a difficult class, or between you and a difficult student, work to develop more positive interactions by using this procedure. First, encourage the class or student to try harder, and be willing to start over yourself. Tomorrow *is* another day. Second, ignore counterattacks (if possible), and try to establish ways for students to escape aversive consequences by investing themselves in further academic work. Check on homework or note taking to ensure attentiveness. Keep comments positive by focusing on improvements in class and on assignments. Provide opportunities to earn bonus points on exams or to raise past exam scores. An early disaster may become a reinforcing experience for you and your student.

Behavior Management

Many educational applications of behavioral learning principles fall under the category of behavior modification, or **behavior management,** a general procedure for changing behaviors through their consequences. Although often used with students who require special educational services, behavior management can also be used with any learner who is asked to achieve an objective that has been defined in behavioral terms. Behavior management requires that you *set a behavioral objective, identify potential reinforcers, establish a contingency, and monitor the effectiveness of the contingency.* Let's look at each of these steps in turn.

Set a Behavioral Objective

Setting a behavioral objective is the first step in a simplified behavior management procedure. Such objectives may have already been established in local curriculum guides or state courses of study. Alternatively, you may want to write the objective yourself, defining an instructional problem in behavioral terms. This behavioral objective often needs to be supplemented by a learning analysis. The analysis should include your estimate of what your students can already do, which gives you an idea of what behaviors are attainable from current performance levels.

Identify Potential Reinforcers

Often one of the more challenging aspects of behavior management is identifying appropriate reinforcers. Although reinforcers often include grades, they are not always the most effective reinforcers available to you. Remember that reinforcers are determined by their effect on behavior; what may strengthen the behavior of one child may not affect that of another or may even weaken it.

Reinforcers. Table 8.2 presents a list of thirteen reinforcers other than grades that are commonly used by elementary teachers. As you can see, teachers appear to use a wide variety of consequences to strengthen behavior, many of them quite natural. Potential reinforcers in general use include a range of social rewards (such as praise, hugs, or notes home), activities (such as use of special equipment/objects), tokens (such as bonus points), tangible rewards (such as stickers), and edibles (such as candy). Of potential reinforcers on the elementary level, only praise is reported in universal use.

If you were to construct a table of potential reinforcers other than grades for secondary students, you would probably find edibles and tangibles less often useful, and tokens (such as points) and activities more often useful, than at the elementary level. Decreased reliance on certain categories of reinforcers and increased reliance on others can be traced to both developmental changes and the increasingly academic nature of the subject matter (Forness, 1973).

s t r a t e g i c   s o l u t i o n s ,   c o n t i n u e d

Table 8.2   *Potential Reinforcers Used by Elementary Teachers*

Positive Reinforcer	% Using	Freq. of Use
Give praise or compliment	100	2.6
Post progress/work	93	1.9
Hug, pat on back, wink, etc.	89	1.8
Show others the good work	87	1.5
Act friendly, tease good-naturedly	85	1.7
Give happy face, star, or other symbolic reward	82	1.9
Send note or call parents	79	1.3
Allow child to tutor	78	1.2
Provide special time with teacher	76	1.1
Give sticker, food, or other material reward	71	1.5
Use special materials/objects	66	1.2
Give bonus points/extra credit	61	1.1
Allow to run errands	59	1.0

3 = very much, 2 = pretty much, 1 = just a little.

Source: Rosen et al., 1990

Premack Principle.   In addition to your own actions, you can also use student activities to reinforce behavior. One way to discover which activities reinforce student behavior is to observe what students do during free time or ask them what they like to do in class. Known as the **Premack Principle** after its discoverer, David Premack (1965), this rule states that the most frequently chosen activities during free time can be used as reinforcers for less frequently chosen activities at any time.

For example, commonly preferred activities for most elementary school children might include use of a classroom computer, time at the listening center, or a nature walk. These activities can be reinforcers for successful completion of less desirable activities, such as practice exercises to increase skill proficiency. Popular group-learning activities, such as a subject-relevant Trivial Pursuit or Jeopardy!, might be chosen by groups of secondary students. Although the specific reinforcers change with age and environment, the Premack Principle can help you identify reinforcing activities for students at any age in any learning environment.

Removal of aversive consequences.   Although we have focused on positive reinforcement here, removal of aversive consequences (negative reinforcement) can also be a very powerful tool for strengthening behavior. Recall

One preferred activity of most elementary students is a nature walk. Desirable learning activities like this one can be used as reinforcers for successfully completing less desirable activities. *(Nita Winter)*

how Mrs. Olive's freeing the students from fear of failing permitted them to become more actively and openly involved in the estimation lesson. You might also *occasionally* let students skip ahead in work or exempt them from tests if they have performed well on quizzes. I even knew one teacher who cleverly gave a practice test on Friday and exempted anyone who demonstrated mastery on the practice test from taking the "real" test on Monday!

During this process of generating a behavior management strategy, you may also wonder about the other side of the coin—that is, should you be identifying aversive consequences as well as or even in lieu of reinforcers? Because punishment can have the unwanted effects we discussed earlier, the answer is "Probably not." In fact, there is a very short list of aversive consequences commonly used by elementary teachers to manage academic learning (Brophy, 1981). A note or call home, a private reprimand, negative comments on work, and undesirable grades are probably the only aversive consequences in general use. Even among these only a note home and a private reprimand are reported in frequent use (Rosen et al., 1990), and they should be balanced by positive notes home and praise for improved behavior when it occurs.

Establish a Contingency

After you identify behavioral objectives and potential reinforcers, you will be ready to make the reinforcers contingent on achievement of the objectives. We will focus here on contingencies of reinforcement rather than of punishment since the former are—and should be—used far more frequently. Reinforcing contingencies can be arranged for individuals, entire classes, or groups within classes. Let's look at individual and class-oriented contingencies here and save our discussion of small-group contingencies for the chapter on motivation.

There are two rules of thumb for establishing reinforcement contingencies: (1) *economically match reinforcers to behaviors,* and (2) *make the terms of the contingency clear.* We'll explore each of them separately.

Economically match reinforcers to behaviors.   An "economical" approach to contingencies means expending the least resources to achieve the greatest effect, particularly in choosing reinforcers that flow most easily from the activity and in timing the delivery of the reinforcers efficiently. Sometimes, progress alone is a sufficient reinforcer to promote learning. At such times, reinforcement is *intrinsic,* or a natural consequence of the learning activity. Swinging higher or reading for pleasure is intrinsically reinforcing. At other times, reinforcement must be *extrinsic,* or a contrived consequence of the learning activity. Not all contrivance is on a par, however. You will find that there is a range of contrivance and that some extrinsic reinforcers (such as offering the "Tower of Hanoi" math game for finishing math work) are more related than others to the behavior. Reinforcers should be matched as economically, or naturally, to behaviors as possible.

When you do need to use extrinsic reinforcement, distribute it most economically to preserve motivation. **Scheduling** is a technique that will help you do this. A *continuous* schedule reinforces each instance of appropriate behavior (such as points awarded for each homework assignment completed). Continuous schedules are generally used to get behavior started, but they require a lot of resources.

An *intermittent* schedule reinforces behavior according to either time intervals or ratios of response. Generally, teachers use schedules that are *fixed interval* (such as points on a quiz each Friday) or *fixed ratio* (such as points on a chapter test). Fixed schedules result in predictable reinforcement and, consequently, high rates of appropriate behavior just before reinforcement is delivered. Most teachers used fixed schedules, and the predictable result is a great deal of study just before points or grades are distributed and little study at other times.

If you assign a lot of daily work (as many teachers in elementary grades do), you might consider *variable* schedules. A *variable interval* schedule involves reinforcement once per time period (say, once a week), but its timing during that period is unpredictable (for example, randomly recording scores on one set of daily papers each week). Work is sustained until the reward is administered. A *variable ratio* schedule (an average of one recorded score per so many assignments) sustains the most work at the least expense, however, because the recipient does not know when reinforcement will be administered. Scores on two sets of papers in a row may be recorded, or a dozen sets of papers may be turned in without scores being recorded. Work will diminish, however, if too many scores go unrecorded.

Make the terms of the contingency clear.   You learned in Chapter 3 that behavioral objectives are most effective when they are shared with students. Contingencies should also be shared, in either oral or written form. One effective way to write a contingency is to draw up a contingency contract with the student (see Figure 8.5).

A **contingency contract** is an agreement composed of a behavioral objective and a statement of what the student will receive for attaining the objective. The drawing up of a contract can involve negotiation between you and your student(s), or the terms can be set by either you *or* your student(s). In general practice, it is best to include only one or two specific behaviors, be concise, utilize readily available rewards, and shift from teacher to student control (Murphy, 1988).

With or without formal contracts, contingencies can be shared quite successfully with students and can operate very informally and effectively in a classroom. For example, in Mrs. Olive's class the students who worked diligently on their homework during the final minutes of class were working under a contingency. If they finished their worksheets and homework, they would not have to carry the math book home and study it that evening. Students were busy at their seats at the end of class, working hard to lighten their anticipated workload after school.

Monitor the Effectiveness of the Contingency

Contingencies sometimes need to be changed because learning—relatively permanent change in behavior—is not occurring. Monitoring the effectiveness of a contingency involves constructing and revising both behavioral objectives and reinforcers so that contingencies are as clear, realistic, and natural as possible. Let's look here at four kinds of monitoring you can do.

First, look at the behavioral objective. If it is not clear, the contingency might be confusing from the start. You learned in Chapter 3, for example, that behavioral objectives should specify activities. If they do not, the student will not know what is expected of him or her. If the objective is unclear, rewrite it for clarity.

Second, even if the behavioral objective is clear, it may still not be attainable. Prerequisites may need to be taught first. In Chapter 4, you learned that "to serve a volleyball overhand" first requires adequate arm strength. If the objective cannot be attained because it is too difficult, conduct a learning analysis to discover attainable behaviors that can lead to achievement of the objective.

Third, the consequence used as a reinforcer might not be sufficiently valued by the student to strengthen the behavior. You may have to change the consequence because it has no effect, or a punitive effect, on behavior. It is

Contract between ___Erin Watson___ (student) and ___Mrs. McCreary___ (teacher)

Fill in agreed-upon behavior and consequence:

If _Erin hands in 4 complete math homework sheets with 80% correct to Mrs. McCreary_
by 11:30 Friday,
then _she can be first in line when her class goes to lunch on Friday_.

If _Erin_ does not _hand in 4 complete math homework sheets with 80% correct to_
Mrs. McCreary by 11:30 Friday,
then _she does not get to be first in line when her class goes to lunch on Friday_.

I agree to this deal.

___Erin Watson___   ___March 18___
(Student's signature)   (Date)

___Mrs. McCreary___   ___March 18___
(Teacher's signature)   (Date)

Figure 8.5   A Contingency Contract *(Adapted from Murphy, 1988, p. 258)*

not uncommon to hear a teacher complain that "reinforcement doesn't work" when actually an appropriate reinforcer has not been identified. Look to the Premack Principle to help you discover what reinforces groups and individuals when the old and overused standbys of praise and grades fail (see Reflection on Practice: Application of the Premack Principle). Also, do not overlook potential intrinsic reinforcers, such as a sense of progress or an opportunity for a student to make a personal decision.

Finally, the contingency can be too contrived or unnatural to result in the desired behavior change or in learning. In these cases, either the sought-for behavior is unrealistic, the reinforcer is unnatural, or both are the case. In the early days of behavior management, several critics suggested that unrealistic behaviors were being sought. For instance, frequently the way for a child to earn tokens was to "be still, be quiet, be docile" (Winett & Winkler, 1972, p. 499)—none of which was realistic for a child, who is an active learner. Too often in these early days reinforcers were unnatural, and obtaining the contrived reinforcer, rather than performing the behavior, became the objective.

Evaluation: Behavior Management

Research on the use of reinforcement to promote learning in schools was widely conducted in the late 1960s through the 1970s. A summary of this research (Lysakowski & Walberg, 1981) suggested that reinforcement is generally highly effective. One measure of its effectiveness was the highly significant gain in achievement of experimental groups (taught with reinforcement) over control groups (taught without reinforcement). Although students in special schools experienced somewhat greater effects of reinforcement than did students in regular schools, the effects of reinforcement in regular schools at all levels were appreciable when compared with the effects of no reinforcement.

Because of the wide use of teacher praise, it was analyzed separately for its effects on student learning (Brophy, 1981). Results of studies on the effects of praise were far more variable than the results of studies on effects of reinforcement, leading researchers to conclude that praise was not often used as a reinforcer contingent on a specific behavior. Praise does appear to affect achievement if it (1) is contingent on the appearance of some behavior, (2) specifies what behavior is praiseworthy, and (3) is genuine, or natural in the situation. When these conditions are absent, almost no relationship exists between praise and achievement. When these conditions are present, however, praise is effective as a reinforcer (Elawar & Corno, 1985; Emmer, 1988; Hopman & Glynn, 1988; Krampen, 1987).

If positive reinforcement is so effective, why is it not used more systematically? Behavioral psychologists have puzzled over this question in light of needed educational reforms (Axelrod, Moyer & Berry, 1990; Lindsey, 1992; Skinner, 1984), but the question cannot be approached in terms of effectiveness alone. Behavior management represents such a powerful technique to control student learning that it raises other issues whenever it is used. Most of these issues focus on the potentially negative side effects of reinforcement, such as inordinate attention to the teacher, points, or grades; insufficient attention to important behaviors, such as free reading, that are inherently and naturally reinforcing; and reward for unethical behaviors such as cheating, stealing tokens, or finding "loopholes" in contracts (Balsam & Bondy, 1983).

The negative side effects spring from two sources. One is the lack of learner control over the contingencies of reinforcement. When control is restricted to the teacher, students do not discover intrinsically reinforcing behavior, such as reading for pleasure. Permitting students to *countercontrol* during the development of reinforcement contingencies is one way to balance your control with that of your students (Axelrod, Moyer & Berry, 1990). Provision can be made to negotiate objectives, reinforcers, and contingencies with students. Such negotiation can occur at the beginning of a term or when a contract is being formulated.

If negotiating contingencies is not possible, you can still make provisions for feedback from students. What are some objectives related to a topic that

strategic solutions, continued

reflection on practice

Application of the Premack Principle

Over the past two years I have collected different math games to use in my math classes. Generally, I have found them to be a great positive reinforcer in my classroom. I remember one student, Brian, who became fascinated with one particular game.

Brian was one of thirty-three students in an afternoon summer-school session I taught. Not only was the large number of students a problem but also the class was a mixture of students from six different junior high schools. As a very energetic fourteen-year-old, Brian was in the midst of a rather distracting situation.

Because of this situation, it was quite difficult to keep Brian on task. He wanted to talk and watch the other students instead of doing his work. Brian knew I had some games, and he wanted to play with them. I told Brian that if he completed his work, then he could play with his favorite, the Tower of Hanoi.

From that time on, I had no trouble with Brian. He was always eager to play with his favorite game.

Kim Bell

Discussion Questions

1. How do you think this teacher discovered that Brian's favorite game was the Tower of Hanoi? How would you discover which activities are rewarding to students in your classes?

2. What do you think motivated the teacher to collect math games? Name some comparable individual and group activities in your teaching field.

3. Why would "recess" or letting class out not be a good positive reinforcer? Give more than one reason. What makes the Tower of Hanoi problem particularly valuable?

they would like to pursue? Do they prefer individual or group rewards? Do they prefer earning points to indicate progress or receiving written feedback? You can ask these questions at almost any point in the term. Responses can give you ideas about appropriate adjustments to increase student satisfaction.

The other source of negative side effects is the artificiality of contrived contingencies. An early mistake of many behavioral psychologists was to conduct interventions that were artificial demonstrations rather than practical modifications to improve the conditions of learning (Fantuzzo & Atkins, 1992). Under such circumstances, token reinforcement led to token learning (Levine & Fasnacht, 1974). Contingencies need to be as natural as possible to avoid drawing inordinate attention to the reinforcers; otherwise obtaining the reinforcers becomes more important than attaining the objective.

In the future, behavior management may best be considered a descriptive term for some of what successful teachers do, each in his or her own way. Both behavioral psychologists and their critics compare behavior management to a versatile and valuable tool (Brophy, 1983; Greer, 1983, 1992). Used indiscriminately, most tools can be destructive, but used by a skilled worker, they make constructive work efficient. Throwing one of these tools away would be as thoughtless as its indiscriminate use. Behavior management can help you structure your teaching so that learning in your classes is more efficient. The promise of the future is closer cooperation between behavior analysts and teachers whenever behavioral learning principles would help teachers meet their objectives, whatever those objectives might be.

The solution may involve a strategy to attain a simple behavioral objective, or a series of them, sequenced for learning through a learning analysis. The solution may involve planning for a term or a single lesson. The solution may take considerable thought or be a part of your moment-to-moment responses in class to keep students on task.

PROGRAMS OF REINFORCEMENT: IMPLEMENTING A SOLUTION

Skinner defined teaching as "the arrangement of contingencies of reinforcement" under which students learn (1968, p. 5). He believed that teaching calls for the skillful arrangement of contingencies to minimize error. In this section we will first look at the general purpose for arranging contingencies, which is "shaping" new behavior; then we will investigate how shaping occurs through a strategy known as computer-assisted instruction.

The Process of Shaping

We have already seen how teachers can use contingencies of reinforcement informally in the classroom through simple frameworks set up verbally or accompanied by written contracts. When contingencies govern an entire course of learning, however, more than simple learning is going on. Behavior is being changed systematically through a process known as **shaping,** which is the reinforcement of successive approximations of a behavior: as the learner's behavior increasingly matches the desired behavior, he or she is rewarded. By skillfully using principles of discrimination and generalization, a teacher can shape behavior much as a sculptor creates a sculpture. Skinner considered the arrangement of contingencies to shape a new behavior very much an art, but one assisted by analysis. A learning analysis permits the discovery of a series of prerequisites to the final behavior, and behavioral analysis supplies effective contingencies to motivate progress.

Shaping means rewarding the learner for behavior that more closely matches the goal.

reflection on practice

Shaping Cursive Handwriting

I was working in a third-grade classroom with an eight-year-old named Chip. Cursive handwriting was one of his least favorite school tasks, and his letters were very poorly formed. I decided to see what I could do to help him improve his handwriting and his idea of his abilities in that area.

The first thing I did was to design a new cursive handwriting worksheet. I used larger spaces than regular notebook paper, and I put in a midline. I also added a small, whimsical character to the corner to make the worksheet more attractive. On each page, I placed one letter and the directional arrows for correct flow of the letter. I also followed each letter with several "broken character" examples. I gave instructions to the entire class and modeled the correct procedure. I then asked students to trace the broken characters on their paper, then continue to copy the letter as space provided.

The new sheets were very popular. Each day during handwriting exercises, I circled the room, paying special attention to Chip. At first, his handwriting was awkward, but together we began to work on his letter formation. I praised his efforts and improvements each time by writing "Good job!" on his paper. Sometimes, I simply gave him a pat on the shoulder and verbalized the praise as I corrected his work. He began to enjoy handwriting.

Each day, I continued to draw him a little closer to the desired form. He began to ask for extra sheets to practice more. I provided the sheets and some extra assistance. I praised his improvements while still correcting his work, along with that of the class. After several days, Chip had progressed to the point where he needed less assistance. He had mastered most of the basic strokes and needed less attention, but he continued to work just as hard.

At this point, I began to select the best work out of three or four days. On this paper, I would put a motivational sticker that said, "Great work!" or "Super." You could see him swell up with pride. Then Chip transferred to another school, so I could not continue to monitor his progress. When I saw him at the new school several months later, he informed me that he was doing all his written work in cursive handwriting.

Linda Matthews

Discussion Questions

1. Analyze the steps in Chip's progress in terms of the contingencies set by the teacher. What do you think eventually sustained his use of cursive handwriting rather than printing?

2. Note that the teacher provided more attention early in the process of shaping rather than later. What are some of the reasons for the change in the teacher's behavior?

3. Attitude, motivation, and achievement are related to one another. Try to puzzle out what that relationship is using the events recounted here as evidence for your theory.

Arranging contingencies of reinforcement so that they shape new behavior into a final form is sometimes known as *programming* because the outcome is a specific sequence of behaviors. The term **programmed instruction** was coined to describe systematically arranged instructional material that is written and set up to teach through contingencies of reinforcement. Some of these materials have involved workbooks and other instructional materials. If you would like to see how a relatively simple skill is shaped through programming, read Reflection on Practice: Shaping Cursive Handwriting. There you will see how a sequence of objectives, plus reinforcement for progress, can result in the development of a new skill in a relatively short amount of time.

> Programmed instruction is systematically arranged material that teaches by reinforcement.

strategic solutions

Computer-Assisted Instruction (CAI)

Although there have been some paper-and-pencil materials created in a programmed instruction format, in most cases this arrangement works best and most efficiently when it is presented by a machine rather than by a teacher. In fact, Skinner believed that a student assisted by a computer could learn twice as much as a conventionally taught student in the same amount of

Shaping involves the reinforcement of successive approximations of a desired behavior, and often occurs through computer-assisted instruction. *(George White Location Photography)*

time with the same effort. The application of programmed instruction through a machine is known as **computer-assisted instruction (CAI).**

Before looking at the natural fit between computers and the implementation of programmed instruction, let's consider for a moment the prevalence of computers and their growing position in schools. Since the mid-1980s, powerful, yet inexpensive microcomputers have fit easily on a table top and require only an ordinary electric outlet and appropriate software to run instructional programs. As of 1989, all but 2 percent of schools in the United States owned microcomputers—a total of 2.4 million machines (Becker, 1991). The typical elementary school had about twenty, and they were occasionally used for instruction by about two-thirds of classroom elementary teachers. The typical high school had between forty and fifty microcomputers, and they were used by about one-third of secondary teachers who taught core academic subjects.

There are basically two uses of a computer; one as a tool and the other as a means of instruction. As a tool, a computer most often processes information. The most common use of the computer by students as a tool is as a word processor, but computers are also used to process numbers (as in spreadsheet programs). Our concern here will be with the other use of a computer—as a means of instruction.

Program Types

As a means of instruction, a computer can be used in at least three ways: for *drill and practice,* for *tutorials,* and for *simulations.* The vast majority of the over thirteen thousand educational programs available today are either drill-and-practice or tutorial programs. These two types are most closely related to behavioral learning principles and will be the focus of our attention here. (Simulations of real-world environments are less common, but their potential is developing rapidly. Learning that occurs through simulations is more easily described through cognitive, rather than through behavioral, learning principles, so simulations will be discussed in Chapter 10.) Figure 8.6 summarizes the different types of computer programs available.

Drill-and-practice programs are display sequences that are designed not to teach but to provide reinforcement for what has already been learned. Speak and Spell, for example, is a common drill-and-practice program in spelling. It does not teach the rules of spelling, but it does provide reinforcement for the correct application of spelling rules. Its unique feature is that it consists of its own unit: a brightly colored, portable keyboard with electronic display and voice. When the unit is turned on, a voice tells the child to spell a given word, and the child types in the letters, which appear in the display.

Letter pressing is reinforced by the display and the voice, which calls the letters out. If the child spells the word correctly, the voice says, "That is right. Now spell [another word]." Incorrect spellings are mildly punished ("Wrong—try again"), but letter pressing is continuously reinforced. The material is not programmed, but different inserts for the machine present words

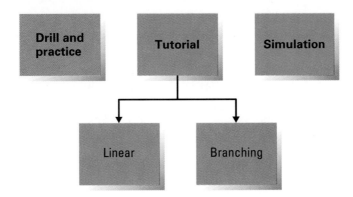

**Figure 8.6
Computer-Assisted
Instruction Programs**

at different levels of difficulty so a parent or teacher can change the skill level. A similar machine can help a child practice arithmetic skills, presenting addition, subtraction, multiplication, or division problems one at a time.

Drill-and-practice programs may seem like electronic worksheets, but unlike worksheets, they can take advantage of three key features of the computer (Bright, 1987). First, the audio-visual display presents only one item at a time. Worksheets sometimes lead to multiple mistakes before the mistakes can be corrected. Second, drill-and-practice programs give the student immediate feedback, whereas a worksheet is often returned the next day. Third, some of these programs use the "computing" capacity of the microcomputer to provide a variety of reinforcers, to provide multiple opportunities to try again, and to generate new practice sessions from a large pool of items—all of which are beyond the capacity of a worksheet.

Tutorial programs are display sequences designed to teach students new information or skills. Sequences generally shape a student's understanding using the principles of discrimination and generalization described earlier. The two types of tutorials in existence are called linear and branching programs. Linear programs lead all students through the same sequence of displays. Branching programs may give a pretest to assess the entry level of the learner and then lead the learner through a sequence of displays that is responsive to the student's errors (hence, the program "branches"). Errors that indicate an absence of understanding lead to remediation within the program. Remediation may take the form of a "looping" back to repeat a series of displays or a provision of additional information.

Because tutorial programs require greater skill to develop than do drill-and-practice programs, they are more difficult to construct and less common. Tutorial programs now exist, however, for virtually all fields at all levels— from naming simple shapes, to doing grammar in a first or second language, to learning rules for volleyball. Programs even exist for entire core curricula in grades K–6. As a computerized curriculum, a series of tutorials can be used to meet behavioral objectives in core subjects at least through the sixth grade. Particularly on the elementary grade levels, tutorial software is

strategic solutions, continued

Table 8.3   *Sample Drill-and-Practice (D&P) and Tutorial Programs*

Elementary Level

Mathematics (D&P)

Coordinate Math (MECC)[1]

Jumping Math Flash (Mindscape/SVE)[1]

Measure Works (MECC)[1]

Mathematics (Tutorial)

Adventures with Fractions (MECC)[1]

IBM Math Concepts Series: Levels I, II, & III (IBM)[2]

Math Blaster Mystery (Davidson)[1,2]

Science (D&P)

Circulation-Organs (Micro Power and Light Co.)[1]

Systems of the Human Body (Little Shaver Software)[1]

Systems of the Body-Game Format (Orange Juice Software Systems)[1]

Science (Tutorial)

Cells and Tissues (Educational Activities)[1,2]

Earth: The Inside Story (Educational Activities)[1,2]

Muscles and Bones (Bare Bones Software)[1]

Social Studies (D&P)

Family Life (Little Shaver Software)[1]

U.S. Geography (Amidon Publications)[1]

U.S. History (Demi-Software)[2]

Social Studies (Tutorial)

Famous Inventors (Little Shaver Software)[1]

Farm Life (Right on Programs)[1]

Time Machine Traveller (Orange Cherry Media)[1]

Language Arts (D&P)

End Punctuation (GAMCO)[1]

Eureka! Following Directions (GAMCO)[1,2]

Wizard of Words (Advanced Ideas)[1,2]

Language Arts (Tutorial)

Grammar Package II (Micro Learningware)[1]

Language Arts Sequence (Milliken Publishing Co.)[1]

Word Quest—Binary Search Strat's (Sunburst Communications)[1]

---

available from state-sponsored computing consortia at nominal prices. Most of these inexpensive tutorials are provided to teachers for remedial services. Other tutorials can be purchased from vendors to provide enrichment for individuals in subjects of interest.

The continuing challenge for teachers will be to select appropriate drill-and-practice or tutorial programs for their classes. Only about 8 percent of the thousands of programs available have been judged excellent (Neill & Neill, 1994). A few highly regarded drill-and-practice and tutorial programs in common use at different grade levels and in different subject areas are

Table 8.3   *continued*

Secondary Level

Mathematics (D&P)

Alge-Blaster Plus (Davidson)[1,2]

Fractions: Multiplication and Division (GAMCO)[1,2]

Micromath (Sheridan College)[1]

Mathematics (Tutorial)

Algebra Concept Vol. 1 (Ventura Educational Systems)[2]

Algebraic Proposer (Tree Basic)[2]

Math for Successful Living: Timecards and Paychecks (GAMCO)[1,2]

Science (D&P)

Chemical Vocabulary Building I (Resource Software International)[1,2]

Earth Science I and II (Focus Media)[1]

Plant Biology Keyword (Focus Media)[1]

Science (Tutorial)

Digestion (J&S Software)[1]

Geological History; Geologists at Work (Sunburst Communications)[1]

Minerals (MECC)[1]

Social Studies (D&P)

Countries and Capitals (Micro Learningware)[1,2]

Foreign Governments and United Nations (Sliwa Enterprises)[1,2]

Knowledge Master—American History I, II, and III (Academic Hallmarks)[1]

Social Studies (Tutorial)

American History: 1760–1970 (Focus Media)[1,2]

The Assembly Line (Media Materials, Inc.)[1]

Discovering America: Parts I, II, & III (Center for Educational Exper/Dev/Evaln)[1]

Language Arts (D&P)

Alphabetize (M. D. Fullmer and Assoc.)[1]

End Punctuation (GAMCO)[1]
Wordy: Common Forms of Wordiness (COMPress)[1]

Language Arts (Tutorial)

Finding the Reasons: Unit III (Center for Educational Exper/Dev/Evaln)[1]

MECC Write Start (MECC)[1]
Writing with a Micro (DCH Software)[1]

Note: Title of program followed by name of supplier
[1]Program for Apple computers
[2]Program for IBM-compatible computers

Source: Compiled from *Only the Best*, courtesy of Michele R. Walker

---

listed in Table 8.3. Most districts have computer consultants available to assist teachers in their initial selections of software.

Program Usage

Typically, all that the student needs to use a computer is prerequisite knowledge or skill in whatever she or he wishes to practice or learn and preliminary instruction in how to turn the machine on and use a few keys, such as the space bar or the "enter" key. More complex keyboarding skills (such as positioning of hands and fingers to type) can be learned through a tutorial program, a computer education class, or both. Before asking students to use a given CAI program, *determine whether they possess prerequisite skills.*

Of teachers involved with computers, more report using drill-and-practice programs than any other kind, with the exception of secondary English teachers, who use word-processing programs more frequently than drill and practice. Figure 8.7 shows the percentage of computer-using teachers at different grade levels who utilize drill-and-practice or tutorial programs more than five times during the year. Drill-and-practice programs are particularly popular among elementary teachers. The key to all such use, however, is that it be done in the context of ongoing instruction—in other words, *use computer-assisted instruction when it is an appropriate supplement to other class activities.*

What instructional function do drill-and-practice and tutorial programs serve? It appears that they are used most often for enrichment of instruction. As you can see from Table 8.4, which shows the function of most computer

Figure 8.7   Select Program Usage by Teachers *(Becker, 1991)*

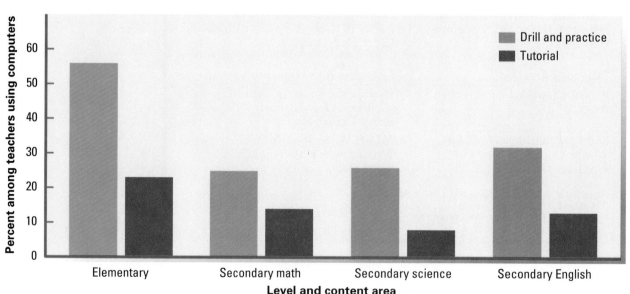

work in the schools, half of elementary-level teachers involved with computers use them most often for enrichment and one-third use computers for regular instruction. On the secondary level, teachers in different subject matters use computers differently: math and science teachers use them most often for enrichment, but English teachers use them most often for regular instruction (related to word processing). The key here is to *use computer-assisted instruction to adapt instruction to learner needs.*

A survey of teachers who were accomplished at integrating computers into their classes (Sheingold & Hadley, 1990) reveals another key to wise, strategic, and optimal computer use in your classroom. Typically, the teachers selected for the survey had taught for between three and eight years, practiced in schools with more computers than average, and used computers for multiple purposes. These teachers were well experienced and well supported. One elementary teacher in this survey reported (p. 10):

Table 8.4 *Most Common Functions of Computer Use by Teachers*

	Elementary	Secondary		
	Grades 3–6	Math	Science	English
Enrichment	50	46	60	24
Regular instruction	34	26	35	62
Remediation	16	28	5	14

Percentage among teachers using computers

Source: Becker, 1991

I currently teach Chapter I and have found drill-and-practice games (i.e., Microzine Math Mall) excellent for reinforcing basic facts. I have also used Microzine Monitor Mysteries and "adventure" stories as motivators in reading for meaning. I have used a spelling program with mazes and a joystick for one very low, reluctant fourth grade remedial speller. We do not have much software, but I have ordered quite a bit for next year. Computers have taken over the "drill and practice" of basic skills, allowing me more time to develop problem solving and higher level thinking skills with my classes.

Like teachers in general, these accomplished teachers used computers more often for drill and practice or tutorials than for any other activity (with the exception of word processing). What was notable, however, was their use of computers in a wide variety of activities. Computer time was not limited to drill and practice or tutorial, remediation or enrichment. Therefore, to use computers effectively, you should *integrate CAI into a number of activities, each of them embedded within an instructional strategy.*

Evaluation: Computer-Assisted Instruction (CAI)

Skinner (1968, 1984) repeatedly claimed that schools have not made sufficient use of technology to accelerate student learning and increase teacher productivity. Some evidence suggests that CAI may accelerate learning, but even if this accelerative effect exists, it does not do so equally for all students at all grade levels in all subject areas.

Almost all older studies of the effect of computers on instructional time focused on drill-and-practice and tutorial programs because those were the primary early applications in the classroom. Since these two types of programs are so related to behavioral learning principles, these studies can answer questions about the effectiveness of behavioral learning as presented by a machine. One analysis of twenty-eight studies (mostly before 1980) collected data on the time it took to learn by computer versus conventional instruction and found an average savings of 32 percent of instructional time with computers (Kulik & Kulik, 1987). Evidence from thirty-two studies at the elementary level and forty-two at the high school level also suggested that students learned somewhat better through computers than through conventional instruction (Bangert-Drowns, Kulik & Kulik, 1985; Kulik, Kulik & Bangert-Drowns, 1985). These relatively early results seemed to support the claim that drill-and-practice and tutorial programs increased learning efficiency.

Educators need to be cautious, however, in reading too much into these findings because early studies were generally short. The largest effects of CAI on achievement were found in studies that measured student learning over less than nine weeks; smaller effects were obtained in studies that lasted longer than nine weeks (Kulik & Kulik, 1987; Niemiec et al., 1987).

This added finding suggests that the novelty of the experimental situation affected achievement gains. In research, the effect of novelty is known as the **Hawthorne effect,** after a General Electric factory in Hawthorne, Illinois, where industrial psychologists discovered that *any* change in the working environment led to a temporary increase in worker productivity. The implication for computer use is that if teachers were to rely extensively on computers for instruction of students over a prolonged period, the "new" would wear off, and long-term gains over conventional instruction might become much smaller than originally reported.

A consensus seems to be emerging from more recent studies (Becker, 1990; Roblyer, Castine & King, 1988), many of which control for the Hawthorne effect. Drill-and-practice and tutorial programs lead to significant achievement gains over conventional instruction for some students at some grade levels in some subject areas. These areas of effectiveness are:

1. disadvantaged or low-ability students, who have often gained more from drill and practice and tutorials than have advantaged or average-ability students

2. elementary students, who have often gained more from drill and practice and tutorials than have older students

3. students learning mathematics computation and vocabulary, who have often gained more from drill and practice and tutorials than have students learning mathematical reasoning and reading

These findings suggest that drill-and-practice and tutorial programs have an optimal effect with disadvantaged elementary students who are learning basic subject matter. Other profitable uses can of course be made of these programs, but chances are that over the long run such uses will not lead to substantially greater learning than will conventional instruction.

OBSERVATIONAL OR SOCIAL LEARNING

An extensive revision of the behavioral approach to learning has been developed by Albert Bandura (1969, 1986) in order to describe how learning occurs through observation as well as through direct experience. Bandura began his career as a psychologist in the behavioral tradition, but over the years he has progressively modified his approach to develop a more comprehensive learning theory that is by now independent of its clearly behavioral origins (Bandura, 1969; Malone, 1990). He believes that **observational or social learning**—acquiring the potential for a behavior by watching someone else perform it—is a more realistic approach than operant conditioning to describe the way many complicated behaviors develop, including speaking, driving a car, and even thinking.

Observation is an important way to learn many complex behaviors.

Observational Learning Versus Operant Conditioning

If we were to wait for complex behaviors to be shaped by an instructor or experience, we would have to wait a long time, and we would risk many inappropriate responses (which in some circumstances could be dangerous) in the course of learning. Thus, according to social learning theorists, a more efficient means of learning complex behavior is to watch someone else perform it. In a series of experiments with children in the 1960s, Bandura demonstrated that small children can learn specific aggressive acts merely by watching them acted out on film. Research by others in the 1970s demonstrated that *prosocial* behaviors, or altruistic and self-controlling activities, can also be learned simply by watching them (Liebert & Sprafkin, 1988; Van Evra, 1990).

Learning occurs through observing both positive and negative behaviors.

Observational learning includes what is commonly called "learning through imitation," although Bandura demonstrated that no actual imitation needs to occur for learning to take place. Society's interest in observational learning has revolved around the psychological effects of television viewing on children, but the educational implications have included many different uses of observational learning in the classroom. We shall explore these uses after first looking at observational learning theory.

Observational learning theory creates a bridge between behavioral learning theory, with its emphasis on reinforcement, and cognitive learning theory, with its emphasis on human thought processes, by explaining that reinforcement creates expectations of future rewards (Bandura, 1986). Expectations in humans are beliefs, which are cognitive, rather than behavioral, in nature. According to Bandura, these expectations or beliefs often exert a more powerful influence on behavior than does the offer of a reward or an incentive.

The core question about learning is transformed from "What behavior do we need to reinforce?" to "How are expectations or beliefs created?" Observational learning theorists believe that expectations are created both through direct experience (such as a history of reinforcement) and through **vicarious experience,** which involves observation of someone else's behavior and its consequences. Vicarious experiences create beliefs and expectations on the part of the observer.

> One can acquire beliefs and expectations from vicarious experience.

How much does vicarious experience affect a particular individual's learning? The answer to that question depends on the "functional value," or anticipated use, for the observer of the behavior. Let's look at just what this means.

Prerequisite to Learning: Functional Value

> Students learn faster when they can see how the learning will help them.

Functional value is the anticipated gain or advantage from learning a behavior. If the functional value is high, the behavior will be learned more quickly and easily than if the functional value is low. High functional value of a behavior is a prerequisite for learning the behavior.

We can use Mrs. Olive's classroom to understand better this concept of the functional value of a behavior. Recall how Mrs. Olive asked students to call out which mental math homework problems they wanted worked on the board? In doing so, she was assuming that students would choose problems whose solutions would involve high functional value. That is, she assumed students would choose to view behavior that might have some *use* to them, helping them to understand their errors and improve their performance on the quiz later that week.

Similarly, when Mrs. Olive called students to the board to write their answers to the in-class mental math problems, she asked them to explain how they arrived at the answers. The explanations, which were also examples of problem-solving behaviors, had high functional value because the problems resembled those that students would encounter on the quiz. Again, these problems had some use to the other students. You've probably had many similar experiences yourself. Your attention focuses when you feel you're learning something that you're going to use (see Deepening Your Knowledge Base: The Functional Value of Behavior on Television).

deepening your knowledge base

The Functional Value of Behavior on Television

A lot of interest today focuses on what children learn from television (Liebert & Sprafkin, 1988). In total, they will spend more time watching television than they will spend in K–12 classrooms. In fact, they will spend more time watching television than they will in any other activity except sleep. So what is the effect of viewing on their knowledge, attitudes, and behavior?

The answer depends partly on how closely they are watching. Break out into your discussion groups, and appoint a recorder to write down your answers to the following questions. The questions should lead you as a group to some insights about what children learn from television and the types of programs you might want children to watch or not watch. After your group has addressed each of these five questions, reassemble with the larger group to compare answers.

Discussion Questions

1. What kinds of shows do children like to watch? Name several favorite shows of children in the age group you will teach.

2. Do these shows contain characters whose behavior has high functional value in the world of the child? Does the child have a *use* for that type of behavior? If so, describe the use briefly. If not, explain why.

3. Have you ever seen the observed behavior acted out in any way, either verbally or physically? If so, recount the incident briefly. If not, explain why.

4. Generalize for all shows: What kinds of behavior portrayed on television are most likely to be acted out by children?

5. Characterize the type of aggression and the type of prosocial behaviors portrayed on television that are most likely to be acted out by children.

The Components of Observational Learning

Four components—attention, retention, production, and motivation—make up the process of learning as defined by observational learning theorists (Bandura, 1986). As we walk through these components, you will notice that one word—*model*—keeps reappearing. It has two different meanings within this theory that need to be distinguished.

To model primarily means to perform or describe a behavior for the benefit of another, who is expected to learn it. Sometimes modeling involves only *demonstration* of a behavior: showing someone how to play a game, solve a puzzle, work cooperatively, take care of a child, dance a new step, or draw an angle with a protractor. Other times modeling involves only *describing* a behavior: telling someone specific instructions for a grammatical composition, the rules for a group activity, or the regulations for an athletic competition.

> Observational learning includes attention, retention, production, and motivation.

think it through

Consider this problem that a novice preservice teacher has **IDENTIFIED** and **REPRESENTED**.

Responding to the Victim of Abuse

Knowing how the world is today, I expect that I will most likely have a child in my classroom who is a victim of violence or child abuse. Suzi comes to class the majority of the time withdrawn from me and her peers. She is a pretty seven-year-old with fear and shame written all over her face. When I try to reach out to her, she withdraws even more. She doesn't seem to trust anyone. Suzi comes from a well-known family, and her mom and dad can't explain her actions either. On the day of the annual school physical, the school nurse can't help but notice that Suzi's body is covered with bruises.

What actions should I take?

Observe how experienced practicing teachers GENERATE SOLUTIONS to this problem.

Unfortunately, violent acts are a part of today's classroom. A caring classroom teacher will greet all kids with a smile and caring attitude. All students should be taught (skills) in an atmosphere that is peaceful and approaches problems in a positive way. Teachers should continue to model behaviors that will form a trusting relationship with all students.

One way that we minimize violence is by teaching a peer mediation program that promotes shared responsibility in learning to solve conflict situations. If students are trained to listen to one another and seek their own solutions to problems, they may feel more positive in reporting violent behavior.

There will be times in your teaching career when you will be required to call your local social service agency to report such abuse situations. By law any suspected incidents such as this must be reported.

Our continued goal as educators will always be to provide a trusting environment for all students.

Pat Tippin and Mitzi Eyestone, Team Teachers
Manhattan Schools
Manhattan, Kansas

This problem involves the issue of responsibility. Having observed the child's behaviors and having discovered, based on physical examination by a professional that physical signs of possible abuse are present, you must deal with that evidence responsibly.

There are several actions you may take: talk with parents, which you have done already; share your suspicions with an authority at your school, probably the principal or guidance counselor; or report the evidence to the local Department of Social Services.

In my state, we have but one alternative: any school employee who reasonably suspects abuse has the legal responsibility to report directly to the Department of Social Services. The consequence of not sharing information is that a teacher could be found guilty of neglect in a court of law.

I must therefore report my concerns to the Department of Social Services and then inform my principal of that decision. The problem of child abuse and neglect has become very serious; the legal implications for teachers are equally serious.

Susan Bounds
North Salisbury School
Salisbury, Maryland

think it through, continued

EVALUATE this problem's possible multiple solutions while you think about the dynamic process of problem solving.

Child abuse involves physical or psychological injury and generally develops out of an unchecked desire to punish a child. Earlier in the chapter, you learned that punishment has psychological side effects and that these effects (such as fear and anger) interfere with learning. In fact, they may be so severe that they are socially and academically debilitating. In Suzi's case, withdrawal (a behavior that accompanies fear) appears to result from highly punitive interactions in the home with one or both parents. If Suzi withdraws from you and her peers, she is also probably having difficulty relating to her schoolwork.

All of the experienced teachers focus on the response required from teachers given the situation: you must report your suspicions to an appropriate authority. State law or district policy will establish to whom you should report. There is more that you can do for the child than report your suspicions, however, because a great deal is now known about the origins of abuse and how to break what appear to be recurring cycles of it.

As the teachers suggest, what you can do in the classroom is provide Suzi with a trusting environment and rational models of conflict resolution. If she withdraws from others, try building rewarding relationships between her and others, including yourself, the school counselor, and peers. You might facilitate these relationships by introducing Suzi to activities that involve others extending trust to her. These activities could include cooperative work of some kind before, during, or after school, such as running errands or assisting you. If Suzi begins talking to you, listen. That should help mitigate the isolation she undoubtedly feels.

Positive relationships with others do not address the long term, however, which includes the potential for victimization when Suzi grows up. We do not know that any given child who is abused will become an adult victim of abuse, but we do know that children who are victims of abuse often lack models for resolving conflicts through rational means. Learning rational methods of conflict resolution should help prevent future victimization.

Finally, it is unlikely that Suzi will become abusive herself (given her pattern of response to abuse), but it is a fact that half of all those adults who abuse children were themselves once abused as children. Observational learning theory explains how a child might learn abusive ways of resolving conflicts in the home. These injurious behaviors might not be acted out until much later, when a similar conflict occurs, but the "child" is now the spouse or the parent. Unthinkingly, the former child might play out a script learned much earlier. The surest way to intervene in this potential cycle of abuse is to have the child learn rational methods of conflict resolution, such as those developed by the experienced teachers. Their peer mediation program sounds right on target. Other suggestions include teaching social problem-solving skills (Chapter 6).

Most of the time, however, a model of performance combines a demonstration and a description of the desired behavior.

A secondary meaning of the verb *to model* refers to the constructive activity of the learner in producing a behavior based on what he or she has perceived. Bandura (1986) has increasingly emphasized this secondary meaning to highlight the cognitive aspect of his theory and to account for variance in the behaviors of different learners who have the same performance model. For example, right-handers who are learning to serve a tennis ball from someone who is right-handed have quite a different task from left-handers in the same class. Both are trying to model their behaviors after what they have seen, but their tasks are quite different. Although technically accurate, this secondary meaning of the verb *to model* can be confusing, so in the description of the observational learning process, I will use a synonym—*match*—whenever the secondary meaning of *model* is intended. *To model* will be used only in its original and primary sense—to perform or describe a behavior for the benefit of another.

Students can learn complex social behaviors by watching a teacher model them.
(Richard Howard/Black Star)

Attention

Attention, or focused awareness on a *model of performance,* is a product of many factors, the most important being the functional value of a behavior. When a model of performance is competent, the behavior of the model has higher functional value. In fact, a highly competent model, even one unlike the learner in many respects, often seems to draw the attention of a learner to the task at hand. Children's heroes and heroines, such as Michael Jordan or gymnast Shannon Miller, are models from whom children learn something because they are competent. Older siblings, parents, and teachers can act as other models of competence.

Competence makes a model more valuable.

Retention

Retention, or the encoding of an act and its consequences in memory, occurs as the learner transforms observations to store them in memory. Called *symbolic transformation,* this encoding results in an image (not a picture of events but a selection of what was sensed) or a verbal representation (rules or procedures that are committed to memory). Even relatively simple events—such as writing the letter *A* or tying a shoe—are often initially retained as both images (tactile and visual) and verbal representations (rules). These representations of behavior form a *mental model* in the learner's mind of the behavior even before it is ever acted out.

Production

Production of a behavior occurs as the learner first *matches* his or her behavioral responses to the mental model. (Remember that this mental model is itself based on observation of the original model of performance.) A second part of production is receiving *performance feedback,* which helps the learner revise the mental model as learning occurs. In softball, the feel of a hit

Performance feedback is important in developing the mental model.

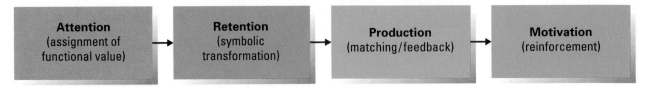

Figure 8.8 **The Observational Learning Process**

or the sound of the ball hitting the bat or, in social studies, a written comment by the teacher on a paper is a form of feedback. Performance feedback is always *informative* in nature.

Motivation

Motivation is generated through various forms of reinforcement. Perhaps the earliest involves *vicarious reinforcement,* which occurs when the behavior of the model of performance is reinforced. For example, if Michael Jordan is named MVP in a game, or Shannon Miller wins a gymnastics competition, an observer who is thinking about practicing basketball or gymnastics skills might be more motivated to go out and practice than if the hero or heroine is not rewarded. An observer learns reinforced behavior more readily than unreinforced behavior (Bandura, 1986).

> Different kinds of reinforcement produce motivation to learn.

The next form of reinforcement is often *direct reinforcement,* which is simply positive or negative reinforcement of the learner's new behavior. Direct reinforcement is sometimes supplemented by a third form of motivation, *self-reinforcement.* That occurs when the learner recognizes the achievement of an internal standard of performance. All three forms of reinforcement can overlap to create a powerful motivational effect. Figure 8.8 summarizes these four components and lists the central concept of each.

Although the entire process is necessary to account for observational learning, the most critical component is retention. Behavior that is attended to and encoded is learned, even though it may never be produced! For example, Mrs. Olive did not ask everyone to recite the explanations she or the model students offered for their solutions of mental math problems. She assumed that students learned from what they saw and heard, given the prospect of future quizzes and tests.

strategic solutions

Models of Performance

Social learning involves a model of performance, whether the performance is cognitive, social, physical, or some combination of the three. What leads to efficient learning from observation? We can answer this question strategically by teasing out the general implications of the four components of observational learning and then by looking more specifically at cognitive modeling.

General Implications

Four general strategic implications follow from social learning theory. First, high functional value of demonstrated behavior—rather than similarity to whomever is demonstrating a skill—is what draws attention and results in observational learning. Consequently, a teacher should *demonstrate only behavior or skills with high functional value.* Models of performance need to be presented only when students are motivated to learn from them (see Reflection on Practice: Recognizing When to Model).

Second, not all models of performance present information that is easily transformed by the learner. Therefore, a teacher should *facilitate symbolic transformation of observed behavior or skills.* In particular, younger learners need visual demonstrations ("Let me show you"). Older learners can profit from both demonstrations and verbal models of performance (rules to follow). Any presentation should be tailored to the age of the learner and the type of information to be learned.

Third, feedback should be used to monitor matches between the mental model and the learner's performance. Therefore, *provide and encourage use of informational feedback.* Learners need to know how to improve performance from their own experience and from the feedback that you provide them.

Fourth, vicarious or direct reinforcers have a short-term motivational effect, but in the long term self-reinforcement offers more enduring satisfaction (Bandura, 1986). Accordingly, develop motivation rather than simply providing incentives or rewards. More specifically, *encourage learners to develop internal standards as they increase in proficiency.* A demonstration can be motivational for a beginner, and reward can help sustain practice, but the achievement of internal standards represents a more fully developed sense of motivation.

Cognitive Modeling

Considerable interest has developed in recent years around models of performance of cognitive behavior. This interest suggests you can *use cognitive modeling to teach specific process skills and problem solving.* Let's see why.

In **cognitive modeling,** the usual technique is for the model to talk him- or herself through a procedure, making "covert" speech overt and stopping to describe mental operations (e.g., Fish & Pervan, 1985; Guevremont, Osnes & Stokes, 1988; Snyder, 1987). Reading skills, which are frequently modeled, are one illustration of this technique.

For instance, a teacher might read aloud a passage that requires cause-effect reasoning and interrupt the reading strategically to demonstrate and

strategic solutions, continued

reflection on practice

Recognizing When to Model

Generally, I don't think there's a piano teacher anywhere who hasn't encountered at least one student who just "doesn't get it." Over the past fifteen years, I have seen many of these students who at one time or another run into difficulty—particularly with rhythm. Now of course the more advanced students play more difficult music, but I have found that the trouble with rhythm occurs most often with beginning or intermediate students. They play notes but pay little or no attention to the counts for notes. Because I was taught to figure out rhythm for myself, I used to believe that there was something taboo about *demonstrating* rhythm rather than having the student clap or count it out.

Over the years, I have come through many a lesson frustrated, fed up, and worn out just because a student couldn't count or feel the beat. A couple of years ago I was ready to throw in the towel! It was time to start putting together a recital, and I had a child who couldn't count straight rhythm. I decided to play for her a few bars of a song that I thought she would like. She wrote in the counts, and I played the song over and over for her as we counted aloud together. She struggled to imitate what she heard. Though her imitation was barely recognizable by note, she began to faintly understand the rhythm. I decided to do something even "more extreme." I taped the entire song five times and sent her home to listen to and play along with the cassette. She didn't practice another tune for a month, but she did learn her recital piece well. I was so proud of her!

I still encourage my students to try counting out rhythm on their own first, but I am not at all hesitant to demonstrate after they attempt to play.

Adina Stone

Discussion Questions

1. Our own teachers often serve as our models for how to teach. What difficulty does that cause us when we encounter students who "don't get it"?

2. Why is it important that the teacher still asks students to play and attempt to count the rhythm before she resorts to a demonstration?

3. How else could demonstration be helpful in the curriculum?
   a. Math: in counting for children?
   b. Reading: in recorded books?
   c. Science: in experiments?

4. What are the possible negative consequences of demonstration?

explain relevant thought processes as he or she figures out the cause-effect relationships. If for several sessions a teacher (1) thinks aloud during oral reading and (2) simultaneously explains the strategies being modeled, students perform better on measures of reading achievement than if they simply watch a model think aloud or have no model at all (Bereiter & Bird, 1985; Miller, Giovenco & Rentiers, 1987). Specific reading strategies that can be taught through cognitive modeling include restatement (paraphrasing and summarizing), backtracking (rereading), demanding relationships (questioning self and making inferences), and problem formulation (developing hypotheses or predictions).

Cognitive modeling is also effective in teaching problem solving, especially when the modeling involves both demonstrating and describing. When contrasted with didactic instruction (in which students read textbook presentations), cognitive modeling of problem-solving skills followed by practice can increase accuracy of problem solving more than didactic instruction followed by practice (Reid & Stone, 1991; Schunk, 1981).

Evaluation: Models of Performance

The strategic implications of observational learning theory are difficult to evaluate because the theory has undergone a number of revisions. Early research on practices related to observational learning—modeling, learner participation, and corrective feedback—demonstrated all such practices to be highly effective (Lysakowski & Walberg, 1981). More recent research has focused on the conditions under which modeling practices are most effective.

For example, should you use students to demonstrate skills? A review of studies found that learning from similar models resulted in greater learning in only some cases (Schunk, 1987). The functional value of the model's behavior was more important for learning than the similarity of the model to the learner. Learners seemed to gain more from similar models than dissimilar models only when the functional value of the behavior was unclear or when the similar model was more competent than the dissimilar model.

Should you use experts as models for beginners? A novice can watch an expert perform and be unable to match the behavior observed. A study that compared learning through observation of "coping" models as opposed to highly competent models found that novices learned more from models who were coping than from those who were highly proficient (Schunk & Hanson, 1985). Modeling how to overcome obstacles or deal with mistakes can have great value for the novice, who is not yet proficient at the skill. In other words, modeling needs to occur in stages, and even in phases within stages, as discussed in Chapters 4 and 5.

Research has also found that generalization of skills learned by observation does not occur easily. This limitation has been a particular concern of psychologists who have advocated cognitive modeling as an approach to the teaching of thinking (Ryan, Short & Weed, 1986). Thus, cognitive modeling represents a useful but context-bound way to teach thinking.

CONCLUSION

The behavioral learning approach to solving instruction problems is complete and quite detailed. It begins with identifying and defining the problem in terms of behavior or setting a behavioral objective. Next, information about activities is gathered through a learning analysis. A learning analysis results in a learning hierarchy composed of many objectives sequenced so that the terminal objective is attainable. Next, a solution to the instructional problem is devised using a sequence of contingencies of reinforcement based on the objectives. Instruction based on behavioral learning principles can be implemented through your own design or through the use of computers. Error analysis, which is a form of evaluation, is a technical procedure employed by developers of CAI to revise programs. It involves monitoring the effectiveness of programs.

Observational learning theory presents a variation of this approach. The focus of observational learning is not on the consequence of behavior but on the antecedent, or what comes before a response is learned. Although an instructional problem may be identified and defined as a behavioral objective, the solution is less likely to be a sequence of activities (as it would be for behaviorists). Instead, it will most likely involve a model of the behavior, opportunity for learners to practice, and informative feedback, with appropriate consequences supplying continued motivation.

The key to understanding behavioral approaches to learning and instruction is their common focus on behavior. In the next two chapters, we will be exploring cognitive learning theories, which are markedly different from behavioral approaches and have in common a focus on thought processes. The application of these theories to the solution of instructional problems is more recent and less complete than is the application of behavioral theories to learning and instruction.

concept paper

Evaluation of a Computer-Assisted Instructional Program

Purpose of the assignment

To evaluate a computer-assisted instruction program according to criteria derived from behavioral learning principles.

Directions for the assignment

1. Your task will be to evaluate a piece of instructional software in your teaching field for the effectiveness of its application of behavioral learning principles. Follow this initial procedure to get started:

a. Find a CAI program designed for use in your teaching field. Make sure that the program is in a format that can be viewed by your instructor.
b. Set aside some time to become familiar with the program. If you have never turned on a computer before, now is your chance to familiarize yourself with this instructional tool. If you need help, ask for it.

2. As you familiarize yourself with the program, begin to analyze it using the following questions (adapted from Vargas, 1986). Not all questions may be relevant to the program that you have chosen.

   a. Does the software require a high frequency of responding (as opposed to screens of material to read)?
   b. Is the responding relevant to the goals or objectives of the program? (You may have to ask for the documentation that accompanied the program or estimate its purpose or goals.)
   c. Do students have to respond to the critical parts of the problems?
   d. Is most of the screen content necessary for the response?
   e. Does each screen require students to discriminate between at least two possible responses?
   f. Can students see their progress from session to session as they work through the program?
   g. Do you think that students would be mostly successful as they go through the program? Would they enjoy using the program?
   h. In the case of series or lessons to be used repeatedly, does the program adjust according to the performance level or the progress of the student?

3. Write a three- to four-page typed, double-spaced paper (six to eight pages handwritten) of your evaluation of the program. Begin with an introductory paragraph that specifies the name of the program, indicates where and how it can be viewed, and presents your overall evaluation. In the body of the paper, support your evaluation with your answers to the specific questions. In your concluding paragraph, summarize your overall impressions and indicate whether you would recommend this software.

SUMMARY

1. Behavioral theories define learning as a relatively permanent change in behavior due to experience. This definition leads to a systematic approach to instructional problem solving.

2. The most important behavioral learning theory in this century is that of psychologist B.F. Skinner. His principles, collectively known as operant conditioning, fall into two major categories: learning processes and consequences.

3. The most important educational application of behavioral learning processes is learning analysis. When you perform a learning analysis, you break down a learning task into its component parts and prerequisite steps in order to create a learning hierarchy. With a learning hierarchy in place, you know precisely how to sequence learning for a given task.

4. The most important educational application of behavioral consequences is behavioral analysis.

When you perform a behavioral analysis, you examine a particular behavior to determine what happens before (the antecedent) and what happens after (the consequence).

5. A consequence relates to behavior in one of four ways: as positive reinforcement, negative reinforcement, presentation punishment, or removal punishment.

6. Behavior management or behavior modification is a strategy that results from a behavior analysis. Within this strategy, a teacher implements a particular relationship between a behavior and a consequence—for example, giving the positive reinforcement of a gold star when a student finishes a homework assignment.

7. Learning analysis and behavior analysis can be combined to produce programmed instruction. The best example of programmed instruction is computer-assisted instruction (CAI).

8. Observational or social learning theory was developed by Albert Bandura as an extensive revision of behavioral learning theory. It is often considered a bridge between behavioral and cognitive learning theories. A basic principle of this theory is that an individual can best learn a behavior by watching someone else perform it.

9. Cognitive modeling is one important technique of observational learning. As a teacher you can use cognitive modeling to "self-talk" your way through, for example, the solving of a math problem, so that students can observe your thought processes.

KEY TERMS

SUGGESTED RESOURCES

Bandura, A. (1986). *Social Foundations of Thought and Action.* Englewood Cliffs, N.J.: Prentice-Hall. This book is a complete statement of Bandura's theory of observational learning. Included are many applications, both in and outside of education.

Gagné, R. M. (1985). *The Conditions of Learning.* New York: Holt, Rinehart & Winston. This textbook is a nontechnical introduction to Gagné's approach to instruction, which includes his analysis of domains of learning and description of learning analysis.

Neill, S. B., and G. W. Neill. (annual). *Only the Best: Annual Guide to Highest-rated Education Software/multimedia for Preschool–grade 12.* Carmichael, Calif.: Education News Service. This annual guide lists all types of education software (including drill-and-practice and tutorial programs) that won awards during the year. A cumulative version (with over 1,000 programs listed) exists in disk format.

Skinner, B. F. (1968). *The Technology of Teaching.* Englewood Cliffs, N.J.: Prentice-Hall. This classic text sketches the many implications of programming instruction for education. Although computers have replaced the "teaching machines" Skinner describes, they often function as teachers through the application of operant conditioning principles.

Cognitive Learning Theories, Part 1: Knowledge Acquisition

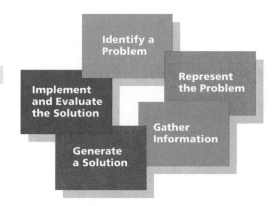

What is knowledge, how do we acquire it, and how do we use it to solve problems and think? These questions form the basis of our exploration of cognitive learning, which is divided into two parts—this chapter and the next one. The goal of this chapter is to introduce you to cognitive processes and structures, and to focus on the basic operations of knowledge acquisition and memory. You will learn about the basic components of the information-processing model of memory and discover how this model represents a cognitive theory of learning. You will also discover numerous strategies to help students develop the fundamental cognitive processes called control processes. As you read, consider these questions:

- **What is a simple definition of knowledge?**

- **In what specific situations might a teacher best teach knowledge directly to students?**

- **When might a teacher better teach learning strategies to students so that they can acquire knowledge on their own?**

- **In human cognition, what element is analogous to computer hardware? To computer software?**

- **What are the three memory structures?**

- **In which memory structure does conscious thought take place?**

- **What is the role of control processes?**

- **Why is the arrangement of information when it is stored in memory so critical to its retrieval?**

learning journal

Principles of Knowledge Acquisition

While reading about knowledge acquisition, make Learning Journal entries about specific experiences in which principles of knowledge acquisition apply. Tell what led up to the experience, name the principles of knowledge acquisition involved, describe how the principles were involved, and describe any relevant outcome. This chapter contains descriptions of the following principles of knowledge acquisition:

- learning strategy
- focusing attention
- enhancing recognition
- chunking
- practice of cognitive skills

- episodic memory
- semantic memory
- schemata
- increasing meaningfulness
- improving organization

KNOWLEDGE ACQUISITION AS A GOAL OF INSTRUCTION

The computer has had a major impact on education, affecting not just the techniques of instruction but also learning theory itself. During the 1940s, psychologists began to realize the potential of the computer as a model of the brain. As computer science became more sophisticated and computers shrank in size, the analogy became even more compelling. Eventually, a new approach to learning theory was developed to explain how the brain processes information.

The analogy of the brain to a computer has suggested some cognitive processes that lead to the goal of knowledge acquisition. **Knowledge** is any organized body of information (Wittrock, 1992). *Knowledge acquisition*, then, involves processes that transform data from experience into organized information. Since the 1940s, models of information processing by machines have been used to identify cognitive processes by which an individual can acquire knowledge. Some of these cognitive processes are derived from similarities between the brain and a computer, but others are derived from an understanding of well-defined differences (Dreyfus & Dreyfus, 1986).

From your experiences with study strategies, you probably know something already about processes used to acquire knowledge. One time-honored strategy taught to high school and college students is SQ3R: *Survey, Question, Read, Recite,* and *Review* (Robinson, 1961). Surveying, questioning, and so on are examples of cognitive processes. Thus, SQ3R is a strategy composed of cognitive processes sequenced to achieve the goal of knowledge acquisition.

How can a teacher sequence cognitive processes to help students learn? To answer that question in an insightful way, we need to approach it from two

> Models of knowledge acquisition can be based on computerized information processing.

directions. First, let's look at how an expert teacher strategically directs the cognitive processes of first graders to help them learn—specifically, by making information memorable. Then, we'll look at the challenge of helping students to become strategists themselves. To empower students as learners, teachers have to help students learn to solve the problem of knowledge acquisition.

Mrs. Bratton's Lesson on Printing

Mrs. Bratton, a first-grade teacher with eighteen students, was just beginning her lesson on how to print the letters S and T. She began by handing out oversized pieces of paper, reminding the children that it was time to do a page of the "alphabet book" that each was making. She told them, "Let's have a pencil box and a pencil ready."

The desks were arranged six across and three deep, all facing the board. Mrs. Bratton had put extra space between the middle rows so that the entire seating arrangement was really composed of six groups of three desks. From time to time during the next twenty minutes she circulated around the seated children, quietly directing the attention of individual students when direction was needed. At the beginning of the lesson, she was at the front, demonstrating against the blackboard how to fold the blank paper in half, from the bottom up. She then turned the paper sideways and told the children to draw a line down the middle, where the crease was.

"Let's look at the left bottom of your paper. Write your name at the left bottom. Try to make it look just like your name tag."

She paused as the children followed instructions. Construction-paper hands labeled "left" and "right" were posted on the blackboard just above her demonstration, and name tags were taped to the top of each desk.

"What letter comes next in our alphabet book?"
"S."
"Right. Now watch me as I make a big S on the board."

Mrs. Bratton carefully positioned herself so that no one had a view that was blocked. She used two different strokes to draw the capital S: a forward C, then a backward one. She knew that students drew letters before they learned to print them, just as most of them drew (rather than printed) their first names. She then drew a lower-case s, explaining that it was a "small s." Finally, she invited the children to draw a big and a small S on the left side of their papers, demonstrating on her paper against the board how to do it. The children had all watched two demonstrations before they attempted their Ss.

Mrs. Bratton circulated as the children drew their letters. When they finished, she walked to the front of the room and began singing words to the tune of "Are You Sleeping": "Listen closely, listen closely, to the sound, to the sound: ssss." The tune gained the attention of the children, and on invitation, they made the sound of S with her. Soon, the whole class was hissing. She told them that she was going to draw a sssnake to go with the S. She drew

> Instructional strategies can make it easier for students to learn.

Young learners cannot construct learning strategies for themselves, but with a teacher's guidance their learning can be strategic. How is this first grader learning to associate the letter F with its sound? *(Frank Siteman/Stock Boston)*

an S-looking snake on the board, then drew it again on her paper, still held against the board so that all of the children could see. "Now you draw a snake on your paper, and you decide what color you want it to be." For the next two or three minutes she circulated, giving the children time to finish drawing and coloring their snakes. Later, Mrs. Bratton called on volunteers to describe their snakes to the class. She held up their artwork (and their Ss) as they described the snakes that they had drawn. Finally, she shifted their attention to the right side of the paper and began work on teaching how to draw the letter T.

The problem that Mrs. Bratton's instructional strategy was designed to solve was the goal of *acquiring knowledge of how to print letters of the alphabet*. Students were learning information in such a way that they could recall it easily. What were the components of her strategy? Clearly, her instruction was filled with devices designed to focus attention, enhance recognition, practice skills, and make material meaningful. Although these cognitive processes often overlapped, they each served a different function.

Learning Strategy Instruction

Assemblages of cognitive processes to achieve some learning goal are known as **learning strategies** (Derry, 1990). Learning strategies differ from instructional strategies in that (1) they focus on knowledge acquisition and (2) they use cognitive processes as learning activities. These processes may be under the control of the teacher, of the student, or of both the teacher and the student. In Mrs. Bratton's class, she was clearly the primary strategist, exercising considerable control over students' processing of information.

Very young learners frequently cannot construct learning strategies by themselves. As you learned in Chapter 5, the short-term memory of a four-year-old is about half that of an adult. Because there is less "space" in the short-term memory of a young child, a teacher of young children must often assume the role of strategist for them. Older children who are slower learners may also require that this role of strategist be fulfilled by the teacher.

Teachers may need to devise learning strategies for young children.

Can learners devise strategies on their own to acquire knowledge? They not only can but often do. Older or more capable learners frequently become skilled at devising learning strategies by themselves (Scruggs & Mastropieri, 1990). Such strategies rely heavily on *metacognitive* knowledge and skills. Students with low levels of these skills might simply use one strategy (such as underlining) over and over, regardless of the nature of the material to be learned or the purpose for learning it. By contrast, students with high levels of these skills are aware of cognitive processes involved in control of perception, memory, and thought. They use problem solving to identify learning goals, represent them in ways that allow them to achieve these goals, take stock of cognitive processes at which they are skilled, and assemble a strategy to acquire knowledge efficiently.

If older or more capable students can learn how to solve problems of knowledge acquisition, presumably these skills can be taught to almost anyone. **Learning strategy instruction** teaches the voluntary use of cognitive processes to meet the goal of knowledge acquisition (Dansereau, 1985). In this form of instruction, students learn to construct or apply a learning strategy to meet some learning goal. This approach to instruction is most commonly used at the high school or college level (e.g., Pauk, 1989; Weinstein & Underwood, 1985), but it has also been developed for upper elementary grades (e.g., Jones, Amiram & Katims, 1985) and is applicable even as early as the second grade (Ghatala et al., 1985).

Teachers can help students develop their own learning strategies.

The various solutions to the problem of knowledge acquisition range along a continuum from teacher control to student control (see Figure 9.1). As a teacher, you will sometimes want to make material memorable without focusing the attention of the learners on the problem of knowledge acquisition. You will want to be the strategist. For example, learners might play a matching game without being aware that they are learning to concentrate (that is, to focus attention). In this case, the conscious goal of the students would be to complete matches, not to learn to concentrate. At other times, you will want to empower students as learners either by teaching them a specific strategy for learning or by giving them tools and techniques to construct strategies of their own (Duffy, 1993). You will have to decide on a case-by-case basis how much student knowledge should be acquired through strategies of your design rather than the design of students.

The range of general solutions to the problem of knowledge acquisition is a little like the proverbial solution to the problem of satisfying a person's hunger. If you want to satisfy his hunger for a day, you need to give him a fish, but if you want to satisfy it for a lifetime, you need to teach the person fishing. The youngest learners and, to some extent, all learners need to be "fed" knowledge through learning strategies of *our* design, but we should also be teaching learners to "fish" knowledge *for themselves* the rest of their lives.

Students will ideally learn how to design learning strategies for themselves.

**Figure 9.1
Strategies to Achieve
the Goal of Knowledge
Acquisition**

Teacher control		Learner control
Instructional strategies designed by teacher	Learning strategy instruction designed by teacher	Learning strategies designed by student

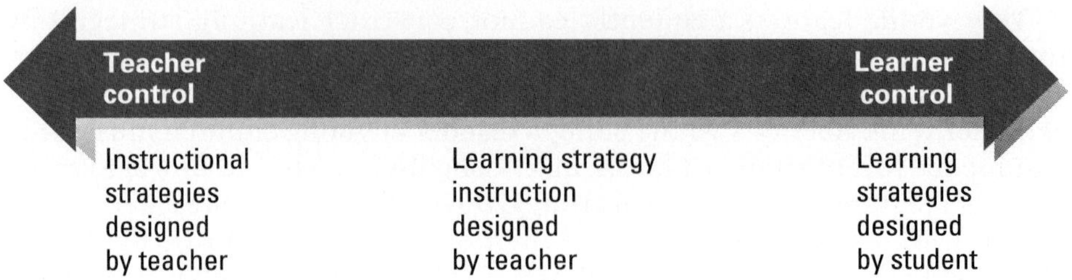

This chapter can serve you well by helping you to identify the various cognitive processes that facilitate knowledge acquisition. The focus of this chapter will be on strategies that incorporate only *one* cognitive process. There are three reasons for proceeding in this way.

First, most recent research has been conducted on simple—as opposed to complex—learning strategies. Many educational psychologists are trying to identify which learning strategies work, and they are having considerable success. The price of this success, however, has been a focus on one cognitive process at a time. Second, the number of possible combinations of cognitive processes is quite large. It is better to study a few of those processes well than to study many poorly. Third, very little is known about effective sequencing of cognitive processes. Traditional study strategies such as SQ3R sequence cognitive processes, but no one knows whether the order makes much difference. At this time, what we do know is that cognitive processes should generally be sequenced to follow the flow of information in memory. This flow is described by an information-processing model of memory.

AN INFORMATION-PROCESSING MODEL OF MEMORY

The key components of both machine and human information processing are (1) *memory structures* that retain information and (2) *control processes*, or procedures that are used to govern the flow of information. In computers, memory structures are identified with fixed capacities and are known as "hardware;" whereas control processes are identified with transitory programs and are known as "software."

Memory Structures

The memory structures of a computer usually involve fixed capacities that are arranged in a sequence to process information. These structures include (1) a "buffer," where information is temporarily stored to keep it for further processing; (2) a "working memory," where information is temporarily stored *while* it is being used for some purpose; and (3) permanent storage (usually on a disk or magnetic tape), where it is stored after use. Information is processed sequentially through these memory structures—from (1) to (2) to (3) and back again from (3) to (2)—it enters the buffer; then it is retained in working memory as long as it is being used; it is "filed" in long-term storage for later use and it is retrieved from storage to working memory when reused.

Psychologists have hypothesized the existence of three types of memory structure in humans, corresponding to the three memory structures in a computer. The most recent of these to be identified is also the first in order of processing. This structure is known collectively as the **sensory registers**, where input is held before we are fully conscious of it (Atkinson & Shiffrin, 1968). The sensory registers act as temporary "buffers" for incoming data, holding it for further processing for only a few seconds.

Information selected for further processing enters the second structure, **short-term memory,** which is approximately the same as consciousness. Short-term memory corresponds to the "working memory" of a computer, or all that the computer can "attend to" when the power is on. The short-term memory of humans, which can hold about seven items of information for a minute or so, is a bottleneck in the flow of information. By contrast, most desktop computers can now hold about a million pieces of information in working memory.

Information selected for permanent storage enters the third memory structure, **long-term memory,** which essentially contains what we know but are not conscious of at the moment. This structure corresponds to the permanent storage of information on "disk" or tape. The fixed capacity of human long-term memory is probably larger than that of desktop computers. There are approximately one *trillion* (or one million million) nerve cells in the brain. When mature, each of these cells (called *neurons*) has about 10,000 connections (called *synapses*) with other nerve cells—a total of 10^{15} possible connections among cells in the brain (Trevarthen, 1987). Neurobiological research suggests that learning has a biological basis in the creation of patterns among these connections (Lynch, 1986). The number of patterns that can be created among such a multitude of cells is virtually endless. (Just think of how many words we can form with the alphabet, which has only twenty-six letters!) Hence, many neurobiologists believe that the capacity of the brain for long-term storage of information is limitless during a lifetime.

If our long-term memories are limitless, why can't we remember more? The answer probably lies in how we *encode* or store information in long-term memory. Much of the information there cannot be *retrieved* or recovered easily because of the way it was encoded when it entered long-term memory. Imagine what would happen if the books in the library had no call numbers and, when a new one was purchased, it was simply added to an unsorted stack of several hundred thousand volumes or more. How would anyone ever retrieve a book on a specific topic? The search would take longer than anyone could afford to spend on it.

> Memory structures in humans may be analogous to those in computer systems.

> Long-term memory seems limitless, but access may be difficult.

Control Processes

A **control process** is any procedure that governs the flow of information in a memory system (Atkinson & Shiffrin, 1968; Herrmann & Searleman, 1990). Control processes are the programs that process information. In a computer,

think it through

Consider this problem that a novice preservice teacher has **IDENTIFIED** and **REPRESENTED.**

Making Learning Memorable and Fun

My major is early childhood, and at this stage in children's development, they are learning many new things, including class rules, vocabulary, and physical skills. I often worry how to make each concept or skill "stick" with my students. What is the best way to help children remember such things?

Observe how an experienced practicing teacher **GENERATES SOLUTIONS** to this problem.

Memory can be aided in a variety of ways in the early-childhood classroom. Basic classroom rules and routines that must be learned will often be forgotten by young children, especially early in the school year. A room full of five-year-olds with classroom rules memorized to perfection on the first day of school does not really meet the basic objective of acceptable and expected behavior. The children will forget because the rules have yet to be applied and experienced. Posting rules, reviewing them often in the first two weeks of the school year, applying them constantly, restating the rules to violators as the consequences are being applied—these are strategies to aid retention.

Routines must be established early and followed consistently during the first month of the school year. At the beginning of each day, the teacher can state the day's activities and then, throughout the day, communicate to the children that "in five minutes we will need to clean up and go to lunch" or "after math we will go to music."

These strategies are consistent with the early-childhood philosophy of "mastery through repetition." As an illustration, consider a scenario in which young children have asked a teacher to read the same short story aloud to them for several days in a row. The perceptive teacher will notice that the children will learn something new from the story each time that they hear it. They learn to master the vocabulary or sequence of events through repetition.

In one of my kindergarten classes, my students and I had almost all of Dr. Seuss's *Green Eggs and Ham* memorized—not through drill and practice but by repeated enjoyable experiences with our favorite book. In fact, we enjoyed it so much that we would read it on a boat, and we would read it with a goat. We would read it here or there; say, we would read it anywhere! We did so like *Green Eggs and Ham.*

Dr. Robert Young
University of North Alabama
Florence, Alabama

think it through, continued

EVALUATE this problem's possible multiple solutions while you think about the dynamic process of problem solving.

Learning takes developmentally appropriate forms that must be considered when you teach any particular age group. Note, in particular, that practice by young children does not take the same form as practice by older children. As the experienced teacher points out, young children should take the lead in initiating practice, and we as adults should follow them by providing the time, materials, and scaffolding for practice of self-selected tasks.

Sometimes these tasks involve physical skills. For example, many children enjoy learning to pour water from one type of container into another. A "water table" with a variety of plastic containers provides children with the opportunity to practice this skill. If a child is practicing pouring, and you are gathering everyone for a story, let the child continue to practice! Too often, we assume that young children should follow our practice schedules rather than their own.

Following rules, primarily a social skill, involves even more integrated development. Like physical skills, social skills must be practiced, but "mastery through repetition" involves (1) practice embedded in natural circumstances—for instance, at the beginning of the year, when rules are new; (2) exemplary behavior, when conscious efforts to follow rules are being made by individuals; and (3) violations of rules, when the need arises to enforce them. Praising children when they adhere to the rules is a good way to restate a rule and encourage others to follow it.

Note the experienced teacher's emphasis on "mastery through repetition." Often, children will ask for a favorite story over and over while you, as a parent or teacher, grow weary of repeatedly reading the same book or telling the same story. What helps is to realize that the children's request has a developmental impetus that should be cherished.

Young children consolidate their physical, social, and intellectual skills in ways that are different from those of older children. During the intermediate phase of skill development, older children can practice through adult-initiated repetition—that is, with end-of-chapter problems, worksheets, practice sessions, exercise routines, rehearsals, and so on. Although a child begins to see these exercises in first grade, they peak in usefulness during the middle elementary years and, again, in high school. Even during these "practice" years, however, new skills are being introduced, and exploration is more appropriate than practice in the beginning phase of any task.

Nevertheless, child-initiated repetition has a special function in infancy and early childhood. It represents consolidation and mastery of a skill—not simply exploration. Piaget observed these repeated actions during early childhood and saw them for what they are: the process of assimilation. Repetitive play with toys (such as trucks or dolls or figurines), like repeated requests for a favorite story (such as Dr. Seuss's *Green Eggs and Ham*), are initiatives that involve assimilation more than accommodation. Play in childhood is often assimilation (or practice) in its purest form.

This is why play during early childhood is so important. It represents extensive and intensive practice of self-chosen skills. The lingering question for me is, Shouldn't most practice in later years be just as fun?

they comprise the software and are stored in permanent memory (on disk or tape); but they are called into working memory whenever needed to transform information. A word-processing program, for example, can be called up to transform keystrokes into words in a document and then to rearrange those words. Alternatively, a spreadsheet program can be called up to transform keystrokes into numbers and to do calculations. *Executive processes* do the "calling up." They correspond with problem solving. This chapter, however, focuses not on executive processes but on lower-order control processes that directly affect the flow of information.

In a human, control processes are the cognitive processes that are used to manage information. Just as there is no fixed number of programs that transform information in a computer, there is no fixed number of control processes that govern memory. Six of these processes are listed in Figure 9.2: attention, recognition, "chunking," practice, meaningfulness, and organization. Each will be discussed in more detail later in the chapter. These processes appear to operate from short-term memory; that is, they are not operative in the sensory registers or in long-term memory. What they have in common is the function of helping information to flow between memory structures.

You might want to take a minute to examine Figure 9.2 carefully or even to make a freehand copy of it for your notes. Though not a complete diagram of all the cognitive processes used to govern memory, it has the virtue of visually organizing most of the information presented in this chapter. Missing from the diagram are "feedback loops," which indicate processes that are self-regulating. Also missing are indications of "decay," the process by which information is lost from the system. Still, the figure is useful as a guide to the general hierarchy of memory governance. As such, it will help you to organize your understanding of the components of human memory and the control processes that are used to govern the flow of information through them.

> Control processes are used to manage information in memory.

Figure 9.2   The Governance of Memory

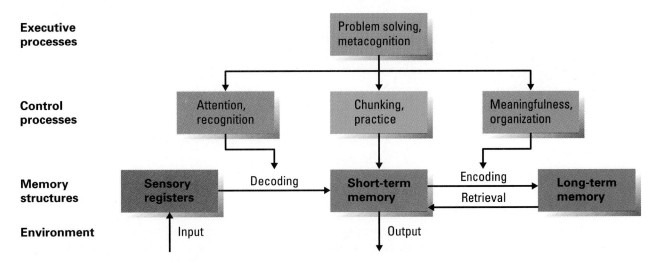

Sensory Registers

Sensory registers hold incoming information for further processing.

"Input," or data from the environment, is stored momentarily in the sensory registers (also called sensory memories). It is thought to be stored here in the form of images—as a visual image of what was seen, an echoic image of what was heard, a tactile image of what was felt, and so on. A sensory register exists for each of the five senses. Many ingenious experiments have been devised to demonstrate that (1) sensory registers exist, (2) sensory images are unprocessed, and (3) sensory images persist for only a few seconds (Klein, 1987).

The importance of the sensory registers seems to lie in the momentary way that images are held for further processing. Sensory registers hold unprocessed images just long enough for recognition of images to occur, but not so long that perception of new images is impeded (Ellis & Hunt, 1989). **Perception,** also known as **recognition,** is the process by which a sensory image is assigned meaning. It occurs through spontaneous comparison of sensory images with knowledge in long-term memory. When the comparison uncovers established associations between sensory images and pre-existing knowledge, meaning is established, and data in the images are *decoded* as information. In other words, data are assigned meaning. The images themselves fade within a second or two.

Perception (recognition) occurs when sensory images are assigned meaning.

All images in the sensory registers are quickly replaced by new images. This replacement is a continuous process, but one of which we are not aware—unless we forget to attend to important input. In that event we must ask someone to repeat what he or she just said, or look twice, or check something again. The important limitation that the sensory registers exercise on learning is related not to their capacity (which is difficult to measure apart from short-term memory) but to the very brief span of time during which input is held for further processing.

strategic solutions

Focusing Attention and Enhancing Recognition

Control processes operate within short-term memory, rather than within the sensory registers, to decode certain aspects of the environment. Decoding generally involves two control processes; attention and recognition. Attention is necessary but not sufficient for recognition, so these two control processes need to be discussed separately.

Focusing Attention

From an information-processing perspective, **attention** entails the allocation of short-term memory capacity. This function, in turn, involves two components: a momentary (and largely involuntary) response and a later (voluntary) prolonging of awareness (Wittrock, 1986). Both the involuntary and voluntary aspects of attention can be controlled.

As a teacher, you can implement several strategies that *focus attention* (Stoiber & Peterson, 1992; Wittrock, 1986). For example, you can take advantage of a largely involuntary (reflex) response to any noise or sudden change in the environment. Specifically, you might *engage the orienting reflex* in young learners by dimming or blinking the lights, or by playing a chord on the piano. And you might engage it in older learners by turning on an overhead projector light or by standing silently. The reason you might decide to engage this response is to switch the attention of students from one source of information (such as auditory input) to another (such as visual input). Many teachers use this reflex to orient attention, but strategic control of the orienting reflex remains with the teacher. By definition, reflex responses cannot be under the voluntary control of the learner.

Strategies that address the second component of attention are sometimes under the control of the teacher, but they can also be taught to learners to enhance self-control. These strategies focus and prolong attention. Mrs. Bratton focused student attention on visual input by saying "Now watch me" and on auditory input by singing, "Listen closely. . . ." As a teacher, you can *use games or enjoyable exercises to focus attention.* The popular game "Simon Says" can be used in early grades to teach children to attend to auditory input apart from visual input. And "concentration" or matching games are sometimes used with older students to focus attention. Indeed, teachers can deliberately employ such games as part of an instructional strategy to train attention.

Other strategies for focusing and prolonging attention are under the control of the learner. To teach them, you need to *instruct students to apply a strategy to focus attention.* Probably the earliest strategy that you learned to focus attention yourself was a variant of "stop, look, and listen." It is a strategy parents teach their children so that they can cross streets safely when their parents aren't around. In this case, the specific problem was to attend to traffic; the strategy was composed of a sequence of three steps to achieve the goal. You were probably taught when and how to apply this strategy.

What academic tasks are similar to crossing a street? Let's take the example of reading an unfamiliar word. If not taught a strategy, children will skip over unfamiliar words in their reading and attend only to the words that they know. To counter this tendency, you were probably taught a three-step strategy similar to "stop, look, and listen." This strategy went something like "Break the word into smaller parts; sound out each part; and put the parts together." When this strategy is applied, a reader learns to pronounce many words that otherwise might be ignored.

Most learning strategy instruction to focus attention follows the form of "stop, look, and listen":

1. Discuss the strategy in terms of its rationale: "Why do we need to stop, look, and listen when we come to a street?"

Standing silently in front of a class is often sufficiently different from what a teacher does normally that it will attract attention for a few moments. This teacher is also modeling her expectations for students. *(Spencer Grant/Liaison International)*

2. Demonstrate application of the strategy to achieve a goal, with students assuming the role of strategist: "Let's pretend this is a street—when I come to it, tell me what to do."

3. Have students apply the strategy in a variety of learning situations: "Show me what you would do to cross a bicycle path (or railroad track) safely."

You can design learning strategies to improve the selective attention of your students in any number of learning situations, such as pronouncing a new word, working word problems in math (which are also often skipped over), or studying. But check to make sure that the strategy is being applied *outside* your direct supervision, because transfer does not always occur. The goal of learning strategy instruction is the independent application of the strategy in any situation that calls for it. You will learn more about how to teach attention-focusing strategies to students in Chapter 13, where we shall consider the topic of behavior management.

Enhancing Recognition

A second category of strategies that influence information in the sensory registers pertains to the enhancement of recognition. You will recall that recognition involves assigning meaning to data. You can enhance recognition in one of two ways: by improving the clarity of information or by progressively increasing the decoding speed. Improving the clarity of information is often assumed to be the responsibility of the teacher, whereas speeding up decoding is often assumed to be a product of extensive practice arranged by either the teacher or the learner.

Direct enhancement of recognition often requires that you *improve the clarity of information.* Many factors affect the clarity with which information is presented to a learner. Mrs. Bratton's demonstration of how to print an *S* illustrates several factors that improve clarity:

- Establish clear lines of sight to the location of the demonstration.
- Use oversized writing and demonstration materials.
- Amplify your voice or signals, and write clearly.
- Use words and examples that are meaningful to your students.

All of these elements were embedded in Mrs. Bratton's instructional strategy. She made sure that all students could see what she wrote *as* she wrote on the blackboard. Her first demonstration of printing (on the blackboard rather than on her paper) was oversized. Her voice and writing were clear. And her vocabulary was understood by all of the children in the class (not just by the average child).

No matter how attentive students are, if images are not clearly recognized in the sensory registers, they cannot be assigned meaning except by default ("I can't see." "Can you read what he wrote?" "What did she say?"). As a beginning teacher, you should *not* assume that what is clear to you is also clear to your students. Typewritten handouts, for example, are acceptable, but the use of typed material with an overhead projector is *not*, even if the overhead seems to enlarge it. If the student in the back of your room cannot read what you have written, consistently hear you, or see crucial signals, or if the student with the smallest vocabulary in the room cannot understand what you have written or said, then the results you achieve will reflect more on the quality of your teaching than on the ability of your students to learn (see Reflection on Practice: Framing Vocabulary to Suit Understanding). Among other things, you must be able to speak loudly or signal clearly, write large, and keep instructions simple if you plan to use whole-group instruction.

Over the years, many other efforts to enhance recognition have involved training students to recognize symbols or images of various kinds (such as numbers, words, or shapes). One of the most effective of these strategies is to *speed up the decoding process*. The general procedure can be illustrated using the example of helping students speed up their recognition of sight vocabulary words (or "instant recognition words"). These are words that a reader immediately identifies on sight:

1. Using a story told by a student or from a reading passage, develop a list of words to be recognized on sight.
2. Present these words to the class on flashcards, one after the other, allowing time for the students to pay attention to critical features.
3. With each presentation of the list, vary the order of items to eliminate accidental cues due to item order (for example, shuffle the "deck" of words).
4. Increase the rate of presentation of items over a number of trials until recognition appears to be automatic (that is, present about one word per second).

After recognition has become automatic, you will want your students to use the symbols in some meaningful context, such as reading material, and to begin to work on reading comprehension skills. Automatic word recognition is a necessary but not sufficient skill for improving reading comprehension (Fleisher, Jenkins & Pany, 1979; Mezynski, 1983).

Although speeding up decoding involves a good deal of teacher control, notice how fundamentally different it is in this regard from the first recognition strategy discussed. By its very nature, improving the clarity of information will always involve the teacher. The flashcard strategy, however, has at least the possibility of becoming "student-owned" and under greater control of the learner. In fact, by upper elementary school, some students make flashcards for themselves as a study device. What we do not yet know is the age at which students can learn this procedure or be taught it, or how students can be led to apply it independently in any appropriate learning situation.

Evaluation: Focusing Attention and Enhancing Recognition

The evaluation of strategies to focus attention and enhance recognition requires that three questions be asked:

strategic solutions, continued

reflection on practice

Framing Vocabulary to Suit Understanding

After teaching tenth- and eleventh-graders biology for several years, I was given a seventh-grade life science class because we had an overload of seventh-graders. I thought, "No problem." I prepared my lesson plans in advance and was ready for the first day of school. Everything was fine for the first three days. I issued books, gave assignments, and tried to learn the names of my students. The first lesson went fairly well. It concerned the metric system and was a review for most of the class.

The next chapter was about science and the scientific method. As I began to talk about scientific method, I had the first inkling of a problem. The students looked at me with big eyes full of empty thoughts. I backtracked, went over the material again, and asked a question. All eyes went to the front, but not a hand went up. Finally I asked, "Does anyone know what the word *systematic* means?" All the students shook their heads "no." "Do you know what *analyze* means?" Again they said no. So I started explaining the meaning of the words and went over the lesson again.

Any time I saw a question in the eyes of the students, I made sure I spoke in simpler terms than I had before. Now when I use a term or word that is over their heads, someone will raise a hand and ask, as I have told them to do.

This experience is an example of failing to use words that students recognize. In preparing my lesson, I forgot to represent the instructional problem in a way that took account of the limited vocabulary of seventh-graders.

Elaine Lauderdale

Discussion Questions

1. What effect(s) might the vocabulary level of students have on the lesson plans of a teacher? For example, how might you approach assignments differently for seven-, thirteen-, and sixteen-year-olds?

2. The teacher sensed a need to monitor her own vocabulary level and developed the strategy of having students raise hands when they did not recognize a word she used. What are some potential strengths of this strategy? Some potential weaknesses?

3. How can the need to monitor one's own vocabulary be minimized by adopting an alternative approach to instruction?

1. Are the strategies to focus attention and enhance recognition effective?
2. Do the goals of focusing attention and enhancing recognition represent the best use of time?
3. Is *learning* strategy instruction effective in these areas?

Let's look at these questions separately. First, are these strategies effective? The answer is "yes, to a degree." Attempts to influence attention and enhance recognition promote knowledge acquisition, particularly among young, moderately capable, and less capable learners (Rosenshine & Stevens, 1986; Walberg, 1986; Wittrock, 1992). You have already discovered (in Chapter 5) that extreme teacher control (as manifested in detailed procedures) can impair the problem-solving abilities of students, but most educators would agree that moderate teacher control over attentional and perceptual processes is appropriate, particularly when knowledge acquisition is the goal.

The objections to teacher control that do exist are made on grounds other than what works to promote knowledge acquisition. For some educators, the lingering issue is whether teachers or students should do the controlling (Duffy, 1993; Weinstein & Meyer, 1986). Those who argue that students should do more of the controlling are highly supportive of learning strategy instruction to supplement, and in many instances replace, teacher influence on student attention and perception.

Second, do the goals of focusing attention and enhancing recognition represent the best use of time? The answer is "sometimes." The time spent in training activities (such as "Simon Says") is time necessarily taken away from other learning activities. Some content (such as knowledge of safety rules or recognition of warning signs) is so important that all students profit from training selective attention to it or rapid recognition of it. But evidence also suggests that we can teach students to be attentive by having them solve interesting problems (Halpain, Glover & Harvey, 1985). Rather than drills to increase speed of decoding, then, why not use a simple problem-solving game (Hirst, 1988)? The decision of whether to train control processes directly, or to develop them in the course of achieving higher-order goals, is not a simple one. You must consider all of the givens in a particular instructional problem, including the maturity and capability of your students, information load, and the criterion of evaluation.

Finally, is *learning* strategy instruction effective in these areas? The answer is that we do not yet know. Some evidence exists that students can learn to attend selectively to information in new settings *if* they are taught to transfer this skill beyond the setting in which it was learned. For transfer to occur, students involved in attention training must be aware of the purpose of the strategy and the strategy must be applied in a wide variety of learning situations (Kendall & Wilcox, 1980).

Less is known about how to teach students to enhance recognition. Students can be taught to use flashcards, but as yet there is very little evidence that teaching students to do so results in effective use of this strategy in a variety of appropriate circumstances. Nevertheless, anecdotal evidence tells us that some students do learn to use flashcards effectively. Presumably, if this skill can be learned, it can be taught.

For the average child, the capacity of short-term memory is fewer than seven items. Why might this young man need to read the phone number while dialing?
(Richard Hutchings)

Short-Term Memory

From the sensory registers, only a small portion of information flows to short-term memory. Information that occupies our attention will be retained in short-term memory up to a minute, but it too will be lost if not processed further. The short-term memory is where the all-important transformation of information must occur.

> The average adult can keep seven items in short-term memory.

The capacity of short-term memory has long been known to be around seven items for an average adult and fewer than that for an average child, depending on the age of the child (see Figure 9.3). It is no coincidence that local phone numbers and license plates throughout North America are no more than seven items long, no matter what state or province one is in. The capacity of short-term memory was discovered by the German scholar Hermann Ebbinghaus (1913/1885) at about the time telephones and automobiles came into existence.

In order to test the accuracy of the averages in Figure 9.3, I spontaneously made up a few short lists of words (all of which were concrete and relatively unrelated in meaning) to ask my son to recite after one reading. At the time he was four-and-a-half years old. According to Figure 9.3, the majority of children this age have a short-term memory capacity of four items. I asked my son to repeat the following four unrelated words after I had finished saying them at the rate of about one per second: *boat, apple, star, dog.* He repeated them without any problem (though he wondered why I had asked him to do this). When I used a string of five new words, however, he tried to begin, realized that he could not repeat them, and asked me to say them again.

Experiments with many individuals (Dempster, 1981) have shown how little variation there is among people in this capacity, but many researchers

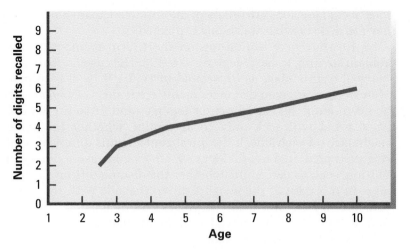

**Figure 9.3
Development of Digit
Span**
(Terman & Merrill, 1973)

believe that such variance is extremely important in the context of learning. The difference between "average" and "superior" short-term memory for an adult is just two items (from seven to nine). The difference between the average short-term memories of four- and ten-year-olds is also just two items (from four to six). These small but reliable differences may actually account for substantial differences in learning capabilities.

> Different capacities in short-term memory may account for different learning capacities.

The Function of Short-Term Memory

The importance of short-term memory lies in the operating space that it provides for thinking—what Robbie Case (1985b) has called **executive processing space.** Executive processing is the equivalent of problem solving (Sternberg, 1984). This space appears to be flexibly divided between operating space and short-term storage space. The more operating space required by thinking, the less room for short-term storage of information, and vice versa.

Since simple recall does not require much operating space, storage of information can be maximized. Being asked to recall, say, a short list of words or numbers just read, or a sentence just heard, does not require the assembly of a problem-solving strategy. But the demands on operating space by tasks that require complex operations can be great enough to prevent short-term storage of adequate information to solve the problem. In short, not enough can be "kept in mind" to solve some reading or mathematics problems without either writing down intermediate steps (as when a word problem is represented symbolically) or practicing a great deal.

> Problem solving requires both strategy and short-term memory.

Limitations on Instruction

We have already discussed (in Chapter 5) the developmental limitations on instructional strategies that flow from cognitive developmental theory. In particular, young children have a short-term memory capacity that is about half that of an adult. One reason complex directions or explanations are developmentally inappropriate for young children is that by the time the directions or explanations are finished, the children can no longer remember what they are to do or what was being explained!

To illustrate how limitations on short-term memory capacity influence problem solving, Robert Siegler (1976, 1986) has used a "balance-beam" task. The goal of this task, as illustrated in Figure 9.4a–c, is to predict whether given weights at given distances on different sides of a balance beam will tip the beam after the experimenter lets go—and, if so, in which direction. A five-year-old will seek only to determine whether the same number of weights are on each side. If the number of weights differs, the side with more weights is predicted to fall (Figure 9.4a). By contrast, a nine-year-old will, in addition, seek to determine whether the distances from the fulcrum are the same. In this case, if the weights differ, the side with the heavier weight is predicted to fall. And if the distances differ, the side with weights farther from the fulcrum is predicted to fall (Figure 9.4b).

But what if both the weights *and* the distances differ? (See Figure 9.4c.) This question is harder, requiring greater executive processing space to answer correctly. Products of weight and distance must be calculated for each side before the two sides can be compared. (The correct answer to the problem in Figure 9.4c is that the beam will balance.) Why are young children unable to solve this problem? One answer seems to be that until adolescence, there is not enough room in executive processing space to assemble and execute a strategy with more than three steps (Case, 1993; Roth, 1991; Siegler, 1986). *Four* steps (listed in Figure 9.5) are required to solve problems in which both the weights and the distances differ.

Teachers intuitively take into account such limitations on short-term memory capacity by simplifying problems or by leading children through complex solution procedures one step at a time. Mrs. Bratton made the problem of drawing letters very simple. And remember in Chapter 3 how the art teacher led kindergartners through the complex procedure for drawing a hamburger? Even young children can be taught complex actions if the proce-

> Lessons must account for the fact that young children have limited short-term memory.

Figure 9.4
Three Balance-Beam Problems
(Adapted from Siegler, 1976)

"Will the beam balance or tip when I let go? If it tips, in which direction will it go?"

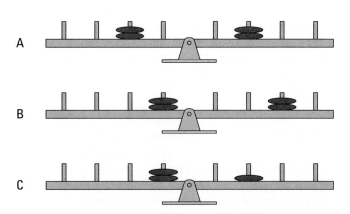

A

B

C

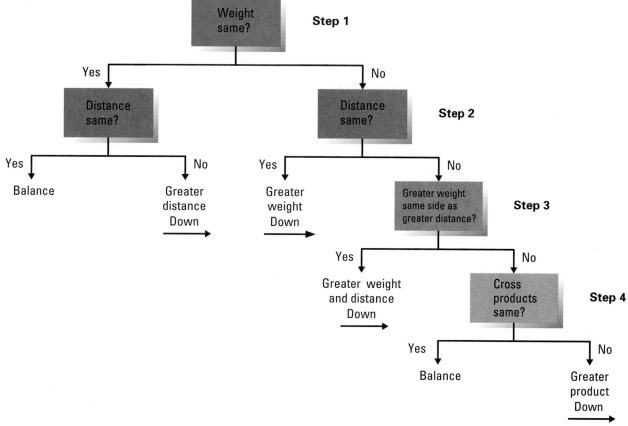

Figure 9.5   Four Levels of Solution to Balance-Beam Problems *(Adapted from Siegler, 1976)*

dures are simplified or if the teacher assumes much of the executive role. What young children cannot do is keep in mind complicated procedures or assemble a problem-solving strategy that has more than a few steps. Demanding that they do so would be developmentally inappropriate.

strategic solutions

Chunking and Practice

Because short-term memory is such a bottleneck, it may appear that there's little we can do as teachers to alter the limitations on instruction imposed by it. Over the past twenty years, however, significant progress has been made on the subject of what a teacher can do to help students use this space more effectively. Let's look at two such strategies: chunking and practice.

The purpose of **chunking** is to integrate smaller units of information into larger wholes, such as words into phrases, or smaller numbers into larger ones (Miller, 1956). Whereas adults can store only about six or seven randomly chosen letters in short-term memory, they can store about nine letters as consonant-vowel-consonant trigrams (such as CAV) and as many as fifty letters in a meaningful sentence (Baddeley, 1990). Accordingly, you might want to *encourage students to chunk information into larger units.*

To develop comprehension, encourage students to read text in phrases rather than in words, or to see objects as mathematical "groupings" rather than as entities in themselves. For students who call out individual words, you might try a strategy as obvious as drawing short lines between meaningful phrases, or asking the students to draw such lines themselves; then reread the passage (Casteel, 1990). Alternatively, to develop number sense, you might ask the students to perceive a particular number of pencils, buildings, or whatever, rather than simply one (singular) or more than one (plural). Chunking encourages students to comprehend meaning through groupings, thereby using short-term memory effectively (see Reflection on Practice: Chunking in Music).

Of even greater significance to efficient use of short-term memory is *practice.* Practice (sometimes called rehearsal) takes different forms, depending on its purpose. A common purpose for practice of a cognitive task is reduction of what is called the **cognitive load,** or the degree to which short-term memory space is occupied by the task. Practice of a cognitive task leads to efficient use of short-term memory by reducing the cognitive load in various ways. The fundamental strategy, however, is the same overall: *reduce cognitive load through practice of a cognitive task.*

You need to decide what type of cognitive task is involved in order to understand how to practice it. If the task requires memorization, practice should be consistent and under stable conditions. Practice under stable conditions is sometimes called *recitation.* Under these conditions, you should *use recitation to support memorization.* For example, you might ask students to recite the letters of the alphabet, or lines from a play or speech, in order to memorize them.

Practice of even simple cognitive skills (such as those used in decoding text or performing mental math), however, requires that the conditions change. New material is thus needed to ensure that cognitive load is reduced through practice of the skill, rather than through memorization. Accordingly, you need to *change material when practicing cognitive skills.* If you don't do so, repeated practice sessions will lead to memorization—and you may find that students who are supposed to be "reading" are actually reciting!

Relatively simple cognitive skills can probably be learned through repeated practice with changing material, but relatively complex cognitive skills (such as solving multistep math problems or writing a critique) require greater cognitive resources. To speed the process of learning them, you can

Practice is designed to reduce cognitive load in various ways. What different skills are being practiced in this band rehearsal? *(George White Location Photography)*

proceduralize them. Recall from Chapter 5 the discussion of *procedural facilitation,* in which procedures are stated as steps in the accomplishment of a task. By following such steps repeatedly, a person can transform rules and facts into "know-how." That know-how, in turn, can be compiled in such a way that operations occur more quickly and efficiently. In short, the strategy is to *proceduralize complex cognitive skills to reduce cognitive load.* You can even proceduralize in a stepwise fashion using skills arranged in a hierarchy (Case, 1985a; Roth, 1991).

Evaluation: Chunking and Practice

Strategies such as chunking and practice help manage information load on short-term memory. They deal with the bottleneck in our memory system by economizing use of executive processing space. That is a very important achievement, and many teachers take advantage of it to help students comprehend meaning and acquire basic skills (cf. Samuels, 1988). Notice, for example, how much practice occurs in the first through third grades to establish proficiency in reading, writing, and arithmetic. These skills are building blocks on which more complex skills often depend. If information is

strategic solutions, continued

reflection on practice

Chunking in Music

Patricia is a smart, musical fourth-grade student who has been coming to piano instruction for the past ten months. She is a quiet, reserved child whose stated goal for piano lessons (as related by her mother) is to achieve her own personal pleasure. Patricia expresses no desire to participate in local and state festivals and auditions. She does, however, want to play in the spring recital.

Patricia's last lesson assignment was to memorize "Water Lilies" for use as a recital piece. After we had started with the theory portion of the assignment, Patricia asked if we could play the piece but skip the theory since she wasn't going to auditions where she would be tested. My previous explanations and examples of the usefulness of theoretical knowledge had obviously not been taken to heart. Using another approach, I asked her to be a detective and find out if theory could be useful or important.

I asked Patricia to play "Water Lilies" by memory. She played with many mistakes and was unable to finish. She was relying on reading and remembering each note rather than relating the music to the theoretical concepts we were working on. We reviewed two basic concepts—the major triad and the use of I, IV, and V chords in a given key. When these two concepts are applied, chunking of information becomes possible and memory is greatly simplified. Relating the piece to these two concepts, Patricia found seven phrases of information. We talked about how chunking provided clues for information in each phrase (what notes to play) and how simple rules actually allowed us to predict what would come in the next "chunk" of information. I had her diagram the basic structure of her piece and then play the piece using the diagram—not the actual music.

After rehearsing the diagram twice, Patricia played the piece by memory with only one small mistake, which she recognized and corrected. We then discussed her detective report, concluding that the theory was a valuable tool that in the long run would enable her to perform many pieces in a more efficient way.

Kay Grubbs

Discussion Questions

1. Chunking is a common practice in musical performance. By chunking information of one type or another, this student can accomplish what goals?

2. What other skills are commonly chunked through theory? Give both academic and nonacademic examples.

3. Either mental or physical skills can be chunked. Which of these categories is the predominant form in this example? Why?

not chunked, or relatively simple cognitive skills are not practiced, the information or skills become a stumbling block to the acquisition of more complex knowledge and skills later on.

If there is any general criticism of strategies such as chunking and practice, it is that they are not necessarily accompanied by corrective feedback. Practice alone does not improve a skill in the sense of correcting it, but strategies such as chunking and practice are used to economize the use of processing space, so that the learner can attend to other matters.

Long-Term Memory

Experiments with individuals who have profound memory loss have convincingly demonstrated that information to be retained beyond a minute must be stored in a long-term memory structure. Psychologists are less certain about the nature of this structure than about that of sensory registers or short-term memory. In fact, long-term memory has been the subject of lively debate for some time.

Agreement, however, exists primarily on two related points. First, long-term memory capacity has no known limit. The defining feature for long-term memory is not the extent of the capacity but how information is arranged. Second, for information to be retrieved, it must be stored in some relation to previously stored information. Isolated bits of information either are quickly forgotten or shortly become inaccessible.

> Long-term memory seems to have no limit.

The more controversial aspects of long-term memory have been an issue for years (Alba & Hasher, 1983; Tulving, 1983). Some philosophers and psychologists have believed that information is stored for the long term in relation to times in our personal lives. In short, they have suggested that memory is primarily **episodic.** Others have believed that information is stored in relation to networks of meaning, and that memory is primarily **semantic.** This word comes from the Greek verb for "to signify"; as an adjective it means "pertaining to meaning." Many psychologists now assume that memories are stored in relation to both events *and* meaning. More particularly, they believe that meaning is abstracted from similarities among events as experience occurs, particularly during the formative years.

> Memories may be stored on the basis of episodes in life or of meaning.

We have all experienced both types of memories. Have you ever heard an old song on the radio and subsequently recollected a specific moment in your past when that song was popular? Perhaps you were even able to figure out the date of the record from your age at the time you first heard the song. This information is contained in episodic memory. Little research has been done on the imagery in episodic memory, but it is probably quite rich given all the information stored as events there. Information about the performer of the song and about other recordings by that artist, however, is contained in semantic memory. Information in semantic memory is probably abstracted from numerous events. It is also comparatively well organized—our definition of *knowledge.*

Perhaps the most important issue for educators has been a debate over the way information is organized in semantic memory. Simply asserting that it is organized as "networks of meaning" does not tell us very much. Many researchers have used the term **schema** (plural: *schemata*) to denote knowledge generalized about a particular domain (Bartlett, 1932; Piaget, 1969). Schemata can be conceived of as *sets of expectations that affect attention and perception as well as other aspects of cognition* (Anderson, 1984).

Schemata are not inert; indeed, they exert an active role in knowledge acquisition. They select information to be retained, encode and abstract it, interpret it, and integrate it into previous knowledge. Schemata in the form of expectations may distort attention and perceptions somewhat (Steffensen, Joag-Dev & Anderson, 1979), but they also provide the advantages of rapid recognition and understanding of information.

> Schemata are expectations that affect how knowledge is acquired and retained.

Expectations explain why memories are not like videotapes of experience but, rather, reflect our interpretations at the time the input was encoded. What they do not explain very well is the effect of new learning on prior knowledge, or changes in expectations. Expectations can be influenced by input, just as input can be influenced by expectations. Piaget referred to this process of give and take in learning as *adaptation* (see Chapter 5).

The Function of Long-Term Memory

The form in which information is stored in long-term memory is largely dependent on our purpose at the time that we acquire it (e.g., Humphreys, Bain & Pike, 1989). If information was not symbolically transformed when initially processed, it was probably associated with an event but only incidentally related to semantic knowledge. Recall of it will tend to be episodic. To find out where we left our keys, for example, we generally try to recollect what happened when we last had them.

On the other hand, if we attended to the information for a specific purpose—such as solving a problem—we probably integrated it with previous knowledge. Memory of it will be both episodic and semantic.

> Long-term memory may be classified as episodic, semantic/declarative, or semantic/procedural.

The flexible and virtually unlimited storage capacity of long-term memory allows us to function efficiently in a variety of situations for a prolonged period of time. Think how differently we use memory to remember where we left our keys (episodic), to remember how to start our car (semantic/procedural), and to remember where we want to go (semantic/declarative). Within less than a minute in each case, we need to be able to use these different forms of memory. How many forms of memory do we possess? Most psychologists have given up the belief that there is only one form. Currently, the most popular assumption is that at least three forms exist (episodic, semantic/declarative, and semantic/procedural). In fact, more than three are possible.

Limitations on Instruction

Given virtually no limit on the capacity of long-term memory, and multiple forms of memory, it would seem that long-term memory storage offers few limitations on strategies to solve instructional problems. But in fact a rather strict limitation exists. Try the following experiment. Take a moment from study to see how quickly you can recite the months in the year beginning with January, using a watch or clock to time yourself. How long did retrieval take? Now try to recite the months of the year in *alphabetical* order, again timing yourself. How long did retrieval take this time? The point of this experiment is that long-term memories are stored in the same way that they were acquired. If we try to retrieve them in a different way, recall can be very difficult.

> Retrieval of a memory is related to how it was stored.

strategic solutions

Increasing Meaningfulness

Virtually all control processes for long-term memory help students elaborate information that they are learning. They are sometimes referred to in the context of **elaborative rehearsal** because they involve relating new information to previously acquired knowledge. The techniques used to elaborate information for storage in long-term memory fall into two categories. The older and better-known category involves *increasing meaningfulness* of information (refer to Figure 9.2 earlier in the chapter).

Meaningfulness is a function of the number and distinctiveness of associations between new information and information stored in long-term memory. As a process to control the storage of information in long-term memory, increasing meaningfulness requires that you help students elaborate relationships between new information and what they already know, and increase the distinctiveness of the new information by contrasting it with what they already know (Ellis & Hunt, 1989).

One general procedure you can use to increase meaningfulness is to *compare and contrast new information with previously acquired information.* Comparison may involve recall of information learned on a previous day or in a previous class (Peterson et al., 1982). Or it may involve an analogy between information to be learned and an event in the life of the learner. Contrast, on the other hand, may involve highlighting dissimilarities between new information and previous learning, or pointing out unique features of material to be learned (see Reflection on Practice: Taking Time to Smell the *Squid?*). In the end, the goal should be to make material meaningful so that it can be retrieved easily and accurately.

Another way to increase meaningfulness is to use **mediation techniques,** which involve creating a specific linkage between input and information already stored in long-term memory. (As you know, a mediator in government

strategic solutions, continued

reflection on practice

Taking Time to Smell the *Squid*?

Sometimes students have difficulty understanding unfamiliar organisms in Biology I. When we study organisms such as invertebrates, for example, the students find them foreign and intangible.

Last week we studied mollusks. We dissected preserved clams, and the students seemed to enjoy the lab. I mentioned that clams had economic importance, food being one aspect. Someone said, "Ugh! Who on earth would eat something slimy that looked like that?" Others seemed to agree. I explained that clams were delicious to many people. Then they wanted to know about "things" like squid. "Who eats *squid?*"

I replied, "Calamari is served in many fine restaurants." About that time, the bell rang. That afternoon I went to the store and bought three pounds of whole squid. Boy, did we have fun the next day! We had a "sensory lab." I took several of the unpreserved squid and baby clams and passed them around on trays. The students observed, touched, and dissected them—and, of course, we all *smelled* them. We talked about functional parts and observed each. This discussion gave the students a better understanding of how the organisms survive.

The following day, I loaded my wok, the remaining squid (which I had cleaned), and other ingredients into my car. In class I demonstrated the preparation of calamari and fried clams. Most of the students enjoyed tasting this food for the first time. Two or three didn't sample it, and only a couple of those who did found it unpleasant. Many students came back for seconds and thirds. One student asked for exact cleaning instructions and the recipe to share with his aunt.

For most, then, it was a positive and meaningful learning experience. Now I know that my students understand how two unfamiliar organisms look, feel, smell, and taste. They can describe the life activities of these organisms as well as their workings. No longer are these organisms foreign and recognizable only by picture. I feel that this learning experience was meaningful because it was represented in several different sensory modalities. It was also memorable because the sensations were different from what my students usually experience.

Adina Stone

Discussion Questions

1. In what ways did this teacher use distinctiveness to increase the meaningfulness of the learning experience?

2. What do you think were the teacher's content objectives, as set by her curriculum guide? How did her lesson meet these objectives?

3. Can you remember a similar experience you had in high school? Describe it in detail. What made it memorable, other than its distinctiveness?

brings together factions that cannot get together on their own to work out an understanding.) **Mnemonics,** the ancient art of improving memory, involves an assortment of mediation techniques known as *mnemonic devices* designed to make input more meaningful both in number and distinctiveness of associations. The rule of thumb is to *use mnemonics for suitable purposes and materials.* Some mnemonic devices are natural language mediators. Examples include *acronyms,* words formed from letters which cue memory; *acrostics,* short phrases in which the initial letter of each word cues memory; and *rhymes.* Each of these devices integrates numerous related pieces of information with something easier to remember, such as a word, short phrase, or rhyming sentence. Accordingly, *use acronyms, acrostics, or rhymes for learning a series of related terms, facts, or actions.* Several examples of natural language mediators suggested by teachers are listed in Table 9.1.

In Reflection on Practice: Teaching History Through Mnemonics, a history teacher describes how, each year, she and her students make an acrostic for the historical steps leading to the American Revolution. Such verbal mnemonics aid memory, but you need to be sure that your students are using them to jog their memory, not as a substitute for understanding. Model their use as "tags" to speed access to procedures or understanding. And when you assess the students' knowledge, do so in a way that cues the use of the natural language mediators but also requires demonstration of procedures or understanding.

Other mnemonic devices are visual images that are highly memorable. They are deliberately associated with images of things that are not as easy to remember. One of the oldest visual mnemonic devices is the *loci method.* Pronounced "low sigh," the word *loci* is Latin for "places." *Use the loci method to access items in a series in their original order.* The items in a series could be the points in a speech, for example. The loci method, which originated in ancient Greece, involves accessing a series of places already stored in long-term memory, such as houses or buildings in a familiar neighborhood, or furnishings in a familiar room. Items on the list to be remembered are then mentally distributed, one to each place. In other words, as a mental tour is taken of the neighborhood or room, the learner visualizes putting an item from the list at each place. Then, when the learner needs to "re-collect" the items on the list, he or she simply repeats the mental tour. The learner may be surprised (and a little unnerved) to "see" each item on the list exactly where it was left.

Pegwords (also called *pegs*) refer to concrete objects that are easily visualized. Usually they rhyme with a number, as in the following list:

one-bun (or gun)	six-sticks
two-shoe	seven-heaven (or oven)
three-tree	eight-gate (or plate)
four-door	nine-line
five-hive (or knives)	ten-hen (or pen)

s t r a t e g i c   s o l u t i o n s ,   c o n t i n u e d

Table 9.1   *Natural Language Mediators*

Acronyms

BANGS: Classes of French adjectives that precede nouns (Beauty, Age, Number, Gender, Size)

FACE: Spaces on the treble clef

FOIL: Order of operations in the multiplication of binomials such as $(x + 2)$ $(y + 3)$ (First by first, Outer by outer, Inner by inner, Last by last)

GRACE'S ADMIRER: Thirteen life functions (Growth, Reproduction, Absorption, Circulation, Excretion, Secretion, Assimilation, Digestion, Movement, Ingestion, Respiration, Egestion, Response)

ROY G. BIV: Colors of the spectrum (Red, Orange, Yellow, Green, Blue, Indigo, Violet)

SEND MR. CURI: Ten systems of the body (Skeletal, Endocrine, Nervous, Digestive, Muscular, Respiratory, Circulatory, Urinary, Reproductive, Integumentary)

Acrostics

"Every Good Boy Does Fine": Lines on the treble clef

"Fat Boys Eat Apple Dumplings Greedily": Number of flat notes in music keys (one flat in the key of F, two flats in the key of B, etc.)

"Kids Have Dropped Over Dead Converting Metrics": Prefixes of metric units (kilo-, hectar-, deka-, origin, deci-, centi-, and milli-)

"On Old Olympus's Towering Top, A Finn And German Viewed Some Hops": Twelve cranial nerves (Olfactory, Optic, Oculomotor, Trochlear, Trigeminal, Abducens, Facial, Acoustic, Glossopharyngeal, Vagus, Spinal accessory, and Hypoglossal)

"My Very Educated Mother Just Served Us Nine Pizzas": Order of the planets, as arranged by distance from the sun, nearest to farthest (Mercury, Venus, Earth, Mars, Jupiter, Saturn, Uranus, Neptune, Pluto)

"Please Excuse My Dear Aunt Sally": Order of operations in algebra (Parentheses, Exponents, Multiplication, Division, Addition, Subtraction)

Rhymes

"Columbus sailed the ocean blue in fourteen hundred and ninety-two."

"*I* before *e* except after *c* and when sounded like *a* as in *neighbor* and *weigh*."

"Thirty days hath September, April, June, and November. All the rest have thirty-one, save February, which has twenty-eight, and one day more every year in four."

Other

"May I have a large container of coffee?" Value for *pi* up to eight digits, using the number of letters in each word (3.1415926)

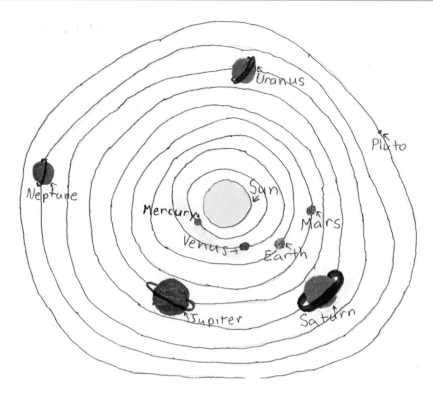

Young students often use the mnemonic "My Very Educated Mother Just Served Us Nine Pizzas" to remember the order of the planets. *(Drawing by Matthew Doeringer and Rachel Gelfand)*

A list of up to twenty pegs has been devised (Bower & Reitman, 1972).

The key is to *use pegwords to access an item in a series based on its location in the series,* such as the fifth item on a list. Pegs involve a simple procedure. First, memorize the pegs. One or two attentive readings of a version of the list above should be sufficient. Second, if you have a list of things to remember (errands or grocery items), take a moment to associate imaginatively each item with one of the pegs, beginning with the first peg and the first item. If the first item on your grocery list is margarine, for example, imagine a bun balanced on a container of your favorite brand of margarine. The more distinctive the image, the better. The result is that you will later be able to recall any item on the list in its sequential order by simply calling up a number, such as "one."

Like pegwords, *keywords* refer to concrete objects that are easily visualized; but unlike pegwords, keywords do not occupy a set list. They are simply chosen to sound like the words to be remembered (Atkinson, 1975). *Use keywords for associating paired information,* such as terms and their definitions, faces and names, or states and capitals. The use of keywords as visual and auditory mediators involves two steps (see Figure 9.6). For example, if the Spanish word *carta* (letter) is to be learned, first try to find an English word that sounds like part of it. *Cart,* for example, is similar to the first syllable. Second, visualize a cart and a letter together. You might imagine a huge

strategic solutions, continued

reflection on practice

Teaching History Through Mnemonics

Our U.S. history textbook did a very good job surveying American history. I have always had a deep personal interest in the Revolutionary period, so I especially appreciated the steps to the Revolution listed by the authors of this book. At the same time, I realized that it was not easy for most of my students to catch all of this in one quick chapter, so I summarized these thirteen steps leading to the Revolutionary War:

1. Proclamation of 1763
2. Sugar Act of 1764
3. Currency Act of 1765
4. Quartering Act of 1765
5. Stamp Act of 1765
6. Declaratory Act of 1766
7. Townshend Duties
8. Writs of Assistance
9. Boston Massacre
10. Tea Acts of 1770 and 1773
11. Intolerable Acts (4)
12. First Continental Congress
13. Second Continental Congress (Declaration of Independence)

Thirteen is an easy number to remember given the number of original colonies.

Thirteen items, however, constitute a long list for high school juniors to master, so I wrote the first letter of each step on the board and had students help me make a sentence out of them. I used this exercise to teach them two things: the thirteen steps and the technique of making up mnemonics that they could use in *any* class they were taking.

Last year's class came up with the following sentence: Patty Sue Could Quit Smoking Dope Today When Billy Thomas Insists Fire Stinks. I had read about this technique in a book by Harry Lorayne and Jerry Lucas (1974) called *The Memory Book,* but I really got excited when I found out how many kids would put this principle to work. The silly sentence didn't mean much to some of them, but those who saw it as a "memory horse" rode it to improved grades. Some of the students picked up the technique and began making up their own sentences. Even some of the weaker students asked for "memory horses" when we moved on to other lists. I tried to provide lists that they could use, but I liked it best when they made up their own.

Lois Williams

Discussion Questions

1. Have you ever constructed a verbal mnemonic similar to the one described by this teacher? Do you have difficulty recalling what the mnemonic stood for? Why or why not?

2. Write a brief essay question that would permit the use of the mnemonic described by this teacher, but would also require the students to demonstrate understanding.

3. Jerry Lucas was a famous professional basketball player. Can you think of a use that mnemonics could be put to in the area of amateur and professional sports? Give a specific example.

letter lying in a grocery cart, for example. Now when you encounter *carta*, the sound of the word should recall the image you have created—your letter in the cart.

Keywords are useful for memorizing many given sets of information, from foreign-language words (Pressley, Levin & Delaney, 1982), to minerals (Levin et al., 1986), to artists and their paintings (Franke, Levin & Carney, 1991). They require insight to locate, but when found, they take advantage of the fact that information coded in two ways—verbally and visually—is more meaningful than information coded in only one way (Paivio, 1986).

Researchers have also developed a mediation technique called *elaborative interrogation,* which seems very promising for use with elementary students. The technique consists of asking "why" questions about new information. *Use elaborative interrogation to make individual events or facts memorable.* Rather than simply teaching elementary students about where an animal lives, for example, you might teach about its habitat, then ask students to explain why the animal lives there rather than elsewhere. In a related application, if students have background information that can be used to explain new information, their construction of an explanation will make the information more memorable (Schneider & Pressley, 1989; Seifert, 1993; Wood et al., 1993). The explanation that a student generates acts as a link between the new information and the previous knowledge, improving memory for the information. It is more effective than both study of information without elaboration and study with explanations already provided.

As a teacher, you'll want to consider the use of mediation techniques to help students with difficult-to-remember information. Some of the experimental ideas, as well as the time-tested ones, are easily adaptable to your classes; others are not. You will have to sort out those of value to you, given your specific goals, resources, subject material, and students. With young learners, you will want to make sure that the environment supports recall

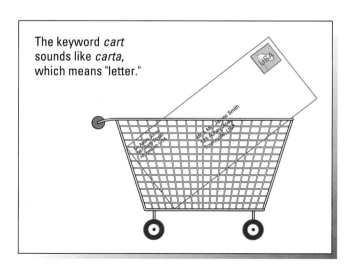

Figure 9.6
Use of the Keyword *Cart* to Recall *Carta*
(Pressley & Levin, 1978)

The keyword *cart* sounds like *carta*, which means "letter."

with cues, such as the "hands" labeled "left" and "right" above Mrs. Bratton's blackboard. With older learners (such as those described in Deepening Your Knowledge Base: What Are Complex Learning Strategies? p. 397), you may want to include instruction on how to generate mediators to increase meaningfulness.

Evaluation: Increasing Meaningfulness

Increasing meaningfulness can be one of the most efficient control processes for storing information in long-term memory in an easily retrievable form. More than a hundred years ago, Hermann Ebbinghaus (1913/1885) discovered that when he memorized highly meaningful material (stanzas of the poem *Don Juan* by Lord Byron) as opposed to meaningless material (lists of nonsense trigrams such as ZUB and SEF), he could learn the meaningful material ten times faster. Rates of learning accelerated by mnemonic devices such as the loci method and pegwords, though not as high, are still significant (Kee & Beuhring, 1978). Rapid acquisition, however, does not necessarily imply slow forgetting.

In comparing forgetting after mnemonic learning to forgetting after equivalent rote rehearsal, researchers have found that the initial advantage of mnemonics for retention is lost after about a week (McDaniel, Pressley & Dunay, 1987; Wang, Thomas & Ouellette, 1992). These results help us to put mnemonic devices in perspective: in short, such techniques seem to have a transitory effect. An equivalent amount of time spent learning to define terms and using them in context, or spent in drill (or rehearsal), appears to result in the same amount of retention, after a week or so, as does the use of a mnemonic device.

This is not to say that mnemonics are ineffective. On the contrary, a teacher can take advantage of the short-term acceleration of learning that mnemonic devices provide, then support retention with exercises designed to have students apply the new information (for example, to solve problems). The elaborative effects of application will result in an increased number of associations of the new information with other material in long-term memory, thus adding to its meaningfulness and memorability.

One last issue concerns whether mediation techniques supplied by the teacher or generated by the student lead to more effective acquisition of information. We might think that student-generated mediators would be more effective, because they are more personally meaningful. Some research supports this view (e.g., Schwartz, 1971), but other research does not (e.g., Hall, 1988). Many variables appear to influence the effectiveness of student-generated mediators, including the concreteness of the material to be learned and the age and ability level of the learner. Meanwhile, although research has yet to examine specific methods of helping students apply mediation techniques effectively on their own, it appears that such skills are likely to involve metacognition and problem solving (Duffy, 1993; Levin, 1993).

deepening your knowledge base

What Are Complex Learning Strategies?

Each of the strategic solutions proposed in this chapter focuses on an individual control process. Hence each is a comparatively simple strategy—simple in the sense that it applies to one cognitive process rather than to several. Real-life studying, however, often calls for the use of more than one process for a given task. Therefore, a likely question is, Shouldn't we be teaching students more complex strategies made up of several component parts?

Research on complex study strategies (such as SQ3R) has yielded mixed results (Adams, Carnine & Gersten, 1982; Cook & Meyer, 1983; Forest-Pressley & Gillies, 1983; Meyer, 1987). Why? It appears that many complex study strategies are not adaptable enough to improve with any consistency the comprehension of different types of text assessed in different ways. Better results seem to be emerging from research on simple learning strategies that have a theoretical base, such as those described in the Strategic Solutions sections of this chapter.

The effectiveness of a study strategy seems to depend on whether the learner has a study procedure suited to a particular purpose, such as "acquisition of second-language vocabulary for a translation quiz." As you will learn in the next chapter, metacognition and problem solving must be used to develop assemblages of control processes for specific purposes. In the long run all-purpose strategies may be of less value than strategic thinking and access to a variety of techniques from which to choose (West, Farmer & Wolff, 1991).

You may find it useful to share strategic thinking examples with other teachers. Divide into groups of four to discuss a study strategy that each of you has developed for a particular study task. The task might involve comprehending a textbook in one of your classes, studying for a specific type of test, or responding to a specific type of assignment.

Begin by having each person in your group describe a *successful* study strategy that you developed for a particular set of circumstances. *Be specific*. For example, explain how you studied for "the Friday quiz in my Spanish III class" rather than for "foreign-language quizzes" in general. After each person has described a successful study strategy, answer the discussion questions for each strategy.

Discussion Questions

1. Briefly explain how you developed this study strategy. Were you taught it? Told about it? Or did you discover it on your own? As a group, discuss the advantages and disadvantages of discovering such strategies.

2. As a group, analyze *each* study strategy for its relationship to one or more of the six control processes described in this chapter: attention, recognition, chunking, practice, meaningfulness, and organization. Which control process(es) does the strategy feature?

3. How old do you think students need to be in order to profit from being taught each of these strategies?

Improving Organization

A second category of elaborative strategies involves active organization of new information by the learner—or, to put it more simply, "improving organization." Knowledge of underlying structures helps the learner relate small bits of new information to an organized whole as it enters long-term memory. You can help your students improve the organization of information in two different ways: through focusing on the *content structure* or on the *formal structure* of information to be learned.

Explicitly teaching content can involve **organizers,** which are statements, expressed in familiar terms, of the concepts to be learned (Ausubel, 1960). When employed *before* reading, as they frequently are, these statements are called *advance* organizers. Providing students with organizers significantly in advance of learning makes learning easier.

Learning is enhanced by organizers because they bridge the gap between what a student already knows and what he or she is about to learn (Ausubel, Novak & Hanesian, 1978). Bridging this gap often requires the activation of a *schema,* a set of expectations that is the internal equivalent of an organizer. By using an advance organizer, you are really activating a set of expectations about what is to be learned. Information can be learned faster and retained better when students know what they are going to learn, how it fits in, and why (Derry, 1984).

Accordingly, you may want to *use organizers to improve the memorability of information to be learned.* There are no specific procedures for creating organizers. They can be short lists of clear statements of principal ideas. They can be longer paragraphs with essentially the same content. They can be schematic diagrams of topics, which are called *graphic organizers,* or *concept maps.* They can even be brief introductory discussions. Figure 9.7a–b provides examples of two different formats for advance organizers.

The following general guidelines apply to the use of advance organizers (Corkill et al., 1988; Dinnel & Glover, 1985; Glover, Bullock & Dietzer, 1990):

1. State fundamental ideas nontechnically.
2. For verbal organizers, include a concrete "bridging" example from student experience.
3. For graphic organizers, locate the fundamental idea at the top or in the center, with subordinate ideas arranged below or radiating outward.
4. Engage students in an active effort to understand the contents of the organizer.
5. Delay further learning for a few minutes.

In comparison to the material to be learned, the organizer should be quite short and state fundamental ideas in familiar terms. A "bridging" example for a verbal organizer can be drawn either from current events or from an

The two recent earthquakes in the Soviet Union have been terrible tragedies with thousands of lives lost and millions of dollars of damage to buildings. It isn't always the earthquake that does the major damage, however. Sometimes, the fires that follow earthquakes do even more harm. In fact, one of the most devastating disasters in American history was the San Francisco earthquake, in which the firestorm that followed destroyed almost the entire city. In an upcoming essay, you'll read a first-hand account of this disaster by a noted American writer, Jack London.

Figure 9.7a
An Advance Organizer for a Seventh-Grade Language Arts Lesson
(Glover, Bullock & Dietzer, 1990, pp. 296–297)

analogy to an experience of the students. Concept maps, which can be distributed before reading a text, are found in some texts themselves. Promote engagement in the reading material by requiring students to summarize or paraphrase the organizer. Further learning of information needs to be delayed a few minutes so that students can access the schema apart from their memory of the event in which the organizer was embedded.

As noted, organizers are frequently used in advance of reading. But they are also useful tools for learning *during* and *after* reading and can aid comprehension. In these instances, students can be taught to acquire knowledge through organizers that they have generated for themselves. Post-reading concept maps drawn up by students, for example, are effective for enhancing comprehension of text (Novak, Gowin & Johansen, 1982). They can be developed by groups or by individuals as a mnemonic after the main lesson, and they have aided reading comprehension in diverse subject fields from elementary school through college (e.g., Ault, 1985; Hanf, 1971). Figure 9.8 is a concept map generated by a previously low-achieving sixth grader as a mnemonic for a history lesson.

Thus far we have been discussing strategies that focus on the structure of content to be learned. A second way of helping students to increase organization of information in long-term memory is to focus on the *formal* structure of the material to be learned. This means literally focusing on the *form* that the material takes.

In a process called **structural schema training**, you can explicitly *teach students about the different kinds of discourse*. There are two general forms of discourse structure: narrative for stories and expository for texts. Narrative structure can be defined in terms of six categories, one for each episode of a story: *setting, beginning* (a precipitating event), *reaction* (of the protagonist), *attempt* (of the protagonist to achieve a goal), *outcome*, and *ending* (Johnson & Mandler, 1980). As you can see, these six categories are an elaboration of "beginning, middle, and end." A teacher can instruct students in the elaborated format to make comprehension and retention easier (Fitzgerald & Spiegel, 1983).

**Figure 9.7b
A Graphic Organizer for
a Seventh-Grade Life
Science Lesson**
(Hawk, 1986, p. 84)

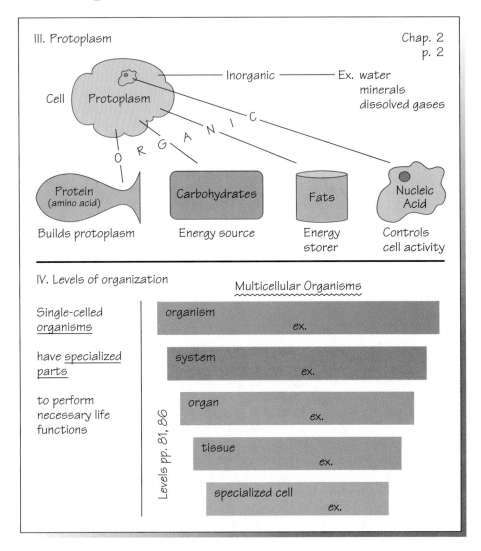

Exposition, the form of most textbooks, is logical, but it is not clearly defined by a single structure. Large expository texts sometimes involve description of an *object*, sometimes analysis of a sequence of *events*, and sometimes an effort to persuade the reader about an *idea* or a thesis (Calfee & Chambliss, 1987). A description of an object might lead to an organization such as "whole to part" or "comparison and contrast." An analysis of a sequence of events might lead to an organization such as "cause and effect." And an effort to persuade a reader about an idea or a thesis might lead to an organization such as "problem and solution." One or more of these structures can be taught to students even before they open a textbook, thus helping to organize their understanding of what they will read.

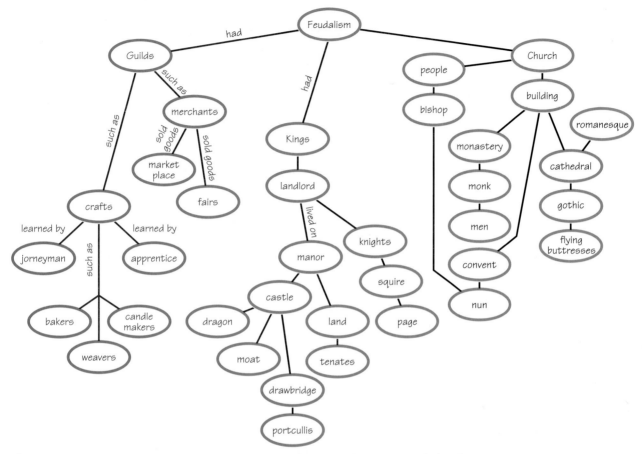

Figure 9.8   A Concept Map Drawn by a Previously Low-Achieving Sixth-Grader
(Novak & Gowin, 1984, p. 41)

How can students be taught to identify discourse structure? There are basically three approaches (Armbruster, Anderson & Ostertag, 1987). One is to *provide direct instruction in the format of a particular type of text.* Direct instruction in a "problem and solution" format, for example, might involve (1) giving students a definition and description of the format (for example, separate definitions of *problem, action,* and *results*), (2) instruction in procedures for how to summarize information within each element of the format, (3) short practice passages to help students learn to analyze text, and (4) formatted sheets of paper with blank lines for students to use (see Figure 9.9). A similar procedure might be used either with another version of the "problem and solution" format just described or with formats for other structures such as "comparison and contrast" or "cause and effect."

The second approach is *teach students to diagram structure* by drawing maps of ideas, with particular attention to identifying the relationships

Figure 9.9
Practice in "Problem and Solution" Analysis
(Armbruster, Anderson & Ostertag, 1987, p. 335)

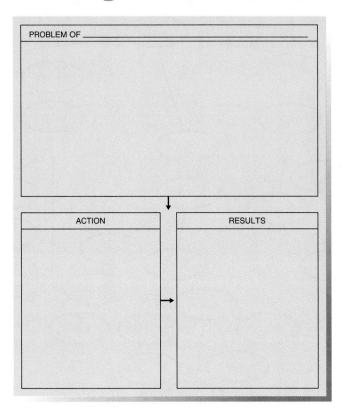

between ideas (Miccinati, 1988). The resulting concept maps are similar to those already discussed, but they put more emphasis on structure than on content.

The third approach is to *teach students to use headings in texts as cues to structure.* For instance, they can be taught to identify the hierarchical heading structure in a textbook, using both visual cues provided by the material (color, size, and so on) and deeper-level cues of concept flow and relationship. Based on their knowledge of headings and chapter organization, they can then develop note-taking skills that reflect the flow of ideas in the material.

Given that the consistent provision of well-organized texts can improve students' comprehension, there is a final strategy for improving organization that you should be aware of (Beck & McKeown, 1989). Here, the key is to steer clear of poorly written materials and *select instructional materials or construct supplementary materials that are well structured in terms of both content and form.* Some teachers construct handouts for this purpose. Note, however, that helping students in this manner requires that a teacher have considerable knowledge of writing composition, so as to be capable of detecting flaws in coherence and structure.

Evaluation: Improving Organization

To what extent do organizers and training in text format affect long-term memory? Intensive evaluative research on advance organizers has been conducted for more than thirty years now, but research on the training of students to recognize format is comparatively recent. Accordingly, the evidence is more conclusive for organizers than for training in text format.

We know that students who carefully attend to a well-structured overview, compared to those who do not, report significantly greater understanding of material to be learned and do better on their seatwork (Peterson et al., 1982). Yet they do only slightly better than these other students on tests of achievement. To be sure, teachers may not always use overviews as effective organizers. But D. P. Ausubel's (1960) original research, many studies conducted in the 1960s and 1970s, and even more recent research suggest that appropriate use of advance organizers generally leads to modest gains in achievement (Kloster & Winne, 1989; Luiten, Ames & Ackerson, 1980). The results of these studies may reflect average effectiveness rather than optimal effectiveness.

As for training in text format, the results of initial research are encouraging; but there is some question as to whether this approach is the most efficient way for students to learn to organize information for better retention. Thus far, almost all of the relevant studies focus on comprehension of experimental reading passages. The problem is that, if the reading that students actually encounter in classrooms is not as well organized as the experimental passages, training in discourse structure may not aid comprehension much. The alternative approach—supplementation of existing materials with handouts (such as logical outlines, or maps that emphasize structure)—may be a more efficient way to improve comprehension of reading materials. In the end, an approach that combines information about text structure with carefully structured supplements may prove to be the most effective way of all to facilitate knowledge acquisition from lengthy texts.

CONCLUSION

In summary, let's reconsider some of the most important questions for learning strategy instruction in light of the problem-solving process:

> The term "strategy" implies that we need to learn more about the conditions under which a particular strategy should be chosen. For example, what strategies are best to use when one is dealing with difficult or unfamiliar material, compared to easy familiar material? What strategies are most effective for different kinds of students? . . . How do we teach students to diagnose both themselves and the situation in order to make effective choices? (McKeachie, 1988, p. 8)

You can increase the meaningfulness of new information by comparing and contrasting it with what students already know. Learning about butterflies, for example, involves identifying the unique features of different species. *(Lawrence Migdale/Tony Stone Images)*

Such questions help us to consider learning strategies as solutions to specific problems. It is illogical to expect students to apply learning strategies without having perceived and defined problems or, in more familiar terms, without having identified goals and resources.

Although educational psychologists do not yet have answers for all of the questions being posed about learning strategy instruction, they are at least asking the right questions. As a teacher, you too will need to consider the same questions as you help students think about how to learn.

Recall from Figure 9.2 (p. 373) that control processes are ultimately governed by metacognition and problem solving. Sometimes called "executive processes" because of this "governing" role, problem-solving skills must be applied to the selection and use of control processes if the learner is to acquire knowledge effectively and efficiently. These skills will be the focus of study in the next chapter on cognition and learning.

concept paper

Building a Concept Map

Purpose of the assignment

To solve the problem of building a concept map for understanding strategies to enhance the use of long-term memory.

Directions for the assignment

Your task is to construct a concept map for the section of this chapter headed "Long-Term Memory" (pp. 387–403). Follow this problem-solving procedure (Ault, 1985, p. 41):

1. Reread the entire section of this chapter on "Long-Term Memory." Choose concepts in the form of key words and phrases, and underline them. Copy each of these words and phrases onto a card for easy rearrangement. (Problem identification)

2. Rank the list of concepts from abstract and inclusive to concrete and specific. You should find fewer abstract/inclusive concepts than concrete/specific ones. (Problem representation)

3. Cluster concepts that (a) function at the same level of abstraction or (b) interrelate closely. These clusters should reflect *your* judgment of the organization of ideas presented in this section of the chapter. To regroup, simply rearrange cards. (Information gathering)

4. Arrange the concepts on a table or desk top in an array resembling a road map. There is no one correct arrangement, but make sure to include all of the important concepts. Draw this map on a single piece of paper. (Solution generation)

5. Link related concepts on the map with lines and label each line with a verb or a preposition. Lines can branch and cross each other, so that the map becomes a paragraph that reads in any direction. Keep in mind the analogy to a road map. (Solution implementation and evaluation)

If you have followed this procedure carefully, you should have a completed map occupying a single page that can be turned in to your instructor. Perhaps more important, you have generated an example and learned a procedure that can help you teach concept mapping to your students.

SUMMARY

1. Knowledge is any organized body of information. Knowledge acquisition involves processes that transform data from experience into organized information.

2. There is a continuum of solutions to the problem of knowledge acquisition. At one end of the continuum, teachers directly influence how students acquire knowledge; in the middle, teachers instruct students in use of learning strategies; at the far end of the continuum, students develop learning strategies themselves in order to gain knowledge independently.

3. An information-processing model can be applied to both the way computers operate and the way the human brain acquires knowledge. In the human brain, memory structures are analogous to computer hardware and control processes are analogous to computer software programs.

4. There are three memory structures: sensory registers, short-term memory, and long-term memory. Information is processed in relation to each of these structures.

5. While information is in the sensory registers, it is assigned meaning. This process is known as perception or recognition. Teachers can develop students' perception and recognition skills using a variety of strategies.

6. From the sensory registers, recognized information goes to short-term memory (STM). Because STM can hold only a few items, strategies such as chunking and practice can be used to reduce memory load.

7. The nature of long-term memory (LTM) is still being debated. Information is probably stored in LTM both episodically (by events) and semantically (according to networks of meaning).

Strategies to store information focus on retrieval cues that increase meaningfulness and improve organization. Mnemonics is a strategy for increasing meaningfulness, and advance organizers and concept maps are strategies for improving organization of information.

KEY TERMS

knowledge p. 364

learning strategies p. 366

learning strategy instruction p. 367

sensory registers p. 369

short-term memory p. 369

long-term memory p. 369

control process p. 369

perception p. 374

recognition p. 374

attention p. 374

executive processing space p. 381

chunking p. 384

cognitive load p. 384

episodic memory p. 387

semantic memory p. 387

schema p. 388

elaborative rehearsal p. 389

meaningfulness p. 389

mediation techniques p. 389

mnemonics p. 391

organizers p. 398

structural schema training p. 399

SUGGESTED RESOURCES

Duffy, G. G. (1993). Teachers' Progress Toward Becoming Expert Strategy Teachers. *Elementary School Journal, 94,* 109–120. This article outlines the issue of whether we should teach specific learning strategies to students, or teach students to construct their own strategies.

Novak, J. D., and B. Gowin. (1984). *Learning How to Learn.* New York: Cambridge University Press. This pioneering book describes concept mapping and its various uses.

Weinstein, C. E., and R. E. Mayer. (1986). The Teaching of Learning Strategies. In M. C. Wittrock (Ed.), *Handbook of Research on Teaching* (3d ed.). New York: Macmillan. This chapter is a useful overview of efforts to teach students how to learn.

West, C. K., J. A. Farmer, and P. M. Wolff. (1991). *Instructional Design: Implications from Cognitive Science.* Englewood Cliffs, N.J.: Prentice Hall. This book provides a useful summary of control processes and a template or pattern for designing complex learning strategies.

10

Cognitive Learning Theories, Part 2: Achieving the Goal of Higher-Order Thinking

Orientation

The goal of this chapter is to build upon the knowledge you gained about cognitive learning from the previous chapter and to use this knowledge as a basis from which to explore the other major element of the information-processing model: the executive powers of higher-order thinking. You will discover three different instructional approaches for helping students develop higher-order thinking skills. As you read, look for answers to these questions:

- **Why is developing a disposition to think in your students an important teaching goal?**

- **What are the three major approaches to teaching higher-order thinking skills?**

- **Why are classification, deduction, and induction considered skills that enable thinking?**

- **What is the defining feature of a dual-agenda approach?**

- **What is "situated cognition"?**

- **What different roles can technology play in situating cognition?**

- **How can we teach students that all knowledge is constructed?**

learning journal

Principles of Higher-Order Thinking

While reading about higher-order thinking, make Learning Journal entries about specific experiences in which principles of higher-order thinking apply. Tell what led up to the experience, name the principles of higher-order thinking involved, describe how the principles were involved, and describe any relevant outcomes. This chapter contains descriptions of the following principles of higher-order thinking:

- disposition to think
- enabling skills
- mediated learning
- internalization of deliberation
- near transfer/far transfer
- bridging

- process skills
- heuristics
- self-regulation of learning
- guided discovery
- simulation fidelity
- situated cognition

HIGHER-ORDER THINKING AS A GOAL OF INSTRUCTION

In the last chapter, you learned that *higher-order* thinking skills led students to acquire knowledge strategically. Just what are higher-order thinking skills? Can they be taught? If so, how should we teach them? Answers to these questions are being developed in research on "teaching thinking." Knowledge about how to teach higher-order thinking is making rapid progress—on at least three fronts. Each of these approaches contributes to our understanding of what higher-order thinking skills are and the extent to which they can be taught.

What Is Higher-Order Thinking?

> Higher-order thinking skills are complex cognitive processes used for problem solving.

A **thinking skill** can be defined as any cognitive performance or action that (1) leads to the attainment of some goal and (2) is subject to improvement in proficiency. You are already familiar with *lower-order* thinking skills. These are the skills that we focused on in the previous chapter—those directly involved in knowledge acquisition, comprehension, and even application. As you know, lower-order thinking involves procedures that can be applied in routine or mechanical ways (Lewis & Smith, 1993).

Higher-order thinking skills are quite different in this regard. Although routines may develop out of their use, these skills *cannot* be applied routinely or mechanically. They are relatively complex cognitive performances, the ultimate purpose of which is not efficient use of memory but problem solving. Although there is no fixed list of higher-order thinking skills, the categories of analysis, synthesis, and evaluation in Bloom's Taxonomy (presented in Chapter 3) are generally considered representative of them. These categories collectively correspond to a procedure for solving problems (see Figure 10.1).

The outcome of higher-order thinking is now increasingly being referred to as **generative learning,** or the construction of knowledge. The assumption behind generative learning is that all knowledge is constructed. Process is emphasized as much as, if not more than, product. The focus of teaching shifts from content learning (discussed in Chapter 9) to cognitive skill learning (covered in this chapter). Educators generally agree that there's a trade-off between the two types of learning, but we can also assume that they exist in a dynamic balance that depends upon the particulars of each situation.

> Higher-order thinking leads to the construction of knowledge.

This brief, introductory discussion of higher-order thinking—and its relation to lower-order thinking—is not meant to be comprehensive. Identifying higher-order thinking with analysis, synthesis, and evaluation, or with problem solving, is only a point of departure for further consideration of the subject. In fact, the nature of higher-order thinking is so actively debated among philosophers and psychologists that several overlapping categories and definitions have been created. Deepening Your Knowledge Base: Alternative Terms for Higher-Order Thinking presents an overview of some of the most common terms and their definitions. This lexicon will contribute to your understanding of how higher-order thinking is sometimes discussed in other classes, in journal articles, in curriculum guides, and in school textbooks.

Psychologists are increasingly realizing that instruction in higher-order thinking includes development of a **disposition to think,** or an abiding tendency to use higher-order thinking skills (Baron, 1985). As a general category, this disposition to think can be broken down into more specific dispositions, such as tendencies to be broad-minded and adventurous, to be intellectually curious, to seek understanding, to be deliberate and strategic, to be intellectually careful, to seek and evaluate reasons, and to be aware of one's own thought processes (Tishman, Jay & Perkins, 1993). Although psychologists are a long way from knowing how to teach such dispositions, they can be thought of as the enduring outcomes of efforts to teach thinking, just as a "disposition to learn" (described in Chapter 5) is an enduring outcome of compensatory education programs.

> Higher-order thinking develops a disposition to think in the individual.

Figure 10.1   Taxonomy Categories and Problem Solving

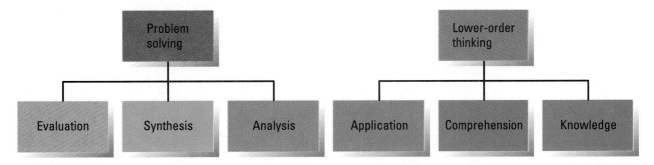

d e e p e n i n g   y o u r   k n o w l e d g e   b a s e

Alternative Terms for Higher-Order Thinking

If you were to ask a philosopher what higher-order thinking is, you would likely be told that it is *critical thinking.* If you asked a psychologist the same question, the answer would probably be *problem solving,* or *metacognition.* How do these terms differ in meaning? At the risk of being circular, I offer the following guidelines for their use.

- *Higher-order thinking* is a general, all-encompassing term for complex thinking skills (Lewis & Smith, 1993). Depending on the context, it can refer to critical thinking, problem solving, or metacognition.
- *Critical thinking* refers primarily to evaluative skills, but these vary widely in definition. Some philosophers use the term *critical thinking* to refer to contemplation of moral and ethical implications. Others use it to refer to logical thinking. When used to refer to moral and ethical issues, *critical thinking* is frequently considered to be more inclusive than *problem solving,* but when used to refer to logical thinking, it pertains to a specific type of problem solving.
- *Problem solving* refers to a stagelike process for attaining a goal. Occasionally, it is still used in the narrow sense of solving a well-defined problem (coming up with a correct answer); but, increasingly, the term refers to finding as well as solving any kind of problem—an unending process involving analysis, synthesis, and evaluation. As used in this text, *problem solving* is functionally equivalent to higher-order thinking.
- *Metacognition* refers to awareness of one's own thought processes. It can also pertain to the skills involved in the conscious use of such thought processes. Problem-solving skills are a form of metacognition, so *metacognition* is sometimes considered to be a more inclusive term than *problem solving.*

Efforts to develop a disposition to think must begin early. Reflection on Practice: Even First Graders Can Develop Higher-Order Thinking describes how one teacher began to teach first graders how to solve problems. As you read through the rest of this chapter, remind yourself from time to time that what may endure following sustained efforts to teach higher-order thinking skills is a disposition to think—rather than to react impulsively or aversively—when faced with problems-as-challenges.

Mrs. Webb's Small-Group Science Lesson

To see how a teacher solves the problem of developing higher-order thinking among somewhat older students, let's return to the sixth-grade lesson about light that began Chapter 5. After Mrs. Webb finished her whole-group development-oriented activity, she began a small-group inquiry-oriented activity. Recall that she told the class, "We're going to work in groups of four, working with a partner." The class of twenty-four students was divided by the teacher into six groups, with two pairs (four students) in each group.

reflection on practice

Even First Graders Can Develop Higher-Order Thinking

In his book *Teaching for Thoughtfulness,* John Barell (1991, pp. 108–109) gives this account of problem solving by first graders:

I was once asked by teachers to demonstrate problem solving in a first-grade classroom. Having spent only one year as a first grader, I felt the need to call upon one of my graduate students, a teacher of first grade, for her assistance. Diane said, "Why don't you tell them one of Aesop's Fables? I just finished doing that with my first graders."

So I selected "The Fox and the Grapes" and told it to the children. My strategy was to tell the story of the hungry fox wandering down the lane until he spied the grapes hanging from a vine over his head. He leaped up, attempting to pull some grapes down, but failed. Here I stopped the story and asked the children, "What would you do to get the grapes, if you were the fox?"

They responded: "Climb the tree!" "Get a long stick." "Find some rocks to climb on top of." "Shake the tree hard." "Call other animals to help me."

I accepted all their answers, listed them on the board with the child's name beside them, and then asked them to decide which solution was best and why. As I recall, they said that using a stick was probably the easiest to do, since other animals and rocks might not be around. Finally, I asked them, "How did you come up with all these answers?"

One girl, Betsy, said, "I remembered what we did at home [in a similar situation]." So Betsy was using her background knowledge, and her comment convinced me that some youngsters, even first graders, could reflect on their own thinking processes. This experience suggested to all of us that we could, indeed, present students with problems to solve and challenge them to become more aware of the kinds of intellectual processes they used: for example, background knowledge.

John Barell

Small-group, inquiry-oriented activities like this one are frequently used to teach cognitive skills in science. *(Bob Daemmrich)*

Discussion Questions

1. Analyze the classroom event in terms of the five-stage model of problem solving in Chapter 1. How do the variations in the applied process reflect a sensitivity to the context?

2. Barell focuses on "background knowledge" as a subprocess of problem solving about which even first graders are aware. At what stage of problem solving is this subprocess engaged?

3. Barell suggests that some first graders are aware of their own thought processes. What might short-term memory span have to do with the development of this awareness?

Although the pairing proceeded rapidly and approximated the seating arrangement, it was the more capable students who tended to be paired with other students. Mrs. Webb said, "Each pair, take out a pencil and eight sheets of paper. [Pause.] Write your names at the top of each sheet. [Pause.] I want you to work with your partner. You are going to be asked to *infer*, or to come up with some conclusions. Use one sheet of paper at each center to write down your conclusions." Small groups were then assigned to most of the eight "centers" that Mrs. Webb had set up around the room. The room began to buzz with activity.

Before they started work at their stations, the students were told to write on their first sheet of paper the number of the center at which they found themselves, and to follow the directions on the board:

1. *Move* from station to station in numerical order.
2. *Record* observations in a comprehensive manner.
3. Remember to *brainstorm* with your partner.

At the first center, the activity was labeled "Symmetry—Integrating science, math, and art." The materials listed were the instruction sheet, the paper, a pencil, a straight edge, and a small mirror. The instructions were as follows: First, "place a mirror on each dotted line [see Figure 10.2]. Write down your observations. What can you *infer* about symmetry, or the fact that two sides are in equal proportion to each other?" Second, "list all the capital letters of the alphabet that have symmetry. *Classify* each letter according to its balance—up-and-down, side-by-side, or both." Third, "how many words can

> **Thinking can be taught in the context of specific tasks.**

you list that are made up of only letters with up-and-down balance?" The first part of the activity called for reaching a conclusion about symmetry from the information given. The second and third parts of the activity emphasized other thinking skills, such as classification and synthesis.

At other centers, students worked on tasks relating to an understanding of light and images. They studied refraction by placing a pencil in water or passing light through a prism. They studied magnification by using a drop of water on a bit of wax paper over print as a magnifying lens. And they classified common materials—construction paper, wax paper, water in a jar, and a bottle of lotion—according to whether the materials were opaque, translucent, or transparent. As I circulated from station to station, I noticed many students making careful observations. A few, however, were engaged in off-task activities. Mrs. Webb called these students back to their observations; then she explained to me that "working in small groups at this age requires a lot of monitoring." It was Friday, and the drift of conversations into weekend activities was almost irresistible.

As you can see from this lesson, teaching thinking often fits best within the context of a specific lesson. This kind of instruction encompasses goals such as the skills found in Bloom's Taxonomy. But note that these goals are contextualized; that is, they are achieved within a specific task or subject matter. In this case, the skills taught by Mrs. Webb—inference, brainstorming, classification, and synthesis—represented a selection of skills appropriate to scientific experimentation.

> **The teacher must choose which thinking skills to teach and how to teach them.**

Mrs. Webb's strategy was a carefully developed solution to the problem of teaching thinking in a real-world context. Her solution reflected not only selection of which skills to teach but selection of a way to teach them. Let's turn now to an array of possibe ways in which *you* can teach thinking skills

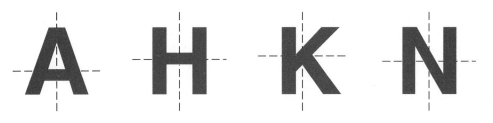

Figure 10.2
Symmetry and Letters of the Alphabet
Directions: Place a mirror along the dotted lines drawn through each letter. What observations can you make? How do the letters differ in their symmetry?

and encourage a disposition to think in *your* students. You will see that two of the three major ways to teach thinking are indeed embedded in the content and context of subject matter, just as Mrs. Webb's lesson was.

THREE WAYS TO TEACH THINKING

Three different approaches, or cognitive designs for instruction, commonly frame instruction of thinking skills (Jones, 1992). You should consider each possibility as you develop a strategy to teach thinking.

> Three approaches are available for teaching how to think.

1. The **stand alone** mode of teaching thinking involves an independent course of instruction. A stand alone course might be a class on logic or a study skills workshop.
2. The **dual agenda** mode of teaching infuses thinking skills into the regular, text-based curriculum. Examples might include a history lesson taught with an emphasis on reading/thinking skills or a science lab involving activities related to experimentation.
3. **Situated cognition** supplements text-based instruction with an activity that embeds or situates higher-order thinking within a real-world task. In this way, higher-order thinking is approached through an authentic cognitive task, such as a computer simulation exercise or a student-generated project.

Which approach did Mrs. Webb use? To answer this question, you need to look at the relationship between the thinking skills that she taught and the context of the lesson. Thinking was taught in the context of a science lesson (rather than a stand alone course), but the lesson did not involve an authentic cognitive task (so it was something other than situated cognition). It did, however, require experimentation along lines established by the teacher and the curriculum guide. In short, Mrs. Webb used a *dual agenda* mode to teach thinking.

Mrs. Webb's lesson represents an example of one solution to the problem-as-challenge of developing higher-order thinking. In the remainder of this chapter we will look at several such solutions to help you design instruction that is appropriate to different circumstances.

In doing so, you will need to consider the distinctive strengths of stand alone, dual agenda, and situated approaches to teaching thinking in light of the "givens" in each particular teaching situation. After selecting your approach, you will need to consider which thinking skills to teach within it.

> Different approaches are appropriate in different circumstances.

You may also combine approaches, or mix higher-order and lower-order thinking skills as needed to achieve your goals. What's important is that you use resources to teach thinking in a way that is itself thoughtful.

Stand Alone Programs

By their very label, it is obvious that stand alone programs do not involve the contextualized learning, used by Mrs. Webb, that is being advocated to teach higher-order thinking. Sometimes, for reasons that will be described, it is preferable to teach thinking skills out of context.

> Stand alone programs generally try to teach fundamental skills for problem solving.

In general, stand alone programs do not focus on teaching students complex or composite higher-order thinking skills. More typically they target **enabling skills,** or *prerequisites* to problem solving. These programs operate on the assumption that improvements in such fundamental skills will ultimately have a profound and enduring effect on a child's ability to solve real problems of various kinds. Indeed, there is considerable hope and some evidence that if problem solving is approached by teaching enabling skills first, virtually everyone can become a better problem solver.

Some enabling skills, such as those described in the last chapter, involve knowledge acquisition. Other enabling skills involve well-defined cognitive processes—such as inference and classification—for solving relatively simple problems. Instruction in prerequisite skills should permit (1) faster and better acquisition of knowledge and (2) higher forms of thinking. After identifying and exploring three of the most common enabling skills, we'll walk through and discuss two stand alone programs.

Enabling Skills: Classification, Induction, and Deduction

> Classification, induction, and deduction are important enabling skills.

Psychologists and educators do not agree on a common list of enabling skills. Accordingly, you need to bear in mind that any list contains some overlap, is necessarily incomplete, and may be supplemented as further consensus about enabling skills develops. Nevertheless, three skills seem to wind up on virtually every list (Nickerson, Perkins & Smith, 1985): classification, induction, and deduction. These skills are simple enough that they are often used routinely. Their routine use enables higher-order thinking.

Classification

One of the most fundamental activities of cognition is **classification,** or the act of grouping things into categories based on shared characteristics. Objects, events, people, and ideas are placed into classes in order to "render things equivalent" (Bruner, Goodnow & Austin, 1957). Why should people assign things to categories, or render them equivalent? There are basically two reasons. First, classification helps people to identify things. Through classification, young children learn to distinguish dogs from cats, many from

> Classification skills help one identify and think about things.

one, and big from little. Almost all abstract as well as concrete concept learning requires classification.

The second reason is that classification enables other forms of thinking. Two skills that it enables are definition and deduction. An identification becomes an informal definition when a child adds information that distinguishes a thing from its class. "Our cat is a calico." "A million is a lot more than ten." "Cool is between cold and lukewarm." A more advanced skill that classification enables is deduction. For example, if a child knows that all cats are born, and the family pet is a cat, then the child can deduce that the cat was born, without ever having seen or been told that it was born. Throughout childhood, such use of relations between classes depends on accurate classifications (for example, born animals include cats, and cats include the family pet).

Because classification is such a fundamental type of thinking, many educators use classification exercises to help students (1) identify concepts and (2) arrange concepts into hierarchies or taxonomies. Such exercises can be as simple as sorting objects by sizes or colors or shapes, but they can be made more difficult by combining categories, such as sorting by sizes *and* colors *and* shapes (as in the case of large red squares). Natural objects in "collections" that a child has gathered (such as pebbles, leaves, crayons, toys, dolls, bottle caps, baseball cards, or "pogs") can be used to develop classification skills, but more structured materials can also be provided.

> Children can learn to identify concepts and arrange them into taxonomies.

Induction

A second skill that enables thinking is **induction,** the process of generalizing beyond the information given. The ability to arrive at a generalization from observation of particular cases is essential for deriving rules and hypotheses from experience. For example, young children may see a number of small purchases made with money and conclude that all buying involves an exchange of money for something else. They are led to many accurate generalizations based on what they see or hear; but they are also led to inaccurate ones, accounting for (among other things) many of their grammatical errors in preschool and kindergarten, and their initial incomprehension when a parent exchanges a purchased item or pays with a credit card.

> Induction is making generalizations from observing particular cases.

Induction enables children to arrive at rules and principles that can be used to guide behavior or, later, reasoning. Some of these rules involve the physical world and others involve the social world. By middle childhood, boys and girls are able to understand the rules of grammar and arithmetic based on many particular experiences. They also understand the rules of quite complex games and the implicit rules of friendship, again based on particular experiences. These rules are often used as working hypotheses to predict what will happen. Only in adolescence are students able to generalize about what they cannot directly experience in some way.

> Children learn rules by induction, based on their experiences.

Our task as teachers may occasionally involve telling (or reminding) children about rules, but rules or principles that are induced by children themselves are valuable for their further intellectual development. Many psychologists and educators believe that too much indoctrination in rules and principles supplants induction, leading a child to depend on authority when observation or independent thinking would be more appropriate.

Opportunities to generalize are provided when teachers permit children to experience many examples. Such examples should be selected so that accurate generalizations are reached. As children learn to generalize, they need to discover the value of considering exceptions to rules, which can lead them to make more accurate generalizations—that is, to consider probability.

> Children should learn to generalize and to recognize exceptions.

Incidentally, one term you will frequently encounter in education is **inference.** You may wonder if it refers to inductive reasoning. The answer is yes—and no! An inference is a conclusion reached by way of *either* inductive or deductive reasoning. When Mrs. Webb asked her class to draw inferences from observations, she was asking them to use inductive reasoning. But the surmises that result from deductive reasoning (as discussed below) are also known as inferences.

Deduction

Classification is a prerequisite for another enabling skill called **deduction,** which is the use of logic to draw conclusions from premises. In deduction, *premises* (such as "all cats are born" and "the family pet is a cat") lead to *conclusions* (such as "the family pet was born"). Sometimes the premises of a conclusion are not completely stated. Concluding that "the family pet was born because she is a cat" would be a deduction, but unstated information (in this case, that "all cats are born") is left understood.

> Deduction is using logic to draw conclusions from premises.

Deduction permits children to use what they know to reason about the world around them. "If the third grade is in Room 9, and this is Room 9, then this must be the third grade." Many psychologists believe that deduction is a skill that enables more complex forms of thinking, including authentic problem solving and process skills such as experimenting or synthesizing. For example, it is doubtful that an experiment could be conducted, or a painting created, without some skill in logic. Pursuit of scientific discoveries requires systematic consideration of alternative hypotheses, and art requires logical composition of elements. Deduction does appear to enable insightful and creative thinking, even though, by itself, it is insufficient for such thinking to occur.

> Deduction may be a skill that can be taught.

In the past, educators often assumed that logic was a by-product of either biological intelligence or subject-specific skills, such as the analysis of causes and effects in science, or the adoption of perspective in art. What psychologists and educators are now coming to realize is that deductive logic can be taught through exercises designed to lead children to an understanding of its basic principles. In such learning situations, teachers can make deduction an explicit goal of instruction.

Two Examples of Stand Alone Programs

In the next few pages, only two of an increasing number of stand alone programs to teach enabling skills will be discussed: *Instrumental Enrichment* (Feuerstein et al., 1980) and *Philosophy for Children* (Lipman, Sharp &

Oscanyan, 1980). Both the hopes and the doubts that these programs raise parallel those evoked by alternative stand alone attempts to enable higher-order thinking. Thus, a detailed comparison of these two programs should be fruitful.

Reuven Feuerstein, the Israeli psychologist who designed Instrumental Enrichment, developed his program in the context of assisting culturally disadvantaged adolescent immigrants to Israel. And Matthew Lipman, the philosopher who designed Philosophy for Children, developed a curriculum to teach philosophy in the schools. Instrumental Enrichment and Philosophy for Children are not necessarily more effective than other alternatives, but they are certainly as fully documented. From an examination of these two programs, you can learn how stand alone courses are used to teach enabling skills.

Instrumental Enrichment

If you were to walk into a classroom where Feuerstein's Instrumental Enrichment program was in use, you would find students identified as having learning deficits at their desks completing a page in a workbook of exercises designed to remediate a specific deficit. The teacher would be circulating among the students to provide clues or assistance, and when the students had finished the page, he or she would lead a group discussion about it.

If you picked up one of the workbooks, you would notice on the front cover a picture of a child in thought (the program logo), a symbol for that particular type of exercise, and the program slogan: "Just a Minute . . . Let Me Think!" The program is used with students in the fifth grade or above. About 500 pages of exercises in this program are devoted to fifteen or more "instruments" (see Table 10.1)—enough material for three to five sessions per week for two or three years. Each instrument contains exercises designed to remediate a cognitive skill deficit that has been identified by a special test given before instruction.

> The Instrumental Enrichment program offers exercises to improve cognitive skill deficits.

This test is called the Learning Potential Assessment Device, or LPAD. On it, a student can progress through a series of problems only to the extent that he or she has learned how to solve them (Feuerstein, Rand & Hoffman, 1979). Subsequently, a teacher trained in the program matches instruments for teaching thinking skills to any deficits in learning that are discovered through the student's responses to the LPAD.

Each instrument is structured so that easy problems precede more difficult ones; thus students can learn how to solve progressively more difficult exercises of any given type. Take the twenty-six-page instrument entitled *Organization of Dots*. Completion of this task does not require verbal skills, but some guidance from the teacher may be helpful.

In addition, each instrument has four phases: an introduction, in which students are asked to verbalize the task; individual work on a page of problems; class discussion; and a summary of the concepts developed or the strategies used to solve the problems. The introduction to the first lesson in *Organization of Dots* is conducted using the cover, which (in addition to the

Table 10.1   Feuerstein's Instrumental Enrichment Exercises

Instruments	Brief Description of Task
Nonverbal	
Organization of Dots	Student connects dots to represent multiple geometric figures (e.g., two triangles and one square)
Analytic Perception	Student systematically analyzes wholes into parts, according to different needs
Illustrations	Student solves problems of interpretation posed by sequences of drawings
Limited vocabulary	
Orientation in Space I–III	Student differentiates among spatial frames of reference (e.g., on, above, up, between)
Comparisons	Student discriminates among relational characteristics (e.g., big, bright)
Family Relations	Student identifies multiple roles of any individual in relation to other family members
Numerical Progressions	Student identifies order and rhythmic appearance of relationships in sequences of numbers or events
Syllogisms	Student performs exercises in formal propositional logic
Independent reading vocabulary	
Categorization	Student organizes data into hierarchies of categories (prerequisite: comparisons)
Instructions	Student reads, understands, and carries out verbal instructions
Temporal Relations	Student develops capacity to register relations in time (e.g., before, after, fast, slow)
Transitive Relations	Student makes inferences about relations of "greater than," "less than," and "equal to"
Representational Stencil Design	Student mentally constructs a portrayed design by combining stencil overlays

Source: Adapted from Feuerstein et al., 1980

standard picture and logo) shows stars in a night sky, some of which are connected by lines to form the Big Dipper.

Figure 10.3 portrays three exercises similar to the ones on a page of *Organization of Dots*. Note that the first item is a demonstration, and that the second item is easy whereas the third is more difficult. These tasks require the perception of geometric patterns that are progressively more difficult to identify without practice. Using the same figures as in the demonstration, you might want to connect the dots in the two trial exercises—but in a different configuration each time.

Students typically find these exercises difficult to complete—and, indeed, discussion of difficult exercises is an integral part of Instrumental Enrich-

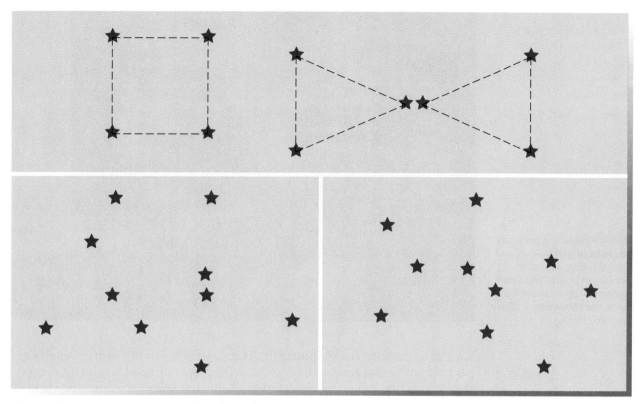

Figure 10.3   Exercises Similar to *Organization of Dots*

ment. Feurestein's program was founded on the belief that deficits in cognitive skills are the result of the absence of mediated learning experiences. **Mediated learning** supplements learning that occurs directly from the environment; it normally takes place between parents and children within the family unit. The parent acts as a mediator between the child and problems posed by the environment, transmitting culturally defined skills that assist the child in solving problems. In the Instrumental Enrichment program, the materials, the teacher, and even other students serve to mediate the learning of the individual with specific deficits so that higher-order thinking can be developed.

> Mediated learning helps the student learn more than he or she could pick up alone.

Mediated learning was conceived by Lev Vygotsky (1978), whom you will recall from Chapter 5. The materials, teacher, and other students in an Instrumental Enrichment class represent **scaffolded instruction** for skill development by the learner. They help the learner take advantage of his or her potential for learning beyond what could be accomplished by working alone.

Evaluation of Instrumental Enrichment

Does Instrumental Enrichment work? Study after study has shown that adolescents and youth who are exposed to at least eighty hours of Instrumental Enrichment improve their scores on intelligence tests that pose problems

Mediated learning normally occurs between parents and their children, as in this Pittsburgh home. Teachers and peers can mediate learning in the classroom. *(Steve Mellon)*

similar to those in the IE materials. The most consistent positive results appear on nonverbal tests of deduction. What has not been so clearly demonstrated is the effect of Instrumental Enrichment exercises on school achievement. Reports of closely supervised studies in Israel were positive, but studies in other countries have indicated mixed results (Savell, Twohig & Rachford, 1986; Shayer & Beasley, 1987).

Philosophy for Children

In Philosophy for Children, students learn by discussing issues under a teacher's guidance.

If you were to enter a classroom where students were participating in the Philosophy for Children program, you would see the implementation of a very different mode of instruction to achieve the same general end of enabling thinking. Desks would be arranged in a circle to facilitate discussion. Students might be taking turns reading aloud from a specially written novel about a child their age, or they might be discussing issues raised by an episode from the novel. The role of the teacher would be to raise relevant issues from a teacher's guide and, then, to direct the discussion. More specifically, the role of the teacher would be to provoke and monitor classroom dialogue, including dialogue among students.

The Philosophy for Children program was initiated in grades 5 and 6 with *Harry Stottlemeier's Discovery* (Lipman, 1982), a novel about a boy who accidentally discovers rules of logic in ordinary experiences. Other novels have been written for other grade levels and subject emphases, from kindergarten through twelfth grade (see Table 10.2). Typically, students discuss episodes three times a week under the supervision of a teacher who has been trained in the use of Philosophy for Children by teachers who themselves were

Table 10.2   The Philosophy for Children Program

Novel/ Teacher's Manual	Grades/Subject
Elfie/Getting Our Thoughts Together	1/Thinking
Kio and Gus/Wondering at the World	2–3/Contrasting concepts
Pixie/Looking for Meaning	3–4/Meaning acquisition
Harry Stottlemeier's Discovery/ Philosophical Inquiry	5–6/Logical reasoning
Lisa/Ethical Inquiry	7–8/Ethics
Suki/Writing: How and Why	9–10/Written expression
Mark/Social Inquiry	11–12/Social studies

trained at the Institute for the Advancement of Philosophy for Children at Montclair State University in New Jersey.

In *Harry Stottlemeier's Discovery*, questions of logic and philosophy are raised in the context of events in the novel. The discovery that Harry makes in Chapter 1 is that logical "all" statements cannot be reversed. "All planets revolve about the sun," he notes after his science class one day, but "not everything that revolves around the sun is a planet" (Lipman, 1982, p. 2). With each episode, the discussion of logical relations becomes more complex as Harry discovers more principles of deduction, all in the context of ordinary events and everyday language. The teacher's manual (Lipman, Sharp & Oscanyan, 1979) contains extensive exercises designed to spark thought and discussion.

The original purpose of the Philosophy for Children program was to improve the basic reasoning skills of students after one year, or approximately eighty hours of instruction. Overall, the program is expected to develop more than thirty skills related to reasoning (Nickerson, Perkins & Smith, 1985). Matthew Lipman (1988) has stressed that learning about logical thinking must be accompanied by discussion if logical thinking is to be practiced in the form of deliberation. The issues are generally related to the content of philosophy, which encompasses not only logic but also ethics and feelings related to the situations in the novel. (One such situation is exemplified by the question "Are there times when it is right to get angry?")

> Logical thinking is enhanced by practice during discussion.

The process by which logical thinking skills are transformed into higher-order thinking applies a second concept of Vygotsky (1978), also discussed in Chapter 5; that of the transformation of dialogue into **inner speech** through internalization. Over time, rational dialogues between adults and children—or among the children themselves—become internalized by the children, who transform them into deliberation. In *Harry Stottlemeier's Discovery*, we can listen in on "inner speech" developing in the mind of the hero as he discovers how logic works. His encounters with adults and other children provide not just challenges to his thinking but alternative points of view that he internalizes in order to discover and test principles of logic.

> Inner speech helps the learner develop higher-order thinking.

External dialogue, which is stimulated by the teacher, is expected over time to internalize during participation in the Philosophy for Children program.

deepening your knowledge base

A Discussion of "Where Do Thoughts Come From?" by First Graders

First, organize the class into groups of four students. Next, to each of these students, assign the role of teacher, all female speakers (one person), all male speakers (one person), and the discussion leader, who is responsible for reporting back to the class as a whole. Then, read the opening excerpt from *Elfie* out loud together. After you finish your discussion, re-assemble into the larger group to compare your answers to the questions.

Then I [Joanna] said to myself, "At this moment, am I thinking?" I really wonder. And I answered myself, "Dummy, if you can wonder, you must be thinking. And if you're thinking, then, no matter what Seth says, you're for real." ...

Adelle: I agree with Joanna because your brain is for learning and powerful.

Teacher: So you agree with Joanna that your brain thinks, and you don't agree with Clarissa who said it's you that thinks.

Adelle: What's Clarissa say?

Teacher: She says it's you that thinks and not your brain. That's an interesting thing to say, Clarissa.

Christian: It's a connection.

Teacher: That's a connection. You're right, Christian. Philip?

Philip: Well, I disagree with Clarissa because if you didn't have a brain, you wouldn't even be thinking about the words that I am talking right now, so it would be impossible without your brain.

Clarissa: I think it could be possible without your brain because you have a heart, and your heart can beat, and it could think that it's beating. ...

Teacher: You think that ...

Clarissa: ... and I disagree with Joanna and Adelle.

Teacher: Bradley?

Bradley: I disagree with Clarissa because you could have ... if your heart beats, that's just because your heart is thinking, and you don't know if your heart thinks. ...

Teacher: You don't know if your heart thinks. ...

Bradley: ... and if your, if you have your brain like we really do, you would know all of your thoughts.

Teacher: Okay. Lauren?

Lauren: I agree with Clarissa because you think, like, and your brain stores your thoughts.

Teacher: So it's really you that's doing the thinking. [Lauren nods.]

Teacher: Okay. Robbie?

Robbie: Well, if we didn't have a brain, we'd say "what's that poem?" [points] "what's that?" [points] "what's this?"

Philip: How would you know what was happening, and how would you know how to spell the word if you didn't think about the word?

Patrick: You don't know anything, so you won't know what you're saying and like, you like, don't know it.

(Continued on next page)

Teacher: So you can't even say "What's that?" Is that what you're saying? Ricky?

Ricky: So then if you don't know it, it's like "Well, I don't know what that is," and you don't even know where you are.

Patrick: You can't even say "What's that?"

Ricky: I know, you can't even talk because you don't even know what the words are.

Teacher: Christian?

Christian: Um, well, I think I can sort of answer them because if you didn't have a brain, I know why they say you would die, because you wouldn't have a brain, so you would keep falling down, you would keep falling down into the street and you would get run over. So you would just be immediately dead if you didn't have a brain.

Clarissa: I disagree with Christian because you would walk, and I disagree with Patrick. . . .

Christian: But your brain wouldn't tell you to walk. I'm thinking that I gotta talk. And if I didn't have a brain, I wouldn't be talking. Or if I didn't have a brain, I couldn't hear you, and I wouldn't be here, and I wouldn't be at school. I wouldn't be doing anything. I wouldn't be alive.

Discussion Questions

1. What skills are being developed in this discussion? Be as specific as possible in terms of both enabling skills and other skills.

2. What skills are being used by the teacher to lead the discussion? Again, be as specific as possible.

3. You may have noticed that one or more issues of *equity* emerged in the dynamics of this discussion. What are these issues? How should the teacher follow up in order to deal with them?

Source: British Broadcasting Corporation, 1990

Deepening Your Knowledge Base: A Discussion of "Where Do Thoughts Come From?" by First Graders gives you an example of this kind of dialogue among first graders. The teacher provides some scaffolding for the discussion.

Evaluation of Philosophy for Children

The major achievements of the Philosophy for Children program appear to be the instruction of school-age children in principles of logical reasoning as well as the facilitation of their development of reading skills and their oral expression of ideas (cf. Sternberg & Bhana, 1986). These are not small accomplishments for a program that occupies only a few hours each week. Together, over the long term, they may contribute to the development of a disposition to think and to higher-order thinking skills. As yet, however, evidence of such developments is only anecdotal.

strategic solutions

Using Stand Alone Programs to Enable Thinking

Now that you have read about two specific stand alone programs in some detail, some general conclusions can be drawn regarding the overall possibilities of these kinds of programs for your strategic planning. Two issues stand out in the analysis of both Instrumental Enrichment and Philosophy for Children. One concerns "lateral" transfer, particularly to traditional school subjects such as arithmetic, language arts, social studies, or science. The other pertains to "vertical" transfer, or long-term effects. These issues provide some tentative guidance for the use of stand alone courses or units to enable thinking.

The first issue is directly related to the key aspect of context that we discussed earlier. Because stand alones are not connected to most subject-matter learning, lateral transfer to such learning is of particular concern. In other words, will the thinking skills that students have learned truly prove useful, or will they turn out to be abstract exercises? The answer is that stand alones are generally successful for **near transfer,** the generalization of skills that have been taught to similar skills that are being tested. Stand alones have had much less success in the realm of **far transfer,** the generalization of skills that have been taught to different subject or skill areas.

Given these findings, you should *use a stand alone course to enable thinking of a specific type.* Thinking skills exercises are much more likely to result in near transfer than in far transfer. Instrumental Enrichment, for example, seems to bring about nonverbal skills related to deduction and insight. Such skills are of value in technical and scientific careers. Philosophy for Children, by contrast, seems to result in verbal skills related to formal argument and persuasion. These skills are valued in the humanities. The program you choose, then, depends not so much on which program is more effective in enabling higher-order thinking but on which *type* of higher-order thinking you wish to enable.

Ever mindful of the importance of context for learning, you should also, whenever possible, *"bridge" thinking skills taught in stand alone courses to thinking skills taught in related subject areas.* Difficulties in transfer of skills might not be eliminated by this means, but they can be reduced.

Bridging consists of the application of thinking skills in the context of subject-matter learning. For example, enabling skills taught through a scientifically oriented stand alone program need to be identified when they occur in math, science, or any other subject. Make the link explicit. ("Look for a pattern in this table of results. Remember when you searched for a pattern in the dots? Now try to find a pattern in the data.") Linkages that are too subtle will probably not lead to transfer of skills.

The second issue concerns long-term effects. Although it is doubtful that participation in any thinking skills program for *less* than a year has significant long-term effects, there is no guarantee that longer involvement in thinking skills programs will increase IQ scores. The lesson learned from Head Start (see Chapter 5) is that through early educational intervention, many students at risk for dropping out actually avoid special education and remain in school. They persist because they think of themselves as learners. By analogy, we might expect students who receive prolonged instruction in fundamental thinking skills to persist in their efforts to solve problems, both in and out of school. This persistence appears to be at the heart of a disposition to think.

As students learn to think of themselves as thinkers and develop reflective habits of thought, they may become less impulsive and more persistent in the face of cognitive challenges. Accordingly, you might *use a long-term thinking skills intervention to develop a disposition to think.* The development of such a disposition requires both intensive and extensive involvement on the part of the student. You, in turn, will need either to participate in a thinking skills program with other teachers or to teach the same group of students in consecutive years. Transitory approaches to teaching thinking are less likely to have an enduring effect than a stand alone program that is bridged to subject-matter fields over a number of years.

Dual Agenda Approaches

Cognitive processes that are specific to a domain of learning, or that are closely associated with a particular content area such as history, mathematics, or science, are generally known as **process skills.** In dual agenda approaches to teaching thinking, process skills are taught along with content—frequently through parallel sets of objectives.

> Dual agenda approaches teach thinking along with content area information.

One implementation of this approach is commonly known as "reading in the content areas" or "reading across the curriculum." In this case, higher-order processes of reading (such as making predictions or asking questions) are taught at the same time that content of a history or science textbook is presented. A second implementation of the dual agenda approach is to teach mathematics by simultaneously teaching **heuristics,** defined as a set of strategies for discovering how to solve problems that can be expressed in terms of numbers. Students are expected to work with these higher-order thinking techniques *at the same time* that they learn math content. A third implementation of the dual agenda approach is **guided discovery,** in which scientific process skills are taught along with scientific principles and laws. In each of these three examples, neither thinking-skill objectives nor content objectives predominate; instead, they coexist to form the dual agenda.

We start this section with an exploration of content area reading; then we will move on to heuristics in mathematics and finally to guided discovery in science. After these approaches are described and evaluated, they will be analyzed for strategic information about how to teach *any* higher-order think-ing skill through a dual agenda. The lessons learned from these three ap-proaches appear to apply equally to process skills in other areas, such as the teaching of writing (Hayes & Flower, 1983).

Teaching Reading Process Skills in the Content Areas

Since reading is a dynamic process aimed at constructing meaning from text, we know that higher-order thinking skills lie at its core. Specifically, **metacognitive skills**—skills that are used by an individual to appraise or monitor his or her own cognition—are fundamental to successful reading.

Psychologists have drawn up varying lists of metacognitive skills, but three broad types are commonly described: planning, regulating, and evalu-ating (see Table 10.3). *Planning* is the process of coordinating a means to achieve a cognitive goal, such as adjustment in the rate of reading or in stan-dards of comprehension to match different purposes. *Regulating* is the process of monitoring demands of the task and modifying plans or strategies to enhance success. Finally, *evaluating* is the process of estimating the qual-ity of cognition, such as depth of understanding as a student reads. One goal of many metacognitive training programs is self-regulated learning (Paris & Newman, 1990).

Can metacognitive skills be taught in the context of subject-matter learn-ing? The answer is that they can be and, indeed, are being taught in this con-text. Although educators once believed that the metacognitive skills used in reading (as when one monitors ongoing comprehension) were best taught in-dependently in workbooks, it is now understood that deep-level reading skills can be developed only in the context of subject matter (Templeton, 1995). A linkup—known as *integration*—between the teaching of process skills and content-area instruction is therefore natural.

Integrating the process skills of reading with content-area learning can take many shapes and forms, but the one that we'll examine in detail here is known as reciprocal teaching. When used as part of a content lesson, recipro-cal teaching is a good example of a dual agenda approach to developing metacognitive skills.

One uses metacognitive skills to monitor one's own thinking.

Sophisticated reading skills can be taught in the con-text of subject matter.

Table 10.3   Three Metacognitive Skills

Skill	Application to Reading
Planning	Adjusting reading to recall rather than just to recognize
Regulating	Monitoring reading speed or selectively rereading to preserve understanding
Evaluating	Estimating depth of understanding during reading

Source: Adapted from Jacobs & Paris, 1987, p. 259

Teaching metacognitive skills (such as self-regulation) in the context of subject matter learning is an example of a dual agenda mode of teaching thinking. *(Lawrence Migdale/ Tony Stone Images)*

Reciprocal Teaching

Reciprocal teaching is a cooperative learning procedure for improving reading comprehension (Palinscar & Brown, 1984). To benefit from the procedure, children must be able to decode words proficiently. In reciprocal teaching, elementary and junior high pupils are given small-group instruction in four metacognitive strategies: *prediction* (finding clues about what will happen next), *clarification* (taking steps to restore meaning), *generation of questions* (focusing on the important details), and *summarizing* (stating the important ideas in a sentence or two). These strategies aid readers in the larger metacognitive skill of regulating their own understanding.

After several sessions in which the four strategies are presented and modeled by the adult teacher, using portions of any text read aloud, the adult asks each member of the group to "teach" by practicing in turn what the adult has been doing. Typically, the leader "begins the discussion by asking a question on the main content and ends by summarizing the gist" (Brown & Palinscar, 1989, p. 413). The discussion consists of requests for clarifications, the clarifications themselves, or predictions of what will happen next in the reading. The teacher intervenes only as necessary to model the strategies (including requests for clarifications) and to provide feedback.

The entire training procedure requires about twenty sessions. Intervention is "faded" over these sessions as students improve in their practice of the strategies. Eventually the children read the text silently; in the final sessions, the teacher interrupts only to remind the group to pause occasionally and to use the four metacognitive strategies. Because the training procedure is labor intensive, a version involving the use of peer tutors has been developed to increase the efficiency of the adult (Palinscar, Brown & Martin,

Reciprocal teaching allows students to practice metacognitive reading strategies.

1987). Another version of the program teaches listening comprehension to children in their early elementary years (Brown & Palinscar, 1989).

Reciprocal teaching represents another application of Vygotsky's (1978) idea of a zone of proximal development. More proficient readers (the teacher or peer tutors) scaffold learning by modeling metacognitive skills for less proficient readers. As these latter readers become more practiced in the skills of self-regulated learning, overt questioning drops out, and the use of metacognitive skills becomes silent and efficient.

Although reciprocal teaching was originally conceived as a method of training metacognitive skills for reading, rather than as a content-area reading technique, it can be successfully implemented within content areas such as history or biology. When used in this way, the technique functions as a dual agenda approach because it enhances both deeper-level processing of text and comprehension of specific concepts within content-area materials that students are reading. Deepening Your Knowledge Base: A Reciprocal Teaching Lesson for Science Content (Day 13 of 20) provides a good illustration of reciprocal teaching within a science lesson.

> Reciprocal teaching works well in content areas.

Evaluation of Reciprocal Teaching

Instructional strategies such as reciprocal teaching work best with students who have already automatized their decoding skills. Automaticity in decoding frees up working memory for the development of strategies. Even so, the adoption of such strategies may not occur without the scaffolding or mediation of teacher and peers.

How effective is reciprocal teaching? No claim is made of general expertise in reading comprehension by the end of the program, but gains of about six months in reading comprehension have been found in independent applications of reciprocal teaching involving children in the fourth to seventh grades (Lysynchuk, Pressley & Vye, 1990). These gains in comprehension are not greater than those associated with other metacognitive skill training programs (Haller, Child & Walberg, 1988), but they are substantial.

Teaching Heuristics in Mathematics

The word *heuristic* comes from the Greek verb meaning "to discover" or "to find." As defined earlier, heuristics are strategies for discovering how to solve problems, often in math. They are often contrasted with **algorithms,** which are routine or mechanical procedures for solving math problems. Heuristics were popularized in a book entitled *How to Solve It,* by mathematician George Polya (1957). Since the National Council of Teachers of Mathematics (1989) mandated instruction in heuristics, problem-solving procedures such as these are increasingly taught in the context of instruction in math.

> Strategies for finding how to solve problems are called heuristics.

Heuristics are generally divided into four categories of strategies: (1) understanding a problem, (2) making a plan, (3) solving the problem, and (4) looking back. Numerous lists of heuristics have been developed for each of these areas. Some of the lists are developed for high school or college mathematics (e.g., Schoenfeld, 1985), whereas others are useful for upper elemen-

A Reciprocal Teaching Lesson for Science Content (Day 13 of 20)

Text [read silently]: In the United States salt is produced by three basic methods: solar (sun) evaporation, mining, and artificial heat evaporation. For salt to be extracted by solar evaporation, the weather must be hot and dry. Thus, solar salt is harvested in the tropiclike areas along our southern coasts and at the Great Salt Lake.

C (student as teacher): Name three different methods about how salt is produced.

A (student): Evaporation, mining, evaporation—artificial heat evaporation.

C: Correct, very good. My summary on this paragraph is "about ways that salt is being produced."

T (adult teacher): Very good. Could you select the next teacher? [Student selects L, another student.]

Text: The second-oldest form of salt production is mining. Unlike early methods that made the work extremely dangerous and difficult, today's methods use special machinery, and salt mining is easier and safer. The old expression "back to the salt mines" no longer applies.

L (student as teacher): Name two words that often describe mining salt in the old days.

K (student): Back to the salt mines?

L: No. Angela?

A: Dangerous and difficult.

L: Correct. This paragraph is all about "comparing the old mining of salt and today's mining of salt."

T: Beautiful!

L: I have a prediction to make.

T: Good.

L: I think it might tell when salt was first discovered; well, it might tell what salt is made of and how it's made.

T: Okay. Can we have another teacher?

Text: Table salt is made by the third method—artificial evaporation. Pumping water into an underground salt bed dissolves the salt to make a brine that is brought to the surface. After purification at high temperatures, the salt is ready for our tables.

K: After purification at high temperatures, the salt is ready for what?

C: Our tables.

K: That's correct. To summarize: After its purification, the salt is put on our tables.

T: That was a fine job, Ken, and I appreciate all that work, but I think there might be something else to add to our summary. There is more important information that I think we need to include. This paragraph is mostly about what?

A: The third method of artificial evaporation.

(Continued on next page)

your knowledge base, continued

B: It mainly tells about pumping water from an underground salt bed that dissolves the salt to make a brine that is brought to the surface.

T: Angela hit it right on the money. This paragraph is mostly about the method of artificial evaporation and then everything else in the paragraph is telling us about that process. Okay. Next teacher.

Source: From Brown & Palinscar, 1989, p. 421

tary school (e.g., Krulik & Rudnick, 1988). Many items on both types of list trace back to Polya's work.

Understanding a Problem

> The first strategy for solving a problem is to understand it.

Listed below are thirteen heuristics designed to help students *understand* a math problem (Kersh & McDonald, 1991, p. 39). Not every problem will require all of these heuristics; rather, they should be thought of as a "tool kit" or set of resources for a student who needs to develop an understanding of a problem before attempting to solve it. This list was developed from the methods that math experts often use when representing math problems.

Make a sketch, drawing, or figure.

Act out the problem.

Create an image or a mental picture.

Identify relevant data.

Identify irrelevant data.

Construct other questions that *could* be asked about your data.

Construct a physical model.

Restate the problem.

Try to recall the problem by memory.

Clarify the language of the problem.

Make a graph.

Make up stories around a theme.

Collect data and make up questions and problems.

Now let's apply a few heuristics to a simple math problem involving a "convoy." *An army bus holds 36 soldiers. If 1,128 soldiers are to be bused to their training site, how many buses are needed?* When given this problem, most junior high students know that they are to use division to solve it, but applying a division algorithm before understanding the problem leads about half of them to err (Kersh & McDonald, 1991).

Which heuristics should students use to understand this problem? Well, they might visualize soldiers getting into buses in a convoy. The soldiers obviously need to be grouped first. How many groups will there have to be? That question involves the number of soldiers (1,128), and the capacity of each bus (36). Where they are going is irrelevant. Visualizing the problem,

One of the best ways to solve a problem is to construct a model of its solution, as these potential architects are doing in a Chicago classroom. *(Richard Howard/ Black Star)*

identifying relevant information, and identifying irrelevant information are three heuristics that can help students understand this problem.

Making a Plan and Solving the Problem

Presented below is a list of thirteen more heuristics useful for making a plan and solving the problem (Kersh & McDonald, 1991, p. 40). Among the most commonly taught heuristics for making a plan are creating a simpler problem, using a picture, guessing and checking, identifying a pattern, and working backward (Taback, 1992).

Numerous strategies can be used to plan how to solve a problem.

Create a simpler problem, and solve it; then solve the harder problem.

Translate the problem into mathematical symbols.

Match the problem with the problem type.

Describe the problem verbally.

Use a physical model.

Use a picture or a figure.

Break down the problem into smaller problems.

Use a table, list, or chart.

Identify a pattern.

Work backward.

Guess and check.

Make systematic guesses.

Use logical reasoning.

The strategy of using a picture might involve drawing circles to represent buses—but considering that more than 30 buses are required, this strategy would not be economical. Working backward might be helpful in the case of a multistep problem, but this "convoy" problem involves only one step. What *does* work, however, is the strategy of identifying the pattern. In this case, the "pattern" involves the grouping of soldiers in such a way that the division problem can be solved.

Looking Back

This last category of heuristics is often the most neglected. Because it involves reflecting on the problem-solving process, it presents an opportunity for further learning, not just verification of the solution. Eight heuristics for looking back are listed below (Kersh & McDonald, 1991, p. 41).

> Find another way to solve the problem.
> Make your assumptions explicit.
> Change your assumptions.
> Check the reasonableness of your answer.
> Check the accuracy of your answer.
> Construct variations of the problem.
> Generalize to a class of problems.
> Identify the heuristics involved in solving a problem.

The most useful heuristic for arriving at a correct answer to the "convoy" problem is checking the reasonableness of the answer. The result of dividing 1,128 by 36 is 31, with a remainder of 12. What does this remainder represent? It represents 12 soldiers; but in terms of the problem, it also represents another bus, bringing the total number of buses necessary to 32. That number, of course, is the correct answer.

Instruction in Heuristics

How should heuristics be taught? Many educators agree that they should be taught in the context of mathematical inquiry (e.g., Davis, Maher & Noddings, 1990; NCTM, 1989; Schoenfeld, 1989). Simply providing lists of heuristics and defining them does not help students learn to apply them. What will help is the following short list of suggestions for teaching heuristics (adapted from Stacey & Groves, 1985):

- Assist children in accepting the challenge of solving mathematical problems.
- Build a supportive classroom atmosphere in which children will be prepared to tackle the unfamiliar.
- Allow children to pursue their own paths toward a solution and assist them when needed, without giving them the answer.
- Provide a framework within which children can reflect on the *processes* involved.
- Talk to the children about the processes involved in solving problems, explicitly drawing their attention to heuristic strategies.

A dual agenda approach to teaching heuristics keeps heuristics in the context of mathematics, rather than isolating them in a specialized course. In Reflection on Practice: Word Problems and Heuristics, a teacher considers the effectiveness of heuristics that are taught in this way.

Margin notes:

Problem solving involves reflecting on the solution process.

Heuristics should be taught as part of math instruction.

reflection on practice

Word Problems and Heuristics

In most math classes, word problems are an important part of the curriculum. At the beginning of the school year, it was apparent that my students hated word problems. If they thought that they could pass a test without even trying them, they would just skip them. They must not have done well with them in the past.

I thought that the students needed some *successful* experience with word problems. So I tried to come up with some definite steps they could use in solving them. Their textbook had a plan that presented the following five steps for guiding their thinking:

1. Read problem carefully. Decide what unknown numbers are asked for and what facts are known. Making a sketch may help.
2. Choose variables to represent the unknowns.
3. Reread problem, and write an equation that represents relationships among the numbers in the problem.
4. Solve the equation for the unknown.
5. Check your results against the wording of the problem. Evaluate your answer to make sure it is logical.

Using this five-step plan, I worked many examples step by step on the board to show my students how fun and solvable word problems can be.

I feel that my instruction prepared many of them to succeed with some of the more complex problems. In fact, I notice now that most of my students will try the word problems instead of leaving them blank. I give them credit for every step of the problem that they attempt.

Karen Eddy

Discussion Questions

1. **The problem-solving suggestions in the first three "steps" are similar to the heuristics for *understanding* a problem; identify these parallels. Why is there such an emphasis on understanding in the case of word problems?**

2. **Identify the parallel between the problem-solving suggestions in the fifth step and one of the heuristics for *looking back*. Is this heuristic effective for word problems? Why?**

3. **What other types of math problems do students typically "skip over"? Do you think that the same heuristics as those discussed here would be applicable in these situations?**

Evaluation of Instruction in Heuristics

The strongest support for instruction in heuristics comes from a recent summary of research on problem solving in mathematics (Hembree, 1992). This summary reports the effects of teaching heuristics on math achievement. On average, such techniques were of significant benefit to students after grade 5, especially those in high school. This limitation is developmentally consistent with Piaget's formal operations stage, involving the ability to reason abstractly. Special training of secondary teachers in the heuristics of mathematics was also of substantial benefit to their students' math achievements.

Which heuristics were most effective? The research summary indicated that diagramming or picturing problems, translating a problem into mathematical symbols, and identifying irrelevant data were of greatest benefit. Of least help were using a guess-and-test strategy and describing math problems verbally. The results suggested that different heuristics were of different value in helping students solve mathematical problems.

Guiding Discovery in Science

Over the years, several carefully studied attempts have been made to teach thinking processes in science. Perhaps the most ambitious has been **discovery learning,** a mode of inquiry adapted to scientific investigation. Although some valid and important discovery learning is of the situated type, most attempts to promote discovery learning have been dual agenda modes of instruction in which process objectives parallel content objectives. These dual agenda approaches rely heavily on guidance offered by the teacher, the textbook, or the curriculum guide; accordingly, they are often referred to as *guided discovery* lessons.

> Discovery learning helps students think about how to make scientific investigations.

The process objectives in science have been more thoroughly investigated than those in any other domain. Although more specific lists of such objectives exist for some of the sciences (such as biology), they can be classified overall into three categories: describing phenomena, formulating hypotheses, and testing hypotheses (Marzano et al., 1988). Dual agenda approaches to process skills in science generally involve the teaching of each category of skills discretely. After a brief look at all three categories, we'll consider one example of guided discovery programs so that you can get a better sense of their components and purposes.

Describing Phenomena

> The description of phenomena is an important skill in science.

The description of phenomena or events builds on the enabling skill of classification, and if an explanation is offered for a phenomenon, it requires inference. More specific skills involved in describing phenomena include observing, measuring, and comparing. Most of the activities in Mrs. Webb's guided discovery lesson were of this descriptive type, calling for inferences from observation.

In a high school biology lab, a process objective of the same type might be "to identify a given set of single-cell organisms in a drop of pond water through a microscope." The purpose of this descriptive exercise would be to relate new information to existing knowledge—in this case, to a list of single-cell organisms described in a textbook or a lab manual. How does what is seen though a microscope relate to categories of single-cell organisms presented in a text or manual? The outcome is not only better understanding of the phenomenon (that is, single-cell organisms) but also skill in using a dropper, slides, and a microscope.

Formulating Hypotheses

The formulation or setting of hypotheses builds on the enabling skills of induction and deduction. Induction allows the student to generate a prediction on the basis of observations. Deduction allows the student to infer a prediction from a principle. Because observations are always guided by rules, and because principles require observations in order to result in inferences, the two enabling skills of induction and deduction cannot be neatly separated in this process of formulating hypotheses. They are inextricably intertwined. In an earth science class, a process objective of this type might be "to predict the relative hardness of rocks." The purpose of this exercise would be to develop a model of hardness similar to the Mohs scale, which is described in the textbook. Gypsum, feldspar, and quartz (with known Mohs values) might be scratched against each other to develop a model; then predictions might be made about the relative hardness of other rocks.

> Induction and deduction are involved in forming hypotheses.

Testing Hypotheses

A test of a hypothesis relies on enabling skills in at least two ways. Deduction (inference) enables a student to control for alternative explanations in the design of an experiment. Classification enables a student to collect and interpret data. In an elementary science class, a process objective that involves testing hypotheses might be "to determine whether a pin, carefully placed on water, can float." The purpose of this exercise would be to confirm or disconfirm a hypothesis about surface tension. Here, after presenting (or discovering) a model of surface tension, the teacher might encourage students to test a prediction from the model.

> Enabling skills are used in testing a scientific hypothesis.

In addition to describing phenomena, formulating hypotheses, and testing hypotheses, scientists must select a method of reporting their results and communicating their findings. This, too, is a scientific process skill, but it is often taught only in advanced courses.

A Guided Discovery Program: "Science . . . A Process Approach"

Although guided discovery lessons are widely used, only a few such programs exist—and of those, only Science . . . A Process Approach (SAPA) has been reviewed recently (Nickerson, Perkins & Smith, 1985). SAPA is a guided discovery program specifically designed to teach process skills in the domain of science. The program consists of 105 modules for use either in chains or by grade levels (15 per level) in grades K–6 (Gagné, 1967). The goals of the program focus on eight processes of science: observing, using space/time relationships, using numbers, measuring, classifying, communicating, predicting, and inferring. At least two of these processes—classifying and inferring—could be categorized as enabling skills that are taught concurrently with process skills. Of the other six skills, some (such as using numbers and measuring) are specific to mathematics and science, but others (such as communicating) are not. Taken together, they represent a sampling of skills involved in scientific problem solving; they do not, however, include problem solving itself.

Guided discovery programs teach scientific process skills, but not problem solving.

Evaluation of Guided Discovery

In theory, what distinguished early discovery learning programs from more traditional approaches to science was the emphasis on problem solving by the student. When discovery curricula were first implemented, the hope was that the more practice one has at discovery, "the more likely is one to generalize what one has learned into a style of problem solving or inquiry that serves for any kind of task one may encounter" (Bruner, 1961, p. 31). However, because many discovery programs focused on highly structured "confirmatory" activities, rather than on scientific problem solving, this hope was not realized.

In practice, guided discovery curricula do not teach problem solving as effectively as they teach individual processes of scientific inquiry. By the mid-

Guided discovery classes teach psychomotor skills as well as process skills. Their "hands-on" aspect of learning also improves attitudes toward science. *(David Ulmer/Stock Boston)*

1970s, it was clear that although students were participating in the *processes* of describing phenomena, formulating hypotheses, and testing hypotheses, they were doing relatively little authentic problem solving or discovery (Shulman & Tamir, 1973). Subsequent revisions of guided discovery programs and models have tended to increase "hands-on" experience in learning scientific processes (Igelsrud & Leonard, 1988), but most text-based science activities today still focus on confirmation rather than on genuine discovery (Pizzini, Shepardson & Abell, 1991; Staver & Bay, 1987).

What do students learn in guided discovery science classes? This question resulted in more than 300 evaluation reports in the 1960s and 1970s. A recent summary of results in 81 of these reports (Shymansky, Hedges & Woodworth, 1990) revealed that students in guided discovery science programs significantly outperformed other students in traditional science curricula in terms of (1) science achievement and (2) functional knowledge of scientific process skills (such as observing, measuring, and experimenting). They did not outperform other students in terms of analytical skills or skills in unrelated activities such as reading nonscientific materials, which requires far transfer.

> Guided discovery increases science achievement and functional knowledge of process skills.

Should we abandon guided discovery because far transfer does not occur? The answer is no. Guided discovery lessons not only improve science achievement and functional knowledge but also achieve the following important objectives:

1. Guided discovery lessons *teach process skills* that are important prerequisites of problem solving in the sciences. These process skills, such as observing, formulating hypotheses, and interpreting data, are explicitly identified in the module being taught. Having been made explicit in this way, they are generally learned.

2. Guided discovery classes *teach psychomotor skills*, as students learn to handle and operate scientific equipment and conduct scientific procedures (Shulman & Tamir, 1973). It is easy to overlook the fact that manipulation of equipment achieves implicit psychomotor and procedural objectives. Learning how to look through a microscope and examine a slide, or even how to use a thermometer, is not an insignificant achievement.

3. Guided discovery methods seem to *improve attitudes* of students toward the sciences. We know that in traditional classrooms, which do not use any form of discovery, attitudes toward science grow less favorable as students progress through school (Yager & Yager, 1985). By contrast, the experience that guided discovery programs offer students to explore scientific procedures results in at least some improvement in such attitudes (Ajewole, 1991; Weinstein, Boulanger & Walberg, 1982). Of even greater promise for promoting positive attitudes toward science are revisions in guided discovery curricula that increase the amount of hands-on experience while students are learning scientific processes (Kyle, Bonnstetter & Gadsen, 1988).

> Guided discovery teaches important skills and promotes a positive attitude toward science.

think it through

Consider this problem that a novice preservice teacher has IDENTIFIED and REPRESENTED.

Developing the Disposition to Think

When I was in high school, I had a beginning teacher for geometry. I often noticed that she had a difficult time answering questions that were not related to the subject matter that we were covering at the time. She would get very apprehensive because she did not know how to handle the situation. This caused several of us to wonder if she was very knowledgeable in her field of study. She failed to answer the majority of the questions. If and when a similar situation occurs when I begin teaching, what are some helpful hints in dealing with answering questions from students that I am unsure of, and how can I prepare to answer these questions in order to keep the students' confidence in me as a teacher?

Observe how an experienced practicing teacher GENERATES SOLUTIONS to this problem.

Inevitably students will ask questions to which teachers have no knowledgeable answers. I don't always find it necessary to announce my ignorance. Teachers have several response options. The teacher can

A. ignore the question.

B. honestly state that he or she does not know the answer, but will find it.

C. treat the question as unimportant or ridiculous so further discussion is discouraged.

D. reprimand the student for straying from the exact lesson objectives to prevent similar questions from occurring.

E. acknowledge the question, allow for relevant student input, then guide students to find the answer at an appropriate time.

Generally, I would choose option E. It is important that teachers react to questions in a manner that facilitates learning for both teachers and students. Discovery learning and the teaching of critical thinking skills are instructional strategies that can be employed across the curriculum, whether the subject matter is well known or relatively new to the instructor. Handling both familiar and unfamiliar questions in this manner allows for the intellectual growth of all those involved, while preserving confidence in the teacher's abilities. Students are encouraged to develop responsibility for their own learning while being actively involved in locating information, processing facts, and making observations, comparisons, or predictions. The teacher acts as a facilitator, not a dispenser, of knowledge.

During a recent life science unit, my students brought in an assortment of small pets and critters. I was unexpectedly asked if frogs eat dead bugs. I replied by smiling, raising my eyebrows, and saying, "How can we find out?" Immediately, the class chorused, "Put a dead bug in there!" My students are used to this type of scenario. They delight in taking charge of their own learning. I am comfortable and confident that together we can learn about any topic.

Robin Gillespie
Powell Elementary School
Florence, Alabama

think it through, continued

EVALUATE this problem's possible multiple solutions while you think about the dynamic process of problem solving.

The response of this experienced teacher suggests an important point about dual agenda approaches to teaching thinking—namely, that they can be adopted spontaneously, whenever the opportunity arises. Specifically, this response demonstrates "reflection in action" to solve an instructional problem when she *doesn't* know the answer. That is the kind of behavior you must develop to become a reflective practitioner.

In short, you need to develop a disposition to think in both yourself and your students when you and they encounter a problem-as-challenge. The experienced teacher makes that point in a clever way by giving us options A through E as alternative ways of responding to students' questions. Option A ("ignore the question") would indicate an unwillingness by the teacher to reflect or think. An option A teacher would eventually extinguish the curiosity of children. Option B ("honestly state that he or she does not know the answer, but will find it") is a bit better, but it should be used sparingly. Option B is the best option when a teacher *should* know an answer but has a momentary lapse of memory. Teachers are human, and students may need to be reminded of that.

Both option C ("treat the question as unimportant or ridiculous") and option D ("reprimand the student for straying from the exact lesson objectives") punish the curiosity of children. They are responses born of insecurity. What is the source of such insecurity? My guess is that it comes from a situation in which a teacher has never learned to reflect in action. At the beginning of the 1980s, many reports on education converged on the finding that elementary, high school, and even education students were not being taught to think.

Justly or unjustly, the blame fell on undergraduate teacher education programs. Reforms are just now beginning to take hold through innovative teacher education programs, curriculum guides, and textbooks. Indeed, there is a great experiment under way in education to develop confident thinking in large numbers of teachers and students (not just among an elite).

The experienced teacher accurately acknowledges that thinking in students can develop only if the teacher possesses (1) a disposition to think, (2) a willingness to continue to develop as a thinker along with his or her students, and (3) skills to teach thinking. These characteristics are all implicit in option E ("acknowledge the question, allow for relevant student input, then guide students to find the answer at an appropriate time"). Guiding students to find an answer requires both patience and skill at teaching higher-order thinking.

Although student questions can be points of departure for sustained investigations or projects, they more often provide opportunities to teach process skills—here, by testing a hypothesis ("frogs eat dead bugs") through guided discovery. Small forays into process skills allow you to stay close to content objectives while teaching thinking. Content objectives are often mandated by the curriculum (in this case, the life science unit).

Ideally, dual agendas should be sustained efforts to teach process skills, but they can also serve as solutions to the problem of teaching thinking whenever students ask questions that you cannot answer.

strategic solutions

Using Dual Agendas to Teach Process Skills

What lessons can be learned—from reciprocal teaching of reading in the content areas, teaching of heuristics in mathematics, and use of guided discovery in science—that apply to most dual agenda modes of teaching thinking?

First, you can *use a dual agenda approach to teach process skills along with content.* With parallel sets of objectives, one for content and another for process skills, dual agendas are appearing more frequently in curriculum guides and textbooks. Many dual agendas are successful in developing specific skills because applications are often immediate. Content provides a *context* for skill learning.

Second, *always define the process skills that you expect students to learn, and discuss these definitions with students.* Teachers cannot expect students to acquire thinking skills when these skills are left implicit. To be learned, process skills must be the *explicit* objective of instruction. Recall, for example, that Mrs. Webb named inference as the objective of her guided discovery lesson.

Third, *take into account the developmental issues and prerequisite skills that are the foundation for content and process objectives.* Some children lack the enabling skills that are prerequisite to acquiring more complex process skills. They may be less proficient decoders of text than other students, or they may think on a concrete level when formal reasoning is required (Lawson, 1985; Mulopo & Fowler, 1987). Developmental goals might include development of thoughts from concrete to abstract, or practice to increase the proficiency of a given skill such as decoding words.

Situated Approaches

Situated approaches to teaching thinking feature authentic cognitive tasks, such as solving a problem situated in the context of a "real-world" activity. They include the *whole-language* approach to developing literacy (Goodman, 1986), as well as an authentic inquiry mode of teaching science. In situated cognition, the role of the teacher is often like that of the master of a craft, with students in the role of apprentices (Brown, Collins & Duguid, 1989). Together, they conduct a "real-world" activity, often as a supplement to more conventional instruction.

Situated approaches involve teaching by real-life activity.

Situated problems vary in terms of the degree to which they are realistic. At one extreme, *simulations* present problems in simplified contexts for novice problem solvers. At the other extreme, *projects* involve solving a problem developed out of the interests of the teacher and students. Both simulations and projects provide a clear view of situated cognition because they are frequently used and have been thoroughly studied.

Simulations as Situated Cognition

| Many subjects can be taught using simulation.

Simulations are operational models that use selected components of a real or hypothetical process, mechanism, or system (Keiser & Seeler, 1987). In the past, simulations were employed primarily to teach skills that involve some risk or high cost, such as driving, flying, managing a business, engaging in military battle, or providing first aid. But they are increasingly being used to teach thinking skills in virtually every academic subject, from history to chemistry. Some of these simulations involve gamelike conditions, in which students enact specified roles; others call for videodisc players or computers; still others involve both. Table 10.4 lists some computer simulation programs that are now being used to teach thinking in mathematics, science, and social studies, at appropriate grade levels.

| Simulations differ in fidelity in terms of appearance and function.

A critical dimension of any simulation is its **fidelity,** which is a description of how closely the simulation imitates reality. Fidelity varies along several dimensions, including perceptual appearance, manipulation, and function (Levin & Waugh, 1988). *Perceptual appearance* refers to whether the simulation looks or feels real; *manipulation* refers to whether realistic actions are involved in responses; and *function* refers to whether the operation of the model is similar to that of the real system.

A common error is to think that "high" fidelity is always desirable, but in fact it is not necessarily appropriate for novice learners, who often learn best in a simplified learning situation (Alessi, 1988). For example, "real time" (an aspect of functional fidelity) might be problematic for novices who cannot perform as quickly as real time requires. Note, however, that degrees of speed or difficulty are offered by some programs as a form of *dynamic support,* which in turn provides operational scaffolding to develop expertise in problem solving. In such cases, speed of operation can be increased to real-time demands as expertise develops. Fidelity and dynamic support are important considerations in the construction or choice of a simulation; but as a teacher you must base your decisions on what enhances learning, not on what is most realistic.

Example of a Simulation: *The Oregon Trail*

One of the best-known computer simulations designed to teach higher-order thinking in a realistic context is *The Oregon Trail* (Minnesota Educational Computing Corporation, 1986). This simulation (included among the listings in Table 10.4) is a social studies computer program that is designed to teach students (from fifth grade up) to solve problems similar to those encountered by pioneers who traveled from Missouri to Oregon in 1848. The traveler(s) can set some of the initial parameters of the program, including the role of the wagon leader (banker, farmer, or carpenter), the month of

Table 10.4   Sample Computer Simulation Programs by Subject and Grade Level

Subjects, Program Titles, and Suppliers	Grade Level
Mathematics	
Taking Chances (Wings/Sunburst)[1,3]	3 and up
Problem-Solving with Nim (MECC)[1]	3 to 8
Hot Dog Stand: Survival Math Skills (Wings/Sunburst)[2,4]	6 and up
Science	
Woolly Bounce (MECC)[1]	K to 2
Paper Plane Pilot (MECC)[1]	3 to 9
Sun and Seasons (MECC)[1]	3 to 9
The Great Solar System Rescue (Tom Snyder)[5]	5 to 8
Sim Ant (Broderbund)[2,4]	5 to 12
Biosolve: Toxicology (Wm. Bradford)[1,3]	7 to 12
Dr. Know-It-All's Inner Body Works Senior Version (Tom Snyder)[1,2,4]	7 to 12
Physics Explorer: Harmonic Motion (Wings/Sunburst)[4]	8 to 12
Projectiles (Vernier)[1,2]	8 to 12
Beaker: An Expert System for the Organic Chemistry Student (Brooks/Cole)[4]	10 to 12
Social studies	
Bluegrass Bluff (MECC)[1]	5 to 9
Lewis and Clark Stayed Home (MECC)[1]	5 to 9
The Oregon Trail (MECC)[1,4]	5 to 12
Wagon Train 1848 (MECC)[4,6]	5 to 12
Election 1912 (Eastgate Systems)[4]	6 to 12
Where in America's Past Is Carmen Sandiego? (Broderbund)[1,2,4]	6 to 12
Who'll Save Abacaxi? (Focus Media)[1]	7 to 12
Hidden Agenda: Scholastic Edition (Scholastic)[2,4]	9 to 12

[1] Program for Apple II computers
[2] Program for IBM-compatible computers
[3] Program for IBM PCs
[4] Program for Macintosh
[5] Videodisc player required
[6] AppleTalk-based network required

Source: List compiled from *Only the Best*, courtesy of Michele R. Walker

departure, and the quantity of supplies. The learner works through the program with minimal preparation. Over repeated attempts to travel the trail, he or she develops a strategy to solve problems within the simulated experience.

On their way to learning how to solve problems in the context of a simulated trip to Oregon, students are expected to achieve the following objectives (Minnesota Educational Computing Corporation, 1986, n.p.):

Simulation games teach problem-solving skills in context.

1. Understand and discuss the experiences of nineteenth-century American pioneers.
2. Consider alternative solutions to problems and their consequences.
3. Make and justify decisions, and act on them.
4. Recognize the legitimacy of values within groups different from their own by studying a community from the past.

The second and third objectives indicate precisely which skills in solving problems are developed by the program. These core objectives essentially require students to gather information, generate thoughtful solutions, and implement them. Together, the objectives support the development of problem solving within the context of the simulation.

You will notice that there are no knowledge-level objectives for this program. Why? Educational researchers have discovered that knowledge-level objectives can be "skipped" when students are willing and able to use higher-level cognitive skills (Halpain, Glover & Harvey, 1985). But how does knowledge and comprehension develop? Apparently, obstacles to the learner's understanding are removed by problem solving within the simulated context. Knowledge is constructed as these obstacles are removed.

For example, an individual with the goal of getting to Oregon might discover *false* assumptions about pioneer travel—that fast, early, or late travel makes no difference (departure time does make a difference); that guns are used for shooting people (instead of hunting for food); or that a store owner's advice about supplies to a one-way traveler is to be trusted (rather than weighed against other options). The discovery of false assumptions requires problem solving. Consequently, problem solving becomes the vehicle by which knowledge is generated—so long as the problems do not overwhelm and discourage the learner.

Evaluation of Simulations

Does engagement with simulation exercises develop higher-order thinking skills? The answer depends on the extent to which students are prepared for responding to these exercises. *If* they are given appropriate background information to make rational decisions, and *if* they are coached in problem-solving strategies, their problem-solving skills may improve. Inadequate information or insufficient awareness of efficient problem-solving strategies may lead students to attempt to progress through simulations by haphazard guesswork (Bransford et al., 1986). Preliminary research on the effectiveness of simulations in which problem-solving strategies are explicitly taught indicates that there is no loss of achievement in relation to traditional classes *and* that there are gains in domain-specific problem-solving skills (Cognition and Technology Group at Vanderbilt, 1992).

Simulations have their limitations. They tend to be expensive and time-consuming, as well as inadequate to the task of leading students to achieve all goals, particularly those related to knowledge acquisition. Most advocates of learning through simulations recommend their use as a supplement rather than as a replacement for other modes of instruction (Cognition and Technology Group at Vanderbilt, 1993). Accordingly, you might want to limit experiences with simulations to supplementary learning, rather than relying on them as the sole or even principal form of instruction.

> Simulations may be best used as supplementary materials.

Student Project Learning as Situated Cognition

A **project** is an extended inquiry into various aspects of a real-world topic that is of interest to participants and judged worthy by teachers (Katz & Chard, 1992). Because of its real-world appeal, students are motivated to investigate, record, and report their findings. The hallmark of project learning is greater independence of inquiry and "ownership" of the work on the part of students. When contrasted with more formal instruction, it allows students a greater degree of choice and capitalizes on internal motivation.

> Doing a project allows the student greater independence and requires motivation.

A teacher of young children might help them organize a project related to some theme of interest to them such as "a visit to the hospital," "building a house," or "the bus that brings us to school." Lillian Katz and Sylvia Chard (1992) recommend that the title of the project should reflect the research effort. Accordingly, the teacher might name the project *What Happens on a Visit to the Hospital?* or *Who Builds Houses?* In early childhood, the project should integrate learning from a number of domains, such as science, literacy, and art.

For older students, projects should supplement text-based instruction; they should also be organized around the interests of the learners related to problem solving in a particular subject matter, such as social studies (VanSickle & Hoge, 1991) or science. In many ways, science projects fulfill the original *intentions* of discovery learning, which, as you'll recall from our earlier discussion, are not usually realized within a dual agenda approach.

One increasingly well-known project approach to science in elementary school is called Search, Solve, Create, and Share, or SSCS (Pizzini, Shepardson & Abell, 1989). Let's look at this approach in some detail to see how student projects can be designed to teach higher-order thinking.

Example of Student Project Learning: Search, Solve, Create, and Share

In Search, Solve, Create, and Share, a text-based lesson is used as a point of departure for a project. There are four phases in the development of each project.

Projects may involve representing a problem, solving it, and creating a product to share the result.

1. *Searching* requires the identification and representation of a scientific problem. Students studying the environment in the sixth grade might suggest, for example, air pollution, rainfall last year, and energy from the sun as suitable topics for a project. They might then divide into groups by interest area and narrow their focus, putting their ideas into a question format. As they do so, they are identifying and representing a problem. A "solar energy" group, for example, may decide to measure "how solar energy can be used to heat buildings."

2. *Solving* the problem involves gathering information and generating a solution. In this phase, the groups collect and analyze data. The sixth-grade solar energy group, for example, might gather information about the ways solar energy is used to heat buildings, or about the number of hours of sunshine in different regions. Another group might gather information to predict rainfall in the state or county this year, based on comparisons with previous years. A third group might conduct a survey of students concerning what they believe to be the most important source of air pollution. Use of the SSCS model with higher grade levels might involve computers as tools for recording or manipulating data. Each group may require some guidance in determining how to gather information and answer research questions but, given this guidance, will be capable of solving the problem.

3. *Creating* refers to the creation of a product, such as a presentation to class members or the school. In this phase, the solar energy group might devise an oral report with visual aids about how different buildings are heated with solar energy. In addition, group members might construct models or make bar graphs on posters.

Projects can supplement textbook-based learning, requiring that teachers and students be both resourceful and creative. *(James Schnepf/Gamma Liaison)*

4. *Sharing* involves the actual communication of findings. It should also result in the generation of future search questions, such as "Can heat from the sun be stored?"

A particular project, whether on the preschool, elementary, or secondary level, may extend anywhere from a few days to several weeks. What's important is not how long it lasts but that it situates higher-order thinking in some authentic task and encourages independent learning. Because projects rely not on textbooks as resources but on teachers and students, they require both the teacher and the students to be resourceful and creative. For younger students, parents can also be of great assistance. They can contribute expertise, donate objects to examine, assist on field trips, or help children investigate aspects of a topic on a weekend (Katz & Chard, 1992).

> A project should stimulate higher-order thinking and encourage independent learning.

For older students, technology can serve as a tool of inquiry. Some computer programs assist students by scaffolding scientific inquiry or report writing with prompts (Hawkins & Pea, 1987; Scardamalia et al., 1989). Others help students gather information by permitting them to conduct searches of encyclopedic databases. When the cost of portable computers falls below a few hundred dollars, their accessibility, like that of the calculator, will become universal.

Evaluation of Student Project Learning

Student projects have a long history in education, but they have not often been evaluated as an approach to teaching higher-order thinking. Recently, however, the SSCS model has been compared with alternatives in terms of several outcomes (Pizzini & Shepardson, 1991; Shepardson & Pizzini, 1993; Shepardson & Pizzini, 1994). These outcomes have generally favored the project approach to teach higher-order thinking.

Does a well-structured project-based approach to science develop higher-order thinking? The answer is yes if higher-order thinking is measured according to the number and level of questions asked. In the initial large-group, text-based component of SSCS (the search phase), questions asked by students do *not* differ from those asked in conventional instruction, but in the small-group (solve and create) sessions, significantly more questions of a higher order are asked than in either worksheet or confirmatory lab activities. Long-term studies will be required to determine whether higher-order thinking actually develops out of this phenomenon, but the engagement of students in higher-order thinking is a significant development in itself.

> Science projects can develop higher-order thinking.

Does a project-based approach to science develop positive attitudes toward science, as well as a disposition to think? Again, the answer is yes—and for a very interesting reason. When various groups of eighth-grade students participating in science worksheet, confirmatory lab, and SSCS project-based activities were asked about their perceptions of science activities, the group experiencing SSCS indicated more often than the other groups that the activities were enjoyable and that they wished to do more of them (see Figure 10.4)—clear evidence of positive attitudes toward science and a disposition to think.

> Science projects can develop positive attitudes and a disposition to think.

Figure 10.4
Perceptions of Science Activities
(Shepardson & Pizzini, 1993, p. 129)

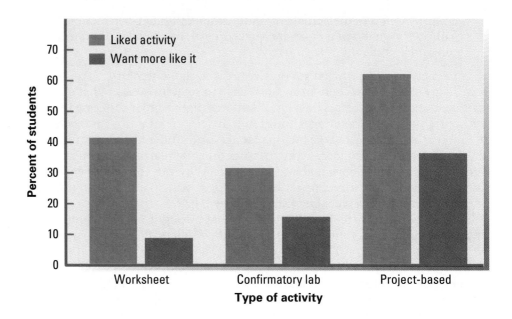

---

strategic solutions

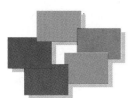

Using Situated Cognition to Teach Thinking

Simulations and projects do not represent all modes of situated cognition, but they provide enough information to suggest how to use situated approaches to teach higher-order thinking. The prerequisite that must be achieved by a teacher before thinking can be taught in this way is the realization that all knowledge is constructed. Knowledge is *not* encyclopedic, objective, and unrelated to inquiry—contrary to the impression that students often receive from textbooks and teachers.

Knowledge is built by the learner. Once you have examined the design of a particular concept or theory, you will see that the process of knowledge construction is at least as important as its outcome.

Once you decide to develop thinking in an authentic context, you need to determine what degree of realism is needed for a learner to acquire a higher-order skill. As discussed, high fidelity is not always best, as it can actually lead to a great deal of frustration. Accordingly, you should first *situate higher-order thinking in a context with appropriate dimensions and degrees of realism.* The learner may become overwhelmed if the situation is so unstructured as to be confusing or the problems you present are too difficult.

Second, you should *train the learner in the necessary prerequisites prior to situating student cognition.* These prerequisites can include background information (usually from a textbook), information on problem-solving procedures, or skills related to computer use.

Third, you should *supply guidance and information only as the learner needs them.* Your role is to circulate among learners, providing guidance and information—but only when needed. In situated approaches to teaching higher-order thinking, students are like apprentices who, when given a task, can often function on their own or in small problem-solving groups, but who sometimes need specific guidance or support to accomplish the task.

The critical question remains: Do students develop knowledge as efficiently through a project-based approach as through more traditional alternatives? If we're drawing a comparison to SSCS, the answer is that the amount of knowledge acquired is about the same. Keep in mind, however, that SSCS uses a textbook lesson as a point of departure, rather than engaging students in a project unrelated to textbook content. Thus, as with simulations, this project-based approach should probably be used as a supplement to text-based instruction—except when texts themselves are generated by the learners as a project (see Chapter 11).

CONCLUSION

Your strategies for teaching thinking should involve *your* constructs, produced by problem solving. They should develop from your understanding that all knowledge is constructed, including constructs designed to teach thinking. As you plan how to teach thinking, consider *stand alone* programs, *dual agenda* approaches, and *situated cognition,* and the ways in which they represent different constructs. To consolidate your understanding of these constructs, Perkins (1986) recommends that you ask four "design questions" about each one: What is its purpose? What is its structure? What are model cases of it? What arguments explain or evaluate it?

First, consider the *purposes* of the different approaches to teaching higher-order thinking. In general, stand alone programs are used to teach *enabling* skills, dual agendas are used to teach *process* skills, and situated cognition is used to teach *problem solving.*

Second, consider their different *structures.* Stand alone programs *separate* thinking skills from specific content learning, dual agendas *parallel* thinking skills with content learning, and situated cognition develops thinking skills *embedded* in content learning.

Third, consider the *model cases* of each approach. Instrumental Enrichment and Philosophy for Children are model cases of stand alone programs. Reciprocal teaching of reading in the content areas, heuristics in mathematics, and guided discovery in science are model cases of the dual agenda approach. And *The Oregon Trail* and Search, Solve, Create, and Share are model cases of situated cognition.

Fourth, consider the *explanations* and *limitations* of these different approaches. Stand alone programs developed out of the need to *remediate* students' thinking, but skills must be "bridged" to the regular curriculum. Dual agendas developed out of the need to teach *subject-specific* skills, but prerequisites must often be mastered first. Finally, situated cognition developed out of the need for *authentic* learning, but it must often be supplemented by text-based instruction to meet curriculum requirements.

Having built an understanding of these different ways to teach thinking, you will be in a better position to construct your own design—one that will almost certainly mix instruction in enabling skills, process skills, and problem solving. There are no easy solutions to the problem of how to teach higher-order thinking. The best solutions, however, are thoughtful ones.

concept paper

Analysis of a Design for Teaching Higher-Order Thinking Skills

Purpose of the assignment

To analyze a design or construct for teaching thinking in one of your subject fields.

Directions for the assignment

1. Identify a *discussion* of how to teach higher-order thinking in one of your subject fields at a level that you will teach (for example, elementary social studies). Higher-order thinking skills generally include levels in Bloom's Taxonomy (1956) above application (that is, analysis, synthesis, or evaluation), *or* critical thinking, *or* reflection, *or* decision making, *or* problem solving. You can find this discussion in many professional journal articles, subject textbooks, curriculum guides, and methods textbooks published since 1990.

2. Copy the discussion, which should be no more than a few pages in length. *Bring the copy to your instructor, who can then verify that you have found a discussion of a design to teach higher-order thinking.*

3. Analyze the *design or construct of how to teach thinking* by asking yourself the four "design questions" recommended by Perkins (1986).

   a. *What is its purpose?*
   Ask yourself, What do the discussion authors mean by their term(s) for higher-order thinking? If the authors do not explain their key terms, you may need to perform a literature search to find out what the terms mean. What purpose is served by this design to teach thinking?

   b. *What is its structure?*
   Ask yourself, What are the organizing principles of the design? Are students expected to be active? To cooperate with other students? Are they capable of thinking when they enter the course? Do thinking skills

need to be modeled by the teacher? Approached in a sequence? Taught concurrently? Do different subjects need to be integrated?

c. *What are model cases of it?*

Ask yourself, What are examples or applications of the design? What illustrations or applications of the construct for teaching thinking are provided? These model cases do not have to be included in the discussion itself; they can appear instead in a feature box or appendix. Remember, a *model* is just a good example. Try to provide more than one.

d. *What arguments explain or evaluate it?*

- What do the authors say or imply is the motive for their design? Why did they develop it? Try to pick up on any reference to the quality of thinking in our schools, professional thinking skills in the subject matter, thinking across the curriculum, and so on, that you might quote in your paper.
- Try to identify the strengths and weaknesses of this approach to teaching thinking. (The evaluations sections in this chapter 10 provide some suggestions.) For example, does the design for teaching thinking take into account the need for enabling skills? Content objectives? Innovative evaluation procedures?

Remember to focus on the design to teach higher-order thinking, not on the design of the discussion. (The purpose of the latter is to inform the reader about the former.)

4. If you have addressed all of the design questions, you are in a position to formulate a thesis sentence about the design for teaching thinking that you have analyzed. How would you characterize, in a few words or a phrase, the approach that you analyzed? Locate this comment at the end of a very short introductory paragraph in which you describe the design, identify who discussed it, and explain the class level and subject for which it is intended.

5. If typewritten, your paper should be four to six pages long. You may organize your paper any way you like—to reflect your understanding of a specific approach to teaching thinking. One common form of organization is to discuss each of the design questions in turn; but if you adopt this format, try not to do so mechanically. Be sure to turn in a copy of the discussion authors' publication along with your paper.

SUMMARY

1. Higher-order thinking skills are relatively complex cognitive performances, the ultimate purpose of which is problem finding and solving. Analysis, synthesis, and evaluation are representative of these thinking skills.

2. To help students develop higher-order thinking, teachers facilitate and foster their students' disposition to think, which is an abiding tendency to use higher-order thinking when faced with a problematic solution.

3. There are three different approaches, or cognitive designs, that commonly frame instruction for thinking skills: stand alone programs, dual-agenda approaches, and situation cognition.

4. Stand alone programs are independent courses of instruction that focus on thinking skills. They typically target skills such as classification, induction, and deduction, which are fundamental to the development of higher-order thinking. Examples of stand alone programs are Instrumental Enrichment and Philosophy for Children.

5. Dual-agenda programs infuse the teaching of thinking skills into the regular, text-based curriculum. They usually have two sets of parallel objectives—one for thinking skills and one for content to be learned. These thinking skills are generally known as process skills because they are related to procedures for conducting activities related to specific content-area learning. Examples of dual-agenda programs are reciprocal teaching of reading in a content area, the use of heuristics in mathematics, and the use of guided discovery in science.

6. Situated cognition features the use of authentic cognitive tasks, such as solving a real problem in the context of a real-world activity. All aspects of problem-solving skills can be developed through this approach. Examples of situated cognition are computer-simulation programs such as *The Oregon Trail* and student-generated projects.

KEY TERMS

thinking skill p. 408
generative learning p. 409
disposition to think p. 409
stand alone p. 413
dual agenda p. 413
situated cognition p. 413
enabling skills p. 414
classification p. 414
induction p. 415
inference p. 416
deduction p. 416
mediated learning p. 419
scaffolded instruction p. 419

inner speech p. 421
near transfer p. 424
far transfer p. 424
process skills p. 425
heuristics p. 425
guided discovery p. 425
metacognitive skills p. 426
reciprocal teaching p. 427
algorithms p. 428
discovery learning p. 434
fidelity p. 442
project p. 445

SUGGESTED RESOURCES

Barell, J. (1991). *Teaching for Thoughtfulness.* New York: Longman. This book is filled with practical strategies for teaching thinking at all grade levels.

Jones, B. F. (1992). "Cognitive Designs in Instruction." In M. C. Alkin (Ed.), *Encyclopedia of Educational Research* (Vol. 1, pp. 166–177). New York: Macmillan. This article is a good overview of the different ways that exist to teach thinking.

Minnesota Educational Computing Corporation. (1986). *The Oregon Trail.* Minneapolis: Author. This award-winning program can provide a very interesting introduction to simulations, particularly when it is accompanied by its documentation.

Perkins, D. N. (1986). *Knowledge as Design.* Hillsdale, N.J.: Erlbaum. David Perkins has written several books that deal with the teaching of thinking. This one is perhaps most helpful for developing an understanding that knowledge is constructed.

11

Cognition and Creativity: Achieving the Goal of Creative Thinking

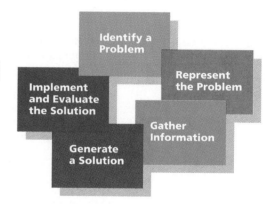

Orientation

The purpose of this chapter is to take a closer look at creative thinking. **Creative thinking** can be defined as *the ability to deal with a problem in an original way.* Creative thinking differs from other forms of cognition because it involves finding new solutions to given problems, finding new problems to solve, and solving those problems in an aesthetic way. As you read, look for answers to the following questions:

- **In what ways is the rational approach to developing creativity different from other approaches?**

- **What are three goals for developing creative thinking?**

- **What are effective strategies for solving open-ended problems and problems with multiple solutions?**

- **In what ways can the rational approach to teaching creative thinking help students become better at identifying problems?**

- **How is problem finding related to cognitive development?**

- **How can teachers help students develop aesthetic sensibility and expression? Why is this important?**

- **What roles can computers play in the development of creative thinking? What are authoring programs, and why do you need to know about them?**

THE RATIONAL APPROACH TO TEACHING CREATIVE THINKING

The rational view of creativity stresses finding and solving problems.

Creativity can be developed in several ways. One approach, which emphasizes problem finding and solving, is known as the **rational view of creativity** (Clark, 1992). In this view, *everyone has the ability to be creative,* but the frequency of creative thinking fluctuates in most people, particularly as a function of age. It appears to rise during preschool and early grades and to level off or even decline in third and fourth grades. Whether or not creative thinking recovers and even increases for a second time, in upper elementary grades or high school, may be related to the learning environment. If a student's early creative initiatives were not met with encouragement from the teacher, that student may not be inclined to experiment with creative thinking later on.

Young children can think creatively.

For that reason, we'll begin this chapter with a look at creative thinking in a kindergarten class. Although you may teach in higher grades throughout your career, you will find no better view of the wellsprings of creative thought than from the floor of a kindergarten in which developmentally appropriate teaching and learning occur. What five-year-olds lack in terms of systematic thinking they make up for in terms of fresh associations. A look at what happens in a creative kindergarten class will help all of us understand better what kinds of teaching practices facilitate creative thinking and what kinds do not.

Ms. Taylor's Kindergarten Class

As I entered Cindy Taylor's kindergarten class, I noticed that the children had settled in a rug area over at one end of the room. Ms. Taylor had a "big book" out—it was sitting open on an easel at the front of the rug area, so all of the children could see the words and pictures. The teacher had begun to sing the words. The book and song were titled "Down by the Bay," and the children were clearly familiar with it:

Down by the bay,	For if I do,
Where the watermelons grow,	My mother will say,
Back to my home	"Did you ever see a pig
I dare not go.	Wearing a wig,
	Down by the bay?"

As she sang each word of this song, Ms. Taylor pointed to it with a wand. At the end of each short phrase, she pointed to the words again and let the children echo her. The phrases were short enough for them to remember easily. Ms. Taylor was using music to teach children to read.

Each verse of the song contained a rhyme describing an absurd image: "Did you ever see a baboon/holding a balloon?" "Did you ever see a llama/wearing pajamas?" and so on. At the end of the book, Ms. Taylor began a new rhyme: "Did you ever see a cow, with . . . ?" A child completed it with "one eyebrow," and everyone delighted in the thought.

Ms. Taylor next asked a boy and a girl to pass around white plastic writing boards, erasable felt pens, and tissue paper. As they distributed the materials, she played a tape with the verses of "Down by the Bay." Even the student teacher and I sang along. After each child had materials, Ms. Taylor said, "We're going to make some of our own rhyming words. We're going to start with *cat*." Everyone in class had already learned to spell *cat* through a computer-assisted instruction (CAI) program called Writing to Read. She and the children wrote *cat* on their writing boards.

Ms. Taylor: How can we change it so that we can make a word that rhymes with it?

Students: Change the first letter.

Ms. Taylor: So what should we change the *c* to?

Michael: *h.*

Ms. Taylor: Good. That spells *hat.* Let's write *hat* under *cat.* [Ms. Taylor pauses until the children have finished writing.] What else?

Students suggested *b* and wrote *bat, f* and wrote *fat, m* and wrote *mat, r* and wrote *rat,* and *t* and wrote *tat.* As students developed their list, Ms. Taylor motioned to the student teacher, who went to help one or two students who were having trouble with their letters. After everyone had a chance to write the last word, Ms. Taylor asked the students to read the list and to tell her what the words had in common. ("They all end with the same letters.") Then she told them to erase their boards completely with the tissue paper.

Now she asked, "What word do you want to start with?" Someone suggested *dog,* so she said, "Let's write *dog.*" She spelled it slowly. Children either wrote the word or copied the letters. She asked students what words rhymed with it, and different children suggested *hog, mog,* and *log.* Students began to fill their plastic slates with real and invented words. She hinted, "We have something in the science center that rhymes with *hog.*" A child said, "frog." "How would we write *frog?*" The challenge was momentarily too great, so Ms. Taylor sounded out the word carefully, and the children attempted to write out the blended letters. Ms. Taylor asked them to read their lists together, then told them to erase everything. "What's the next word?" Someone suggested *fish,* and the class developed a third list of rhyming words.

After the reading/music and spelling/poetry lessons, students went to their tables (while the "Down by the Bay" tape played one last time) to complete an art activity in which they would compose their own pages for a book. Each child was given an oval piece of paper with two blanks:

> Did you ever see a _____
> Wearing a _____
> Down by the bay?

Ms. Taylor asked them to fill in the blanks with their own rhyming words and draw a picture. Many of the children would use a rhyme that they had recalled from the song, but the groundwork was set for those who were motivated by the challenge to be original. Ms. Taylor had already drawn and laminated the front and back covers for a book that would contain the children's compositions. The front cover was the red inside of half a watermelon, and the back cover was its green skin. Ms. Taylor circulated around the tables and helped children as they happily tackled this challenging assignment—to create a "big book" of their own.

Ms. Taylor taught reading through song, spelling through poetry, and composition through art. She did all of this before snack time, when a real watermelon was devoured. (The class saved the seeds for a science lesson.) Not only did Ms. Taylor gently introduce the kindergartners to language arts, she did it in a way that challenged a typical group of five-year-olds to be creative.

> Teaching strategies can challenge students to be creative.

Three Goals for Developing Creative Thinking

Three goals for developing creative thinking have been outlined by Elliot Eisner (1985), a professor of education and art. These goals are to help students (1) solve problems with multiple solutions, (2) identify new problems, and (3) develop aesthetic sensibility. These goals define the aims of developing creative thinking in most schools.

The first goal is to help students generate multiple solutions to problems. Many practical problems do not have just one correct solution. Such problems may occur in the natural and social sciences, in the arts, or in math. They include the following:

- creating variations on a musical theme or thinking of new stanzas for a poem (multiple solutions in the arts)

Problems with multiple solutions can be found in the sciences as well as in the arts. What different hypotheses, for example, might these third-graders generate to explain a change in water quality? *(Bob Daemmrich)*

- discovering multiple causes of an event or developing new arguments to persuade people to a position on an issue (multiple solutions in the social sciences)
- generating alternative hypotheses or imagining ingenious ways to recycle materials (multiple solutions in the sciences)
- identifying different ways to divide a space or generating several ways to arrive at an estimate (multiple solutions in mathematics)

Creative solutions need not be new to humanity, only to one individual. What is important is for children to discover that many everyday problems have more than one solution.

In Ms. Taylor's class, the children were challenged to find new solutions to a given problem when she asked them to find words that rhymed with *cat*. The problem was given, but it had no uniquely correct solution. Students were challenged to come up with *multiple* solutions. As a result, they generated a list of six words that rhymed with *cat*—each a different solution to the same problem.

Children should learn that many problems have multiple solutions.

Originality is expressed not only in finding new solutions to old problems but also in formulating new problems that require solutions. Therefore, the second goal of creative education within the rational model is to help students formulate new questions or problems. In the arts, new problems often take the form of feelings or ideas to be expressed, portrayed, or composed in logical relation to each other. In the social sciences, new problems often take the form of social imbalances or inequities. In the natural sciences, they often take the form of unknown causes of events. In math, new problems often stem from unexplained equivalencies or relationships.

Creativity includes coming up with new problems.

A goal of creative education is to help children perceive and symbolically express properties of experience, as in the arts. *(Globe Staff Photo/Wendy Maeda)*

Aesthetic expression in all areas can enhance creativity.

When Ms. Taylor asked the children to tell her what word they wanted to use for their next list, she asked them to find a *new problem.* One student suggested *dog,* and later, another suggested *fish.* These words were not solutions but new problems that would require them to generate new lists of solutions.

A third goal of creative education is to help students perceive and symbolically express properties of experience. **Aesthetic expression** can be defined as the representation of properties through symbols such as lines, figures, colors, words, movements, or tones (Goodman, 1976). In the arts, these properties are often ideas or feelings. They can be represented by simple or quite complex combinations of visual or auditory images. For example, a kindergarten student might learn how the shape of a line can communicate feeling (such as a "flat" line representing calmness). Using much more complex imagery, a high school English student might express a conflict between security and adventure in a story about beavers forced by a new real estate development to move to a new pond. We know much more about teaching students how to perceive and symbolically express properties of experience in the arts than we do about teaching the same skills in the sciences or mathematics.

In the composition/art activity, Ms. Taylor presented children with an *aesthetic problem* or challenge: to complete the sentence with rhyming words that were comic. Rhymes that evoked a funny image were encouraged. Her overarching goal was to help children create a "big book" of their own, representing a property of *their* experience.

As you can see, Ms. Taylor's lesson developed creative thinking in three distinct yet interrelated ways. Each was part of a larger strategy. In developing this strategy, she had taken into account the age and abilities of her students, their background experiences, her resources, the curriculum guide, and her own personal goals. Unless you had the same students, resources,

A teaching strategy for creativity takes account of the entire situation.

curriculum objectives, and personal goals as Ms. Taylor, you would almost certainly not arrive at the same strategy. Nevertheless, Ms. Taylor gives us a valuable example of a teacher helping *all* students to develop their creative potential within the boundaries of the rational model. She attained her larger goal by working at subgoals that built on each other. The remainder of the chapter will present information about each of these subgoals and suggest broad sequences of activities to attain them.

SOLVING PROBLEMS WITH MULTIPLE SOLUTIONS

Modern research within the rational view of creativity originated with the work of psychologist J. P. Guilford (1950, 1967). In a speech to the American Psychological Association, Guilford drew attention to the *absence* of research on creative thinking. Much of his own research in the 1950s focused on the ability to solve "open-ended" problems. In **open-ended problems,** the givens are well defined, but the goal is not specified.

Open-ended problems have well-defined givens but no specified goals.

The key to identifying open-ended problems is to recognize that the problem has already been found and framed, but that the remaining steps of gathering information, generating a solution, and evaluating the solution will not occur according to well-defined procedures. Many everyday challenges are like this. Suppose you are making out your schedule for next term's classes, and you need an art or a music elective to complete your program of studies. The "givens" of the problem are clear: limitations on your time schedule (such as other classes or work), specific course offerings, and the need for a specified number of credit hours in music or art. The solution, however, is not clear. Given these limitations, which art or music elective you choose is up to you.

Every subject matter at every level can present open-ended problems. Let's take mathematics, because it is often associated with *well-defined problems*—problems that have only one correct solution. Suppose a teacher has been given the objective in the curriculum guide of having students "determine areas of different polygons." Perhaps this objective falls under the goal of developing ability to solve open-ended problems. To achieve both the curriculum objective and the goal of open-ended problem solving, the teacher might give each student twelve toothpicks and ask them to develop polygons. She might begin, "How many square units are in a square with three toothpicks on each side?" The question poses a well-defined problem (solution: nine square units). The teacher might then ask students to make different polygons with an area of five square units. Three different solutions are pictured in Figure 11.1. Perhaps you can think of another. Many open-ended problems are beginning to "open up" creative thinking in mathematics for children.

Open-ended problems can inspire creativity in every subject.

There is really not much doubt that the ability to solve open-ended problems is related to creative thinking. On the face of it, students who develop their own solution to open-ended problems have produced something original, at least in their own experience. If they develop their *own* solutions

**Figure 11.1
Solutions to the
Toothpick Problem**
(Pehkonen, 1992, p. 4)

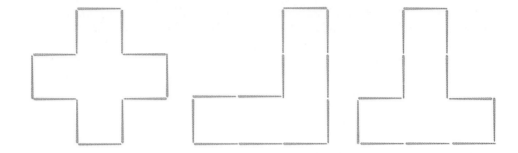

frequently enough, it becomes more likely that they will also produce something that is original in the experience of others, which can be recognized by the outside world as a creative performance or product.

There are several ways to solve an open-ended problem, but not all of them are related to creative thinking. For example, if you needed to find an elective course, you could simply ask someone else for advice about what to take, or schedule the same elective as a roommate or friend. Neither of these solutions is creative, because it is not original. There are, however, two well-established paths for solving open-ended problems in a creative manner. One is "divergent thinking" and the other is "analogical thinking."

Divergent Thinking

> Divergent thinking finds multiple solutions to an open-ended problem.

Divergent thinking is the ability to generate alternative solutions to an open-ended problem. For example, how many uses can you think of for a brick? Take a minute to think of some uses, the more the better. The ability to develop *multiple* solutions for brick uses in a given amount of time is one measure of divergent thinking (Guilford, 1967).

Divergent thinking contrasts with **convergent thinking,** which is the ability to generate necessary solutions to problems that are well defined. Convergent thinking corresponds with deductive logic, which you studied in the last chapter. To illustrate the difference, let's consider a newspaper. Why do people commonly *read* a newspaper? This question is a "right answer" or a convergent question because there are only a few reasons people commonly read a newspaper—for news, ads, opinions, or entertainment. Thought converges on these few answers, ruling out alternatives. Now consider the question, "What are some *possible uses* for a newspaper, other than reading it?" This question is open ended because there are many possible uses. Newspaper is used to pack material, catch drops, start fires, clean windows, wrap fish, insulate against the cold, and to generate cash as a recyclable, to mention just a few uses. Divergence of thought results in transfer of knowledge from one domain to another.

> Convergent thinking finds the right answer to a well-defined problem.

Although many researchers have investigated divergent thinking, perhaps Paul Torrance (1965) has investigated it most intensively and extensively. Torrance developed the *Torrance Tests of Creative Thinking,* which measure divergent thinking with words or with figures. These tests extend the work of Guilford and are scored for *fluency,* or the number of solutions provided for a given problem; *flexibility,* or the number of categories into which these solutions fall; *originality,* or how unusual an individual's solutions are; and *elaboration,* or how complex the solutions are.

Some forms of divergent thinking are related to the ability to develop creative products or performances. Perhaps the most convincing evidence of this is a longitudinal study by Torrance (1988) in which he and his colleagues found some forms of divergent thinking in elementary and junior high school to be related to creative achievements over twenty years later. Recent studies of divergent thinking have continued to verify a relationship between divergent thinking and creative achievements in most domains (e.g., Hocevar & Bachelor, 1989; Runco, 1991).

> Divergent thinking seems to be related to creative achievements.

strategic solutions

Brainstorming

One well-known strategy for solving open-ended problems with divergent thinking is called **brainstorming,** which is a group procedure for generating a quantity of solutions to a given problem. Brainstorming was originally developed by an advertising executive named Alex Osborn (1963) and is closely related to divergent thinking. In brainstorming, only two rules prevail: (1) judgment and criticism are deferred, and (2) quantity of ideas breeds quality solutions (Osborn, 1963). In a brainstorming session, criticism of ideas is ruled out so that group members are not inhibited in their suggestions. "Freewheeling," or the production of wild ideas, is encouraged. Friendly competition may also develop to increase the number of ideas for a solution to a problem, or to combine and improve them to produce better solutions (a process called "piggybacking"). Quantity is expected to result in the development of high quality ideas. In a follow-up session, group members evaluate ideas according to criteria.

To guide your students in brainstorming the solution to an open-ended problem, you can follow four steps. First, *demonstrate brainstorming with a practice problem.* The practice problem may be related to your lesson, but it does not have to be. This demonstration helps students understand that in brainstorming, evaluation is temporarily suspended and all relevant ideas are welcome. Second, *present students with an open-ended problem to solve.* This problem should relate to your lesson. It might involve developing rules for the class (on the first day), generating topics to write about, coming up with ideas for science projects, suggesting different movement activities, and so on. Provide enough information about givens (including limitations on time or resources) so that suggestions will be relevant in terms of the assignment or project.

Third, *ask students to brainstorm individually and silently.* Involvement is at a maximum when everyone is thinking about a problem divergently. For example, you might give students a couple of minutes to write down a short list of class rules, or ideas for specific topics, projects, or activities. Fourth, *ask the group members to pool ideas in a nonevaluative discussion.* Write the list on the board, or have a student act as secretary. The total number of ideas generated separately by group members will often be greater than the number of ideas that they could have generated together (Mullen, Johnson & Salas, 1991; Thornburg, 1991). A brainstorming session may be followed by a session where you evaluate ideas or "map" relations between ideas, depending on your purpose (see Deepening Your Knowledge Base: Brainstorming Uses for a Paper Cup).

Some of the most useful applications of brainstorming are to help students fulfill writing assignments, not just in English class but in any class at any level. In general, a writing assignment presents an open-ended problem. One use of brainstorming in this situation is to help students create a list of potential topics (Pfotenhauer, 1982; Roop, 1990). Brainstorming can help students participate in the development of a group topic or, alternatively, encourage them to find a topic of their own about which to write. A second use for brainstorming is to generate information to be arranged in an outline once a topic is chosen (Blackey, 1988; Phelps, 1992). The teacher can have students brainstorm answers to a practice essay exam question, for example, to show how to produce content during prewriting.

Brainstorming is the central component of a specific program of creative education called Creative Problem Solving (Parnes, 1981). This procedure, which is widely taught in seminars, has six steps:

1. Mess finding—identifying an area of concern
2. Data finding—gathering information about the problem
3. Problem finding—brainstorming subproblems and further defining the problem
4. Idea finding—brainstorming to find as many solutions as possible
5. Solution finding—developing and applying criteria to identify a "best" solution
6. Acceptance finding—developing a plan to implement the best solution.

The Creative Problem Solving procedure incorporates brainstorming at the "problem-finding" and "idea-finding" substages. Although it can be applied to any situation, it appears to be most frequently used to solve open-ended problems.

Creative Problem Solving is at the heart of an educational program called Future Problem Solving, which now attracts over 200,000 students each year (Crabbe, 1989). Future Problem Solving requires students to work in groups of four to develop solutions to problems presented by five "fuzzy situations," or futuristic scenarios. These scenarios involve an open-ended problem selected by children the previous year, such as "consequences of the breakup of the Soviet Union," or "the effects of robotics in the year 2010." The first two of the five situations are used for practice, but the remaining ones are used for

deepening your knowledge base

Brainstorming Uses for a Paper Cup

If you would like to try a brainstorming exercise, divide into small groups. Decide on which member of your group is to be the timekeeper. The tasks of the timekeeper will be to allow your group only four minutes to do the first part of the exercise, and to compile the group list in the second part of the exercise. Now each member of the group (except the timekeeper) should take out a piece of paper and number blank lines from 1 to 20. Do not read further until you are ready to begin.

When you are ready to begin, each member will write down on the numbered lines as many uses as possible for a paper cup, *other than to hold liquid*. Think of practical uses, not impossible or unrealistic ones. List one use on each line as you think of it. You have four minutes. Begin now.

When four minutes are up, hand your lists to the timekeeper, whose task is to compile a group list, adding uses to the longest individual list from shorter lists. The timekeeper should not list duplicate answers on your group list. After the group list has been compiled, reassemble in the larger group to discuss your findings.

Discussion Questions

1. On your individual list, did you find the most original uses mentioned first, or last? Why?

2. Your group list was longer than each individual's list. In terms of a percentage, how much more effective was brainstorming than individual divergent thinking?

3. Did you and your group enjoy this exercise? Is there any relationship between your individual enjoyment (or frustration) and the length of your individual or combined list?

state and international competitions in grade-related divisions (grades 4–6, 7–9, and 10–12).

Evaluation: Brainstorming

Brainstorming serves several useful functions in teaching and learning. First, it facilitates communication of ideas. In brainstorming groups, participation improves, criticism decreases, social support increases, and humor increases (Firestein & McCowan, 1988). Second, it generally improves the ability of individuals to *transfer* information to solve a given problem. That is, participants can more easily retrieve the information stored in their memory for use in problem solving. Programs such as Creative Problem Solving and Future Problem Solving improve divergent thinking (Schack, 1993; Tallent-Runnels, 1993).

Training students in brainstorming techniques increases the quantity of their ideas, but it does not always increase the quality of their ideas, and little evidence suggests it has an impact on creative achievements.

Unfortunately, the principal evidence of success in most of the studies of programs that utilize brainstorming is higher scores on divergent thinking tests (e.g., Rose & Lin, 1984). Because divergent thinking is related to creative thinking but is not the *same* as creative thinking, there is some concern about whether programs that teach brainstorming have taught creative thinking (Feldhusen & Clinkenbeard, 1986). There is little doubt, however, that programs like Creative Problem Solving and Future Problem Solving improve students' communication skills and their ability to transfer information to solve open-ended problems.

Analogical Thinking

Analogical thinking uses comparisons to help solve an open-ended problem.

A second way to solve open-ended problems is **analogical thinking,** which is the use of an extended comparison, or *analogy.* Analogical thinking is used to solve problems that are considerably more complex than paper cup uses. For example, how can the gas mileage of luxury cars be improved? This problem is harder to solve than paper cup uses; nevertheless, it is an open-ended problem (Mayer, 1992; Reitman, 1965).

An analogy can provide a solution that fits a complex problem situation better than many other potential solutions. One analogy that comes to my mind is a comparison between cars and dinosaurs. Large dinosaurs consumed massive amounts of food because of their size. Some large dinosaurs must have eaten all day just to survive. Like large dinosaurs, large luxury cars are inefficient. What kinds of "dinosaurs" could have survived a food shortage (analogous to a price rise in gasoline)? Smaller and lighter ones could have survived, such as the ancestors of today's lizards and birds. How might the analogy of cars to dinosaurs help improve the gas mileage of luxury automobiles? The answer is to "downsize" cars and to make them of lighter materials. Luxury automobiles can use energy more efficiently this way. Such analogies can help solve a problem that has no obvious single solution.

What, you might ask now, makes for analogical thinking? It is not merely establishing the similarity of two situations. For example, car manufacturers might compare their large, luxury models to the luxury model of a competitor that has better gas mileage, and simply copy gas-saving features of the competitor's model. Although that solution is achieved by comparison, the comparison is not an analogy but a literal similarity: the one luxury car is like the other in both its physical characteristics and its relationships to other things.

Analogical thinking involves comparing relationships, not attributes.

Analogical thinking occurs when only relationships and not physical characteristics are transferred from one situation to another (Gentner, 1983). In the automotive example, a relation would be "high energy consumption," whereas attributes would be the physical characteristics of cars or dinosaurs, which are not at all alike.

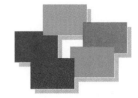

Synectics

There are fundamentally two uses for thinking in analogies. One is to increase comprehension (making the strange familiar). The other is to develop new solutions to old problems (making the familiar strange). Both uses of analogies develop solutions to open-ended problems, but only the second seems to be directly related to creative thinking.

Synectics (a term coined from the Greek roots for "together" and "connecting") is a procedure to solve problems creatively through the use of analogies and imagery. Synectics was originally developed by William Gordon (1961) to solve complex problems in industry. He designed the procedure to help small groups develop creative solutions to persistent technical problems in manufacturing, but its adaptability to school settings has made it a model for developing the creative thinking of students.

The procedure is relatively simple. First, *explore a difficult, open-ended problem in a group discussion.* You may find that a significant amount of frustration also gets expressed. After the group of students has explored the open-ended problem, *invite the group to put the problem aside and focus on something else.* This second step is called the "excursion." Almost anything will do, but you might want to focus discussion on enjoyable things—where students would like to go on vacation, or what their hobbies or favorite class activities are. Third, *return the group to the problem to solve it by finding similarities to what they have been thinking about during the excursion.* These comparisons are called "forced fits." The excursion should have distanced the thinking of the group far enough from the problem that some forced fits will suggest creative solutions. These three steps offer a simplified procedure to stimulate creative writing, to explore social problems, or to create a design or a product (see Deepening Your Knowledge Base: An Example of an Excursion by Fourth Graders).

Evaluation: Synectics

Many creative mathematicians, scientists, and inventors have used analogical reasoning in their discoveries, but the analogies are almost always generated spontaneously by an adult person. Below are some questions that often arise in the course of evaluating procedures to develop analogical thinking in students.

Do these techniques work with children? One important prerequisite for analogical thinking is the ability of the learner to think in terms of relationships rather than physical similarities. According to structure mapping theory (Gentner, 1988), the ability to appreciate relationships apart from physical similarities develops with age. Not until adolescence is this ability fully established (as noted by Piaget). The sometimes strikingly creative statements of young children are not based on analogies but on similarities in

An Example of an Excursion by Fourth Graders

Problem: To invent a grizzly-bear repellent to keep bears in British Columbia from destroying electrical transformers.

Facilitator: Okay. We are going to use the Synectics invention process to work on this problem for a little while.

John: Mine has already sort of been invented.

Facilitator: That's okay. Let's have it.

John: Honey!

Facilitator: What are you wishing?

John: Wish we could use honey to . . . wish we could use like liquid honey. Sort of make it a little wetter so that it would blend in and then put it around the transformer, like near trees and stuff; spray it on trees and the bear will go for those.

Facilitator: [writing down exactly what John said] So, attract the bear away from the transformers by spraying the honey on other things . . . Am I right?

John: Right.
[The students come up with several more ideas.]

Christine: Put . . . something that makes a ray around the whole electrical thing. And when the bear goes through it there would be a closed circuit.

Jeremy: When the bear goes through . . . what would happen is that it would send out like a small shock and it'll immediately tell the bear that this is no place for the bear.

Elliot: Possibly put the transformer underground.

Lisa: Invent something that you could spray on the transformer so that the bear could smell it, and it would smell bad.

Jeremy: It's not keeping the bears away from the transformers. It's keeping the transformers away from the bears. You could put a Styrofoam tree over the transformer, and the bear wouldn't attack a tree.
[The facilitator then takes the students on an excursion.]

Facilitator: We're going to put the problem out of our minds . . . and just to symbolize that, I'm going to cover up the problem, and, to the extent that you possibly can, I want you to forget about the problem that we are working on. The place you can go on your imaginary trip can be anywhere in the world. It doesn't matter where it is.
[Students select several places—Disney World, London, Honolulu, a cheese factory—and describe how they imagine them.]

Jeremy: I would see the guards at Buckingham Palace.
[The facilitator takes the students back to the problem. Christine immediately has an idea.]

Christine: There would be a circle that would turn around when the bear steps on it [and gets], you know, like dizzy.

Facilitator: Where did you get that idea?

Christine: [pointing to the light fixtures in the ceiling] I saw the circles around on the ceiling, so I got the idea.

Facilitator: I love that idea. So the bear would step on this thing, and he would get dizzy.

Jeremy: I got this idea from the Queen's guards marching back and forth. You would have things to distract the bear by moving around and around. Things moving in front of each other with their arms waving. [Jeremy gestures with his arms.]

Source: Weaver & Prince, 1990, p. 385

appearance (such as calling a crescent moon a "banana"). Even young children are capable of solving problems in which similarities in appearance form the basis for developing a solution (Holyoak, Junn & Billman, 1984). Recent revisions in synectics downplay the role of *analogies* and focus on *imagery* generated in excursions as a basis for developing creative solutions to given problems (Weaver & Prince, 1990).

Are excursions sufficient to perceive creative solutions to problems? The answer is that sometimes they are. Fatigue and negative affect (frustration, discouragement, or sadness) are well known to inhibit transfer in problem solving (Jausovec, 1989). A change in mood can explain why the perception of a creative solution may be difficult at first but easier after a pleasant excursion. What appears to be important for the success of the excursion is both the imagery and the lighthearted mood that it creates. An excursion does the double duty of generating images to suggest creative solutions and dispelling any negative affect (such as initial frustration or discouragement in solving a problem) that would inhibit transfer.

There is no single best way to solve an open-ended problem creatively; perhaps there never will be, due to the nature of open-ended problem solving. But brainstorming and analogical thinking are two strategies that have been widely recommended and practiced. Both facilitate transfer of information. Brainstorming allows a student to transfer information from many closely associated domains. Analogical thinking allows a student to transfer information from a few remotely associated domains. The evidence that these techniques develop students' originality is less persuasive, but any new solution to an open-ended problem is more original than a solution to a well-defined problem.

IDENTIFYING PROBLEMS

The second goal of the rational approach to teaching creative thinking is to help students identify problems—also called "problem posing" and "problem finding." The relationship between originality and the ability to identify

think it through

Consider this problem that a novice preservice teacher has **IDENTIFIED** and **REPRESENTED.**

Seizing the Teachable Moment

It is mid-January and very snowy. The class has just returned from lunch and is settling down for spelling. The principal comes to the door and quietly informs the teacher that schools are turning out at 1:30, approximately $1\frac{1}{2}$ hours away. The teacher has to tell the class because some children may have to contact their parents. The class goes wild at the news and all hopes for continuing the spelling lesson are lost.

How should a teacher handle the class during this situation?

Observe how an experienced practicing teacher GENERATES SOLUTIONS to this problem.

What a fantastic opportunity you have just been given! Seize the moment! Bring out all your creative juices and teach snow.

You can go outside and take a thirty-second snow sample and, if possible, count the flakes, then figure out how many billions fall in a certain area in a given time. You can compute driving time home or talk about how many snowflakes would need to fall before a snowman could be built. The list is endless.

In science, you can look at flakes under a microscope or do a mini-lesson on what makes snow and act out the process. Involve art by talking about the fact that each snowflake is unique and then cut them out in an art setting. Label the snowflakes with characteristics of each student—either individually or as a group—and you have a story starter on "what makes me." Talk out likenesses and differences in a cooperative group setting and then discuss how the class is a community and the strengths people bring to class. In language arts, write poems about snow or have a snow spelling bee where words relate to the weather. In social studies, talk about snow routes or possible creative uses of piles of snow, or build a community out of snow (or sugar cubes). Talk about the environmental issues of global warming or annual snowfall in the United States and how people accommodate. Talk about clothes to wear, layering, mountain-climbing clothing, and how wool keeps you warm because it lets out the moisture.

Have hot chocolate on hand and talk about your favorite snow memories. Do a graph of what activities members of the class will be doing for the rest of the day. If possible, get outside and play follow-the-leader, make snow angels, play fox-and-goose, or stick out your tongue and catch the flakes. Join hands and spin. Then hug your kids, tell them to remember the hug when they are cold, and send them on their way. They will remember this day for a long time and respect you as a teacher who took advantage of a "teachable moment."

Barbara Peterson
Lincoln Schools
Lincoln, NE

think it through, continued

EVALUATE this problem's possible multiple solutions while you think about the dynamic process of problem solving.

This creative response to the situation primarily involves problem *finding* by the teacher, but open-ended problem *solving* by the students. What cognitive challenges can a heavy snowfall represent? The experienced teacher begins to think of some possibilities by considering "snow" problems suitable for teaching math, science, art, language arts, social studies, and physical education. Almost all of these activities involve open-ended problem solving.

For example, take the social studies problem of "creative use of piles of snow." Students might use brainstorming to develop a list of uses, much as you developed a list of uses for a paper cup. You might give students an idea or two to help them get started (use piles of snow for a water source, or to make a hill for sledding). Students acting alone might then think divergently about the problem before pooling responses. This activity would take advantage of not only the snowfall but the lighthearted mood that it would create.

Even the math problems suggested by the experienced teacher are open ended. There is no "right" answer for how many snowflakes have fallen in a given area over a given period of time, or how long it will take to travel different distances in the snow by car. The experienced teacher is highly adept at finding open-ended problems for students to explore—an indication of considerable creativity.

The creative challenge that remains is to stimulate problem finding by students. You will learn more about it in the next part of the chapter, but in this case, it would involve asking students to generate their own questions about snow. What would they like to find out about snow? You may need to hold on to your hat—quite literally—as you discover that their interests will probably take you outside. How cold is snow? Can it be colder than freezing? Asking students to find problems is quite different from asking students to solve them. For one thing, they are liable to ask questions difficult enough that you must discover the answers together!

Nevertheless, it is quite clear that if your goal is creative thinking, you cannot stop with open-ended problems. They can be challenging and a lot of fun to solve, but they structure the learning situation in such a way that the teacher is more creative than the student. Open-ended problems are a valuable point of departure for students' creative thinking, but they are only a point of departure.

Einstein once said, "To raise new questions, new possibilities, to regard old questions from a new angle, requires creative imagination and marks real advance in science."[1] If we take the liberty of interpreting "science" as individual knowledge, we can apply this principle not only to the field of science but to progress in the understanding of an individual child. For a *child* to raise new questions requires creative imagination and marks a real advance in understanding.

To the rich and abundant opportunities to find new solutions created by the experienced teacher, let's add some opportunities for students to identify problems.

[1]A. Einstein & L. Infeld, *The Evolution of Physics* (New York: Simon & Schuster, 1938), p. 92

new problems was described by a French philosophy teacher named Paul
Souriau (1881) more than a hundred years ago. He said, "The truly original
mind is that which finds problems" (p. 17). **Problem finding,** or the activity of
identifying problems, is close to the heart of originality in the sciences and
the arts. It also appears to account for much everyday creative thinking that
you and I are likely to do. In the next few pages, we will examine this activity
of problem identification more closely for what it says about how to develop
creative thinking in your students.

> The ability to find new
> problems is closely linked
> to originality.

What Is Problem Finding?

Although the idea of problem finding goes back more than a hundred years,
the investigation of it as an approach to creative thinking is relatively recent.
The first studies of problem finding were conducted by Jacob Getzels and
Mihalyi Csikszentmihalyi (1976). Initial studies focused on college-age art
students, but subsequent studies have been conducted with elementary
school children (e.g., Moore, 1985). One of the consistent findings is that like
divergent thinking, *problem finding is relatively independent of logic*
(Hoover & Feldhusen, 1990; Runco & Okuda, 1988; Smilansky, 1984;
Wakefield, 1985). Since logic is a type of problem solving, questions arise as
to how problem finding and problem solving are and are not related.

The Source of Problem Finding

First, what is the source of problem finding? From a cognitive perspective,
problem finding most nearly matches Piaget's concept of *cognitive disequilibrium.* As you will recall from Chapter 5, cognitive disequilibrium involves
the perception of something that you do not understand. It is greatest during
stage transitions.

> Problem finding is related
> to not understanding
> something.

For example, say that you mention to a child the fact that the earth spins
around once each day. The child skeptically asks, "How fast is it going?"
Instead of dismissing the question with "I don't know," why not demonstrate that it is a good question by pursuing it? If you look in an encyclopedia
under *Earth,* you will find its diameter, circumference, mass, and so forth,
but not how fast it is spinning. From its circumference at the equator (24,902
miles), and the observation that it turns once each day, you can calculate that
it must be spinning about 1,037 miles per hour at the equator—as fast as a fast
jet. Now new questions can arise, and the child asks, "How can the earth
travel so fast and we not feel it?" "Why don't we fly off into outer space?"
"Could a jet always stay in daylight?" When we value the questions of children, we value problem finding.

The Interdependence of Problem Finding and Problem Solving

The relationship between problem finding and problem solving is not a simple one. Some researchers have supposed that problem solving precedes problem finding. How can you find a problem if you do not know how to solve it?

Bringing ideas to school from home involves everyday problem finding and sense making. What measurement problems have these children discovered in making cookies? *(Bob Daemmrich)*

Other researchers have supposed that problem finding precedes problem solving. How can you solve a problem if you have not identified it first? There is no consensus among psychologists about how to characterize the relationship between problem finding and problem solving, but the question of which comes first is likely to be a "chicken-and-egg" question. The answer depends on the scope of inquiry.

Problem finding may or may not precede problem solving.

Everyday Problem Finding

One hypothesis that accounts for the complex interrelatedness of problem finding and problem solving is that their development is cyclical. Problem finding appears to occur both during the initial phase of learning and after the learner has become expert at problem solving. Posing problems that are encountered routinely has been labeled **everyday problem finding.** Everyday problem finding is the kind of activity that you or I engage in when learning a new skill, even before we practice much. This type of problem finding is most frequently studied in relation to school tasks by psychologists interested in the development of mathematical understanding and reading comprehension—or what has recently been called "sense making."

Posing everyday problems is part of initial learning.

Everyday problem finding in mathematics often focuses on daily situations that are familiar to children including home life. Young students might decide to measure rainfall or the size of their classroom, as they study units of measurement; to guess the number of marbles a jar will hold, as they study estimation; and so on. At home, they may decide to count fingers or toes of family members when learning to count; find groups of three things at home when learning about sets; or classify and count objects purchased on a trip to the food store when learning elements of logic. Bringing to school ideas for math problems from home is part of everyday problem finding.

In reading and writing, as in mathematics, everyday problem finding can improve understanding. Reading comprehension, for example, has been conceptualized as a problem-solving activity (Mulcahy & Samuels, 1987). Problem finding involves identifying when the goal of comprehension is not being met so that a strategy such as summarizing, interpreting, or extrapolating can be used to meet it. Written composition has also been used as a problem-finding and -solving activity (Flower & Hayes, 1980). Everyday problem finding in composition requires the writer to identify thoughts or feelings that need to be composed, in order to understand them better (Liggett, 1991). In mathematics, reading, writing, and other subjects, everyday problem finding is the first step in sense making. If you respond to a child's question about how fast the world is spinning, you are modeling sense making.

Expert Problem Finding

Posing problems of extraordinary depth or scope is **expert problem finding.** Expert problem finding is harder than everyday problem finding because (1) it presumes expertise at some type of problem solving, which takes time to develop; and (2) it requires finding significant or important problems. In Chapter 5, you learned that expertise develops only after extensive practice. Such developments take time and sustained effort. Furthermore, once a learner has achieved competence in a domain of learning, he or she may not be motivated to develop into an expert problem finder.

> Expert problem finding requires expert problem solving and works on significant problems.

Why do some, but not all, experts become expert problem finders? There are at least three hypotheses. One is that not all experts were once everyday problem finders. Some learners do not conduct much everyday problem finding during the *initial* phase of learning; consequently, they fail to base expertise on their own understanding of a domain of knowledge (see Chapter 5). They cannot progress beyond highly competent performance. Other experts, who have developed their own understanding all along, can develop new knowledge by simply extending their understanding beyond what is commonly known by experts in their field.

> Expert problem finding may require experience in everyday problem finding.

A second hypothesis to explain why relatively few expert problem solvers become expert problem finders is that not all people have the personality and the motivational characteristics to carry them beyond expertise. While persistence is valuable to develop expertise, the characteristics that carry learners beyond expertise include curiosity, independence, and the courage to overcome pressures to conform. Many students appear to possess enough of these characteristics to progress through early developmental plateaus, but at some point, many also appear to stop developing. Social and intellectual pressure to conform can be intense, and it often comes from both teachers and peers. Whether to conform or not in a given situation is a major issue for creative thinkers (Albert & Runco, 1986).

> Curiosity and independence may contribute to expert problem finding.

A third hypothesis that explains why expert problem finders are relatively rare after adolescence is that most learners have few opportunities to observe or participate in finding "deep" problems as they further develop expertise. Apprenticeship to an expert problem finder has been described by several

Mentors can help develop expert problem finding.

Nobel Prize winners as crucial to the development of their own problem-finding ability (Zuckerman, 1979). Similarly, mentors in or out of school seem to have helped Westinghouse Science Talent Search winners acquire expert problem-finding and -solving abilities (Subotnik, 1986). Finding a master or a mentor who is an expert problem finder can facilitate the development of expertise in problem finding.

strategic solutions

Teaching Problem Finding

Much more is known about how to develop everyday problem finding than expert problem finding. As a consequence, everyday problem finding has begun to enter the curriculum, particularly in mathematics. For example, the *Curriculum and Evaluation Standards for School Mathematics* of the National Council of Teachers of Mathematics (NCTM) (1989) mandates the teaching of everyday problem finding in grades K–4, and problem formulation in grades 5–8 and 9–12. Specific techniques and examples to teach problem finding or formulating are appearing in journals such as *Arithmetic Teacher* and *Mathematics Teacher*.

Four general suggestions may help you turn problem solvers into problem finders. The first is to *teach students to solve problems of a particular type*. You saw in Chapter 10 how goals for students in any subject at any level can present problems for students to solve. At the beginning of the present chapter, you read about Ms. Taylor exercising kindergarten students in problem solving by giving them the word *cat* and asking them for rhyming words. She set the open-ended problem, and students solved it divergently.

You can also present problems that have only one right answer (or are well-defined problems) to students in order to prepare them for problem finding. A fifth-grade teacher, for example, rotated students through problem-solving and -finding sessions during each math period (Winograd, 1992). During problem-solving sessions, students worked on textbook story problems or story problems posed by other students. During the problem-finding session, students worked in small groups on story problems that *they* generated. To teach everyday problem finding, teachers generally must teach problem-solving skills first, but problem finding can be introduced as the final learning activity in a sequence or as homework.

A second implication of everyday problem finding is to *ask students to identify uncertainties in a problematic situation of your choice*. Share with students a situation that you've experienced, and with which your students can identify. Ms. Taylor simply asked students what word they wanted to write to develop the next list of rhyming words. She asked students to find problems for the class exercise, and that was sufficient to produce uncertainty. The fifth-grade math teacher used this "snack" situation to introduce problem finding (Silverman, Winograd & Strohauer, 1992, p. 8):

Last night I was at the library doing some work. After a few hours, hunger set in, and I remembered that there were some candy machines in the basement. I walked downstairs and looked at the selections in the machines. Oh boy! Grandma's Cookies, my favorite brand, were for sale! All right! I noticed that it cost $0.60 for a package of two cookies. I reached into my pocket and pulled out $2.75.

The teacher asked students to start generating questions based on the "snack" situation, and they did: "How many packages could I have bought?" "How much change would I have received if I had bought one package [two packages, three packages, etc.]?" "If I had bought as many cookies as I could, would I have had enough money to make a phone call [to buy mints, etc.]?" These questions reflect various states of uncertainty developed by students who identified with the "snack" situation.

A third implication of everyday problem finding is to *ask students to identify uncertainties in a problematic situation of their choice.* Consistent advice from teachers of everyday problem finding is to have students identify problematic situations of their own. Ownership of the problematic situation is a key to creative thinking because it ensures a connection between the resolution of uncertainty and the development of understanding. It also ensures that the problem of each student will differ from that of the teacher and other students.

There are a few common strategies to help students identify problematic situations, but the list is far from complete. Free writing, analogy, generalization, alternative interpretation, contradiction, and compiling a "bug" list (a list of things that bother you) have all been suggested as techniques to identify problematic situations (Brown & Walter, 1990; Hayes, 1989; Kilpatrick, 1987; Liggett, 1991). Some of these techniques are highly specialized to a given domain, such as math. Perhaps what is more important than a technique is the ability to sense that some situations generate more uncertainty than others do. There may be no logical path to this ability. It seems to require openness to experience, particularly to one's own doubts and uncertainties (Wakefield, 1994).

A final implication of everyday problem finding is that you *help students to redefine their problems so that they can solve them.* Everyday problems are not always represented in a way that can be solved routinely by the students who identify them. Students who generate story problems, for example, sometimes write problems that are too difficult because they require knowledge of concepts, knowledge of procedures, metacognition, or skill proficiencies that the student does not yet possess (Winograd, 1992). This finding confirms that everyday problem finding is a sense-making activity, but it also tells us that students sometimes find problems that exceed the grasp of their current skill levels.

In such cases, you can do a number of things. First, adopt a "whole to part" sequence of instruction. Once students have begun to formulate a problem, do not expect or demand the first statement of it to be its final statement

Computers can be used to help students refine the problems they have found, whether the problem involves calculation or word processing. *(Paul Conklin)*

(Fennell & Ammon, 1985). Extensive redefinition of problems is a characteristic of talented problem finders (DeLorenzo, 1989). To facilitate the process of problem redefinition, you might want to ask students to submit problems to each other for feedback, even as they go about solving the problems. Simplifications of a math problem or several drafts of a topic sentence or paper outline may be needed before a path to a solution becomes clear. Second, screen problems to save for use later in the year. Prerequisite concepts or procedures may be introduced in the meantime. Third, provide tools to aid problem solving, such as calculators or word processors. Computational errors or the need for recopying should not prevent students from arriving at satisfactory solutions to the problems that they have found.

The outcome of everyday problem finding can be a book of new verses and illustrations (as created in the "Down by the Bay" sequence), a collection of student-generated story problems (see Deepening Your Knowledge Base: Sample Worksheet of Story Problems by Students), or other original products or performances. As students become more practiced in such activities, you can expect the products and performances from everyday problem finding to resemble increasingly the outcomes of expert problem finding. More needs to be discovered about the support, talent, and dedication necessary to develop expert problem finding from everyday problem finding, but the two kinds of problem finding appear to be developmentally related.

deepening your knowledge base

Sample Worksheet of Story Problems by Students

1. My dad drives 30 miles every day. How many days would it take for him to drive 3,000 miles?   *Larry*

2. I have a dog whose name is Max. He just ripped up my neighbor's garden. There were 61 flowers in all. There were 20 marigolds, 17 tulips, 18 roses, and 6 puffs. Each marigold cost 25 cents, each tulip cost 50 cents, each rose cost $1.00 and each puff cost 75 cents. How much money will I need?   *Amy*

3. I take tap and jazz at Lynn Bassett. I learn 3 new steps in each lesson. I take 1 lesson a week. How many steps do I learn in 1 year?   *Dana*

4. Stardate: 09/12/89

   Entry: We have just escaped a Klingon vessel. The ship has been damaged in these ways:

   1. 15 of the 500 people on the ship are injured.
   2. 50% of the warp drive was damaged. The max speed of the ship is warp 14. It would take 281 days at that speed to get to the nearest star base. We can now only go warp 7. How long will it take us?   *Luke*

5. I had an invitation to attend a Star Trek convention. Gate tickets cost $3 per person. Trekkie stuff is available and my mom gave me a $50 bill. I spent 1/2 of my money on Trekkie stuff. The fee for entrance to the gift shop is $2.50. I was hungry and I spent $3 on plain ordinary food. How much money did I have left to give back to my mom?   *Joshua*

6. My brother has 32 baseball cards. He was getting 2 more packs today. There's 8 in a package. At Christmas, he bought 3 packages. How many baseball cards will he have?   *Misty*

Source: Silverman, Winograd & Strohauer, 1992, p. 7

Evaluation: Teaching Problem Finding

There is little doubt that problem finding is a real phenomenon, and that it is only indirectly related to problem-solving ability, particularly when problems are posed by the student rather than imposed (directly or indirectly) through the designs of the teacher. Furthermore, there is a growing consensus that there are at least two levels of problem finding, one that we engage in every day and the other that some experts engage in to think creatively. Educators are now developing specific ideas about how to teach everyday problem finding, particularly in light of the curriculum and evaluation standards of the NCTM, which have received widespread support. What remains unclear is the relationship between everyday problem finding, expert problem finding, and creative thinking.

Studies of individual elementary school classrooms have found that everyday problem finding improves comprehension of mathematics. Lauren Resnick and colleagues (1991) implemented an experimental curriculum for at-risk first and second graders that emphasized an inquiry approach to mathematics and everyday problem finding and solving. Before entry into the program, two groups of students scored well below average for their age on a math achievement test (about the 25th percentile). After a year of intervention, the students scored well above average (70th to 80th percentile). Similar results have been reported for students in an average fourth-grade classroom (Larkin, 1986). Not all improvements in problem solving can be attributed to practice in everyday problem finding, but improved understanding of basic math concepts is a likely outcome.

As yet, there is very little evidence that everyday problem finding improves cognitive skills more complex than comprehension or application. Between everyday problem finding and expert problem finding lies a great deal of practice and effort. Does everyday problem finding in first or second grade ultimately lead to expert problem finding (or to increases in cognitive disequilibrium) in fifth or sixth grade? Are there such things as "breakthrough" problems at that age that can lead to greater understanding and lay the foundation for further developments in adolescence? As yet, there is no clear answer, but these questions pose interesting problems for future research.

DEVELOPING AESTHETIC SENSIBILITY

The third goal of the rational approach to creative thinking is to help students develop aesthetic sensibility and expression. Aesthetic sensibility is expressed in reactions to a beautiful painting, a parsimonious formula in physics, or a gracefully turned double play in baseball. Aesthetic sensibility is one of the most difficult goals of education to represent, let alone attain. If it is not represented, however, it cannot be attained. To understand how to develop aesthetic sensibility, we might begin with the question of what people "get out of" art. This question goes to the heart of aesthetic sensibility because art, unlike science or even athletics, appears to many people to have no practical value (Greene, 1991).

Aesthetic sensibility contributes to creative thinking but is difficult to teach.

Why Do People Value Art?

There are basically three psychological theories of why people value art. One is the theory of *emotional catharsis,* which is a therapeutic purging of feelings. This theory goes back to the Greek philosopher Aristotle, who believed that tragedy purged feelings of fear and pity in the audience. A second theory

Brighter hues are more pleasing than duller ones; reds are more pleasing than most other colors. What are the colors of flowers the young lady has already chosen? *(Owen Franken/ Stock Boston)*

is that art allows people to fulfill a need for beauty quite apart from other needs. In this view, art arouses an *aesthetic emotion,* which is a form of pleasure derived from the contemplation of beauty. Contemplation of a statue of an idealized figure, for example, might bring pleasure because of the beauty of its proportions. A third view of why people value art is that it serves perceptual preferences. *Perceptual preferences* range from the barely measurable appeal of some colors or shapes over others, to identification of structures or configurations (such as themes or patterns) that facilitate understanding. The measurement of perceptual preferences is called **experimental aesthetics.**

If our goal is to develop aesthetic sensibility and expression, we must have a common definition of the goal. The theory of aesthetics as emotional catharsis is incomplete because it focuses only on the pleasure caused by purging undesirable feelings, such as fear. The theory of aesthetic emotion is also incomplete. It accounts for pleasure from viewing what is ideal or romantic, but it does not easily account for pleasure from viewing what is tragic or unromantic. Perceptual preferences currently seem to explain best why art that depicts an attractive subject and art treating an unattractive subject can be equally enjoyable.

> Perceptual preference is thought to best explain enjoyment of art.

Perceptual Preferences and Aesthetics

The measurement of perceptual preferences began in 1876 with the work of Gustav Fechner, a German psychologist interested in developing a science of aesthetics from its elements. Fechner devised a simple experimental method to test perceptual preferences that was popular well into the twentieth century. He presented two stimuli to many individuals and asked each individual which stimulus was more pleasing. The stimulus that received more votes was assumed to have greater aesthetic value.

What Fechner and other psychologists found is that certain colors, amplitudes, patterns, and cognitive states are preferred over others (Winner, 1982):

- brighter hues are preferred to duller ones
- green-blue colors and reds are more pleasing than other colors
- yellow-green colors are the least pleasing
- patterns of contrasting colors are preferred to patterns of similar colors
- moderate levels of loudness are more pleasing than low or high levels

> Research in aesthetics has found certain preferred colors and patterns.

Other findings in this tradition have discovered that many of the same preferences exist among people from different backgrounds and cultures. In other words, most of these perceptual preferences appear to be valid across cultures. Finally, psychologists in this tradition have discovered that moderate levels of novelty and complexity are preferred over high or low levels. These findings account for interest or curiosity (see Chapter 12).

Although experimental aesthetics has led to many findings, some of which explain individual artistic effects, its results have not always been closely related to the complexity of experiencing a work of art. More relevant in this respect have been the principles of **Gestalt psychology,** an approach to cognition that finds meaning in the configuration of elements rather than in their individual significance. For a Gestalt psychologist, any whole is greater than the sum of its parts. Rudolf Arnheim, a Gestalt psychologist and professor of art, suggests that relationships between elements of a painting become clear only when a person has found a "structural pattern that fits the configuration of shapes and colors" (1986, p. 299). This structural pattern is a Gestalt.

Gestalt Psychology

Four principles of Gestalt psychology explain perceptual preferences that determine aesthetic responses to artworks (cf. Kohler, 1970/1947; Pickford, 1972; Wertheimer, 1982/1945). These principles are known as (1) figure and ground, (2) differentiation, (3) closure, and (4) the "good Gestalt." Each of these principles represents a different perceptual preference.

Figure and Ground

> Gestalt psychology finds a preference for a pattern rather than background.

The perceptual preference for a pattern (the figure) apart from other related experiences (the ground) is a basic principle of Gestalt psychology. Viewing Vincent van Gogh's painting titled *The Starry Night* (Figure 11.2), we are drawn to the large, dark cypress in the foreground, because of our preference for distinguishing figure from ground. We are also drawn to the stars as opposed to the sky, and the town as opposed to the hills, by the same preference.

Figure 11.2
The Starry Night
*(Vincent van Gogh, 1889, oil on canvas, 29 x 36 ¹/₄".
New York, Museum of Modern Art, Lillie P. Bliss Bequest)*

Differentiation

The principle of differentiation refers to our tendency to associate elements perceptually on the basis of characteristics such as similarity or proximity. In *The Starry Night*, the houses are perceived as a town rather than individual houses because of their proximity to each other. Also, the moon, the stars, the night sky, and the dawn over the hills are all perceived in relationship to each other because of the similarity of their portrayal. This similarity differentiates them from the town or cypress.

> In differentiation, elements are perceived together because of similarity or proximity.

Closure

A third principle of Gestalt psychology, known as closure, is a perceptual preference for complete rather than incomplete figures. Closure leads us to understand that the town and its surrounding fields in *The Starry Night* pass behind the cypress, even though we do not see actual continuity of color. Taken one step further, closure also gives us the perception of dawn—we anticipate that the lightening sky over the hill will be followed by the appearance of the sun. Closure is a preference for completion in our understanding, even if completion is not what we see.

> Closure represents a preference for completeness.

The Good Gestalt

A fourth principle of Gestalt psychology that explains our perception of properties is the "good Gestalt," or the principle of *Pragnanz* (conciseness). According to this principle, a stronger or more adequate pattern tends to dominate weaker patterns in perception. The three major elements of *The Starry Night* are the town, the cypress, and the sky, and they are configured in a circular way. The cypress points to the stars, and the sky and hills roll down over the town. The good Gestalt does not let any major element of the

> The good Gestalt means that a pattern of elements dominates perception.

painting escape our attention, despite the possibility that contrasting feelings and movements are expressed by different elements.

What is the good Gestalt of this painting? Not long ago, I asked educational psychology students who were viewing *The Starry Night* what feeling or feelings they thought the artist was trying to communicate. I asked them to write down their answers anonymously and hand them in. You might take a moment to examine the painting and write down what feelings you think it expresses before you read the results in the next paragraph.

What I found was not too surprising (see Table 11.1). Sixty-nine students turned in eighty-seven responses. Seventy-five of them could be classified in one of seven categories: calmness, sadness, loneliness, mystery, chilliness, turmoil, and fear. Many students listed only one feeling, such as "a peaceful feeling in the city" (calmness) or "like a Halloween night—kind of spooky" (fear). Note in the table, however, that the number of responses peaked at extremes of calmness and fear.

There is much evidence that the different elements in the painting express conflicting feelings in a dynamic relationship. Students appeared to focus on either the town or the night sky, but not both. Several sensed that contrasting feelings were expressed by the painting, but they resolved the tension as a "calm before the storm" or "quiet that is going to be interrupted by turbulence." Another student wrote, "This picture communicates a feeling of tranquility, yet unrest from the sky." Anne Sexton (1981), the poet, noted a similar unresolved tension: "The town is silent. The night boils with eleven stars." As for the cypress, it points to the stars. The elements of the painting express emotional conflict—the excitement of the sky opposed to the comfort of the town, with the cypress bridging the two. Professional art criticism, which may focus on the symbolism of the painting or on letters van Gogh wrote at the time (e.g., Soth, 1986), gives this conflict a particular context, but the point is clear enough to the viewer. A strong case can be made for identifying the good Gestalt of *The Starry Night* as an emotional conflict that cannot be resolved in the world of the painting.

Table 11.1   Responses to *The Starry Night*

Feeling	Responses	Examples of Variants
Calmness	22	Quiet, mellow, comfort, security
Sadness	13	Gloomy, depressing, somber
Loneliness	7	Solitude, alone
Mystery	6	Suspense, anticipation
Chilliness	4	Cold
Turmoil	9	Restless, anxiety, confusion
Fear	14	Spooky, eerie, scary

Note: Of 87 responses from 69 students, 75 were classifiable in one of seven categories.

Do such perceptual biases guide aesthetic response outside the visual arts? The answer is that we do not yet know. At present, Gestalt psychology is not an active area of research, but it has come closer than any other approach to an accurate description of how properties are expressed through sometimes-complex combinations of symbols. The appreciation of these properties requires more than "reading" the meaning of symbols. It requires a sensibility to their interrelationships. What follows in art is frequently a feeling or an idea (cf. Arnheim, 1986). Educators are only beginning to understand how to develop aesthetic sensibility in arts education. Perhaps we can all learn something from their experiences.

> Gestalt psychology concerns complex interrelationships.

strategic solutions

Developing Aesthetic Response

If aesthetic response is the product of perceptual preferences such as those investigated in experimental aesthetics and Gestalt psychology, it makes sense to *challenge students to interpret symbols and their relationships in terms of properties of experience.* One approach is to begin with relatively simple and well-defined aesthetic problems. For example, an art teacher might show students one or more paintings of two people caring for each other (see Figures 11.3 and 11.4), explain the subject of the two paintings, and ask students, "How did the artist show caring?"

Figure 11.3
The Banjo Lesson
(Henry O. Tanner, Hampton University Museum, Hampton, Virginia)

Figure 11.4
The Lovers
(Pablo Picasso, The National Gallery of Art, Washington, D.C.)

To focus on the relation of artistic elements to caring, the teacher might ask students what kinds of lines, shapes, colors, and space they see. A discussion might follow on how different lines, shapes, and so forth are used to establish moods and feelings (Alexander & Day, 1991). A similar lesson could be designed for literature or music.

Another way to achieve the same goal would be to have students describe aesthetic responses to their own art. An art teacher might ask students to create a drawing of themselves and someone or something for whom they care. The teacher might use student drawings to ask why the use of more than one figure in the foreground expressed caring (figure versus ground), how contact or overlapping of figures expressed caring (nondifferentiation and closure), or why warm colors helped to communicate caring (good Gestalt). The teacher might point out how symbols used in drawings by different students might represent the property of caring. By using students' own artwork, the teacher in a sense is asking them to pose their own aesthetic problems.

Most art programs that develop aesthetic sensibility combine appreciation of works of art with artistic production. Discipline-Based Art Education (Clark, Day & Greer, 1987), for example, has aesthetic and production components that are not always separable. The challenge to develop aesthetic sensibility is greatest for teachers outside the arts, where aesthetics are neither well defined nor often studied. Teachers might look to parsimony (sciences), elegance (mathematics), and gracefulness (physical skills) for properties that are symbolically expressed. It is likely that the perception of these characteristics is brought on by some of the same perceptual preferences that govern the communication of feelings and ideas in the arts.

Evaluation: Developing Aesthetic Response

Aesthetic education has meant different things to different people. To some, it has meant appreciating art for its therapeutic value. To others, it has meant using art to enhance perception of beauty. To still others, it has meant using perceptual preferences to explain art. This third approach to aesthetic education appears to be gaining in popularity with cognitive approaches to instruction. With popularity, however, comes scrutiny and sometimes criticism.

In particular, Discipline-Based Art Education has relied upon principles such as those of Gestalt psychology to explain why people value art. This approach to aesthetics has been criticized for its excessive emphasis on cognition (Arnstine, 1990). Thinking about art, the critics say, is not the only pleasure art affords. Implicit in such criticism is the idea that the pleasure of art comes not from its appeal to perceptual preferences but from other sources. Elliot Eisner (1990) has defended the cognitive view of aesthetics by noting that it does not conform to a narrow conception of cognition, such as information processing, or even the procedures of problem solving. Cognition can involve holistic perception or the apprehension of *feeling*, as well as information processing or problem solving.

The principles of Gestalt psychology are out of favor with psychological researchers, and as yet there is no clear substitute for their capacity to explain holistic responses such as aesthetics. As psychology progresses, researchers will undoubtedly return to the subject of holistic perception, perhaps with renewed interest in Gestalt psychology, or perhaps with renewed interest in one of the alternative approaches to aesthetics.

CREATIVE THINKING IN YOUR CLASSROOM

So far, this chapter has introduced you to three goals of creative thinking: open-ended problem solving, problem finding, and aesthetic response. These goals go a long way toward explaining why Ms. Taylor's lessons in reading, writing, and composition developed creative thinking. Creative education may address all three goals, or only one. Creative people in the arts and sciences tend to be adept at achieving all three goals simultaneously (Kay, 1991; Root-Bernstein, 1989; Wakefield, 1992).

Creativity, however, involves more than achieving the three goals mentioned above. Robert Sternberg (1988) has pointed out that creativity also involves tolerance for ambiguity, willingness to surmount obstacles, willingness to grow, intrinsic (or internal) motivation, moderate risk taking, desire for recognition, and willingness to work for recognition. A surprising number of these characteristics involve motivation, which is the subject of the next chapter.

Creativity involves many characteristics related to motivation.

Along the same lines, the social climate of the classroom can have an impact on creative thinking. Teresa Amabile (1985) has written about how a focus on external evaluation and reward can be detrimental to creative thinking. In her studies of artists, she found that an environment that emphasizes external evaluation or reward often inhibits creativity. By way of contrast, an environment that emphasizes doing work for its own sake tends to facilitate creative thinking.

External evaluation and reward can inhibit creativity.

In the past, "creative" motivation and climate have been hard to develop in schools because of teaching techniques that were oriented toward transmitting knowledge rather than toward generating it. Yet a revolutionary change is occurring in some classrooms to make their climate more conducive to creative thinking. This ongoing change in classroom climate is associated with the use of the computer as a tool of students' thought rather than as a stand-in teacher (Nix, 1988).

Computer Tools and Creative Thinking

Computers have different uses, but the fastest-growing one in schools is not for drill and practice (Chapter 8), or for simulation (Chapter 10), but as a tool

(Becker, 1991). Use of the computer as a tool includes *word-processing programs* with which to write; *paint programs* with which to draw in color; *spreadsheet programs* or *database programs* with which to record, manipulate, and present data; and *languages* or *authoring programs* with which to create entire new computer programs. Although word-processing, painting, and spreadsheet or database programs can facilitate some dimensions of creative activity (such as saving multiple versions of a work in progress), there is little evidence that they develop originality any more than other tools do. There is some evidence, however, that authoring programs *are* developing originality. For that reason, you need to know about them, even though your students may not have access to them yet.

> Some computer programs can facilitate creativity.

LOGO: A Programming Language

In the late 1970s, a group led by Seymour Papert invented a language to program computers that was much simpler than other languages previously developed by computer scientists (such as BASIC or Pascal). They called this language LOGO, and proponents claimed that its use by school-age children could enhance their problem-solving abilities and creativity, especially in an environment that emphasized inquiry (e.g., Papert, 1980).

Students from kindergarten up are generally introduced to LOGO with a simple goal: to make a square. They are taught how to turn the computer on, call up a triangular-shaped "turtle," and make the turtle move, leaving a trail in the shape of a square. Movements are the result of simple commands typed in at the keyboard, such as "forward 10" or "right 90," telling the turtle to move forward 10 steps, or turn to the right 90 degrees. Four such commands make the square. Students are then taught more of the command language so that they can make quite complex designs of their own (see Figure 11.5).

Since the early 1980s, over 40,000 teachers have taught their students to use LOGO in one of its many variants, and several research studies have been undertaken to assess whether or not students in LOGO environments develop creative thinking. The results of these studies suggest that outcomes are closely related to the preparation and goals students have for using LOGO, rather than use of the language in and of itself. If students are well prepared and problems are open ended, using LOGO to solve them can enhance divergent thinking (Clements, 1991; Roblyer, Castine & King, 1988). Since the computer screen tends to call for integrated solutions (solutions in the form of one figure), originality and elaboration are enhanced more than fluency or flexibility.

> The LOGO program can enhance divergent thinking in children.

LOGO has its critics, who have contended that it does not develop thinking skills more than any other tool. They suggest that it needs to be supported by some problem-solving strategy in order to develop thinking (e.g., Kinzer, Sherwood & Bransford, 1986). There is merit in this criticism, but there is also evidence that LOGO provides a medium for developing expression, much as brainstorming or even synectics does. Unlike brainstorming and synectics, however, LOGO provides a *visual* medium for increasing expressiveness. Brainstorming and synectics provide a predominantly *verbal* medium.

Figure 11.5   LOGO Drawings *Pictures produced by third-grade children using basic LOGO shapes (in left box) as building blocks. (Clements, 1991, p. 184)*

Authoring Tools

In the late 1980s, authoring tools became available for both the Apple Macintosh and IBM personal computers. These tools allow a person to link segments of text, graphics, animation, voice, music, movies, or video in a network of information. The product of such networked linkages of information is known as **multimedia** (see Deepening Your Knowledge Base: A Brief Introduction to Multimedia Operation).

Multimedia constructions were once developed only by teams of adults working in production studios, but authoring tools such as HyperCard for Macintosh, mentioned above, and the similar LinkWay for IBM PCs can give students as early as elementary school access to such production facilities in their schools. Special accessories such as *scanners* (for transforming printed pictures into computer images), *video digitizers* (for transforming video pictures into computer images), and *CD/ROM drives* (for storing large amounts of information) are needed to supplement more familiar accessories such as printers, video cameras, and videotape players. Obviously, such technology is expensive, but prices are falling and packages are becoming more integrated, so you increasingly will see such equipment in the classroom.

As yet, there are only anecdotal and unpublished reports of the transformation in the learning environment that such production entails (Dwyer, Ringstaff & Sandholtz, 1991). What seems to occur is a change in focus from student as *learner* to student as *teacher*. Students are initially taught how to create linkages between different types of media using HyperCard, LinkWay, or some other authoring program. After such initial instruction (which may last no longer than a week), students embark on a project, such as developing multimedia folders for information on chemical elements in the periodic table, designing storybooks for younger children, or composing tunes to

> Multimedia involves linking computer text, graphics, music, and other facilities.

> Working with multimedia can put students into the role of teachers.

Multimedia projects involve networking linkages of text and graphics, video, or music. These students in Apple's Classroom of Tomorrow program are linking text and video. *(James D. Wilson/Gamma Liaison Network)*

accompany their own limericks (Davidson, 1990; Havice, 1994; O'Connor & Brie, 1994).

Multimedia projects are usually carried out in small groups, with the teacher acting as a consultant. After an initial orientation, students tutor each other in computer operations while they construct representations of knowledge from which others can learn. Several psychologists have noted that in constructing linkages between segments of information (such as graphics and text), students are creating networks of meaning similar to the semantic structure of human memory (Kozma, 1991). If you have students develop multimedia projects, you may see them develop representations or models of constructed knowledge. It is too early to say how authoring tools will affect creative thinking, but they may develop it in an even more profound way than LOGO.

Contrasting Approaches to Developing Creative Thought

Whether or not you use computers to facilitate creative thinking, you still face the question of how to sequence activities in your instructional strategy. How should teachers sequence activities to develop creative thinking? Howard Gardner (1989) has noted that throughout history, societies have tended to accentuate one of two approaches. One approach, which focuses on imitation before freedom to create, approaches creative thinking "from the bottom up." The other, which focuses on free exploration, approaches creativity "from the top down." Which sequence of activities you choose for your classroom depends largely on your situation.

deepening your knowledge base

A Brief Introduction to Multimedia Operation

Multimedia is the product of networked linkages of text, graphics, animation, voice, music, movies, or video. Text is only one medium; by enhancing computer's presentation of text, a *multimedia program* can present added information (such as a further explanation of a word, or a recording of its sound) at the touch of a button, which is a designated location on the screen. To touch the button, the user moves a *cursor* (a probe on the screen) over that button with the aid of a *mouse* (the small, hand-held device that guides the cursor). The user then *clicks* the mouse (by pressing on the mouse) to reveal the added information on the screen. Some screen buttons are constructed so that they can be activated with a *light pen* rather than a mouse.

Authoring tools allow children to construct multimedia projects themselves, not just *navigate,* or move interactively, through an existing program. Students may work alone or in small groups to create media products, using a set of rather simple procedures represented on the screen as a *toolbox* (in a program called HyperCard). The toolbox contains a pen, paintbrush, eraser, and other useful tools. Pieces of information in each medium are put on *nodes* or "cards," which are connected by screen buttons. One of the most useful tools is the *button tool,* because it allows the student to create links between nodes. Linked nodes are stored in a *folder* or file, which is also stored and accessed with a click of the mouse.

The world of multimedia sounds complex, but in an authoring environment, students can supplement the teacher's instruction by demonstrating procedures to each other. What currently limits multimedia is the cost, which depends on how many accessories are involved, ranging from a minimum setup at several thousand dollars to a complete system costing about twenty thousand dollars.

Bottom-up Sequencing

"You have to crawl," the expression goes, "before you can walk." The bottom-up approach to sequencing activities is represented by this philosophy, in which creative thinking is permitted only after development of basic skills. In North America, moderate use of this approach to creative thinking is represented by programs that emphasize a disciplined foundation for the expression of originality.

The bottom-up approach generally has well-defined objectives arranged in a hierarchy. Knowledge and discrimination are taught before comprehension or concepts; comprehension or concepts are taught before intellectual skills or applications; intellectual skills or applications are taught before analysis, synthesis, and evaluation or problem solving. Preparatory exercises may also include the development of technical abilities, such as computer-operation skills, before creativity is allowed. Creative thinking is exercised at or near the end of any sequence of learning activities.

Bottom-up sequencing teaches basic skills before creative thinking is introduced.

Top-down Sequencing

Top-down sequencing puts free exploration before basic skills.

"Creativity cannot be taught," the saying goes; "it has to be expressed." The top-down approach to sequencing activities focuses on coaching or facilitating creative thinking with minimal attention to basic skills. This approach emphasizes free exploration. In free exploration, originality and independence are highly valued, and constraints on activities are minimized to avoid suppressing curiosity. Scaffolding can be provided through structure in the menu of choices (such as "select one activity from each subject area"), the directions for conducting an activity (such as steps in a general procedure), the materials themselves (such as the pages with blanks provided by Ms. Taylor), or on an as-needed basis (such as additional training in computer-operation skills).

The top-down approach often has general goals, but objectives are not arranged in a hierarchy. Rather, instruction is organized around global themes or the creation of original performances and products. At the center of the top-down approach is generally a project. Students themselves take the lead in conceiving, planning, executing, and sometimes even evaluating the project.

You might want to look back one last time at the description of the lesson Ms. Taylor taught at the beginning of the chapter. Was her approach bottom up, top down, or a combination of both?

CONCLUSION

The bottom-up and top-down approaches are not necessarily antagonistic. Each has its strength. The solution to the dilemma of which approach to use lies in treating the development of creative thinking as an instructional problem that you must frame flexibly.

You may want to consider using a cycle to teach creative thinking, in which you allow exploration at the beginning and end of the cycle, but require practice at problem solving in the middle. In this manner, *everyday* problem *finding* (sense making) can provide a foundation for the practice of problem *solving*, and problem *solving* (including open-ended problem solving) can provide a foundation for *expert* problem *finding*. The philosopher Alfred North Whitehead (1929) long ago observed that mental development tends to occur in cycles, with exploration at the beginning and end, but with a great deal of practice in the middle.

This philosophy matches the apparent relationship between everyday problem finding and expert problem finding. The best way to combine bottom-up with top-down sequencing of activities may be cycles of problem finding and solving. As you embark on your teaching career, however, remember that despite this prescription, there is no one way to develop creative thinking. The problem of how to develop creative thinking invites *your* creative solution.

concept paper

Analysis of a Creative Education Program

Purpose of the assignment

To analyze a creative education program for its relation to components of creative thinking.

Directions for the assignment

1. Obtain a printed description of a creative education program that you might use to enhance the creativity of your students. Creative education programs are typically described in books of teaching methods. *Do not use one of the programs described in this chapter.* The program does not have to be supported by research, but it does have to provide a method or procedure to enhance creative thinking.

2. Analyze this program in relation to the components of creative thinking described in this chapter.

    a. Does the program develop open-ended problem solving? Compare and contrast its methods for open-ended problem solving with brainstorming and analogical thinking. How are its methods similar? How do they differ?

    b. Does the program develop problem finding? Compare and contrast its methods for problem finding with the general procedure for teaching everyday problem finding recommended in this chapter. How are its methods similar? How do they differ?

    c. Does the program develop aesthetic sensibility or expression? Compare and contrast its methods for developing aesthetic sensibility with the approaches to aesthetics mentioned toward the end of this chapter.

    d. How does the program sequence activities to develop creative thinking? Does it use a bottom-up sequence, a top-down sequence, or a mixture of both?

3. Write a three- to four-page paper in which you describe how the creative education program addresses each of the three goals of creative education. You may find that the program addresses all three goals, one or two goals better than another, or none of the goals. This finding should be expressed as a thesis sentence near the beginning of your paper. Note in the introduction to your paper the source of the program description, and where the description may be located. Attach a copy of the description, if necessary.

SUMMARY

1. The rational view of creativity is an approach that emphasizes problem finding and problem solving. Within this view, everyone has the ability to be creative.

2. The three goals for creative education within the rational model are to help students solve problems with multiple solutions, identify new problems, and develop aesthetic sensibility and expression.
3. Open-ended problems, which have well-defined givens but no specified goals, encourage students to generate multiple solutions. There are two ways students can learn to solve these problems: by using divergent thinking, which involves generating alternative solutions, or by using analogical thinking, which involves creating an extended comparison.
4. Problem finding, or the activity of identifying new problems, is closely related to originality in thinking. It involves the perception of something that is not understood. Everyday problem finding refers to routine, familiar situations. Expert problem finding requires finding significant or important problems.
5. Aesthetic sensibility and expression result from an individual's perceptual preferences. Four principles of Gestalt psychology identify these perceptual preferences as figure and ground, differentiation, closure, and the good Gestalt.
6. The increasing use of the computer in the classroom as a tool of students' thought makes the classroom climate more conducive to creative thinking. When students use computers to solve open-ended problems or they author computer programs, they are enhancing their creative abilities.
7. Activities to encourage creative thinking can be sequenced in either a bottom-up manner, which stresses a skills hierarchy, or a top-down manner, which emphasizes free exploration.

KEY TERMS

creative thinking p. 453
rational view of creativity p. 454
aesthetic expression p. 458
open-ended problems p. 459
divergent thinking p. 460
convergent thinking p. 460
brainstorming p. 461
analogical thinking p. 464
synectics p. 465
problem finding p. 471
everyday problem finding p. 472
expert problem finding p. 473
experimental aesthetics p. 479
Gestalt psychology p. 480
multimedia p. 487

SUGGESTED RESOURCES

Amabile, T. M. 1992. *Growing Up Creative: Nurturing a Lifetime of Creativity.* Buffalo, N.Y.: Creative Education Foundation. In this book, Teresa Amabile distills her many discoveries about the social influences that promote creativity at different ages.

Gardner, H. 1991. *The Unschooled Mind.* New York: Basic Books. This is a thought-provoking analysis of schools in light of what we know about the development of understanding.

Grabe, M. and C. Grabe. 1996. *Integrating Technology for Meaningful Learning.* Boston: Houghton Mifflin. This new text discusses the "how-tos" of using multimedia for creative learning experiences.

Sternberg, R. J. 1988. *The Nature of Creativity.* New York: Cambridge University Press. This impressive collection focuses on theories of creativity, including chapters by most of the major researchers in the field.

Solving Motivational Problems

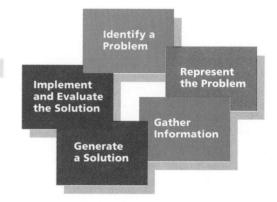

Orientation

The goal of this chapter is to provide you with a strong background in identifying, representing, and solving motivational problems in your students' learning. In building your knowledge base about motivational problems, you will learn how to identify the sources of motivational problems, how to stimulate your students' interest in learning, how to build confidence in students, how to increase their satisfaction in learning, and how to design motivational strategies. As you read, look for answers to these questions:

- **Where do motivational problems come from?**

- **What is the relation between personal needs and interests?**

- **How do you create situational interests?**

- **Why is interest stimulated if learning is useful?**

- **What are personal determinants of confidence?**

- **How can students' lost confidence be restored?**

- **How much do expectations of teachers affect confidence?**

- **Why does personal choice develop satisfaction?**

- **How do cooperative groups and mastery goals motivate learning?**

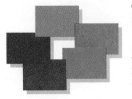

MOTIVATIONAL PROBLEMS

Motivation is the collection of causes that engage someone in an activity. The origin of the word *motivation* is Latin for "a moving cause" (*motivus*). Motivation is not the same as learning, but it accounts for engagement in learning activities. In other words, motivation enables learning in somewhat the same way that fuel enables travel in a car. Its principal visible effect is to permit learning to progress at a slower or faster rate, for a longer or shorter period; but as you will learn later in the chapter, motivation also affects the quality of learning.

> Motivation makes learning possible and affects its quality.

As you may remember, motivational problems are one of four types of teaching problems we identified in Chapter 1 (see pages 6–9). A **motivational problem** is a situation in which a teacher wishes to engage students in an activity but does not immediately know how to do so. What are some motivational problems that you might encounter? Consider the following possibilities:

- Students can be expected to be tired at the end of a day, week, or term. How can you obtain or maintain students' interest at these times?
- Students who switch from one school to another due to grade promotion or a family move often become uncertain about their acceptance by new classmates. How can you boost their confidence?
- Students who do not perceive a benefit from doing homework often lose their motivation to do it. How can you make homework more satisfying?

If students are tired, they will easily become bored or indifferent. If students are new to a school or class, they will often feel anxious. If students believe that homework is not beneficial, they will become dissatisfied, grumble about how much they have to do, and perhaps not do it.

> Developing a motivational strategy is like solving any problem.

Because you can often anticipate motivational problems, you can also plan to solve them. **Motivational strategies** are plans to engage students in activities. The process of devising a motivational strategy parallels the process of solving any other teaching problem. It involves (1) finding a motivational problem, (2) representing it in such a way that it can be solved, (3) gathering information about motivational techniques, (4) generating a solution by devising a motivational strategy, and (5) evaluating the solution's effectiveness. The problem is recycled through this process until it is solved.

Where Do Motivational Problems Come From?

The possible sources of motivational problems are limitless, but educators have recently classified such problems in an effort to understand them better and solve them more efficiently (Keller, 1987; Wlodkowski & Jaynes, 1990). Fortunately, there seem to be only a few sources for motivational problems related to learning. These are (1) boredom or indifference, (2) anxiety or a sense of inadequacy, and (3) frustration or a lack of satisfaction. Teachers often perceive boredom and indifference as a "don't care" attitude, anxiety and a sense of inadequacy in "I can't" statements, and frustration in complaints or "giving up."

These problems can be important. If you look back at the concerns of beginning teachers described in Chapter 1 (Table 1.2), you will find that "relevance of subject matter to students" is the third most important concern of elementary teachers and the *most* important concern of secondary teachers. Demonstrating relevance of subject matter is a motivational problem. Which motivational goal is it related to—developing interest, confidence, or satisfaction? Most of us would agree that demonstrating subject-matter relevance is a problem primarily related to developing interest. This problem increases with grade level for reasons that will be discussed later in this chapter.

How do you prevent or help students overcome motivational problems? The answer is that you set a motivational goal and devise a strategy to meet it. Specific goals tend to fall into the same categories as motivational problems: *stimulating interest, building confidence,* and *increasing satisfaction.* These goals may exist independent of one another, or they may be combined. If you are able to solve problems in all of these areas, either alone or in cooperation with others, you will be able to solve most motivational problems that you will encounter during your career.

> Motivational problems are usually caused by boredom, anxiety, or lack of enjoyment.

> Teachers should stimulate interest, build confidence, and increase satisfaction for students.

Mrs. Eck's Basic Math Class

To begin our exploration of how to solve motivational problems, let's look at how one teacher addresses a difficult case. It is 12:30 P.M. on Friday, and fifteen eleventh graders are entering their fifth-period math class. All failed to pass the mathematics competency test last fall. They are now enrolled in Mrs. Eck's basic math class. Mrs. Eck has won several national awards and is recognized as one of the best math teachers around. She is seen as the teacher most likely to be capable of motivating these fifteen students to learn the skills that will allow them to pass the competency test later in the spring. If they fail it again, they will have two more attempts to pass the test in their senior year. If they fail those attempts, they will graduate with a certificate of attendance rather than with an academic diploma.

Mrs. Eck does not "teach to the test" but, rather, develops the problem-solving skills of her students. In this way, she treats her basic math students just like her advanced-placement (AP) calculus students—with respect for their thinking. The class has just finished studying formulae for calculating areas and volumes, and is beginning a small-group project to apply some of that information. The project will be evaluated for a grade that is equivalent to that of a chapter test. Mrs. Eck divides the class into five groups of three students each, unobtrusively balancing race and gender. To save time, she describes the general procedure that all groups should follow to complete the project, tells each group what general problem it must solve, and explains that a report describing what each group member contributed to completion of the task is due next Wednesday.

The task requires that the students solve a problem by using information about how to calculate area and volume: group 1 is to calculate the surface

> An assignment can be interesting and relevant to students.

area and volume of the "class rock" that stands in front of the school, group 2 is to calculate the proportion of the parking lot covered by cars that day, group 3 is to estimate the number of bricks on the outside wall of the school, group 4 is to calculate the area of the stadium's oval track in square feet, and group 5 is to calculate the area of the grounds around the school in acres. Each portion of the task is designed to present a problem that must be solved in at least two steps. Mrs. Eck stresses that each group's explanation of the problem-solving process it used to complete its task will be more important for the report than a correct answer. The students are surprised and delighted that they will have a chance to work outside.

An assignment can build confidence by rewarding effort and the problem-solving process.

Mrs. Eck sets some final ground rules for behavior, then releases the class. Soon she will follow them to check on their progress. In the meantime, I follow the group headed toward the class rock. Just before we leave the building, someone remembers that we need a measuring tool, and a student returns to the classroom for a yardstick, emerging moments later. When we approach the rock, we see that it has a split in it, and that its surface is curved and irregular (see photo). The yardstick is clearly inadequate, and for a moment the group is frustrated.

Another group member suggests that a string might help us measure some of the concave areas and protrusions. Everyone agrees, and she goes back into the classroom to find some string. When she returns, the students begin to go about their work. One uses the string to measure irregular dimensions, another uses the ruler to measure the string and regular dimensions, a third makes a sketch and takes down measurements. Everyone is taking part. Mrs. Eck stops by on a walk around the building to ask how the students are doing. She asks, "Are you taking account of the split?" They are. The surface area and volume of the rock are now only a matter of careful recording of measurements today, of calculating by formula on Monday, and of constructing a report on Tuesday.

The assignment for students in group 1 of Mrs. Eck's class was to calculate the surface area and volume of the "class rock" that stood in front of the school. *(John F. Wakefield photo)*

Mrs. Eck anticipated motivational problems in all three areas described earlier—stimulating interest, building confidence, and increasing satisfaction. First, many students—not just those who have failed a basic math test—tend to be indifferent to mathematical formulae. How could she relate the formulae that the students had just learned for calculating area and volume to their interests? Second, these particular students had failed a test that most of their peers had passed. How could she increase the students' confidence in their problem-solving skills? Finally, success had been rare in their past math classes. How could she make learning more enjoyable or satisfying?

The motivational problem that Mrs. Eck encountered required a multistep solution. First, she stimulated interest through the assignment. Students applied formulae for calculating area and volume to familiar objects outside: the class rock, cars in the parking lot, and so on. This first part of her strategy made learning more meaningful or relevant. Second, she built confidence by rewarding the *process* of problem solving rather than the "right answer." She did not change the rate of reward, but she did link the reward more directly to effort than it had been in the past. Third, she increased the opportunity for satisfaction by putting students in groups where each was accountable in the report for contributing to completion of the task. This way, they could pool their resources to generate a solution to a problem far more complex than they thought they could handle.

> Motivational problems may require multistep solutions.

I joined Mrs. Eck as she left the class-rock group. During our walking tour of the other sites, Mrs. Eck explained that her Friday project had proven highly motivational in the past. In fact, she deliberately assigned it on Fridays and specifically devised tasks that could be completed outside school hours. One cold weekend afternoon last November, she had seen a group working on the school-grounds task after a snowfall! For her, the persistence of those students was evidence that her motivational strategy had worked.

A Note About Unexpected Problems

So far, we have discussed motivational problems for which a solution can be planned. Other motivational problems, however, appear unexpectedly. Consider this example from Chris Zajac's fifth-grade math lesson one day (Kidder, 1989, p. 42):

> Chris had seen progress in this group. They would start long division fairly soon. But today even the well-behaved ones, such as Margaret, looked sleepy. . . .
>
> Chris considered telling them she couldn't teach *celery*, but the eyes that were open and looking at her seemed to say that they didn't want to hear it all from her again: they'd need to know this if they wanted to move on to something new; if they didn't want to get cheated at the grocery store; if they wanted to learn how to design cars and rocket ships. They did not want to hear that Mrs. Zajac couldn't drill holes in their heads and pour in information, that they had to help, which meant, first of all, paying attention. Jimmy yawned. He didn't even bother to cover his mouth. A paper fell off a child's

desk and floated down, gently arcing back and forth like a kite without a tail. She'd try something different. An old trick might work.

This account is a good portrayal of what might go through the mind of a teacher when motivational problems unexpectedly develop.

The first reaction is likely to be anger and a temptation to project the motivational problem onto the class (as when Mrs. Zajac referred to her students as *celery*). A second reaction is likely to be a "scramble" or quick search for any strategy that might work. Rather than reacting to the problem in anger or with a solution that did not fit the problem, however, Chris Zajac defined the problem in such a way that she could manage it and solve it. The solution that she chose was "an old trick": she called Jimmy to the board, made him the teacher, and asked him to show her (in her role as student) how to solve a multiplication problem. She took his seat, and then she hammed it up, pretending to be sleepy and bored. The interest of the class was quickly rejuvenated through humor at the incongruity of the situation: one of them was trying to show their sleepy, bored, unmotivated teacher how to do a math problem.

The rest of this chapter will focus on three areas of motivational problems—both expected and unexpected—in school. Related to each area are a number of psychological "micro-theories" that tell us something about (1) how motivational problems come about, (2) how they can be solved, and (3) what research says about the effectiveness of the solutions. A concluding section will then help you design motivational strategies for complex problems, such as those Mrs. Eck and many other teachers face every day.

> Motivational problems may arise suddenly and require interesting solutions.

STIMULATING INTEREST

Most children begin school as eager learners. They enjoy learning about Africa, zithers, and almost anything else in between. Their interests tend to be concrete but very general. Beginning about the third or fourth grade, however, learning becomes very difficult for some children. Successfully stimulating their interests is crucial to their continued motivation to learn.

Interests are motivational effects of values and knowledge. There are different ways to stimulate interests based on the distinction between personal and environmental determinants of interest. Personal determinants of interest are variable influences *within* the learner. That is, interest is personally determined by such factors as the learner's values or knowledge. Personal determinants are relatively easy to understand. In contrast, environmental determinants of interest are more difficult to understand. They are variable influences *outside* the learner. Interest is environmentally determined by values temporarily imposed by others. Although environmental determinants—such as reinforcement—are more difficult to understand than personal determinants, teachers tend to use them more often (Marshall, 1987; Newby, 1991).

> Interests are determined by personal and environmental factors.

Personal Determinants of Interest

Personal determinants of interest currently fall into two categories. On the one hand are interests that develop from the values of the learner. They are brought to a learning situation by the learner. Their foundation often appears to be an unmet *need* of some kind. On the other hand are interests that develop from a particular situation. They are provoked by novelty, complexity, or incongruity in the learning environment. Their foundation appears to be the cognitive process of *equilibration*—that is, the cognitive need to understand what we perceive. Both these sources of interest lie within the learner.

Needs and Values of the Learner

Although unmet needs are not the only source of values, they undeniably influence them, just as values influence interests. In a school situation, these needs are sometimes as fundamental as the need for food: a child may come to school without breakfast, or an adolescent may skip meals to diet or try to live on soda, candy, and chips. Sometimes the unmet need is for esteem, in which case learning is fueled by the desire to achieve or be recognized for achievements. On the surface, the need for food seems unrelated to the need for esteem, but Abraham Maslow (1970) theorized that human needs are related to each other in a hierarchy. **Maslow's hierarchy of needs** is a theory that establishes a taxonomy of needs, listed according to the order in which they motivate an individual (see Figure 12.1 on p. 500).

Maslow's theory suggests that the "lowest" unmet needs in the hierarchy influence the values of an individual until they are met, at which time the needs in the next highest category begin to influence these values. The lowest category is composed of *physiological* or survival needs. Physiological needs include the biological demands for air, food, water, elimination of waste, and sleep. As long as a physiological need is unmet, a person values highly whatever will fulfill that need.

The next higher category consists of *safety* needs. These include freedom from anxiety or fear, as well as the needs for protection (shelter, clothing, etc.) and structure (law or order). Then, once the individual feels secure, needs for *love and belongingness* emerge. These include the need for family and friends and for a place in the group. Once love and belongingness needs are met, needs for *esteem* emerge, including needs for recognition (esteem of others) and a favorable judgment of self-worth (self-esteem). Needs for esteem are related to valuation of the self.

Survival, safety, love and belongingness, and esteem together constitute "deficiency" needs. According to Maslow, deficiencies are prerequisites that must be satisfied before an individual can be motivated by **self-actualization,** or "full use and exploitation of talents, capacities, potentialities, etc." (1970, p. 150). Maslow (1971) believed that self-actualization occurs through moments of insight called *peak experiences* of joy or beauty in which one "learns one's identity." What appears to take place in such moments is the

> Unmet needs may influence a student's interest.

> Maslow's hierarchy arranges human needs in order of urgency.

> Self-actualization is the highest need in Maslow's hierarchy.

Figure 12.1
Maslow's Hierarchy of Needs *(Summarized from Maslow, 1970, pp. 35–47)*

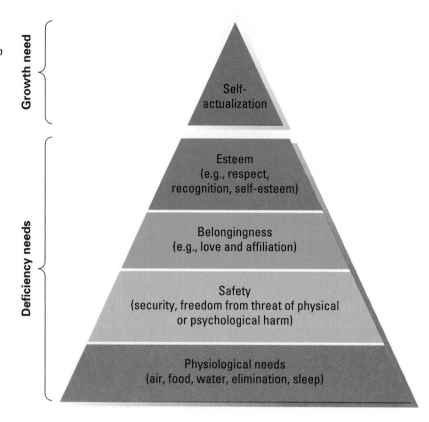

integration of several previously unrelated values into a value complex. (Recall from Chapter 3 that we encountered the concept of a value complex as an instructional objective in the affective domain.) The value complex of a self-actualizing person integrates acceptance of different values, but in such a way that perception of reality is not distorted. As a consequence of this integration process, many value conflicts within the individual disappear.

Maslow (1970) found that only very few people have been motivated by needs to actualize the self. Examples include such historical public figures as Thomas Jefferson, Abraham Lincoln, Albert Einstein, and Eleanor Roosevelt. Each of these individuals had a set of characteristics identified with self-actualization (see Table 12.1). Interviews with more than three thousand college students located only one self-actualizer and one or two dozen students with potential for motivation at this level. Maslow speculated that opportunities for self-actualization before one becomes established in life are relatively rare. Most students exhibit, at one time or another, various levels of deficit need. No one, not even a self-actualizer, is motivated by only one level of need all of the time.

It is clear that needs affect values, but how do values affect interests or a student's motivation to learn? The answer to this question depends on what we mean by values (Maslow, 1971). *Value* can be defined as worth—and in this sense, values have everything to do with interests. Unmet needs assign temporary values to goals. These temporary values prioritize goals in a hier-

Few people reach the level of self-actualization.

Interests reflect the value placed on unmet needs.

Table 12.1   Characteristics of Self-Actualizing Individuals

More efficient perception of reality (perspicuity)

Increased acceptance of self, others, and nature

Increased spontaneity, simplicity, naturalness

Increased problem centering (as opposed to ego centering)

Increased detachment and desire for privacy

Increased autonomy (independence)

Continued freshness of appreciation

Higher frequency of peak experiences

Increased identification with the human race

Improved interpersonal relations

More democratic character structure

Discrimination between means and ends

Discrimination between good and evil

Development of a philosophical, unhostile sense of humor

Increased creativity

Transcendence of any particular culture

Tolerance of imperfection in self and others

Source: Adapted from Maslow, 1970, pp. 153–176

archy. People are motivated to achieve more fundamental goals first because they are more highly valued. Interests become an expression of these temporary values. A hungry person is interested in food, a frightened person is interested in safety, a lonely person is interested in belonging to a group, and so on. These interests are deactivated when the need is met.

strategic solutions

Needs and Values of the Learner

Maslow would *not* have a teacher "reinforce [students] or shape or teach [them] into a prearranged form, which someone else had decided upon in advance" (1968, p. 688); rather, he would have the teacher help students meet deficiency needs so that the students would work up the hierarchy toward self-actualization. As students' deficit needs were fulfilled, they would increasingly make choices that uncovered their identities or core talents rather than revealing further deficits. To change the motivational level of students, then, the teacher should (1) help students meet deficiency needs that

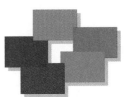

interfere with achievement, (2) provide personally relevant means to achieve esteem, and (3) create opportunities for self-actualization. Let's consider some ways to accomplish these ends.

1. *Help students meet deficiency needs*

Physiological, safety, and belongingness needs block interest in achievement because they often motivate a child to pursue other interests. A child who is tired, thirsty, or hungry, for example, may have difficulty paying attention in class. A child who is feeling insecure because of a home situation, a school bully, or the threat of failure cannot easily be interested in a task unrelated to reestablishing a sense of security. Finally, a child who is lonely or simply different from other children may not be interested in individual achievement, but, rather, just want to "fit in."

There is much that you can do within your role as a teacher to help students meet these needs and reestablish an interest in school achievement. If you are teaching on the preschool or elementary levels, you will want to establish procedures for getting a drink and for going to and returning from the bathroom. If a child seems listless or tired, you might remark that "you seem tired today," providing the child with an opportunity to explain why. At this point, you may learn that the child is being allowed to stay up as late as the parent(s). In a routine parental conference, tactfully share your perception that the child often seems tired. Then point out that children, on average, need more sleep than adults.

Personally relevant and interesting tasks improve the quality of learning and increase perseverance. These students are packing boxes to send to American soldiers during the Gulf War. What academic subjects are integrated by this project?
(Steve Leonard/Black Star)

Children may be hungry for many reasons. Inadequate nutrition can be the direct or indirect result of poverty. Free breakfast and lunch programs are often available for students whose parents qualify. Inadequate nutrition can also be the result of self-set diets to lose weight. If any of your students tell you that they are on a diet, remind them not to skip meals.

Children may be lonely for many reasons. You may recall from Chapter 6 that an average of one child in every class reports having no friends there. Loneliness may be the result of recent enrollment in a new school, lack of social skills, or a sense of being different from other children. You can conduct exercises to help students get to know each other, to feel that they're part of a group, and to develop social skills (again, as described in Chapter 6). You can also counsel peers and talk with parents about the necessity of accepting differences more readily.

There is no end to the strategies for helping children meet deficit needs (Richardson, 1985). Such strategies range from asking parents' permission to give a child a coat long ago left in the Lost and Found, to using a small fund set aside by the school to hire a student as a lab assistant or a student worker. Indeed, it is quite possible for teachers to nonintrusively help individual students meet deficiency needs that block interest in achievement (see Reflection on Practice: Diagnosing Personal Needs).

2. Provide personally relevant means to achieve

Many students come to school interested in gaining recognition from their parents, peers, and teachers. They will be oriented to achievement. You can help such students toward self-actualization by providing them with personally relevant means to achieve. Perhaps the best way to begin is to provide students with meaningful choices that help them identify interests *other than grades or scores on tests.* Psychologists, for example, identify interests by asking people to express their preferences for one activity as opposed to another. In a classroom, you may not always be able to give children a choice of learning activities, but within a given learning activity, you can almost always give children a choice of ways to participate. Letting students choose *topics* to investigate, *problems* to solve, or *roles* to play are three common ways to incorporate choice in activities.

3. Create opportunities for self-actualization

You may not be able to plan your students' peak experiences, but you *can* create the conditions under which they might occur. These conditions involve (1) the satisfaction of deficit needs and (2) the development of a goal that can be used to organize personal values and interests into a value complex. One of the most useful ways to do this is to present students with opportunities to explore career images. You can list such images on the board and discuss them in class—but, more important, you can continually serve as a resource person while your students are developing vocationally related goals and plans to achieve them. Self-actualization requires the teacher to be

reflection on practice

Diagnosing Personal Needs

I have a student in my fourth-period p.e. class who, in the beginning, seemed to have trouble fitting in or being accepted by her peers. Gina was quiet, but not shy, and very standoffish toward her peers. Every day, as soon as she dressed out, she'd come to my office and "hang out." At the end of class, after she dressed back in, she'd do the same. During class, she was always by herself, and if a particular drill called for partners, I'd either have to be her partner or assign one to her.

As Gina seemed to spend more time with me than with anyone else, and as she didn't seem to be very happy, I began casually asking questions that gave me insight as to how to deal with her. I knew that money was a problem because she didn't have things other teenagers had. I learned that her parents had recently divorced. Her mother did not qualify for a high-paying job and was working part-time as a cashier at Kroger. They lived in low-rent housing, and from time to time, I noticed that Gina did not eat lunch. Her grades were low Cs in my class, and lower than that in others.

Gina craved my attention; however, she never created a disturbance to get it. This semester, because I was registered for two university night classes (Mondays and Wednesdays) and had ball games on Tuesdays and Fridays (I am cheerleader sponsor), I asked Gina if she "would like to baby-sit—it would really help me out." Others wanted the job, but I offered it to Gina first because I knew that she needed it most.

Gina took the job. She has been very dependable as well as responsible; but she has also been a very different person these past few weeks. She bought new clothes, got a new hairdo, and has had spending money to go places after school with other children her age. Others accept her now that she baby-sits for me. She laughs with the other students and participates more in class. And during our fitness testing last week, Gina ranked first in the one-mile walk/run. She finished in 8 minutes, 10 seconds. She's even mentioned running track next year. I attended a meeting after school concerning her request to move from special education math to a regular math class. She has also requested a move from basic English to grade-level English. The desire to improve has made a remarkable change in Gina.

Erlene Entrekin

Discussion Questions

1. Social acceptance led to many changes in Gina, but what was the underlying deficiency need?

2. Analyze the development of motivation in this student. What stages did it go through? Use Maslow's hierarchy to describe this progression.

3. Suppose you are on the committee to reevaluate Gina's placement in English and math. What further information would you want in order to make a decision? Why?

nonintrusive, permitting the genuine interests of a student to emerge in relation to a subject. Your role is that of a helper, presenting and re-presenting how professionals in a given domain solve problems.

Evaluation: Needs and Values of the Learner

Maslow's hierarchy of needs anchors a discussion of how to stimulate interests. In doing so, it provides a way of understanding the source of interests. Since Maslow's death in 1970, competing explanations of self-actualization have emerged from research on emotional development (Piechowski, 1991) and *flow* or optimal experience (Csikszentmihalyi & Nakamura, 1989; Schiefele, 1991). These alternatives are more focused on *affect,* or feelings, as a source of motivation than is Maslow's theory. Flow, for example, is a feeling of total engagement in an activity, so that time seems to pass quickly.

Maslow's theory draws strength from its relation to everyday experiences. We all know how important a drink of water is to someone who has become very thirsty or how threats from a bully can interfere with concentrating on a reading assignment. Yet, although Maslow's hierarchy of needs has great intuitive appeal, it also has some weaknesses. For example, it does not assign a clear role for cognitive needs in motivation. Maslow (1970) identified the "desires to know and understand" as cognitive needs, but he never clearly conceptualized their relation to the other needs in his hierarchy. All of these other needs are *conative*; that is, they are related to striving or purposeful action. Maslow suggested that cognitive needs belonged within another hierarchy, implying that they did not always lead to overt action.

In addition to this theoretical limitation, there are two practical limitations on the development of self-actualization in schools. First, the needs and values of students are often difficult to diagnose. It is not easy to determine the needs and interests of an individual, let alone those of a roomful of students. Second, beginning teachers often face pressures from their own unmet needs for security, belonging, and esteem (Nelli & Atwood, 1986), leading them to choose safe, conforming, or prescribed goals or teaching methods. As you will recall from Chapter 2, the interests of teachers often change to focus on the needs of individual students after threats to survival have diminished.

Despite these shortcomings, Maslow's theory and its implications for the classroom often appeal to teachers, who are cast in the role of helpers. We are all too aware that some students come to class burdened with problems that limit their responsiveness to incentives and to opportunities for growth. Maslow's hierarchy offers us a framework for understanding these problems and, perhaps to a lesser extent, for resolving them. Furthermore, efforts to teach to the values and interests of students are educationally effective. Personally relevant and interesting material improves attention, memory, comprehension, and inferences. It also facilitates perseverance in learning (Renninger, 1992).

Equilibration

Not all interests are brought to the learning situation by the learner. Some interests can be created as responses to the learning situation (Berlyne, 1960). Interests that are provoked by the learning situation have historically been referred to in the context of "curiosity," but they are increasingly defined as **situational interests,** or personal determinants of motivation that stem from novelty, complexity, or incongruity in the environment. Their origin is a self-regulatory mechanism of learning that Piaget labeled equilibration. In Chapter 5, you came to know *equilibration* as the self-regulatory mechanism through which we are driven to understand what we perceive. In short, thought must accommodate or adjust whenever people perceive something they do not fully understand.

> Situational interests are created by the novelty or complexity of the lesson.

Situational interests are evoked in a rather well-defined way. Once a child perceives that something is new to his or her experience, disequilibrium occurs. Disequilibrium motivates the mind of the child to revise existing understanding (or expectations) to account for what has been perceived. When the object of this perception has been understood, equilibrium is restored. Interest ceases because what was novel has now come to be expected. Interest in the object or event is restored only when equilibrium is upset again (that is, when something unexpected is perceived).

> Interest results from situations that create disequilibrium.

Consider what happens when an infant discovers that a rattle makes a noise. Let's say the infant knows how to shake things, but thus far, things have not made a noise when shaken. When she shakes the rattle, it *does* make a noise (thus producing a novel experience). At first, the infant cannot understand that shaking makes the noise (a case of disequilibrium). The rattle seems to make the noise, but when it is not shaken, it makes no noise. Only through repeated experience, and with a revised understanding of shaking (as a means to an end), does the child begin to understand that shaking the rattle makes the noise. At this point, shaking the rattle to make a noise is no longer new (equilibrium). The infant may shake the rattle to make a sound, but she is not motivated by the novelty of it. If the rattle is then shaken and *fails* to make a noise, however, interest will recur (disequilibrium).

Small children are alive with interests in objects that are moderately new to them. They pick up small rocks, sticks, and whatnot out of curiosity; they bend over to stare at a flower or a worm; they pull out pans in the kitchen and climb on chairs to see what is on top of tables. Their curiosity seems insatiable. When they become older, their curiosity will seem more adultlike because disequilibrium caused by things has been reduced. Their interest will then often turn to the causes or effects of events.

Developing Situational Interests

Several recent studies have shown that situational interests have more than one component (e.g., Henderson & Wilson, 1991). Interests in *novelty* and *complexity*, for example, appear to have different developmental courses (Henderson & Moore, 1979; Vandenberg, 1984). Interest in novelty of objects declines during the early school years, whereas interest in complexity of stimuli increases. As children get older, they seem to become less curious about objects and more curious about complexities or incongruities in the world around them. As they move from early childhood into middle childhood, "share time" interests them less and "puzzles" interest them more.

These changes can be understood by reference to developmental theory. Young children, ages two through seven, can be expected to be more interested in novel objects because disequilibrium occurs on a preoperational level. Such children are interested in learning about different *things* that are new to them—the reason for their many "collections." Disequilibrium on a concrete operational level generally cannot be resolved until the children are seven or eight. At this age, they are more likely to want to "figure things out" than to identify what things are. They are more likely to seek explanations of complexities or incongruities ("Where do birds go in the winter?" "Why do trees lose their leaves?") rather than just to seek more novel objects. In sum, situational interests are influenced by the developmental stage of the learner.

> Younger children are interested by novelty, older children by complexity.

strategic solutions

Developing Situational Interests

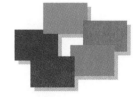

As a teacher, you can draw four implications from this research. First, *take advantage of a variety of techniques to stimulate situational interests.* Novelty, complexity, and incongruity can take many different forms. In the classroom, novelty often translates into interesting objects, displays, and facts, but it can also take the form of surprise. To interest her basic math students, Mrs. Eck announced that their project was to begin *outside.* Complexity often takes the form of phenomena that call for explanation, but it can also be found in puzzling questions. Incongruity may take the form of either inconsistency or humor.

Second, *use novel things to stimulate the interest of younger children.* Younger children are more likely than older children to be curious about novel things. Schedule "share time" for young children to develop this form of motivation to learn. Also, take advantage of "teachable moments" created by objects that children spontaneously bring to you on the playground or from home. Try to appreciate their surprise the first time that they see a cocoon, for example, and use their surprise to teach a science lesson. Put the cocoon in a jar with holes in the lid to see what develops. You can also bring novelties to class to initiate a lesson. Novel things that younger children can touch or hold work best because the examination can be "up close and personal."

Third, *introduce complexities to stimulate the interests of older children and adolescents.* Older children are more likely than younger children to be curious about complexities in their environment, and their curiosity is often reflected in puzzlement. Whereas "what" questions seem to peak before the school years, "why" and "how" questions frequently indicate puzzlement that begins about the time a child enters school. "Why is it raining?" "How do trees grow?" "Why do people sing at holiday time?" The form of the question is not as important as its significance. It is a search for the cause of some complex phenomenon. Children can answer a few of their own causal questions at four or five, but not until about seven or eight can they figure out the answers to similar questions posed to them.

Fourth, *arrange an optimal level of novelty or complexity to motivate learners.* Keep in mind that novelty, complexity, and incongruity are variable. That is, objects can be more or less novel, phenomena more or less complex, and relationships more or less incongruous or discrepant. Objects of moderate novelty, problems of moderate complexity, and relationships of moderate discrepancy seem to work best to stimulate interests. Researchers have long hypothesized that too much novelty, complexity, or incongruity can overwhelm a child, resulting in a loss of motivation to learn (Lepper & Hoddell, 1989).

Evaluation: Developing Situational Interests

Most recent research on the influence of situational interests on learning has been conducted through the study of reading (Hidi, 1990). Reading provides an almost ideal environment for research on curiosity in the learning situation because the situation can be highly controlled. Surprising content, for example, can be introduced at the same point for many different individuals acquiring the same knowledge. Research tells us that this type of motivation is difficult to create; but when created, it has a significant, positive impact on recall and comprehension (Hidi & Baird, 1986).

Novelty, complexity, and incongruity must be used skillfully to enhance learning rather than distract from it. For example, it may be interesting for a student to learn that Washington wore false teeth in his later years, but is that fact important for understanding the American Revolution, or Washington's presidency? Probably not. When techniques to stimulate situational interest are used carelessly, they distract from important points. Important rather than trivial details need to be made interesting to affect achievement (Garner, Gillingham & White, 1989; Wade & Adams, 1990; Wade et al., 1993).

Environmental Determinants of Interest

At first glance, we might think that a purely "environmental" determinant of interest is a contradiction in terms, but let's consider some examples:

- A book falls in a classroom, making a loud sound, and everyone turns around to see what happened.

- Just after the bell rings, a teacher taps her hand rapidly a few times on her desk to get the attention of the class.
- A child watches other children of the same age ride bicycles and is motivated to learn to ride, too.
- Foreign-language students watch attentively as their teacher demonstrates how to position lips, teeth, and tongue to produce the correct sound.

These examples illustrate interests that are determined by the environment: interest in "what happened," interest in attending to the teacher, interest in learning to ride a bicycle, interest in how to position one's mouth to make a sound. In each case, the control of the environment over responses is rather complete. In the first two cases, learners cannot help paying attention; and in the second two, their responses would have to be actively inhibited.

Environmentally determined interests, like personally determined interests, fall into two categories. On the one hand are interests caused by the *orienting response* (as discussed in Chapter 9). On the other hand are interests that are due more directly to the *functional value* of observed behavior (as discussed briefly in Chapter 8). Both of these sources of interest can be used to engage learning.

Interest may be aroused by environmental causes.

The Orienting Response

Why do most people turn around to look when a book falls? Similarly, why do teachers develop signals—such as flicking the lights or tapping on a desk—to gain the attention of students? The answer to both questions is very practical: humans, like animals, possess an **orienting response**—namely, a reflex reaction that involves both physiological arousal and a turning of the head for optimal perception of a new stimulus. This reflex has been studied by psychologists around the world (e.g., Berlyne, 1960; McGuinness & Pribram, 1980; Siddle, 1983; Sokolov, 1963) but has rarely, if ever, been examined in the classroom.

An orienting reflex compels people to pay attention to a new stimulus.

About seventy years ago, the Russian physiologist Ivan Pavlov discovered the orienting response in his experiments on reflexes in dogs—they perked up their ears and turned their heads toward any new sound. He informally called it the "'What-is-it?' reflex," which, though not a very scientific term, is certainly an accurate description of the reaction of a human or an animal to something in the environment that it is not fully positioned to perceive (Pavlov, 1927/1960, p. 12). Pavlov speculated that this response had strong survival value for any organism.

There are many examples of this response in people. Meetings, for example, are called to order with a gavel. When a speech is about to commence at a dinner, someone taps a water glass. A referee blows a whistle to distract players momentarily from their game. Lights dim for a moment in a theater to indicate that intermission is almost over. School bells ring to signal the beginning and end of the school day, and alarms buzz to signal fire drills. Watches sometimes beep in the middle of class, distracting everyone. What these sounds have in common is that they cause a slight disruption in activity as well as a momentary orienting of interest toward the sight or sound.

The orienting response is useful in many situations.

Using the Orienting Response

The fact that the orienting response is not normally under conscious control is what makes it so useful to teachers. It is so often used, and in so many different ways, that we generally do not think about it until it's our turn to direct the attention of a group. The stimulus does not have to be very loud or bright, just different from stimuli in the environment. In fact, some teachers find that they can attract the attention of a group by standing silently. Critical to the effectiveness of the stimulus is that it is (1) socially acceptable, (2) perceptibly different from other stimuli, and (3) not overused.

For example, a particular tune might be socially acceptable in the first grade but not in the third. A small bell might be socially acceptable in the third grade, but not in high school, where you might use a variety of more natural stimuli, such as closing the door to start the period, turning on a projector light to start the lesson, or standing quietly in front of the class. Your voice is typically what children hear, so try to use new stimuli to elicit the orienting response—visual signals, for example. Finally, make sure that your signals are not overused. You can use a specific stimulus to gain momentary attention, but if you use it too often, your students will become *habituated* to it and thus no longer react to it. The overall strategy is *to stimulate momentary interest* by *eliciting the orienting response.*

Evaluation: Using the Orienting Response

Gaining attention is essentially a problem of *motivation*. You can either plan to use the orienting response as a part of a motivational strategy, or you can use it to deal with spontaneous difficulties as they arise. Unfortunately, the research to date gives us very little information on the effective use of these stimuli to interest students, but you might want to reflect about how your grade-school teachers used them—whether appropriately or inappropriately.

Functional Value of Observed Behavior

> People are interested in things that may be useful to them.

In Chapter 8 you learned that the functional value of any behavior is the *use* it has for the learner. From a motivational perspective, functional value is no different from other values because it leads to interest. A belief in the usefulness of any behavior leads to interest in it, and interest, in turn, engages attention and motivates observational learning.

Let's take the example of a child learning to ride a bicycle. Many events lead up to riding a bicycle for the first time—riding "Hot Wheels" or tricycles as a preschooler, riding a bicycle with training wheels, and so on. But a crucial step occurs when the training wheels are removed. What leads a child to

Interest can be stimulated by creating a functional value for a skill. The girls in the foreground are interested in learning how to stake a tent because they have an immediate use for the skill— setting up the tent they will sleep in. *(Nita Winter)*

persist through the bangs and bumps that follow? Albert Bandura (1986), who developed observational learning theory, might say that it is "the functional value of riding a bicycle." Bandura defined *functional value* as the anticipated consequences of prospective actions. The anticipated consequences of riding a bicycle are many—being able to do what adults or older siblings can do, playing with friends on bikes, riding faster than you can run, and so on. *All* of the anticipated consequences stimulate interest in learning to ride a bicycle.

> Learning is motivated by its anticipated consequences.

Three influences, in particular, seem to determine the functional value of observed behavior. First, the observer must anticipate that performance of the behavior will result in a reward of some kind. This reward may be a natural consequence, or it may be supplied by a teacher. Second, if the functional value (or use) of a behavior is unclear, the observer will use "symbols" to infer it (Bandura, 1986). Prestige, for example, often symbolizes competence (that is, behavior with high functional value). When functional value is unclear, the behavior of a high-status model becomes more interesting to the observer than the behavior of a low-status model. Third, if functional value is unclear, and if the observer is uncertain of achieving a given behavior, he or she may become more interested in the behavior of a model who matches the self in age, sex, or background characteristics (Schunk & Hanson, 1985). In this situation, the behavior of the model who is most similar to the observer is assumed to have the highest functional value (or use) for the observer.

> Children are motivated to learn what they value.

All of these principles explain what motivates young children to adopt "heroes" and influences older children and adolescents to conform to peer pressure. Children are learning acceptable social behaviors, and their heroes and peers often serve as their models. Social skills do not develop easily or naturally, and they often have to be quite developed in order to be rewarding. Heroes demonstrate to younger children which behaviors are valued by society. When children become older, they demonstrate to each other as peers what is valued. Heroes are highly motivating to young children, whereas older children and adolescents look to each other for models—thus readily conforming to peer expectations of dress, hairstyles, and values.

All of these principles also explain why a child learns to ride a bicycle, despite the pain and awkwardness involved in doing so. After watching adults, older children, or peers ride bicycles, the child infers that bicycle riding has value. Soon after that, the child takes interest in a more than casual way. In the process, interest has been engaged and sustained by the *expectation* of enjoyment as well as by progress and praise.

Much learning by novices appears to be motivated in this way. Some learning is inherently enjoyable, but for novices much learning has to be based on anticipated consequences. Otherwise, people would never learn to ride bicycles; read books, magazines, or newspapers; tell time by analog clocks; or do long division by hand. A learner has to become quite good at these and many other skills before they become more rewarding than frequently available alternatives (such as walking or running, listening to others talk, reading a digital clock, or using a hand-held calculator). Beginners, in particular, often need models of skilled performance to become interested in learning. Without models to establish functional value, many beginners would show insufficient interest to engage in many learning activities.

Models can inspire beginners to learn new skills.

strategic solutions

Creating a Functional Value for Behavior

In Chapter 8, you learned that the one implication of observational learning for gaining and holding attention was "to demonstrate only behavior or skills with high functional value." We can now derive strategies for stimulating interest so that functional value does not interfere with personal determinants of interest. First, *when personal determinants do not stimulate interest in learning, create a functional value for behavior.* Personal determinants include individual needs and cognitive equilibrium. Ideally, you should rely on personal determinants to stimulate interest in all learning activities; but note that when a learner is a beginner, personal determinants are often weak—personal relevance is unclear, and progress is sometimes not perceptible. At such times, you should create a functional value for behavior to stimulate interest. You can create functional value by demonstrating the usefulness of some skill—that is, by showing "what it is good for." Grades and scores are time-honored ways of creating functional value, but they tend to be overused.

Second, *when the functional value of a behavior is unclear, stimulate student interest by selecting competent models.* Since parents and teachers are believed by most children to be competent at most skills, their behavior stimulates interest when competing values and interests do not interfere. In some circumstances, however, you might want to use other high-status models—adults or even older children who are renowned for achievement, popularity, and so forth—to stimulate interest. For example, a popular political figure could be invited to speak before a junior high class to stimulate interest in government.

Third, *when functional value is unclear, and the learner lacks confidence, stimulate interest by using a model similar to the learner.* At such times, either you can demonstrate coping skills to help the learner (for example, by saying, "Here's where I need to be careful . . . "), or you can use a peer model. Both are ways to create similarities between the model and the learner. The model most similar to the learner is the learner him- or herself, an observation that has led to the study of self-modeled behavior. Viewing one's own performances on videotape can lead to even greater improvements in skill and confidence than viewing the performances of a peer model (Schunk & Hanson, 1989).

Evaluation: Creating a Functional Value for Behavior

Observational learning is most helpful for beginners (Schunk, 1991). The same might be said of the use of functional value to attract interest or hold attention. It's often the case that, by the time learners have reached the intermediate phase of a physical or cognitive skill, they enjoy the learning activity enough to value it and take some interest in it. Beginners, however, often need an incentive to pay attention and learn. Functional value provides the incentive to engage in activities that are not naturally appealing.

BUILDING CONFIDENCE

Interest by itself is not always sufficient to engage learning. For example, children may be interested in learning to swim, but because they are frightened of the water, or believe they cannot learn, they do not try. The same may be said of any skill. The motivational effects of interest may be disrupted by fear or a lack of belief that a goal can be attained. As a consequence, building **confidence,** or a belief in one's power to affect outcomes, can be as important a motivational issue for teachers as stimulating interest.

Confidence is an important part of motivation to learn.

How do teachers build confidence? They can do so by drawing on the revolutionary insights offered by psychologists in the last twenty years. Like interest, confidence has both personal and environmental determinants. Personal determinants include *self-efficacy,* or the belief in one's power to affect outcomes, and *causal attributions,* or explanations for outcomes in life. Environmental determinants include the *expectations of teachers.* Each of these sources of confidence can contribute to motivation to learn.

Personal Determinants of Confidence

Personal determinants of confidence grow out of the belief that hard work is necessary for success. How is this belief built up? What can undermine it in the course of learning? How can teachers help reestablish it when a learner gives up trying? Questions such as these have occupied many researchers in education in the past decade, and their findings provide some useful answers.

What Is Self-Efficacy?

Efficacy, which is a synonym for "effectiveness," refers to the power or capacity to produce a desired effect. **Self-efficacy** is the perception of one's own power to do so (Bandura, 1986). We might call it a belief in one's own effectiveness or a "can-do" attitude. Self-efficacy is a source of confidence and, consequently, a source of motivation.

> Self-efficacy is a belief in one's ability.

Causes of Self-Efficacy

The outcomes of a learner's actions have the greatest effect on self-efficacy. Success generally increases self-efficacy whereas failure generally decreases it. Exceptions occur, however, when a task is easy; then success does not raise self-efficacy. Success at moderately difficult tasks seems to work best to build confidence.

> Self-efficacy is raised by success.

A learner's self-efficacy is also influenced by what happens to other people. Beginners frequently compare themselves with others like themselves to decide whether they are capable of performing an action or a skill (Schunk, 1991). That is why teachers frequently have competent students "lead off" in learning activities that require taking turns. Less proficient students who follow the leader are encouraged by the success of a peer, and their own subsequent success builds self-efficacy.

> Watching models can increase one's self-efficacy.

Finally, persuasion and changes in physiological states may cause temporary changes in self-efficacy. Persuasion, a positive influence, can come from parents, peers, or teachers, often in the form of encouragement. Discouragement, of course, can lower self-efficacy. Physiological states (such as being nervous) are sometimes interpreted by a learner as indications of low or high self-efficacy. Information—whether from personal accomplishments, from observation of others, from persuasion by others, or from physiological states—is often interpreted before a change in belief is made about one's own effectiveness.

> Persuasion can increase self-efficacy.

Effects of Self-Efficacy

The most important effects of self-efficacy are participation in an activity, effort, and task persistence (Bandura, 1986; Schunk, 1991). Some researchers have defined *engagement* as the involvement in tasks that derives from high self-efficacy (Skinner, Wellborn & Connell, 1990). Engagement appears to be specific to domains in which self-efficacy is high. When self-efficacy in a domain of activity is low, learners tend to avoid participating in that activity,

> Self-efficacy increases effort and engagement and decreases anxiety.

even if they express interest in it (cf. Wigfield & Karpathian, 1991). Low self-efficacy is associated with anxiety (Meece, Wigfield & Eccles, 1990; Mizelle, Hart & Carr, 1993), which suggests that increases in self-efficacy are accompanied by decreases in anxiety.

strategic solutions

Building Novices' Confidence

Three teaching strategies can be derived from the three causes of self-efficacy. First, *build students' confidence by providing them with opportunities for success at tasks of moderate difficulty.* Novice learners who in the past have been successful will perceive moderately difficult goals as *challenges*. Such students will put forth reasonable efforts to achieve these goals. You should allow expert learners to set their own goals in tasks that are appealing to them. These learners tend to prefer challenges of moderate difficulty rather than tasks that are either too easy or too hard to develop confidence.

Second, *build novices' confidence by using competent peer models.* Novices face the special problem of overcoming the initial anxiety that they bring to a learning task. Watching others like themselves perform successfully can help them cope with uncertainty about their own capabilities. In general, the greater is the degree of similarity of model to learner, the better the effect on self-efficacy. *Coping models,* or students just slightly more proficient than beginners, increase self-efficacy of beginners. For this reason, you might want to "scaffold" learning tasks so that less proficient learners are paired with slightly more proficient learners (see Reflection on Practice: Building Confidence Through Peer Models).

Third, *build novices' confidence through persuasion and attention to improved physiological states.* Indicate to students who seem to lack confidence that you have confidence in them. Remember to *persuade* (which has the same origin as "sway") rather than cajole, ridicule, or embarrass. Persuade through situational humor ("No extra credit for nervousness"), encouragement ("Give it a try!" "You can do it!"), and supportive reasoning ("There is no such thing as a dumb question; we're all learners here"). As students experience success and gain confidence, magnify both by pointing out physiological change ("You're not nervous anymore"; "Hey, you're really enjoying driving now"). Good teachers have a good grasp of how to boost confidence in these small ways.

Evaluation: Building Novices' Confidence

Self-efficacy represents a coherent explanation of the origins of confidence and is one of the most rapidly growing areas of research on motivation in education. Its portrayal of success as a source of confidence, and confidence as a source of success, has much support in research and in our own experi-

reflection on practice

Building Confidence Through Peer Models

I teach after-school art classes to children in our school. On Tuesdays, I teach a beginners pastel and drawing class to grades K–3. On Thursdays, I teach watercolor and drawing to advanced students in grades 4–6. The beginners class is very basic because some of the students have not yet mastered coordination or confidence in using a drawing or coloring instrument. It is very hard to overcome the "I can't" idea that children have when they first begin the class. It is also imperative that the idea be eliminated and that patience take its place.

When I first began teaching art, I tried to help the children overcome this idea by making an analogy between learning to run and learning to be a good artist. We all had to go through developmental stages to finally be able to run. I tried to help them understand that we were going to learn some basic "crawling" skills and that, before they knew it, we would be "running away" with our artwork. I didn't understand at first why they didn't believe me. However, as I listened to them talk as they drew, I realized that the age difference between us was a reason. They felt that I could do art only because I was older! I knew that somehow I needed to convince them that they could do it at their ages.

The second year that I taught, two of my former art students were not able to take the advanced class on Thursdays and asked if they could stay in the beginners class. I agreed since the objects I planned to use would be different from the ones I had used the previous year. During the first few class sessions, I noticed that the beginners seemed to be paying more attention to the two former students than they were to me. When I demonstrated a technique, the beginners would watch me, turn to watch the two former beginners, and finally practice the technique themselves.

As the class developed and an occasional "I can't" popped up, the two former students would remark that they had felt the same way. One shared that he had decided right at the beginning to put the "I can't" in his pocket and try anyway. With great delight the two students would describe to the younger ones how excited they were to be able to say, "I can!" The younger students believed them and were able to put away their "I can'ts." I was not able to provide the kind of model that these two students did. I have realized the importance of observational learning from peers and strive to incorporate a mix of beginners and advanced students in our art classes.

Beth Vinson

Discussion Questions

1. Why did the behaviors of the peer models have greater interest for the learners than the behaviors of the teacher?
2. In terms of self-efficacy, what does "I can't" represent?
3. The teacher explains that one model said "he had decided right at the beginning to put the 'I can't' in his pocket and try anyway." How does what he said help build confidence in the younger students?

ences. Self-efficacy as a component of observational learning theory has its greatest educational implications for novice learners rather than intermediate or advanced learners.

Causal Attributions

What explanations other than effort do people offer for outcomes in their lives? The systematic analysis of how people relate causes to significant outcomes is known as **attribution theory,** and it has much to tell us about what types of experience can undermine confidence and what types can restore it. The "attribution of causes" might seem an unlikely focus for modern notions of how to rebuild student confidence, but this idea is well supported by a great deal of research. The study of attributional processes began with the realization that *explanations* are not facts; rather, they are inferences often based on perceptual relationships (Heider, 1958). A cause and effect tend to be inferred by a person when she or he perceives that two events *covary* or are positively related.

Sometimes covarying events are causally related, but many times they are not. Particularly when failures occur, we want to know "why" and we will invent an explanation. Bernard Weiner (1992) developed a means for classifying causal attributions or explanations along two dimensions: *internal/external* and *stable/unstable.* The result of combining the two dimensions was a two-by-two classification of attributions (see Figure 12.2 on p. 518).

The *internal/external* dimension was first studied as *locus of control* (Rotter, 1966): people who felt in control of outcomes in their lives were distinguished from those who did not. A student who received a good grade on a test, for example, might explain it as a result of *internal* factors (such as skill or ability) or *external* factors (such as lucky guesses or an easy test). A preference for internal explanations was called an "internal locus of control," and a preference for external explanations was called an "external locus of control."

One significance of the internal/external dimension lies in its relation to self-esteem. All other things equal, when children (or adults) experience success, they tend to make *internal* causal attributions. "I received a B on the test because I studied hard," or "I received a B because I am relatively smart." Internal attributions of success boost self-esteem. Similarly, when they experience failure, they tend to make *external* causal attributions. "I received a *D* on the test because I was unlucky," or "I received a D because this teacher gives hard tests." External attributions of failure protect self-esteem. This tendency to ascribe success to internal factors (skill or ability) and failure to external factors (luck or other people) is called the *hedonic*

> Attribution theory can explain how people believe outcomes are caused.

> Results may be ascribed to internal or external causes.

Figure 12.2
Four Types of Attributions
(Adapted from Weiner, 1992, p. 250)

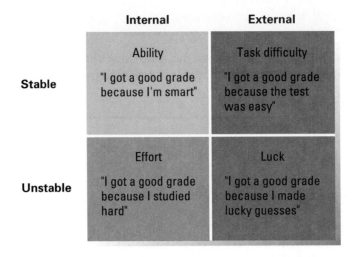

	Internal	External
Stable	Ability "I got a good grade because I'm smart"	Task difficulty "I got a good grade because the test was easy"
Unstable	Effort "I got a good grade because I studied hard"	Luck "I got a good grade because I made lucky guesses"

bias (Weiner, 1992). It maximizes the pleasure of success and minimizes the pain of failure.

The *stable/unstable* dimension was added by Weiner and others (1971), who observed that, while some internal causes (such as effort) change, others (such as ability) do not. The student who received the good test grade might attribute success either to effort in studying (internal-unstable) or to ability in the subject (internal-stable). As for external causes, they too seem divisible between those that readily change (such as luck) and those that do not change (such as the difficulty of a given task). The student who received the good test grade might attribute success to good luck (external-unstable) or to easy tests (external-stable). The significance of adding the stable/unstable dimension was to permit analysis of attributions that lead away from self-esteem.

Self-Esteem versus Helplessness

What are the consequences when students attribute failure to an internal cause? The answer depends on which internal cause. Students with a history of success typically attribute failure to lack of effort, but students with a history of failure typically attribute failure to lack of ability. If students attribute failure to lack of effort, they preserve self-esteem and continue expectancy of future success because they can always try harder. Their confidence remains undiminished. If students attribute failure to low ability, however, their self-esteem is undermined, and their expectancy of future success decreases. There is very little that can be done about limits on one's own abilities. Confidence is diminished.

If students explain failures by low ability often enough, they begin to experience what Weiner (1992) called "hopelessness." Hopelessness, or what is more often referred to as **learned helplessness,** is a motivational state acquired through consistently internal and stable attributions of causes for failure (Abramson, Seligman & Teasdale, 1978). Such attributions are not

Results may also be ascribed to stable or unstable conditions.

Self-esteem remains high if failure is attributed to lack of effort rather than lack of ability.

Learned helplessness comes from repeatedly blaming one's failure on low ability.

generally made during the elementary years, perhaps because children do not distinguish effort and ability as clearly as adolescents do (Fincham & Cain, 1986; Nicholls & Miller, 1984). By early adolescence, however, children's attributional patterns are similar to those of adults. If failure is repeatedly experienced, and if it becomes attributed to stable internal causes (low ability), confidence (the belief in one's power to affect outcomes) diminishes, and a learner feels he or she might as well not try (see Reflection on Practice: Helplessness in Math).

Goal Theory

Why do some students repeatedly experience failure and lose confidence in their ability to learn? The answer to this question, which is crucial to our understanding of the origins of helplessness, has been provided by Carol Dweck (1986), along with a number of other researchers (Ames, 1992; Anderman & Maehr, 1994; Blumenfeld, 1992; Dweck & Leggett, 1988; Elliott & Dweck, 1988; Nicholls, 1989). A major cause for repeated failures, and attributions of failure to low ability, is the pursuit of "performance goals" rather than "learning goals" (see Table 12.2).

A **performance goal** is a purpose for striving that primarily involves the approval of others. Performance goals are very common in interpersonal competitions, where "winning" or pleasing others is a criterion of success. In contrast, a **learning goal** is a purpose for striving that involves building competence through completion of some task (Elliott & Dweck, 1988). Learning goals involve striving to master knowledge or skills. These goals are common in situations where progress and task mastery are criteria of success.

> Performance goals are based on approval from others, whereas learning goals focus on mastery for its own sake.

When students with *performance* goals fail, they often attribute failure to low ability. Why is this so? One reason may be that these students fail repeatedly, but researchers have theorized that beliefs about self and others are also involved. Winners often magnify feelings of success through **ego involvement,** or the desire to enhance oneself by establishing superiority relative to others (Nicholls, 1989). How often have we heard victors chant, "We are number one"? Ego involvement requires attributing success to ability rather than to effort. Because of ego involvement, performance goals often result in a belief that success requires high ability. Consequently, when

> Ego involvement magnifies the effect of failure.

Table 12.2   Selected Characteristics of Performance and Learning Goals

Performance goal:	Focus is on approval of others.
	Student believes that success requires high ability.
	Success leads to attributions of ability.
	Failure leads to sense of helplessness.
Learning goal:	Focus is on task mastery.
	Student believes that effort is related to outcomes.
	Success leads to attributions of effort.
	Failure leads to persistence.

reflection on practice

Helplessness in Math

One of the students whom I tutor is a seventh grader named Vickie. She is taking pre-algebra and came to her first tutoring session in tears. She kept saying she just couldn't do math. After working with Vickie for a while, I realized that one of her main problems was in remembering the order of operations and the rules for simplifying expressions. I taught Vickie a mnemonic device that I use with my classes for the rules of order of operations.

The acrostic Please Excuse My Dear Aunt Sally gives the order of operations for doing algebra: parentheses, exponents, multiplication, division, addition, and subtraction. When Vickie would miss a problem because of order, I would remind her simply by saying, "Remember Aunt Sally," and she would usually find her mistake.

Vickie told me that on test papers she writes "Aunt Sally" at the top to help her remember now. Vickie's attitude about her ability to do math has been harder to correct, however. I have encouraged and praised her successes and have tried to find problems that she can do well so that she will begin to see she can do math. Her grades have improved a little, and that helps, but each time she makes a low grade, she slips back into the "I can't do math" routine. We are working on maintaining a positive attitude and breaking the problems down into tasks that she can do, but it is a battle to overcome her negative attitude.

Jackie Griffith

Discussion Questions

1. **What aspects of this student's unstated experiences before she came to the tutor led her to feel helpless?**

2. **The tutor rightly gives her a learning strategy and praises her successes, but what keeps this approach from being very effective?**

3. **If you were the tutor, how would you adapt your teaching strategy in light of what you have discovered about the attributions of this student?**

performance-oriented students fail, they begin to believe that their ability is not high enough to succeed. Ego involvement traps them into the belief that low ability causes failure.

The demoralizing situation in which some students find themselves may not be entirely of their own making. Although a student may adopt performance goals independently of the teacher ("What d'ya get?"), the teacher is likely to create a learning situation that favors either performance goals or learning goals. A teacher who focuses not on learning (process and content) but on performance (grades and competition) may be partly responsible for the development of helplessness in some students. Students who repeatedly experience failure in competitive situations eventually wonder, "Why try, if I can't win?"

> Teachers should focus on learning rather than performance to avoid creating helpless students.

Helping Students Overcome Helplessness

Attribution theory tells us that the way to build confidence in students is to *establish learning goals that relate outcomes to effort.* Define success as improvement, value effort, view mistakes as part of learning, model appropriate strategies to deal with mistakes and failure, and keep attention focused on the task and learning. Recall that Mrs. Eck announced to students that she would evaluate their individual contributions to their project, not whether they had found the "right answer" or how each group did in comparison with the others. However you implement learning goals, they should result in a belief that effort affects outcomes. Students will become more persistent and less susceptible to helplessness.

What should you do if students enter your class helpless? You will find these students in almost any class. First, give them a chance to respond to your learning goals. Second, if they fail an initial task because they do not try, ask them why they think they failed. Third, *explain that they failed because they did not work hard enough; then give them a chance to try again.* This strategy, which is consistent with learning goals and establishes the belief that outcomes are related to effort, is called **attribution training** (Fosterling, 1985).

Attribution training does not always work because "helpless" students who try and succeed sometimes attribute their successes to external factors, such as "You made the assignment easier," or "It was a lucky day." *When helpless students begin to succeed, remind them that their success was due to their efforts.* If they thank you for their improved grade, remind them that they earned it.

Evaluation: Helping Students Overcome Helplessness

The recent distinction between performance and learning goals has been a major achievement of motivational research. It explains *why* some children ignore the hedonic bias and attribute failure to internal causes such as low ability. In other words, it explains why some children give up easily. It also suggests a strategy to restore lost confidence and motivation.

Despite the value of this strategy to restore confidence, it has limitations that you also need to consider. First, attributional interpretations of student failure need to be made cautiously. Learned helplessness offers *one* explanation for student failure, but it does not explain everything. Not all insufficient effort is due to attributions of low ability. When some students perceive themselves failing, they may deliberately reduce effort to preserve a belief in high ability (Covington, 1992). Other students give up on tasks because the tasks really are beyond their present ability levels, are uninteresting, or are not satisfying. When a student fails in your class, you as a teacher need to make a judgment about why that student failed and respond accordingly.

Second, we do not as yet know a great deal about performance goals. Their identification gives us hope of more progress, but currently they raise several unanswered questions. For example, how do performance goals develop? Do students bring them to class, are they patterns of behavior that emerge when teachers grade competitively, or are both true? Are performance goals ever acceptable? Some aspects of performance goals seem adaptive to competitive situations, but other aspects (such as ego involvement) do not. Goal theory is still incomplete, but it has already contributed to our understanding of how confidence is built.

An Environmental Determinant of Confidence: Teacher Expectations

You have studied how the self-expectations of the learner affect motivation, but what about the expectations of others? Significant research has been conducted on **teacher expectations,** or anticipations of student ability and achievements by their instructors. Teacher expectations became a focus of attention when Robert Rosenthal and Lenore Jacobson published a study of teacher expectations titled *Pygmalion in the Classroom* (1992/1968). In Roman mythology, Pygmalion was a king of Cyprus who fell in love with a statue, and in answer to his prayers, the gods made her come to life. Rosenthal and Jacobson hypothesized that teacher expectations of student ability and achievements could actually raise scores on IQ and achievement tests.

Teacher expectations about students have been extensively studied.

To conduct their study, Rosenthal and Jacobson created in elementary-school teachers false expectations that specific pupils in their classes would be "early bloomers" and have high ability by the end of the year. Actually, the pupils had been randomly selected. At the end of the year, the researchers found that the IQ and achievement scores of these students were higher than the scores of the other students. This effect came to be known as a "self-fulfilling prophecy" because teachers' anticipations (like Pygmalion's love) seemed sufficient to bring about the changes.

Seven or eight *hundred* research studies followed. When the results were reviewed, researchers generally agreed that (1) most expectancies of teachers are realistic and based on experience, (2) unrealistic expectations tend to have a significant effect on student achievement only in the first two grades, and (3) teacher expectancy effects can account for only about 5 percent of achievement score differences among pupils (Brophy, 1983; Good, 1987; Raudenbush, 1984). (See Deepening Your Knowledge Base: Why Do Teacher Expectations Affect Younger Students More than Older Students? on p. 525.)

Achievement is affected by teacher expectancy in some limited respects.

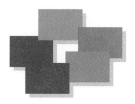

Teacher Expectations

As a teacher, your effectiveness will be based partially on whether students perceive you as unbiased or fair. Consequently, *learn to recognize and neutralize your biases.* You will have some positive expectations for the whole class, and individual expectations based on student needs, but you will be more fair and effective if you identify and neutralize expectations based on stereotypes. For example, you might use a checklist to monitor whom you call on to answer questions in a reasonable period of time. Did you call on everyone? In elementary grades, you might change seating periodically so that no individual student feels disfavored. You might also change student helpers weekly to give everyone a chance to feel favored.

Many teachers informally adopt a "proactive" policy to monitor the achievement of students they believe to be less capable. That is, they watch these students work and provide more assistance to them than to other students. This strategy may backfire. Receiving help from the teacher is perceived by students to be an indication of low ability. Both self-expectations and peer expectations may be negatively affected (Graham & Barker, 1990; Weinstein, 1989). To minimize these effects, circulate through the whole class when you offer help, hold conferences with students for a variety of reasons, and in conference discuss past progress as well as future achievement.

The evidence on teacher expectations also suggests that you should *expect each student to be capable of success.* Communicate to students that if they work hard, they can succeed. If they should fail, continue your expectation of

In order to prevent students from perceiving extra help as an indication of low ability, teachers need to circulate throughout the class. Note that this teacher has arranged desks so that he can move through the entire class to offer assistance. *(Bob Daemmrich/Stock Boston)*

success, and rededicate yourself to helping them achieve. The most profound effect of high expectations appears to be on teachers themselves. Those with high expectations are more likely to persist in attempts to teach low-achieving or difficult students (Meyer, 1985). If you follow this strategy, you will almost certainly find that some students whom you know to have given up in the past ("I can't/I'm just no good at . . .") will flourish in your class.

Evaluation: Teacher Expectations

Although many expectancy effects can be demonstrated to be significant in groups of students, they are limited in how much they affect an individual student's confidence and motivation. Achievement seems to be the best source of confidence and motivation (Brophy, 1983; Jussim, 1989; West & Anderson, 1976) and in most cases quickly overrides false expectations. Most experienced teachers simply set aside biasing information. Positive expectations are often motivational for a teacher but by themselves are unlikely to motivate students much.

Positive expectations can sometimes *undermine* achievement, as illustrated in a case study of two first-grade Hispanic- American girls in the same bilingual classroom (Goldenberg, 1992). At the end of August (the second month of school), the teacher did not expect Marta to read well but did expect Sylvia to read at an above-average level. The teacher intervened with Marta because she saw her beginning to fail in the lowest of five reading groups. The teacher talked with her about her lack of effort ("I told her that if she didn't try she wasn't getting anywhere"). Sylvia was in the next higher reading group, and though she worked slowly, she seemed to be making adequate progress.

In September, the teacher had a conference with Marta's mother over a report card, and the mother began to work with Marta on language skills at home. Sylvia's unfinished work was beginning to pile up, but the teacher did not intervene. October was a month of vacation. By November, increases in Marta's language skills and motivation led the teacher to promote her to a reading group at Sylvia's level. Sylvia, however, was falling further behind because of her slow and deliberate pace of work. By March, Marta was again at the top of her group, but Sylvia was so far behind that an aide mentioned this to the teacher. The teacher didn't intervene in this decline ("I always thought she'd pull out of it") until April, when the year was almost over. At the end of the year, Marta was in one of the top reading groups, but Sylvia was in the same group in which she had begun.

In Marta's case, the teacher's low expectations resulted in a series of interventions that led to success rather than failure. In Sylvia's case, the teacher's initially above-average expectations resulted in no intervention until the end of the year, when failure appeared imminent. Such paradoxical outcomes illustrate how limited our generalizations about expectancies must be and how important the intervening efforts of teachers are.

deepening your knowledge base

Why Do Teacher Expectations Affect Younger Students More than Older Students?

Research on expectancy effects has broadened to include teacher expectations of achievement based on various personal characteristics (such as physical appearance, social class, race, and gender), social expectations possessed by teachers (Brophy, 1987), emotional cues and helping by teachers, achievement expectations in ability-grouped classes, achievement expectations possessed by schools, and a host of related topics (Dusek, 1985; Good, 1987). In general, expectancies follow stereotypes (for example, a middle-class child should achieve more highly than a lower-class child), but not all research on such expectancies has followed through with measurement of effects on achievement.

Teachers' expectation-related behaviors appear to affect learners' self-perceptions of ability (Barker & Graham, 1987; Graham & Barker, 1990; Weinstein, 1989). In other words, they raise or lower the confidence of learners in their abilities to succeed at a task. Interestingly, the most recent research on expectancies (Jussim, 1989) does not suggest that changes in self-perception of ability automatically translate into motivational changes. Rather, teacher expectancies appear to have their primary motivational effect on the actions of teachers. An expectation of high ability, for example, might lead a teacher to offer a student greater challenge, and to interact with a student more frequently, than if the teacher expected low ability.

Whether the effects of teacher expectancy on achievement are due to sterotypes of one kind or another, or whether they influence teacher perceptions of students more than students' perceptions of themselves, the effects are often found to be relatively small—accounting for 5 percent or less of achievement. An important question to discuss is, Why do studies show that such expectancies affect younger students (first and second graders) more than they do older students? Break up into small groups to answer the following questions, then reassemble in the larger group to compare answers.

Discussion Questions

1. What do teachers represent for younger students that they do not represent for older students? Be specific.

2. How might the *structure* of learning in elementary schools cause elementary teachers to have greater influence on learners than secondary teachers do?

3. If not teachers, who would influence older students' self-perceptions of academic ability? Why? (Give more than one reason.)

INCREASING SATISFACTION IN LEARNING

Interest and confidence can engage learning, but they do not always sustain it. In particular, novices can experience frustrations that overwhelm their interest in a learning activity and undermine their confidence. Such frustrations may indicate that they are not ready to learn, or that the challenge needs to be reduced, but they may also indicate that *incentives* or rewards are lacking. The learner becomes uninterested and easily distracted. Doubts seem to increase about whether the activity is worthwhile. Motivation flags.

The *incentive value* to succeed at any task has been analyzed as a function of task difficulty (Atkinson, 1964). To be motivated by a task with a small probability of success, the incentive must be great. We understand this rule from watching game shows. The more difficult the task, the greater the prize must be to make the task worthwhile, and vice versa. What is particularly interesting here, however, is that incentives can be either *extrinsic* (or external) to a task, such as winning a game show prize, or *intrinsic* (internal) to a task, such as making a puzzle match. Satisfaction results from either winning the prize, making the match, or both.

> Motivation can be intrinsic (for its own sake) or extrinsic (for a reward).

Research on incentives or rewards in education has recently focused on **intrinsic motivation,** or engagement in an activity through curiosity, challenge, or enjoyment of the activity itself (Deci, 1975; Gottfried, 1985, 1990). In terms of challenge, increasing one's knowledge or skill is a bit like completing a puzzle. Until 1975 or so, research on incentives or rewards in education focused on **extrinsic motivation,** or engagement in an activity for a reward apart from the activity itself.

> Extrinsic motivation should be used only when intrinsic motivation is absent.

Comparatively recent research suggests that extrinsic motivation is used too often. Susan Harter (1981) found that third graders tend to learn out of curiosity, work for their own satisfaction, and prefer challenging work. They approach school with an *intrinsic orientation.* Upper elementary and junior high school students, however, increasingly tend to learn in order to please the teacher or to get good grades, and they tend to prefer easy to challenging work. They exhibit an *extrinsic orientation.* As children move through elementary grades and into secondary school, they increasingly expect the teacher to motivate them to learn. We can minimize this expectation on the students' part by using *extrinsic* motivation only when *intrinsic* motivation is absent.

Personal Determinants of Satisfaction in Learning

What determines satisfaction in learning? There is widespread agreement that *intrinsic motivation* is the single greatest personal determinant of satisfaction in learning. Intrinsic motivation can have many sources (such as any of the personal determinants of motivation discussed thus far), but one that is related to satisfaction is *self-determination* or *autonomy* (Deci, 1975; Deci & Ryan, 1985). People are often more satisfied with an activity that they have chosen. A school cafeteria worker once told me that complaints went down dramatically when the cafeteria began offering a choice for lunch. The same is true of learning experiences. Most people like to choose, and given the same learning experience, they are more satisfied if they choose it than if they do not choose it.

> Autonomy increases satisfaction in learning.

Self-Determination and Classroom Learning

How does self-determination or autonomy affect the *quality* of learning in the classroom? Edward Deci and Richard Ryan suggested that autonomy has two important effects (Deci et al., 1991). First, autonomy improves conceptual learning or understanding. How? Learners process information more deeply when they do not feel controlled. Second, autonomy seems to favor optimal psychological adjustment in school. Autonomous learning is positively related to enjoyment of school and learning activities.

> Self-determination favors learning and adjustment in school.

One experiment illustrates why researchers believe that self-determination is satisfying (Grolnick & Ryan, 1987). In the experiment, researchers gave fifth graders a passage to read from a social studies book and one of three directions designed to represent different degrees of experimenter control, from high to low: *controlling directed* ("After you've finished, I'm going to test you on it. . . . I'll be grading you on the test"), *noncontrolling directed* ("After you've finished, I'm going to ask you some questions about the passage. . . . You won't be graded on it"), and *nondirected* ("After you've finished, I'm going to ask you some questions"). After reading the passage under one of the three conditions, students rated interest and enjoyment of the reading and were tested for understanding (conceptual learning), immediate recall of facts, and (a week later) delayed recall of facts.

The results are summarized in Table 12.3. Interest in and enjoyment of the reading activity were comparatively high when experimenter control was low. The less experimenter control there was, the more students enjoyed the reading. They did not enjoy reading to be tested. Understanding (conceptual learning) fit the same pattern. Students understood more of what they read when experimenter control was low. They understood better when they were not going to be tested. However, immediate recall of facts was comparatively low when experimenter control was low. The less external control there was, the fewer were the facts that students immediately recollected. When students took a recall test one week later, however, those who had experienced low experimenter control remembered more than those who had experienced high experimenter control. Students who had experienced high

> Long-term recall may be greater when teacher control of learning is low.

Table 12.3 Results of Experimenter Control over Student Learning

Dimension of Motivation or Learning	Outcome in Groups with Less Experimenter Control
Interest/enjoyment	Higher*
Understanding	Higher*
Immediate recall	Lower
Delayed recall (after 1 week)	Higher*

Source: Grolnick & Ryan, 1987, p. 895

*Result favors group with less experimenter control.

experimenter control seemed to "dump" facts from memory shortly after the first test.

The findings suggest that teacher control and student autonomy affect the quality of student learning. Low teacher control and high student autonomy lead to greater enjoyment and understanding (conceptual learning) than do high teacher control and low student autonomy. These results echo the cumulative results of dozens of studies that have compared achievement results under behavioral approaches to education (high teacher control and low student autonomy) with achievement results under open education (low teacher control and high student autonomy). Students typically have acquired more knowledge through behavioral approaches, but they have demonstrated improved attitudes toward school and higher levels of thinking through open education (Horowitz, 1979; Peterson, 1979).

strategic solutions

Providing Choices for the Learner

The strategic implications of the self-determination approach to intrinsic motivation are relatively straightforward (Deci et al., 1991). First, *increase learner satisfaction by giving your students a choice of tasks and letting them determine how much time they want to spend on them.* A sense of choice is a precondition for self-determination and intrinsic motivation. Choice in learning can be introduced in those ways discussed under stimulation of interest. You can either offer students a choice of learning activities or, when that is not possible, offer them a choice within a learning activity. Other choices involve time, extending it or limiting it. Choice allows students' needs and values to stimulate interest and leads to increased satisfaction for many students.

Second, *when you are requiring an uninteresting task or procedure, acknowledge students' feelings of dissatisfaction.* This acknowledgment can be subtle ("Let's make the review painless"; "Let's get our warm-ups finished"). You can take the same opportunity to underscore the instrumental value of the activity ("Once we finish, we can take a break"; "You have to know the safety rules before you can use the equipment"). The acknowledgment of mild dissatisfaction permits students to feel self-determined and makes the internalization of necessary constraints easier.

Third, *develop a noncontrolling style to direct activities and communicate feedback to your students.* Focus on information rather than authority. For example, when giving directions, supply reasoning in support of them ("Clear your desks so that we can move on to math now" as opposed to "Clear your desks!"). Reasons imply consideration of alternatives and a rationale for a decision. When giving feedback, emphasize its informational value ("You're really doing some fine work now"; "You're really improving") rather than its judgmental aspect ("Excellent!" "You did okay"). An informational focus implies continued, independent learning, whereas a summary judgment implies that learning is over. Sadly, many times after a summary judgment, learning *is* over.

Evaluation: Providing Choices for the Learner

There are generally two qualifications to be made about the use of intrinsic motivation to increase satisfaction. First, a limit exists on how much freedom benefits most students in terms of their cognitive functioning. In Chapter 6, for example, you learned that an *authoritative,* rather than an authoritarian or a permissive, parental style results in children who are self-reliant, self-controlled, and explorative (Baumrind, 1973). Moderate, rather than extreme, student control seems best for autonomy. This finding has been confirmed in the classroom, where problem solving occurs best under conditions of *moderate,* rather than radical, freedom (Prawatt & Anderson, 1988). These results are not inconsistent with the reading experiment because even in the low experimenter control condition, students were presented with a specific task (to read a passage from a social studies text) and could infer a purpose to their activity (to understand the passage).

Second, a teacher cannot institute student options, choice, or freedom in the classroom without a web of supportive educational practices (Ames, 1990). For example, you cannot suddenly ask students to decide what they want to learn about long division, require them to design their own weather projects, or permit them to assign themselves grades in a unit on Reconstruction because such action is inconsistent with the expectations that they have developed from the learning context (see Chapter 13). Often intrinsic motivation can be introduced only insofar as your personal beliefs and goals, your students, and your context allow such motivation to function. We shall address this matter of coordinating strategies in greater detail at the end of this chapter and in the next. It is my experience, however, that teachers have more opportunity than they use to incorporate student input in instructional decisions. In other words, student autonomy is currently undervalued in most classrooms because of an overemphasis on coverage of curricula.

Environmental Determinants of Satisfaction in Learning

Extrinsic reinforcers such as praise, points, and grades *can* serve a constructive, motivational function in education. What has been established in the last twenty years, however, is that they do not *always* do so. What is now being formulated is a more sophisticated approach to their use in the classroom to supplement, rather than replace, intrinsic motivation. Briefly, teachers should use rewards in a way that does not create competition. They should use rewards that reinforce behaviors, are contingent on achieving standards, and are attainable by everyone. When these principles of application are followed, rewards generally increase motivation (Dickinson, 1989).

> Rewards should only supplement intrinsic motivation.

In Chapter 8, you learned how to identify reinforcers, what a contingency was, and how to schedule rewards. You also learned about vicarious motivation and the way observed reinforcement or punishment can facilitate or inhibit learning. What we have not yet discussed are *competition* and its alternatives, *cooperation* and *individual reward*.

Competition

When was the last time you played Monopoly? Or bridge? Or a pickup game of basketball? What was the incentive for this activity? If you think about it, we play very few games for a reward other than winning. This fact is obvious to a small child, and as the child grows, he or she almost always plays games to win. Winning is the fundamental motive for competition in our society.

As you have learned from attribution theory, those who win (or lose) competitions often attribute the outcome to their ability (or lack of it). Ego involvement often magnifies feelings of satisfaction for the winners and dissatisfaction for the losers. Sometimes those who lose competitions deflect these feelings to maintain their sense of self-worth (Covington, 1992). In classroom competitions, losers begin to resent victors, calling them "nerds" or "teacher's pets." Or perhaps they feel that the learning activity was not worthwhile anyway. Over time, they learn that one purpose in school is to avoid losing—a game that is played not only with the teacher and grades but also with peers and peer approval, particularly in junior high school. Some secondary students deliberately underachieve to avoid the disapproval of their peers for "winning" at the academic game.

> Competitive learning situations can spoil motivation to learn.

Losing, perhaps even more than winning, begins to explain a lot of behavior in school. The high school student who ambles down the hall hat backward, or who comes to school wearing a T-shirt advertising cigarettes or cutoffs slit up the sides, is not just exercising freedom of expression. He or she may be simultaneously losing the academic game but winning the peer approval game.

Research on motivation has advanced to the stage where we know enough now to issue a warning to teachers: *avoid competitive motivational practices in situations where the same students are repeatedly forced to lose.* These practices include, but are not limited to, display of only the best work, progress charts posted next to each other, racing or social comparison to determine individual grades (rather than to challenge students), compulsory spelling contests, and so on. A complete list of commonplace competitive practices would be quite long. Realize that each of these activities currently has its advocates. Almost to a person, the advocates were winners in these types of learning competitions. You do not have to debate these practices, but you should be able to defend alternatives by pointing out that satisfaction in learning competitions occurs at the expense of others' motivation to learn.

> Teaching practices should not set up the same students to lose repeatedly.

Not all competitions undermine motivation to learn, however. Voluntary learning situations, meaning those in which students are not compelled to participate, may have different motivational effects. Indeed, losses are mitigated even in compulsory situations when the same students are not forced to lose. Some motivational strategies use competition, but the level of competition ensures some wins for each team, and after a few periods teams change. Even on teams with higher achievers, however, low achievers attribute loss to low ability and express dissatisfaction (Chambers & Abrami, 1991). Thus, in most competitions the winner takes all the motivational gains.

> Voluntary competition may not hurt motivation.

Cooperation

Cooperative reward structures can make learning satisfying for more students than competition does. Cooperation involves more intrinsic motivation and a **group norm,** or criterion of performance set by individuals acting together (Johnson & Johnson, 1989; Slavin, 1987). In the view of Robert Slavin, rewarding groups based on group achievements "creates an interpersonal reward structure in which group members will give or withhold social reinforcers (such as praise and encouragement) in response to groupmates' task-related efforts" (1990, p. 14). Satisfaction in cooperative learning flows from a mixture of intrinsic motivation, social reinforcement, and group reward.

> Cooperative reward systems may make learning more enjoyable.

Slavin believed that group norms favor achievement when three preconditions are met: (1) reward is contingent on group performance, (2) members of the group are individually accountable for their achievements, and (3) equal opportunities exist for success. In the presence of these conditions, group achievement seems to exceed achievement averages in competitive conditions. If one (or more) of these conditions is absent, group norms do not necessarily emerge, or if they do, they do not necessarily favor achievement.

> A group norm system may favor achievement.

A study group, for example, does not meet any of these criteria. Study groups have not been found to be advantageous (or disadvantageous) for achievement. Their benefits seem to be primarily social. Even if the group is formed around a common goal, such as a committee might be, individuals are not necessarily accountable for their contributions to the success of the whole. We have all been on a committee in which one or more members took a "free ride." Group norms emerge only when everyone is making a contribution to efforts that will receive group reward. Finally, even if the group has a common reward, and members are individually accountable and contributing, there may be unequal opportunity for success. Unequal individual or group abilities often lead one person to contribute more than others or one group to have an advantage over others. That is why group reward strategies often base rewards on *gains* over past achievements to ensure equality of opportunity for success.

Rewards, whether intrinsic or extrinsic, are not the only source of satisfaction. The benefits of well-designed cooperative strategies include social and attitudinal outcomes (Slavin, 1990). In addition to achievement, cooperative strategies have been found to increase acceptance of racial and ethnic differences, acceptance of mainstreamed students, self-esteem (probably through peer liking), and enjoyment of school. Increased enjoyment of school, however, is not as consistent an outcome as improvements in either achievement or interpersonal attitudes.

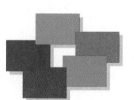

s t r a t e g i c   s o l u t i o n s

Using Cooperative Reward Structures

There are many formal and informal cooperative learning reward structures. Two formal strategies are Student Teams–Achievement Divisions (STAD) and Jigsaw. In STAD, students are assigned to four-member teams mixed in terms of performance level, sex, and ethnicity. The teacher presents a lesson, and then students study in assigned groups, making sure that every group member has mastered the lesson. A lot of peer teaching occurs in these groups because improvements in the achievement of weaker students help the group as much as or more than improvements in the achievement of stronger students. All students then take an individual quiz, but they cannot help each other on it. Points are awarded to individuals based on their meeting or exceeding previous individual averages (see Table 12.4). Finally, points are summed for each team, and totals are compared with criteria for certificates or awards. This cycle takes three to five classes. Individual grades are computed at intervals on the basis of actual quiz scores, not gain scores. Slavin and his colleagues developed this strategy, other cooperative strategies for grades 3–6 mathematics (Team Assisted Individualization, or TAI)

Table 12.4   *Point Awards for Improvement in STAD*

Scoring Individual Quizzes for Improvement Points	
More than 10 points below base score (prior quiz average)	0
Ten points below to 1 point below base score	10
Individual average to 10 points above base score	20
More than 10 points above base score	30
Perfect paper	30

Recognizing Team Accomplishments	
Criterion	**Award**
Team average of 15 improvement points	Goodteam
Team average of 20 improvement points	Greatteam
Team average of 25 improvement points	Superteam

Notes:
1. All teams can achieve awards.
2. To be a Greatteam, most team members scored above their base scores.
3. To be a Superteam, most team members scored at least 10 points above their base scores.
4. Public recognition should be given to all Greatteams and Superteams.

Source: Adapted from Slavin, 1990, p. 63

and language arts (Cooperative Integrated Reading and Composition, or CIRC), and a strategy that mixes cooperation and competition (Teams-Games-Tournaments, or TGT).

In Jigsaw (Aronson et al., 1978), material to be learned is divided into five or six parts. Then five- or six-member groups give a part to each member to learn. The class regroups so that members with the same part in different groups get together in "expert" groups (typically three or four members) to discuss their part. After discussion, research, and so forth, the original groups reassemble, and each group member teaches the group about his or her part. All students then take an individual quiz on all of the material. Grades are often set on the basis of mastery criteria (described in Chapter 14).

In addition to formal structures, informal arrangements such as peer tutoring, peer teaching, peer response groups, and various forms of collaboration on projects are often used by teachers to boost achievement and increase satisfaction. Mrs. Eck adopted a cooperative design using groups of three to motivate students to work together on a short-term project. The students in each group had a common goal, and they were held individually accountable

Sometimes a back is good for more than bending over. Cooperative groups create interpersonal reward structures, enhancing satisfaction from learning. *(Bob Daemmrich)*

through the report, which detailed individual contributions. Equal opportunity to succeed was not a problem because all were relatively low achievers.

Because cooperative designs provide a social intervention for motivating students to achieve, *increase satisfaction of group work by using a cooperative reward structure.* Implementation of this structure requires (1) a reward contingent on group performance, (2) individual accountability, and (3) equal opportunity for success. Gains in both achievement and interpersonal attitudes occur often enough through such strategies to warrant their serious consideration as a means for increasing student satisfaction.

Evaluation: Using Cooperative Reward Structures

Evaluative research in the 1970s focused on the question of which goal structure—competition or cooperation—led to the greatest gain in achievement. The clear answer was that cooperation led to better overall test results than did competition, which appeared to promote the achievement of a few at the expense of the many (Walberg, 1986). Perhaps more important, cooperative designs strongly influenced social development and affect. Students learned to accept interpersonal differences in small-group situations—a social outcome of substantial value in a heterogeneous culture.

The key question seems to be not whether to use cooperative motivational strategies, or even how to use them, but *when* to use them to increase student satisfaction. There is no simple answer. Your decision should be based on whether students need extrinsic rewards to increase satisfaction and on what your instructional problem is. Recall that an instructional problem is defined in relation to givens such as the characteristics of the students and the task they are to accomplish (such as achieving curriculum objectives). For example, young children cannot be depended on to cooperate with each other to accomplish an assigned task. In addition, some tasks, such as most art projects, are often better accomplished by students working individually rather than collectively. There are other situations, however, when you may want to use cooperative designs to increase the satisfaction of group work, as in the case of social goals. Some objectives, such as learning team games, can be achieved only in groups. Finally, limitations imposed by equipment or supplies can be circumvented by grouping students to match resources. Such situations favor the use of a cooperative structure as part of a motivational strategy.

Using Individual Reward Structures

Another alternative to a competitive reward structure is an individual reward structure. Under such structures, individuals are rewarded for making progress or achieving mastery. These structures can be designed for individually paced instruction (usually through a computer) or for group-based instruction. We shall look only at the implications of individual reward structures for instruction in class-sized groups.

The fundamental assumption of individual reward structures is that "the learner will succeed in learning a given task to the extent that he spends the amount of time that he *needs* to learn the task" (Carroll, 1963, p. 725). **Mastery learning** is an approach to instruction that allows a student time and opportunity to achieve a criterion of success on a task.

> Mastery learning allows students enough time to learn the material.

The prototype of mastery strategies, called Learning for Mastery, was developed by Benjamin Bloom (1981). Students differ in ability to learn subject matter, but, as John Carroll suggested, ability can be defined in terms of the time required to master a subject. Bloom believed that over 90 percent of students can master what we teach given (1) clear objectives and standards, both of which are shared with students; (2) multiple opportunities to take tests and receive feedback over given material; and (3) alternative resources, including additional time and study materials. Bloom argued that his program is fundamentally motivational because it makes individual progress rewarding. Grades are based not on the performance of other students but on the achievement of mastery criteria.

think it through

Consider this problem that a novice preservice teacher has **IDENTIFIED** and **REPRESENTED**.

Holding Kids' Interest

One of the many challenges I expect to encounter as a new teacher is holding kids' interest and motivating them. I worry that in a class of general students I might lose the kids who are above average and the ones who need remedial help. I want to find a way to help them all and keep them from being bored with math. I realize that today's students face many outside pressures, and I'm not sure how to compete with them. The question I have is, How do you teach to different levels of students while not leaving anyone behind or bored?

Observe how an experienced practicing teacher GENERATES SOLUTIONS to this problem.

Captivating, motivating, and instructing students of varying ability levels is a challenge, even for veteran teachers. To meet this challenge, know your students' academic abilities, disabilities, and possibilities. Consider the full range of instructional materials available (textbooks, media, resource speakers, etc.); then plan appropriately. Modify what is taught and how it is taught to meet the needs of individual learners. Allow for frequent student responses. Give feedback, prompts, and cues to encourage student participation. Continually assess each student's progress. Provide clarity about how to get help and what options are available for activities when work is finished.

Several approaches have been identified as appropriate for adapting instruction:

1. Mastery learning
2. Cooperative learning
3. Ability grouping
4. Learning style adaptations
5. Learning centers
6. Self-paced instruction
7. Computer-assisted instruction
8. Content options

I usually employ all of these approaches during the course of a school year. My students and I like variety and enjoy the change of pace and style. The needs of the class dictate which strategy is used most often. Low-achieving students need more structuring from their teachers, more active instruction, feedback, repetition, and small steps in instruction. This means exposure to less material with an emphasis on mastery of what is taught. Higher-ability students seem to learn under both structured and unstructured settings. Independent units of study or work as a peer tutor is a valuable learning experience for them. The primary concern is to use the most suitable teaching strategy, provide clarity about how students can get help, and ensure that meaningful, stimulating options are available for students who finish their work.

Robin Gillespie,
Powell Elementary School
Florence, Alabama

think it through, continued

EVALUATE this problem's possible multiple solutions while you think about the dynamic process of problem solving.

As the experienced teacher points out, changing your approach to motivation can itself be motivational. Change as a motivational technique was discovered by industrial psychologists in the 1930s (Roethlisberger & Dickson, 1940). You learned about it in Chapter 8 as the "Hawthorne effect," an increase in productivity due to changes in working conditions that are not accompanied by other improvements.

Researchers wanted to determine whether increasing the wattage of light bulbs in three departments of the Western Electric factory in Hawthorne, Illinois, would increase the productivity of assembly workers. They found it did for a while, but only for a while. When they reduced the wattage to see if productivity would decline, productivity went up again! It seems that the attention and concern for the workers' well-being were sufficient to increase motivation.

Does the Hawthorne effect motivate students when you change teaching methods? It probably does. The enthusiasm that you show for the new method and the effort you expend to implement it probably stimulate interest and motivate learning. This effect, which is an example of *situational interest*, should not discourage you but lead you to change motivational strategies now and then.

Most of the techniques listed by the experienced teacher have been described in this book: ability grouping, in Chapter 7; computer-assisted and self-paced instruction, in Chapters 8 and 10; content options (or choices), mastery learning, and cooperative learning in this chapter. Two methods of instruction that have not been described are *learning centers* and *learning style adaptations*. Let's briefly look at them.

Learning centers are a common way to supplement whole-group instruction in elementary classrooms. They are areas designed to contain materials and activities from themes and units being pursued. Usually, they present the child with a choice of activities to capitalize on children's interests and desire for self-determination.

The extent of choice among centers and within each center depends on how many centers a teacher can manage. Centers for young children might include block play, language arts, fine arts, home living and dramatic arts, scientific investigation, people and places, sand and water play, and woodworking, as well as movement and outdoor play "centers" or areas. Centers for older children might include reading and writing (sometimes combined), math, art (or music), and science. You will want to start with a few centers, adding new ones as you feel comfortable.

As for learning style adaptations, you will have opportunities for advanced study of them later in your career. There are well-researched cognitive styles that need to be studied by teachers who are focused on helping individual students, but frequently these styles are confused with sensory modes, such as visual, auditory, and tactile (or kinesthetic). As a beginning teacher, you should be aware that changing the modality of learning can increase everyone's situational interest (students become bored with talk), but Piaget's stage theory of development (described in Chapter 5) still offers the best explanation of why younger or delayed learners assimilate information by touching or seeing more easily than by listening.

Using Individual Reward Structures

Many variations of the Learning for Mastery model now exist. They share several features with the original strategy: (1) feedback, correctives, and enrichment and (2) congruence among components of instruction, such as objectives, learning activities, feedback, corrective activities, and evaluation (Guskey, 1990). Individual reward structures that do not have these features are not mastery strategies.

In a typical mastery strategy, students are given objectives and engage in learning activities matched to the objectives (Chapter 3). At the end of the sequence of activities, they take a quiz matched to the level and content of the objectives. If an individual achieves a preset criterion of mastery (such as 80 or 90 percent correct), that individual is given an enrichment activity (such as computer lab time or independent reading). Those individuals who do not achieve the mastery criterion on the test receive feedback from the quiz and corrective activities. The correctives do not repeat the original learning activities but involve new activities designed to help students achieve the same objectives. At the end of the second activity period, the students who received the correctives take another version of the quiz. At this point, all of the students generally move on to the next unit, most having mastered the material on their first or second try.

Bloom (1981) asserted that lower-achieving students (who in the past earned grades of C, D, or F) strive harder than normal to achieve under mastery conditions because they no longer believe that their ability limits their achievements. The strategic implication is clear: *to increase the satisfaction of lower-achieving students, adopt the principles of mastery learning.* These principles include (1) feedback, correctives, and enrichment activities and (2) alignment of instructional components so that quizzes and activities match objectives. Mastery learning appears to be advantageous for lower-achieving students. As long as teachers plan enrichment activities, mastery strategies are not detrimental to higher-achieving students.

Evaluation: Using Individual Reward Structures

Evaluative research on mastery learning has focused on whether it leads to greater gains in achievement than traditional (competitive) instruction does. The findings are that it does. In particular, mastery learning programs have been found to improve the achievement of low-ability students. They also improve student confidence and attitude toward the subject (Guskey & Pigott, 1988). Unlike cooperative learning, however, gains in attitude are generally smaller than gains in achievement.

Again, what remain are questions about when to use mastery learning. You should make this decision in light of your instructional problem. Some circumstances, such as inadequate preparation time, a large number of high-achieving students, or loosely structured curricular materials (as in social studies or English literature), do not favor this approach. Other circumstances, such as extra preparation time, a large number of low-achieving students, or well-structured curricular materials (as in science or math), do. Mastery learning strategies generally take extra time to plan and prepare, but your investment in time is likely to return in the form of enhanced student achievement.

A description of mastery learning is not a comprehensive treatment of individual reward structures, but it gives you an idea for another alternative to a competitive reward structure in the classroom. Mastery and cooperative structures can even be combined to offer a third alternative (Guskey, 1990).

CONCLUSION

The design of a motivational strategy is not a simple process, but neither is it an impossible one. Deliberate designs are necessary because the application of many motivational techniques is counterintuitive. Massive doses of success, for example, do not build confidence when students perceive success to be the result of easy tasks. By setting out to design a motivational strategy, a teacher sets out to solve a problem rationally rather than by simply applying principle.

Motivational problems are less complex than instructional problems because motivational problems tend to occur in only a few areas: stimulating interest, building confidence, and increasing satisfaction. Whenever you solve an instructional problem, you can identify a motivational problem by asking these questions:

- Will the learning activities stimulate interest?
- Will the outcomes build confidence?
- Will the activities or outcomes be satisfying?

Problems may be found to exist in just one area, two, or all three areas. They may be large problems, such as the lack of confidence of Mrs. Eck's students, who failed a test that most other students passed, or they may be temporary problems, such as the lack of interest brought about by sleepiness one morning in Chris Zajac's class. They may be group problems or individual problems. Motivational problems come in all sizes, but they tend to come in only three shapes—interest, confidence, and satisfaction.

Like instructional problems, motivational problems must be represented so that you can solve them. Many of the defining limitations are the same as those found in instructional problem solving: your personal goals, curriculum objectives, the characteristics of the learners, and your resources. For example, what are your personal motivational goals for your students? Do you want them to rely more on personal than on environmental determinants of motivation? If so, your problem needs to be framed so that you can focus on personal determinants of interest, confidence, and satisfaction. ("Will the learning activities address the needs and values of students?") Curriculum objectives and the characteristics of your students, however, may limit the extent to which you can achieve your personal goals. The material that you are to teach may (or may not) be intrinsically interesting. The learners may be novices (or experts), low achievers (or high), and those who require more (or less) extrinsic feedback. Preparation time, equipment, materials, and class size can also affect the design of a motivational strategy.

After you identify a problem and represent it in a way that you can solve it, you will want to gather information about motivational techniques. Some of this information will be provided by your previous experience—what have you seen to be effective motivational practices? Remember that what motivated you in an academic situation may *not* have motivated others or may even have been at their expense. Try to recall a range of motivational techniques and strategies that were successful for most, if not all, students.

Other information will be provided by your teacher education program and the concepts presented in this chapter. Table 12.5 summarizes motivational problems and information used to develop strategic solutions. Use this table as an index to find strategies to solve your problem.

Finally, some aspects of your teaching situation will suggest motivational techniques. For example, how can you use the school grading policy for motivational purposes? Most grading policies do not specify the form of evaluation. As a result, you can sometimes be creative. Notice that Mrs. Eck substituted a report for a test and based the report grade on the process of solving a problem rather than on a correct answer. She announced the criterion of evaluation *before* the students began the assignment, using it for motivational purposes. Other aspects of your situation—such as a computer and educational software—can also be used to motivate students. Your motivational strategy will develop from a creative synthesis of techniques suggested by past experience, your teacher education program, and your situation.

You need to evaluate your motivational strategy both during instruction and after instruction is over. Sometimes you can adjust a motivational strategy while teaching, but other times you cannot. Two questions are particularly important: Are students motivated to learn? Are they motivated to achieve the objective? When you evaluate your motivational strategy, consider how students feel about their learning. Do they find what they are learning interesting? Is it building their confidence? Are they satisfied with what they are learning? You can ask older students to answer questions like these anonymously during the term, but you have to watch younger students to see their reactions. If they really enjoy learning in your class, both older and younger students will let you know in many ways. They will come early, spontaneously ask questions, bring things to you, leave reluctantly, see you after school, and so on. Time will fly for you as well as them, and teaching will take on the characteristics of optimal experience or "flow."

Nevertheless, in evaluating a motivational strategy, you also have to determine whether it helped you achieve your goals. Quality experiences in the classroom can be reservoirs of motivational supply, but you must also ask

To meet a motivational goal, a teacher needs a motivational strategy. What strategy does this teacher use to stimulate first graders' interest in brushing their teeth? *(David Young-Wolff/ PhotoEdit)*

Table 12.5   Summary of Motivational Strategies

Problem Type	Personal Determinants	Environmental Determinants
Stimulating interest	Needs and values	Orienting response
	Equilibration	Functional value of observed behavior
Building confidence	Causal attributions	Teacher expectations
	Self-efficacy	
Increasing satisfaction	Self-determination	Cooperative reward structure
		Individual reward structure

whether they helped you realize your intentions. Students can leave class interested, confident, and satisfied but without the information they needed to learn. You should ask yourself, Did the motivational strategy help students get somewhere they needed to go? Abundant interest can be created rather easily in a classroom, but abundant interest in a designated task is a greater challenge.

Educators are just beginning to think about such matters as the design of motivational strategies. Frankly, our profession has not thought about them very much before, and the result has been neglect of an important area. As more is learned about how to tailor motivational strategies to particular motivational problems, we shall increasingly realize that motivational strategies are the products of reflection, not of being "a born teacher" or possessing charisma. Motivational problem solving is *learned*, just as other forms of problem solving are learned. What makes the study of motivational problem solving so interesting is that it is a new field; consequently, we are all learning together, making some mistakes, but also making a good deal of progress.

concept paper

Case Study of a Motivational Problem

Objective of the assignment

To analyze a motivational problem in light of information presented in this chapter and to synthesize a motivational strategy based on this analysis.

Directions for the assignment

1. Make a personal copy of the case of an individual motivational problem that your instructor has provided to you.

a. Analyze the case in light of the three areas of motivational problems discussed in this chapter (stimulating interest, building confidence, and increasing satisfaction).

b. Rank the three problem areas in terms of their importance in this case. Do *not* indicate that all three areas are equally involved—the equivalent of grading papers by awarding them all Cs.

c. Explain the rationale for your ranking. Why did you decide that interest, confidence, or satisfaction was the most important problem in this case? Why did you decide the second area you listed was of secondary importance? Why did you decide the third area you listed was of least importance?

2. Develop a motivational strategy that you would use if you were the teacher in this case. Consider your personal goals, the characteristics of the student(s), any existing objectives, and any indications of limits on resources given with the case.

a. Use the organization of the chapter to identify strategic implications of the number one problem area. Identify whether personal or environmental determinants should play a greater role in your solution; then decide which strategic implications are best suited to the situation. Do the same with number two and number three problem areas.

b. Design a motivational strategy that addresses all three problem areas—interest, confidence, and satisfaction. You may incorporate any element of the existing situation that indicates a "no-problem" area (why the student is sufficiently interested, confident, or satisfied).

3. Explain why this strategy should solve the problem or how it achieves your motivational goal(s) of stimulating interest, building confidence, or increasing satisfaction. Anticipate any long-term problems that may arise, or any changes to the problem that may occur, as a result of your strategy. What long-term strategy may be needed to address these changes?

4. Write up your case study of the motivational problem as a three- to four-page paper. If you like, you can follow the format of your investigation: presenting the problem (the first point of these directions), offering your solution to it (the second point), and stating your rationale for this solution (the third point).

SUMMARY

1. Motivation is the collection of causes that engage an individual in a particular activity. In the classroom, motivation is the force that enables a student to engage in learning.

2. There are three primary sources of motivational problems related to learning: boredom or indifference, anxiety or a sense of inadequacy, and lack of enjoyment or satisfaction. The three primary goals of motivational problem solving target those sources by stimulating interest, building confidence, and increasing satisfaction.

3. Interests that develop from personal values are brought to a learning situation by the learner. Their foundation often appears to be an unmet need. According to Maslow's hierarchy, deficiency needs must be satisfied first before an individual can be interested in self-actualization, the full use of his or her capacities.

4. Other personal determinants of interest are called situational interests. These stem from a self-

regulatory mechanism of learning called equilibration. They are evoked by the novelty, the complexity, or the incongruity of a particular task or experience.

5. Interest can also be environmentally determined, in two different ways: by the orienting response, a reflexive action that causes an individual to focus attention on an environmental stimulus; or by the functional value of a new behavior—an anticipated reward, such as enjoyment or usefulness.

6. Confidence has two related personal determinants. Self-efficacy is the perception of one's power to produce desired effects and affect outcomes in one's life. Success generally increases self-efficacy and failure decreases it. The other determinant is described by attribution theory. Students with a history of failure typically attribute failure to a lack of ability. This undermines confidence and can result in learned helplessness.

7. An important environmental determinant of confidence is teacher expectations or anticipations of student ability. High expectations of teachers tend to increase confidence, particularly in young learners, and increase the willingness of a teacher to persevere in efforts to help students.

8. The single greatest personal determinant of satisfaction in learning is intrinsic motivation, or motivation that comes from engaging in a learning activity. Self-determination, or choice of activity, increases intrinsic motivation.

9. Satisfaction in learning can also have environmental determinants. Extrinsic reinforcers, such as praise, points, and grades, can be used to supplement intrinsic motivation. Goal theory suggests that these rewards can increase satisfaction for more students if offered in cooperative or mastery learning situations than if offered in competitive learning situations.

KEY TERMS

motivation p. 494
motivational problem p. 494
motivational strategies p. 494
interests p. 498
Maslow's hierarchy of needs p. 499
self-actualization p. 499
situational interests p. 506
orienting response p. 509
confidence p. 513
self-efficacy p. 514

attribution theory p. 517
learned helplessness p. 518
performance goal p. 519
learning goal p. 519
ego involvement p. 519
attribution training p. 521
teacher expectations p. 522
intrinsic motivation p. 526
extrinsic motivation p. 526
group norm p. 531
mastery learning p. 535

SUGGESTED RESOURCES

Ames, C. 1990. "Motivation: What Teachers Need to Know. " *Teachers College Record*, 91, 409–421. This article is a brief summary of goal theory that provides helpful suggestions for teachers.

Keller, J. M. 1987. "Development and Use of the ARCS Model of Motivational Design." *Journal of Instructional Development*, 10, 2–10. Motivation is a complex topic, but this article presents a theoretical model of it that is very useful for further inquiry.

Slavin, R. E. 1990. *Cooperative Learning: Theory, Research, and Practice.* Boston: Allyn and Bacon. This practical guide was written by a leading designer of cooperative learning techniques.

Wlodkowski, R. J., and J. H. Jaynes. 1990. *Eager to Learn.* San Francisco: Jossey-Bass. This book was written by counselors, and it has many useful suggestions for teachers' conferences with parents and students about motivational problems.

Classroom Management: Establishing and Keeping a Climate for Learning

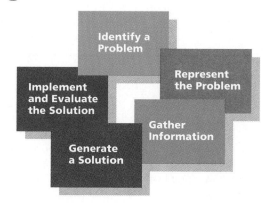

The goal of this chapter is to help you learn how to identify and represent management problems, find ways to understand and gather information about them, and know about some strategies for solving them. If you as a teacher achieve *motivational* goals, you will have fewer situations in which the behavior of students does not meet your expectations. Nevertheless, the behavior of even motivated students will not always be what you expect. In a whole-class discussion, for example, most students can be motivated to participate, but what if a participant repeatedly interrupts others or does not give others a chance to respond? As you will find, realizing behavioral expectations involves motivation and management. As you read, look for answers to these questions:

- **How do classroom management and classroom discipline differ?**

- **How is a teacher's choice of instructional goals and objectives related to management planning?**

- **How are the rules and procedures of effective classroom managers different from those of less effective ones?**

- **What managing skills do teachers use to prevent misbehavior?**

- **What is the role of effective communication in establishing positive learning environments?**

- **What are two types of discipline policies? How are they used?**

- **What are some effective coping strategies, and what do they help teachers do?**

IDENTIFYING AND REPRESENTING MANAGEMENT PROBLEMS

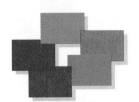

> Classroom management involves prevention and promotes self-control.

Management consists of establishing and maintaining a climate conducive to learning. Classroom management includes what is often called "discipline," but it differs from discipline through inclusion of preventive measures, a positive emphasis, and promotion of self-control. You discovered in Chapter 1 that classroom management is among the top three concerns of beginning teachers. It is also one of the top concerns of school administrators and the public. A **management problem** exists when an individual wants to create or maintain a climate conducive to learning but does not immediately know how to do so. Management problems, like other kinds of educational problems, are solved by planning and by reflection-in-action. The solution to a management problem is a **management strategy**, or a procedure to create and maintain a climate conducive to learning.

Representing Management Problems

> Some behavior problems can be prevented.

Management problems can be represented in various ways, but two of the most common are in terms of *prevention* and *intervention*. You might ask, "What can I do to *prevent* students from coming late to class?" or "What can I do to *prevent* a student from interrupting others?" Sometimes prevention just involves motivation (Chapter 12), but you can also set up the learning environment—by carefully arranging the seating or formulating and teaching class rules—so that many problematic situations never occur.

Sometimes misbehavior will occur despite your best efforts to create a climate conducive to learning. Then you must intervene. "What can I do *after* a student comes late to class so that next time the student will arrive on time?" "What can I do *when* a student interrupts so that the student develops greater respect for others?" The need for intervention springs from the absence of any academic consequences for misbehavior (Alexander, Entwisle & Dauber, 1993; Gaddy, 1988; Hinshaw, 1992). Accordingly, follow the school discipline policy and develop practices to cope with different kinds of misbehavior. Discipline policies and coping strategies represent what you can do to solve a problem once intervention becomes necessary.

A second distinction involved in representing management problems is between *teacher control* and *self-control*. A teacher's authority often has to be asserted to limit disruptions of learning, but to develop student thinking and improve personal adjustment, you need to help students develop self-control. To this end, psychologists are reexamining the value of strategies that are based on teacher control and are developing new strategies to promote self-control.

> Student involvement in rule making may improve self-control.

One goal of these new strategies is to assist in the development of thinking. Discussions that involve students in formulating class rules and in talking about misbehavior attempt to develop a rational basis for appropriate

Some behavior problems can be prevented by the way that you set up the learning environment. **Posting rules and procedures (including the daily schedule) can help create a climate conducive to learning.** *(David Young-Wolff/PhotoEdit*

behavior and supplement or even replace teacher control. Reasoning about rules, for example, can support the teaching of thinking, whereas denying students the opportunity to reason outside content areas is inconsistent with the development of thinking as a goal (McCaslin & Good, 1992). For that reason alone, facilitating student self-control is preferable to asserting teacher control.

Behavior can become more controlled either through compliance with authority or through development of self-control. Development of compliance does *not* prepare children for self-governance, however, which is the basis for social control in democracies. By way of contrast, development of self-control *does* prepare children for self-governance. Consequently, self-control leads to better adjustment in a democracy than does compliance. This reason, too, supports development of self-control over assertion of authority.

> Self-control helps prepare students for democratic self-government.

Although at first glance distinctions between prevention and intervention and between teacher control and self-control may seem to complicate classroom management, this is not so. Rather, they help you represent management problems more deeply than was the case thirty years ago, when there was much less interest in preventive measures and student thinking. Deep, rather than superficial, representation of management problems offers the promise of strategies that are better suited to the classrooms and students of today.

Distinguishing between prevention and intervention, and teacher control and self-control, also helps structure the discussion of management strategies. This chapter will examine prevention strategies before intervention strategies and will evaluate each strategy in light of its capacity to enable self-control. To begin the discussion of management strategies in the context of a real learning situation, let's see how one highly skilled fourth-grade teacher deals with management problems in her classroom.

Management in Ms. Romine's Fourth-Grade Class

In Ms. Romine's fourth-grade class, roll call immediately follows the 8:00 bell. Ms. Romine then asks for "permission slips" from students absent the day before who have checked in with the office with notes from their parents. Although the school sets the discipline policy, Ms. Romine sets the class rules, which she has posted at the front of the room. Students learned them through rehearsal and examples given during the first week of class:

1. Keep your hands and feet to yourself.
2. Follow directions quickly and quietly.
3. Be kind and courteous; speak in turn.
4. Be prompt and prepared.
5. Be neat.
6. Complete your work.

It is now October, and the six written rules have become embedded in classroom routines. For example, students know that they are to turn their homework in as they arrive each morning (Rule 4). A pile of homework papers (yesterday's unfinished seatwork in science) accumulated on a corner of Ms. Romine's desk between 7:50 and 8:00. Later, Ms. Romine will check that all homework from the previous day was completed satisfactorily (Rule 6).

Even before Ms. Romine takes class roll, students are working on their first learning activity, part of their daily routine. They begin to define the "word for the day" that Ms. Romine has written on the board—*gnash*. After they hand in their homework, and while others are still arriving, they go to their desks, pull out their dictionaries, write out the definition in a notebook, and use the word in two sentences. Ms. Romine, having taken attendance and posted names of absentees at the door, addresses the group and briefly discusses what gnash means, asking for a few sample sentences. Early arrival or timely work is rewarded by her use of these sentences as examples to the class.

After the brief discussion of gnash, Ms. Romine announces the seatwork assignment for the day, which students may carry home to complete. With seatwork assigned, Ms. Romine now directs the class to break into previously arranged groups. The classroom has three major activity areas (see Figure 13.1). Twelve children (group 1) go to a teacher-led reading lesson on the rug area within the U-shaped arrangement of desks, eight children (group 2) go to learning centers (art, math, language, or listening) at the sides of the classroom, and five (group 3) remain at their desks to do assigned seatwork. Ms. Romine surveys the classroom from a chair in the rug area next to the front of the room. She monitors concentric rings of activity—from the rug, to the seats, to the centers.

This particular arrangement of groups lasts from 8:15 to 8:45, at which time groups rotate, while Ms. Romine stays in her chair on the rug. The directions for rotation are posted at the back of the room. Group 1 (rug) will go to seatwork, group 2 (learning centers) will go to the rug, and group 3 (seatwork) will go to centers. Students will rotate a second time at 9:15, so that by

Class rules let students know what is expected.

Routines help establish orderly classroom behavior.

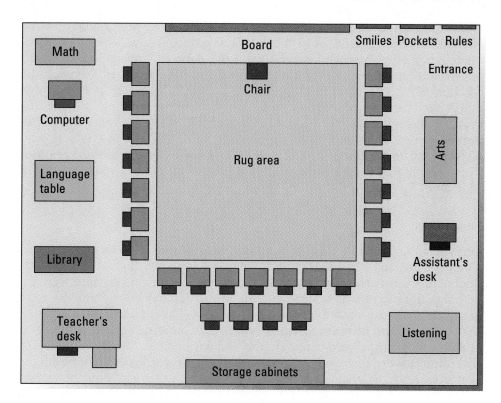

Figure 13.1
The Organization of One Fourth-Grade Classroom

9:45 all students will have had a small-group language arts lesson, will have worked at a learning center of their choice, and will have begun their seatwork for the day.

At the learning centers, each student is held accountable for following directions (Rule 2) and completing the assignment (Rule 6). Because it is mid-October, the theme at all the centers is autumn. At 8:30, two students are at the art center helping each other cut out varieties of leaves to post on barren trees on the bulletin board, three are at the math center working on fall word problems, two are at the language center developing fall stories that use specified words, and one is listening to a record.

Conforming with the school discipline policy, Ms. Romine applies rewards or punishments according to a program known as "Assertive Discipline" (see Strategic Solutions: Assertive Discipline). Ms. Romine awards "smiley faces" to the group for good behaviors. Each day, the class begins with four smilies posted on a bulletin board at the front. Orderly work through the rotation periods, a favorable written comment by the librarian or physical education teacher later in the day, exceptional adherence to the rules, or exemplary demonstration of them can each earn a smiley for the class. At the end of the day, Ms. Romine puts a marble in a jar for each smiley on the board. When the jar is full (120 marbles), the class will have a special treat, such as an educational movie.

Punishments (also known as "sanctions") are signaled through a bulletin board at the front of the classroom that contains a pocket for each of the

Class rules apply to students' independent work time.

Students receive rewards for good behavior.

Rule violations bring reminders and sanctions.

twenty-five children in class. All of the pockets are empty at 8:00, but if a child should break a rule, he or she will be asked to put a yellow "marker" in his or her pocket. A second infraction on the same day means the child will be asked to put a red marker in the pocket and have a conference with the teacher. With a third infraction, the child will be asked to put in a blue marker and have a conference with the teacher and the principal. No one this year has had a blue marker. Ms. Romine records who earns markers in her notebook. On Friday, she awards good conduct certificates to students who have not put any markers in their pockets and sends these home with the students' completed work folders (which are signed by parents and returned on Monday).

Prevention

Planning results in the prevention of behavior problems.

Perhaps you missed in this account any violation of rules or misbehavior. There weren't any while I was there. This classroom presented a climate conducive to student learning. Many of the conditions of this climate were established through *management planning* in which behavior problems were anticipated and prevented before the class met. This planning resulted in a seating arrangement that indicated appropriate activities and in class rules and procedures that were taught on the first day of class. Other conditions of this climate were the result of *managing skills* in which behavior problems that could not be anticipated were prevented through specific practices. Managing skills resulted in Ms. Romine's locating herself so that she could survey the situation to prevent incipient misbehavior. She also created smooth transitions between activities to minimize opportunities for misbehavior. Management planning and managing skills prevented most problems from developing in the classroom.

Intervention

Discipline and coping strategies let the teacher intervene when behavior problems occur.

By way of contrast, the school *discipline policy* and a repertoire of *coping strategies* available to the teacher focused on intervention. The discipline policy anticipated that rules would be either followed or broken. Consequences of following or breaking rules conformed to the school's Assertive Discipline policy. The evidences of this policy to any visitor were the smiley faces posted on the board and the set of behavior pockets, a few of which (later) would probably have markers in them. Coping strategies were invisible procedures used by Ms. Romine over and above the planned procedure to respond to different misbehavior. Most teachers spontaneously adapt their response to misbehavior by using somewhat different strategies to cope with persistent misbehavior.

A set of components such as management plans, managing skills, a school discipline policy, and coping strategies make up a **management system,** which is an assemblage of strategies to create and maintain a climate conducive to learning. In the rest of this chapter, you will have an opportunity to look at separate strategies that can be combined to form management systems. This survey should provide you with enough general information about management systems to help you understand how different strategies can work in support of each other. Later, as you enter your first year of teaching, the chapter should also provide you with enough specific information to help you build a management system to promote self-control in your classes.

MANAGEMENT PLANNING

Many new teachers wonder about how they will arrange their instructional setting, what rules they will use, or what procedures and routines they will adopt. Such thoughts are the beginning of management planning. Your decisions in these and related matters should fall into place as you make *instructional* plans. Your choice of instructional goals and objectives, for example, should affect your choice of learning activities, and your choice of learning activities should, in turn, affect your arrangement of the instructional setting, choice of rules, and so on. Thinking through the implications of your instructional plans will help you make management decisions.

> Instructional goals affect management decisions.

Seating Arrangements

Desks were once bolted to the floor and uniformly arranged in rows to permit teachers to survey groups at a glance, to facilitate recitation and testing, to inhibit communication between students, and to make the sweeping of floors efficient. Many rooms today are still arranged in this pattern, but the bolted chairs have been replaced by movable furniture. Most teachers today can arrange their instructional setting to facilitate different learning activities.

How you arrange your instructional environment depends on what you want your students to do and what helps them do it. *Environmental psychologists* study how settings affect activities, and several studies of alternative classroom settings suggest that the thoughtful arrangement of furniture or equipment can help students learn in expected ways (see Table 13.1). Expected behavior in activities is known as **on-task behavior.** Traditional rows promote more on-task behavior in lecture, seatwork, or recitation than do tables or clusters of desks (Bennett & Blundell, 1983; Wheldall & Lam, 1987). Desks arranged in a circle, however, promote more on-task behavior in a whole-group discussion than do clusters of desks or traditional rows (Rosenfield, Lambert & Black, 1985). Tables, clusters of desks, and designated group areas appear to be the best arrangements for promoting cooperative learning. Finally, casual interaction of young pupils with the teacher is better facilitated by a rug area than by a desk area (Zifferblatt, 1972).

> Different seating arrangements are best for different learning tasks.

On-task behavior in one seating arrangement is often considered *off task* in another arrangement. Let's take the example of students seated at their desks. If they are given seatwork, a group discussion would be distracting, cooperative activity would often be suspect, and casual interactions between students would probably be interpreted as socializing. Ms. Romine expected seatwork to be completed independently. Extensive cooperative work, which was encouraged by the tables at the learning centers, was *not* expected at the

Table 13.1   Learning Activities and Seating Arrangements

Learning Activity	Seating Arrangement	Student Behaviors
Lecture/seatwork	Rows	Individual work, listening, note taking
Whole-group discussion	Circle	Student-to-teacher, student-to-student communications
Cooperative groups	Clusters/tables/areas	Work shared by students independently of teacher
Small-group discussion	Rug area	Informal communication of young students and teacher

desks, where students were to work alone. Research tells us that expected behaviors occur more often when seating arrangements are matched to the learning activity than when they are mismatched.

The situation is complicated by the findings of research on effective classroom management. This research suggests that one characteristic of effective managers is that they engage students in a variety of learning activities (Emmer, Evertson & Anderson, 1980; Evertson & Emmer, 1982). But such variation can pose a significant problem for the design of an instructional environment because it has to change to facilitate these activities and change itself can be disruptive. Change in the instructional environment needs to occur routinely if it is to result in effective management.

strategic solutions

Designing Seating Arrangements

The implication of the research on seating arrangements is that you should *design the seating arrangement to suit your learning activities.* Such designs can help you achieve your educational objectives. However, the design of seating arrangements is complicated by the need to accommodate changes in the learning activity that you have chosen for a particular time.

You can implement change in the seating arrangement in one of two ways. You can either designate different "activity areas" or adopt a "home base" arrangement. Activity areas require students to move around. Note how in Ms. Romine's class students were grouped and then, during the first two hours, rotated through three different activity areas—the rug, the desks, and the learning centers. Activity areas may enable a high school teacher to use limited equipment efficiently. In contrast, the home base arrangement requires moving the desks, but it allows the whole class to participate in every activity at the same time. A math teacher, for example, might normally seat students in rows (the home base) but ask students on a given day to rearrange their desks into groups of four for a lesson requiring cooperative learning.

Because preschool and elementary teachers have students who are often located in the same room for several hours at a time, they are more likely than secondary teachers to divide their rooms into different activity areas. And because secondary teachers have students for only forty-five minutes or less each day, they are more likely than preschool and elementary teachers to use a home base arrangement from which they depart from time to time. The more often students change instructional environments during the day, the more attractive the home base arrangement becomes.

Finally, some characteristics of the seating arrangement should not change with changes in the learning activity. First, according to Edmund Emmer (1987), you should always be able to survey the entire group from where you stand or sit. If you can see all of your students, they all can see you, and you can monitor all activities. Second, heavy traffic areas—such as at the room entrance, around the pencil sharpener, or around your desk—should not be congested. You and your students need to be able to move easily about the room when movement is appropriate. Third, you should store frequently used materials in easily accessible but uncongested areas. Ms. Romine stored materials in cupboards lining the back of her room and kept several feet of free space in front of them.

The seating arrangement represents only the most visible and thoroughly researched aspect of the environmental setting. Other aspects you may need to consider are storage or placement of equipment, glare on the chalkboard, unevenness of heating or cooling, and special arrangements for special learners (cf. Tessmer & Harris, 1992; Zabel & Zabel, 1996). Management planning can prevent the emergence of off-task behavior due to any one of these environmental conditions.

Rules and Procedures

At the beginning of the 1980s, a number of researchers studied effective classroom managers in order to identify how their instructional approach differed from those of less effective managers (Emmer, Evertson & Anderson, 1980; Evertson & Emmer, 1982). They focused on teachers' use of **rules,** or explicit expectations for participation in an activity, and **procedures,** or sequences of steps in courses of action.

Effective classroom rules are clear and enforceable.

Most teachers gave their students four to six rules at the beginning of the year. The researchers discovered that effective classroom managers did *not* differ from less effective managers in the number of rules that they taught students or in how long they spent doing so. Rather, effective managers differed from less effective ones in two ways. First, the rules and procedures of effective managers were *clear* and *enforceable*. Examples of clear and enforceable rules are provided in Table 13.2.

An example of an *un*clear and *un*enforceable rule is "Students may not talk without permission." This rule contains a double negative ("not . . . without") and is therefore unclear. It also is unenforceable. Should a student who asks someone for the loan of a pencil be punished? Is silence of all but one or two students appropriate to a variety of learning activities? In general, rules must be reasonable to be enforceable.

Students should learn and understand rules at the beginning of the year.

Second, effective classroom managers made *comprehension* of rules and procedures one of their first instructional objectives at the beginning of the school year or term. In the elementary grades, comprehension of rules and procedures was often taught through rehearsal and discussions of example situations. Students learned not only what the teacher meant by a rule such as "Respect others" but also how to follow routine procedures, such as where and when to hand in homework, how to take turns by raising hands, and so on. On the secondary level, many of the basic rules and procedures taught in elementary school had already been mastered, but effective classroom managers still provided students with a handout or expected them to take notes on the rules and procedures for their class (see Deepening Your Knowledge

Table 13.2   Some Common Class Rules

Elementary Level
1. Be polite and helpful.
2. Respect other people's property.
3. Listen quietly while others are speaking.
4. Do not hit, shove, or hurt others.
5. Obey all school rules.

Secondary Level
1. Bring all needed materials to class.
2. Be in your seat and ready to work when the bell rings.
3. Respect and be polite to all people.
4. Listen and stay seated when someone is talking.
5. Respect other people's property.
6. Obey all school rules.

Source: for elementary, Evertson, Emmer et al., 1994, pp. 21–22; for secondary, Emmer, Evertson et al., 1994, pp. 22–23.

deepening your knowledge base

An Experienced Math Teacher Introduces Class Rules

Divide into small groups and read out loud the following script, each person in turn reading aloud one statement. When you are finished, appoint a secretary, and answer the discussion questions for your group (with each person other than the secretary answering a question). After your small group has finished, reassemble in the larger group to comparc and contrast answers.

T1:   Okay, now I'm going to pass out some classroom rules to you.

T2:   Be sure to keep these.

T3:   You'll be required to keep them in your folder all year long.

T4:   I'm going to hand them out to you today, and I know that this is asking a lot to keep them from the first day of school, but hang on to these.

T5:   Okay, did everybody get a set of classroom rules?

T6:   Now I'm going to go over these, and if you have any questions at any time, please be sure to ask me.

T7:   Also, after we go over these, I'm going to ask you to sign your name on the back of the card telling me that you have read these rules, that you understand them, and that you realize what's going to happen if you don't follow them.

T8:   Any time you sign your name to something, that's very, very important.

T9:   Does anybody have a checking account? No?

T10: Does anyone have a car?

T11: Okay, did you have to sign a title or anything for a loan?

T12: Any time you sign your name to something, make sure that you know what you are signing for because you could be held liable for that.

T13: Okay, let's start at the first.

T14: Number one—follow school standards.

. . .

T33: Okay, part two—follow classroom standards.

T34: First of all, be in your seat when the last bell rings in order not to be tardy.

T35: After the third unexcused tardy, you will receive one daily grade of zero.

T36: Now, when the bell rings and you're running through this door, are you tardy?

Class: Yes.

T37: Yes, you are because you're supposed to be in your seat when the bell rings.

T38: If you are up there sharpening your pencil when the bell rings, are you tardy?

Class: Yes.

T39: Yes, because you're supposed to be in your seat when the bell rings.

(Continued on next page)

T40: So make sure that in that five-minute period during which you come in that you sharpen your pencil and are ready for class to begin.

Source: Brooks, 1985, p. 66

Discussion Questions

1. What statements give students the impression that this teacher is organized?

2. What signals you that comprehending the rules is the teacher's objective?

3. Does this introduction to classroom rules support the development of self-control? Why or why not?

Base: An Experienced Math Teacher Introduces Class Rules). On the first or second day, comprehension of rules and procedures was one of the instructional objectives of effective classroom managers at all levels, and students participated in learning activities to achieve this goal.

Should students help formulate the rules? Educators are divided on this issue. On the one hand, research by Jean Piaget and Lawrence Kohlberg (reviewed in Chapter 6) suggested that reasoning about rules is related to moral development. More specifically, opportunities to *formulate* rules help develop students' self-control. On the other hand, research by Diana Baumrind and Daniel Hart (also reviewed in Chapter 6) suggested that an authoritative teacher (who is controlling but reasonable and communicative) promotes reasonableness by example. More specifically, understandable *explanations* and *discussions* of rules should develop self-control. It appears that alternative ways of developing self-control may complement, more than contradict, one another.

> Self-control may be developed in different ways.

Effective classroom managers make comprehension of rules and procedures one of their first instructional objectives. These children in Santa Ana, California, are learning to come back quietly from the library.
(Spencer Grant/Liaison International)

Developing Rules and Procedures

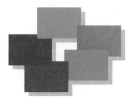

Strategies that apply research on management planning are relatively straightforward. First, *develop a clear and enforceable set of rules and procedures.* These should suit the learning activities in which students will participate, the age of the learners, and the subject matter. Keep rules positive and reasonably specific. You may occasionally use a particular prohibition ("No eating in class"), but almost all prohibitions can be stated positively as goals. "Don't be late" can be stated as *"Be on time"*; "Don't forget paper and pencil," as *"Be prepared"*; "Don't interrupt," as *"Speak in turn"*; and so on. Keep the list short. More than six rules signal that behaviors are too specific and should be grouped under a more general behavior.

Rules have to be reasonable in order to be enforceable. At a minimum, you should indicate why a rule is needed and discuss examples of its application. One of the best ways to ensure that rules are reasonable is to invite students to participate in a rule-setting discussion on the first day of class. Accept most suggestions, and feel free to make a suggestion or two of your own. When your students have finished, edit the list with them to ensure that it is short and that rules are stated positively. After the list is finalized, post an oversized version of it where everyone can read the rules. If the students are in elementary school, also send the list home with other general information.

In addition to developing rules, you should plan procedures for conducting specific activities and for handling academic work (Emmer, 1987). Students may need to be introduced to expectations in various types of activities. For example, elementary students need to know if they should raise their hand to participate in a discussion. Students also need to be made aware of the procedures that you use for handling academic work, from homework paper formats, to grading policies, to make-up work (see Table 13.3).

Second, *develop students' comprehension and acceptance of rules and procedures.* Rules are easier to teach through a discussion than through a demonstration. Explanation or discussion of rules should have the cognitive objective of comprehension and the affective objective of acceptance. Students are much more likely to follow rules they understand and accept than rules they merely understand. Procedures, in contrast, are often more easily taught through a demonstration than through a discussion. To show elementary students how to line up, for example, you may decide to orient them to the library or gym, ask them to line up, and remind them about being quiet in the halls so as not to disturb other classes. To introduce secondary students to your routines for handling homework, you may ask them to take out a sheet of paper and format it (name, class, and so on) in the manner that you want homework formatted.

Table 13.3   *Some Common Class Procedures*

Routine Activity Procedures

How to participate in one or more learning activities:

   Reading circle (small-group oral reading and discussion)

   Seatwork (written responses during independent work)

   Two-way presentations (whole-group discussions)

   One-way presentations (lecture)

   Mediated presentations (such as filmstrips)

   Silent reading

   Construction (building a product from materials)

   Games (with learning goals, rules, and strategies)

   Play (fun with no obvious instructional goals)

   Transition (into and out of other activities)

   Housekeeping (cleaning up)

How to obtain assistance from the teacher

Routine Work Procedures

Communication of assignments and work requirements

Make-up work and absences

Teacher monitoring and student completion of assignments

Feedback on progress and failure to complete work

Grading and record keeping

Source: Adapted from Berliner, 1983, pp. 4–11; and Emmer, 1987, pp. 237–238

Evaluation: Developing Rules and Procedures

Management planning has traditionally been the responsibility of the teacher. Long before the first day, a teacher will often work out the managerial implications of activities planned to achieve academic goals. Evidence from research on a program to improve management planning suggests that teachers trained to plan in this way have classrooms more ready for school, use space more effectively, and have more appropriate and suitable procedures and routines than do teachers not trained to be effective management planners (Evertson, 1985).

Nevertheless, many educators have recently questioned whether management planning promotes students' self-control. A teacher can plan the instructional environment and classroom rules in great detail, but if her or his managerial style is authoritarian, obedience to the rules does not develop self-control, but compliance, based on a belief in authority. The development of self-control requires a degree of autonomy or independence.

So it is not enough for students to accept and follow rules if the goal is to develop self-control. To achieve that, students must independently judge rules as reasonable and enforcement as fair. They can be assisted in their judgment by the teacher modeling reason and consideration. They can also be assisted in their judgment if they propose rules, supply reasons for them, and discuss them. In other words, teachers have to plan for the development of self-control.

MANAGING SKILLS

After management planning, managing skills are necessary to prevent the occurrence of misbehavior. To identify managing skills in Ms. Romine's class, let's take another look at student activities during the first two hours. Figure 13.2 presents a time line, running from 7:50 to 9:45. We might call the first activity, which lasts from 7:50 to 8:04, "settling in." Students enter, greet

Managing skills help make the classroom run smoothly.

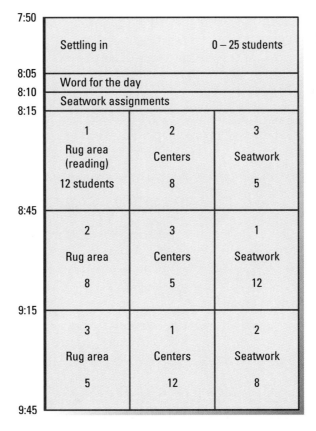

**Figure 13.2
A Time Line of Fourth-Grade Activities**

7:50			
	Settling in		0 – 25 students
8:05	Word for the day		
8:10	Seatwork assignments		
8:15	1 Rug area (reading) 12 students	2 Centers 8	3 Seatwork 5
8:45	2 Rug area 8	3 Centers 5	1 Seatwork 12
9:15	3 Rug area 5	1 Centers 12	2 Seatwork 8
9:45			

think it through

Consider this problem that a novice preservice teacher has **IDENTIFIED** and **REPRESENTED.**

What to Expect

My biggest fear about teaching is not being prepared. I worry that when I find a teaching job, I may have to begin immediately without being able to look at textbooks or curriculum guides. I think that I would probably panic trying to think of things to do the first day of class. My question to experienced teachers is, "How did you prepare yourselves for your very first day of teaching, and how did you know what to do and say?"

Observe how an experienced practicing teacher **GENERATES SOLUTIONS** to this problem.

Most of my secondary school colleagues agree with me that it is not the first day that is tricky; it's the next! I used to teach music in elementary school, and the first day was extra challenging. Teaching an elective in elementary school can present some real problems because you have to take into account such a mix of maturity and attention span levels. You can't take very much for granted with children this age, and you're always on your toes because you don't want to lose anyone's attention. That can cause behavior problems. With elementary school children, I always planned to spend some time getting to know the students' names and doing some activities to help them start to know each other's names, too. Sometimes I tried pairing students randomly and having them interview each other. Then after a few minutes, I had each pair introduce the other to the whole class. This usually worked well, but not always—it's true that with some classes there were students who didn't pay attention during the "introductions" and who snickered and could make other children feel bad. That's why you really always need a backup plan or activity. Every class is different. What works wonders in one group might be a disaster with another group. Write down your plans and backup plans so that if you get nervous, you can just glance down and remind yourself that yes, you can try something else! Colleagues are a great source of ideas. And everybody gets nervous the first day. Even teachers who have taught for many years. Just try to be yourself.

Besides an introductions activity, I always did two other things the first day with elementary students. I explained my expectations and did something basic like have the students understand about tuning their instruments so we could play together. Some little kids really didn't know much about their instruments, and with string players especially I had to look at how they held their bow and lots of other things. I tried to be really encouraging. I think music education is very important and meaningful for children in lots of ways, and it helps them in their school subjects, so encouragement and accomplishment are key.

In middle and secondary school, the first day is pretty much eaten up by my statements of rules and expectations. With this age group this could easily take up one class, if not two, with explanations and discussions, but it's a good idea not to spend too much time on expectations before getting right to learning and preparing for a concert. I think it's the same in all classes, math or history or phys ed. Be clear about your rules, and get right into some work. The students need this kind of focus. I have also always had several days of in-services with teacher planning days before the students actually arrive, and this is a big help for getting prepared. You can also spend some time with these older students letting them get to know each other's names, and you also need to learn their names, of course.

Overplan so that you have confidence that there is no way you will run out of activities. And remember, everyone can get nervous, so it's okay.

Eugénie Edmonds
Covington Middle School
Austin, Texas

think it through, continued

EVALUATE this problem's possible multiple solutions while you think about the dynamic process of problem solving.

Let's begin by looking at the teacher's response to the general question "What do you do on the first day?" The answer was to have elementary students introduce themselves, and at all levels, to teach your rules and procedures, among other expectations. How do we evaluate this response from a problem-solving perspective? Let's focus on teaching rules and procedures.

It helps to realize that rules are often goals and as such represent instructional problems. Even if you are not familiar with content or curriculum, you can develop a plan to achieve these goals. Your plan may even involve the students in a discussion to set the goals or rules for the class.

Let's say that Rule 1 is, "Keep your hands and feet to yourself." You may have suggested it, or your students may have suggested it. What does this rule mean? Why is it needed? These are good questions for discussion.

As an example of teaching a procedure, the experienced teacher suggests tuning instruments, but you might teach any other important procedure on the first day. Teaching a procedure generally involves a demonstration rather than a discussion. Discussing how to tune an instrument, for example, is not as instructive as seeing and hearing it tuned and then trying to tune it oneself. Important procedures exist for every learning situation from kindergarten through grade 12 and for every teaching field. What are the important procedures in your setting? The answer to this question will provide you with abundant material for the first day's lesson, regardless of the curriculum.

The experienced teacher emphasizes that it's okay to be nervous and to overplan. That is good advice. As Chapter 3 mentioned, planning will boost your confidence. My only advice is to set your notes aside when you begin to teach. Have them there for moral support, but trust what remains in your head to provide most of the guidance for what you will say and do. If you need to refer to your notes to make sure you didn't forget something important, they are always there, but try to speak spontaneously. You will find that your awareness of an audience will help you adapt what you have to say to suit your listeners' needs. You may even find yourself asking questions rather than doing most of the talking—a bit daring, but a move that will get you off to the right start as a teacher of thinking.

If you decide to ask questions, and you are not ready to discuss the content or curriculum of the year ahead, consider asking about what your students have learned. The experienced teacher pursues this line of questioning a little, but you can pursue it further. Be honest with your students. Explain to them that you need a little more information about them to decide what and how to teach. Students generally do not mind telling you about what they already know, and the younger they are, the more eager they will be to tell you. If any problems arise, they too provide you with information about how to plan for the next day.

Next consider what they tell you, and how they act, in relation to what you anticipate teaching on the second day. With these "givens" in mind, you will have begun your problem-solving journey into teaching.

their friends, turn in their homework, settle in their seats, and begin work on the word for the day. Ms. Romine participates in routines of her own: greeting students, collecting permission slips, and taking attendance. From 8:05 to 8:10 she leads the class in a brief discussion of the word for the day, ending the initial task. From 8:10 to 8:14 she goes over the morning seatwork activity while students listen. From 8:14 to 8:16 students move to their activity areas and begin work. For the next ninety minutes, students' time is distributed among three activities. How does Ms. Romine manage all this? She does so through strategies for (1) managing students' use of time, (2) managing demands on attention, and (3) communicating effectively.

Research on Managing Skills

Research on managing skills has developed significantly since the first studies of managing behaviors were conducted by Jacob Kounin (1970). Kounin used videotapes of classroom practices of effective and less effective teachers to identify managing skills that seemed to prevent misbehavior. Since his work, researchers from a variety of disciplines (psychology, sociology, anthropology, and linguistics) have investigated in great detail what keeps students on task (Cazden, 1986; Green, 1983). The results of this more recent research have confirmed that a set of identifiable skills are used by teachers to guide students in learning activities (e.g., Brooks, 1985; Dorr-Bremme, 1990; Evertson, 1987).

Managing Students' Use of Time

The amount of time that a student spends engaged in an activity depends on the activity itself, but on average, students spend between 50 percent and 75 percent of their class time engaged in learning. At the low end of engagement is seatwork, during which students are engaged in an assigned task only about half of the time. At the high end of engagement is constructive activity (or the making of a product), during which students are engaged three-fourths of the time or more. A significant amount of research has been devoted to how we can increase students' *time-on-task* because greater time-on-task is associated with more appropriate behavior and higher achievement (Doyle, 1986; Gump, 1982; Karweit, 1985).

> Planning can ensure that students spend sufficient time-on-task.

strategic solutions

Increasing Students' Time-on-Task

There are many ways to increase students' time-on-task that are associated with reduction in rates of misbehavior (Stallings, 1985).

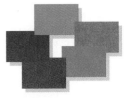

strategic solutions, continued

- One way (which we have discussed in previous chapters) is to *plan instruction well*. Well-planned classes tend to have higher engaged time and less misbehavior than poorly planned classes.

- A second way is to *maintain high rates of interaction with students*. High rates minimize seatwork, which is associated with relatively low time-on-task. Even in activities in which students are relatively autonomous and interacting with each other, your circulation and engagement with students will be reflected in students' engagement with their work.

- A third way is to *maintain a group focus*. Skills for maintaining a group focus include **group alerting,** which is the inclusion of all members of a group in a learning activity (Kounin, 1970). Examples of group alerting are calling on students in a large group in an unpredictable way and asking for a choral response from members of a small group. Whatever the size of the group, group alerting keeps everyone in the group actively learning.

Evaluation: Increasing Students' Time-on-Task

Increasing student time-on-task contributes to students' achievement and prevention of misbehavior (Irving & Martin, 1982; Walberg, 1986). The way a teacher plans instruction, interacts with a group, and focuses on the group can all be important. Failing to plan instruction, assigning large amounts of seatwork, or working extensively with only a few students out of the group decreases overall time-on-task and is likely to increase misbehavior.

Do these efforts to increase time-on-task promote self-control in students? The answer is probably yes. By carefully planning instruction, by interacting with the class, and by maintaining a group focus, you are a model of self-regulation of activity, and this model is not lost on students. Remember back in Chapter 6 how important parental interaction and involvement were to the development of moral reasoning of children? Such parents are models of self-regulation in games and activities. They obey rules of various kinds (which generally enhance safety and enjoyment) as well as teach the rules. Teachers are also models of self-regulation, but our domain is a little closer to the workplace. By regulating your behavior as a teacher, you are a model for students who are learning to regulate their behavior as learners.

Managing Demands on Attention

Teachers may have to give attention to overlapping situations.

If you have ever been in an important conversation and needed to attend to something else—a phone ringing, a baby crying, a child tugging at your sleeve—you have experienced what Kounin (1970) called an **overlapping situation,** meaning your attention was required outside the activity in which you were involved. Overlapping situations occur often during instruction with multiple groups. You may be an elementary teacher in a reading circle, and a boy comes over to have you check his seatwork. Or you may be a phys-

Teachers must often handle overlapping situations by doing two things at once. This teacher is teaching the class while keeping her eye on the board—where an error is being made. *(Michael Newman/ PhotoEdit)*

ical education teacher working with a beginner group in volleyball and notice players in the "advanced" court disagreeing over a call. Or you may be a math teacher in the middle of a lesson and hear a distracting conversation in the hallway. All of these situations need to be managed, but none involves misbehavior.

Another situation that requires your attention occurs when behavior begins to deviate from your expectations but is not yet clearly misbehavior. Many experienced teachers pick up quickly on such deviations from the norm and respond by communicating their expectations. Kounin (1970) used the term **withitness** to describe a teacher's awareness of what is going on in the classroom and communication of that awareness to one or more students. "Jimmy, center time is over—come to the rug area." "Henrietta [who is talking to Angie], it's time to get to work." Sometimes teachers do not pay attention until behavior is so far off task that intervention is required. A teacher who is "withit" will be aware of what is going on when someone is off task and will communicate expectations to prevent a misbehavior from occurring.

> Teachers must be aware of students who are beginning to get off task.

strategic solutions

Handling Overlapping Situations

Your ability to reallocate attention will sometimes determine whether a misbehavior occurs. To avoid the occurrence of misbehavior in overlapping

situations, *monitor groups to detect such situations.* Monitoring all the activities in a class permits you to detect overlapping situations early. For example, Ms. Romine monitored activities of all three student groups from her chair on the rug. She could continue her instruction of the reading group from the chair even as she observed students doing seatwork or participating in the centers. Her view of student activities allowed her to observe any divergence from expected behavior that might require more of her attention.

When an overlapping situation occurs, do not interrupt the students' activity in which you have been involved to attend to the other activity. For example, if you are in a reading circle and notice a girl approaching from her seat, indicate that children are to continue reading, and then attend for a moment to the girl. You might direct her to a classmate for help. For two boys quietly socializing during seatwork across the room, you might wait until someone in the circle has finished reading before sharing a general expectation, such as "I expect everybody at their seats to be working."

When misbehaviors are about to develop, redirect the student by indicating you are aware of the situation and by communicating your expectations. This demonstration of withitness should nip any misbehavior in the bud. You will find that experience will help you identify behaviors that are frequently preludes to misbehavior, such as lingering around the pencil sharpener, wandering when seeking materials, or concealing things (by passing notes or whispering). Rather than confront students and risk real misbehavior ("Let me have that note"), you would be better off redirecting the students by indicating your expectations about what they should be doing. Back up your expectations with a general rule, such as "Follow all directions," so that you do not have to redirect the students repeatedly.

Evaluation: Handling Overlapping Situations

We know that effective handling of overlapping situations and withitness are both associated with effective teaching (Emmer, Evertson & Anderson, 1980; Evertson, 1985; Evertson & Emmer, 1982). The remaining question is, "Do they promote self-control?" The answer is that they probably do. A teacher who is actively monitoring student learning is on task as a teacher and a model of task orientation. Reminders of expectations may support efforts at self-control, but consider asking, "What should you be doing?" to help a younger student remind him- or herself of expectations. Older children and adolescents may need a more detailed procedure to support self-control. (The design of these procedures will be described later in the chapter because it is generally regarded as an intervention.)

Communicating Effectively

Much of what you have already learned about managing skills involves effective communication, but what makes communication effective? Scholars such as Carol Evertson are beginning to discover that an environment conducive to learning is often maintained through communication of expectations in moment-by-moment interactions (Evertson & Weade, 1989). Research on classroom discourse is revealing that routine use of language to signal or cue activity is important, as is appropriate interpretation of such signals or cues. In particular, study has focused on the use of language to signal, or "mark," transitions between activities and on miscommunications that result from misinterpretation of language.

Typically, transitions are not planned; rather, they are marked by the teacher with a routine phrase or action within a specific context. A **marker** is a cue that routinely signals the boundary of a context or activity. It might be as simple as a kindergarten teacher saying, "Let's see who's not here today." Or a high school teacher might stand in front of a class a few seconds after the bell and say, "Okay, let's get started" to cue the beginning of the lesson. Markers are not stimuli to elicit orienting responses (such as a flick of the lights or the sound of a bell), but they are routine uses of language that cue appropriate responses. Teachers typically use markers to signal changes in activities.

Markers often serve to create orderly transitions, but what happens when the activity changes and the appropriate marker is not used? A study of one kindergarten class (Dorr-Bremme, 1990) found the absence of a marker at the end of one activity was itself meaningful, signaling to the children that "the floor is now open to anyone who has something to say" (p. 389). The teacher was unaware that through the absence of a marker, she signaled a transition to an activity that she did not intend, creating what appeared to her to be misbehavior but that actually was an orderly transition in the past experience of her pupils. Appropriate behavior (from the teacher's perspective) was restored only when she happened to utter a marker that in the experience of the students signaled a transition to a listening activity (such as "All right").

Markers can also be a source of miscommunication when they are present but students do not interpret them in expected ways. A white teacher, for example, might use directive language to communicate expectations to an African-American or Asian-American child and expect the child to look him or her in the eye when receiving directions. African-American and Asian-American children, however, are often taught not to look in the eye of an adult who is speaking to them. It is a sign of disrespect. As a result, these children will typically look at the floor or beyond the teacher. A white teacher may interpret this behavior as a sign of inattentiveness, when actually the children are doing their best to indicate respect and a willingness to meet expectations. Other equally significant misinterpretations can occur around expectations of turn taking and what teachers interpret as speaking out of turn (Morine-Dershimer & Beyerbach, 1987).

Transitions can be marked by using routine verbal cues.

Cultural differences may create miscommunication.

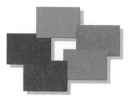

Marking Transitions

The study of how discourse influences classroom behavior is so new that we have only case studies of it. Nevertheless, some conclusions can be drawn. First, *mark transitions routinely and appropriately in order to manage them.* How you mark a given transition is up to you, but the more often that a particular marker is used in a given way, the more it becomes a signal of a specific type of transition. If "okay" followed by a pause is the way you begin a class, omission of this marker can signal that class has not yet begun, even though you have started the lesson! Devising appropriate routines for changing activities, and using them consistently, will smooth the flow of activities.

Second, *be sensitive to the cultural context of some cues.* What you believe to be signals or cues for specific behaviors may sometimes be bound to your particular culture. Children may or may not be reared in a culture that shares these cues. You need to be sensitive to cultural differences on these matters so that, when students fail to respond as expected to culture-dependent cues for behavior, you do not assume that the student is deliberately ignoring you.

Evaluation: Marking Transitions

Research on classroom discourse (also called sociolinguistic research) is opening a valuable perspective on how a positive learning environment is maintained or undermined by the teacher's use of language. In particular, researchers are discovering that effective teachers have better communication techniques than less effective teachers (Evertson & Weade, 1989). This research deepens our understanding of what it means to use smooth transitions between activities, and it has the potential to make other contributions with regard to classroom management. Study of classroom discourse is helping us become aware that misunderstandings often have their source in miscommunications.

This research may have a significant impact on teacher perception of student self-control. Through misinterpretation, teachers sometimes identify what they believe to be a misbehavior when none exists. If a student practicing basketball free throws, for example, does not want to give up the ball to another student after a successful shot, the teacher needs to realize that a successful shot is a cue in "street ball" to continue shooting. The ball will be courteously turned over after the first miss. No misbehavior exists, although the student's behavior might not follow the teacher's expectations for taking turns. An understanding of cultural expectations can help a teacher avoid provoking real misbehavior and appreciate different ways students express self-control.

DISCIPLINE POLICIES

In the context of schools, **discipline** can be defined as an intervention to stop a misbehavior. A *discipline policy* is a plan of intervention to stop misbehavior. Discipline policies are set by teachers, principals, school boards, and state law. Virtually all schools have general discipline policies, and one of your first tasks is to find out the discipline policy of any school where you might work. Usually the principal or an assistant principal is responsible for seeing that the school (and district or state) discipline policy is carried out. From these general guidelines, teachers often have much more specific discipline policies that are translated into consequences for adhering to rules or violating them.

Historically, most disciplinary practices have been punitive. As you learned in Chapter 8, the frequent use of punishment to promote learning is counterproductive. The case against the use of punishment to promote appropriate social behavior is similar but makes two additional points: (1) **corporal punishment,** or any punishment administered to the body (such as paddling), is overused, and (2) alternative techniques to change behavior are underused.

Corporal punishment is widely used as a disciplinary practice to stop misbehavior. Only three states have banned its use, but twenty-one have provision for its limited use (Rich, 1989). In other states, local boards can ban it or set guidelines for its use. In some states and districts, paddling is widely practiced, particularly in elementary schools. Despite widespread practice, corporal punishment has disadvantages that often outweigh its advantages, particularly in schools (see Deepening Your Knowledge Base: The Pros and Cons of Corporal Punishment).

While corporal punishment is overused, alternatives to punishment continue to be underused. A survey of over three hundred teachers, for example, found that their most common method of "behavior change" was a verbal reprimand. Positive comments clearly came in second at all grade levels and tended to decrease as grade level increased (Brown & Payne, 1988). These survey results are confirmed by extensive classroom observations at both primary and secondary school levels (Merrett & Wheldall, 1987; Wheldall, Houghton & Merrett, 1988). Well-known and well-researched alternatives to punishment are underused.

In the next few pages, you will learn about two types of discipline policies that focus not on punishment but on its alternatives. **Positive discipline policies** are plans to stop misbehavior through teaching specific characteristics or skills, and **problem-solving discipline policies** are plans to stop misbehavior through reasoning with students about a situation.

Positive Discipline Policies

Some teachers, schools, and even districts are adopting positive discipline policies, which may or may not be formalized in a discipline program. Such

> Discipline policy is set by the school, district, and state.

> Corporal punishment may do more harm than good.

> Alternatives to punishment are not used often enough.

deepening your knowledge base

The Pros and Cons of Corporal Punishment

In Chapter 8, you learned that punishment leads to emotional responses, such as fear, anger, and resentment, that can interfere with learning. These responses also interfere with learning appropriate social behaviors. Very few educators suggest that a well-ordered classroom can be run without any punishment, but many believe that well-ordered classrooms can be run without *corporal* punishment. The pros and cons of the issue have recently been summarized (Vockell, 1991).

Advantages of corporal punishment. Corporal punishment has three advantages over other behavior control techniques. First, it is almost always perceived as unpleasant. Second, it can be administered quickly and be over quickly. It is relatively easy to administer, although this advantage does not pertain to all situations, particularly when supervision of paddling is required. Third, it is a clear consequence of misbehavior. There is not much room for ambiguity about what will happen if a rule is broken as long as corporal punishment is consistently administered. This last advantage is shared by other forms of punishment if they consistently follow misbehavior.

Disadvantages of corporal punishment. The list of disadvantages is longer than the list of advantages. First, corporal punishment is not likely to be logically related to the misbehavior. For example, paddling is not logically related to smoking in a washroom. Second, corporal punishment does not lead to positive behavior. Being paddled to stop doing something does not direct the child in what to do. Third, corporal punishment can model socially inappropriate behavior. Hitting a student, even if in an approved way, is not a way to show a student how to resolve a problem. Fourth, corporal punishment is often administered in frustration or anger, leading to the practical problem of potential abuse of the child, injury, or litigation. These four disadvantages exist *in addition to* the universal disadvantage of punishment—that it results in emotional side effects that interfere with learning.

The author Edward Vockell concluded that "although the advantages sometimes outweigh the disadvantages among young children in family settings, the disadvantages are often more prevalent in school settings" (1991, p. 283). This reasonable conclusion suggests that if your school allows (or promotes) the use of paddling, you might decide that the disadvantages outweigh the advantages and choose not to paddle your students.

Positive discipline policies aim to develop good social behavior.

policies range from programs like Assertive Discipline to **character education,** which is direct instruction in the moral norms of a culture. They share the goal of rewarding the development of socially useful characteristics or skills such as respect and responsibility. Unlike punitive control, positive discipline policies teach prosocial behaviors.

Assertive Discipline

Assertive Discipline is an intervention program created by educational consultants Lee and Marlene Canter to develop social behaviors through the teacher's communication of wants and needs to students and expression of approval or disapproval of student actions (Canter, 1976). (You read about Assertive Discipline at the beginning of this chapter in the description of Ms. Romine's classroom.) Class rules are special cases of teacher wants and needs. Students who obey the rules receive reinforcement which, according to Lee Canter (1989), is the key to making Assertive Discipline work. Students who act inappropriately are punished, which is also necessary to have credible rules.

Punishment is always preceded by a warning and has several levels. Students who violate a rule typically receive a warning card in an individual behavior pocket posted on a board in the room. Further violations lead to other cards placed in the pocket. Punishments vary according to the policy of the school, the teacher, and the age of the child, but they might involve loss of privileges, time-out, or removal from the room. Teachers should adapt the system to their own needs and circumstances, but Canter did not encourage the use of corporal punishment.

Assertive Discipline incorporates a three-step cycle of positive discipline (Canter, 1989). First, *teach specific behaviors that are to be followed.* Instruction involves determining the rules and procedures for each specific situation and then teaching students how to follow them. You as the teacher must state the rules and procedures or write them on the board, model them, ask students to restate them, question students about them, and engage students in the activity to ensure an understanding of rules and procedures.

Second, *use "positive repetitions" to reinforce students who follow rules and procedures.* This reinforcement should involve a rephrased statement of the original rule or procedure. "Jeremy, just now you moved very quickly and quietly to the rug area." "Sonya, thank you for raising your hand." The behavior is reinforced and serves as a model to other students.

Third, *if misbehavior occurs, apply consequences outlined in the Assertive Discipline plan.* Canter (1989) suggested that the following of directions needs to be reinforced in at least two students before misbehavior is punished. This delay in punishment keeps your focus on the positive, provides models for a misbehaving student, and limits the extent to which misbehavior is used to gain attention. Punishment for misbehavior that continues should follow gradations of intensity.

Evaluation: Assertive Discipline

Lee Canter has expressed his concern that his program is better understood by teachers than by education professors, many of whom have been critical of his discipline program (e.g., Render, Padilla & Krank, 1989). Many examples of classroom behavior in Canter's writings appear simplistic to a veteran teacher, and his claims for research support for the program are broad and unqualified. Nevertheless, the program communicates clearly to teachers, and many have found enough value in it to continue its use.

A summary of fourteen studies between 1980 and 1986 (Emmer & Aussiker, 1990) found that teachers often perceived Assertive Discipline to be effective, but on balance the evidence of effects on the behavior of students was "decidedly mixed." In a dozen studies of the effects of Assertive Discipline, indications of serious student misbehavior (rates of referral for class disruptions, detention, suspension, truancy) went down in only a few cases. In a few cases they even went up—probably as a result of the systematic enforcement of a discipline policy. One unpublished study did suggest that off-task classroom behavior went down with the introduction of Assertive Discipline, but not enough research has yet been conducted to reach a firm conclusion regarding the effectiveness of the program.

Does Assertive Discipline develop self-control? No evidence has been found that, as presented, Assertive Discipline does. Can it develop self-control? The answer is that it probably can. If you use Assertive Discipline, you might consider using a rational form of it (as Ms. Romine did). Reward the group for appropriate behavior, and follow misbehavior with a signal that the student must either (1) exert greater self-control or (2) confer with you, the principal, or parent(s).

Character Education

Direct instruction in the moral norms of a culture has a long history, including extensive experimental implementation during the 1920s. Students read pointedly moral stories or poems, for example, and were expected to improve their character from reading and discussion. The test of whether their character had improved was often their ability to recognize or summarize the rules or moral precepts embedded in such exercises. Most teachers today construct similar lessons as a means of developing understanding of their classroom rules at the beginning of the year. Some teachers, particularly in private schools, conduct character lessons throughout the year using character-oriented readings and discussions.

Even though a few educators continue to recommend interventions based primarily on readings, most educational researchers are finding that *school climate* seems to have a greater impact on student values. In particular, (1) clear rules, (2) student ownership of them, (3) a supportive environment, and

Community service projects are frequently part of character education. These young people are participating in a program known as National Community Service. *(James D. Wilson/ Gamma Liaison)*

(4) satisfaction from conforming with desirable norms seem to have the greatest impact on student values (Leming, 1993; Lickona, 1991).

There is no consensus about how such a climate is best achieved, but one line of thinking (Walberg & Wynne, 1989; Wynne, 1991) emphasizes core practices such as assigning students responsibilities for school activities; engaging students in community service projects; keeping students connected with responsible, caring adults; maintaining high academic standards; and maintaining frequent, high-quality ceremonial activities. These practices all engage students in prosocial *behavior* and for that reason are generally considered a more effective way to develop values than are reading and discussion.

Although no unified theory of character education exists, and interventions are generally conducted on the school level, core practices can be translated into a general intervention strategy for the classroom. A strategy might consist of attempts to engage all students (behaving and misbehaving) in a number of different activities designed to create a classroom climate that fosters character development. To support the development of this climate, you might:

Assign students responsibilities for class academic and service activities

Engage students in a community service project

Sponsor an extracurricular activity and encourage universal participation in such activities

Maintain high academic standards

Incorporate ceremonial activities into class routines

A comprehensive list of practices is available (Lickona, 1993), but this short list represents a positive form of intervention that can supplement, rather than replace, existing policies and practices.

Evaluation: Character Education

Researchers long ago discovered that teaching rules or moral precepts is not enough to produce appropriate conduct. Social psychological research as well as classroom experience repeatedly affirmed that understanding and acting can be quite different, particularly for children (Lockwood, 1991; Pritchard, 1988). Accordingly, modern character education focuses on student participation and involvement in activities to foster characteristics such as responsibility, respect, and caring for others. Although several schools have reported reductions in misbehavior after the adoption of specific character education programs, almost no well-designed research yet exists to tell us whether this intervention technique really works (Leming, 1993).

Will character education promote self-control? The answer is uncertain, partly because practices associated with character education are inconsistent in this respect and partly because the question has not yet been researched (Lockwood, 1993). Some aspects of character education, such as student ownership of rules and involvement by teachers in student activities, probably have a positive impact on the development of self-control. Other aspects of character education, such as adult or peer pressure to engage in service activities, may develop conforming behaviors rather than self-control. There is much room for further research on these matters.

Problem-Solving Discipline Policies

Problem solving in discipline attempts to prevent misbehavior by reasoning with students.

Problem solving is at the heart of several discipline policies and programs designed to end misbehavior through reasoning with students. Two examples of such programs are Reality Therapy and Teacher Effectiveness Training. These programs are not the only ones that use a problem-solving approach to discipline (cf. Watson et al., 1989), but they have been widely discussed and have been the subject of effectiveness research.

Reality Therapy

Reality Therapy is an intervention designed by William Glasser (1965, 1990) to help emotionally distressed children and adults resolve problem behavior.

According to Glasser, a psychiatrist who has written extensively about education and discipline, misbehavior is an unrealistic means of fulfilling five basic needs: survival, love, power, fun, and freedom. Problem solving with students enables them to discover how to fulfill one or more of these unmet needs.

The Reality Therapy strategy of classroom management calls for (1) leading students in a discussion to formulate class rules, (2) holding class meetings to discuss problems related to schoolwork, and (3) following a problem-solving procedure when a student breaks a rule to meet a need.

- *Lead students in a discussion to formulate class rules at the beginning of the year.* You have already learned about leading a discussion to formulate rules. Glasser proposed that students also be asked to suggest consequences if rules are broken. Some will recommend punishment, but explain that you neither believe in nor want punishment, and then ask if students believe someone who has broken a rule has a problem. When they agree, ask them how a problem is solved. Try to lead students to the conclusion that problems are solved when people change what they are doing. Finally, write the rules down; then have everyone sign that they have read them and agree that if they break these rules, they will try to solve the underlying problem.
- *Hold class meetings regularly.* Although often led by the teacher, class meetings offer the teacher the opportunity to listen. Problems related to satisfying needs and doing quality work can be discussed in class meetings, following one of three meeting types. *Social problem-solving* meetings deal directly with problems of satisfying needs (for example, rule-setting meetings). *Open-ended* meetings deal with student interests in relation to the subject. *Educational-diagnostic* meetings provide feedback on student understanding of important concepts in the curriculum. Glasser (1986) recently modified Reality Therapy to deemphasize the role of class meetings and to emphasize the use of cooperative learning as a mode of instruction.
- *When a student breaks a rule, follow a problem-solving procedure.* First, ask the student to acknowledge that he or she has broken a rule ("What did you do?" "Did that break a rule?"). Second, try to solve the problem collaboratively with the student by identifying a more appropriate way for the student to satisfy a need ("What's something you could do to prevent this from happening again?"). In other words, gather information for a solution; the student does not have to be aware of needs she or he is trying to satisfy in order to work toward a solution. Third, ask the student to commit to this plan (an oral or written contract). Thus, a solution is established and a foundation laid for evaluating how well the plan works.

Evaluation: Reality Therapy

Reality Therapy did not develop a broad academic emphasis until the mid-1980s, so most evaluation studies previous to that date focused on its use as a discipline program rather than as a total management system. A summary of eleven studies between 1972 and 1985 (Emmer & Aussiker, 1990) found mixed to positive results. Improvements in academic performance and

strategic   solutions,   continued

long-term behavior were least convincing because they occurred with such irregularity. With only a few exceptions, however, referral rates and other short-term indications of misbehavior declined, even though the declines were not always clearly attributable to behavior improvements. Teachers may have been more effectively dealing with misbehavior in the context of their classes, or administrative handling of misbehavior may have changed.

The most convincing evidence was found in relation to students with chronic behavior problems, suggesting that Reality Therapy works best with such students. It may be that problem solving when students break a rule is more effective for establishing a climate conducive to learning than either classroom meetings or student participation in the formulation of rules. If accurate, this conclusion suggests that Reality Therapy works best as a problem-solving intervention strategy. Because the student makes significant contributions to the plan, Reality Therapy may enhance self-control (Heuchert, 1989), but the evidence is not conclusive.

strategic   solutions

Teacher Effectiveness Training

Teacher Effectiveness Training (TET) is an intervention to improve student-teacher relationships through communication skills and problem solving. It was developed by Thomas Gordon (1974), a clinical psychologist who has developed similar training courses for parents and leaders. Gordon posited that most misbehavior is the result of relationships that are not mutually satisfying and that the key to improving these relationships is "problem ownership" and a "no-lose" method of resolving conflicts.

The first step in communicating effectively with students about an unresolved problem is to *determine who owns the problem. Problem ownership* is the assumption of responsibility for a need that is not being met. *If the teacher owns the problem, communicate the unmet need through an "I-message."* An I-message includes three parts: (1) a nonjudgmental statement of student behavior, (2) its tangible effect on you, and (3) how that makes you feel:

> "Jimmy, when you are out of your seat, I have to interrupt what I am doing, and that frustrates me."

> "Clarissa, when you push Connie on the playground, I have to stop watching the little children on the jungle gym because I'm afraid Connie will be hurt."

Gordon suggested that when you own a problem, you need to send an I-message rather than a *you-message,* which accuses the student of misbehavior ("You are roaming around the room again," or "You are going to hurt her"). You-messages make a student feel defensive and cause him or her to protest or deny. Although I-messages can be overused, they are more likely than you-messages to lead the student to restrain his or her own behavior.

If the student owns a problem by sharing a concern, listen actively. Active listening, which is also called "reflective listening" or "empathic listening," involves summarizing the cognitive and affective content of a speaker's message as a way of responding to him or her (see Deepening Your Knowledge Base: An Example of Active Listening). It permits a student to feel understood, explore an unmet need related to the class, and develop a solution for him- or herself. At some point you may want to supply a direction for the conversation, but as you listen actively, you can help a student clarify a problem and develop his or her own solution.

In most cases, neither the teacher nor the student is entirely responsible for the problem. Shared responsibility exists. Gordon suggested that *if a problem is shared, use the no-lose method of conflict resolution.* This is a method of cooperative problem solving in which there is no winner or loser but only an attempt to satisfy the needs of both the teacher and student. The no-lose method often begins with an I-message, after which you actively listen to the student's reply.

Suppose a student comes late to class, and you talk to him briefly after class. You send the I-message, "Albert, when you come in five minutes after the second bell, I have to repeat the assignment, and that's frustrating me." Albert replies, "But Mrs. Jones, Mr. Smith's class is at the other end of the building, and he sometimes keeps us after the bell." You realize that the problem is shared, so you start using the no-lose method of conflict resolution.

The method consists of six steps, and at each step both you and the student need to provide input so that you can arrive at a plan that is likely to satisfy both needs. The six steps, which are simply a cooperative form of problem solving, are listed in Table 13.4, with a continuation of this example. Notice that the steps are almost identical to the problem-solving procedure you learned back in Chapter 1. The only differences are that problem identification has been omitted (it has already occurred) and that solution generation has been split into three steps: evaluating possible solutions, deciding which is best, and figuring out how to implement it.

Evaluation: Teacher Effectiveness Training

Between 1974 and 1982, eleven studies of Teacher Effectiveness Training were conducted (Emmer & Aussiker, 1990) to determine program effectiveness. Results suggested that teachers who were trained in TET implemented its practices and developed a more democratic attitude toward the use of authority. Effects on students were less consistent, and when effects on behavior were found, they tended to be small. Only one study looked at student achievement, and it found a positive effect for both math and reading. Like

Table 13.4   *The No-Lose Method of Conflict Resolution*

1. Define the problem (or conflict).
   Example: Student is late to class, but lateness is due to other teacher (shared problem)

2. Generate possible solutions.
   Example: Either student talks with other teacher, or you talk with other teacher

3. Evaluate the solutions.
   Example: Student will encounter other teacher tomorrow; you do not know other teacher

4. Decide which solution is best.
   Example: Student will have earlier opportunity to explain situation to other teacher

5. Determine how to implement the decision.
   Example: Student to talk to other teacher *before* other class begins

6. Assess how well the solution solved the problem.
   Example: Student will see you after class if late to class again tomorrow

Source: Gordon, 1974, p. 228

Reality Therapy, TET might be expected to influence self-control, but despite some indications that it improves attitudes toward class and even self, there has been little evidence yet that it improves self-control. Its greatest impact appears to be on the attitude of the teacher.

Positive discipline minimizes punishment and problem-solving promotes reasoning.

TET, Reality Therapy, character education, and Assertive Discipline are just four of the many programs for implementing intervention procedures when misbehavior occurs. Discipline policies and programs are often enacted schoolwide to develop some consistency in the expectations of students. According to an extensive study of secondary school disciplinary practices (Rutter et al., 1979), such general expectations may be more important than the particular rules or consequences developed by individual teachers for creating a climate conducive to learning. Most schools have discipline policies and programs that afford you an opportunity to set your own rules and consequences, giving you the decision of how or whether to punish and how or whether to reason with students. Although punitive practices are widespread, positive practices have greater instructional merit than punishment, and cooperative problem solving is more likely to develop discipline based on reasoning than is simple assertion of authority.

deepening your knowledge base

An Example of Active Listening

Student: I came in to see you to get your ideas about what I should write about in my theme.

Teacher: You're uncertain about what topic to choose, is that right?

Student: I sure am. I've stewed about this now for days, but I still haven't come up with anything. I knew you'd have an idea.

Teacher: You've really struggled with this, but no progress yet.

Student: What have other students written on that made a really good theme?

Teacher: You want a topic that would make an exceptionally good theme, right?

Student: Yeah. I just have to get an A on the theme so that I can make an A in the course.

Teacher: It sounds like you're feeling some strong pressures to get an A in the course.

Student: I'll say! My parents would really be upset if I didn't. They always want me to do as well as my older sister. She's really a brain.

Teacher: You feel they expect you to be just as good as your sister in school.

Student: Yeah. But I'm not like her. I have other interests. I wish my parents would accept me for what I am—I'm different from Linda. All she ever does is study.

Teacher: You feel you're a different kind of person than your sister, and you wish your parents recognized that.

Student: You know, I've never told them how I feel. I think I will now. Maybe they'll stop pushing me so hard to be a straight-A student.

Teacher: You're thinking maybe you should tell them how you feel.

Student: I can't lose. And maybe it'd help.

Teacher: Everything to gain, nothing to lose.

Student: Right. If they stopped pushing me, I wouldn't have to worry so much about my grades. I might even learn more.

Teacher: You might get even more out of school.

Student: Yeah. Then I could write a theme on a topic I'm interested in and learn something. Thanks for helping me with my problem.

Teacher: Anytime.

Source: Gordon, 1974, pp. 9–10

COPING STRATEGIES

So far, we have looked at management planning, managing skills, and discipline policies. We have not examined *coping strategies* that teachers use to deal with the problems presented by the behavior of individual students. For example, if you use Assertive Discipline, you will probably find that the same few students have to receive punishments despite your best efforts to "catch them being good." What should you do with such students? Coping

Coping strategies are used to deal with continuing misbehavior.

strategies allow you to continue to teach and offer students with behavior problems a measure of hope. Coping strategies are what you can use after you have done everything in your power to prevent and to be prepared for misbehavior.

How many students present troublesome behaviors in any class? Rates differ depending on the age of the students, the location of the school, and even techniques for identifying problems. Furthermore, what is a troublesome behavior for one teacher is not for another. Nevertheless, when asked to identify how many students were troublesome, one group of British elementary teachers indicated that about 15 percent of their students consistently posed problem behaviors, or about four per class (Wheldall & Merritt, 1988). Most of these students were boys, but then again most of the teachers were women. The interpretation of such studies is always difficult and subject to challenge, but you need an idea of what to expect.

Behavioral Control Strategies

Recently, Jere Brophy and Mary McCaslin published results from the Classroom Strategy Study (Brophy & McCaslin, 1992), a survey of disciplinary practices of ninety-eight elementary teachers nominated as average to outstanding in classroom management. The teachers were each observed to determine which of twenty-one interventions correlated with compliance. They were then surveyed about their use of forty-one ways to cope with eleven types of "problem students." The result was a large and revealing body of data on coping strategies, some of which involved teacher control and some of which supported self-control.

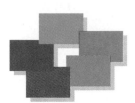

strategic solutions

Behavioral Control Strategies

Except perhaps for strategies that involved praise of students (a component of positive discipline policies), none of the observed practices of effective classroom managers was based on a discipline program. Most of the time, effective classroom managers used strategies that supported self-control:

- *Cue appropriate behavior*, or make a statement of what a child should be doing ("Matt, let's get to work").
- *Look for a chance to praise*, or catch students being good.
- *Praise peers*, or reward a peer model of behavior ("Thank you, Thomas, for raising your hand").
- *Make eye contact*, or watch a misbehaving student until he or she sees you.
- *Use humor* ("Susie [who has just called out an answer without raising her hand], your arm must be asleep this morning").

reflection on practice

Supporting Self-Control

This situation began when a new child transferred in from another school. The first day he was in my room, he sat at his desk very quietly. I did notice, however, that he needed constant encouragement about the work he was doing. This got to the point where he was coming up to me every few minutes to check if he was doing it right. I tried to reassure him and explain that he could not continue this way and that he would have to stay in his seat and raise his hand.

The next day he stayed in his seat, but he talked and blurted out any comment that crossed his mind. I again explained to him the rules we had in our classroom, but he continued to do this and became more vocal. I realized that he was trying to get my attention, so I decided to ignore him whenever he talked without raising his hand.

At first he would repeat his questions or comments several times, until he realized he would have to raise his hand before I would call on him. I made sure that I called on the other students as soon as they raised their hand, and I did the same for him. I also praised them for following the rules. This worked. Later that day, I noticed that he raised his hand almost every time he had something to say. He still "forgets" sometimes, but I do my best not to encourage that type of behavior anymore, and he realizes he will get my attention only if he is following the rules.

Jennifer Garrison

Discussion Questions

1. **What management strategies seemed to prevent most misbehaviors in this class?**
2. **Identify several techniques to support self-control that this teacher used.**
3. **The teacher suggested that the student needed attention. What underlying problem might his desire for attention signal? Use the list of student problem types in the Classroom Strategy Study (Table 13.5) to help you decide.**

- *Control through physical presence,* or move to the proximity of a misbehavior.

All of these techniques involved only mild forms of intervention—the type that you can observe in the class of any effective teacher (see Reflection On Practice: Supporting Self-Control). They did not intrude on learning because none of them was punitive.

Table 13.5 describes eleven categories of problem behavior. The only punitive strategy mentioned frequently was time-out, which was reserved for students who were aggressive or defiant. **Time out from reinforcement** (also

strategic solutions, continued

Table 13.5 *A List of Problem Behaviors and Coping Strategies*

- *Underachievement due to failure syndrome:* (1) support through physical presence, voice control, or eye contact; (2) praise, encourage, communicate positive expectations; (3) build self-concept; (4) change task; (5) provide academic help.

- *Underachievement due to perfectionism:* (1) appeal/persuade, (2) model coping with error, (3) use peer models of coping, (4) comfort or reassure, (5) treat with kid gloves.

- *Low achievement:* (1) reward, (2) make contracts.

- *Hostile aggression:* (1) time-out student to calm student down, (2) make behavior contracts, (3) counsel to produce insight, (4) engage student in group work, (5) involve parents or school authority figures to provide support or help.

- *Passive aggression:* (1) extinguish or ignore undesirable behavior, (2) get peers to pressure or punish.

- *Defiance:* (1) inhibit through physical presence, voice control, or eye contact; (2) time-out student to extinguish the behavior or simply to remove the student from the situation; (3) threaten with punishment; (4) involve parents or authority figures to pressure or punish.

- *Hyperactivity:* (1) intervene to redirect attention; (2) inhibit through physical presence, voice control, or eye contact; (3) eliminate external source of problem; (4) change physical environment or isolate; (5) involve medical experts.

- *Distractibility:* (1) intervene to redirect attention, (2) eliminate external source of problem, (3) change task, (4) change physical environment or isolate, (5) provide academic help.

- *Immaturity:* (1) criticize, (2) encourage or provide positive expectations.

- *Shyness:* (1) minimize stress or embarrassment; (2) provide support through presence, voice control, or eye contact; (3) treat with kid gloves; (4) build and use a personal relationship; (5) change the social environment.

- *Peer rejection:* (1) use peer models of social behavior, (2) eliminate source of problem, (3) counsel to produce insight, (4) change social environment, (5) engage in group work, (6) involve peers to support or help.

Source: Adapted from Brophy & McCaslin, 1992, pp. 29–30

known as "time-out" or "isolation") is a commonly used intervention to punish a misbehavior, extinguish the misbehavior, and reinforce appropriate behavior in its place. *Reserve time out from reinforcement for defiant or aggressive students.*

Time-out involves achieving three goals in sequence (Brantner & Doherty, 1983). The first goal is to *punish a misbehavior by removing the reinforcement that is sustaining it.* This first goal is usually accomplished by removing the student from a reinforcing activity or from his or her seat in the class

Parents sometimes need to be called in for a conference as part of a teacher's strategy to cope with hostile or defiant behavior. *(George White Location Photography)*

to a "time-out" seat or location. Participating in an activity, sitting where one wants, and even being in class should be privileges (reinforcers) that can be withdrawn. The second goal is to *extinguish the misbehavior*. If the misbehavior is no longer being reinforced in the new location, the misbehavior should die out in a few minutes. If it does not, you may need to remove the student to a quieter place or eventually isolate the student. Isolation generally requires a person other than yourself—a monitor, a teacher's aide, or an assistant principal—to supervise the student (see Reflection on Practice: Defiant Dave [High School]).

The third goal, after the student has calmed down and has begun to listen, watch, or study, is to *reinforce appropriate behavior by allowing the student to rejoin the activity*. You will probably need to alter the learning environment to ensure that the misbehavior does not recur. You may need to return the student to another location or to another role in the activity. You should also monitor the situation to determine whether the student is receiving enough reinforcement for on-task behavior. If not, develop an instructional or a motivational strategy for this student (see Chapters 8 and 12). For example, make a contract with the student, or use praise to reinforce appropriate behavior.

Because aggressive or defiant students are generally the most challenging to cope with, time-out is an important strategy, but it does not fit all misbehavior. Time-out does not suit students who are trying to escape an embarrassing situation or a boring class. In such cases, time-out reinforces misbehavior rather than punishes it. Time-out is also ineffective for responding to nonaggressive misbehaviors, such as repeated failure to follow directions. It is better to find another consequence that suits the misbehavior.

strategic solutions, continued

reflection on practice

Defiant Dave (High School)

Dave was perhaps the most troubled (and troublesome) student in any of my classes last year. He had been in trouble with the law and had lost his driver's license because of alcohol and marijuana use. While most kids his age think that having a driver's license is a necessity of life, Dave told the class quite proudly about losing his and apparently saw no great problem in the fact that he would not be able to get his license again until age nineteen.

Dave had a natural gift of memory, so he could pass practically any test that I gave without putting much effort into it. Perhaps my greatest concern was the effect that Dave was having on two other students, Jim and John. Neither of them was quite as sharp as Dave, and they could not afford to be distracted by his antics. I could almost count on hearing his undertone, and the other two boys would occasionally show laughter and amusement.

Finally, I decided that Dave's behavior was having consequences for the class that had to be challenged. Our school has a program of ISS (In-School Suspension) and an Alternative School. Dave had been in both of them, though I had nothing to do with his being there. I knew that he did not seem to like either of these placements.

On this occasion, I could not catch Dave in his disruptions, but I knew that they were coming from him, and the reactions of the other boys confirmed to me that I would have to do something. I reminded Dave that I could have him sent to ISS if he preferred it that way. He blurted out to the whole class that he would be kicked out of school for the rest of the year if he was sent there again. Apparently his last visit there had put some fear in his heart, so I decided to use that in my approach to him.

We went into the hall where we could discuss the matter privately. I told him that we had only a few more weeks of school left, and it would be of no benefit to either of us to send him to ISS, but if he persisted, I was fully prepared to do that. I told him that I felt he had much to lose by being out of school for the rest of the year, so I'd like him to cooperate for the short time left.

The outcome of this was that Dave saw that I was serious about the matter, and that the consequences of misbehaving outweighed the rewards, so he cooperated with me for the last few weeks. He did not go to ISS, and he passed the course with a 71 (a low C). He was not put out of school. By the way, the two other boys also barely made it.

Lois Williams

Discussion Questions

1. **What tells you Dave is intelligent and has a sharp sense of reality? A poorly formulated conscience?**

2. **What happens when teachers try to appeal to such students' conscience or sense of fairness?**

3. **What does this teacher use to get Dave on track again? How do the coping strategies of this teacher compare with the coping strategies of teachers of defiant students in the Classroom Strategy Study?**

Evaluation: Behavioral Control Strategies

The Classroom Strategy Study is especially useful for its perspective on discipline as a problem-solving process and for its data on coping. You need to know what effective teachers do when confronted with difficult students. The Classroom Strategy Study represents the collective wisdom of a large number of experienced teachers.

It is, however, wisdom suited to the conditions of a previous generation. The researchers acknowledged that the data were collected between 1977 and 1981 and that most teachers who participated in the study had a minimum of ten years' experience. During their own education, little emphasis would have been placed on student reasoning, let alone reasoning with students to develop self-control. The consequence may be a behavioral bias in the results of the study due to what psychologists call a *cohort effect,* or the results of developmental experiences within a specific historical period. The possibility of a cohort effect does not invalidate results, but it does require that we put them in perspective, either by looking for more recent research or by taking account of social change.

Have students' problems changed much since 1981? Elementary teachers report that student behavior problems have become worse, but secondary teachers report that they have remained about the same (Brown & Payne, 1992). What *has* dramatically changed in the past ten to fifteen years is not the problem of establishing a climate conducive to learning but the priority of developing students' thinking and self-control. The Classroom Strategy Study did not take into account this priority. As several educators have noted (Duke & Jones, 1985; Jones & Jones, 1990), positive discipline practices work to control student behavior, but they need to be blended with problem-solving approaches if they are to develop students' thinking as a basis for self-control.

Toward Self-Control: Cognitive Behavior Modification

In the 1970s, researchers began to search for management techniques that would develop self-control. Donald Meichenbaum (1977) proposed a strategy, **cognitive behavior modification,** for teaching self-management that relies on internalization of verbal instructions (Vygotsky, 1978). Cognitive behavior modification is relatively simple. A teacher develops a verbalized procedure for a student to follow in order to cope with frustration. The procedure is first modeled by the teacher during the task ("Okay, I'm getting frustrated, but all I need to do is be patient with myself, and try, try again"), then rehearsed by the student during the task, and eventually incorporated through practice as a routine in the behavior of the student.

Cognitive behavior modification teaches the student to verbalize self-control procedures.

This method of teaching self-control is similar to cognitive strategy instruction (described in Chapter 9), but cognitive behavior modification focuses on coping with frustration. Most of us have adopted sayings to cope with frustration through patience and persistence. As a child, you may have learned "Slow and easy does it," "If at first you don't succeed, try, try again," and so on. Strategies to cope with frustration are learned as a form of self-management or self-control. Bear in mind that if they can be learned, they can also be taught.

strategic solutions

Cognitive Behavior Modification

Cognitive behavior modification is now the behavioral strategy recommended by many psychologists to develop self-control in response to frustration. *When a student becomes frustrated by a task and has difficulty maintaining self-control, use cognitive behavior modification.* A generic set of steps (Manning, 1991; Meichenbaum & Goodman, 1971) would probably include the following:

1. Talking to yourself aloud while you perform the task that requires self-control (cognitive modeling)
2. Having the student perform the task under your instructions (overt, external guidance)
3. Having the student perform the task while instructing self aloud (overt self-guidance)
4. Having the student whisper instructions to self while performing the task (faded, overt self-guidance)
5. Having the student perform the task while guiding self through private speech (covert self-instruction)

Strategies to cope with frustration are easily modeled when students have an authentic task that requires a relatively great amount of self-control. Rather than abandon the task or become angry as a result of frustration, they can watch you model a way to cope with the situation. The procedure for handling frustration becomes internalized as a form of self-talk, which the student can then use to regulate behavior.

Evaluation: Cognitive Behavior Modification

When students encounter frustrating tasks on their own, do they use strategies for self-control provided by their teachers? Early concerns focused on whether this form of strategy training could generalize. It now appears that at least in some cases, cognitive behavior modification can be used to reduce impulsive reactions to frustrating situations outside the specific training task (Gerber, 1987). Cognitive behavior modification does not teach students to design strategies for coping with frustration, but it does teach them to implement strategies designed by the teacher. If these strategies are sufficiently general, and if students implement them, they represent a significant step toward the development of self-control.

CONCLUSION

You have now surveyed management planning, managing skills, discipline policies, and coping strategies to achieve the goal of establishing and maintaining a climate conducive to learning. Each type of strategy actually addresses a subproblem of management, so when you teach, you will need to assemble strategies into a management system. Decisions related to your management system should be based on a number of circumstances, including your curriculum, the discipline policy of your district and school, the nature of your students, and your beliefs regarding the purpose of control. Your beliefs about control are themselves founded on your experience as a child growing up in a family and as a student.

Before you teach, examine your beliefs in light of what we now know about the development of self-control. There is no serious dispute among educators that self-control should be the ultimate goal of management. Sometimes you need to exercise control of a class to maintain a climate conducive to learning, but educators generally agree that in the long run the imposition of control is valuable in a democratic society only in the service of developing self-control. If schools do not graduate self-controlled citizens, then they have failed to achieve an important social goal.

The consensus is not complete, but few disagree with Piaget's argument that self-control based on reasoning requires a certain amount of independent thought. The question now, as when Piaget wrote, is how to balance the need to maintain the learning climate with the need for decision making by the student. There is no easy answer. Some educators have suggested that the balance requires a set of reasonable rules that are fairly enforced. Other educators have suggested that the balance requires helping students meet needs and solve problems of behavior.

These two suggestions are not incompatible. An effective teacher ensures that class rules are reasonable and fair. If a student has a need or a problem that is an underlying cause of misbehavior, the same teacher generally wants to know about it and is willing to help the student meet that need or solve that problem within available resources. The principal limitation on your ability to provide conditions that promote self-control may not be your beliefs but your time. You can always take time for those students in each class who need you the most.

Analysis of a Discipline Policy

Objective of the assignment

To analyze a discipline policy for its capacity to support the development of a rational basis for self-control.

Directions for the assignment

1. Explain to a teacher of a grade level (and subject) that you plan to teach that you are doing an assignment for your educational psychology class, and ask if he or she would mind being interviewed about his or her discipline policy. Most teachers will be glad to cooperate because they explain their discipline policies to students and parents all the time. The teacher may even have a handout to give you.

2. In your interview, try to identify the following:

   a. Rules, rewards, and sanctions. At a minimum, the classroom policy should consist of rules and sanctions. If a teacher posts these, write them down word for word.
   b. The schoolwide discipline policy. This policy may take the form of a discipline program or sanctions for serious misbehavior.
   c. The schedule of sanctions for increasingly serious misbehaviors. Make sure you identify these.

   After you have finished the interview, be sure to thank the teacher for his or her cooperation.

3. Compare and contrast the policy of this teacher with general characteristics of positive discipline policies and problem-solving discipline policies:

   a. Positive discipline policies develop prosocial skills and characteristics through reward, modeling, or reasoning.
   b. Problem-solving discipline policies use reasoning to develop a plan to satisfy needs.

4. Given the policy as it exists, *elaborate it* to support the development of a rational basis for self-control. What *additions* might you make to enhance student reasoning? Make only minor deletions.

5. Develop a thesis that characterizes the policy's capacity to support the development of a rational basis for self-control. The thesis might simply indicate that the capacity is high, moderate, or low.

6. Write a three- to four-page paper to support your thesis.

   a. Begin an introductory paragraph by identifying the grade level of the policy and offering a general description of the students, but not the teacher, subject, or school. State your thesis at the end of this paragraph.
   b. Describe the discipline policy in as much detail as possible. Be sure to hand in a copy of the policy with your paper.
   c. Support your thesis with details from your analysis (step 3) and ideas for elaboration (step 4). For example, if the capacity is moderate, explain why it is neither high nor low.
   d. Try to reach an insightful conclusion about the adaptive capacity of any discipline policy to support the development of reasoning.

SUMMARY

1. Classroom management is the process of establishing and maintaining a climate conducive to learning. It includes both prevention and intervention strategies.
2. Prevention measures are aimed at anticipating potentially troublesome situations and preventing problematic situations from arising. Intervention strategies focus on what a teacher can do when, despite prevention attempts, management problems do develop.
3. Management planning is a key prevention strategy. It involves decisions about such matters as seat arrangements and classroom rules and procedures. Because instructional goals have important implications for management decisions, they are the guiding force behind management planning.
4. Knowing how and when to use managing skills is a second critical element of prevention. Managing skills involve activities such as increasing students' on-task time, handling overlapping situations in which there are multiple demands competing for your attention, and communicating effectively with students about, for example, transitions between classroom activities.
5. One element of intervention is the use of discipline. While discipline is often assumed to involve punishment, it does not have to. Corporal and verbal punishment have more disadvantages than advantages. Positive discipline policies and problem-solving policies are two alternative discipline strategies that emphasize rewards and reasoning rather than punitive measures.
6. Coping strategies are the second major means of intervention. They are useful when troublesome behaviors erupt or persist. Behavioral control strategies such as shaping or time out from reinforcement are one example of coping strategies. A second example includes cognitive behavior modification, in which a teacher models for a student how to handle frustrating situations.
7. Each type of strategy presented in this chapter actually addresses a subproblem of management. When assembled together, they will form your own particular management system.
8. At the foundation of a management system is a core of beliefs about the role and importance of students' development of self-control. Most educators agree that in a democratic society the ultimate goal of classroom management should be self-controlled citizens.

KEY TERMS

management p. 546

management problem p. 546

management strategy p. 546

management system p. 550

on-task behavior p. 551

rules p. 553

procedures p. 553

overlapping situation p. 564

withitness p. 565

marker p. 567

discipline p. 569

corporal punishment p. 569

positive discipline policy p. 569

problem-solving discipline policy p. 569

character education p. 570

Assertive Discipline p. 571

Reality Therapy p. 574

Teacher Effectiveness Training (TET) p. 576

time out from reinforcement p. 581

cognitive behavior modification p. 585

SUGGESTED RESOURCES

Emmer, E. T. 1987. "Classroom Management and Discipline." In *Educators' Handbook: A Research Perspective* (pp. 233–258). Ed. V. Richardson-Koehler. New York: Longman. This chapter is a very useful summary of the findings of teacher effectiveness research.

Glasser, W. 1990. *The Quality School: Managing Students Without Coercion.* New York: Harper & Row. This book focuses on how to develop self-management through a collaborative problem-solving approach.

Lickona, T. 1993. "The Return of Character Education." *Educational Leadership,* 51(3), 6–11. This article is useful for contemporary information about character education.

Zabel, R. H., and M. K. Zabel. 1996. *Classroom Management in Context.* Boston: Houghton Mifflin. This new text focuses on how to create a classroom climate that fosters learning.

Evaluating Learning

Part IV shows you how designing assessment strategies and attaining your assessment goals follow the problem-solving process demonstrated throughout this text. You will learn about problems of assessment and aligning tasks with learning outcomes. You will also learn about different types of psychological research in education, ethical considerations that should guide research, and how you as a teacher can get started as a researcher.

Assessment Design

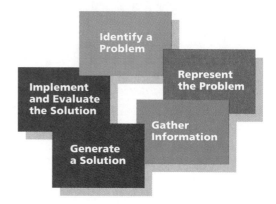

The goal of this chapter is to help you understand that "assessment" or "evaluation" means more than "test." **Testing** is the administration of an evaluation instrument, but testing is not the same as **assessment**— the process of gathering information to meet a variety of evaluation needs (Chittenden, 1991). The design of **assessment strategies,** or means to attain assessment goals, follows a problem-solving process much like the one you have studied throughout this book. This process involves identifying a problem, representing it in a way that you can solve it, gathering information relevant to the solution, generating a solution, and trying it out and evaluating it. As you read, look for answers to the following questions:

- **What is the main goal of assessment? How is it related to the technical goals of reliability and validity?**

- **What are several examples of objectively scored assessment items?**

- **How does choice of item type reflect your goals and objectives?**

- **What are several examples of performance-based assessment exercises?**

- **When might a teacher use performance-based exercises?**

- **What is the function of marking standards, and what role should they play during assessment design?**

- **In what three ways can assessment results affect teaching decisions?**

PROBLEMS OF ASSESSMENT

For a teacher, the general purpose of assessment design is to *evaluate learning accurately.* This goal ensures that assessments by teachers serve instructional goals and do not exist as ends in themselves.

A great deal in teaching depends on an accurate evaluation of learning. For example, consider three related but different effects of grades. First, a grade often has a motivational effect. An inaccurate grade will lead to an inappropriate sense of satisfaction or dissatisfaction. Second, a grade almost always provides informational feedback to students, parents, and administrators. An inaccurate grade results in miscommunication about a student's accomplishments and needs for improvement. Third, grades of the entire class can be used by a teacher to improve instruction. Inaccurate grades will misdirect the teacher's efforts to teach better. In short, inaccurate grades impair efforts by *everyone* to progress.

> Accurate grading assists in motivation, feedback, and planning.

Stages of Assessment Design

Designing an assessment strategy involves a smaller problem-solving cycle within the larger problem-solving cycle of instruction. Assessment design usually occurs *after* you have set instructional goals because the goals for learning establish a purpose for the assessment. If you were to teach a unit on parts of the human body, for example, you might interpret your instructional objectives as a list of *anticipated learning outcomes* when you think about making up a test. Learning outcomes are generally restatements of objectives of the type that you considered in Chapter 3. Anticipated outcomes such as "describe functions of various internal organs" or "locate different organs on a map of the human body" help you select relevant assessment tasks.

> Assessment design is related to instructional goals.

We can outline the process of assessment design in a cycle that begins with specification of learning outcomes and ends with decisions based on the results of an evaluation. This cycle might include the following:

1. Specifying learning outcomes (as previously described)
2. Specifying assessment tasks and scoring criteria
3. Using standards to evaluate scores
4. Using results to make decisions

This sequence of steps is portrayed as a cycle in Figure 14.1. It resembles the problem-solving cycle because it is a specialized form of problem solving.

Identifying and *representing* particular assessment problems require you to specify learning outcomes. These two initial stages of problem solving are combined in assessment design because teachers often come to assessment relatively late in their planning. Instructional objectives and strategies should be considered *before* assessment so that it is aligned with those objectives and strategies.

> Assessment design is a process that resembles the problem-solving cycle.

Gathering information about a solution to an assessment problem requires you to specify assessment tasks and criteria for scoring responses.

**Figure 14.1
Assessment Design by
Teachers**

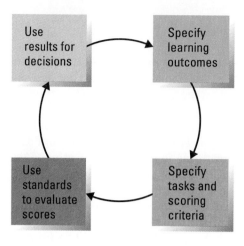

Ideas for assessment tasks and criteria for scoring them are often found in learning activities—questions, discussion, experiences to develop process skills, and criteria followed to develop products. It is no accident, for example, that many tests consist of questions that are similar to those asked by the teacher during instruction.

Developing a solution to an assessment problem requires you to connect scores with standards. A score of 80 out of 100 on an assessment exercise is relatively meaningless until it is matched to a standard of excellence. This match links the task of scoring with the task of assigning grades and generally signifies a completed strategy.

Trying out and evaluating the solution to an assessment problem require you to actually apply your strategy and use the results to set new goals. Some of these goals may relate to future assessment, but for a teacher they must also relate to instruction. The results of an evaluation should provide feedback into your instructional planning decisions.

The process of assessment design or planning is relatively easy to understand when presented in a stagelike way, but in reality it interacts with other forms of planning. For example, you read about mastery learning in Chapter 12 as a motivational strategy. In comparison to traditional instruction, mastery learning involves added learning opportunities. These require you to administer tests to diagnose learning deficits and verify remediation of them. Mastery learning requires a different assessment strategy than traditional instruction does.

Stages in assessment design often receive unequal emphasis. For example, scoring criteria do not pose much difficulty on a test that is scored by machine. Responses are relatively easy to identify as correct or incorrect. By way of contrast, scoring criteria are more difficult to establish in an assessment that involves rating an original performance. You may have to develop a scoring guide, practice scoring, and revise the guide before you are comfortable with the criteria.

> Assessment may need to be modified for certain forms of learning.

Technical Goals of Assessment Design

The main goal of assessment—evaluating learning accurately—is related to two technical goals known as reliability and validity. **Reliability** is *consistency* in the results of an assessment. **Validity** is the *appropriate interpretation* of assessment results. Reliability is necessary but not sufficient for a valid interpretation, such as an accurate grade according to districtwide standards.

> Reliability involves consistency; validity involves appropriate interpretation.

Reliability

Reliability is generally established through collection of an adequate sample of what has been learned. What is an adequate sample? In general, it is a sample that is large enough to limit inconsistencies in assessment results.

The more observations there are of a given type of learning, the higher is the reliability of assessment results. Say that a second-grade teacher wants to assess students' pronunciation and fluency in reading. This teacher will want each child to read more than one paragraph, or better yet, read a paragraph on more than one occasion. Distributing observations so that inconsistencies in results are reduced might well involve conducting three reading sessions and calling on children in a random, rather than in a predictable, order during each session.

> Reliability is higher when a sufficient number of cases is considered.

The number of observations needed in any assessment is limited by the phenomenon of diminishing returns for added observations. That is, increases in reliability become smaller as you add observations (Cronbach, 1990). For example, having students read on three occasions will greatly increase the reliability of a reading assessment in comparison to one occasion, but having students read on six occasions will not further increase the reliability of the assessment much. Similarly, increasing the length of a machine-scored test from thirty to sixty items will greatly increase the reliability of results, but doubling its length again will further increase reliability only a little. The rule of *diminishing returns* holds for all types of assessment, from opportunities to read, to length of a machine-scored test, to tryout sessions for the basketball team.

> More than enough samples will not enhance reliability.

Validity

If assessment results are *not* reliable, they cannot be said to represent any learning outcome. However, once you have established reliability, validity comes into the picture. Like reliability of results, valid interpretations contribute to accuracy in evaluation. Somewhat different procedures are used to gather evidence for the validity of different kinds of interpretation.

Content Validation.   **Content validation** involves gathering evidence that assessment tasks adequately represent the "domain" of knowledge or skills to be assessed. Observations should not only be adequate in number (to establish reliability) but they should also represent whatever is to be assessed and do so in proportion to instruction. The result of a paper-and-pencil test of

> Content validity means testing only the skills that were taught.

Construct validation involves verifying that responses are based *only* on intended learning and not some other factor. This Brockton, Massachusetts, science teacher is listening to a group's explanation to clear up any confusion or misunderstanding about a problem or a proposed solution. *(Rick Friedman/ Black Star)*

soccer rules, for example, can represent knowledge of soccer rules, but it cannot represent soccer *skills*, which are in the psychomotor domain. If you *teach* psychomotor skills, you must *test* psychomotor skills in proportion to instruction in these skills for the results to be interpreted as indications of them. Evidence of content validity is usually gathered by matching assessment tasks to anticipated learning outcomes.

Construct Validation. **Construct validation** involves gathering evidence that assessment results represent *only* what is to be assessed. A "construct" is a meaningful interpretation of observations. An interpretation has construct validity if it matches expectations based on *theory*. For example, suppose you build a fifth-grade life science test to assess *understanding of systems of the human body* (the instructional objective or learning outcome) using multiple-choice items. After the test, which you intended to assess comprehension of *systems*, you discover that some students did not know some of the general vocabulary words in some of the test items (unrelated to understanding systems of the human body). Factors such as limited vocabulary, testwiseness, test anxiety, fatigue, or dishonesty can change the meaning of test results so that they do not signify what was intended. Evidence of construct validity can be gathered by finding ways to verify that assessment results are the consequence of *only* what the test was intended to assess and not of some other factor.

> Construct validity means that unrelated factors do not affect the test results.

Criterion-Related Validation. **Criterion-related validation** involves gathering evidence that assessment results have some value for estimating a standard of performance (the criterion). Classroom teachers are often interested in criteria of performance known as "benchmarks." Benchmark performances can sometimes be impractical to assess, however. You may be interested in developing skills of interpersonal understanding in a civics course, for example, but find the only practical way to assess the attainment of such an objective is by evaluating written responses to hypothetical situations. To

> Criterion-related validity means comparing results with a benchmark performance.

gather evidence of the criterion-related validity of this interpretation of written responses, you must at some point compare performance of at least some students on the test with the benchmark performance, which is behavior that demonstrates interpersonal understanding.

You need general information about how to attain reliability and validity because you will often have to assess anticipated learning outcomes through your own designs for assessment. How do you know that your interpretations of scores are reliable and that your grades are valid indications of intended learning? Those are the specific questions that you will want to answer or the technical problems that you will want to solve as you design assessments.

Evaluating Learning in Ms. Gist's Class

Let's think about reliability and validity in light of a classroom example. It's 2:10 in the afternoon, and twenty-one juniors and seniors are filing into Mary Gist's human physiology class for a test. Ms. Gist has prepared a thirty-one item test of a textbook chapter on glands and hormones. The test consists of twelve multiple-choice questions (each 4 points), six short-answer questions (each 4 points), a map of the human glandular system with eight short-answer blanks (each 1 point), five discussion questions (each 4 points), and one bonus question (2 points). The test totals 100 points without the bonus question. Clearly, the test has been designed to measure a variety of learning outcomes and to provide meaningful feedback in terms of a score.

Later, I return to interview Ms. Gist to find out how students did. Table 14.1 presents the results of this test (T4) among a series of scores and point totals. Students averaged 73 points on the test, or what in the marking system of the high school would have been a middle C, but the test itself was not graded. One student scored as high as 101 points, but another scored as low as 49. Ms. Gist explains to me that the test is just one among four 100-point tests for the six-week marking period. Before students will receive a six-week grade, she will average the four tests with points for homework (100 points minus 5 points for each missing assignment) and points for six written summaries of science articles (100 points). The homework and written assignments tend to bring grades up, particularly for those students who do not do well on tests but who are diligent and demonstrate an awareness of the value of science.

How does Ms. Gist's assessment strategy solve the core problem of accurately evaluating learning? First, let's look at reliability because assessment results that are unreliable cannot be interpreted as an indication of anything in particular.

Ms. Gist did not assign grades to scores on the test, largely because the test consisted of relatively few items. Students could interpret their point total on the test in terms of the school grading system, but the teacher reserved assignment of a grade until she had an adequate sample of responses. To be reliable, an evaluation of scores has to be based on a relatively large number of responses, often made on different occasions.

An average of several test scores should be more reliable.

Table 14.1   Scores for Six Weeks in Human Physiology

Name	T1	T2	T3	T4	Homework	Articles	Average	Grade
Aday, Caroline	72	80	78	73	100	100		
Balot, Jennifer	55	60	65	64	90	100		
Barnes, Marcus	60	63	82	61	100	100		
Dean, Gina	49	60	61	59	95	100		
DuBois, Angeline	68	73	68	61	100	100		
Eccles, Derrick	80	86	87	83	100	100		
Hewlett, Peter	71	73	82	76	100	100		
Iseli, John	54	50	48	49	65	0		
Jarmon, Chloe	78	82	87	80	100	100		
Lipsett, Sam	82	85	89	87	100	100		
McMurtrey, Jenny	82	83	86	85	100	100		
Murdock, Alex	92	94	89	90	100	100		
Muse, Sally	48	67	72	70	100	100		
Oberlies, Kevin	95	81	85	96	40	100		
Qualls, Maria	97	100	102	101	100	100		
Richards, Jeff	68	70	75	76	95	100		
Sanchez, Ramon	65	48	70	71	90	100		
Smith, Traci	65	63	63	52	85	100		
Talbot, Nicole	39	43	57	60	100	100		
Warren, Matt	85	68	70	62	85	100		
Yu, Connie	79	83	83	78	100	100		
Averages								

Now let's look at validity. Mrs. Gist's tests were the products of a design cycle in which assessment tasks for the students were developed in relation to objectives or outcomes. The achievement of cognitive objectives was measured through tests of the type previously described. The achievement of affective objectives (attitudes toward work and science) was assessed through a cumulative record of homework and of written summaries of science articles. Her final grade was based on a 2 to 1 ratio of cognitive outcomes to affective outcomes. Her careful design of the content of assessments to match cognitive and affective learning outcomes was evidence of content validity.

Evidence of construct and criterion-related validity of test results was visible in the way Ms. Gist tested students and in the match between test tasks and classroom performance. Test were announced, testing was focused on individual achievement, and students had adequate time to respond. All of these conditions contributed to interpretation of results as the product of individual learning (construct validity). Furthermore, the test, with its empha-

Test validity should be related to classroom performance.

sis on information but inclusion of discussion, mirrored her expectations for performance in class (criterion-related validity).

As teachers' expectations for classroom performance change with the increasing emphases on realistic contexts for problem solving, we can expect the face of assessment to change as well. Concerns over criterion-related validity are leading many educators to develop tests that contain tasks that are much closer to "authentic" performances than are responses to objectively scored tests (Stiggins, 1991). Later in this chapter we will consider the assessment of authentic or realistic performances in some detail. For now, it is sufficient to understand that, even though the face of assessment will change with changing goals for learning, the core problem of evaluating learning will remain the same. Teachers will always have to evaluate learning, and because the results of such evaluations are important to students, their parents, teachers, administrators, and even communities, evaluations will have to be accurate.

SPECIFYING TASKS AND SCORING CRITERIA

Your decisions about the assessment techniques you will use depend to a large extent on your goals and objectives for learning. As you discovered in Chapter 3, some goals and objectives can be met through many types of learning activity, whereas others can be met only through a few types of activity. The situation is much the same for learning outcomes and assessment tasks. Some outcomes can be assessed through many different types of task, whereas others can be assessed through only a few types of task. In this section you will learn about how to match assessment tasks to anticipated outcomes using the cognitive, affective, and psychomotor domains of objectives you learned about in Chapter 3.

> Testing must be matched to learning objectives.

The face of assessment will change with increasing emphasis on realistic problem solving. Standardized testing, as shown in this picture, will remain with us, but assessments designed by teachers will resemble standardized testing much less often than they do now.
(Bob Daemmrich)

think it through

Consider this problem that a novice preservice teacher has **IDENTIFIED** and **REPRESENTED**.

Keeping Your Distance

This is a situation that I have previously encountered, and I am certain that I will encounter this in the future. I was a student assistant at a local high school, helping teach the high school band. I had noticed a particular young man who had missed the first three days of rehearsal and finally showed up, only to be rowdy and raucous while others were trying to learn. I did my best to be patient with this young man, and we ended up getting along pretty well. One afternoon we were all gathering our things to go. Most of the students had cleared out, and I leaned over to get a drink of water as I had done several times before. This particular young man walked up behind me and jabbed me in both sides, meaning to tickle me.

My question is, Although this may seem rather trivial, how does one handle an unprovoked touch from a student, especially if this had been a more "serious" situation?

Observe how an experienced practicing teacher GENERATES SOLUTIONS to this problem.

The problem you describe is a very difficult one to talk about and try to solve. It doesn't seem trivial at all. A group of us talked about it for a while and came up with these suggestions.

The first time an incident such as this happens, try not to panic. Try to take the event lightly since you can assume that this particular type of unprovoked touch is likely to be a spur-of-the-moment touch and not an attack. Say something clear, such as "Be careful." The idea is to give the student a low-key but unambiguous warning.

If the warning doesn't work or the student just doesn't take you seriously and pokes you again, it is very important to do something more emphatic. Make an appointment to talk with the student. As is true with all serious discipline problems, it's best not to discuss the event in front of other students because then the student needs to save face and you'll have an entirely different problem to solve.

In the private appointment with the student, be clear about what is and is not appropriate behavior. Explain that in some situations, words and actions may not be hurtful, but in certain other situations and contexts those same words and actions may be very hurtful. And they may be completely inappropriate. Make sure that the student understands what you are saying and knows that his or her action was inappropriate and must not happen again.

There are, of course, situations of touching and commenting that are very serious. There are miles and mountains of difference between a poke and a sexual touch. In any such situation, you should go directly to the principal or a guidance counselor—someone in authority whom you trust and can speak with easily. No situation that crosses these fuzzy boundaries should be ignored.

Some Members of the English Department
Belmont High School
Belmont, Massachusetts

EVALUATE this problem's possible multiple solutions while you think about the dynamic process of problem solving.

The experienced teachers have some excellent suggestions for how to deal with this situation and with other, more serious ones that might arise in your teaching career. What I wonder is, Why did this situation arise, and why did the assistant or intern teacher expect it to happen again?

Different teachers will give the incident at the drinking fountain different readings. If we assume that the intern teacher is female, the behavior of the student is more difficult to understand than if we assume that the intern is male. A poke in the ribs at the drinking fountain between classes is fairly common among boys in (junior) high school—a little like being told that your shoe is untied, just to see if you will look. A boy learns not to look at his shoe—and not take a drink of water around certain people.

Not knowing the sex of the intern, let's suppose that the intern is male, if for no other reason than to explore why the intern teacher was perceived as a student. This is sometimes a concern of intern teachers—that they will be treated by high school students as fellow students and not as teachers. Students will be disobedient, disrespectful, and so on because they do not perceive the intern as a "real teacher."

The solution to the problem is to assess how you want to represent yourself as teacher. Anyone who is a college student in a preservice teacher education program will probably conform to expectations of how to dress, act, and talk as a college student. That is fine as long as that person is

in the role of a student; but when entering a school as an intern, that person's peer group changes from students to teachers, and often her or his dress and demeanor must change. You, along with the other teachers, will be trying to communicate to students and each other expectations of work.

An intern does not need to be excessively formal but should dress to communicate expectations of work. Clothing should be neat (that is, orderly in appearance). If work may soil neat clothes, wear an apron, a lab coat, or an exercise uniform. If an event involves representing the school or other people, put on a tie, suit, or dress.

Similar expectations must be communicated for language and deportment. Teachers should use good grammar because our work involves teaching apt language use. We may offer some students the only models of good grammar that they have. Similarly, we should conduct ourselves in ways that are appropriate to a workplace. For example, teachers should follow school rules and refrain from socializing when they should be working. To communicate expectations of work, how you act is just as important as how you talk and what you wear.

Whether the advice of the experienced teachers, or the preceding advice, is most helpful depends on how someone reads the problem. If the problem belonged to the misbehaving student, the advice from the experienced teachers is helpful. If it belonged to the intern teacher, the advice about demeanor and dress is helpful.

Traditionally, assessment of learning has rested on either **objectively scored tests,** which are evaluation instruments that are accurately and efficiently scored either by machine or by hand, or **performance-based exercises,** which evoke responses that the teacher or some other expert then appraises. In the past ten years the gap between these two approaches has narrowed so that both can serve the same general goal of assessment: an accurate evaluation of learning. This development has challenged teachers to solve the problem of accuracy in creative ways.

In general, scoring criteria have been developed to help teachers accurately evaluate performance. Criteria are not difficult to establish with objectively scored test items. Responses are relatively easy to judge as correct or incorrect. Scoring criteria are much more difficult to establish with performance-based exercises, however. These criteria often involve guidelines for judging one or more qualities of response on each exercise. For that reason, we will discuss scoring criteria in relation to performance-based exercises rather than in relation to objectively scored test items.

> It is easier to define scoring criteria for objectively scored tests than for performance-based tests.

Objectively Scored Test Items

From your own experiences as a student, you are probably familiar with objectively scored test items such as *matching, alternative response* (true-false, fact-opinion), *short answer* (or "fill in the blank"), and *multiple choice.* These items made up most of Ms. Gist's human physiology chapter test.

Although each of these item types has its own definition, they share several characteristics:

> Objectively scored items have several characteristics in common.

1. They are all used to assess learning in the cognitive domain rather than the development of attitudes or psychomotor skills.
2. They are primarily used to assess knowledge and lower-order thinking skills.
3. They can be efficiently and objectively scored either by machine or by hand.

These shared characteristics often lead objectively scored items of different types to be included on the same test.

Matching

Matching items on a test contain two lists of approximately the same length between which the student must recognize associations of some sort: names-achievements, compositions-composers, terms-definitions, places-characteristics, and so forth. One list consists of item stimuli called *premises,* and the other list consists of *responses.* In general, the instructions are the following: in the line to the left of each item in column A record the correct match from column B. Students should be informed of the basis of the match and whether responses may be used more than once. Matching items are used only to assess knowledge of a particular type (see Deepening Your Knowledge Base: Matching Items).

> Matching tests ask students to recognize associations.

strategic solutions

Using Matching Items

The implication for an assessment strategy is to *use matching items to assess knowledge of a specific type.* Knowledge of definitions or knowledge of facts can be assessed through matching items in a number of ways. The most common format is a column of premises and a column of responses, but premises may be listed underneath a pool of potential responses or listed beside a diagram labeled *A, B,* and so forth. Finally, a popular format for children in lower elementary grades is to have them draw a line from each item in column A to match the correct response (such as an associated picture) in column B.

Evaluation: Using Matching Items

Matching items are particularly common in sections of tests that assess knowledge of definitions and terms. They do not often stand as tests alone because of the confusion created by lists more than ten items long. The advantages of matching items are (1) ease of construction, (2) economy of presentation, and (3) ease of scoring. To facilitate the scoring of matching items, you might want to construct a short *strip key,* which lists the correct answers vertically on a piece of paper so that you can read the correct answers horizontally adjacent to responses.

The major limitation of matching items is that they cannot assess cognitive skills. As you will recall from Chapter 3, cognitive skills range from comprehension to evaluation. A matching item is restricted to assessing knowledge outcomes such as a set of names, facts, terms, processes, or generalizations.

deepening your knowledge base

Matching Items

The following are examples of matching items used to assess knowledge of different kinds. Notice that the lists are of varying length to avoid cuing correct responses and that responses are very short.

In the line to the left of each location in column A record the appropriate description from column B. Use descriptions only once.

COLUMN A	COLUMN B
_____ 1. dry and windy with few plants	a. tundra
_____ 2. ground covered by grasses	b. jungle
_____ 3. tree-covered land	c. desert
_____ 4. cold and damp with mosses	d. prairie
_____ 5. wet and hot with many plants	e. forest

Match the letters on this map of North America with the location of the Indian cultures listed below.

_____ 1. Anasazi

_____ 2. Hopewell

_____ 3. Mississippian

_____ 4. Northwest Coast

_____ 5. Eskimo

Source: Map test is adapted from Perry, *History of the World*, Houghton Mifflin Company, 1993, p. 321

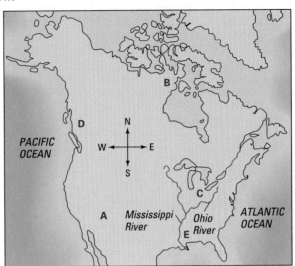

Alternative Response

Alternative response items on a test contain *stems*, which represent problems, and the same set of options for selecting solutions: true-false, fact-opinion, agree-disagree, yes-no, and so on. The instructions for true-false items are generally as follows: circle T if the statement is true, and circle F if the statement is false. But there are many variations of this instruction to suit different alternatives. Furthermore, there may be more than two alternatives. Alternative response items are generally used to assess knowledge or comprehension (see Deepening Your Knowledge Base: Alternative Response Items).

> Alternative response tests assess knowledge or comprehension.

strategic solutions

Using Alternative Response Items

There are two implications of alternative response items for an assessment strategy. First, *use alternative response to assess knowledge.* Alternative response items often present an adequate way to test knowledge of specifics,

strategic solutions, continued

deepening your knowledge base

Alternative Response Items

The following are examples of alternative response items used to assess knowledge or comprehension. Note that the statements are clear and short and generalities (such as "always" or "never") that cue correct responses are avoided.

A. Knowledge

Circle *T* if the statement is true, or circle *F* if the statement is false.

Planets give off their own light.   T   F

Write *Axis* beside each Axis country during World War II, write *Allied* beside each country allied against the Axis, and write *Neutral* beside each neutral country.

Germany: _____   Russia: _____   Japan: _____

Sweden: _____   U.S.: _____   Italy: _____

B. Comprehension

Circle *fact* if the statement is a fact, or circle *opinion* if the statement is an opinion.

George Washington was the best U.S. president.   Fact   Opinion

Circle *yes* if the conclusion is valid, or circle *no* if the conclusion is not valid.

Given:

John works after school only if he has his parents' permission.

John works after school.

Then, would this conclusion be valid?

John has his parents' permission.   Yes   No

ways of dealing with specifics, and generalizations. Second, *use alternative response items to assess comprehension.* Some logical distinctions (such as fact-opinion, valid-invalid, or relevant-irrelevant) can be assessed through alternative response items. Also, interpretation of a passage or diagram can be assessed in this format. You should not use alternative response items simply because they are the preferred item type of the teacher or student, because they "cover" a lot of material, or because they are easy to score. They are designed to assess whether students have acquired knowledge or understanding of a specific type.

Evaluation: Using Alternative Response Items

Alternative response items are valuable for testing comprehension, particularly to assess understanding of distinctions. For example, they are a valuable way to test understanding of the distinction between fact and opinion or between appropriate and inappropriate interpretations. In addition, scoring is relatively easy when compared to short-answer and essay items.

Chance can play such a large role in scores when there are only two options, however, that short true-false quizzes are not very reliable indicators of achievement. If failure on a true-false quiz is set at 50 percent, then students who answer randomly and have any luck at all will pass. If you decide to use alternative response items, consider the possibility of more than two alternatives, or a lot of items, to increase the reliability of results on this portion of a test.

Short Answer

Short-answer items on a test require a student to fill in the blank with a number, word, or phrase, regardless of whether the blank is within a sentence (completion) or at the end of a statement or question (short answer). Generally, the directions for such items are as follows: fill in the blank with the appropriate word or phrase. Short-answer items test recall of knowledge, comprehension, or application of information (see Deepening Your Knowledge Base: Short-Answer Items).

> Short-answer tests ask for knowledge, comprehension, or application of facts.

strategic solutions

Using Short-Answer Items

There are three major implications for using short-answer items for assessment. First, *use short-answer items to assess recall of knowledge.* Recall requires that the student fill in the blank with required information. Second, *use short-answer items to assess comprehension of certain types of information.* Short-answer items require students to translate from graphic to numeric forms, as in geometry, algebra, or physics, or to interpret a passage. Third, *use short-answer items to assess application skills in math and science.* Short-answer items require students to apply formulae to solve problems presented in graphic form, numeric form (such as an algebra equation), or verbal form (such as a word problem).

Evaluation: Using Short-Answer Items

Short-answer items are very common on tests. For example, Ms. Gist used fifteen of them (including the bonus question) on her chapter test. Their advantages in comparison to other objectively scored items include (1) relative

strategic solutions, continued

deepening your knowledge base

Short-Answer Items

The following are examples of short-answer items used to assess recall, comprehension, or application. Notice that each item is carefully stated so that only one answer is possible and unintended cues to the correct response are avoided.

A. Knowledge

Fill in the blank with the appropriate term or phrase.

What is the capital of British Columbia? _____

Problem solving begins with problem _____ .

The first ten amendments to the American Constitution are called _____ .

B. Comprehension: Translation

Refer to the graph at the right.

1. The coordinates of point *A* are _____ .
2. The point whose coordinates are (0, −2) is _____ .

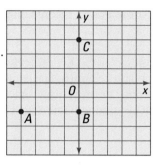

Use the correct form of *avoir* to make a complete sentence.

Vous _____ anglais à dix heures.

C. Comprehension: Interpretation

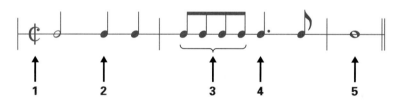

Identify as fully as possible:

1. _____
2. _____
3. _____
4. _____
5. _____

D. Application

Fill in the blank with the correct solution to the problem.

Given: $12 - x = 7$, $x =$ _____

A bus with an average of 30 people aboard traveled 200 miles in 5 hours, making 4 stops. What was its average speed in miles per hour? _____

Refer to the graph of *CDE* on the next page.

1. The coordinates of the midpoint of *CE* are _____ .
2. The coordinates of the midpoint of CD are _____ .
3. The slope of the line joining the midpoints of *CE* and *CD* is _____ .
4. The slope *ED* is _____ .

Source: Graph tests are adapted from Jorgensen, 1988, p. 62

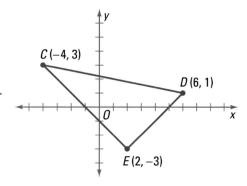

ease of construction and (2) minimal effect of student guessing on the score. Their disadvantage is the occasional difficulty in scoring responses. You should decide beforehand whether you will accept incorrect spellings, synonyms, and the like. Your scoring decisions should rest on whether the response is a valid indication of the type of knowledge that you wish to assess rather than an absolute standard of precision.

Multiple Choice

Multiple-choice items on a test contain a problem and at least three plausible solutions to the problem. Multiple-choice items differ from alternative response items in (1) *new* response options for each multiple-choice item and (2) number of response options, which is never less than three. The plausible but incorrect solutions to each item are called *distractors*. The directions for multiple-choice items are generally as follows: Choose the *best* response to each of the following items. Multiple-choice items can be used to assess knowledge, comprehension, application, analysis, or evaluation (see Deepening Your Knowledge Base: Multiple-Choice Items).

Multiple-choice tests can assess several types of cognition.

Using Multiple-Choice Items

There are three implications for using multiple-choice items for assessment design. First, *use multiple-choice items to assess knowledge when matching is not an appropriate format and recall is not necessary.* If you want to assess

strategic solutions, continued

deepening your knowledge base

Multiple-Choice Items

Following are examples of *multiple-choice* items that are used to assess all levels of cognition with the exception of synthesis. Notice that the stems are worded to avoid unintended cues to the correct response, that responses are relatively short, and that one response is always clearly better than the others.

A. Knowledge

Choose the best response to each of the following items.

The normal temperature of the average adult human is _____ degrees Fahrenheit.

    a. 99   c. 98.6
    b. 96.8   d. 100.6

Generally, what parts of dinosaurs became fossils?

    a. skin and muscles   c. internal organs
    b. bones and teeth   d. fatty tissues

B. Comprehension

What time is shown on the clock?

    a. 11:30
    b. 10:30
    c. 6:50
    d. 6:30

    Steve bought a pretty vase to send to his grandmother with money that he had saved from his allowance. The vase was a birthday present. He knew that she liked to keep flowers in the house. His mother helped him wrap the vase. Then his father took him in the car to the post office, where Steve gave it to the mailman. He imagined his grandmother's reaction when she opened the package.

1. What is the best title for this story?
    a. Going to the Post Office
    b. Flowers in the House
    c. A Pretty Vase
    d. A Present for Grandmother

C. Application

Which sentence is declarative?
    a. What a great show it was!
    b. Who was the star?

    c. Andy went to the movies.

    d. Buy the tickets.

D. Analysis

Refer to the preceding story about Steve. From the details, what would you assume to be his age?

    a. younger than 6   c. from 13 to 15

    b. from 6 to 12   d. 16 or older

E. Evaluation

Jenny went to listen to Bill, her next-door neighbor, make his first presentation at the mall as a salesman for a company that sells food processors. Bill claimed that his company's product was better than all the other food processors on the market. What fact might most lead Jenny to doubt Bill's claim?

    a. Bill never cooked at home.

    b. He was not being paid on commission.

    c. This was his first day on the job.

    d. This food processor was comparatively expensive.

recognition of a variety of facts, for example, you might prefer multiple-choice over matching or short-answer items. Second, *use multiple-choice items to assess comprehension when alternative response is not an appropriate format.* Although you can accurately assess some comprehension of distinctions (such as fact-opinion) through alternative response items, you may find multiple choice a better way to assess comprehension of statements and the like. Third, *use multiple-choice items to assess application, analysis, and evaluation skills when short answer is not necessary.* Even math and science problems can often be put in multiple-choice format, which is easier to score than short answer.

Evaluation: Using Multiple-Choice Items

Multiple-choice items are as common as short-answer items on tests—for example, Ms. Gist used twelve of them on her thirty-one-item test. Together, these items counted for almost half of all possible points. The advantages of multiple-choice items over other item types are that they are (1) flexible enough to address a wide range of objectives, (2) relatively reliable indicators of ability compared with other item types, and (3) more easily scored than short-answer items and performance exercises. These advantages often lead test makers to prefer them over other item types.

    The limitations on multiple-choice items are that they (1) are difficult to construct and (2) do not assess abilities related to synthesis or affective and psychomotor outcomes. Their difficulty of construction is largely due to how hard it is to invent plausible distractors. Nor can multiple-choice items assess abilities related to synthesis (such as originality), expression of a value, or demonstration of a physical skill. Despite these limitations, multiple-choice items remain very useful because of their advantages over other item types and exercises.

Objectively scored test items are most often used to assess lower-order cognitive outcomes, but multiple choice can also be used to assess analysis and evaluation. Performance-based exercises are generally used to assess outcomes involving synthesis or the affective or psychomotor domain.

Performance-Based Exercises

> Demonstration of a skill is an increasingly popular method of assessment.

Education has recently seen a great increase of interest in **performance assessment,** which is a direct appraisal of a skill through a demonstration of some kind. The demonstration of the skill may involve engaging in an activity or creating a product (Haertel, 1992). Performance-based exercises include *essay questions, simulations,* and various forms of *work sample.* An essay question is often used to assess complex thinking in a subject field. A simulation is used to assess a range of outcomes when the learner is operating with a model of a process, mechanism, or system. A work sample is used to assess authentic or realistic performances.

Essay Questions

> Essay questions can assess a variety of skills through a relatively long response.

Essay questions are items that contain a statement that requires the student to supply a response of greater length than a few specific words. Essay items that require only a brief response (from a phrase to a paragraph in length) are known as *restricted response questions.* Essay items that require more than a short paragraph in response are known as *extended response questions.* There are no standard instructions for either type of item. Essay questions are generally used to assess a wide variety of cognitive skills (see Deepening Your Knowledge Base: Essay Questions).

Using Essay Questions

There are two major implications for using essay questions for assessment planning. First, *use restricted response essay items to assess thinking skills when you want the student to construct a response, short answer is inappropriate,*

deepening your knowledge base

Essay Questions

Following are examples of restricted response and extended response essay questions. Note how each question is formulated in terms of a task for the student to accomplish.

A. Comprehension

Write a short paragraph describing what could happen if a person did not follow the drug safety skills that we talked about in class. (restricted response/health)

Give three examples showing how the history of Canada is tied directly to the history of the United States and of Great Britain. Describe two ways in which Canada is tied to Britain today. Write your answer below. Use complete sentences. (extended response/history)

B. Application

Henry is much smaller than the other fourteen-year-old boys in his class. Should he be concerned? In a few sentences, explain why or why not. (restricted response/home economics)

In an essay, discuss how each of the following principles of design is used in building a room: balance, proportion, scale, rhythm, and emphasis. (extended response/home economics)

C. Analysis

James knows that half of the students from his school are accepted at the public university nearby. Also, half are accepted at the local private college. James thinks that this adds up to 100 percent, so he will surely be accepted at one or the other institution. Explain why James may be wrong. If possible, use a diagram in your explanation. (restricted response/math)

Using the tales of King Arthur, Sir Lancelot, and Sir Gareth studied in this unit, discuss the type of hero and story patterns typically found in Arthurian romance. (extended response/English)

D. Synthesis

Plan a healthful meal using foods from each of the four food groups. (restricted response/health)

Imagine that you are an advisor to the leaders of Puerto Rico. You have been asked to write a brief report on the political status of the commonwealth. The report should (1) describe the advantages and disadvantages of various options for changing the political status of Puerto Rico and (2) make recommendations for action by Puerto Rico's leaders. (extended response/world history)

E. Evaluation

Imagine yourself an admiral charged with evaluating the punishment Billy Budd received for striking his ship's captain. In a paragraph, describe what (if any) punishment you think the *captain* should receive and why he should (or should not) receive it. (restricted response/English)

(Continued on next page)

strategic solutions, continued

your knowledge base, continued

Choose one of the ancient societies that we have studied, and explain why you think it was superior to the other societies. Support your answer by including information about the following components: (1) geographic location, (2) form of government, (3) type of economy, (4) contributions to other societies. Your answer will be graded in terms of organization, ability to support your answer, and inclusion of the listed components. (extended response/world history)

Source: Essay about James's thinking is from California State Department of Education, 1989, p. 21; essay about Puerto Rico is adapted from Perry, *History of the World* (Boston, MA: Houghton Mifflin Company), 1993, p. 815

and extended response is unnecessary. Sometimes we are interested in the ability of students to construct a response by explaining something in their own words or describing how they would apply a procedure in a specific situation. As long as the response does not require extended discussion, restricted response items are appropriate. Second, *use extended response essay items to assess thinking that requires extensive integration or organization of information or ideas.* When students are asked to put together several different ideas or pieces of information to form a whole (the definition of *synthesis*), an extended response essay item is necessary to assess learning.

One of the most common difficulties in the use of essay questions is the establishment of scoring criteria. For restricted response essay items, you might address this problem by using **analytic scoring,** which involves identifying different dimensions of a response and awarding points based on a rating scale for each dimension (Herman, Aschbacher & Winters, 1992). For extended response items, you may prefer **holistic scoring,** which involves sorting essay responses as they are read into one of five or so categories of quality.

You can enhance the reliability of scoring by using a **rubric,** or scoring guide. Rubrics involve descriptions of criteria for scoring, examples of responses that meet different criteria, or both. Rubrics can be constructed for either restricted response or extended response essays. The rubric in Figure 14.2 is for an extended response essay to assess the development of mathematical understanding.

Evaluation: Using Essay Questions

In the past, essays were used as a "last resort" to assess the attainment of objectives. Techniques have now been developed to improve the reliability of scoring so that essay items can be used to obtain reliable indications of learning (Dunbar, Koretz & Hoover, 1991). Despite the development of techniques to improve the reliability of scoring, essay responses are still time-consuming to mark. And whereas responses to objectively scored tests can almost al-

Demonstrated competence	Satisfactory response	Inadequate response
Exemplary response ... rating = 6	**Minor flaws but satisfactory ... rating = 4**	**Begins, but fails to complete problem ... rating = 2**
Gives a complete response with a clear, coherent, unambiguous, and elegant explanation; includes a clear and simplified diagram; communicates effectively to the identified audience; shows understanding of the open-ended problem's mathematical ideas and processes; identifies all the important elements of the problem; may include examples and counterexamples; presents strong supporting arguments.	Completes the problem satisfactorily, but the explanation may be muddled; argumentation may be incomplete; diagram may be inappropriate or unclear; understands the underlying mathematical ideas; uses mathematical ideas effectively.	Explanation is not understandable; diagram may be unclear; shows no understanding of the problem situation; may make major computational errors.
Competent response ... rating = 5	**Serious flaws but nearly satisfactory ... rating = 3**	**Unable to begin effectively ... rating = 1**
Gives a fairly complete response with reasonably clear explanations; may include an appropriate diagram; communicates effectively to the identified audience; shows understanding of the problem's mathematical ideas and processes; identifies the most important elements of the problem; presents solid supporting arguments.	Begins the problem appropriately but may fail to complete or may omit significant parts of the problem; may fail to show full understanding of mathematical ideas and processes; may make major computational errors; may misuse or fail to use mathematical terms; response may reflect an inappropriate strategy for solving the problem.	Words do not reflect the problem; drawings misrepresent the problem situation; copies parts of the problem but without attempting a solution; fails to indicate which information is appropriate to problem. **No attempt ... rating = 0**

Figure 14.2   A Rubric for an Essay Test of Mathematical Understanding
(California State Department of Education, 1989)

ways be marked by a machine or by a nonexpert, responses to essay items must almost always be marked by an expert.

Simulation Exercises

In Chapter 10, you learned that a **simulation** is an operational model of a process, mechanism, or system. Simulations have frequently been used to teach skills that involve some risk or high cost, and with the advent of the computer, they are also being used to teach thinking skills in academic subjects. Because performance in simulated experiences can often be more

Simulation creates a good situation for assessment.

Simulation exercises are sometimes the best way to assess skills as well as develop them. For example, what skills are better assessed on a simulator in CPR training than on a paper-and-pencil test, or on a real-life partner? *(Frank Siteman/Stock Boston)*

easily monitored than in actual experiences, simulation lends itself to evaluation (see Deepening Your Knowledge Base: Assessments Through Simulation).

strategic solutions

Using Simulation Exercises

The implication of simulation exercises for assessment design is straightforward: *use simulation exercises to assess a skill when assessment of actual performance is not as safe, efficient, or appropriate.* Sometimes the actual performance would be too risky to be made an assessment exercise. Chess, it is said, had enough realism to inspire the first war games with wooden figures and battlefield maps (Cohen & Rhenman, 1961). Simulations with dangerous chemicals or equipment, investment strategies, and so on are considerably less risky ways to develop strategic reasoning than actual performances. At other times simulations are a more efficient way to evaluate the acquisition of a skill than actual performance. Opposing players do not have to be present, for example, to demonstrate an accurate overhand serve in volleyball. Finally, a novice might benefit most from learning through a simulation that simplifies performance conditions (Alessi, 1988). In all cases, scoring guides can be helpful for establishing reliability.

Evaluation: Using Simulation Exercises

Simulations have a couple of advantages over their alternatives: (1) they can be less risky, more efficient, and more appropriate than assessments that would utilize actual performance; and (2) they are often more effective at developing skills than any other alternative short of actual performance (Salomon, 1992). Simulations also have a couple of limitations: (1) they are

deepening your knowledge base

Assessments Through Simulation

Following are assessments through simulation. Notice that appropriate dimensions and degrees of realism are established, that assessment exercises resemble instructional exercises, that scoring or rating criteria are keyed to the dimensions of performance being trained, and that an adequate number of observations are collected to ensure reliability of results.

Assessment of Volleyball Serve

Purpose: To measure consistency and accuracy in serving.

Equipment: Standard inflated volleyballs, net $(7'11\frac{5}{8}'')$, court, and tape for indicating the target area.

Administration:

- Subject serves ten times (40 possible points) from the service area (see figure).
- Subject may serve overhead or underhand.
- Tape lines mark the court and outline the target areas with values from 2 to 4 points.
- Balls hitting on line score the higher point value.
- Balls contacting the net or antennae or landing out of bounds receive no score.

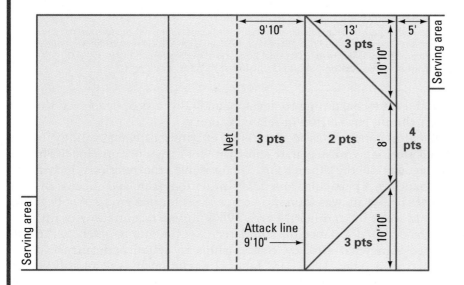

Assessment of Business Management Skills

You are the chief executive officer of an established firm. Your firm has always captured a major share of the market because of good use of technology, understanding of the natural laws of constraint, understanding of

(Continued on next page)

strategic solutions, continued

your knowledge base, continued

market systems, and maintenance of a high standard for your product. However, in recent months your product has become part of a new trend in public tastes. Several new firms have entered the market and have captured part of your sales. Your product's proportional share of total aggregate demand is continuing to fall. When demand returns to normal, you will be controlling less of the market than before.

Your board of directors has given you less than a month to prepare a report that solves the problem in the short run and in the long run. In preparing the report, you should (1) define the problem, (2) prepare data to illustrate the current situation, (3) prepare data to illustrate conditions one year in the future, (4) recommend action for today, (5) recommend action over the next year, and (6) discuss where your company will be in the market six months from today and one year from today.

The tasks that must be completed in the course of this project include:

- Deriving formulae for supply, demand, elasticity, and equilibrium
- Preparing schedules for supply, demand, costs, and revenues
- Graphing all work
- Preparing a written evaluation of the current and future situation for the market in general and for your company in particular
- Preparing a written recommendation for your board of directors
- Showing aggregate demand today and predicting it for a year later
- Showing the demand for your firm's product today and a year later

Source: Volleyball: This article is reprinted with permission from the *Journal of Physical Education, Recreation & Dance*, February, 1991, p. 20. JOPERD is a publication of the American Alliance for Health, Physical Education, Recreation and Dance, 1900 Association Drive, Reston, VA 22091. Business: Wiggins, 1989, p. 707

costly and time-consuming to develop, and (2) the skill developed through them might not have criterion-related validity.

Of greatest concern has been the issue of criterion-related validity. Is simulated performance an adequate substitute for actual performance? This answer depends on the simulation. For example, the relationship between performance in a particular business simulation game and success in business after five years was found to be near zero for one group of college students and weak for another (Norris, 1986). In one recent study of fifth and sixth graders' performance on simulated experiments in science, the data suggested somewhat stronger relationships to actual performance (Shavelson, Baxter & Pine, 1991, 1992), but the relationships were still weaker than what would be desirable for a performance substitute. There is no doubt that simulations can be a valuable tool for learning and assessment, but you should look for evidence of criterion-related validity before adopting a simulation as a learning or assessment tool.

Work Samples

A **work sample** is a portion of an actual performance that represents the whole to be assessed. Work samples are collected either through observation of some activity or through evaluation of some product of the activity. If the activity is observed, it is often observed under controlled conditions, such as a driving test or student teaching. If the product of an activity is to be assessed, samples of the product are often selected to meet a set of goals to be attained, such as in a portfolio.

> A work sample is part of an actual performance to be assessed.

Observational Techniques

The means to assess student actions directly are known as **observational techniques.** In theory, you could assess anything or everything that a student does in class, but in practice assessment of student behavior is limited by constraints on your time. An important feature of an observational technique is that it can make assessment of student behavior efficient. Accordingly, observational techniques are generally designed with learning outcomes in mind. Sometimes the outcome is predominantly affective, such as expression of spontaneous interest in a learning task. At other times the outcome is predominantly cognitive or psychomotor, such as solving homework problems at the chalkboard, setting up a scientific experiment, or singing skillfully. Although observational techniques are typically used to assess activities, they are sometimes used to assess products of activities, such as work shown on a math problem or understanding of a story that was read.

> Observational techniques should make assessment of learning outcomes more efficient.

There are four types of observational techniques: anecdotal records, rating scales, checklists, and cumulative records.

- *Anecdotal records* are written accounts of the behavior of a particular student at a particular time. They are frequently placed on cards to be filed or are logged into a notebook.
- *Rating scales* are lists of characteristics with a means to indicate the degree or frequency of each characteristic. They may be composed of a continuous scale (such as a line from high to low, seldom to always, or ineffective to effective, with intermediate ratings marked off) or an intermittent scale (with numbers or letters to indicate different response categories).
- *Checklists* are lists of characteristics with a means to indicate whether each characteristic is present. Checklists usually present one, two, or, at most, three response categories (such as a blank for a checkmark, yes and no, or agree, disagree, and no opinion). Checklists with more than three response categories are typically rating scales.
- *Cumulative records* are indications of the total response during any period in time. Cumulative records often consist of dots, checkmarks, pluses, or minuses and are frequently used for recording attendance or homework.

Most teachers use one or more of these observational techniques (see Deepening Your Knowledge Base: Observational Techniques).

Using Observational Techniques

There are two major implications for employing observational techniques. First, *use observational techniques to assess affective and psychomotor outcomes.* Such outcomes include attendance in class; attitudes toward a subject or other students; development of values such as citizenship, honesty, cooperation, and fair play; and development of skills in the psychomotor domain (see Chapter 3).

Second, *use observational techniques to assess cognitive outcomes when other forms of assessment are inappropriate.* For example, you may find that young children's understanding of a story is more appropriately assessed through a checklist you keep during an interview or a small-group discussion than through a written exercise of some kind. Or suppose you are interested in *typical,* rather than optimal, cognitive performance. The unobtrusive use of observational techniques can help you assess the routine attainment of cognitive, affective, and psychomotor objectives (Norris & Ennis, 1989).

The key to reliable interpretation of performance is collecting a number of observations under similar performance conditions. If observations are made by more than one person, validity as well as reliability of interpretation often increases.

Evaluation: Using Observational Techniques

Teachers have always used observational techniques because they represent an assessment of authentic performances. The advantages of observational assessments over paper-and-pencil tests are (1) improved accuracy of assessment and (2) meaningful feedback to the teacher, student, and parents. Methods now exist to make the results of observations as reliable as those from any objectively scored test, and if an effort is made to train raters, the validity of observational assessments is seldom questioned. Comments by teachers who use observational techniques as opposed to objectively scored tests indicate that they learn more about their students this way and are in a better position to give the student (and parents) meaningful feedback about the student's strengths and needs.

The meaningfulness of feedback from direct observation has a high price, however, in the time and effort required to make repeated observations of individual performance. Furthermore, ratings of one performance may not generalize to ratings of other similar performances. Success at one science experiment or multistep math problem, for example, does not necessarily lead to success at another. If you adopt observational techniques of assessment for your classes, be careful to structure observations so that you are not overburdened by the work required to make reliable and valid interpretations.

deepening your knowledge base

Observational Techniques

Following are illustrations of rating scales and a checklist. Notice that what is to be observed has been determined in advance, that terms are descriptive, and that on rating scales a small number of positions is used.

A. Numerical Rating Scale

Indicate how often the student exhibits the behavior described by circling the appropriate number. 1 = always, 2 = frequently, 3 = occasionally, 4 = seldom, and 5 = never.

1. Demonstrates self-control   **1**   **2**   **3**   **4**   **5**

2. Works and plays well with others   **1**   **2**   **3**   **4**   **5**

B. Graphic Rating Scale

Indicate how often the student exhibits the behavior described by making an X at the appropriate point on the line under each item.

1. Demonstrates self-control

always   frequently   occasionally   seldom   never

C. Descriptive Graphic Rating Scale (same instructions for B)

1. Demonstrates self-control

| Self-controlled even when provoked | Needs reminding of rules but follows them | Unable to control self even when reminded of rules |

2. Works and plays well with others

| Cooperates routinely with adults and children | Cooperates with some children and needs occasional guidance | Never wants to cooperate and is very shy or aggressive |

Checklist for a Pourquoi Tale[1]

Name of student: _____   Story title: _____

	Yes	No
1. Is the main character of the story an animal?	____	____
2. Does the animal in the story have an unusual characteristic?	____	____
3. Does the story answer *why* the main character has an unusual characteristic?	____	____
4. Does the story have a beginning, middle, and end?	____	____
5. Does the story begin with a purposely vague setting ("Long, long ago . . . ")	____	____

[1]A *pourquoi* tale is a "why" tale that explains how something people do not understand came into being. Courtesy of Nancy Draper.

Portfolio Assessment

> Portfolios of students' work can be used to assess their progress.

Portfolios are systematic collections of work samples. They are typically used by artists, photographers, and journalists to represent their capabilities to potential customers or employers. Recently, interest has developed around the use of portfolios by teachers and students to represent capabilities of various kinds.

The *showcase portfolio*, for example, is often a collection of from three to six samples of work that represent optimal performance in one or more subject areas. The *working portfolio* may include examples of typical performance or work in progress. Sometimes both showcase and working portfolios are kept in the same location—typically a place where students have access to their own work for any number of reasons (Tierney, Carter & Desai, 1991).

> Students who select items for their portfolios will reflect on their work.

In the context of a portfolio, the word *item* takes on a very different meaning from what it does on a test. An item on a test is a stimulus to which a student responds, but an item in a portfolio is evidence of previous performance and a stimulus to future performance. The item may take the form of an actual product (such as a best piece of writing, a response to a multistep math problem, or successive representations of a scientific problem) or a record of a product or performance (such as a tape cassette of a musical performance, a picture of a papier-mâché mask, student-teacher writing conference notes, or a reading log). These items are usually chosen by the student. They are subject to reflection as the student gains proficiency and revises the contents of the portfolio to represent the attainment of new goals (see Deepening Your Knowledge Base: Possible Items in a Portfolio).

strategic solutions

Using Portfolio Assessment

The implications of portfolios for assessment design are just beginning to emerge, particularly in elementary reading and writing, where they have caught on rapidly (e.g., DeFina, 1992; Flood, Lapp & Monken, 1992; Glazer & Brown, 1993; Tierney, Carter & Desai, 1991; Valencia, 1990). Because a portfolio is a dynamic collection always accessible to the student, you should *use portfolios to integrate assessment with instruction*. Portfolio assessment is unique among assessment techniques because it is conducted with a continuing representation of the student's work and is almost always done with the student in a conference. The use of portfolios to integrate assessment with instruction has recently been described in both the arts and sciences as development of a *portfolio culture* (Duschl & Gitomer, 1991; Gitomer, Grosh & Price, 1992). A portfolio culture can be developed on the level of a class, program, or school.

deepening your knowledge base

Possible Items in a Portfolio

The following items are sometimes found in a portfolio. If you use portfolio assessment, phase in the use of portfolios one subject at a time; negotiate the purpose, goals, and criteria for including items in the collection; require that each portfolio contain a summary sheet that describes its contents; and develop a collaborative assessment procedure.

Poetry and other creative writing	Essays and reports
Sequels/spin-offs from texts	Letters
Problem statements/solutions	Response logs/reviews
Posters/artistic media	Journal entries
Workbook pages, quizzes, and tests	Interviews
Attitude surveys	Collaborative works
Reading lists and reviews	Teacher comments
Self-assessment checklists	Teacher checklists
Self-assessment statements	Peer reviews
Parental observations and comments	

Source: DeFina, 1992, pp. 23–27

Evaluation: Using Portfolio Assessment

Like observational techniques, portfolio assessment can improve the quality of feedback to student, teacher, and parents. And like observational techniques, it requires a fair amount of time, perhaps five to fifteen minutes per portfolio review conference (Tierney, Carter & Desai, 1991). Unlike time spent observing performance, however, time spent in portfolio review has instructional value. The collaborative dimension of portfolio assessment is believed to develop metacognitive skills (see Chapter 10), although there is no scientific evidence as yet to support this claim.

The limitations of portfolio assessment are that (1) reliability of assessment needs to be carefully established and (2) validity of an interpretation can be questioned if it does not match the conditions under which work was accomplished. Reliability can be enhanced through rating scales and checklists, and teachers can meet regularly to discuss how they would rate the contents of a sample portfolio with regard to the attainment of a given set of goals. Validity of interpretation is a matter of reflecting conditions under which work was accomplished. Work accomplished with the help of teachers, peers, or parents, for example, does *not* represent what the student can accomplish independently (Herman & Winters, 1994).

Teachers frequently indicate significant concern over how to initiate portfolio assessment (Johns & Leirsburg, 1992). Some ways of structuring portfo-

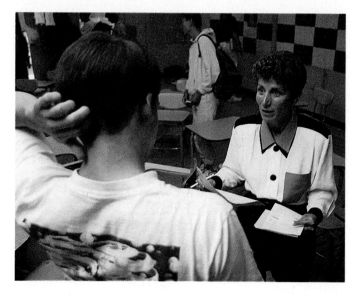

Portfolios can include a wide range of items. Both a student's essay and a teacher's written comments are potential items. *(Elizabeth Crews)*

lios are more reflective than others, and you might find an instructional module by the National Council on Measurement in Education (Arter & Spandel, 1992) a useful guide should you decide to develop a portfolio approach to assessment. The full module can be photocopied for instructional purposes.

Aligning Assessment Tasks with Learning Outcomes

Test questions should reflect what was learned in class.

Perhaps the best way to ensure that your assessment tasks match anticipated learning outcomes is to design an assessment in which learning activities and assessment tasks are similar. For example, if you organize your lessons around questioning as an activity, you can use questions of the type employed in class to structure a test. Test questions, including discussion questions, should be a version of what has actually gone on in class, with the understanding that the same questions used for learning cannot be used to assess cognitive skills. You may want to construct a *table of specifications* to ensure that the content of the test questions is representative of what you expected students to learn in class (see Table 14.2).

In a table of specifications, learning processes such as those described in the taxonomies of cognitive, affective, and psychomotor objectives are typically arranged along one dimension, and content units are typically arranged along the other. Goals or learning outcomes fill the cells created by the combination of the two dimensions. A number of test tasks or items can then be developed in proportion to the relative importance of goals or outcomes.

Table 14.2   Table of Specifications for an Objectively Scored Test on Assessment Design

Unit Contents	Knowledge	Comprehension	Application	Analysis	Evaluation
Problems of assessment (20%)	Define reliability and three kinds of validity (2 items)	Interpret assessment activities in terms of problem solving in assessment (2 items)	Classify specific assessment conditions using goals of assessment (2 items)	Analyze assessment activities for problem solving (2 items)	Evaluate cases of design in terms of problem-solving goals (2 items)
Specification of tasks and scoring criteria (40%)	Identify examples of assessment tasks by name (4 items)	Predict effects of changing assessment conditions on accuracy (4 items)	Use Bloom's hierarchy to identify appropriate assessment tasks, given outcome (4 items)	Analyze test descriptions for probable learning outcome (4 items)	Evaluate matches of test task with learning outcomes (4 items)
Use of standards to evaluate scores (30%)	Define standard, norm, and terms for different grading systems (3 items)	Interpret different scores as grades, given absolute grading standards (3 items)	Apply mastery learning criteria to set of test scores to determine grades (3 items)	Analyze grading methods for effects on motivation (3 items)	Evaluate appropriateness of procedures to assign grades, given scenario (3 items)
Use of results for teaching decisions (10%)	Identify decisions based on assessment (1 item)	Predict effect of grades on future learning (1 item)	Use set of results to identify appropriate decisions (1 item)	Analyze set of scores for gender fairness (1 item)	Evaluate appropriateness of intervention strategies based on assessment results (1 item)
Total: 100%	10 items	10 items	10 items	10 items	10 items

The natural relationship between many learning activities and performance-based exercises provides an opportunity for assessment that is closely related to instruction, but to take advantage of this situation, you must assess performances in terms of desired outcomes so that you can assess whether students have achieved them. Outcomes may be so many, or assessment opportunities so few, that you may want to use the same assessment task to assess the attainment of multiple outcomes. If so, specify how each outcome is to be assessed on the task. These specifications can be listed in a table much like a table of specifications, except that brief descriptions of performances replace descriptions of unit contents. Goals or outcomes become descriptions of dimensions for assessing particular performances (constructing rating scales or checklists). Tables such as these systematize the process that most teachers use intuitively to align assessment with instruction.

USING STANDARDS TO EVALUATE SCORES

Teachers must establish a way to make judgments about students' responses on assessment tasks. Scoring criteria help teachers make these judgments accurately but do not represent evaluation. At some point or other, scoring criteria must bridge assessment of responses with **standards,** or general expectations for scores that teachers, schools, and communities hold. This bridging of scores with standards should occur during assessment design—that is, long before the design is implemented.

> Grades interpret student performance according to a standard of excellence.

Standards form the basis for evaluating scores and eventually for assigning **grades,** which are interpretations of performance by a standard of excellence. Even in kindergarten, the practice of assigning grades is widespread (Freeman & Hatch, 1989). By middle school years, students are assigned letter or number grades for each subject in *99 percent* of schools (MacIver, 1990). Long before you give a test or even introduce your students to objectives, examine the grade reporting system of your school for grading standards. Although there is generally no "correct" way to assign grades, there is usually a correct way to report them, accompanied by an explanation of standards to permit interpretation of the grade report. Figure 14.3 presents a typical elementary school report card.

Normed Excellence

> Grades are related to where scores fall on a normal curve.

Almost all standards are based on a concept of **normed excellence,** or a set of criteria for evaluating scores that is based on the normal curve. You encountered the concept of a normal curve in Chapter 7 when you learned about the range of what is "normal." Normal curves are used to describe many scores that are distributed around an average value, such as the scores of an unselected group of third graders on a test of reading achievement. The average score is known as the *norm* or *mean.* In terms of grading standards, scores around the norm are generally interpreted as average or fair. Scores immediately above these are interpreted as above average or good. Scores immediately below them are interpreted as below average or poor. *Excellence* is generally defined in terms of scores far above the norm, whereas *failure* is generally defined in terms of scores far below the norm.

> Grades may reflect students' achievement or progress.

The characteristic of learning that is scored can vary from one school policy to another. Some reports focus on *achievement,* which is often correlated with scores on standardized tests (see Deepening Your Knowledge Base: Standardized Tests). A student receives a grade that reflects the standing of his or her score in relation to the norm or the mean. Other reports focus on *progress,* which is often defined as improvement over past performance. A student receives a grade that reflects a degree of improvement in scores over past performance in a subject.

The contents of report cards are largely a matter of school policy, but you have some flexibility as to how you assign grades within this policy (cf. Ornstein, 1989). There are three recommended ways to grade student performance: *absolute grade standards, contracting for grades,* and *continuous*

Name	1st nine weeks	2nd nine weeks	3rd nine weeks	4th nine weeks
Attendance				
Days present				
Days absent				

Marking Key

A – Excellent progress	(90–100)
B – Good progress	(80–89)
C – Average progress	(70–79)
D – Poor progress	(60–69)
F – Failure to make progress	(below 59)

I – Above level	+ Mastery
II – On level	– Nonmastery
III – Below level	

Reading	1st	2nd	3rd	4th
1. Reads with understanding				
2. Uses word attack skills				
3. Reads well orally				
4. Recognizes vocabulary words				
5. Locates needed information				
6. Reads for enjoyment				
7.				

Spelling	1st	2nd	3rd	4th
1. Spells assigned words				
2. Spells correctly in written work				
3.				

Language	1st	2nd	3rd	4th
1. Listens with understanding				
2. Expresses ideas well orally				
3. Expresses ideas well in writing				
4. Uses correct writing skills				
5. Writes neatly and legibly				
6.				
7.				

Mathematics	1st	2nd	3rd	4th
1. Addition				
2. Subtraction				
3. Multiplication				
4. Division				
5. Fractions				
6. Place value				
7. Estimation				
8. Measurement				
9. Geometry				
10. Reading problems				
11. Money				
12.				
13.				

Social Studies

Science and Health

Work and Study Habits	1st	2nd	3rd	4th
1. Uses time wisely				
2. Follows directions				
3. Prepares assignment on time				
4. Is attentive — listens				
5. Works well independently				
6. Does work carefully				
7. Puts forth effort				
8. Takes care of materials				
9. Shares information and participates in group activities				
10. Works well in cooperative groups				
11.				
12.				
13.				

Citizenship	1st	2nd	3rd	4th
1. Observes accepted rules				
2. Is courteous				
3. Exhibits self-control				
4. Works and plays well with others				
5. Respects authority				
6. Respects the rights and property of others				
7.				
8.				

Figure 14.3   An Elementary Grade Report Card

deepening your knowledge base

Standardized Tests

A **standardized test** is an evaluation instrument that has fixed directions for administration and scoring and that has been administered to a representative sample of the population for whom the test is intended. Scores from the representative sample, which is known as the *norm group,* are used to calculate *norms,* or average scores, which serve as estimates of averages for the population. Scores of individual students do not typically represent *raw scores,* or actual number of items answered correctly on the test, but are expressed as *derived scores,* which take into account the need to interpret individual scores in relation to the norm.

An **achievement test,** which is an evaluation instrument designed to measure knowledge, skill, or accomplishment in any area, is either standardized or teacher made. Several well-known standardized achievement tests are the *Stanford Achievement Tests,* the *Iowa Tests of Basic Skills,* and the *California Achievement Tests.* These and other standardized tests are reviewed in *Mental Measurements Yearbooks* and *Test Critiques.* Teacher-made achievement tests are found in resources that accompany textbooks or are constructed by classroom teachers themselves to accompany units of instruction. Results of teacher-made tests are generally less reliable than results of standardized achievement tests, which have been constructed by test experts to meet standards of reliability and validity. Somewhat paradoxically, standardized achievement test results are not always given as valid an interpretation by educators as teacher-made test results. A teacher-made test generally conforms more closely in content than a standardized test to what was actually taught.

Standardized achievement test scores are very useful, however, for a range of purposes. Probably the best-known purpose is to compare average achievements by students in local schools with state and national norms. A second purpose is to place students in grade levels or groupings, particularly if they have recently moved into the local school system. A third purpose is to identify students for individual diagnostic or intelligence testing, the results of which are generally more accurate than the results of group-administered tests.

Now that you know something about standardized tests, break out into small groups to discuss the following questions. Appoint someone to record your answers. After you answer the questions, reassemble in the larger group to compare your findings.

Discussion Questions

1. What influences might account for changes in a person's scores on the same standardized test from one time to another? Make a short list.

2. Identify several types of achievement that cannot be easily measured by standardized tests. What do standardized tests measure best? What do they measure poorly or not at all?

progress assessment. Absolute standards are the most common, with a perfect score at 100 and cutoff percentages for grades established at regular intervals below 100. Contracting for grades involves establishing a work agreement with individual students. Continuous progress assessment involves periodic appraisal of performance without the assignment of a grade until the end of a course of study.

Absolute Grade Standards

Many teachers, like Ms. Gist, use **absolute grade standards,** which are evaluations of scores in comparison to established percentages of a perfect score. A perfect score is usually 100, and absolute standards are sometimes set so that 90 percent or higher of a perfect score is an A, 80–89 percent is a B, 70–79 percent is a C, 60–69 percent is a D, and less than 60 percent is an F. Higher criteria are also used.

> Absolute grade standards use established percentages to figure grades.

Absolute grade standards rest on the general assumption of normed excellence, but they do not attempt to apply the normal curve directly to a set of scores to assign grades. Direct application of the normal curve to set grades, or use of *relative grade standards,* was once widespread, but it is no longer widely practiced. Relative grade standards forced the lowest *obtained* scores to be assigned the lowest *possible* grades (such as D or F), even if those scores were high enough to indicate mastery of the material.

> Relative grade standards are uncommon because they may be unrelated to mastery.

It might be useful at this point to use absolute grade standards to calculate a six-week grade in Ms. Gist's human physiology class. A hand-held calculator is as important for this task as a pencil. The school where Ms. Gist taught used 90 percent as a cutoff score for an A, 80 percent for a B, and so on. After calculating grades for this class, you might try recalculating them with slightly higher cutoffs (such as 94–100 percent as an A) to determine the effect of higher standards on class grades. Many teachers use absolute grade standards because assigning a grade is just a matter of converting the percent obtained of a perfect score over a given number of tests or exercises to the appropriate letter (or number).

strategic solutions

Using Absolute Grade Standards

Absolute grade standards can facilitate the achievement of more than a few students. With absolute standards, every student can earn an A, but in reality scores tend to distribute themselves normally if the test is of intermediate difficulty. The key to using absolute standards is to *gauge the difficulty level of the test so that top performances are perfect scores, or nearly so, and scores distribute through a range of grades.* Such calibration tends to come with experience. Ms. Gist knew the capabilities of her students well enough to judge accurately the difficulty level of a test so that a top test performance was always 100 or very nearly so.

What happens if no one scores 90 percent or higher on a test? In theory, no one should receive an A. If no one earns a near-perfect score, however, you might want to consider the possibility that some items on the test were too difficult for any of your students. Rather than trying to sort through the items, or throwing the test scores out, consider *scaling scores*, a process by which the highest obtained score is assumed to be perfect. *If no one scores well on a test, consider the highest obtained score to be perfect (100 percent), and use revised standards to assign grades.* In scaling, score equivalents of 90–100 percent of the highest score are interpreted as an A, score equivalents of 80–89 percent of the highest score are interpreted as a B, and so on. Scaled scores remove from consideration that portion of the test that was too difficult. The technique of scaling is particularly useful whenever you introduce a new test and have no benchmark by which to gauge expected performance. No one will object to the revised standard, which raises most grades by removing the "top" of the test, where no one scored.

You also might want to consider the possibility of awarding a few bonus points on tests or assignments. Bonus points are motivational, and they serve to compensate for minor inconsistencies. These inconsistencies cause even the highest-scoring student to earn less-than-perfect scores by the end of a marking period. Bonus points tend to raise point totals to eliminate such inconsistencies, reducing the need to scale total scores at the end of a marking period.

Evaluation: Using Absolute Grade Standards

Two advantages cause absolute grade standards to be popular. First, they are relatively easy to compute. Ms. Gist, for example, awarded up to 100 points for every test (not including 2 bonus points), up to 100 points for homework, and 100 points for article summaries. A total of 600 points was possible during a marking period, making conversion to grades a simple matter of setting score cutoffs for the marking period, summing points for each student, and matching the sums to the cutoffs.

Second, and perhaps more important, absolute grade standards give students a measure of control over their grades. Regardless of whether they respond to these standards, they are aware of them. Students' motives for obtaining a given grade may be a mixed bag of extrinsic reasons, but to some extent they need to decide what they must do to earn the grade they want.

The two disadvantages of absolute grade standards are both related to an inappropriate level of difficulty of tests or assignments. First, an overly easy test does not lead to discrimination of degree or quality of learning. A spelling test on which everyone receives 100 may be a legitimate cause for celebration, or it may signify that students spelled words that they did not have to learn to spell. We cannot tell much about performance from grades if there are no distinctions.

Second, an overly difficult test or assignment can discourage students if no one does well. You may compensate for the difficulty by scaling scores, but then the advantage of ease of interpretation is lost. Receiving a 65 on a test (which would usually be interpreted as a D) and learning that it is an A (by re-

Grades are interpretations of performance by a standard of excellence. Assigning grades is almost universal and often involves hard work, but to ease the task you can usually pick a comfortable location.   *(Robert Brenner/PhotoEdit)*

vised standards) sends mixed signals to a student. With experience, however, you are likely to improve your judgment of student capabilities so that the actual scores students receive on tests are reasonably matched to preset standards.

Contracting for Grades

You have briefly looked at the subject of learning contracts in the context of gifted education (Chapter 7) and in the context of behavioral approaches to learning (Chapter 8). As mentioned in Chapter 7, a contract is an agreement among the learner, the teacher, and any other relevant parties. **Contracting for grades** is a process for establishing a work agreement between the learner and the teacher for assessment purposes. It is not new to education (Edwards, 1991), but it provides choice and flexibility in grading.

In general, students are given performance criteria and grade standards and agree to a set of criteria and standards before they begin to work. The standards generally relate progressively higher grades to increasing expectations for quantity and quality of work. Some students may opt for doing just the required work for a minimum pass (usually a C), but others will attempt to meet the higher standards that usually define a B and an A. Because contracting for grades requires a significant amount of self-knowledge as well as self-direction, this approach is not recommended for most elementary students in most learning situations (Ornstein, 1989).

Teachers and students agree on standards for work when they contract for grades.

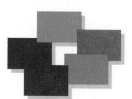

Using Contracting for Grades

Contracts can be more negotiable or less negotiable, depending on ability and age of the learner and on constraints imposed by the curriculum and by the grade reporting system. If you choose this approach, however, you should *begin contracting with relatively short time periods.* Students need to accustom themselves gradually to this approach by contracting for a grade over only a few weeks' time. The contracting approach requires more responsibility than more traditional learning does. Second, *negotiate revised contracts for students who do not perform as well as expected.* The revision may impose more structure on learning during the next contract period, or it may modify the options available to the student. Part of responsible learning involves a realistic assessment by the learner of what he or she can do well within a specified period of time.

Evaluation: Using Contracting for Grades

The strength of contracting lies in the control exerted by students over their own learning and assessment (White & Greenwood, 1992). Students know exactly what is expected of them because to some extent they choose a set of criteria and a standard. As you learned in Chapter 12, choice and self-determination are important for the development of motivation.

The limitation of contracting lies in the opportunity it gives students to do the minimum necessary to obtain a minimum passing grade. Most high school students have very full and busy lives, which include demanding courses, after-school jobs, extracurricular activities, and social commitments. As a consequence, some are likely to contract for minimally acceptable grades to invest themselves in activities of more immediate importance to them.

To compensate for such distractions, a teacher who contracts with students for grades must require *more* work for a minimally acceptable grade than for higher grades. A C should require the greatest *quantity* of work of acceptable quality. By way of contrast, a B should require less quantity but higher-quality work and an A, less quantity still but even higher quality. With such criteria, students motivated to economize their time cannot escape work by choosing a lower grade.

Continuous Progress Assessment

Continuous progress assessment is the periodic appraisal of performance without the assignment of a grade until the end of a course of study. Its most common use is in mastery learning, which was discussed in Chapter 12. Continuous progress assessment relies on the distinction between **formative**

Continuous progress assessment uses frequent appraisals but defers grades to the end of the course.

evaluation, which is an assessment of the degree of mastery of a given learning task, and **summative evaluation,** which is an assessment of the degree to which learning outcomes have been attained over an entire course or at least a substantial part of it (Bloom, Hastings & Madaus, 1971). Continuous progress assessment involves both formative and summative evaluation but in different ways, depending on the teacher.

---

strategic solutions

Using Continuous Progress Assessment

Formative evaluation often involves the administration of **criterion-referenced tests,** which are evaluation instruments constructed to align with goals. The goals are identified through tables of specification for each unit. An important implication of continuous assessment, then, is to *construct and administer criterion-referenced tests to provide feedback on progress toward the attainment of goals.* A criterion-referenced test is administered at the end of every unit, and students who take the test receive feedback regarding mastery (or nonmastery), but *they do not receive a grade.* Rather, students might study their test responses with a feedback booklet, and parents might receive midterm grade reports with only a list of goals marked with some combination of pluses (mastery) and minuses (nonmastery).

In the version of continuous progress assessment used in Learning for Mastery, formative evaluation every week or two provides students who do not achieve mastery on a test with a diagnosis of strengths and weaknesses. Corrective learning activities (such as programmed instruction) are keyed to the weaknesses. Students who do achieve mastery on the formative test are provided with enrichment activities until instruction on the next unit. The grade for the course is based on a comprehensive final examination with absolute grade standards. Teachers do not always include a comprehensive final examination in their assessment designs.

Table 14.5 presents an example of what a portion of the grade book for Ms. Gist's human physiology class might look like had she used this technique in her assessment design. Average gains in achievement in science classes due to the mastery approach are about half a standard deviation (Guskey & Pigott, 1988), which would translate into 5 to 10 points on tests in this course. Note also that the motivational effect of continuous progress assessment reduces the need for motivational assignments.

Evaluation: Using Continuous Progress Assessment

There is some disagreement over whether score gains due to continuous progress grading are the result of increased motivation or of a narrowed focus of attention on achievement of objectives. Good arguments have been offered

s t r a t e g i c   s o l u t i o n s ,   c o n t i n u e d

Table 14.5 *An Example of Continuous Progress Assessment*

Name	T1[1]	T1[2]	T2[1]	T2[2]	T3[1]	T3[2]	T4[1]	T4[2]	Average	Grade
Aday, C.	72	81	80		78	83	73	77	80	B
Balot, J.	55	65	60	68	65	75	64	80	72	C
Barnes, M.	60	76	63	78	82	89	61	75	80	B
Dean, G.	49	58	60	64	61		59		61	D
DuBois, A.	68	71	73	75	68	70	61	73	72	C
Eccles, D.	80	85	86	91	87	96	83	92	91	A
Hewlett, P.	71	80	73	81	82	87	76	84	83	B

Note: [1] refers to form A and [2] refers to Form B of the unit test. Student names are fictitious.

for both sides, but there is common agreement that programs such as Learning for Mastery do lead students to spend greater time on task.

Some critics point out that continuous progress assessment requires a great deal of time and other resources to implement. At a minimum, teachers must prepare (1) tables of specification to link goals with test structure, (2) tests over units of relatively short duration, (3) diagnostic feedback, (4) corrective learning activities for those who do not achieve mastery, (5) enrichment activities for those who do, and (6) either a second set of tests to retest students or a comprehensive final examination. The list of special tasks is relatively long, but all of these are legitimate teaching tasks, and a dedicated teacher can raise test scores significantly through investment of time and effort in this approach to assigning grades.

CONCLUSION

Accurate evaluations of learning enable students, parents, teachers, administrators, and communities to make many types of decisions (Herman, Aschbacher & Winters, 1992), but among the most important of these for the teacher is setting new goals for student learning. A table of scores like the one you might find in a teacher's grade book seems dry and uninviting, but to a teacher these scores represent a wealth of information as long as learning has been evaluated accurately. If you know what students have learned and what they have not learned at any given point in time, you are in a position to set new goals for instruction.

The use of evaluation for instructional decisions can be analyzed in terms of three time frames: individual assessments, sequences of assessments, and assessment strategies. Individual assessments occur in the most limited time frame, from as short as ten to fifteen minutes for an entire class to as long as ten to fifteen minutes per individual (a total of four to six hours). They encompass individual quizzes, tests, written assignments, sets of homework papers, portfolio conferences, and the like. Individual assessments provide valuable information about learning at any given point in time.

Let's take the first test in Ms. Gist's human physiology class as an example. What information can it provide for instructional decisions? You might want to turn back to Table 14.1 to refer to student scores in the column labeled "T1." How did the students do on this 100-point test? Let your eyes run down the column of figures. It is clear that some students did well and some did not do so well. To find out how well the class did, average the scores. The average score on the test was 71, which, according to school marking standards, would be a low C.

Why did the class not do better? Was the test too hard? If you look again at the individual scores, you find that some students scored near the top of the test, an indication that the test was *not* too hard. Experience will tell you that students typically do not perform as well on initial assessments as on later assessments. The reason is probably lack of study, so Ms. Gist might decide to mention a study strategy to the group while reviewing performance on the test. She might also write "Please see me" on the test papers of the five students who failed the test and set up individual conferences with them.

Additional information for instructional decisions becomes available through a sequence of assessments. For example, let's look at the scores on the second test in human physiology (T2) and compare them with the scores on the first test. The average score (72) is not much improved, but one student scored 100, and there were only three failing scores this time. As Ms. Gist reviews the test results with students, she might decide to build motivation by reminding the class that homework turned in on time and article summaries can reap rewards above and beyond test results.

The improvements at the lower end of the range of scores represent real progress by several students, so Ms. Gist might write motivational comments on their papers and confer again with the three who are still at risk for failing the course. During the conferences, she might individualize instruction as follows:

- Suggest a study strategy to John Iseli and set him up with a tutor
- Ask Ramon Sanchez why his score dropped so dramatically from the first test
- Encourage Nicole Talbot by noting that, despite the low score, she is making real progress

Finally, the results of an assessment strategy for a marking period can provide a teacher with still more information for instructional decisions. At the end of a marking period, you should have sufficient results from assessments to set reliable and valid grades for learning. Based on this evaluation, you can make plans for the next marking period. In the human physiology class, Ms. Gist might ask Maria Qualls (who scored over 100 on the last two tests) if she would like to tutor or do a project for enrichment. Ms. Gist might try to encourage Nicole Talbot further and find out why tutoring did not help John Iseli.

These are just three ways that the results of assessment might help you make instructional decisions. There are others. For example, in the next chapter we shall explore how teachers sometimes design assessments to help them conduct research on teaching. A description of this use of assessment, however, belongs in a general discussion of research, our next topic.

Analysis of an Examination

Purpose of the assignment

To analyze an examination for its cognitive level(s).

Directions for the assignment

1. Select a written examination containing various items for a grade level that you might teach within your teaching field.
   a. The examination may be found in the teacher's edition of a textbook or your personal test files or obtained from a schoolteacher, but it should not be one that you constructed for another course.
   b. Make sure that the test contains at least two of the following item types: short answer, alternative response, matching, multiple choice, interpretive, short essay. These item types are defined in the chapter.
   c. Copy the entire test unless it is from your personal files, in which case you can hand in your copy. Submit the test with the paper. All materials will be returned.

2. Analyze the test items to identify their *cognitive* level(s) according to Bloom's Taxonomy of objectives for the cognitive domain (see Chapter 3).
   a. Classify each item by its cognitive level. If an item explicitly calls for more than one level of response (such as an essay test item that requires the inclusion of specified facts or sequences), classify the item at both levels.
   b. Within each level, classify items by sublevel if sublevels are specified in the taxonomy. Knowledge, for example, has three sublevels, as does comprehension.

3. Write a three- to four-page paper that identifies the cognitive level(s) of the test as specifically as possible.
   a. An introductory paragraph should specify (1) the grade level and subject of the test, (2) the source of the test, and (3) the predominant cognitive level of the test.
   b. Organize your paper from lower- to higher-order thinking, using items from the test as examples. You do not need to repeat the item if it is numbered on the test. You do not need to list levels or sublevels for which there are no items.
   c. Conclude with a paragraph about what *higher* levels of cognition are *not* included on the test. In this paragraph, provide two specific test items that you might add to the test to address at least one of these levels. The items do not need to be of the same type as the rest of the test. Remember to turn the test in with your paper.

SUMMARY

1. Assessment is a process for gathering information in order to evaluate learning accurately. Testing is often confused with assessment, although it is actually only one small part of the whole process.

2. The assessment process can be outlined in a cycle that begins with specifying learning outcomes and ends with making decisions based on the results of an evaluation. The stages of the cycle resemble those of the problem-solving model used throughout this book.

3. The main goal of assessment—to evaluate learning accurately—is related to the two technical goals of reliability and validity. Reliability refers to consistency in the results of an assessment; validity is the appropriate interpretation of assessment results.

4. There are two major approaches to the assessment of learning: objectively scored items and performance-based exercises. Within the last decade, the gap between the two approaches has narrowed.

5. Objectively scored items fall into four common formats: matching, alternative response (such as true-false), short answer, and multiple choice. All are used primarily for assessing knowledge and lower-order thinking skills within the cognitive domain.

6. Performance-based exercises include essay questions, simulations, and various forms of work samples. Essay questions assess complex thinking, simulations are used for assessment when actual performance would not be safe or appropriate, and work samples are portions of actual performances that represent the whole.

7. Work samples can be assessed either through observation or through a representative collection. There are four observational techniques: anecdotal records, rating scales, checklists, and cumulative records. The collection method is known as portfolio assessment. Both observation and portfolio methods are increasingly popular because they allow particularly close links between instruction and assessment.

8. Standards are general expectations that teachers, schools, and communities hold for assessment scores. Almost all standards are based on the concept of normed excellence—the normal curve that describes the distribution and range of what is normal.

9. Standards form the basis for evaluating scores and eventually for assigning grades. There are three recommended ways to grade student performance: absolute grade standards, contracting for grades, and continuous progress assessment.

KEY TERMS

testing p. 592

assessment p. 592

assessment strategies p. 592

reliability p. 595

validity p. 595

content validation p. 595

construct validation p. 596

criterion-related validation p. 596

objectively scored tests p. 603

performance-based exercises p. 603

matching items p. 603

alternative response items p. 605

short-answer items p. 607

multiple-choice items p. 609

performance assessment p. 612

essay questions p. 612

analytic scoring p. 614

holistic scoring p. 614

rubric p. 614

simulation p. 615

work sample p. 619

observational techniques p. 619

standards p. 626

grades p. 626

normed excellence p. 626

achievement test p. 628

standardized test p. 628

absolute grade standards p. 629

contracting for grades p. 631

continuous progress assessment p. 632

formative evaluation p. 632

summative evaluation p. 633

criterion-referenced tests p. 633

SUGGESTED RESOURCES

Guskey, T. R. (1994). "Making the Grade: What Benefits Students?" *Educational Leadership*, 52(2), 14–20. This article by an advocate of continuous progress assessment presents a good critique of existing marking practices. Most of this issue of *Educational Leadership* deals with issues related to innovative marking practices and reporting procedures.

(Continued on next page)

(Suggested Resources continued)

Herman, J. L., P. R. Aschbacher, and L. Winters. (1992). *A Practical Guide to Alternative Assessment.* Alexandria, Va.: Association for Supervision and Curriculum Development. This book describes how to use performance-based exercises, and is consistent with a problem-solving approach to assessment design.

Linn, R. L., and N. E. Gronlund. (1995). *Measurement and Evaluation in Teaching* (7th ed.). New York: Macmillan. This text by two highly respected measurement experts provides detailed procedures for how to construct different kinds of test items.

15

The Teacher as Researcher

Identify a
Problem

Represent
the Problem

Implement
and Evaluate
the Solution

Gather
Information

Generate
a Solution

In this chapter, you will be introduced to different types of psychological research in education and to ethical considerations that should guide research activities. This chapter cannot tell you what you might want to research, but it can help you learn about how research is used to address some of the issues that develop around teaching practices. As you read, look for answers to the following questions:

■ **What are some questions that research processes can help you answer?**

■ **How do qualitative and quantitative research methods differ?**

■ **What are four characteristics of qualitative studies?**

■ **What are four characteristics of quantitative studies?**

■ **Why do qualitative and quantitative techniques often complement each other?**

■ **Why is it necessary to minimize risk to participants, and how is that done?**

GETTING STARTED

Throughout this textbook, you have been reading about psychological research as it applies to education. What about research processes themselves? What can an understanding of them offer to you at the beginning of your career as a teacher?

Research has a unique mission in education: to develop the professional knowledge base of teachers. Without such a base, we have very little knowledge that we can share. We begin to rely entirely on customs, the opinions of others, and our own experiences to guide us. All of these can be useful, but they do not guarantee progress, particularly over the long term. With a knowledge base that is not only put into practice but also developed further, however, we can make steady progress in devising teaching practices that are more effective, congruent, and ethical than practices of the past.

Research can help teachers develop better teaching practices.

Using Research Processes to Answer Questions

Knowledge of research processes can also help you answer three specific kinds of question related to practice. The better you understand how educational research is conducted, the more accurately you can

1. evaluate claims about the effectiveness of strategies
2. discover which strategies work best for you
3. conduct inquiries of your own related to wider issues

Let's look more closely at each of these in turn.

First, an understanding of research processes can help you evaluate claims about the effectiveness of strategies that you hear about during your career. These claims are like product advertising. Some strategies are not very well known, but they have been found to be quite effective in meeting specified goals. These strategies have been "undersold." Other strategies may be very popular, but research on their effectiveness is not supportive. They have been "oversold." Some strategies have been found to have effectiveness with limited groups. They need to have a "limited market." Still others are new, and there is very little known about their effectiveness. They need to be "field tested." You can learn to ask whether there is a scientific basis to claims of effectiveness.

Teachers should evaluate strategies in light of research findings about them.

Second, you can use an understanding of the research process to view teaching as a form of experimentation. **Action research** is a disciplined inquiry conducted in a specific field setting, such as a classroom or school, where conditions cannot be completely controlled. You may wonder if one of the many strategies discussed in this text works for *you*. For example, if you are a high school teacher, does the performance of the class improve when you use a short list of objectives or questions announced at the beginning of each class? Formal research on these matters has yet to reach a consensus, but opinions abound, some better informed than others. You can conduct ex-

Teachers can improve their effectiveness by experimenting.

periments of your own, adopting a new technique for one term (or class) and informally comparing results from this term (or class) with results from comparable terms (or classes) when you did not use this technique. In this way, you can improve your effectiveness as a teacher.

Third, you might use research to help you answer questions related to wider issues, such as those related to ethics. For example, you might be interested in whether your teaching materials are biased by gender or race. This question is related to equity, an ethical or moral issue. Using action research, you can analyze teaching materials (such as the representation of gender in textbooks) for the purpose of selecting new materials or creating supplementary materials if gender or racial bias is found.

You can evaluate scientific claims of effectiveness, conduct informal inquiries about strategies in your classroom, or address wider issues in a systematic way only if you know something about how research is conducted. To see how the research process can be used, let's turn to one research question and look at various ways a teacher might pursue it.

> Research may address broad issues of ethics.

Sample Question: Can I Teach Science in a Gender-Equitable Way?

Research generally begins with an ill-defined problem of genuine interest to the researcher. Suppose that you are going to teach science at either the elementary or secondary level, and you want to teach in a way that is equitable to both boys and girls. You are aware that boys generally score higher than girls on assessments of scientific knowledge (e.g., U.S. Department of Education, 1992), but you are not convinced that this difference is due to anything other than the ways science is taught and knowledge is assessed. In short, you wonder, *How can I teach science in a gender-equitable way?*

If a persistent question arises in relation to your teaching, chances are it has arisen in the practices of other teachers. These questions provide problems for researchers, many of whom are or have been teachers just like yourself. How do you find out whether someone else has asked the same question as you have? The answer is usually as near as a local college library.

Library Resources

Getting started in research is often a matter of doing a little reading at a college library. You will have many tools there at your disposal. These include reference works (such as the *Encyclopedia of Educational Research* and the *Handbook of Research on Teaching*), document indexes of various kinds (such as the *Education Index* and the *Educational Resource Information Center* [ERIC] index), and journals in your teaching field. You might begin with reference works, document indexes, or recent journal articles to find out if others have asked the same question.

> Teachers can approach research through references, indexes, or journals.

Each approach has its strengths and limitations. If you begin with reference works, you can sometimes obtain a brief summary of research related to your question by looking up key words in the index. You need the commonly

One hypothesis of a science teacher-as-researcher might be that hands-on science activities improve girls' attitudes toward science. If you observed this scene, what slight change might you suggest in the teacher's practices to develop a more equitable form of teaching? How would you measure the effect of this change on attitudes toward science? *(Janice Rubin/Black Star)*

used term (such as *sex fairness* or *gender equity*), but often this is only a matter of cross-reference or of finding a larger, more inclusive term. Reference works generally give you quick access to brief summaries, but they often do not refer to the most recent work related to your question.

To find recent work, you must use either document indexes or journals. If you use document indexes, you can often quickly find a set of recent articles on your topic—if you have the right term(s). A common experience is a search of the index (now often on computer disk) that seems fruitless, but only because you have not found the right term(s). You can find it through an index of descriptors. For example, the ERIC document index lists several terms related to gender equity, but the one that you probably want is *sex fairness*. If you search for documents on this or related topics, you will find so many that you will need to narrow your search to only those involving *science education*.

You will generally find two types of journal. One is oriented to practitioners; the other, to researchers. Table 15.1 lists a sample of the many journals in common teaching fields that predominantly contain either discussion articles, research articles, or a mixture of both. Some journals not on this list (such as *Teaching K–8*) span more than one teaching field. Other journals (such as the *Journal of Educational Psychology* and the *Journal of Educational Research*) are more generic, and results often apply more widely than to a single teaching field.

For example, in science education a journal such as *The Science Teacher* is oriented to practitioners, but the *Journal of Research in Science Teaching* is oriented to researchers. Either type of journal might contain articles related to the question of gender equity in science teaching. Chances are, however, that the question answered in the journal article(s) will not have been asked in the same way that you asked it or for the same subject or group of students.

Table 15.1 Sample Journals Associated with Teaching Fields

Business and Office Education

Business Education Forum (discussion and research)

Early Childhood

Young Child (discussion)

Merrill-Palmer Quarterly (discussion and research)

Research in Early Childhood Education (research)

Elementary Education

Arithmetic Teacher (discussion)

Science and Children (discussion)

Elementary School Journal (discussion and research)

Childhood Education (discussion and research)

The Reading Teacher (discussion and research)

Table 15.1 Continued

English

English Teacher (discussion)

Research in the Teaching of English (research)

Foreign Languages

Hispania (discussion and research)

Foreign Language Annals (discussion and research)

Home Economics

Journal of Home Economics (discussion)

Home Economics Research Journal (research)

Mathematics

Mathematics Teacher (discussion)

Journal for Research in Mathematics Education (research)

Music

Music Educators Journal (discussion)

Journal of Research in Music Education (research)

Physical Education

Journal of Physical Education, Recreation, and Dance (discussion)

Journal of Teaching in Physical Education (discussion and research)

Research Quarterly for Exercise and Sport (research)

Science

The Science Teacher (discussion)

Science Education (discussion and research)

Journal of Research in Science Teaching (research)

Social Studies

Journal of Geography (discussion)

The Social Studies (discussion and research)

Theory and Research in Social Education (discussion and research)

Special Education

Teaching Exceptional Children (discussion)

G/C/T (discussion)

Remedial and Special Education (discussion and research)

Mental Retardation (research)

Exceptional Children (research)

Journal of Special Education (research)

Gifted Child Quarterly (research)

Education journals may be oriented toward practitioners or toward researchers.

Do not become discouraged—the way that you asked the question, the specific subject you teach, or the group for whom you asked it may indicate the possibility of a new contribution. No one before may have asked the question in just the way that you need it answered!

Library resources will also include journals that are more generic in nature. Occasionally, one or two of these journals may feature articles related to your question, but these will generally not address questions as specifically as those related to individual teaching fields. They can provide you with valuable background information, however, which will supplement the information that you gain from more specialized journals.

Books can provide general background information on a desired topic.

Perhaps you have noticed that I have not yet mentioned anything about books among library resources. Books are sometimes written on the basis of research, but often they are not as recent as articles. In the case of gender equity in science teaching, a relatively recent report by the American Association of University Women (1992) and a chapter on "Women and Minorities in Science and Math" in a recent volume of research reviews (Oakes, 1990) might provide you with sufficient general background information to begin your inquiry. Specific documents, articles, or books that you need but that your college library does not own can usually be ordered from another library for a small fee through the interlibrary loan department of your college library.

PRINCIPLES OF PSYCHOLOGICAL RESEARCH

Let's also look at what you might do by way of psychological research to answer your research question. (If you are engaged in the development of a research project, you will want more detailed procedural instructions than are contained here. Consult textbooks specifically designed to introduce you to educational research, some of the suggested resources at the end of this chapter, or your faculty advisor.) Psychological research encompasses the broad domains of human development, learning, motivation, management, and assessment—the same areas that you have studied in this textbook. The question of gender equity in strategies to teach science, for example, is related to the topic of human development.

Psychological research covers development, learning, motivation, and other topics.

Psychological research is generally conducted in one of two ways—qualitative or quantitative—depending on whether information is in nonnumerical or numerical form. An increasing number of studies include both types of information, but separating qualitative from quantitative work remains a useful way to distinguish broad categories of research activity, even if they occur within the same study.

Qualitative Methods of Research

Qualitative research in volves data that are not numerical.

Qualitative research is any disciplined inquiry that does *not* employ numerical data as its principal means of representing information. Among the categories of qualitative research are document analysis, case study, and

Action research, conducted in a field setting, can help you figure out what strategies—in this case, peer tutoring—work best for you. *(Nita Winter)*

semistructured interview. These types of qualitative research have a long history in psychology. Document analysis was developed as a scientific procedure over fifty years ago (cf. Allport, 1942), and case studies go back to the early twentieth century (cf. Freud, 1963/1917), as does the semistructured interview, which Jean Piaget often used. Other forms of qualitative research exist (cf. Jacob, 1988), but they tend to be more closely associated with anthropology or sociology than with psychology. Let's look at examples of each type to see how qualitative psychological research is done.

Document Analysis

Qualitative research that involves **document analysis** primarily uses original written or visual material as a source of information. This material can include literary and artistic works, reports, records, transcripts, portfolios, personal documents (logs, journal entries, letters), and the like. Contents of these sources are analyzed using some systematic form of observation to develop a generalization of psychological significance.

> Various documents can be analyzed to develop psychological theories.

For example, if you were interested in testing a gender-equitable strategy to teach science, you might develop a detailed list of key questions focused on whether specific practices met the psychological needs of girls, who have fewer out-of-school experiences with science than boys (U.S. Department of Education, 1992) and who often receive less encouragement to develop scientific careers (AAUW, 1992). You might give the questions to female students to answer anonymously. You might use these same questions to analyze your teaching materials, lesson plans, and even videotaped lessons to provide some additional documentation of your findings.

Obviously, the success of document analysis rests on the focus questions and the extent to which documents can be used to address them. Focus questions need to be developed carefully from readings on your topic in relation to your central question. Many document analyses train evaluators, but if you are teaching, you can ask your students to answer focus questions about teaching materials, lesson contents, and patterns of interaction. Particularly by high school, many students are keen "teacher watchers," and if you ask the right questions in the right way, they can be quite good evaluators. Conclusions from document analysis should be expressed in terms of generalizations that can be reached by way of examples.

Case Study

In **case study,** a researcher analyzes a social unit as a whole as a source of information (whether it be a person, a class, a program, or an organization), usually over a prolonged period of time. In case study, a "whole" is studied using some systematic form of observation, such as interviews structured by questions related to key issues. Observations are reported as narratives or descriptions that center on the questions or issues. Case study differs from document analysis because it is generally conducted by a single individual (the case researcher) and generalizations do not necessarily extend beyond the unit being studied.

> A case study is observation of a social unit, usually over time.

Several case studies have been conducted on gender equity in science teaching. In particular, these studies have focused on female high school valedictorians and how their career aspirations develop or are deferred (Arnold, 1991) and on programs aimed at encouraging girls in math, science, and technology (Nicholson & Frederick, 1991). Although concern for objectivity may prevent you from doing a case study of your own teaching, you can use case studies of the achievement of individual students to illustrate effects of teaching when they are primarily assessed in other ways.

Semistructured Interview

Semistructured interview (also known as *clinical method* or *clinical interview*) is a technique that uses a series of questions to evoke responses that manifest specific knowledge, skills, or attitudes. Like case study, semistructured interview relies on observation, but unlike case study, the researcher focuses not on a social unit but on discovery of generalizations that are not limited to the individual(s) being studied.

> The semistructured interview uses questions to uncover knowledge, skills, or attitudes.

A number of studies of gender equity in teaching science have been conducted using semistructured interviews. In one recent study, researchers looked at the responses of a total of forty girls in grades 2, 5, 8, and 11 to questions about learning science (Baker & Leary, 1995). Researchers addressed just three "threads" of inquiry—school science, social factors, and equity—and used multiple evaluators to categorize responses. With regard to equity, they reached the generalization that older girls often seem "caught in a paradox" between "establishing and standing up for who they are and the cultural feminine ideal" (p. 23). If you taught science, you might conduct a similar study with your female students to determine to what extent this generalization might apply to them.

> Semistructured interviews may be used to reach generalizations.

The challenge of the semistructured interview is to use your responses to reach broad generalizations in an unbiased way. The key lies in the selection of the sample of individuals whom you interview. Often semistructured interviews are involved in exploratory studies—that is, they are followed by *structured* interviews with a larger number of individuals and *quantitative* studies. Such follow-ups are not immediately necessary, however, if the responses to semistructured interviews have been used to generate theory.

Document analysis, case study, and semistructured interview may be used separately, but they can be found together and also combined with the results of quantitative studies. In a study by Jane Kahle (1983) of schools where teachers successfully encouraged their female students to pursue interests in science, the primary method was case study of individual schools (each by a different case researcher), but the results at eight sites were pooled to achieve generalizations across sites (see Table 15.2). Because the resources required to conduct this study were great in comparison to those available to you, you would not be expected to conduct such research as a beginning teacher, but later on you might have the opportunity to participate in a larger study like this one.

Research techniques may be used separately or together.

Four Characteristics of Qualitative Research

There is not much doubt that educational psychology now includes well-designed qualitative studies. At this point, we are in a position to make four generalizations about those characteristics that well-designed qualitative studies possess in common.

Qualitative research studies have four characteristics in common.

1. *Qualitative research uses objective means to study behavior.* All research attempts to investigate phenomena in an unbiased way. Unbiased focus questions, audiotaped or videotaped documentation, multiple observers, and elaborate techniques for analyzing "protocols" (records of interviews) are just a few signs that qualitative research is developing objective methods to observe and interpret events.
2. *Qualitative research employs nonnumerical description.* The distinguishing feature of qualitative research (as opposed to quantitative research) is that it

Table 15.2   Characteristics of Gender-Equitable Science Education

Teachers who successfully encourage girls in science:

- Maintain well-equipped, organized, and perceptually stimulating classrooms
- Are supported in their teaching activities by the parents of their students and are respected by current and former students
- Use nonsexist language and examples and include information on women scientists
- Use laboratories, discussions, and weekly quizzes as their primary modes of instruction and supplement those activities with field trips and guest speakers
- Stress creativity and basic skills and provide career information

Source: Kahle, 1983, p. ii

reaches generalizations about some phenomenon by way of examples (such as excerpts from interviews) rather than by way of numerical analysis.

3. *Qualitative research emphasizes the natural setting.* Most qualitative research is conducted in a "field" setting, often under realistic conditions. Sometimes qualitative studies are called *naturalistic* because in education they often collect information in authentic settings, such as in the classroom or on the playground, rather than in a laboratory or under the conditions of a standardized test.

4. *Qualitative research acknowledges a subjective dimension of behavior.* Qualitative researchers frequently view students' knowledge of topics as constructed, and the quality of these constructions (e.g., cause-effect relations, students' ability to reconstruct a narrative account of events in history) is often a central interest.

Qualitative studies may share other characteristics, but these four seem to be of greatest importance.

Quantitative Methods of Research

Quantitative research is any disciplined inquiry that employs numerical data as its principal means of representing information. Although document analysis and case studies *can* be conducted as quantitative research, they infrequently are.

> Quantitative research uses numerical data to represent findings.

Generally, studies that consist of quantitative research fall into three categories: statistical description, statistical correlation, and experimentation. All three categories originated when psychology separated from philosophy in the late nineteenth century. A closer look at examples of each type of quantitative research will help you understand them better.

Statistical Description

In **statistical description,** characteristics are summarized in numerical form. These characteristics are not limited to *demographics,* or data that describe general attributes of participants in a study (such as number of males and females and their average ages), but include attributes of psychological significance. These attributes may belong to people (such as abilities, achievements, or attitudes), or they may belong to objects (such as the content of teaching materials) or events (such as a focus on career awareness).

> Statistical description reports characteristics of research interest in numerical form.

Many studies have documented the differences between males and females on test scores in science, particularly after elementary school. Statistics exist to "test" the differences between scores of any two groups to determine if they are significant in terms of probability. Most studies have found the sex differences in scores on science tests to be "statistically significant," that is, it is highly improbable that they are due to chance.

The possible causes of these differences have been the impetus for further descriptive analysis. For example, these differences are more likely to be found in older students than in younger ones (U.S. Department of Education, 1992), suggesting that the cumulative effect of experience plays a role. They are also more likely to be found on items that assess knowledge than on items that assess scientific thinking, suggesting that experience outside class plays a role. Males often have significantly more in-school *and* out-of-school experiences with science than females have (Kahle, Matyas & Cho, 1985)—apparently a key cause of this pattern in test results.

Although statistical descriptions often suggest cause-effect relationships, they cannot test such relationships. Consequently, if you wanted to assess the effectiveness of a technique designed to produce gender-equitable teaching in science, you could *not* use descriptive statistics alone. You could compare one or more groups (or sets of materials) with respect to one or more characteristics, and you could even summarize the statistical results of many descriptive studies, a statistical technique called *meta-analysis* (Weinburgh, 1995). But you would have to conduct an experiment to test a cause-effect relationship.

> Statistical description can suggest but not prove cause-effect relationships.

Statistical Correlation

A *correlation* is any association or correspondence between two characteristics, such as attitude and achievement. A **statistical correlation** is a procedure used to measure the degree of association between two or more characteristics. A statistical correlation results in a *correlation coefficient,* or a number ranging from +1 to –1 that indicates the strength of the association.

> Statistical correlation measures the degree of association between characteristics.

Generally, educational psychologists look for correlations that are significantly different from zero and that have a theoretical significance. Can there be a correlation that differs significantly from zero but is theoretically *in*significant? The answer is yes. For instance, attendance at professional baseball games and the U.S. gross national debt rose together from 1983 to 1992 (the debt more steadily than attendance). The two columns of figures statistically correlate quite highly (above 0.9). No one, however, would suggest that the increase in baseball attendance ties in with the national debt, let alone causes it to rise. We have to be very careful about interpreting a statistical correlation, which may alternatively signal a direct relationship between a cause and an effect, an indirect relationship, or no meaningful relationship at all!

Nevertheless, correlational studies can sometimes provide valuable information in response to well-defined research questions. For example, how do females respond to multiple-choice tests in science when they don't know the answer? They are more likely than boys to indicate that they "don't know" when the content of the items is physical science, a fact established by statistical correlation (Linn et al., 1987). The cause of this phenomenon is uncertain, but its effect is to disadvantage girls in relation to boys when "don't know" is an option on a multiple-choice test.

> Statistical correlations may or may not be significant.

An interesting study for a science teacher would be to correlate out-of-school science experiences (reported by students on a simple questionnaire) with scores on a multiple-choice science test, then compare this correlation with one for another group that experienced hands-on activities and a more authentic form of assessment than a multiple-choice test. A higher correlation for the first group than for the second might be expected. Such a finding would demonstrate that the second group had been taught in a more equitable way than the first. Before conducting this study, however, the teacher would have to determine how to do it with regard for the welfare of the first group. For example, the teacher would not want to teach these students or assess their achievements in a way that he or she believed to be inequitable.

Experimentation

> Experiments manipulate causal factors in order to determine effects.

Well-designed correlational studies begin to resemble experiments. In **experiments,** events are designed so that causes can be systematically manipulated to determine effects. Experiments are generally designed to rule out ("control for") alternative explanations. Ethical constraints are stringent on such manipulations in education because they often involve the welfare of schoolchildren. In general, only causes thought to have a beneficial effect on the welfare of children, teachers, and other educators are ethically permissible to study in an experiment.

Only a couple of experiments have been conducted on gender-equitable teaching in science, but they provide the most convincing evidence that differences in science test scores are a reflection of inequity in teaching. One study (Mason & Kahle, 1989) trained teachers to use teaching techniques that were described earlier in Table 15.2: hands-on activities, group discussion, career information, and awareness of female as well as male role models. The researchers hypothesized that student outcomes for these specially trained science teachers (the *treatment group*) would be more gender-equitable than those for teachers who had not been specially trained (the *control group*). The outcomes for attitudes toward science, perceptions of science, experiences with science, and career interests in science all favored the girls *and* the boys in the treatment group. In the area of greatest gender difference—science career interests—the gender differences were found to be smaller in the treatment group than in the control group (see Figure 15.1). The experiment showed that gender-equitable methods of teaching science benefit *all* students.

**Figure 15.1
Career Interest in
Science** *(Mason & Kahle,
1988, p. 35)*

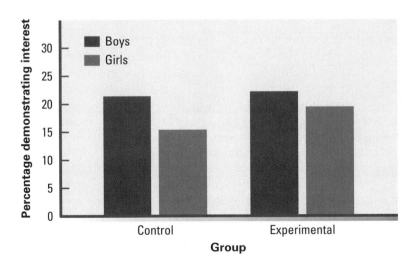

This teacher is using news-papers to develop critical reading skills. How might she test the effectiveness of this activity as opposed to an alternative activity to achieve the same goal?
(Paul Howell/Gamma Liaison)

Four Characteristics of Quantitative Research

Since the inception of educational psychology, it has included well-designed quantitative studies. Like qualitative studies, quantitative studies share a set of distinctive characteristics.

> Quantitative studies share four characteristics.

1. *Quantitative research uses objective means to study behavior.* Special care is taken in the design of a quantitative study so that the process of gathering information is not biased by the researcher's personal expectations. Others are trained to intervene, information is coded in numerical form, and results are often calculated statistically to minimize bias in observations.
2. *Quantitative research employs numerical data and statistical analysis.* Information is gathered through rating scales, checklists, test scores, and so on. It is then generally subjected to statistical analysis, from averages to elaborate statistical procedures, in order to verify any hypothesis or expectation.
3. *Quantitative research emphasizes a controlled situation.* The situation may be controlled in a laboratory setting, but more often in education it is controlled through the administration of tests or treatments under well-specified conditions.
4. *Quantitative research focuses on manifest behavior.* Behavior includes all types of performance, from physical activities to paper-and-pencil test performance. Attention is focused on the researcher's interpretation of behavior rather than on the subject's interpretation of experience.

Quantitative research shares with qualitative research a concern for objectivity in the study of behavior but otherwise is quite different.

Patterns of Inquiry

Qualitative and quantitative research may seem worlds apart, but they are related in several ways. Both, for example, employ objective means to study behavior. Qualitative research may collect less numeric information, emphasize a more natural setting, and give greater attention to the interpretations of participants, but both types of research set out to be objective. Objectivity is their "common denominator."

> Both qualitative and quantitative research must be objective.

In addition to sharing the value of objectivity, qualitative and quantitative research increasingly coexist in the same studies. For example, your question about gender-equitable teaching might call for an experiment, but if no control group were available, you could analyze documents (such as student journals and special course evaluations) for answers to focus questions, then test your generalizations with quantitative data from another source (such as male and female averages on a series of quiz scores). More and more research studies are combining qualitative and quantitative approaches. Such studies are like stereoscopic vision: they allow the reader to perceive the phenomenon studied in greater depth. They also appear to interest and involve male and female researchers more equitably than do studies that are only quantitative in nature (Rosser, 1993).

> Studies increasingly use both qualitative and quantitative techniques.

A third similarity between qualitative and quantitative research is that they both are forms of inquiry. They involve aspects of the problem-solving process. Qualitative research, with its focus on the development of questions, emphasizes problem *finding*. The generalizations that sometimes emerge as hypotheses are *solutions*, but they are not always tested in the study. They are the point of departure for further investigation. Quantitative research, in contrast, focuses on verification of hypotheses, emphasizing problem *solving*. The scope of quantitative research may be entirely restricted to testing hypotheses, which is the last stage of our problem-solving model. Where the theory came from to generate these hypotheses is often considered peripheral to the study.

> Qualitative and quantitative methods both contribute to problem solving.

When the two types of research in any area are viewed in historical relationship, qualitative investigations appear to come first because they are generally exploratory in nature and out of them emerge generalizations that serve as hypotheses for further investigation. For example, Jane Kahle's (1983) work on gender equity began with case studies, and out of these studies emerged ideas for teaching techniques, which were tested through an experimental design (Mason & Kahle, 1989). Quantitative studies, however, can eventually lead back to qualitative investigations because through the latter important new questions can be raised. Which should come first—qualitative or quantitative research—is likely to be a "chicken and egg" issue. Which comes first depends on *when* you enter a cycle of inquiry.

ETHICAL CONSIDERATIONS IN RESEARCH

Whatever the type of research you become involved in, its conduct must be ethical. One of the first principles of research is that an investigator must make an evaluation of the *ethical acceptability* of any proposed study. Ethical acceptability generally involves respect for principles of human rights, privacy, and dignity and the seeking of ethical advice for studies in which ethical principles may be compromised. In terms of specific procedures, the three principles of *minimizing risk, obtaining informed consent,* and *ensuring confidentiality* encompass most of the specific recommendations of the American Psychological Association (1992) and the American Educational Research Association (1992) for ethical practice in research.

> Ethical principles must be part of every educational research project.

Research on learning activities within the normal range—such as computer-assisted instruction—minimizes risk to the participants. *(Lawrence Migdale/Stock Boston)*

Minimizing Risk

Whether a participant will be physically or psychologically "at risk" or "at minimal risk" must be determined prior to the conduct of research. Research that entails activity within the range of normal classroom activities (participating in group or individual instruction within the curriculum, taking a standardized achievement test) would put a child at minimal risk. Research that leads to participation in activities outside the normal range, or in activities thought to have a undesirable effect (naively witnessing a staged crime, taking a logic test with emotionally provocative items, enduring a teaching technique that is intentionally unfair) put children at risk. Risks are always to be minimized.

Obtaining Informed Consent

Regardless of whether a participant is at risk, she or he must ordinarily be fully informed and allowed to decline to participate in a study. Deception is discouraged, but when deception is required by the nature of the study (as in research on naive responses to the researcher), or when the participant is unable to give informed consent (such as an infant), other safeguards (such as approval by the site supervisor or parent) are necessary. In addition, participants (or those who have consented for them) have the right at any time to withdraw themselves (or those for whom they have consented) from further participation in the research.

> Researchers must minimize risk and obtain informed consent.

Ensuring Confidentiality

Participants have the right to remain anonymous, and knowledge of their participation should remain confidential unless otherwise agreed on in advance. If other researchers are allowed access to the data, procedures for maintaining confidentiality (such as assigning case numbers to replace

> Confidentiality is an important principle in research.

names) are to be explained as part of the process of obtaining informed consent from participants. Participants also must be informed that, despite every effort of the researcher to preserve their anonymity, it may still be compromised.

As a student of education with an interest in ethical questions, you should be aware that researchers go to some trouble to avoid harming their participants. Only rarely now do we hear cases of human rights violations in educational research. In fact, many studies adopt higher standards than these minimal ones, providing a reasonable benefit of participation (such as payment or informative feedback), which is described during the process of obtaining informed consent.

CONCLUSION

As you develop your career as a teacher, you may want to consider the benefits of conducting research as a teacher/researcher. These benefits will extend to you, your students, and society. Discoveries related to teaching not only improve your teaching but also lead to a better education for children in your classroom. Furthermore, if your discoveries have application beyond your classroom, they can contribute to progress in education.

Education has come a long way in the last few decades. The 1960s were a highly creative period. In the 1970s, the emphasis swung "back to basics." By the early 1990s, we were seeing reforms to teach thinking beginning to take hold. What lies ahead? Reforms under way are far from complete. Teachers and researchers are still learning how to become problem solvers. The problems that we address may never fully be solved, but as new problems emerge, we learn to formulate new goals, and we progress.

If we become tired or frustrated, all we have to do is take a moment to look at how much education progressed in the twentieth century. As you look forward to the next century, seek to define new challenges not only for your own development as a teacher but also for the progress of our profession.

concept paper

Contrast of Research with Discussion

Purpose of the assignment

To contrast a research article with a discussion article in order to characterize a central difference between the two types of discourse.

Directions for the assignment

1. Select two articles from professional journals in your teaching field. They must both have been published within the past two years and be about the same general subject.

a. One should be a short *discussion* article on some development in teaching in your field. It might have as its subject a particular idea about goals, students, learning, motivation, management, or evaluation—any subject generally falling within the context of educational psychology.

b. The other should be a short *research* article in your teaching field that follows a distinct format of problem, method, results, discussion, and conclusion. It might be an experiment, a correlational study, or a qualitative study on a subject in the same general area (goals, students, learning, motivation, management, or evaluation) as that of the other article.

c. Photocopy each article for use in writing your paper. Then turn in the photocopies with your paper.

2. *Seek approval of your articles from your instructor. This approval is a critical check over whether you have accurately identified examples of different modes of discourse.*

3. After you have gained approval of your articles from your instructor, analyze each article for characteristics related to its mode of discourse.

a. *Audience.* For whom is the article intended? What background in terms of general education, specific training, and present experience does the author assume about the reader?

b. *Format.* How do the formats of the two articles compare and contrast? What does the design or structure of each article assume about the reader's purpose for reading the article?

c. *Style of writing.* What style or manner of writing (vocabulary, manner of presenting evidence, use of references, and so on) does the author adopt? What does the style communicate about the author's purpose?

d. Other points of comparison or contrast that you find reveal significant details about the mode of discourse of the article. Do not focus on the topic of the articles but on the different ways they present information.

4. In a thesis sentence, characterize the different purposes of the two types of discourse—research and discussion. *Do not describe the content of the two articles:* research and discussion are modes of discourse that are quite general, and your articles are only illustrations or examples of them. Place your thesis sentence at the end of an introductory paragraph that identifies the two articles (author, title, journal, month/year of publication).

5. Support your thesis sentence in a three- to four-page paper, drawing on your analysis (step 3) for examples and details to support your thesis. Papers that are handwritten should be five to six pages.

6. Feel free to organize your paper either by discussing each mode of discourse separately or by discussing them together according to different points of contrast. (You might want to consult a composition handbook for further information about how to organize a comparison/contrast theme.) Try to reach an insightful conclusion about a broad difference between the *purposes of research and of discussion.*

7. Remember to hand in your articles with your paper. By the end of this assignment, you will have completed an exercise in formal operational thought. It should improve your understanding not only of the differences between research and discussion but also of formal operational thinking, which focuses on *form* rather than content.

SUMMARY

1. Research has a unique mission in education—to develop the professional knowledge base of teachers. Only by building upon a solid knowledge base can we progress in developing teaching practices that are increasingly effective and ethical.

2. There are three specific ways in which classroom teachers can use educational research: to better understand claims about strategies and programs; to conduct action research, or on-the-spot inquiries, in their own classrooms about what works and what doesn't; and to address wider issues, such as gender equity, in a systematic way.

3. The library is an invaluable resource in getting started on a research question. There are three primary tools a teacher will find helpful: reference works, document indexes, and recent journal articles.

4. There are two basic kinds of psychological research: qualitative research and quantitative research. Each stresses objectivity and includes aspects of the problem-solving process.

5. In addition to using objective means to study behavior, qualitative research has three other characteristics: it always employs non-numerical analyses, it emphasizes natural settings, and it acknowledges a subjective dimension to behavior.

6. The three primary methods for carrying out qualitative research are document analysis, case studies, and semistructured interviews.

7. The main characteristics of quantitative research, in addition to objectivity, are the use of numerical data and numerical analysis, an emphasis on controlled situations, and a focus on observable behavior.

8. The three primary methods for carrying out quantitative research are statistical description, statistical correlation, and experimentation.

9. All research, no matter what approach or method it employs, must be conducted in an ethical manner. There are three widely accepted principles that govern ethical acceptability: minimizing risk to participants, obtaining informed consent from participants, and assuring all participants' confidentiality.

KEY TERMS

action research p. 640
qualitative research p. 644
document analysis p. 645
case study p. 646
semistructured interview p. 646
quantitative research p. 648
statistical description p. 648
statistical correlation p. 649
experiments p. 650

SUGGESTED RESOURCES

American Psychological Association. (1994). *Publication Manual of the American Psychological Association* (4th ed.). Washington, D.C.: Author. This manual describes the professional standards for writing style, writing format, and manuscript preparation in psychology and related fields.

Best, J. W., and J. V. Kahn. (1989). *Research in Education* (6th ed.). Englewood Cliffs, N.J.: Prentice-Hall. This textbook presents a good introduction to research emphasizing quantitative methods.

Le Compte, M. D., W. L. Millroy, and J. Preissle. (1992). *The Handbook of Qualitative Research in Education.* San Diego: Academic Press. This collection of summaries has developed into a standard reference for conducting qualitative inquiry.

Sternberg, R. J. (1993). *The Psychologist's Companion* (3rd ed.). New York: Cambridge University Press. This highly readable book provides helpful guidelines for writing library research papers as well as experimental research papers in psychology.

Glossary

absolute grade standard   An evaluation of scores in comparison to established percentages of a perfect score.

achievement test   An evaluation instrument designed to measure knowledge, skill, or accomplishment in any area.

action research   A disciplined inquiry conducted in a specific field setting, such as a classroom or school, where conditions cannot be completely controlled.

activity level   Any organism's expenditure of energy through movement.

adaptation   The process of adjusting to the environment.

aesthetic expression   The representation of properties through symbolic forms, such as patterns of variables, lines, figures, words, movements, and tones.

affective domain   The area of values, attitudes, and feelings.

age effect   A difference in skill levels based on age apart from experience.

algorithm   A routine or mechanical procedure for solving a problem.

alternative-response item   A test item containing a stem, which represents a problem, and a set of options for selecting solution. (Also called *true-false item*)

analogical thinking   Open-ended problem solving by extended comparison.

analytic scoring   An evaluation model that requires identifying different dimensions of a response and awarding points based on a rating scale for each dimension.

antecedent   The events that immediately precede a behavior.

aptitude-treatment-interaction (ATI) research   A procedure that matches student characteristics with specific instructional strategies based on achievement outcomes.

Assertive Discipline   An intervention that communicates the teacher's wants and needs to students and expresses approval or disapproval of student actions.

assessment   A process for gathering information to meet a variety of evaluation needs.

assessment strategy   A means to attain assessment goals.

attention   Focal awareness that involves the allocation of short-term memory capacity.

attribution theory   A systematic analysis of how people relate causes to significant outcomes.

attribution training   A strategy to establish the belief that outcomes are related to effort.

automaticity   The capacity to respond without attention.

aversive stimulus   An undesirable consequence that weakens the probability of a behavior when it follows that behavior.

behavioral analysis   A correlation of an activity with its antecedents and consequences.

behavior management   A general procedure for changing behaviors through their consequences.

bilingual education   A strategy for teaching students of limited English proficiency, which may include instruction in two languages, the use of the two languages as mediums for instruction in any or all subjects, and study of the history and culture associated with each language. (Also called *bilingual instruction*)

brainstorming   A group procedure for generating a quantity of solutions to a given problem.

case study   A qualitative form of investigation in which a researcher analyzes a social unit as a whole as a source of information, usually over a prolonged period of time.

cephalocaudal sequence   The tendency for maturation to occur from the top of the body to the bottom of the trunk. (Also called *head-to-tail sequence*)

character education   Direct instruction in the moral norms of a culture.

chunking   A control process in which smaller units of information are integrated into larger wholes, such as words into phrases.

classification   The act of grouping things into categories based on shared characteristics.

cognition   The process of knowing in its broadest sense, including perception, memory, and thinking.

cognitive behavior modification   A procedure for internalizing verbal instructions to develop self-control.

cognitive development   Progressive change in processes of knowing.

cognitive domain   The area of knowledge, intellectual skills, and intellectual abilities.

cognitive load   The degree to which short-term memory space is occupied by a given task.

cognitive modeling   The demonstration and description of the use of mental skills as a means to teach those skills.

compensatory education program   An intervention designed to reduce educational disadvantages resulting from poverty.

computer-assisted instruction   The application of programmed instruction through a machine.

concept   A class or collection of things that share one or more characteristics.

concrete operations period   A stage of cognitive development that corresponds to middle childhood and involves the development of knowledge through applied reasoning.

confidence   A belief in one's power to affect outcomes. (*See* **self-efficacy**)

consequence   The effects that immediately follow a behavior.

conservation   An understanding that equivalencies underlie all changes in appearance.

constructivism   The philosophical position that a child builds his or her own knowledge.

construct validation   The gathering of evidence that assessment results represent only what is to be assessed.

content validation   The gathering of evidence that assessment tasks represent the domain of knowledge or skills to be assessed.

contingency   A dependent relationship between a behavior and its consequence.

contingency contract   An agreement composed of a behavioral objective and a statement of what the student will receive for attaining the objective.

contingency of reinforcement   The relationship between a behavior and the consequence that strengthens the behavior.

continuous progress assessment   The periodic appraisal of performance without the assignment of a grade until the end of a course of study.

contract   An agreement between individuals, such as a learner and the teacher.

contracting for grades   A process to establish a work agreement between the learner and the teacher for assessment purposes.

control processes   A procedure that governs the flow of information in the memory system.

convergent thinking   The ability to generate necessary solutions to problems that are well defined.

corporal punishment   Any punishment administered to the body (such as paddling).

creative thinking   The ability to deal with problems in original ways.

crisis   As defined by Erikson, a critical period in the formation of the personality.

criterion-referenced test   An evaluation instrument constructed to align with goals.

criterion-related validation   The gathering of evidence that assessment results have some value for estimating a standard of performance.

critical reflection   Evaluation of practices in terms of their moral and ethical implications.

curriculum guide   A statement of goals and objectives for learning.

declarative knowledge   Information consisting of facts and rules.

deduction   The use of logic to draw conclusions from premises.

development   Progressive change, specifically in the body, cognition, and social relations.

developmentally appropriate practice   An instructional strategy that matches the age and individual needs of the learner.

differentiation   The tendency for maturation to begin with large areas and muscle groups and extend to smaller. (Also called *gross-to-specific trend*)

discipline   An intervention to stop a misbehavior.

discovery learning   A mode of inquiry in which students acquire the processes of scientific investigation.

discrimination   The ability to recognize the difference between one thing and another.

disequilibrium   A discrepancy between what is perceived and what is understood.

disposition to learn   A tendency to exhibit a pattern of behavior that is directed toward a broad goal.

disposition to think   Persistence in the face of problem-solving tasks.

divergent thinking   The ability to generate alternative solutions to an open-ended problem.

document analysis   Qualitative research that primarily uses original written or visual material as a source of information.

drill-and-practice program   A computer display sequence that provides reinforcement for what has already been learned.

dual agenda   A mode of instruction in which content objectives are often paralleled by objectives for teaching thinking skills.

early maturers   An individual whose body develops full functioning before peers of the same sex.

educationally disadvantaged student   A student who has insufficient background experience for school success due to poverty.

ego involvement   The desire to enhance oneself by establishing superiority relative to others.

egocentric knowledge   Knowledge derived by a child from his or her own experience as a norm for all experience.

elaborative rehearsal   A global term that describes strategies for relating new information to previously acquired knowledge.

emotional development   Progressive change in attitudes and values.

empathy   The capacity to share the perceived emotion of another person.

enabling skills   An intellectual process (such as a technique for acquiring knowledge) that is prerequisite to more complex forms of problem solving.

epigenesis   As defined by Erikson, the planful, stagelike development of capacities before and after birth.

episodic memory   An event stored in long-term memory.

equilibration   The self-regulatory mechanism through which accommodation is activated and terminated.

essay question   A test item that requires the student to supply a verbal response that is longer than a few words.

ethnic group   A collection of individuals who identify with a differentiated social and cultural heritage passed from one generation to the next.

ethnic minority group   A collection of individuals with all the characteristics of an ethnic group but also unique physical or cultural characteristics that are easily identifiable.

evaluation of a solution   The step of the problem-solving process in which one judges how well a strategy has worked.

everyday problem finding   The process of posing problems that are encountered routinely.

executive processing space   Short-term memory capacity, divisible into operating space and storage space.

experiment   The designing of an event so that causes can be systematically manipulated to determine effects.

experimental aesthetics   The measurement of perceptual preferences.

expertise   A high degree of skill or knowledge in a specific domain.

expert problem finding   The process of posing problems of extraordinary depth or scope.

extrinsic feedback   Information that indirectly results from the performance of an activity or is artificially added to the situation.

extrinsic motivation   The desire to engage in an activity for a reward apart from the activity itself.

far transfer   The generalization of taught skills to other subject areas or skills.

fidelity   A description of how closely a simulation imitates reality.

fine motor skills   The proficient use of small muscles near and in the eyes, hands, and feet.

formal operations period   A stage of cognitive development that corresponds with adolescence and adulthood and involves the development of knowledge through systematic reasoning.

formative evaluation   An assessment to demonstrate the degree of mastery of a learning task and to identify the portion not mastered.

functional value   The anticipated gain or advantage from learning a behavior.

gender difference   A contrast between the sexes.

gender role   A sense of what is appropriate for males or females.

generalization   The transfer of a specific response to features of the environment that have not been responded to before.

general objectives with specific learning outcomes   Nonspecific statements of what a learner should be able to do, with subordinated examples or illustrations.

generative learning   The process of constructing knowledge.

Gestalt psychology   An approach to cognition that finds meaning in the configuration of elements rather than in their individual significance.

giftedness   High performance capability in intellectual, creative, artistic, or leadership areas, or in specific academic fields.

givens   The range of limiting circumstances that accompany a problem.

goal   A broad statement of purpose regarding what a community has decided its citizens should learn.

grade   In assessment, an interpretation of performance by some standard.

gross muscle activity   Use of large-muscle groups such as those in the arms and legs.

group alerting   The inclusion of all of the members of a group in a learning activity.

group norm   A criterion of performance set by individuals acting together.

growth spurt   The period of most rapid increase in height and weight.

guided discovery   A text-based approach to teaching science that emphasizes process skills.

Hawthorne effect   A temporary sense of novelty that affects the results of research.

heterogeneous grouping   Classification of learners by age without regard to ability or skill levels.

heuristics   A strategy for discovering how to solve math problems, based on building a model.

higher-order rule   A statement to regulate behavior that is composed of more than one rule. (*See* **rule**)

holistic planning model   A planning model in which multiple factors involved in solving teaching problems are considered at the same time.

holistic scoring   An assessment model in which essay responses are sorted as they are read into one of several categories of quality.

homogeneous grouping   Classification of learners into ability or skill levels.

identity   As defined by Erikson, "a feeling of being at home in one's body, a sense of 'knowing where one is going,' and an inner assuredness of anticipated recognition from those who count" (1968, p. 165).

ill-defined problem   A problem for which the limiting circumstances, the solution procedures, or the goals have not been specified. (*See* **well-defined problem**)

implementation of a solution   The step of the problem-solving process in which one tries out a strategy to achieve a goal.

inclusion   A reform movement aimed at educating disabled learners in regular classrooms.

induction   The ability to generalize beyond the information given.

inference   A conclusion reached by way of either inductive or deductive reasoning.

information gathering   The step of the problem-solving process in which one collects and analyzes data needed to solve a problem.

information processing   Procedures for transforming data into organized information.

inner speech   Internalized dialogue.

integration   In physical development, the coordination of movements.

interest   The motivational effects of values and knowledge.

internalization   The process by which social discourse is transformed into thinking.

intrinsic feedback   Information that directly results from the performance of an activity.

intrinsic motivation   The desire to engage in an activity because of curiosity or the challenge or enjoyment the activity presents.

knowledge   Any organized body of information.

knowledge base   A clearly defined body of information and set of values.

learned helplessness   A motivational state acquired through consistently internal and stable attributions for failure.

learning   Relatively permanent change in behavior due to experience.

learning analysis   A procedure for discovering prerequisites to the achievement of a behavioral objective. (*See* **learning hierarchy**)

learning cues   A word or phase that communicates critical features of a movement.

learning goal   The purpose or end of increasing competence through completion of some task.

learning hierarchy   A logically arranged sequence of activities intended to achieve the goal of behavior change. (*See* **learning analysis**)

learning strategy   An assemblage of cognitive processes aimed at achieving some learning goal.

learning strategy instruction   Teaching based on the voluntary use of cognitive processes to meet the goal of knowledge acquisition.

least restrictive environment   A set of conditions that includes the disabled child in as many mainstream activities as possible.

long-term memory   The structure that contains what we know but are not conscious of at the moment, and which has a virtually unlimited capacity.

management   The act of establishing and maintaining a climate conducive to learning.

management problem   A situation that exists when an individual wants to create or maintain a climate conducive to learning but does not immediately know how to do so.

management strategy   A procedure for creating and maintaining a climate conducive to learning.

management system   An assemblage of strategies to establish and maintain a climate conducive to learning.

marker   A cue that routinely signals the boundary of a context or activity.

Maslow's hierarchy of needs   A theory which establishes both a taxonomy of needs and an order in which they motivate an individual.

mastery learning   An approach to instruction that allows a student time and opportunity to achieve a criterion of success on a task.

matching items   A test format containing two lists of approximately the same length, between which the student must recognize associations of some kind.

maturation   The development of full functioning of the body.

meaningfulness   The number and distinctiveness of associations between input and information stored in long-term memory.

mediated learning   Learning that is supported directly or indirectly by others who are more knowledgeable or skilled.

mediation technique   A way of creating specific linkages between input and information already stored in long-term memory. (*See* **meaningfulness**)

mental retardation   Significantly subaverage intellectual functioning, existing concurrently with related limitations in two or more adaptive skill areas.

metacognitive skill   A skill used by an individual to appraise or monitor his or her own thinking processes.

mnemonics   The art of improving memory.

model   To perform or describe a behavior for the benefit of another.

moral development   Progressive change in a child's reasoning about rules and understanding of others.

motivation   The collection of causes that engage someone in an activity.

motivational problem   A situation in which an individual wishes to engage in an activity, but does not immediately know how to do so.

motivational strategy   A plan to engage in an activity.

multicultural education   Teaching that aims to increase awareness and appreciation of cultural diversity, and which is designed to address the problem of discrimination.

multimedia   The product of networked linkages of text, graphics, animation, voice, music, movies, or video.

multiple-choice item   A test item containing a problem and at least three new plausible options to solve each problem.

nature/nurture controversy   A long-standing debate between those who view development as a product of aging and those who view development as a product of experience.

near transfer   The generalization of skills that have been taught to similar skills that are being tested.

negative reinforcement   The effect of removing an aversive stimulus following a behavior.

neo-Piagetians   A school of developmental psychologists who have proposed stages of intellectual development which are revisions of those of Piaget.

norm   The average value of any characteristic or skill.

normal curve   A line that describes a random distribution of values around the average.

normed excellence   A set of standards for evaluating scores that is based on the normal curve.

objectively scored test   An evaluation instrument that can be accurately and efficiently scored by machine or by hand.

object permanence   A milestone in cognitive development that is achieved when a child looks for things not in view.

observational learning   The acquisition of the potential for behavior from a model. (Also called *social learning*)

observational technique   A means to assess student activities directly.

on-task behavior   Expected behavior in an activity.

open-ended problem   A problem with well-defined givens but an unclear goal state.

operant conditioning   A set of behavioral learning principles developed by B. F. Skinner.

organizer   A statement, expressed in familiar terms, of concepts to be learned.

orienting response   A reflex reaction that involves physiological arousal and turning the head for optimal perception of a new stimulus.

outcome-based education   A philosophy of education that emphasizes exit outcomes as the source of instructional objectives, multiple learning opportunities, and performance assessment.

overlapping situation   A set of circumstances in which the instructor must pay attention to something outside the activity in which he or she is involved.

overspecialization   The excessive development of a small set of skills.

peer conformity   The adoption of the norms of a group with similar attributes.

peer tutoring   One-to-one teaching between students.

perception   The process by which a sensory image is assigned meaning. (Also called *recognition*)

perceptual centration   An error of reasoning that occurs when one considers only a single dimension or perspective of a problem before generating a solution.

performance assessment   A direct appraisal of a skill through a demonstration of some kind.

performance-based exercise   An activity designed to evoke responses that must be appraised by the teacher or some other expert.

performance goal   The purpose or end of either obtaining a favorable judgment of competence or avoiding a negative judgment.

perspective taking   The ability to adopt the viewpoint of another as a prerequisite to a sense of right and wrong.

phases   A level of learning that shows relatively continuous change in the direction of increasing proficiency.

physical development   Progressive change in the body.

portfolio   A systematic collection of work samples.

positive discipline policy   A plan to stop misbehavior by teaching specific characteristics or skills.

positive reinforcement   The effect of presenting a reinforcer following a behavior.

practical reflection   Consideration of the relation between values and practice.

Premack principle   The belief that the activities a child most frequently chooses during free time can be used as reinforcers for less frequently chosen activities at any time.

preoperational period   A stage of cognitive development that roughly corresponds to early childhood and involves the development of knowledge through intuition and conceptualization.

presentation punishment   The effect of applying an aversive stimulus following a behavior.

problem   A situation in which an individual wants to attain a goal but does not know immediately how to do so.

problematizing   Problem finding with regard to the social causes of one's own actions.

problem finding   The activity of identifying problems.

problem identification   The recognition of a goal one wishes to attain without having a clear way to achieve it.

problem representation   The stage in the problem-solving process in which one defines a goal in a way that it can be achieved.

problem-solving discipline policy   A plan to stop misbehavior through reasoning with students about a situation.

problem-solving process   A stage-like series of actions intended to achieve a goal.

problem space   The range of choices that a decision maker must evaluate in order to achieve a goal.

procedural facilitation   The initial statement of rules in a way that they can be acted upon.

proceduralization   The process by which declarative knowledge is transformed through experience into "know-how."

procedural knowledge   Solution methods or expert "know-how."

procedure   A set of multiple rules in sequence, forming a course of action.

process skill   A subject-specific cognitive performance.

programmed instruction   Systematically arranged material that teaches through contingencies of reinforcement.

project   An extended inquiry into a topic.

proximodistal sequence   The tendency for maturation to occur from the spinal column out to the extremities. (Also called *near-to-far trend*)

psychomotor development   Progressive change in physical abilities or skills.

psychomotor domain   The area of movement, physical skills, and related mental abilities.

psychosocial development   A theory of directive change in personality that emphasizes relationships with others.

puberty   The onset of sexual maturation.

qualitative research   Any disciplined inquiry that does not employ numerical data as its principal means of representing information. (See **quantitative research**)

quantitative research   Any disciplined inquiry that employs numerical data as its principal means of representing information. (See **qualitative research**)

rational planning model   A linear model in which objectives are specified, activities are considered and sequenced, and evaluation procedures are designed.

rational view of creativity   A philosophy that emphasizes problem finding and original problem solving.

readiness   A set of conditions within an individual and his or her environment that make a task appropriate to master.

readiness hypothesis   The belief that any subject can be taught effectively in some intellectually honest form to any child at any stage of development.

Reality Therapy   An intervention to help emotionally distressed children and adults resolve problem behavior.

reciprocal teaching   A cooperative learning procedure for improving reading comprehension.

recognition   (See **perception**)

reflection   Active, persistent, and careful consideration of any belief or thought in light of its grounds or implications.

reflective practitioner   A skilled professional who resolves problems during the course of work.

reinforcer   A stimulus that increases the probability of a behavior when it follows that behavior.

reliability   Consistency in the results of an assessment.

removal punishment   The effect of removing a reinforcer following a behavior.

routine   A repeated action that does not require much attention.

rubric   A scoring guide.

rule   1.) A simple relationship between concepts. 2.) An explicit expectation for participation in an activity.

scaffolded instruction   A form of teaching in which the student's mental structuring ability is supplemented by the support of more-expert peers or adults.

scheduling   A technique for economizing the distribution of extrinsic reinforcers.

schema   (plural *schemata*) A hypothetical memory structure that contains categories of knowledge.

secondary sexual characteristic   A sex-related physical change that occurs outside the reproductive system.

self-actualization   The full use and exploitation of one's talents, capacities, or potentialities.

self-concept   An individual's assessment of his or her own strengths and weaknesses.

self-efficacy   The perception of one's power to produce a desired effect. (See **confidence**)

self-esteem   A feeling of one's own worth.

semantic memory   A meaning stored in a network of meaning. (See also **episodic memory**)

semistructured interview   A qualitative research technique that uses flexible questioning for investigation. (Also known as the *clinical method*)

sensorimotor period   A stage of cognitive development that corresponds to the first two years of life and involves the development of knowledge through sensing and movement.

sensory register   The initial memory structure in which input is held before we are fully conscious of it.

serious emotional disturbance   An inability to build or maintain interpersonal relationships over a period of time.

sex stereotype   A rigid conception of behavior that conforms to sex roles.

sex typing   The process by which children are identified with one gender or the other.

shaping   The reinforcement of successive approximations to a behavior.

short-answer item   A test item that requires a student to fill in the blank with a number, word, or phrase.

short-term memory   A structure that is approximately the same as consciousness. In an adult, it has a capacity of about seven items.

simulation   An operational model that uses selected components of a real or hypothetical process, mechanism, or system.

situated cognition   The teaching of problem solving through an authentic cognitive task.

situational interest   A personal determinant of motivation that stems from the perception of novelty, complexity, or incongruity in the learning environment.

social development   Progressive change in relationships between an individual and others.

social learning   (See **observational learning**)

solution generation   The creation of a means to achieve a goal from the givens of a situation.

specific learning disability   A disorder in one or more of the basic psychological processes involved in understanding or in using language, which may result in an imperfect ability to listen, think, speak, read, write, spell, or perform mathematical calculations.

specific performance objective   A statement of what a learner will be able to do under certain conditions to a certain degree.

speech and language impairment   An inability to formulate, transmit, or receive information through a conventional symbol system.

stage   A maturational plateau.

stand alone   A mode of teaching thinking that consists of a separate unit or course of instruction in thinking skills.

standard   A general expectation for scores that is held by the teacher, the school, and the community.

standardized test   An evaluation instrument with fixed directions for administration and scoring, which has been administered to a representative sample of the population for whom the test is intended.

statistical correlation   A procedure used to measure the degree of association between two or more characteristics.

statistical description   A summary of characteristics in numerical form.

structural schema training   A process by which students are taught about the format of various kinds of discourse.

student action   A form of learning in which learners are relatively active while teachers function in a supportive role.

student educational objectives   Particular ends for learning. (Also known as *instructional objectives* or *objectives*)

subjectively assessed exercise   A response that must be appraised by the teacher or some other expert.

summative evaluation   An assessment of the degree to which outcomes have been attained over an entire course or some substantial part of it.

synectics   A procedure that solves problems creatively through the use of analogies and imagery.

taxonomy   A set of classifications arranged on the basis of a set of principles.

Teacher Effectiveness Training   An intervention to improve student-teacher relationships through improved communication skills and problem solving.

teacher expectations   An instructor's anticipation of student ability and achievements.

teacher presentation   A form of learning in which the instructor is relatively active during the lesson while the students take a passive role.

teacher-student interaction   A form of learning in which learners are active but the instructor is also an active participant.

technical reflection   Consideration of teaching strategies in light of achieving specified goals or objectives.

testing   The administration of an evaluation instrument.

thinking skill   A cognitive performance or action that leads to the attainment of some goal and is subject to improvement in proficiency.

time out from reinforcement   A commonly used intervention to punish a misbehavior, extinguish the misbehavior, and reinforce appropriate behavior in its place, by temporarily removing a student from a reinforcing situation.

transductive reasoning   Reasoning from particular to particular in experience.

transfer   The generalization of learning. (*See* **generalization**)

tutorial program   A computer display sequence designed to teach students new information or skills.

validity   The appropriate interpretation of assessment results.

variability   A statistical description of the degree of "spread" of values for any given characteristic.

vicarious experience   Observation of someone else's behavior and its consequences.

vocational identity   A clear and stable picture of one's talents, interests, and career goals.

well-defined problem   A problem that is highly specified in terms of its limiting circumstances, solution procedures, and goals. (*See* **ill-defined problem**)

withitness   A teacher's awareness of what is going on in the classroom and communication of that awareness to one or more students.

working memory   A memory structure that roughly corresponds to consciousness and increases in capacity throughout childhood.

work sample   A portion of an actual performance that is representative of the whole to be assessed.

zone of proximal development   The difference between a child's unaided level of thinking and his or her potential level if aided by a more-expert peer or adult.

References

Abramson, L. Y., Seligman, M. E. P., & Teasdale, J. (1978). Learned helplessness in humans: Critique and reformulation. *Journal of Abnormal Psychology, 87*, 49–74.

Achenbach, T. M., & Edelbrock, C. S. (1981). Behavioral problems and competencies reported by parents of normal and disturbed children aged four through sixteen. *Monographs of the Society for Research in Child Development, 46* (1, Serial No. 188).

Adams, A., Carnine, D., & Gersten, R. (1982). Instructional strategies for studying content area texts in the intermediate grades. *Reading Research Quarterly, 18*, 27–53.

Adams, J. A. (1987). Historical review and appraisal of research on the learning, retention, and transfer of human motor skills. *Psychological Bulletin, 101*, 41–74.

Ajewole, G. A. (1991). Effects of discovery and expository instructional methods on the attitude of students to biology. *Journal of Research in Science Teaching, 28*, 401–409.

The Alan Guttmacher Institute. (1994). *Sex and America's teenagers.* New York: Author.

Alba, J. W., & Hasher, L. (1983). Is memory schematic? *Psychological Bulletin, 93*, 203–231.

Albert, R. S., & Runco, M. A. (1986). The achievement of eminence: A model based on a longitudinal study of exceptionally gifted boys and their families. In R. J. Sternberg and J. E. Davidson (Eds.), *Conceptions of giftedness* (pp. 332–357). New York: Cambridge University.

Alessi, S. M. (1988). Fidelity in the design of instructional simulations. *Journal of Computer–Based Instruction, 15*(2), 40–47.

Alexander, K., & Day, M. (1991). *Discipline-based art education: A curriculum sampler.* Santa Monica, CA: The Getty Center for Education in the Arts.

Alexander, K. L., Entwisle, D. R., & Dauber, S. L. (1993). First-grade classroom behavior: Its short- and long-term consequences for school performance. *Child Development, 64*, 801–814.

Allport, D. A., Antonis, B., & Reynolds, P. (1972). On the division of attention: A disproof of the single channel hypothesis. *Quarterly Journal of Experimental Psychology, 24*, 225–235.

Allport, G. W. (1942). *The use of personal documents in psychological science.* New York: Social Science Research Council.

Amabile, T. M. (1985). Motivation and creativity: Effects of motivational orientation on creative writers. *Journal of Personality and Social Psychology, 48*, 393–399.

American Association on Mental Retardation. (1992). *Mental retardation: Definition, classification, and systems of supports* (9th ed.). Washington, DC: Author.

American Association of University Women. (1992). *How schools shortchange girls.* Washington, DC: Author.

American Educational Research Association. (1992). Ethical standards for the American Educational Research Association. *Educational Researcher, 21*(7), 23–26.

American Psychological Association. (1992). Ethical principles of psychologists and code of conduct. *American Psychologist, 47*, n. p.

Ames, C. (1990). Motivation: What teachers need to know. *Teachers College Record, 91*, 409–421.

Ames, C. (1992). Classrooms: Goals, structures, and student motivation. *Journal of Educational Psychology, 84*, 261–271.

Anderman, E. M, & Maehr, M. L. (1994). Motivation and schooling in the middle grades. *Review of Educational Research, 64*, 287–309.

Anderson, J. R. (1982). Acquisition of a cognitive skill. *Psychological Review, 89*, 369–406.

Anderson, J. R. (1995). *Learning and memory: An integrated approach.* New York: John Wiley & Sons.

Anderson, R. C. (1984). Some reflections on the acquisition of knowledge. *Educational Researcher, 13*, 5–10.

Arbogast, G., & Lavay, B. (1986). Combining students with different ability levels in games and sports. *Physical Educator, 44*, 255–260.

Archer, J., & Lloyd, B. (1985). *Sex and gender.* Cambridge, England: Cambridge University Press.

Archer, S. L. (1989). The status of identity: Reflections on the need for intervention. *Journal of Adolescence, 12*, 345–359.

Armbruster, B. B., Anderson, T. H., & Ostertag, J. (1987). Does text structure/summarization instruction facilitate learning from expository text? *Reading Research Quarterly, 22*, 331–346.

Arnheim, R. (1986). *New essays on the psychology of art.* Berkeley, CA: University of California.

Arnold, K. D. (1991). *Gender, race, and academic talent: The postsecondary experiences of high school valedictorians.* Paper presented at the annual meeting of the Association for the Study of Higher Education, Boston, MA. (ERIC Document Reproduction No. ED 339297)

Arnstine, D. (1990). Art, aesthetics, and the pitfalls of

Discipline-Based Art Education. *Educational Theory, 40*, 415–422.

Aronson, E., Stephan, C., Sikes, J., Blaney, N., & Snapp, M. (1978). *The jigsaw classroom.* Beverly Hills, CA: Sage.

Arter, J. A., & Spandel, V. (1992). Using portfolios of student work in instruction and assessment. *Educational Measurement: Issues and Practice, 11*, 36–44.

Atkinson, J. W. (1964). *An introduction to motivation.* Princeton, NJ: Van Nostrand.

Atkinson, R. C. (1975). Mnemotechnics in second-language learning. *American Psychologist, 30*, 821–828.

Atkinson, R. C., & Shiffrin, R. M. (1968). Human memory: A proposed system and its control processes. In K. W. Spence & J. T. Spence (Eds.), *The psychology of learning and motivation* (Vol. 2, pp. 89–196). New York: Academic Press.

Ault, C. R. (1985). Concept mapping as a study strategy in earth science. *Journal of College Science Teaching, 15*, 38–44.

Ausubel, D. P. (1960). The use of advance organizers in the learning and retention of meaningful verbal material. *Journal of Educational Psychology, 51*, 267–272.

Ausubel, D. P., Novak, J. D., & Hanesian, H. (1978). *Educational psychology: A cognitive view* (2nd ed.). New York: Holt, Rinehart and Winston.

Axelrod, S., Moyer, L., & Berry, B. (1990). Why teachers do not use behavior modification procedures. *Journal of Educational and Psychological Consultation, 1*, 309–320.

Baddeley, A. (1990). *Human memory.* Boston, MA: Allyn & Bacon.

Bailey, S. M. (1993). The current status of gender equity research in American schools. *Educational Psychologist, 28*, 321–339.

Baker, D., & Leary, R. (1995). Letting girls speak out about science. *Journal of Research in Science Teaching, 32*, 3–27.

Balsam, P. D., & Bondy, A. S. (1983). The negative side effects of reward. *Journal of Applied Behavior Analysis, 16*, 283–296.

Bandura, A. (1969). *Principles of behavior modification.* New York: Holt, Rinehart and Winston.

Bandura, A. (1986). *Social foundations of thought and action.* Englewood Cliffs, NJ: Prentice-Hall.

Bangert-Drowns, R. L., Kulik, J. A., & Kulik, C-L. C. (1985). Effectiveness of computer-based education in secondary schools. *Journal of Computer-Based Instruction, 12*, 59–68.

Banks, J. A. (1992). Multicultural education: Nature, challenges, and opportunities. In C. Diaz (Ed.), *Multicultural education for the 21st century* (pp. 23–37). Washington, DC: National Education Association.

Banks, J. A. (1993). The canon debate, knowledge construction, and multicultural education. *Educational Researcher, 22*(5), 4–14.

Barell, J. (1991). *Teaching for thoughtfulness.* New York: Longman.

Barker, G. P., & Graham, S. (1987). Developmental study of praise and blame as attributional cues. *Journal of Educational Psychology, 79*, 62–66.

Barnett, M. A. (1987). Empathy and related responses in children. In N. Eisenberg & J. Strayer (Eds.), *Empathy and its development* (pp. 146–162). New York: Cambridge University Press.

Barnes, H. (1989). Structuring knowledge for beginning teaching. In M.C. Reynolds (Ed.), *Knowledge base for the beginning teacher* (pp. 13–22). Oxford: Pergamon.

Baron, J. (1985). *Rationality and intelligence.* New York: Cambridge University Press.

Barrett, K. R., Williams, K., & Whitall, J. (1992). What does it mean to have a "developmentally appropriate physical education program"? *Physical Educator, 49*(3), 114–118.

Bartlett, F. C. (1932). *Remembering.* Cambridge: University Press.

Bartlett, J., Smith, L., Davis, K., & Peel, J. (1991). Development of a valid volleyball skills test battery. *Journal of Physical Education, Recreation, and Dance, 62*(2), 19–21.

Baumgartner, R. N., Roche, A. F., & Himes, J. H. (1986). Incremental growth tables: Supplementary to previously published charts. *American Journal of Clinical Nutrition, 43*, 711–722.

Baumrind, D. (1973). The development of instrumental competence through socialization. In A. Pick (Ed.), *Minnesota symposium on child psychology* (Vol. 7). Minneapolis, MN: University of Minnesota Press.

Baumrind, D. (1986). Sex differences in moral reasoning: Response to Walker's (1984) conclusion that there are none. *Child Development, 57*, 511–521.

Beck, I. L., & McKeown, M. G. (1989). Expository text for young readers: The issue of coherence. In L. B. Resnick (Ed.), *Knowing, learning, and instruction: Essays in honor of Robert Glaser* (pp. 47–65). Hillsdale, NJ: Erlbaum.

Becker, B. J. (1990). Item characteristics and gender differences on the SAT-M for mathematically able youths. *American Educational Research Journal, 27*, 65–87.

Becker, H. J. (1990). *Effects of computer use on mathematics achievement: Findings from a nationwide field experiment in grade five to eight classes.* Baltimore, MD: Center for Social Organization of Schools, Johns Hopkins University.

Becker, H. J. (1991). How computers are used in United States schools: Basic data from the 1989 I.E.A. Computers in Education Survey. *Journal of Educational Computing Research, 7*, 385–406.

Beed, P. L., Hawkins, E. M., & Roller, C. M. (1991). Moving learners toward independence: The power of scaffolded instruction. *The Reading Teacher, 44,* 648–655.

Beilin, H. (1992). Piaget's enduring contribution to developmental psychology. *Developmental Psychology, 28,* 191–204.

Beirne-Smith, M. (1991). Peer tutoring in arithmetic for children with learning disabilities. *Exceptional Children, 57,* 330–337.

Bennett, N., & Blundell, D. (1983). Quantity and quality of work in rows and classroom groups. *Educational Psychology, 3,* 93–105.

Bereiter, C., & Bird, M. (1985). Use of thinking aloud in identification and teaching of reading comprehension strategies. *Cognition and Instruction, 2,* 131–156.

Bereiter, C., & Englemann, S. (1966). *Teaching disadvantaged children in the preschool.* Englewood Cliffs, NJ: Prentice-Hall.

Berliner, D. C. (1983). Developing conceptions of classroom environments: Some light on the T in classroom studies of ATI. *Educational Psychologist, 18,* 1–13.

Berliner, D. C. (1986). In pursuit of the expert pedagogue. *Educational Researcher, 15*(7), 5–13.

Berlyne, D. (1960). *Conflict, arousal, and curiosity.* New York: McGraw-Hill.

Berndt, T. J., Laychak, A. E., & Park, K. (1990). Friends' influence on adolescents' academic achievement motivation: An experimental study. *Journal of Educational Psychology, 82,* 664–670.

Bierman, K. L., & Furman, W. (1984). The effects of social skills training and peer involvement on the social adjustment of preadolescents. *Child Development, 55,* 151–162.

Bierman, K. L., Miller, C. L., & Stabb, S. D. (1987). Improving the social behavior and peer acceptance of rejected boys: Effects of social skill training with instructions and prohibitions. *Journal of Consulting and Clinical Psychology, 55,* 194–200.

Bigelow, B. J., Lewko, J. H., & Salhani, L. (1989). Sport-involved children's friendship expectations. *Journal of Sport & Exercise Psychology, 11,* 152–160.

Blackey, R. (1988). Bull's-eye: A teachers' guide for developing student skill in responding to essay questions. *Social Education, 52,* 464–466.

Bloom, B. S. (1956). *Taxonomy of educational objectives: The classification of educational goals. Handbook I: Cognitive domain.* New York: McKay.

Bloom, B. S. (1981). *All our children learning: A primer for parents, teachers, and other educators.* New York: McGraw-Hill.

Bloom, B. S. (1986). Automaticity: The hands and feet of genius. *Educational Leadership, 43*(5), 70–77.

Bloom, B. S., Hastings, J. T., & Madaus, G. F. (1971). *Handbook on formative and summative evaluation of student learning.* New York: McGraw-Hill.

Blumenfeld, P. C. (1992). Classroom learning and motivation: Clarifying and expanding goal theory. *Journal of Educational Psychology, 84,* 272–281.

Blumenfeld, P. C., Pintrich, P. R., & Hamilton, V. L. (1987). Teacher talk and students' reasoning about morals, conventions, and achievement. *Child Development, 58,* 1389–1401.

Boccia, J. A. (1989, March). *Beginning teachers speak out: A study of professional concerns in the first three years of teaching.* Paper presented at the annual meeting of the American Educational Research Association, San Francisco, California. (ERIC Document Reproduction No. ED 316 555)

Boccia, J. A. (1991, April). *Beginning teachers speak out: A study of professional concerns in the first three years of teaching.* Paper presented at the annual meeting of the American Educational Research Association, Chicago, Illinois. (ERIC Document Reproduction No. ED 332 982)

Borko, H., Lalik, R., & Tomchin, E. (1987). Student teachers' understandings of successful and unsuccessful teaching. *Teaching & Teacher Education, 3,* 77–90.

Borko, H., & Livingston, C. (1989). Cognition and improvisation: Differences in mathematics instruction by expert and novice teachers. *American Educational Research Journal, 26,* 473–498.

Borko, H., & Shavelson, R. (1990). Teacher decision making. In B. Jones & L. Idol (Eds.), *Dimensions of thinking and cognitive instruction* (pp. 311–346). Hillsdale, NJ: Erlbaum.

Boschee, F., & Baron, M. A. (1994). OBE: Some answers for the uninitiated. *Clearing House, 67*(4), 193–196.

Bower, G. H., & Reitman, J. S. (1972). Mnemonic elaboration in multilist learning. *Journal of Verbal Learning and Verbal Behavior, 11,* 478–485.

Bransford, J. D., Stein, B., Delclos, V. R., & Littlefield, J. (1986). Computers and problem solving. In C. K. Kinzer, R. D. Sherwood, & J. D. Bransford (Eds.), *Computer strategies for education* (pp. 147–180). Columbus, OH: Merrill Publishing.

Bransford, J. D., & Stein, B. S. (1993). *The ideal problem solver* (2nd ed.). New York: W. H. Freeman.

Brantner, J. P., & Doherty, M. A. (1983). A review of time-out. In S. Axelrod & J. Apsche (Eds.), *The effects of punishment on human behavior* (pp. 87–132). New York: Academic Press.

Bredekamp, S. (1987). *Developmentally appropriate practice in early childhood programs serving children from birth through age 8.* Washington, DC: National Association for the Education of Young Children.

Bredemeier, B. J., & Shields, D. L. (1993). Moral psychology in the context of sport. In R. N. Singer, M. Murphey, & L. K. Tennant, Eds., *Handbook of research on sport psychology* (pp. 587–599). New York: Macmillan.

Bredemeier, B. J., & Weiss, M. R., Shields, D., & Shewchuk, R. (1986). Promoting moral growth in a summer sport camp: The implementation of theoretically grounded instructional strategies. *Journal of Moral Education, 15,* 212–220.

Bright, G. W. (1987). *Microcomputer applications in the* *elementary classroom.* Boston, MA: Allyn & Bacon.

British Broadcasting Corporation. (1990). *Socrates for six-year-olds.*

Brodkey, J. J. (1993). Learning while teaching: Possibilities and problems. *Teacher Education Quarterly, 20,* 63–71.

Brodkin, P., & Weiss, M. R. (1990). Developmental differences in motivation for participation in competitive swimming. *Journal of Sport & Exercise Psychology, 12,* 248–263.

Brooks, D. M. (1985). The teacher's communicative competence: The first day of school. *Theory Intro Practice, 24,* 63–70.

Brooks-Gunn, J. (1990). Consequences of maturational timing variations in adolescent girls. In R. M. Lerner, A. C. Peterson, J. Brooks-Gunn (Eds.), *Encyclopedia of adolescence* (Vol. 2, pp. 614–618). New York: Garland.

Brooks-Gunn, J., Petersen, A. C., & Eichorn, D. (1985). Special issue: Time of maturation and psychosocial functioning in adolescence. *Journal of Youth and Adolescence, 14*(3/4).

Brophy, J. (1981). Teacher praise: A functional analysis. *Review of Educational Research, 51,* 5–32.

Brophy, J. (1983). If only it were true: A response to Greer. *Educational Researcher, 12*(1), 10–13.

Brophy, J. (1983). Research on the self-fulfilling prophecy and teacher expectations. *Journal of Educational Psychology, 75,* 631–661.

Brophy, J. (1987). Synthesis of research on strategies for motivating students to learn. *Educational Leadership, 45*(2), 40–48.

Brophy, J., & McCaslin, M. (1992). Teachers' reports of how they perceive and cope with problem students. *Elementary School Journal, 93,* 3–68.

Brown, A. L., & Palinscar, A. S. (1989). Guided, cooperative learning and individual knowledge acquisition. In L. B. Resnick (Ed.), *Knowing, learning, and instruction* (pp. 393–451). Hillsdale, NJ: Erlbaum.

Brown, B. B., Clasen, D. R., & Eicher, S. A. (1986). Perceptions of peer pressure, peer conformity dispositions, and self-reported behavior among adolescents. *Developmental Psychology, 22,* 521–530.

Brown, D. S. (1988). Twelve middle-school teachers' planning. *The Elementary School Journal, 89,* 69–87.

Brown, J. S., Collins, A., & Duguid, P. (1989). Situated cognition and the culture of learning. *Educational Researcher, 18*(1), 32–42.

Brown, S. I., & Walter, M. I. (1990). *The art of problem posing* (2nd ed.). Hillsdale, NJ: Erlbaum.

Brown, W. E., & Payne, T. (1988). Policies/practices in public school discipline. *Academic Therapy, 23,* 297–301.

Brown, W. E., & Payne, T. (1992). Teachers' views of discipline changes from 1981 to 1991. *Education, 112,* 534–537.

Bruer, J. T. (1993). *Schools for thought.* Cambridge, MA: MIT Press.

Bruner, J. (1960). *The process of education.* Cambridge, MA: Harvard.

Bruner, J. (1975). The ontogenesis of speech acts. *Journal of Child Language, 2,* 1–40.

Bruner, J. S., Goodnow, J. J., & Austin, G. A. (1956). *A study of thinking.* New York: Wiley.

Bruner, J. S. (1961). The act of discovery. *Harvard Educational Review, 31,* 21–32.

Bukatko, D., & Daehler, M. W. (1995). *Child development: A topical approach* (2nd ed.). Boston, MA: Houghton Mifflin.

Bulkeley, R., & Cramer, D. (1990). Social skills training with young adolescents. *Journal of Youth and Adolescence, 19,* 451–463.

Bullough, R. V. (1989). *First-year teacher.* New York: Teachers College.

Burden, P. R. (1990). Teacher development. In W. R. Houston (Ed.), *Handbook of research on teacher education* (pp. 311–328). New York: Macmillan.

Burts, D. C., Hart, C. H., Charlesworth, R., DeWolf, D. M., Ray, J., Manuel, K., & Fleege, P. O. (1993). Developmental appropriateness of kindergarten programs and academic outcomes in first grade. *Journal of Research in Childhood Education, 8,* 23–31.

Burts, D. C., Hart, C. H., Thomasson, R. H., Charlesworth, R., Fleege, P. O., & Mosley, J. (1992). Observed activities and stress behaviors of children in developmentally appropriate and inappropriate kindergarten classrooms. *Early Childhood Research Quarterly, 7,* 297–318.

Calderhead, J. (1984). *Teachers' classroom decision-making.* New York: Holt, Rinehart and Winston.

Calderhead, J. (1988). The development of "knowledge structures" in learning to teach. In J. Calderhead (Ed.), *Teachers' professional learning* (pp. 51–64). New York: Falmer Press.

Calderhead, J. (1989). Reflective teaching and teacher education. *Teaching & Teacher Education, 5*(1), 43–51.

Calderhead, J. (1993). The contribution of research on teachers' thinking to the professional development of teachers. In C. Day, J. Calderhead, & P. Denicolo (Eds.), *Research on teacher thinking: Understanding professional development* (pp. 11–18). London: Falmer Press.

Calfee, R. C., & Chambliss, M. J. (1987). The structural design features of large texts. *Educational Psychologist, 22,* 357–378.

California State Department of Education. (1989). *A question of thinking.* Sacramento, CA: Author.

Canter, L. (1989). Assertive discipline—More than names on the board and marbles in a jar. *Phi Delta Kappan, 71*(1), 57–61.

Canter, L. & Canter, M. (1976). *Assertive discipline.* Santa Monica, CA: Canter and Associates, Inc.

Carnine, D. W. (1993). Effective teaching for higher cognitive functioning. *Educational Technology, 33,* 29–33.

Carroll, J. (1963). A model of school learning. *Teachers College Record, 64,* 723–733.

Carter, J., & Sugai, G. (1989). Survey on prereferral practices: Responses from state departments of education. *Exceptional Children, 55*, 298–302.

Carter, K., Sabers, D., Cushing, K., Pinnegar, S., & Berliner, D. C. (1987). Processing and using information about students: A study of expert, novice, and postulant teachers. *Teaching & Teacher Education, 3*(2), 147–157.

Case, R. (1985a). A developmentally-based approach to the problem of instructional design. In S. F. Chipman, J. W. Segal, & R. Glaser (Eds.), *Thinking and learning skills* (Vol. 2, pp. 545–562). Hillsdale, NJ: Erlbaum.

Case, R. (1985b). *Intellectual development: Birth to adulthood.* Orlando, FL: Academic Press.

Case, R. (1991). *The mind's staircase.* Hillsdale, NJ: Erlbaum.

Case, R. (1993). Theories of learning and theories of development. *Educational Psychologist, 28*, 219–233.

Casteel, C. A. (1990). Effects of chunked text material on reading comprehension of high and low ability readers. *Reading Improvement, 27*, 269–275.

Cazden, C. B. (1986). Classroom discourse. In M. C. Wittrock (Ed.), *Handbook of research on teaching* (3rd ed., pp. 432–463). New York: Macmillan.

Chamberlin, C., & Lee, T. (1993). Arranging practice conditions and designing instruction. In R. N. Singer, M. Murphey, & L. K. Tennant (Eds.), *Handbook of research on sport psychology* (pp. 213–241). New York: Macmillan.

Chambers, B., & Abrami, P. C. (1991). The relationship between student team learning outcomes and achievement, causal attributions, and affect. *Journal of Educational Psychology, 83*, 140–146.

Chambers, S. T. (1991). Factors affecting elementary school students' participation in sports. *Elementary School Journal, 91*, 413–419.

Chi, M. T. H., & Cesi, S. J. (1987). Content knowledge: Its role, representation, and restructuring in memory development. *Advances in Child Development and Behavior, 20*, 91–142.

Chi, M. T. H., Feltovich, P. J., & Glaser, R. (1981). Categorization and representation of physics problems by experts and novices. *Cognitive Science, 5*, 121–152.

Chi, M. T. H., & Koeske, R. D. (1983). Network representation of a child's dinosaur knowledge. *Developmental Psychology, 19*, 29–39.

Chittenden, E. (1991). Authentic assessment, evaluation, and documentation of student performance. In V. Perrone (Ed.), *Expanding student assessment* (pp. 22–31). Alexandria, VA: Association for Supervision and Curriculum Development.

Clark, B. (1992). *Growing up gifted* (4th ed.). New York: Macmillan.

Clark, C. M. (1988). Asking the right questions about teacher preparation: Contributions of research on teacher thinking. *Educational Researcher, 17*(2), 5–12.

Clark, C. M., & Peterson, P. L. (1986). Teachers' thought processes. In M. C. Wittrock (Ed.), *Handbook of research on teaching* (3rd ed., pp. 255–296). New York: Macmillan.

Clark, G. A., Day, M. D., & Greer, W. D. (1987). Discipline-based art education: Becoming students of art. *Journal of Aesthetic Education, 21*(2), 129–193.

Clarke, H. H. (1968). Characteristics of the young athlete: A longitudinal look. *Kinesiology Review, 3*, 33–42.

Clark, J. E., Phillips, S. J., Petersen, R. (1989). Developmental stability in jumping. *Developmental Psychology, 25*, 929–935.

Clements, D. H. (1991). Enhancement of creativity in computer environments. *American Educational Research Journal, 28*, 173–187.

Cognition and Technology Group at Vanderbilt. (1992). The Jasper Series as an example of anchored instruction: Theory, program description, and assessment data. *Educational Psychologist, 27*, 291–315.

Cognition and Technology Group at Vanderbilt (1993). Anchored instruction and situated cognition revisited. *Educational Technology, 41*, 52–70.

Cohen, K. J., & Rhenman, E. (1961). The role of management games in education and research. *Management Science, 7*, 131–166.

Coie, J. D., Underwood, M., Lochman, J. E. (1991). Programmatic intervention with aggressive children in the school setting. In D. J. Pepler & K. H. Rubin (Eds.), *The development and treatment of childhood aggression* (pp. 389–410). Hillsdale, NJ: Erlbaum.

Colangelo, N., & Davis, G. A. (1991). *Handbook of gifted education.* Boston, MA: Allyn & Bacon.

Compas, B. E. (1987). Coping with stress during childhood and adolescence. *Psychological Bulletin, 101*, 393–403.

Cook, L. K., & Meyer, R. E. (1983). Reading strategies training for meaningful learning from prose. In M. Pressley & J. R. Levin (Eds.), *Cognitive strategy research* (pp. 87–131). New York: Springer-Verlag.

Cook, V. (1991). *Second language learning and language teaching.* New York: Edward Arnold.

Cooksey, E. C. (1990). Factors in the resolution of adolescent premarital pregnancies. *Demography, 27*, 207–218.

Corkill, A. J., Glover, J. A., Bruning, R. H., & Krug, D. (1988). Advance organizers: Retrieval context hypothesis. *Journal of Educational Psychology, 80*, 304–311.

Cornell, D. G., Callahan, C. M., & Loyd, B. H. (1991). Socioemotional adjustment of adolescent girls enrolled in a residential acceleration program. *Gifted Child Quarterly, 35*, 58–66.

Corno, L., & Snow, R. E. (1986). Adapting teaching to individual differences among learners. In M. C. Wittrock (Ed.), *Handbook of research on teaching* (3rd ed., pp. 605–629). New York: Macmillan.

Côté, J. E., & Levine, C. G. (1989). An empirical test of Erikson's theory of ego identity formation. *Youth and Society, 20*, 388–415.

Covington, M. V. (1992). *Making the grade: A self-worth perspective on motivation and school reform.* Cambridge, England: Cambridge University Press.

Cox, J., Daniel, N., & Boston, B. O. (1985). *Educating able learners: Programs and promising practices.* Austin, TX: University of Texas.

Crabbe, A. B. (1989). The future problem solving program. *Educational Leadership, 47*(1), 27–29.

Crittenden, P. (1990). *Learning to be moral.* New Jersey: Humanities Press International.

Cronbach, L. J. (1990). *Essentials of psychological testing* (5th ed.). New York: Harper & Row.

Csikszentmihalyi, M. (1987). The pressured world of adolescence. *Educational Horizons, 65*(3), 103–105.

Csikszentmihalyi, M. (1990). *Flow: The psychology of optimal experience.* New York: Harper & Row.

Csikszentmihalyi, M., & Getzels, J. W. (1988). Creativity and problem finding in art. In F. H. Farley & R. W. Neperud (Eds.), *The foundations of aesthetics, art & art appreciation* (pp. 91–116). New York: Praeger.

Csikszentmihalyi, M., & Nakamura, J. (1989). The dynamics of intrinsic motivation: A study of adolescents. In C. Ames & R. Ames (Eds.), *Research on motivation in education* (Vol. 3, pp. 45–71). San Diego, CA: Academic Press.

Cushing, K. S., Sabers, D. S., & Berliner, D. C. (1992). Olympic gold: Investigations of expertise in teaching. *Educational Horizons, 70*(3), 108–114.

Damon, W., & Phelps, E. (1989). Strategic use of peer learning in children's education. In T. J. Berndt & G. W. Ladd (Eds.), *Peer relationships in child development* (pp. 135–157). New York: John Wiley & Sons.

Dansereau, D. F. (1985). Learning strategy research. In J. W. Segal, S. F. Chipman, & R. Glaser (Eds.), *Thinking and learning skills* (Vol. 1, pp. 209–239). Hillsdale, NJ: Erlbaum.

Davidson, L. (1990). Tools and environments for musical creativity. *Music Educators' Journal, 76*(9), 47–51.

Davis, R. B., Maher, C. A., Noddings, N. (1990). Suggestions for the improvement of mathematics education. *Journal for Research in Mathematics Education* (Monograph No. 4), 187–191.

Day, J. D., & Cordon, L. A. (1993). Static and dynamic measures of ability: An experimental comparison. *Journal of Educational Psychology, 85*, 75–82.

Day, J. D., Cordon, L. A., & Kerwin, M. L. (1989). Informal instruction and cognitive development: A review and critique of research. In M. Pressley, C. B. McCormick, & G. E. Miller (Eds.), *Cognitive strategy research: From basic research to educational applications* (pp. 83–103). New York: Springer-Verlag.

DeBusk, M., & Hellison, D. (1989). Implementing a physical education self-responsibility model for delinquency-prone youth. *Journal of Teaching in Physical Education, 8*, 104–112.

Deci, E. L. (1975). *Intrinsic motivation.* New York: Plenum.

Deci, E. L., & Ryan, R. M. (1985). *Intrinsic motivation and self-determination in human behavior.* New York: Plenum.

Deci, E. L., Vallerand, R. J., Pelletier, L. C., & Ryan, R. M. (1991). Motivation and education: The self-determination perspective. *Educational Psychologist, 26.* 325–346.

DeFina, A. A. (1992). *Portfolio assessment: Getting started.* New York: Scholastic Inc.

DeLorenzo, L. C. (1989). A field study of sixth-grade students' creative music problem-solving processes. *Journal of Research in Music Education, 37*, 188–200.

Dempster, F. N. (1981). Digit span: Sources of individual and developmental differences. *Psychological Bulletin, 89*, 63–100.

Dennebaum, J. M., & Kulberg, J. M. (1994). Kindergarten retention and transition classrooms: Their relationship to achievement. *Psychology in the Schools, 31*, 5–12.

Derry, S. J. (1984). Effects of an organizer on memory for prose. *Journal of Educational Psychology, 76*, 98–107.

Derry, S. J. (1990). Learning strategies for acquiring useful knowledge. In B. F. Jones & L. Idol (Eds.), *Dimensions of thinking and cognitive instruction* (pp. 347–379). Hillsdale, NJ: Erlbaum.

Deux, K., & Major, B. (1987). Putting gender into context: An interactive model of gender-related behavior. *Psychological Review, 94*, 369–389.

Dewey, J. (1933). *How we think.* Lexington, MA: D. C. Heath.

Dick, W., & Reiser, R. A. (1989). *Planning effective instruction.* Englewood Cliffs, NJ: Prentice-Hall.

Dickinson, Alyce M. (1989). The detrimental effects of extrinsic reinforcement on "intrinsic motivation." *The Behavior Analyst, 12*, 1–15.

Dinnel, D., & Glover, J. A. (1985). Advance organizers: Encoding manipulations. *Journal of Educational Psychology, 77*, 514–521.

Dodge, K. A. (1983). Behavioral antecedents of peer social status. *Child Development, 54*, 1386–1399.

Dorr-Bremme, D. W. (1990). Contextualization cues in the classroom: Discourse regulation and social control functions. *Language in Society, 19*, 379–402.

Doyle, W. (1986). Classroom organization and management. In M. C. Wittrock (Ed.), *Handbook of research on teaching* (3rd ed., pp. 392–431). New York: Macmillan.

Dreyfus, H. L., & Dreyfus, S. E. (1986). *Mind over machine.* New York: The Free Press.

Duchastel, P. C., & Merrill, P. F. (1973). The effects of behavioral objectives on learning: A review of empirical studies. *Review of Educational Research, 43*, 53–69.

Duffy, G. G. (1993). Teachers' progress toward becoming expert strategy teachers. *Elementary School Journal, 94*, 109–120.

Duke, D., & Jones, V. (1985). What can schools do to foster student responsibility? *Theory Into Practice, 24,* 277–285.

Dunbar, S. B., Koretz, D. M., & Hoover, H. D. (1991). Quality control in the development and use of performance tests. *Applied Measurement in Education, 4,* 289–303.

Dunn, T. G. (1984). Learning hierarchies and cognitive psychology: An important link for instructional psychology. *Educational Psychologist, 19,* 75–93.

Duschl, R. A., & Gitomer, D. H. (1991). Epistemological perspectives on conceptual change: Implications for educational practice. *Journal of Research in Science Teaching, 28,* 839–858.

Duschl, R. A., & Wright, E. (1989). A case study of high school teachers' decision making models for planning and teaching science. *Journal of Research in Science Teaching, 26,* 467–501.

Dusek, J. B. (1985). *Teacher expectations.* Hillsdale, NJ: Erlbaum.

Dweck, C. S. (1986). Motivational processes affecting learning. *American Psychologist, 41,* 1040–1048.

Dweck, C. S., & Leggett, E. L. (1988). A social-cognitive approach to motivation and personality. *Psychological Review, 95,* 256–273.

Dwyer, D. C., Ringstaff, C., & Sandholtz, J. H. (1991). Changes in teachers' beliefs and practices in technology-rich classrooms. *Educational Leadership, 48*(8), 45–52.

Dyson, A. H. (1990). Weaving possibilities: Rethinking metaphors for early literacy development. *The Reading Teacher, 44,* 202–213.

Earle, R. S. (1992, February). *The use of instructional design skills in the mental and written planning processes of teachers.* Paper presented at the Convention of the Association for Educational Communications and Technology. (ERIC Document Reproduction No. ED347987)

Eaton, W. O., & Enns, L. R. (1986). Sex differences in human motor activity level. *Psychological Bulletin, 100,* 19–28.

Eaton, W. O., & Yu, A. P. (1989). Are sex differences in child motor activity level a function of sex differences in maturational status? *Child Development, 60,* 1005–1011.

Ebbinghaus, H. (1913). *Memory: A contribution to experimental psychology* (H. A. Ruger & C. E. Bussenius, Trans.). New York: Teachers College. (Original work published 1885)

Eccles, J. S., Jacobs, J. E., & Harold, R. D. (1990). Gender role stereotypes, expectancy effects, and parents' socialization of gender differences. *Journal of Social Issues, 46,* 183–201.

Edwards, J. (1991). To teach responsibility, bring back the Dalton Plan. *Phi Delta Kappan, 72,* 398–401.

Eibl-Eibesfeldt, I. (1989). *Human ethology.* New York: Aldine de Gruyter.

Eisenberg, N., Fabes, R. A., Schaller, M., Carlo, G., & Miller, P. A. (1991). The relations of parental characteristics and practices to children's vicarious emotional responding. *Child Development, 62,* 1393–1408.

Eisenberg, N., & Strayer, J. (1987). Critical issues in the study of empathy. In N. Eisenberg & J. Strayer (Eds.), *Empathy and its development* (pp. 3–13). New York: Cambridge University Press.

Eisner, E. W. (1985). Creative education in American schools today. *Educational Horizons, 63,* 10–15.

Eisner, E. W. (1990). Discipline-based art education: Conceptions and misconceptions. *Educational Theory, 40,* 423–430.

Elawar, M. C., & Corno, L. (1985). A factorial experiment in teachers' written feedback on student homework: Changing teacher behavior a little rather than a lot. *Journal of Educational Psychology, 77,* 162–173.

Elkind, D. (1981). *The hurried child.* Reading, MA: Addison-Wesley.

Elkind, D. (1987). *Miseducation: Preschoolers at risk.* New York: Knopf.

Elliott, E. S., & Dweck, C. S. (1988). Goals: An approach to motivation and achievement. *Journal of Personality and Social Psychology, 54,* 5–12.

Ellis, H. C., & Hunt, R. R. (1989). *Fundamentals of human memory and cognition* (4th ed.). Dubuque, IA: Wm. C. Brown.

Emde, R. N., Plomin, R., Robinson, J., Corley, R., DeFries, J., Fulker, D. W., Reznick, J. S., Campos, J., Kagan, J., Zahn-Waxler, C. (1992). Temperament, emotion, and cognition at fourteen months: The MacArthur longitudinal twin study. *Child Development, 63,* 1435–1455.

Emmer, E. T. (1987). Classroom management and discipline. In V. Richardson-Koehler (Ed.), *Educators' handbook: A research perspective* (pp. 233–258). New York: Longman.

Emmer, E. T. (1988). Praise and the instructional process. *Journal of Classroom Interaction, 23,* 32–39.

Emmer, E. T., & Aussiker, A. (1990). School and classroom discipline programs: How well do they work? In O. C. Moles (Ed.), *Student discipline strategies* (pp. 129–165). New York: SUNY Press.

Emmer, E. T., Evertson, C. M., & Anderson, L. M. (1980). Effective classroom management at the beginning of the year. *Elementary School Journal, 80,* 219–231.

Emmer, E. T., Evertson, C. M., Sanford, J. P., Clements, B. S., & Worsham, M. E. (1994). *Classroom management for secondary teachers* (3rd ed.). Needham Heights, MA: Allyn & Bacon.

Entwisle, D. R., Alexander, K. L., Pallas, A. M., & Cadigan, D. (1987). The emergent academic self-image of first graders: Its response to social structure. *Child Development, 58,* 1190–1206.

Epstein, J. L. (1989). The selection of friends. In T. J. Berndt & G. W. Ladd (Eds.), *Peer relationships in child development* (pp. 158–187). New York: John Wiley & Sons.

Epstein, M. H., & Cullinan, D. (1992). Emotional/behavioral problems. In M. C. Alkin (Ed.), *Encyclopedia of educational research* (Vol. 2, pp. 430–432). New York: Macmillan.

Erikson, E. H. (1968). *Identity: Youth and crisis.* New York: Norton.

Erikson, E. H. (1982). *The life cycle completed.* New York: Norton.

Evans, K. M., & King, J. A. (1994). Research on OBE: What we know and don't know. *Educational Leadership, 51*(6), 12–17.

Evertson, C. M. (1985). Training teachers in classroom management: An experimental study in secondary school classrooms. *Journal of Educational Research, 79,* 52–58.

Evertson, C. M. (1987). Creating conditions for learning: From research to practice. *Theory Into Practice, 26,* 44–50.

Evertson, C. M., & Emmer, E. T. (1982). Effective management at the beginning of the school year in junior high. *Journal of Educational Psychology, 74,* 485–498.

Evertson, C. M., Emmer, E. T., Clements, B. S., Sanford, J. P., & Worsham, M. E. (1994). *Classroom management for elementary teachers* (3rd ed.). Needham Heights, MA: Allyn and Bacon.

Evertson, C. M., & Weade, R. (1989). Classroom management and teaching style: Instructional stability and variability in two junior high classrooms. *Elementary School Journal, 89,* 379–393.

Fagot, B. I., Leinbach, M. D., & O'Boyle, C. (1992). Gender labeling, gender stereotyping, and parenting behaviors. *Developmental Psychology, 28,* 225–230.

Fantuzzo, J., & Atkins, M. (1992). Applied behavior analysis for educators: Teacher centered and classroom based. *Journal of Applied Behavior Analysis, 25,* 37–42.

Feingold, A. (1988). Cognitive gender differences are disappearing. *American Psychologist, 43,* 95–103.

Feldhusen, J. F., & Clinkenbeard, P. A. (1986). Creativity instructional materials: A review of research. *Journal of Creative Behavior, 20,* 153–182.

Fennell, F., & Ammon, R. (1985). Writing techniques for problem solvers. *Arithmetic Teacher, 33*(1), 24–25.

Feuerstein, R., Rand, Y., & Hoffman, M. B. (1979). *The dynamic assessment of retarded performers.* Baltimore, MD: University Park Press.

Feuerstein, R., Rand, Y., Hoffman, M. B., & Miller, R. (1980). *Instrumental enrichment: An intervention program for cognitive modifiability.* Baltimore: University Park Press.

Fillmore, L. W., & Valadez, C. (1986). Teaching bilingual learners. In M. C. Wittrock (Ed.), *Handbook of research on teaching* (3rd ed., pp. 648–685). New York: Macmillan.

Fincham, F. D., & Cain, K. M. (1986). Learned helpless-

ness in humans: A developmental analysis. *Developmental Review, 6,* 301–333.

Fincham, F. D., Hokoda, A., & Sanders, R. (1989). Learned helplessness, test anxiety, and academic achievement: A longitudinal analysis. *Child Development, 60,* 138–145.

Fine, G. A. (1981). Friends, impression management, and preadolescent behavior. In S. R. Asher & J. M. Gottman (Eds.), *The development of children's friendships* (pp. 29–52). New York: Cambridge University Press.

Firestein, R. L., & McCowan, R. J. (1988). Creative problem solving and communication behaviors in small groups. *Creativity Research Journal, 1,* 106–114.

Fish, M. C., & Pervan, R. (1985). Self-instruction training: A potential tool for school psychologists. *Psychology in the Schools, 22,* 83–92.

Fitts, P. M., & Posner, M. I. (1967). *Human performance.* Belmont, CA: Brooks-Cole.

Fitzgerald, J., & Spiegel, D. L. (1983). Enhancing children's reading comprehension through instruction in narrative structure. *Journal of Reading Behavior, 15*(2), 1–17.

Flavell, J. H., Green, F. L., & Flavell, E. R. (1987). Development of knowledge about the appearance–reality distinction. *Monographs of the Society for Research in Child Development, 51*(1), Serial No. 212).

Flavell, J. H., Miller, P. H., & Miller, S. A. (1993). *Cognitive development* (3rd ed.). Englewood Cliffs, NJ: Prentice-Hall.

Fleisher, L. S., Jenkins, J. R., & Pany, D. (1979). Effects on poor readers' comprehension of training in rapid decoding. *Reading Research Quarterly, 15,* 30–48.

Flood, J., Lapp, D., & Monken, S. (1992). Portfolio assessment: Teacher beliefs and practices. In C. K. Kinzer & D. J. Leu (Eds.), *Literacy research, theory, and practice: Views from many perspectives* (pp. 119–127). Chicago, IL: The National Reading Conference.

Flower, L., & Hayes, J. R. (1980). The cognition of discovery: Defining a rhetorical problem. *College Composition and Communication, 31*(2), 21–32.

Forest-Pressley, D. L., & Gillies, L. A. (1983). Children's flexible use of strategies during reading. In M. Pressley & J. R. Levin (Eds.), *Cognitive strategy research: Educational applications* (pp. 133–151). New York: Springer-Verlag.

Forness, S. R. (1973). The reinforcement hierarchy. *Psychology in the Schools, 10,* 168–177.

Fosterling, F. (1985). Attributional training: A review. *Psychological Bulletin, 98,* 495–512.

Franke, T. M., Levin, J. R., & Carney, R. N. (1991). Mnemonic artwork-learning strategies: Helping students remember more than "who painted what?" *Contemporary Educational Psychology, 16,* 375–390.

Freeman, E. B., & Hatch, A. J. (1989). What schools expect young children to know and do: An analysis of kindergarten report cards. *Elementary School Journal, 89,* 595–605.

Freire, P. (1972) *Pedagogy of the oppressed.* Harmondsworth, England: Penguin.

French, K. E., Rink, J. E., Rikard, L., Mays, A., Lynn, S., & Werner, P. (1991). The effects of practice progressions on learning two volleyball skills. *Journal of Teaching in Physical Education, 10,* 261–274.

Freud, S. (1963). Introductory lectures on psycho-analysis. In J. Strachey (Ed.), *The standard edition of the complete psychological works* (Vols. 15 and 16). London: Hogarth Press. (Originally published 1917)

Frey, K. S., & Ruble, D. N. (1987). What children say about classroom performance: Sex and grade differences in perceived competence. *Child Development, 58,* 1066–1078.

Friedman, L. (1989). Mathematics and the gender gap: A meta-analysis of recent studies on sex differences in mathematics tasks. *Review of Educational Research, 59,* 185–213.

Fuchs, D., Fuchs, L. S. (1994). Inclusive schools movement and the radicalization of special education reform. *Exceptional Children, 60,* 294–309.

Fuchs, D., Fuchs, L. S., Bahr, M. W., Fernstrom, P., & Stecker, P. M. (1990). Prereferral intervention: A prescriptive approach. *Exceptional Children, 56,* 493–513.

Fuchs, D., Fuchs, L. S., & Fernstrom, P. (1993). A conservative approach to special education reform: Mainstreaming through transenvironmental programming and curriculum-based measurement. *American Educational Research Journal, 30,* 149–177.

Fuller, F. F., & Brown, O. H. (1975). Becoming a teacher. In K. Ryan (Ed.), *Teacher education, part II* (pp. 25–52). Chicago, IL: National Society for the Study of Education.

Furst, E. J. (1994). Bloom's taxonomy: Philosophical and educational issues. In L. W. Anderson & L. A. Sosniak (Eds.), *Bloom's taxonomy: A forty-year retrospective* (pp. 28–40). Chicago, IL: The National Society for the Study of Education.

Gaddy, G. D. (1988). High school order and academic achievement. *American Journal of Education, 96,* 496–518.

Gagné, F. (1991). Toward a differentiated model of giftedness and talent. In N. Colangelo & G. A. Davis (Eds.), *Handbook of gifted education* (pp. 65–80). Boston, MA: Allyn & Bacon.

Gagné, R. M. (1967). *Science . . . a process approach: Purposes, accomplishments, expectations.* Washington, DC: Commission on Science Education, American Association for the Advancement of Science.

Gagné, R. M. (1985). *The conditions of learning* (4th ed.). New York: Holt, Rinehart and Winston.

Gagné, R. M. (1991). Analysis of objectives. In L. J. Briggs, K. L. Gustafson, M. H. Tillman (Eds.), *Instructional design* (2nd ed., pp. 123–150). Englewood Cliffs, NJ: Educational Technology Publications.

Gallagher, J. J. (1985). *Teaching the gifted child* (3rd ed.). Boston, MA: Allyn & Bacon.

Gallahue, D. L., & Ozmun, J. C. (1995). *Understanding motor development: Infants, children, adolescents, adults* (3rd ed.). Madison, WI: WCB Brown & Benchmark.

Gardner, H. (1983). *Frames of mind: The theory of multiple intelligences.* New York: Basic Books.

Gardner, H. (1989). *To open minds: Chinese clues to the dilemma of contemporary education.* New York: Basic Books.

Garner, R., Gillingham, M. G., & White, C. S. (1989). Effects of "seductive details" on macroprocessing and microprocessing in adults and children. *Cognition and Instruction, 6,* 41–57.

Gelman, R., & Gallistel, C. R. (1978). *The child's understanding of number.* Cambridge, MA: Harvard University Press.

Genishi, C. (1989). Observing the second language learner: An example of teachers' learning. *Language Arts, 66,* 509–515.

Gentner, D. (1983). Structure-mapping: A theoretical framework for analogy. *Cognitive Science, 7,* 155–170.

Gentner, D. (1988). Metaphor as structure mapping: The relational shift. *Child Development, 59,* 47–59.

Gerber, M. M. (1987). Application of cognitive-behavioral training methods to teaching basic skills to mildly handicapped elementary school students. In M. C. Wang, M. C. Reynolds, & H. J. Walberg (Eds.), *Handbook of special education: Research and practice* (Vol. 2, pp. 167–186). Oxford: Pergamon.

Gersten, R. (1985). Direct instruction with special education students: A review of evaluation research. *Journal of Special Education, 19,* 41–58.

Getchell, N., & Roberton, M. A. (1989). Whole body stiffness as a function of developmental level in children's hopping. *Developmental Psychology, 25,* 920–928.

Getzels, J. W., & Csikszentmihalyi, M. (1976). *The creative vision: A longitudinal study of problem finding in art.* New York: Wiley.

Ghatala, E. S., Levin, J. R., Pressley, M., & Lodico, M. G. (1985). Training cognitive strategy-monitoring in children. *American Educational Research Journal, 22,* 199–215.

Gibbs, J. C., Arnold, K. D., & Burkhart, J. E. (1984). Sex differences in the expression of moral judgment. *Child Development, 55,* 1040–1043.

Gibbs, J. C., & Schnell, S. V. (1985). Moral development "versus" socialization. *American Psychologist, 40,* 1071–1080.

Gibson, M. A. (1989). School persistence and dropping out: A comparative perspective. In H. T. Trueba, G. Spindler, & L. Spindler (Eds.). *What do anthropologists have to say about dropouts?* (pp. 129–134). New York: Falmer Press.

Gick, M. L. (1986). Problem solving strategies. *Educational Psychologist, 21,* 99–120.

Gilligan, C. (1982). *In a different voice.* Cambridge, MA: Harvard University Press.

Gilligan, C., & Attanucci, J. (1988). Two moral orientations: Gender differences and similarities. *Merrill-Palmer Quarterly, 34,* 223–237.

Gipe, J. P., & Richards, J. C. (1992). Reflective thinking and growth in novices' teaching abilities. *Journal of Educational Research, 86,* 52–57.

Gitomer, D., Grosh, S., & Price, K. (1992). Portfolio culture in arts education. *Art Education, 45*(1), 7–15.

Glaser, R. (1990). The reemergence of learning theory within instructional research. *American Psychologist, 45,* 29–39.

Glasser, W. (1965). *Reality therapy: A new approach to psychiatry.* New York: Harper & Row.

Glasser, W. (1986). *Control theory in the classroom.* New York: Harper & Row.

Glasser, W. (1990). *The quality school: Managing students without coercion.* New York: Harper & Row.

Glazer, S. M., & Brown, C. S. (1993). *Portfolios and beyond: Collaborative assessment in reading and writing.* Norwood, MA: Christopher-Gordon Publishers.

Glover, J. A., Bullock, R. G., Dietzer, M. L. (1990). Advance organizers: Delay hypotheses. *Journal of Educational Psychology, 82,* 291–297.

Goldenberg, C. (1992). The limits of expectations: A case for case knowledge about teacher expectancy effects. *American Educational Research Journal, 29,* 517–544.

Good, T. L. (1987). Two decades of research on teacher expectations: Findings and future directions. *Journal of Teacher Education, 38*(4), 32–47.

Goodman, J. (1988). The political tactics and teaching strategies of reflective, active preservice teachers. *Elementary School Journal, 89,* 23–41.

Goodman, K. (1986). *What's whole in whole language.* Portsmouth, NH: Heinemann.

Goodman, N. (1976). *Languages of art* (2nd ed.). Indianapolis, IN: Hackett.

Gordon, T. (1974). *T.E.T.: Teacher effectiveness training.* New York: Peter H. Wyden.

Gordon, W. J. J. (1961). *Synectics: The development of creative capacity.* New York: Harper & Row.

Gore, J. M. (1987). Reflecting on reflective teaching. *Journal of Teacher Education, 38*(2), 33–39.

Gore, T. (1991). A portrait of at-risk children. *Journal of Health Care for the Poor and Underserved, 2*(1), 95–105.

Gottfried, A. E. (1985). Academic intrinsic motivation in elementary and junior high school students. *Journal of Educational Psychology, 77,* 631–645.

Gottfried, A. E. (1990). Academic intrinsic motivation in young elementary school children. *Journal of Educational Psychology, 82,* 525–538.

Graden, J. L., & Bauer, A. M. (1992). Using a collaborative approach to support students and teachers in inclusive classrooms. In S. Stainback & W. Stainback (Eds.), *Curriculum considerations in inclusive classrooms* (pp. 85–100). Baltimore, MD: Paul H. Brookes.

Graden, J. L., Casey, A., Christenson, S. L. (1985). Implementing a prereferral intervention system: Part I. The model. *Exceptional Children, 51,* 377–384.

Graham, K. (1987). A description of academic work and student performance during a middle school volleyball unit. *Journal of Teaching in Physical Education, 7,* 22–37.

Graham, S., & Barker, G. P. (1990). The down side of help: An attributional-developmental analysis of helping behavior as a low-ability cue. *Journal of Educational Psychology, 82,* 7–14.

Graham, S., MacArthur, C., & Schwartz, S. (1995). Effects of goal setting and procedural facilitation on the revising behavior and writing performance of students with writing and learning problems. *Journal of Educational Psychology, 87,* 230–240.

Green, J. L. (1983). Research on teaching as a linguistic process: A state of the art. In E. W. Gordon (Ed.), *Review of research in education* (Vol. 10, pp. 151–252). Washington, DC: American Educational Research Association.

Greendorfer, S. L. (1987). Psycho-social correlates of organized physical activity. *Journal of Physical Education, Recreation and Dance, 58,* 69–74.

Greene, M. (1991). Texts and margins. *Harvard Educational Review, 61,* 1–17.

Greer, R. D. (1983). Contingencies of the science and technology of teaching and pre-behavioristic research practices in education. *Educational Researcher, 12*(1), 3–9.

Greer, R. D. (1992). *L'enfant terrible* meets the educational crisis. *Journal of Applied Behavior Analysis, 25,* 65–69.

Griffiths, M., & Tann, S. (1992). Using reflective practice to link personal and public theories. *Journal of Education for Teaching, 18,* 69–84.

Grissom, J. B., & Shepard, L. A. (1989). Repeating and dropping out of school. In L. A. Shepard & M. L. Smith (Eds.), *Flunking grades: Research and policies on retention* (pp. 34–63). New York: Falmer Press.

Grolnick, W. S., & Ryan, R. M. (1987). Autonomy in children's learning: An experimental and individual difference investigation. *Journal of Personality and Social Psychology, 52,* 890–898.

Gronlund, N. E. (1959). *Sociometry in the classroom.* New York: Harper.

Gronlund, N. E. (1995). *How to write and use instructional objectives* (5th ed.). New York: Macmillan.

Guevremont, D. C., Osnes, P. G., & Stokes, T. F. (1988). The functional role of preschoolers' verbalizations in the generalization of self-instructional training. *Journal of Applied Behavior Analysis, 21,* 45–55.

Guilford, J. P. (1950). Creativity. *American Psychologist, 14,* 469–479.

Guilford, J. P. (1967). *The nature of human intelligence*. New York: McGraw-Hill.

Guillaume, A. M., & Rudney, G. L. (1993). Student teachers' growth toward independence and analysis of their changing concerns. *Teaching & Teacher Education, 9,* 65–80.

Gump, P. V. (1982). School settings and their keeping. In D. L. Duke (Ed.), *Helping teachers manage classrooms* (pp. 98–114). Alexandria, VA: Association for Supervision and Curriculum Development.

Guskey, T. R. (1990). Cooperative mastery learning strategies. *Elementary School Journal, 91,* 33–42.

Guskey, T. R., & Pigott, T. D. (1988). Research on group-based mastery learning programs: A meta-analysis. *Journal of Educational Research, 81,* 197–216.

Haan, N. (1977). *Coping and defending: Processes of self-environment organization*. San Francisco, CA: Academic Press.

Haass C. (1988). Task analysis: An exceptional tool for educators. *Forecast for Home Economics,* 40–42.

Habermas, J. (1974). *Theory and practice*. Boston, MA: Beacon Press.

Haertel, E. (1992). Performance measurement. In M. C. Alkins (Ed.), *Encyclopedia of educational research* (6th ed., pp. 984–989). New York: Macmillan.

Hall, C. S. (1954). *A primer of Freudian psychology*. New York: Mentor.

Hall, J. W. (1988). On the utility of the keyword mnemonic for vocabulary learning. *Journal of Educational Psychology, 80,* 554–562.

Haller, E. P., Child, D. A., & Walberg, H. J. (1988). Can comprehension be taught? A quantitative synthesis of "metacognitive" studies. *Educational Researcher, 17*(9), 5–16.

Halpain, D. R., Glover, J. A., & Harvey, A. T. (1985). Differential effects of higher and lower order questions: Attentional hypotheses. *Journal of Educational Psychology, 77,* 703–715.

Hamilton, R. J. (1985). A framework for the evaluation of the effectiveness of adjunct questions and objectives. *Review of Educational Research, 55,* 47–85.

Hanf, M. B. (1971). Mapping: A technique for translating reading into thinking. *Journal of Reading, 14,* 225–230, 270.

Haring, N. E., & McCormick, L. (1990). *Exceptional children and youth* (5th ed.). Columbus, OH: Merrill.

Harris, A. J., & Sipay, E. R. (1990). *How to increase reading ability* (9th ed.). New York: David McKay Co.

Harrow, A. J. (1972). *A taxonomy of the psychomotor domain*. New York: McKay.

Hart, D. (1988). A longitudinal study of adolescents' socialization and identification as predictors of adult moral judgment development. *Merrill-Palmer Quarterly, 34,* 245–260.

Harter, S. (1981). A new self-report scale of intrinsic versus extrinsic orientation in the classroom: Motivational and informational components. *Developmental Psychology, 17,* 300–312.

Harter, S. (1982). The perceived competence scale for children. *Child Development, 53,* 87–97.

Haubenstricker, J. L., & Seefeldt, V. D. (1986). Acquisition of motor skills during childhood. In V. D. Seefeldt (Ed.), *Physical activity & well-being* (pp. 41–102). Reston, VA: National Association for Sport and Physical Education.

Havice, B. (1994). Learning HyperCard through story writing. *The Computing Teacher, 22*(1), 23–26.

Hawk, P. P. (1986). Using graphic organizers to increase achievement in middle school life science. *Science Education, 70,* 81–87.

Hawkins, J. & Pea, R. (1987). Tools for bridging the cultures of everyday thinking and scientific reasoning. *Journal of Research in Science Teaching, 24,* 291–307.

Hayes, J. R. (1989). *The complete problem solver* (2nd ed.). Hillsdale, NJ: Erlbaum.

Hayes, J. R., & Flower, L. S. (1983). Uncovering cognitive processes in writing: An introduction to protocol analysis. In P. Mosenthal, L. Tamor, & S. A. Walmsey (Eds.), *Research on writing: Principles and methods* (pp. 206–220). New York: Longman.

Haynes, N. M., & Comer, J. P. (1990). Facilitating the psychoeducational development of disadvantaged children. In S. S. Goldberg (Ed.), *Readings on equal education* (Vol. 10, pp. 23–33). New York: AMS Press.

Heider, F. (1958). *The psychology of interpersonal relations*. New York: John Wiley.

Hembree, R. (1992). Experiments and relational studies in problem solving: A meta-analysis. *Journal for Research in Mathematics Education, 23,* 242–273.

Henak, R. M. (1984). *Lesson planning for meaningful variety in teaching* (2nd ed.). Washington, DC: National Education Association.

Henderson, B. B., & Moore, S. G. (1979). Measuring exploratory behavior in young children. *Developmental Psychology, 15,* 113–119.

Henderson, B. B., & Wilson, S. E. (1991). Intelligence and curiosity in preschool children. *Journal of School Psychology, 29,* 167–175.

Henshaw, S. K., & Vort, J. V. (1989). Teenage abortion, birth and pregnancy statistics: An update. *Family Planning Perspectives, 21,* 85–88.

Herman, J. L., Aschbacher, P. R., & Winters, L. (1992). *A practical guide to alternative assessment*. Alexandria, VA: Association for Supervision and Curriculum Development.

Herman, J. L., & Winters, L. (1994). Portfolio research: A slim collection. *Educational Leadership, 52*(2), 48–55.

Herrmann, D. J., & Searleman, A. (1990). The new multimodal approach to memory improvement. In G. H. Bower (Ed.), *The psychology of learning and motivation* (Vol. 26, pp. 175–205). San Diego, CA: Academic Press.

Heuchert, C. M. (1989). Enhancing self-directed behavior in the classroom. *Academic Therapy, 24*, 295–303.

Hidi, S. (1990). Interest and its contribution as a mental resource for learning. *Review of Educational Research, 60*, 549–571.

Hidi, S., & Baird, W. (1986). Interestingness—A neglected variable in discourse processing. *Cognitive Science, 10*, 179–194.

Hillerich, R. L. (1990). What does "grade level" mean? *Principal, 69*, 47–48.

Hillocks, G., Jr. (1984). What works in teaching composition: A meta-analysis of experimental treatment studies. *American Journal of Education, 93*, 133–170.

Hillocks, G., Jr. (1986). *Research on written composition.* Urbana, IL: National Conference on Research in English.

Hillocks, G., Jr., Kahn, E. A., & Johannessen, L. R. (1983). Teaching defining strategies as a mode of inquiry: Some effects on student writing. *Research in the Teaching of English, 17*, 275–284.

Hinshaw, S. P. (1992). Externalizing behavior problems and academic underachievement in childhood and adolescence: Causal relationships and underlying mechanisms. *Psychological Bulletin, 111*, 127–155.

Hirst, W. (1988). Improving memory. In M. S. Gazzaniga (Ed.), *Perspectives in memory research* (pp. 219–244). Cambridge, MA: MIT Press.

Hitzing, W. (1992). Support and positive teaching strategies. In S. Stainback, & W. Stainback (Eds.), *Curriculum considerations in inclusive classrooms* (pp. 143–158). Baltimore, MD: Paul H. Brookes.

Hocevar, D., & Bachelor, P. (1989). A taxonomy and critique of measurements used in the study of creativity. In J. A. Glover, R. R. Ronning, & C. R. Reynolds (Eds.), *Handbook of creativity* (pp. 53–75). New York: Plenum.

Hofferth, S. L., Kahn, J. R., & Baldwin, W. (1987). Premarital sex activity among U.S. teenage women over the past three decades. *Family Planning Perspectives, 19*(2), 46–53.

Hoffman, M. L. (1981). Is altruism part of human nature? *Journal of Personality and Social Psychology, 40*, 121–137.

Hoffman, M. L. (1987). The contribution of empathy to justice and moral development. In N. Eisenberg & J. Strayer (Eds.), *Empathy and its development* (pp. 47–80). New York: Cambridge University Press.

Holland, J. L. (1985). *Making vocational choices* (2nd ed.). Englewood Cliffs, NJ: Prentice-Hall.

Hollingsworth, P. M., & Reutzel, D. R. (1988). Whole language with LD children. *Academic Therapy, 23*, 477–488.

Holmes, C. T. (1989). Grade level retention effects: A meta-analysis of research studies. In L. A. Shepard & M. L. Smith (Eds.), *Flunking grades: Research and policies on retention* (pp. 16–33). New York: Falmer Press.

Holyoak, K. J., Junn, E. N., & Billman, D. O. (1984). Development of analogical problem-solving skill. *Child Development, 55*, 2042–2055.

Hoover, S. M., & Feldhusen, J. F. (1990). The scientific hypothesis formulation ability of gifted ninth-grade students. *Journal of Educational Psychology, 82*, 838–848.

Hopman, M., & Glynn, T. (1988). Behavioral approaches to improving written expression. *Educational Psychology, 8*, 81–100.

Horowitz, R. A. (1979). Psychological effects of the "open classroom." *Review of Educational Research, 49*, 71–86.

Hughes, J. N. (1990). Brief psychotherapies. In T. B. Gutkin & C. R. Reynolds (Eds.), *The handbook of school psychology* (pp. 733–749). New York: John Wiley & Sons.

Humphreys, M. S., Bain, J. D., & Pike, R. (1989). Different ways to cue a coherent memory system: A theory for episodic, semantic, and procedural tasks. *Psychological Review, 96*, 208–233.

Hunt, N., & Marshall, K. (1994). *Exceptional children and youth: An introduction to special education.* Boston, MA: Houghton Mifflin.

Hyde, J. S., & Linn, M. C. (1988). Gender differences in verbal ability: A meta-analysis. *Psychological Bulletin, 104*, 53–69.

Igelsrud, D., & Leonard, W. H. (1988). What research says about biology laboratory instruction. *The American Biology Teacher, 50*, 303–306.

Ignico, A. (1994). Early childhood physical education: Providing the foundation. *Journal of Physical Education, Recreation, and Dance, 65*(6), 28–30.

Irving, O., & Martin, J. (1982). Withitness: The confusing variable. *American Educational Research Journal, 19*, 313–319.

Jacob, E. (1988). Clarifying qualitative research: A focus on traditions. *Educational Researcher, 17*(1), 16–24.

'Jacob K. Javits Gifted and Talented Students Education Act of 1988.' SEC. 4101.

Jacobs, J. E. & Paris, S. G. (1987). Children's metacognition about reading: Issues in definition, measurement, and instruction. *Educational Psychologist, 22*, 255–278.

Jantz, R. (1975). Moral thinking in male elementary pupils as reflected by perception of basketball rules. *Research Quarterly, 46*, 414–421.

Jausovec, N. (1989). Affect in analogical transfer. *Creativity Research Journal, 2*, 255–265.

Jenkins, J. R., Jewell, M., Leicester, N., Jenkins, L., & Troutner, N. M. (1991). Development of a school building model for education students with handicaps and at-risk students in general education classrooms. *Journal of Learning Disabilities, 24*, 311–320.

Johns, J. L., & Leirsburg, P. V. (1992). How professionals view portfolio assessment. *Reading Research and Instruction, 32*, 1–10.

Johnson, D. W., & Johnson, R. T. (1989). *Cooperation and competition: Theory and research.* Edina, MN: Interaction Book Company.

Johnson, E. R., Merrell, K. W., & Stover, L. (1990). The effects of early grade retention on the academic achievement of fourth-grade students. *Psychology in the Schools, 27*, 333–338.

Johnson, N. S., & Mandler, J. M. (1980). A tale of two structures. *Poetics, 9*, 51–86.

Johnston, L. D., O'Malley, P. M., & Bachman, J. G. (1991). *Drug use among American high school seniors, college students and young adults, 1975–1990* (Vol. 1). Rockville, MD: National Institute on Drug Abuse.

Jones, B. F. (1992). Cognitive designs in instruction. In M. C. Alkin (Ed.), *Encyclopedia of educational research* (Vol. 1, pp. 166–177). New York: Macmillan.

Jones, B. F., Amiran, M, & Katims, M. (1985). Teaching cognitive strategies and text structures within language arts programs. In J. W. Segal, S. F. Chipman, & R. Glaser (Eds.), *Thinking and learning skills* (Vol. 1, pp. 259–295). Hillsdale, NJ: Erlbaum.

Jones, V. F., & Jones, L. (1990). *Comprehensive classroom management* (3rd ed.). Boston, MA: Allyn & Bacon.

Jorgenson, R. C. (1988). *Resource book for basic geometry.* Boston, MA: Houghton Mifflin.

Jussim, L. (1989). Teacher expectations: Self-fulfilling prophecies, perceptual biases, and accuracy. *Journal of Personality and Social Psychology, 57*, 469–480.

Kagan, D. M. (1992). Professional growth among preservice and beginning teachers. *Review of Educational Research, 62*, 129–169.

Kahle, J. B. (1983). *Factors affecting the retention of girls in science courses and careers: Case studies of selected secondary schools.* Paper presented at the meeting of the National Association of Biology Teachers, Washington, DC. (ERIC Document Reproduction No. ED 244781)

Kahle, J. B., Matyas, M. L., & Cho, H.-H. (1985). An assessment of the impact of science experiences on the career choices of male and female biology students. *Journal of Research in Science Teaching, 22*, 385–394.

Kahn, J. R., Kalsbeek, W. D., & Hofferth, S. L. (1988). National estimates of teenage sexual activity: Evaluating the comparability of three national surveys. *Demography, 25*, 189–204.

Kamii, C. (1984). Autonomy: The aim of education envisioned by Piaget. *Phi Delta Kappan, 65*, 410–415.

Karnes, M. B., Shwedel, A. M., & Williams, M. B. (1983). A comparison of five approaches for educating young children from low-income homes. In Consortium for Longitudinal Studies (Ed.), *As the twig is bent—lasting effects of preschool programs* (pp. 133–169). Hillsdale, NJ: Erlbaum.

Karweit, N. (1985). Time scales, learning events, and productive instruction. In C. W. Fisher & D. C. Berliner (Eds.), *Perspectives on instructional time* (pp. 169–185). New York: Longman.

Katz, L. G. (1992). *What should young children be learning?* ERIC Digest. Urbana, IL: ERIC Clearinghouse on Elementary and Early Childhood Education. (ERIC Document Reproduction No. ED 290 554)

Katz, L. G., & Chard, S. C. (1989). *Engaging children's minds: The project approach.* Norwood, NJ: Ablex.

Katz, L. G., & Chard, S. C. (1992). The project approach. In J. E. Johnson & J. Rooparine (Eds.), *Approaches to early childhood education.* Columbus, OH: Merrill.

Kaufman, J. M. (1993). How we might achieve the radical reform of special education. *Exceptional Children, 60*, 6–16.

Kavale, K. (1990). Effectiveness of special education. In T. B. Gutkin & C. R. Reynolds (Eds.), *The handbook of school psychology* (pp. 870–898). New York: John Wiley & Sons.

Kay, S. I. (1991). The figural problem solving and problem finding of professional and semiprofessional artists and nonartists. *Creativity Research Journal, 4*, 233–252.

Kee, D. W., & Beuhring, T. (1978). Verbal and pictorial elaboration effects on children's long-term memory for noun pairs. *Journal of Educational Psychology, 70*, 745–753.

Keil, F. C. (1986). On the structure-dependent nature of stages of cognitive development. In I. Levin (Ed.), *Stage and structure: Reopening the debate* (pp. 164–190). Norwood, NJ: Ablex.

Keiser, T. C., & Seeler, J. H. (1987). Games and simulations. In R. L. Craig (Ed.), *Training and development handbook: A guide to human resource development* (3rd ed., pp. 457–469). New York: McGraw-Hill.

Keller, J. M. (1987). Development and use of the ARCS model of motivational design. *Journal of Instructional Development, 10*, 2–10.

Kendall, P. C., & Wilcox, L. E. (1980). Cognitive-behavioral treatment for impulsivity: Concrete versus conceptual training in non-self-controlled problem children. *Journal of Consulting and Clinical Psychology, 48*, 80–91.

Kent, K. M. (1993). The need for school-based teacher reflection. *Teacher Education Quarterly, 20*(1), 83–91.

Kersh, M. E., & McDonald, J. (1991). How do I solve thee? Let me count the ways! *Arithmetic Teacher, 39*, 38–41.

Kidder, T. (1989). *Among schoolchildren.* Boston, MA: Houghton Mifflin.

Kilpatrick, J. (1987). Problem formulating: Where do good problems come from? In A. H. Schoenfeld (Ed.), *Cognitive science and mathematics education* (pp. 123–147). Hillsdale, NJ: Erlbaum.

Kinzer, C. K., Sherwood, R. D., & Bransford, J. D. (1986). *Computer strategies for education.* Columbus, OH: Merrill.

Klauer, K. J. (1984). Intentional and incidental learning with instructional texts: A meta-analysis for 1970–1980. *American Educational Research Journal, 21*, 323–339.

Klein, S. B. (1987). *Learning: Principles and applications.* New York: McGraw-Hill.

Klint, K. A., & Weiss, M. R. (1987). Perceived competence and motives for participation in youth sport. A test of Harter's competence motivation theory. *Journal of Sports Psychology, 9,* 55–65.

Kloster, A. M., & Winne, P. H. (1989). The effects of different types of organizers on students' learning from text. *Journal of Educational Psychology, 81,* 9–15.

Kohlberg, L. (1985). The Just Community in theory and practice. In M. Berkowitz & F. Oser (Eds.), *Moral education* (pp. 27–87). Hillsdale, NJ: Erlbaum.

Kohlberg, L. (1987). *Child psychology and childhood education.* New York: Longman.

Kohler, W. (1970). *Gestalt psychology.* New York: Liveright. (Originally published 1947)

Kounin, J, S. (1970). *Discipline and group management in classrooms.* New York: Holt, Rinehart and Winston.

Kozma, R. B. (1991). Learning with media. *Review of Educational Research, 61,* 179–211.

Kozol, J. *Savage inequalities: Children in America's schools.* New York: Crown Publishers.

Krampen, G. (1987). Differential effects of teacher comments. *Journal of Educational Psychology, 79,* 137–146.

Krathwohl, D. R. (1994). Reflections on the taxonomy: Its past, present, and future. In L. W. Anderson & L. A. Sosniak (Eds.), *Bloom's taxonomy: A forty-year retrospective* (pp. 181–202). Chicago, IL: The National Society for the Study of Education.

Krathwohl, D. R., Bloom, B. S., & Masia, B. B. (1964). *Taxonomy of educational objectives: The classification of educational goals.* Handbook 2. *Affective domain.* New York: Longman.

Krulik, S., & Rudnick, J. A. (1988). *Problem solving: A handbook for elementary teachers.* Boston, MA: Allyn & Bacon.

Ku, L. C., Sonenstein, F. L., & Pleck, J. H. (1992). The association of AIDS education and sex education with sexual behavior and condom use among teenage men. *Family Planning Perspectives, 24,* 100–106.

Kuhn, D., & Ho, V. (1977). The development of schemes for recognizing additive and alternative effects in a "natural experiment" context. *Developmental Psychology, 13,* 515–516.

Kulik, J. A., & Kulik, C-L. C. (1987). Review of recent research literature on computer-based instruction. *Contemporary Educational Psychology, 12,* 222–230.

Kulik, J. A., & Kulik, C.-L. C. (1991). Ability grouping and gifted students. In N. Colangelo & G. A. Davis (Eds.), *Handbook of gifted education* (pp. 178–196). Boston, MA: Allyn & Bacon.

Kulik, J. A., Kulik, C-L. C., & Bangert-Drowns, R. L. (1985). Effectiveness of computer-based education in elementary schools. *Computers in Human Behavior, 1,* 59–74.

Kupersmidt, J. B., Coie, J. D., & Dodge, K. A. (1990). The role of poor peer relationships in the development of disorder. In S. R. Asher & J. D. Coie (Eds.), *Peer rejection in childhood* (pp. 274–305). New York: Cambridge University Press.

Kurtzberg, R. L., & Kurtzberg, K. E. (1993). Future problem solving: Connecting middle school students to the real world. *Middle School Journal, 24*(4), 37–40.

Kyle, W. C., Bonnstetter, R. J., & Gadsen, T. (1988). An implementation study: An analysis of elementary students' and teachers' attitudes toward science in process vs. traditional science classes. *Journal of Research in Science Teaching, 25,* 103–120.

LaBoskey, V. K. (1994). *Development of reflective practice.* New York: Teachers College Press.

Ladd, G. W. (1981). Effectiveness of a social learning method for enhancing children's social interaction and peer acceptance. *Child Development, 52,* 171–198.

Ladd, G. W., & Price, J. M. (1987). Predicting children's social and school adjustment following the transition from preschool to kindergarten. *Child Development, 58,* 1168–1189.

Larkin, J., McDermott, J., Simon, D. P., & Simon, H. A. (1980). Expert and novice performance in solving physics problems. *Science, 208,* 1335–1342.

Larkin, S. (1986). Word problems for kids by kids. In M. Driscoll & J. Confrey (Eds.), *Teaching mathematics: Strategies that work* (pp. 51–61). Portsmouth, NH: Heinemann.

Lawson, A. E. (1985). A review of research on formal reasoning and science teaching. *Journal of Research in Science Teaching, 22,* 569–617.

Lee, A. M., Keh, N. C., & Magill, R. A. (1993). Instructional effects of teacher feedback in physical education. *Journal of Teaching Physical Education, 12,* 228–243.

Leinhardt, G. (1988). Situated knowledge and expertise in teaching. In J. Calderhead (Ed.), *Teachers' professional learning* (pp. 146–168). New York: Falmer Press.

Leming, J. S. (1993). In search of effective character education. *Educational Leadership, 51*(3), 63–71.

Lepper, M. R., & Hoddell, M. (1989). Intrinsic motivation in the classroom. In C. Ames & R. Ames (Eds.), *Research on motivation in education* (Vol. 3, pp. 73–105). San Diego, CA: Academic Press.

Lerner, J. W., & Lerner, S. R. (1991). Attention deficit disorder: Issues and questions. *Focus on Exceptional Children, 24*(3), 1–17.

Lever, J. (1976). Sex differences in the games children play. *Social Problems, 23,* 478–487.

Levin, J. A., & Waugh, M. (1988). Educational simulations, tools, games, and microworlds: Computer-based environments for learning. *International Journal of Educational Research, 12,* 71–80.

Levin, J. R., Morrison, C. R., McGivern, J. E., Mastropieri, M. A., & Scruggs, T. E. (1986). Mnemonic facilitation of text-embedded science facts. *American Educational Research Journal, 23,* 489–506.

Levin, J. R. (1993). Mnemonic strategies and classroom

learning: A twenty-year report card. *Elementary School Journal, 94*, 235–244.

Levine, F. M., & Fasnacht, G. (1974). Token rewards may lead to token learning. *American Psychologist, 29*, 816–820.

Lewis, A., & Smith, D. (1993). Defining higher order thinking. *Theory Into Practice, 32*, 131–137.

Liben, L. S. (1987). Information processing and Piagetian theory: Conflict or congruence? In L. S. Liben (Ed.), *Development and learning: Conflict or congruence?* (pp. 109–132). Hillsdale, NJ: Erlbaum.

Lickona, T. (1991). *Educating for character: How our schools can teach respect and responsibility.* New York: Bantam Books.

Lickona, T. (1993). The return of character education. *Educational Leadership, 51*(3), 6–11.

Liebert, R. M., & Sprafkin, J. *The early window: Effects of television on children and youth* (3rd ed.). New York: Pergamon Press.

Liggett, S. (1991). Creativity and non-literary writing: The importance of problem finding. *Journal of Teaching Writing, 10*, 165–179.

Lindsey, O. R. (1992). Why aren't effective teaching tools widely adopted? *Journal of Applied Behavior Analysis, 25*, 21–26.

Linn, M. C., De Benedictis, T., Delucchi, K., Harris, A., & Stage, E. (1987). Gender differences in National Assessment of Educational Progress science items: What does "I don't know" really mean? *Journal of Research in Science Teaching, 24*, 267–278.

Linn, M. C., & Hyde, J. S. (1991). Cognitive and psychosocial gender differences. In R. M. Lerner, A. C. Petersen, & J. Brooks-Gunn (Eds.) *Encyclopedia of adolescence* (Vol. 1, pp. 139–150). New York: Garland Publishing.

Linn, R. L., & Gronlund, N. E. (1995). *Measurement and evaluation in teaching* (7th ed.). New York: Macmillan.

Lipman, M. (1985). *Harry Stottlemeier's discovery.* Upper Montclair, NJ: The Institute for the Advancement of Philosophy for Children.

Lipman, M. (1988). *Philosophy goes to school.* Philadelphia, PA: Temple University Press.

Lipman, M., Sharp, A. M., & Oscanyan, F. S. (1979). *Philosophical inquiry: An instructional manual to accompany Harry Stottlemeier's discovery* (2nd ed.). Upper Montclair, NJ: The Institute for the Advancement of Philosophy for Children.

Lipman, M., Sharp, A. M., & Oscanyan, F. S. (1980). *Philosophy in the classroom* (2nd ed.). Philadelphia, PA: Temple University Press.

Liston, D. P., & Zeichner, K. M. (1987). Critical pedagogy and teacher education. *Journal of Education, 169*, 117–137.

Lloyd, J. W. (1987). Direct academic interventions in learning disabilities. In M. C. Wang, M. C. Reynolds, & H. J. Walberg (Eds.), *Handbook of special education: Research and practice* (Vol. 2, pp. 345–366). Oxford: Pergamon Press.

Lockwood, A. L. (1991). Character education: The ten percent solution. *Social Education, 55*, 246–248.

Lockwood, A. L. (1993). A letter to character educators. *Educational Leadership, 51*(3), 72–75.

Lorayne, H., & Lucas, J. (1974). *The memory book.* New York: Ballantine Books.

Lozoff, B. (1989). Nutrition and behavior. *American Psychologist, 44*, 231–236.

Luiten, J., Ames, W., & Ackerson, G. (1980). A meta-analysis of the effects of advance organizers on learning and retention. *American Educational Research Journal, 17*, 211–218.

Lynch, G. (1986). *Synapses, circuits, and the beginnings of memory.* Cambridge, MA: MIT Press.

Lyons, N. (1989). Seeing and resolving moral conflict: Students' approaches to learning and making choices. In L. P. Nucci (Ed.). *Moral development and character education* (pp. 145–160). Berkeley, CA: McCutchan.

Lysakowski, R. S., & Walberg, H. J. (1981). Classroom reinforcement and learning: A quantitative synthesis. *Journal of Educational Research, 75*, 69–77.

Lysynchuk, L. M., Pressley, M., & Vye, N. J. (1990). Reciprocal teaching improves standardized reading-comprehension performance in poor comprehenders. *Elementary School Journal, 90*, 469–484.

Maccoby, E. E. (1990). Gender and relationships. *American Psychologist, 45*, 513–520.

Maccoby, E. E., & Jacklin, C. N. (1974). *The psychology of sex differences.* Stanford, CA: Stanford University Press.

Maccoby, E. E., & Jacklin, C. N. (1987). Gender segregation in childhood. In E. H. Reese (Ed.), *Advances in child development and behavior* (Vol. 20, pp. 239–287). New York: Academic Press.

Maccoby, E. E., & Martin, J. A. (1983). Socialization in the context of the family: Parent-child interaction. In E. M. Hetherington (Ed.), *Handbook of child psychology: Socialization, personality, and social development* (Vol. 4, pp. 1–101). New York: John Wiley & Sons.

MacIver, D. J. (1990). *A national description of report card entries in the middle grades* (Report No. 9). Baltimore, MD: Center for Research on Effective Schooling for Disadvantaged Students.

MacKinnon, D. W. (1978). *In search of human effectiveness.* Buffalo, NY: Creative Education Foundation.

Maclin, J. P. (1993). The effect of task analysis on sequential patterns of music instruction. *Journal of Research in Music Education, 41*, 48–56.

Mager, R. F. (1975). *Preparing instructional objectives* (2nd ed.). Belmont, CA: Fearon Publishers.

Malone, J. C. (1990). *Theories of learning: A historical approach.* Belmont, CA: Wadsworth.

Manning, B. H. (1991). *Cognitive self-instruction for classroom processes.* Albany: State University of New York Press.

Marcia, J. E. (1980). Identity in adolescence. In J. Adelson

(Ed.), *Handbook of adolescent psychology* (pp. 159–187). New York: John Wiley & Sons.

Marsh, H. W. (1989). Age and sex effects in multiple dimensions of self-concept: Preadolescence to early adulthood. *Journal of Educational Psychology, 81,* 417–430.

Marsh, H. W., Craven, R. G., & Debus, R. (1991). Self-concepts of young children 5 to 8 years of age: Measurement and multidimensional structure. *Journal of Educational Psychology, 83,* 377–392.

Marshall, H. H. (1987). Motivational strategies of three fifth-grade teachers. *Elementary School Journal, 88,* 135–150.

Martin, D. S. (1989). Restructuring teacher education programs for higher-order thinking skills. *Journal of Teacher Education, 40*(3), 2–8.

Marzano, R. J., Brandt, R. S., Hughes, C. S., Jones, B. F., Presseisen, B. Z., Rankin, S. C., & Suhor, C. (1988). *Dimensions of thinking: A framework for curriculum and instruction.* Alexandria, VA: Association for Curriculum and Development.

Maslow, A. H. (1968). Some educational implications of the humanistic psychologies. *Harvard Educational Review, 38,* 685–696.

Maslow, A. H. (1970). *Motivation and personality* (2nd ed.). New York: Harper & Row.

Maslow, A. H. (1971). *The farther reaches of human nature.* New York: Viking Press.

Mason, C. L., & Kahle, J. B. (1989). Student attitudes toward science-related careers: A program designed to promote a stimulating gender-free learning environment. *Journal of Research in Science Teaching, 26,* 25–39.

Mayer, R. E. (1992). *Thinking, problem solving, and cognition* (2nd ed.). San Francisco, CA: Freeman.

McBride, R. E. (1991). Critical thinking—An overview with implications for physical education. *Journal of Teaching in Physical Education, 11,* 112–125.

McCaslin, M., & Good, T. L. (1992). Compliant cognition: The misalliance of management and instructional goals in current school reform. *Educational Researcher, 21*(3), 4–17.

McCormick, L. (1990). Communication disorders. In N. G. Haring & L. McCormick (Eds.), *Exceptional children and youth* (5th ed., pp. 327–363). Columbus, OH: Merrill.

McCutcheon, G. (1980). How do elementary school teachers plan? The nature of planning and influences on it. *Elementary School Journal, 81,* 4–23.

McDaniel, M. A., Pressley, M., & Dunay, P. K. (1987). Long-term retention of vocabulary after keyword and context learning. *Journal of Educational Psychology, 79,* 87–89.

McGarrigle, J., Grieve, R., & Hughes, M. (1978). Interpreting inclusion: A contribution to study of the child's cognitive and linguistic development. *Journal of Experimental Child Psychology, 26,* 528–550.

McGroarty, M. (1992). The societal context of bilingual education. *Educational Researcher, 21*(2), 7ff.

McGuinness, D., & Pribram, K. (1980). The neuropsychology of attention: Emotional and motivational controls. In M. C. Wittrock (Ed.), *The brain and psychology* (pp. 95–139). New York: Academic Press.

McIntyre, J. D., & Pape, S. (1993). Using video to enhance teacher reflective thinking. *Teacher Educator, 28*(3), 2–10.

McKeachie, W. J. (1988). The need for study strategy training. In C. E. Weinstein, E. T. Goetz, & P. A. Alexander (Eds.), *Learning and study strategies: Issues in assessment, instruction and evaluation* (pp. 3–9). New York: Academic Press.

McKeon, D. (1994). When meeting "common" standards is uncommonly difficult. *Educational Leadership, 51* (8), 45–49.

McKey, R. H., Condelli, L., Ganson, H., Barrett, B. J., McConkey, C., Plantz, M. C. (1985). *The impact of Head Start on children, families and communities* (DDDS Publication No. OHDS 85-31193). Washington, DC: U.S. Government Printing Office.

Means, M. L., & Voss, J. F. (1985). Star wars: A developmental study of expert and novice knowledge structures. *Journal of Memory and Language, 24,* 746–757.

Meece, J. L., & Eccles, J. S. (1993). Introduction: Recent trends of gender equity research in American schools. *Educational Psychologist, 28,* 313–319.

Meece, J. L., Wigfield, A., & Eccles, J. S. (1990). Predictions of math anxiety and its influence on young adolescents' course enrollment intentions and performance in mathematics. *Journal of Educational Psychology, 82,* 60–70.

Meichenbaum, D. H. (1977). *Cognitive-behavior modification: An integrative approach.* New York: Plenum.

Meichenbaum, D. H., & Goodman, J. (1971). Training impulsive children to talk to themselves. *Journal of Abnormal Psychology, 77,* 115–126.

Mellard, D. F., & Deshler, D. D. (1992). Learning disabilities. In M. C. Alkin (Ed.), *Encyclopedia of educational research* (Vol. 2, pp. 724–733). New York: Macmillan.

Melton, R. F. (1978). Resolution of conflicting claims concerning the effect of behavioral objectives on student learning. *Review of Educational Research, 48,* 291–302.

Merrett, F., & Wheldall, K. (1987). Natural rates of teacher approval and disapproval in British primary and middle school classrooms. *British Journal of Educational Psychology, 57,* 95–103.

Meyer, R. E. (1987). The elusive search for teachable aspects of problem solving. In J. A. Glover & R. R. Ronning (Eds.), *Historical foundations of educational psychology* (pp. 327–347). New York: Plenum.

Meyer, W. J. (1985). Summary, integration, and prospective. In J. B. Dusek (Ed.), *Teacher expectations* (pp. 353–370). Hillsdale, NJ: Erlbaum.

Mezynski, K. (1983). Issues concerning the acquisition of knowledge: Effects of vocabulary training on reading comprehension. *Review of Educational Research, 53,* 253–279.

Miccinati, J. L. (1988). Mapping the terrain: Connecting reading with academic writing. *Journal of Reading, 31,* 542–552.

Miller, A. T. (1985). A developmental study of the cognitive basis of performance impairment after failure. *Journal of Personality and Social Psychology, 49,* 529–538.

Miller, G. A. (1956). The magical number seven, plus or minus two: Some limits on our capacity for information processing. *Psychological Review, 63,* 81–97.

Miller, G. E., Giovenco, A., & Rentiers, K. A. (1987). Fostering comprehension monitoring in below average readers through self-instruction training. *Journal of Reading Behavior, 19,* 379–393.

Miller, L. J., Kohler, F. W., Ezell, H., Hoel, K., & Strain, P. S. (1993). Winning with peer tutoring. *Preventing School Failure, 37*(3), 14–18.

Minnesota Educational Computing Corporation. (1986). *The Oregon Trail.* Minneapolis, MN: Author.

Mizelle, N. B., Hart, L. E., & Carr, M. (1993). *Middle grade students' motivational processes and use of strategies with expository text.* Paper presented at the annual meeting of the AERA, Atlanta, Georgia. (ERIC Document Reproduction No. ED 360728)

Montessori, M. (1964). *The Montessori method.* New York: Schoken Books.

Moore, M. T. (1985). The relationship between the originality of essays and variables in the problem-discovery process: A study of creative and noncreative middle school students. *Research in the Teaching of English, 19,* 84–95.

Morine-Dershimer, G., & Beyerbach, B. (1987). Moving right along . . . In V. Richardson-Koehler (Ed.), *Educators' handbook: A research perspective* (pp. 207–232). New York: Longman.

Mosher, W. D., & McNally, J. W. (1991). Contraceptive use at first premarital intercourse: United States, 1965–1988. *Family Planning Perspectives, 23,* 108–158.

Mulcahy, P. I., & Samuels, S. J. (1987). Problem-solving schemata for text types: A comparison of narrative and expository text structures. *Reading Psychology: An International Quarterly, 8,* 247–258.

Mullen, B., Johnson, C., & Salas, E. (1991). Productivity loss in brainstorming groups: A meta-analytic integration. *Basic and Applied Social Psychology, 12,* 3–23.

Mulopo, M. M., & Fowler, H. S. (1987). Effects of traditional and discovery instructional approaches on learning outcomes for learners of different intellectual development: A study of chemistry students in Zambia. *Journal of Research in Science Teaching, 24,* 217–227.

Munson, W. W. (1992). Self-esteem, vocational identity, and career salience in high school students. *Career Development Quarterly, 40,* 361–368.

Murphy, G. L., & Wright, J. C. (1984). Changes in conceptual structure with expertise: Differences between real-world experts and novices. *Journal of Experimental Psychology: Learning, Memory, and Cognition, 10,* 144–155.

Murphy, J. J. (1988). Contingency contracting in schools: A review. *Education and Treatment of Children, 11,* 257–269.

Nagy, P., & Griffiths, A. K. (1982). Limitations of recent research relating Piaget's theory to adolescent thought. *Review of Educational Research, 52,* 513–556.

National Council for Teachers of Mathematics. (1989). *Curriculum and evaluation standards for school mathematics.* Reston, VA: Author.

Natriello, G., McDill, E. L., & Pallas, A. M. (1990). *Schooling disadvantaged children: Racing against catastrophe.* New York: Teachers College Press.

Neill, S. B., & Neill, G. W. (1994). *Only the best: Annual guide to highest-rated education software/multimedia for preschool–grade 12.* Carmichael, CA: Education News Service.

Nelli, E. R., & Atwood, V. A. (1986). Teacher education students and classroom teachers: A comparison of conative levels. *Journal of Teacher Education, 37*(3), 46–50.

Newby, T. J. (1991). Classroom motivation: Strategies of first-year teachers. *Journal of Educational Psychology, 83,* 195–200.

Newell, A., & Simon, H. A. (1972). *Human problem solving.* Englewood Cliffs, NJ: Prentice-Hall.

Nicholls, J. G. (1989). *The competitive ethos and democratic education.* Cambridge, MA: Harvard University Press.

Nicholls, J. G., & Miller, A. T. (1984). Development and its discontents: The differentiation of the concept of ability. In J. G. Nicholls & M. L. Maehr (Eds.), *Advances in motivation and achievement* (Vol. 3, pp. 185–219). Greenwich, CT: JAI Press.

Nicholson, H., & Frederick, J. (1991). *The explorer's pass: A report on case studies of girls and math, science and technology.* New York: Girls Inc.

Nickerson, R. S., Perkins, D. N., & Smith, E. E. (1985). *The teaching of thinking.* Hillsdale, NJ: Erlbaum.

Niemiec, R., Samson, G., Weinstein, T., & Walberg, H. J. (1987). The effects of computer based instruction in elementary schools. *Journal of Research on Computing in Education, 20,* 85–103.

Nix, D. (1988). Should computers know what you can do with them? *Teachers College Record, 89,* 418–430.

Norris, D. R. (1986). External validity of business games. *Simulation & Games, 17,* 447–459.

Norris, S. P., & Ennis, R. H. (1989). *Evaluating critical thinking.* Pacific Grove, CA: Midwest Publications.

Nottelmann, E. D. (1987). Competence and self-esteem during transition from childhood to adolescence. *Developmental Psychology, 23,* 441–450.

Novak, J. D., & Gowin, B. (1984). *Learning how to learn.* New York: Cambridge University Press.

Novak, J. D., Gowin, B., & Johansen, G. T. (1982). The use of concept mapping and knowledge vee mapping with junior high school science students. *Science Education, 66,* 211–227.

Nucci, L. P. (1987). Synthesis of research on moral development. *Educational Leadership, 44*(5), 86–92.

O'Connor, J., & Brie, R. (1994). Products, people, performance, and multimedia. *The Computing Teacher, 22*(1), 27–30.

Oakes, J. (1985). *Keeping track: How schools structure inequality.* New Haven, CT: Yale University Press.

Oakes, J. (1990). Opportunities, achievement, and choice: Women and minority students in mathematics and science. In C. Cazden (Ed.), *Review of research in education* (Vol. 16, pp. 153–222). Washington, DC: American Educational Research Association.

Ogbu, J. U. (1982). Socialization: A cultural ecological approach. In K. M. Borman (Ed.), *The social life of children in a changing society* (pp. 253–267). Hillsdale, NJ: Erlbaum.

Ogbu, J. U. (1992). Understanding cultural diversity and learning. *Educational Researcher, 21*(8), 5–14.

"Orel Hershiser" (1991). *Elementary School Journal, 91,* 509–514.

Ornstein, A. C. (1989). The nature of grading. *The Clearing House, 62,* 365–369.

Osborn, A. F. (1963). *Applied imagination* (3rd ed.). New York: Scribners.

Oxendine, J. B. (1984). *Psychology of motor learning* (2nd ed.). Englewood Cliffs, NJ: Prentice-Hall.

Paivio, A. (1986). *Mental representations: A dual coding approach.* New York: Oxford University Press.

Palinscar, A. M., & Brown, A. L. (1984). Reciprocal teaching of comprehension-fostering and monitoring activities. *Cognition and Instruction, 1,* 117–175.

Palinscar, A. M., Brown, A. L., & Martin, S. M. (1987). Peer interaction in reading comprehension instruction. *Educational Psychologist, 22,* 231–253.

Papert, S. (1980). *Mindstorms: Children, computers, and powerful ideas.* New York: Basic Books.

Paris, S. G., & Newman, R. S. (1990). Developmental aspects of self-regulated learning. *Educational Psychologist, 25,* 87–102.

Parke, B. (1989). *Gifted students in regular classrooms.* Boston, MA: Allyn & Bacon.

Parker, J. G., & Asher, S. R. (1987). Peer relations and later personal adjustment: Are low-accepted children at risk? *Psychological Bulletin, 102,* 357–389.

Parkhurst, J. T., & Asher, S. R. (1992). Peer rejection in middle school: Differences in behavior, loneliness, and interpersonal concerns. *Developmental Psychology, 28,* 231–241.

Parnes, S. J. (1981). *The magic of your mind.* Buffalo, NY: Creative Education Foundation.

Patten, J. Van, Chao, C., & Reigeluth, C. M. (1986). A review of strategies for sequencing and synthesizing information. *Review of Educational Research, 56,* 437–471.

Patterson, G. R., DeBaryshe, B. D., & Ramsey, E. (1989). A developmental perspective on antisocial behavior. *American Psychologist, 44,* 329–335.

Patton, J. R., & Polloway, E. A. (1990). Mild mental retardation. In N. G. Haring & L. McCormick (Eds.), *Exceptional children and youth* (5th ed., pp. 195–237). Columbus: Merrill.

Pauk, W. (1989). *How to study in college* (4th ed.). Boston, MA: Houghton Mifflin.

Pavlov, I. P. (1960). *Conditioned reflexes* (G. V. Anrep, Trans.). New York: Dover. (Original work published 1927)

Pehkonen, E. (1992). Using problem fields as a method of change. *Mathematics Educator, 3*(1), 3–6.

Penick, N. I., & Jepsen, D. A. (1992). Family functioning and adolescent career development. *Career Development Quarterly, 40,* 208–222.

Perkins, D. N. (1986). *Knowledge as design.* Hillsdale, NJ: Erlbaum.

Peterson, P. L. (1979). Direct instruction reconsidered. In P. L. Peterson & H. J. Walberg (Eds.), *Research on teaching.* Berkeley, CA: McCutchan.

Peterson, P. L. (1989). Alternatives to student retention: New images of the learner, the teacher and classroom. In L. A. Shepard & M. L. Smith (Eds.), *Flunking grades: Research and policies on retention* (pp. 174–201). New York: The Falmer Press.

Peterson, P. L., & Comeaux, M. A. (1987). Teachers' schemata for classroom events: The mental scaffolding of teachers' thinking during classroom instruction. *Teaching & Teacher Education, 3,* 319–331.

Peterson, P. L., Swing, S. R., Braverman, M. T., & Buss, R. (1982). Students' aptitudes and their reports of cognitive processes during direct instruction. *Journal of Educational Psychology, 74,* 535–547.

Pfiffer, L. J., & O'Leary, S. G. (1987). The efficacy of all-positive management as a function of the prior use of negative consequences. *Journal of Applied Behavior Analysis, 20,* 265–271.

Pfotenhauer, V. (1982). Brainstorming as a prewriting activity. *Childhood Education, 59,* 111–113.

Phelps, T. O. (1992). Research or three-search? *English Journal, 81,* 76–78.

Piaget, J. (1948). *The moral development of the child.* Glencoe, IL: The Free Press.

Piaget, J. (1969). *Psychologie et pedagogie* [The science of education and the psychology of the child]. Paris: Denoel/Garnier.

Pickford, R. W. (1972). *Psychology and visual aesthetics.* London: Hutchinson Educational.

Piechowski, M. M. (1991). Emotional development and emotional giftedness. In N. Colangelo & G. A. Davis

(Eds.), *Handbook of gifted education* (pp. 285–306). Boston, MA: Allyn & Bacon.

Pigge, F. L., & Marso, R. N. (1987). Relationships between student characteristics and changes in attitudes, concerns, anxieties, and confidence about teaching during teacher preparation. *Journal of Educational Research, 81,* 109–115.

Pizzini, E. L., Abell, S. K., & Shepardson, D. S. (1988). Rethinking thinking in the science classroom. *The Science Teacher, 55*(9), 22–25.

Pizzini, E. L., & Shepardson, D. S. (1991). Student questioning in the presence of the teacher during problem solving in science. *School Science and Mathematics, 91,* 348–352.

Pizzini, E. L., Shepardson, D. P., & Abell, S. K. (1989). A rationale for and the development of a problem solving model of instruction in science education. *Science Education, 73,* 523–534.

Pizzini, E. L., Shepardson, D. P., & Abell, S. K. (1991). The inquiry level of junior high activities: Implications to science teaching. *Journal of Research in Science Teaching, 28,* 111–121.

Poest, C. A., Williams, J. R., Witt, D. D., & Atwood, M. E. (1990). Challenge me to move: Large muscle development in young children. *Young Children, 45*(5), 4–10.

Polloway, E. A., & Smith, J. D. (1987). Current status of the mild mental retardation construct: Identification, placement, and programs. In M. C. Wang, M. C. Reynolds, & H. J. Walberg (Eds.), *Handbook of special education: Research and practice* (Vol. 2, pp. 7–22). Oxford: Pergamon Press.

Polya, G. (1957). *How to solve it* (2nd ed.). Garden City, NY: Anchor Books.

Porath, M., & Arlin, P. (in press). Developmental approaches to artistic giftedness. In F. D. Horowitz & R. C. Friedman (Eds.), *The gifted and talented: Theories and reviews* (Vol. 2). Washington, DC: American Psychological Association.

Power, C. F., Higgins, A., & Kohlberg, L. (1989). *Lawrence Kohlberg's approach to moral education.* New York: Columbia University Press.

Prawatt, R. S., & Anderson, A. L. (1988). Eight teachers' control orientations and their students' problem-solving ability. *The Elementary School Journal, 89,* 99–112.

Premack, D. (1965). Reinforcement theory. In D. Levine (Ed.), *Nebraska symposium on motivation* (Vol. 13, pp. 123–180). Lincoln, NE: University of Nebraska.

Pressley, M., & Levin, J. R. (1978). Developmental constraints associated with children's use of the keyword method of foreign language vocabulary learning. *Journal of Experimental Child Psychology, 26,* 359–372.

Pressley, M., Levin, J. R., & Delaney, H. D. (1982). The keyword method. *Review of Educational Research, 52,* 61–91.

Pritchard, I. (1988). Character education: Research prospects and problems. *American Journal of Education, 96,* 469–495.

Quellmalz, E. S. (1987). Developing reasoning skills. In J. B. Baron and R. J. Sternberg (Eds.), *Teaching thinking skills: Theory and practice* (pp. 86–105). New York: Freeman.

Rafferty, Y., & Shinn, M. (1991). The impact of homelessness on children. *American Psychologist, 46,* 1170–1179.

Ramirez, J. D., Yuen, S. D., & Ramey, D. R. (1991). *Longitudinal study of structured English immersion strategy, early-exit and late-exit transitional bilingual education programs for language-minority children.* San Mateo, CA: Aguirre International.

Ramos-Ford, V., & Gardner, H. (1991). Giftedness from a multiple intelligences perspective. In N. Colangelo & G. A. Davis (Eds.), *Handbook of gifted education* (pp. 55–64). Boston, MA: Allyn & Bacon.

Raudenbush, S. W. (1984). Magnitude of teacher expectancy effects on pupil IQ as a function of the credibility of expectancy induction: A synthesis of findings from 18 experiments. *Journal of Educational Psychology, 76,* 85–97.

Reid, D. K., & Stone, C. A. (1991). Why is cognitive instruction effective? Underlying learning mechanisms. *Remedial and Special Education, 12,* 8–19.

Reis, S. M. (1989). Reflections on policy affecting the education of gifted and talented students: Past and future perspectives. *American Psychologist, 44,* 399–408.

Reiser, R. A., & Mory, E. H. (1991). An examination of the systematic planning techniques of two experienced teachers. *Educational Technology Research and Development, 39*(3), 71–82.

Reitman, W. (1964). Heuristic decision procedures, open constraints, and the structure of ill-defined problems. In M. W. Shelley, & G. L. Bryan (Eds.), *Human judgments and optimality* (pp. 282–315). New York: Wiley & Sons.

Reitman, W. R. (1965). *Cognition and thought: An information-processing approach.* New York: Wiley & Sons.

Render, G. F., Padilla, J. M., & Krank, H. M. (1989). Assertive discipline: A critical review and analysis. *Teachers College Record, 90,* 607–630.

Renninger, K. A. (1992). Individual interest and development: Implications for theory and practice. In K. A. Renninger, S. Hidi, & A. Krapp (Eds.), *The role of interest in learning and development* (pp. 361–395). Hillsdale, NJ: Erlbaum.

Renzulli, J. S. (1991). The National Research Center on the Gifted and Talented: The dream, the design, and the destination. *Gifted Child Quarterly, 35,* 73–83.

Renzulli, J. S., & Reis, S. M. (1991). The schoolwide enrichment model: A comprehensive plan for the development of creative productivity. In N. Colangelo &

G. A. Davis (Eds.), *Handbook of gifted education* (pp. 111–141). Boston, MA: Allyn & Bacon.

Resnick, L. B. (1976). Task analysis in instructional design. In D. Klahr (Ed.), *Cognition and instruction* (pp. 51–80). Hillsdale, NJ: Erlbaum.

Resnick, L. B. (1987). Constructing knowledge in school. In L. S. Liben (Ed.), *Development and learning: Conflict or congruence?* (pp. 19–50). Hillsdale, NJ: Erlbaum.

Resnick, L. B., Bill, V. L., Lesgold, S. B., & Leer, M. L. (1991). Thinking in arithmetic class. In B. Means, C. Chelemer, & M. S. Knapp (Eds.), *Teaching advanced skills to at-risk students* (pp. 27–67). San Francisco, CA: Jossey-Bass.

Reuschlein, P., & Vogel, P. (1985). Motor performance and physical fitness status of regular and special education students. In J. E. Clark & J. H. Humphrey (Eds.), *Motor development: Current selected research* (Vol. 1, pp. 147–165). Princeton, NJ: Princeton Book Company.

Rich, J. M. (1989). The use of corporal punishment. *The Clearing House, 63,* 149–152.

Richardson, R. L. K. (1985). Wisdom-based junior high school teaching. *Childhood Education, 61,* 277–281.

Richert, E. S. (1991). Rampant problems and promising practices in identification. In N. Colangelo & G. A. Davis (Eds.), *Handbook of gifted education* (pp. 81–96). Boston, MA: Allyn & Bacon.

Richman, N., Stevenson, J., & Graham, P. J. (1982). *Preschool to school: A behavioral study.* New York: Academic Press.

Rink, J. E. (1993). *Teaching physical education for learning* (2nd ed.). St. Louis, MO: Times-Mirror.

Rink, J. E., French, K. E., Werner, P. H., Lynn, S., & Mays, A. (1992). The influence of content development on the effectiveness of instruction. *Journal of Teaching in Physical Education, 12,* 139–149.

Rito, G. R., & Moller, B. W. (1989). Teaching enrichment activities for minorities. *Journal of Negro Education, 58,* 212–219.

Robinson, F. P. (1961). *Effective study* (Rev. ed.). New York: Harper & Brothers.

Roblyer, M. D., Castine, W. H., & King, F. J. (1988). Assessing the impact of computer-based instruction: A review of recent research. *Computers in the Schools, 5*(3–4), 1–139.

Roethlisberger, F. J., & Dickson, W. J. (1940). *Management and the worker.* Cambridge, MA: Harvard University Press.

Romance, T. J., Weiss, M. R., & Bockoven, J. (1986). A program to promote moral development through elementary school physical education. *Journal of Teaching in Physical Education, 5,* 126–136.

Roop, P. (1990). The magic of writing: How a writer teaches writing. *Childhood Education, 67,* 281–284.

Root-Bernstein, R. S. (1989). *Discovering.* Cambridge, MA: Harvard.

Rose, L. H., & Lin, H. (1984). A meta-analysis of long-term creativity training programs. *Journal of Creative Behavior, 18,* 11–22.

Rosen, L. A., Taylor, S. A., O'Leary, S. G., & Sanderson, W. (1990). A survey of classroom management practices. *Journal of School Psychology, 28,* 257–269.

Rosenfield, P., Lambert, N. M., & Black, A. (1985). Desk arrangement effects on pupil classroom behavior. *Journal of Educational Psychology, 77,* 101–108.

Rosenshine, B., & Meister, C. (1992). The use of scaffolds for teaching higher-level cognitive strategies. *Educational Leadership, 49*(7), 26–33.

Rosenshine, B., & Stevens, R. (1986). Teaching functions. In M. C. Wittrock (Ed.), *Handbook of research on teaching* (3rd ed., pp. 376–391). New York: Macmillan.

Rosenthal, R., & Jacobson, L. (1992). *Pygmalion in the classroom* (Rev. ed.). New York: Irvington Publishers. (Originally published 1968)

Ross, D. D., Johnson, M., & Smith, W. (1992). Developing a professional teacher at the University of Florida. In L. Valli (Ed.), *Reflective teacher education: Cases and critiques* (pp. 24–39). Albany, NY: SUNY Press.

Rosser, S. V. (1993). Female friendly science: Including women in curricular content and pedagogy in science. *Journal of General Education, 42,* 191–220.

Rotella, R. R., Hanson, T., & Coop, R. H. (1991). Burnout in youth sports. *Elementary School Journal, 91,* 421–428.

Roth, W-M. (1991). The development of reasoning on the balance beam. *Journal of Research in Science Teaching, 28,* 631–645.

Rotter, J. B. (1966). Generalized expectancies for internal versus external control of reinforcement. *Psychological Monograph, 80*(1, Whole No. 609).

Routh, D. K., Schroeder, C. S., & O'Tuama, L. A. (1974). Development of activity level in children. *Developmental Psychology, 10,* 163–168.

Royce, J. M., Darlington, R. B., & Murray, H. W. (1983). Pooled analyses: Findings across studies. In Consortium for Longitudinal Studies (Ed.), *As the twig is bent—lasting effects of preschool programs* (pp. 411–459). Hillsdale, NJ: Erlbaum.

Rubin, Z. (1980). *Children's friendships.* Cambridge, MA: Harvard University Press.

Rumelhart, D. E., & Norman, D. A. (1978). Accretion, tuning, and restructuring: Three modes of learning. In J. W. Colton & R. L. Klatzky (Eds.), *Semantic factors in cognition* (pp. 37–53). Hillsdale, NJ: Erlbaum.

Runco, M. A. (1991). *Divergent thinking.* Norwood, NJ: Ablex.

Runco, M. A., & Okuda, S. M. (1988). Problem finding, divergent thinking, and the creative process. *Journal of Youth and Adolescence, 17,* 211–220.

Russell, T. (1988). From preservice teacher education to first year of teaching: A study of theory and practice. In J. Calderhead (Ed.), *Teachers' professional learning* (pp. 13–34). New York: Falmer Press.

Rutter, M., Maugham, B., Mortimore, P., Ouston, J., & Smith, A. (1979). *Fifteen thousand hours: Secondary schools and their effects on children.* Cambridge, MA: Harvard University.

Ryan, E. B., Short, E. J., & Weed, K. A. (1986). The role of cognitive strategy training in improving the academic performance of learning disabled children. *Journal of Learning Disabilities, 19,* 521–529.

Sabers, D. S., Cushing, K. S., & Berliner, D. C. (1991). Differences among teachers in a task characterized by simultaneity, multidimensionality, and immediacy. *American Educational Research Journal, 28,* 63–88.

Sadker, M., Sadker, D., & Klein, S. (1991). The issue of gender in elementary and secondary education. In G. Grant (Ed.), *Review of research in education* (Vol. 17, pp. 269–334). Washington, DC: American Educational Research Association.

Salomon, G. (1992). New information technologies in education. In M. C. Alkins (Ed.), *Encyclopedia of educational research* (Vol. 3, pp. 892–903). New York: Macmillan.

Samuels, S. J. (1988). Decoding and automaticity: Helping poor readers become automatic at word recognition. *Reading Teacher, 41,* 756–760.

Savell, J. M., Twohig, P. T., & Rachford, D. L. (1986). Empirical status of Feuerstein's "Instrumental Enrichment" (FIE) technique as a method of teaching thinking skills. *Review of Educational Research, 56,* 381–409.

Scardamalia, M., & Bereiter, C. (1983). The development of evaluative, diagnostic and remedial capabilities in children's composing. In M. Martlew (Ed.), *The psychology of written language: Developmental and educational perspectives* (pp. 67–95). New York: John Wiley & Sons.

Scardamalia, M., & Bereiter, C. (1986). Research on written composition. In M. C. Wittrock (Ed.), *Handbook of research on teaching* (3rd ed., pp. 778–803). New York: Macmillan.

Scardamalia, M., & Bereiter, C. (1989). Conceptions of teaching and approaches to core problems. In M. C. Reynolds (Ed.), *Knowledge base for the beginning teacher* (pp. 37–46). Oxford: Pergamon.

Scardamalia, M., Bereiter, C., McLean, R. S., Swallow, J., & Woodruff, E. (1989). Computer-supported intentional learning environments. *Journal of Educational Computing Research, 5,* 51–68.

Schack, G. D. (1993). Effects of a creative problem-solving curriculum on students of varying ability levels. *Gifted Child Quarterly, 37*(1), 32–38.

Schiefele, U. (1991). Interest, learning, and motivation. *Educational Psychologist, 26,* 299–323.

Schlaefli, A., Rest, J. R., & Thoma, S. J. (1985). Does moral education improve moral judgment? A meta-analysis of intervention studies using the Defining Issues Test. *Review of Educational Research, 55,* 319–352.

Schmidt, R. A. (1987). The acquisition of skill: Some modifications to the perception-action relationship through practice. In H. Heuer & A. F. Sanders (Eds.), *Perspectives on perception and action* (pp. 77–103). Hillsdale, NJ: Erlbaum.

Schmidt, R. A. (1988). *Motor control and learning* (2nd ed.). Champaign, IL: Human Kinetics.

Schneider, W., Korkel, J., & Weinert, F. E. (1989). Domain-specific knowledge and memory performance: A comparison of high- and low-aptitude children. *Journal of Educational Psychology, 81,* 306–312.

Schneider, W., & Pressley, M. (1989). *Memory development between 2 and 20.* New York: Springer-Verlag.

Schneider, W., & Shiffrin, R. (1977). Controlled and automatic human information processing: I. Detection, search, and attention. *Psychological Review, 84,* 1–66.

Schoenfeld, A. H. (1985). *Mathematical problem solving.* Orlando, FL: Academic Press.

Schoenfeld, A. H. (1989). Teaching mathematical thinking and problem solving. In L. B. Resnick & L. E. Klopfer (Eds.), *Toward the thinking curriculum: Current cognitive research* (pp. 83–103). Washington, DC: Association for Supervision and Curriculum Development.

Schön, D. (1983). *The reflective practitioner.* New York: Basic Books.

Schön, D. (1990). *Educating the reflective practitioner.* San Francisco, CA: Jossey-Bass.

Schunk, D. H. (1981). Modeling and attributional effects on children's achievement. A self-efficacy analysis. *Journal of Educational Psychology, 73,* 93–106.

Schunk, D. H. (1987). Peer models and children's behavioral change. *Review of Educational Research, 57,* 149–174.

Schunk, D. H. (1991). *Learning theories: An educational perspective.* New York: Macmillan.

Schunk, D. H., & Hanson, A. R. (1985). Peer models: Influence on children's self-efficacy and achievement. *Journal of Educational Psychology, 77,* 313–322.

Schunk, D. H., & Hanson, A. R. (1989). Self-modeling and children's cognitive skill learning. *Journal of Educational Psychology, 81,* 155–163.

Schwager, S., & Labote, C. (1993). Teaching for critical thinking in physical education. *Journal of Physical Education, Recreation, and Dance, 64*(4), 24–26.

Schwartz, M. (1971). Subject-generated versus experimenter-supplied mediators in paired-associate learning. *Journal of Educational Psychology, 63,* 389–395.

Schwarz, G., & Cavener, L. A. (1994). Outcome-based education and curriculum change: Advocacy, practice, and critique. *Journal of Curriculum and Supervision, 9*(4), 326–338.

Schwebel, M. (1975). Formal operations in first-year college students. *Journal of Psychology, 91,* 133–141.

Scott, M. S., Perou, R., Urbano, R., Hogan, A., & Gold, S. (1992). The identification of giftedness: A comparison of white, hispanic, and black families. *Gifted Child Quarterly, 36,* 131–139.

Scruggs, T. E., & Mastropieri, M. A. (1990). The case for mnemonic instruction: From laboratory research to classroom applications. *Journal of Special Education, 24,* 7–32.

Searle, D. (1984). Scaffolding: Who's building whose building? *Language Arts, 61,* 480–483.

Seddon, G. M. (1978). The properties of Bloom's taxonomy of educational objectives for the cognitive domain. *Review of Educational Research, 48,* 303–323.

Seefeldt, V. (1980). Developmental motor patterns: Implications for elementary school physical education. In C. H. Nadeau, W. R. Holliwell, & K. M. Newell (Eds.), *Psychology of motor behavior and sport—1979* (pp. 314–323). Champaign, IL: Human Kinetics.

Seefeldt, V., & Haubenstricker, J. (1982). Patterns, phases, or stages: An analytical model for the study of developmental movement. In J. A. S. Kelso & J. E. Clark (Eds.), *The development of movement control and coordination.* New York: John Wiley.

Seifert, T. L. (1993). Effects of elaborative interrogation with prose passages. *Journal of Education Psychology, 85,* 642–651.

Selman, R. L. (1980). *The growth of interpersonal understanding.* New York: Academic Press.

Sexton, A. (1981). *The complete poems.* Boston, MA: Houghton Mifflin.

Shaffer, L. H. (1975). Multiple attention in continuous verbal tasks. In P. M. A. Rabbitt & S. Dornic (Eds.), *Attention and performance V* (pp. 157–167). New York: Academic Press.

Shavelson, R. J., Baxter, G. P., & Pine, J. (1991). Performance assessment in science. *Applied Measurement in Education, 4,* 347–362.

Shavelson, R. J., Baxter, G. P., & Pine, J. (1992). Performance assessments: Political rhetoric and measurement reality. *Educational Researcher, 21*(4), 22–27.

Shavelson, R. J., Hubner, J. J., & Stanton, G. C. (1976). Validation of construct interpretations. *Review of Educational Research, 46,* 407–441.

Shayer, M., & Beasley, F. (1987). Does instrumental enrichment work? *British Educational Research Journal, 13,* 101–119.

Sheingold, K., & Hadley, M. (1990, September). *Accomplished teachers: Integrating computers into classroom practice.* New York: Bank Street College of Education.

Shepardson, D. P., & Pizzini, E. L. (1993). A comparison of student perceptions of science activities within three instructional approaches. *School Science and Mathematics, 93,* 127–131.

Shepardson, D. P., & Pizzini, E. L. (1994). Gender, achievement, and perception toward science activities. *School Science and Mathematics, 94,* 188–193.

Shiffrin, R. M., & Schneider, W. (1977). Controlled and automatic human information processing: II. Perceptual learning, automatic attending, and a general theory. *Psychological Review, 84,* 127–190.

Shuell, T. J. (1990). Phases of meaningful learning. *Review of Educational Research, 60,* 531–547.

Shulman, L. S., & Tamir, P. (1974). Research on teaching in the natural sciences. In R. M. W. Travers (Ed.), *Second handbook of research on teaching* (pp. 1098–1148). Chicago, IL: Rand McNally.

Shure, M. B. (1989). Interpersonal competence training. In W. Damon (Ed.), *Child development today and tomorrow* (pp. 393–408). San Francisco, CA: Jossey-Bass.

Shymansky, J. A., Hedges, L. V., & Woodworth, G. (1990). A reassessment of the effects of inquiry-based science curricula of the 60's on student performance. *Journal of Research in Science Teaching, 27,* 127–144.

Siddle, D. (1983). *Orienting and habituation: Perspectives in human research.* Chicester, England: Wiley.

Siegler, R. S. (1976). Three aspects of cognitive development. *Cognitive Psychology, 8,* 481–520.

Siegler, R. S. (1981). Developmental sequences within and between concepts. *Monographs of the Society for Research in Child Development, 46* (Whole No. 189).

Siegler, R. S. (1986). *Children's thinking.* Englewood Cliffs, NJ: Prentice-Hall.

Silverman, F. L., Winograd, K., & Strohauer, D. (1992). Student-generated story problems. *Arithmetic Teacher, 39*(8), 6–12.

Simmons, C., & Wild, P. (1992). New forms of student teacher learning. *Educational Review, 44,* 31–40.

Simpson, E. J. (1966). The classification of educational objectives, psychomotor domain. *Illinois Teacher of Home Economics, 10*(4), 110–144.

Skeels, H. (1966). Adult status of children with contrasting early life experiences. *Monographs of the Society for Research in Child Development, 31,* no. 3.

Skinner, B. F. (1938). *The behavior of organisms.* New York: Appleton-Century-Crofts.

Skinner, B. F. (1968). *The technology of teaching.* Englewood Cliffs, NJ: Prentice-Hall.

Skinner, B. F. (1984). The shame of American education. *American Psychologist, 39,* 947–954.

Skinner, E. A., Wellborn, J. G., & Connell, J. P. (1990). What it takes to do well in school and whether I've got it: A process model of perceived control and children's engagement and achievement in school. *Journal of Educational Psychology, 82,* 22–32.

Slavin, R. E. (1987). Ability grouping and student achievement in elementary schools: A best-evidence synthesis. *Review of Educational Research, 57,* 293–336.

Slavin, R. E. (1987). Developmental and motivational perspectives on cooperative learning: A reconciliation. *Child Development, 58,* 1161–1167.

Slavin, R. E. (1990). Achievement effects of ability group-ing in secondary schools: A best-evidence synthesis. *Review of Educational Research, 60*, 471–499.

Slavin, R. E. (1990). *Cooperative learning: Theory, re-search, and practice.* Boston, MA: Allyn & Bacon.

Sleeter, C. E., & Grant, C. A. (1987). An analysis of multi-cultural education in the United States. *Harvard Educational Review, 57*, 421–444.

Sleeter, C. E., & Grant, C. A. (1991). *Race, class, gender, and disability in current textbooks.* New York: Routledge and Chapman.

Smagorinsky, P. (1991). The writer's knowledge and the writing process: A protocol analysis. *Research in the Teaching of English, 25*, 339–364.

Smilansky, J. (1984). Problem solving and the quality of invention: An empirical investigation. *Journal of Educational Psychology, 76*, 377–386.

Smith, C. R., Wood, F. H., & Grimes, J. (1987). Issues in the identification and placement of behaviorally disor-dered students. In M. C. Wang, M. C. Reynolds, & H. J. Walberg (Eds.), *Handbook of special education: Research and practice* (Vol. 2, pp. 95–123). Oxford: Pergamon.

Smith, M. L. (1989). Teachers' beliefs about retention. In L. A. Shepard & M. L. Smith (Eds.), *Flunking grades: Research and policies on retention* (pp. 132–150). New York: Falmer Press.

Smyth, J. (1992). Teachers' work and the politics of reflec-tion. *American Educational Research Journal, 29*, 267–300.

Snarey, J. (1985). The cross-cultural universality of social-moral development: A critical review of Kohlbergian research. *Psychological Bulletin, 97*, 202–232.

Snyder, V. (1987). Use of self-monitoring of attention with LD students: Research and application. *Learning Disability Quarterly, 10*, 139–151.

Sokolov, Y. E. (1963). *Perception and the conditioned reflex* (S. W. Waydenfeld, Trans.). New York: Pergamon Press.

Sonenstein, F. L., Pleck, J. H., & Ku, L. C. (1989). Sexual activity, condom use and AIDS awareness among ado-lescent males. *Family Planning Perspectives, 21*, 152–157.

Sonenstein, F. L., Pleck, J. H. & Ku, L. C. (1991). Levels of sexual activity among adolescent males in the United States. *Family Planning Perspectives, 23*, 162–167.

Sosniak, L. A. (1994). The taxonomy, curriculum, and their relations. In L. W. Anderson & L. A. Sosniak (Eds.), *Bloom's taxonomy: A forty-year retrospective* (pp. 103–125). Chicago, IL: The National Society for the Study of Education.

Soth, L. (1986). Van Gogh's agony. *Art Bulletin, 68*, 301–313.

Soto, L. D. (1991). Understanding bilingual/bicultural young children. *Young Children, 46*(2), 30–36.

Souriau, P. (1881). *Théorie de l'invention.* Paris: Librairie Hachette.

Southern, W. T., & Jones, E. D. (1991). *The academic acceleration of gifted children.* New York: Teachers College Press.

Spady, W. G. (1988). Organizing for results: The basis of authentic structuring and reform. *Educational Leadership, 46*(2), 4–8.

Sparks-Langer, G. M, & Colton, A. B. (1991). Synthesis of research on teachers' reflective thinking. *Educational Leadership, 48*(6), 37–44.

Sparks-Langer, G. M., Simmons, J. M., Pasch, M., Colton, A., & Starko, A. (1990). Reflective pedagogical think-ing: How can we promote it and measure it? *Journal of Teacher Education, 41*(4), 23–32.

Spilich, G. J., Vesonder, G. T., Chiesi, H. L., & Voss, J. F. (1979). Text processing of domain-related information for individuals with high and low domain knowledge. *Journal of Verbal Learning and Verbal Behavior, 18*, 275–290.

Spivak, G., & Shure, M. B. (1974). *Social adjustment of young children: A cognitive approach to solving real-life problems.* San Francisco, CA: Jossey-Bass.

Stacey, K., & Groves, S. (1985). *Strategies for problem solving.* Burwood, Victoria (Australia): VICTRACC Ltd.

Stahl, S. A., & Miller, P. D. (1989). Whole language and language experience approaches for beginning reading: A quantitative research synthesis. *Review of Educational Research, 59*, 87–116.

Stainback, W., Stainback, S., & Moravec, J. (1992). Using curriculum to build inclusive classrooms. In S. Stain-back & W. Stainback (Eds.), *Curriculum considerations in inclusive classrooms* (pp. 65–82). Baltimore, MD: Paul H. Brookes.

Stallings, J. A. (1985). Instructional time and staff devel-opment: How useful is the research on time to teach-ers? In C. W. Fisher & D. C. Berliner (Eds.), *Perspectives on instructional time* (pp. 283–298). New York: Longman.

Stallings, J. A., & Stipek, D. (1986). Research on early childhood and elementary school teaching programs. In M. C. Wittrock (Ed.), *Handbook of research on teach-ing* (3rd ed., pp. 727–753). New York: Macmillan.

Staver, J., & Bay, M. (1987). Analysis of the project syn-thesis goal cluster orientation inquiry emphasis of elementary science textbooks. *Journal of Research in Science Teaching, 24*, 629–643.

Steffensen, M. S., Joag-Dev, C., & Anderson, R. C. (1979). A cross-cultural perspective on reading comprehension. *Reading Research Quarterly, 15*, 10–29.

Sternberg, R. J. (1984). Mechanisms of cognitive develop-ment. In R. J. Sternberg (Ed.), *Mechanisms of cognitive development* (pp. 163–186). New York: W. H. Freeman.

Sternberg, R. J. (1985). *Beyond IQ: A triarchic theory of human intelligence.* New York: Cambridge University Press.

Sternberg, R. J. (1988). A three-facet model of creativity. In R. J. Sternberg (Ed.), *The nature of creativity* (pp. 125–147). New York: Cambridge University.

Sternberg, R. J. (1991). Giftedness according to the triarchic theory of human intelligence. In N. Colangelo & G. A. Davis (Eds.), *Handbook of gifted education* (pp. 45–54). Boston, MA: Allyn and Bacon.

Sternberg, R. S., & Bhana, K. (1986). Synthesis of research on the effectiveness of intellectual skills programs: Snake-oil remedies or miracle cures? *Educational Leadership, 44*(2), 60–70.

Stiggins, R. J. (1991). Facing the challenges of a new era of educational assessment. *Applied Measurement in Education, 4,* 263–273.

Stoiber, K. C., & Peterson, P. L. (1992). Attention and classroom learning. In M. C. Alkins (Ed.), *Encyclopedia of educational research* (Vol. 1, pp. 102–107). New York: Macmillan.

Subotnik, R. F. (1986). Scientific creativity: Westinghouse Science Talent Search winners' problem finding behavior. In A. J. Cropley, K. K. Urban, H. Wagner, & W. Wieczerkowski (Eds.), *Giftedness: A continuing worldwide challenge* (pp. 147–156). New York: Trillium Press.

Super, D. E. (1991). Toward a comprehensive theory of career development. In D. H. Montross & C. J. Shinkman (Eds.), *Career development: Theory and practice* (pp. 35–64). Springfield, IL: Charles C. Thomas.

Suransky, V. P. (1982). *The erosion of childhood.* Chicago, IL: University of Chicago Press.

Swanson, H. L., O'Connor, J. E., & Cooney, J. B. (1990). An information processing analysis of expert and novice teachers' problem solving. *American Educational Research Journal, 27,* 533–556.

Taback, S. F. (1992). Enhancing the teaching of mathematical problem solving. *School Science and Mathematics, 92,* 253–256.

Tallent-Runnels, M. K. (1993). The Future Problem Solving Program: An investigation of effects on problem-solving ability. *Contemporary Educational Psychology, 18,* 382–388.

Templeton, S. (1995). *Teaching the integrated language arts* (2nd ed.). Boston, MA: Houghton Mifflin.

Tenenbaum, G., & Goldring, E. (1989). A meta-analysis of the effect of enhanced instruction. *Journal of Research and Development in Education, 22,* 59–64.

Terman, L. M., & Merrill, M. A. (1973). *Stanford-Binet intelligence scale manual.* Boston: Houghton Mifflin.

Tessmer, M., & Harris, D. (1992). *Analyzing the instructional setting.* London: Kogan Page.

Thelen, E. (1981). Rhythmical behavior in infancy: An ethological perspective. *Developmental Psychology, 17,* 237–257.

Thomas, J. R., & French, K. E. (1985). Gender differences across age in motor performance: A meta-analysis. *Psychological Bulletin, 98,* 260–282.

Thomas, J. R., & Thomas, K. T. (1988). Development of gender differences in physical activity. *Quest, 40,* 219–229.

Thomas, J. R., Thomas, K. T., & Gallagher, J. D. (1993). Developmental considerations in skill acquisition. In R. N. Singer, M. Murphey, & L. K. Tennant (Eds.), *Handbook of research on sport psychology* (pp. 73–105). New York: Macmillan.

Thompson, R. A. (1987). Empathy and emotional understanding: The early development of empathy. In N. Eisenberg & J. Strayer (Eds.), *Empathy and its development* (pp. 119–145). New York: Cambridge University Press.

Thorkildsen, T. A. (1993). Those who can, tutor: High-ability students' conceptions of fair ways to organize learning. *Journal of Educational Psychology, 85,* 182–190.

Thornburg, T. H. (1991). Group size & member diversity influence on creative performance. *Journal of Creative Behavior, 25,* 324–333.

Thorndike, R. L., Hagan, E., & Sattler, J. (1986). *Stanford-Binet intelligence scale.* Chicago, IL: Riverside.

Thorne, B. (1986). Girls and boys together . . . but mostly apart: Gender arrangements in elementary schools. In W. W. Hartrup & Z. Rubin (Eds.), *Relationships and development* (pp. 167–184). Hillsdale, NJ: Erlbaum.

Tierney, R. J., Carter, M. A., & Desai, L. E. (1991). *Portfolio assessment in the reading-writing classroom.* Norwood, MA: Christopher-Gordon Publishers.

Tishman, S., Jay, E., & Perkins, D. N. (1993). Teaching thinking dispositions: From transmission to enculturation. *Theory Into Practice, 32,* 147–153.

Tom, A. R. (1985). Inquiring into inquiry-oriented teacher education. *Journal of Teacher Education, 36*(5), 35–44.

Torrance, E. P. (1965). *Rewarding creative behavior.* Englewood Cliffs, NJ: Prentice-Hall.

Torrance, E. P. (1984). The role of creativity in identification of the gifted and talented. *Gifted Child Quarterly, 28,* 153–156.

Torrance, E. P. (1988). The nature of creativity as manifest in its testing. In R. J. Sternberg (Ed.), *The nature of creativity* (pp. 43–75). New York: Cambridge University Press.

Towers, J. M. (1992). Some concerns about outcome-based education. *Journal of Research and Development in Education, 25,* 89–95.

Trevarthen, C. (1987). Brain development. In R. L. Gregory (Ed.), *Oxford companion to the mind* (pp. 101–110). Oxford: Oxford University Press.

Tulving, E. (1983). *Elements of episodic memory.* New York: Oxford University Press.

Tyler, R. W. (1950). *Basic principles of curriculum and instruction.* Chicago, IL: University of Chicago Press.

U.S. Department of Education. (1987). *Elementary and secondary civil rights survey: National summaries.*

Arlington, VA: DBS Corporation. (ERIC Document Reproduction No. 304485)

U.S. Department of Education (1992). *The 1990 science report card: NAEP's assessment of fourth, eighth, and twelfth graders.* Washington, DC: Government Printing Office.

U.S. Department of Education (1992). *Language characteristics and academic achievement: A look at Asian and Hispanic eighth graders in NELS:88.* Washington, DC: Government Printing Office.

U.S. Department of Education (1993). *NAEP 1992 reading report card for the nation and the states.* Washington, DC: Government Printing Office.

U.S. Department of Education. (1994a). *The condition of education, 1994.* Washington, DC: U.S. Government Printing Office.

U.S. Department of Education. (1994b). *Digest of education statistics, 1994.* Washington, DC: U.S. Government Printing Office.

U.S. Department of Education. (1994c). *Implementation of the Individuals with Disabilities Education Act: Sixteenth annual report to Congress.* Washington, DC: U.S. Government Printing Office.

U.S. Department of Education (1994d). *NAEP 1992 trends in academic progress.* Washington, DC: Government Printing Office.

Vacc, N. N., & Cannon, S. J. (1991). Cross-age tutoring in mathematics: Sixth graders helping students who are moderately handicapped. *Education and Training in Mental Retardation, 26,* 89–97.

Valencia, S. (1990). A portfolio approach to classroom reading assessment: The whys, whats, and hows. *The Reading Teacher, 43,* 338–340.

Vandenberg, B. (1984). Developmental features of exploration. *Developmental Psychology, 20,* 3–8.

Van Evra, J. (1990). *Television and child development.* Hillsdale, NJ: Erlbaum.

Van Manen, M. (1977). Linking ways of knowing with ways of being practical. *Curriculum Inquiry, 6*(3), 205–228.

VanSickle, R. L., & Hoge, J. D. (1991). Higher cognitive thinking skills in social studies: Concepts and critiques. *Theory and Research in Social Education, 19,* 152–172.

Vargas, J. S. (1986). Instructional design flaws in computer-assisted instruction. *Phi Delta Kappan, 67,* 738–744.

Varnon, C. J., & King, R. L. (1993). A tidal wave of change—OBE in the USA. *Outcomes, 12*(1), 16–19.

Veeman, S. (1984). Perceived problems of beginning teachers. *Review of Educational Research, 54,* 143–178.

Vitz, P. C. (1990). The use of stories in moral development. *American Psychologist, 45,* 709–720.

Vockell, E. L. (1991). Corporal punishment: The pros and cons. *The Clearing House, 64,* 278–283.

Vondracek, F. W. (1992). The construct of identity and its

use in career theory and research. *Career Development Quarterly, 41,* 130–144.

Voss, J. F. (1989). On the composition of experts and novices. In E. Maimon, B. Nodine, & F. O'Connor (Eds.), *Thinking, reasoning and writing.* New York: Longman.

Voss, J. F., & Post, T. A. (1988). On the solving of ill-structured problems. In M. T. H. Chi, R. Glaser, & M. Farr (Eds.), *The nature of expertise* (pp. 261–285). Hillsdale, NJ: Erlbaum.

Vygotsky, L. S. (1978). *Mind in society.* Cambridge, MA: Harvard.

Vygotsky, L. (1976). *Thought and language.* Cambridge, MA: MIT Press.

Vygotsky, L. S. (1987). Thinking and speech. In R. W. Rieber & A. S. Carton (Eds.), *The collected works of L. S. Vygotsky* (Vol. 1, pp. 39–285). New York: Plenum Press.

Wade, S. E., & Adams, B. (1990). Effects of importance and interest on recall of biographical text. *JRB: A Journal of Literacy, 22,* 331–353.

Wade, S. E., Schraw, G., Buxton, W. M., and Hayes, M. T. (1993). Seduction of the strategic reader: Effects of interest on strategies and recall. *Reading Research Quarterly, 28,* 93–111.

Wakefield, A. P. (1993). Developmentally appropriate practice: Figuring things out. *Educational Forum, 57*(2), 134–143.

Wakefield, J. F. (1985). Problem finding in a divergent-thinking exercise. *Child Study Journal, 15,* 265–270.

Wakefield, J. F. (1992). *Creative thinking: Problem-solving skills and the arts orientation.* Norwood, NJ: Ablex.

Wakefield, J. F. (1994). Problem finding and empathy in art. In M. A. Runco (Ed.), *Problem finding, problem solving, and creativity* (pp. 99–115). Norwood, NJ: Ablex.

Walberg, H. J. (1986). Synthesis of research on teaching. In M. C. Wittrock (Ed.), *Handbook of research on teaching* (3rd ed., pp. 214–229). New York: Macmillan.

Walberg, H. J., & Wynne, E. A. (1989). Character education: Toward a preliminary consensus. In L. P. Nucci (Ed.), *Moral development and character education* (pp. 37–50). Berkeley, CA: McCutcheon.

Wang, A. Y., Thomas, M. H., & Ouellette, J. A. (1992). Keyword mnemonic and retention of second-language vocabulary words. *Journal of Educational Psychology, 84,* 520–528.

Waterman, A. S. (1989). Curricula interventions for identity change: Substantive and ethical considerations. *Journal of Adolescence, 12,* 389–400.

Watson, M., Solomon, D., Battistich, V., Schaps, E., & Solomon, J. (1989). The Child Development Project: Combining traditional and developmental approaches to value education. In L. P. Nucci (Ed.), *Moral develop-*

ment and character education (pp. 51–92). Berkeley, CA: McCutcheon.

Weaver, W. T., & Prince, G. M. (1990). Synectics: Its potential for education. *Phi Delta Kappan, 71*, 378–388.

Wechsler, D. (1991). *Wechsler intelligence scale for children—III.* San Antonio, TX: Psychological Corporation.

Weinburgh, M. (1995). Gender differences in student attitudes toward science: A meta-analysis of the literature from 1970 to 1991. *Journal of Research in Science Teaching, 32*, 387–398.

Weiner, B. (1992). *Human motivation: Metaphors, theories, and research.* Newbury Park, CA: Sage.

Weiner, B., Frieze, I. H., Kukla, A., Reed, L., Rest, S., & Rosenbaum, R. M. (1971). *Perceiving the causes of success and failure.* Morristown, NJ: General Learning.

Weinstein, C. E., & Mayer, R. E. (1986). The teaching of learning strategies. In M. C. Wittrock (Ed.), *Handbook of research on teaching* (3rd ed., pp. 315–327). New York: Macmillan.

Weinstein, C. E., & Underwood, V. L. (1985). Learning strategies: The how of learning. In J. W. Segal, S. F. Chipman, & R. Glaser (Eds.), *Thinking and learning skills* (Vol. 1, pp. 241–258). Hillsdale, NJ: Erlbaum.

Weinstein, R. S. (1989). Perceptions of classroom processes and student motivation: Children's view of self-fulfilling prophecies. In C. Ames & R. Ames (Eds.), *Research on motivation in education* (Vol. 3, pp. 187–221). San Diego, CA: Academic Press.

Weinstein, T., Boulanger, F. D., & Walberg, H. J. (1982). Science curriculum effects in high school: A quantitative synthesis. *Journal of Research in Science Teaching, 19*, 511–522.

Weiss, M. R., & Bredemeier, B. J. (1990). Moral development in sport. In K. B. Pandolf & J. O. Holloszy (Eds.), *Exercise and sport science reviews* (Vol. 18, pp. 331–378). Baltimore, MD: Williams & Wilkins.

Weisz, J. R., Sigman, M., Weisz, B., & Mosk, J. (1993). Parent reports of behavioral and emotional problems among children in Kenya, Thailand, and the United States. *Child Development, 64*, 98–109.

Welker, R. (1991). Expertise and the teacher as expert: Rethinking a questionable metaphor. *American Educational Research Journal, 28*, 19–35.

Wertheimer, M. (1982). *Productive thinking.* Chicago, IL: University of Chicago. (Originally published 1945)

Wertsch, J. V., & Tulviste, P. (1992). L. S. Vygotsky and contemporary developmental psychology. *Developmental Psychology, 28*, 548–557.

West, C. K., & Anderson, T. H. (1976). The question of preponderant causation in teacher expectancy research. *Review of Educational Research, 46*, 613–630.

West, C. K., Farmer, J. A., & Wolff, P. M. (1991). *Instructional design: Implications from cognitive science.* Englewood Cliffs, NJ: Prentice-Hall.

Westcott, W. L. (1992). High school physical education: A fitness professional's perspective. *Quest, 44*, 342–351.

Wheldall, K., Houghton, S., & Merrett, F. (1988). Natural rates of teacher approval and disapproval in British secondary school classrooms. *British Journal of Educational Psychology, 59*, 38–48.

Wheldall, K., & Merrett, F. (1988). Which classroom behaviours do primary school teachers say they find most troublesome? *Educational Review, 40*, 13–27.

Wheldall, K., & Lam, Y. Y. (1987). Rows versus tables II: The effects of two classroom seating arrangements on classroom disruption rate, on-task behavior, and teacher behavior in three special school classes. *Educational Psychology, 7*, 303–312.

White, G. P., & Greenwood, S. G. (1992). Empowering middle level students through the use of learning contracts. *Middle School Journal, 23*(5), 15–20.

White, R. (1959). Motivation reconsidered: The concept of competence. *Psychological Review, 66*, 297–323.

Whitehead, A. N. (1929). *The aims of education.* New York: Macmillan.

Whitehead, J. (1989). Creating a living educational theory from questions of the kind, "How do I improve my practice?" *Cambridge Journal of Education, 19*(1), 41–52.

Wigfield, A., & Karpathian, M. (1991). Who am I and what can I do? Children's self-concepts and motivation in achievement situations. *Educational Psychologist, 26*, 233–261.

Wiggins, G. (1989). A true test: Toward more authentic and equitable assessment. *Phi Delta Kappan, 70*(9), 703–713.

Winett, R. A., & Winkler, R. C. (1972). Current behavior modification in the classroom: Be still, be quiet, be docile. *Journal of Applied Behavior Analysis, 5*, 499–504.

Winn, M. (1983). *Children without childhood.* New York: Pantheon.

Winner, E. (1982). *Invented worlds: The psychology of the arts.* Cambridge, MA: Harvard.

Winograd, K. (1992). What fifth graders learn when they write their own math problems. *Educational Leadership, 49*(7), 64–67.

Wittrock, M. C. (1986). Students' thought processes. In M. C. Wittrock (Ed.), *Handbook of research on teaching* (3rd ed., pp. 297–314). New York: Macmillan.

Wittrock, M. C. (1992). Knowledge acquisition and comprehension. In M. C. Alkin (Ed.), *Encyclopedia of educational research* (Vol. 2, pp. 699–705). New York: Macmillan.

Wlodkowski, R. J., & Jaynes, J. H. (1990). *Eager to learn.* San Francisco: Jossey-Bass.

Wood, D., Bruner, J., & Ross, G. (1976). The role of tutoring in problem-solving. *Journal of Child Psychology and Psychiatry, 17*, 89–100.

Wood, D., Wood, H., & Middleton, D. (1978). An experimental evaluation of four face-to-face teaching strategies. *International Journal of Behavioral Development, 1*, 131–147.

Wood, E., Miller, G., Symons, S., Canough, T., & Yedlicka, J. (1993). Effects of elaborative interrogation on young learners' recall of facts. *Elementary School Journal, 94*, 245–254.

Wynne, E. A. (1991). Character and academics in the elementary school. In J. S. Benninga (Ed.), *Moral, character, and civic education in the elementary school* (pp. 139–155). New York: Teachers College Press.

Yager, R. E., & Yager, S. O. (1985). Changes in perception of science for third, seventh, and eleventh grade students. *Journal of Research in Science Teaching, 22*, 347–358.

Yinger, R. J. (1980). A study of teacher planning. *Elementary School Journal, 80*, 108–127.

Yoder, D.E., & Crais, E. R. (1992). Speech-language services. In M. C. Alkin (Ed.), *Encyclopedia of educational research* (Vol. 4, pp. 1248–1252). New York: Macmillan.

York, J., Vandercook, T., MacDonald, C., Heise-Neff, C., & Caughey, E. (1992). Feedback about integrating

middle-school students with severe disabilities in general education classes. *Exceptional Children, 58*, 244–258.

Zabel, R. H., & Zabel, M. K. (1996). *Classroom management in context.* Boston, MA: Houghton Mifflin.

Zahn-Waxler, C., Robinson, J. L., & Emde, R. N. (1992). The development of empathy in twins. *Developmental Psychology, 28*, 1038–1047.

Zahorik, J. A. (1975). Teachers' planning models. *Educational Leadership, 33*(2), 134–139.

Zaichkowsky, L. D., Zaichkowsky, L. B., & Martinek, T. J. (1980). *Growth and development: The child and physical activity.* St. Louis, MO: Mosby.

Zifferblatt, S. (1972). Architecture and human behavior: Toward increased understanding of a functional relationship. *Educational Technology, 12*, 54–57.

Zuckerman, H. (1979). *The scientific elite: Nobel laureates' mutual influences.* New York: Free Press.

Zumwalt, K. K. (1989). Beginning professional teachers: Need for a curricular vision of teaching. In M. C. Reynolds (Ed.), *Knowledge base for the beginning teacher* (pp. 173–184). Oxford: Pergamon Press.

(Credits continue p. A-53)

Author/Source Index

Subject Index

Text Credits *(continued from p. A-34)*

International Reading Association. Reprinted by permission. **p. 411,** *Box:* From *Teaching from Thoughtfulness* by John Barell. Copyright © 1995, 1991 by Longman Publishing. Reprinted with permission. **pp. 429–430,** *Box:* Excerpted from *Knowing, Learning, and Instruction: Essays in Honor of Robert Glaser,* edited by Lauren B. Resnick, p. 421. Hillsdale, New Jersey: Lawrence Erlbaum Associates, Inc. Copyright © 1989 by Lawrence Erlbaum Associates, Inc. Reprinted by permission. **p. 460,** *Figure 11.1:* Reprinted from Pehkonen, E. (1992). "Using Problem Fields as a Method of Change." *The Mathematics Educator 3* (1), p. 3–6. **pp. 466–467,** *Box:* "Synectics®: Its Potential for Education" by W. Timothy Weaver and George M. Prince, *Phi Delta Kappan,* January 1990, p. 385. Reprinted by permission of the authors. **p. 477,** *Box:* From "Student-Generated Story Problems," by Frederick L. Silverman, Ken Winograd, and Donna Strohauer. Reprinted with permission from *The Arithmetic Teacher,* copyright April 1992 by the National Council of Teachers of Mathematics. **p. 486,** *Figure 11.5:* "Enhancement of Creativity in Computer Environments" by Douglas H. Clements. *American Educational Research Journal,* Spring 1991, Vol. 28, No. 1, p. 184. Copyright 1991 by the American Educational Research Association. Reprinted by permission of the publisher. **pp. 497–498,** Excerpts from *Among Schoolchildren* by Tracy Kidder. Copyright © 1989 by John Tracy Kidder. Reprinted by permission of Houghton Mifflin Co. and Macmillan London. All rights reserved. **pp. 555–556,** *Box:* Douglas M. Brooks, "The Teacher's Communicative Competence: The First Day of School," *Theory into Practice,* 1985, Vol. 24, pp. 63–70. Reprinted by permission. **p. 578,** *Table 13.4:* From *Teacher Effectiveness Training* by Thomas Gordon. Copyright © 1974 by Thomas Gordon. Reprinted by permission of David McKay Company, a division of Random House, Inc. **p. 582,** *Table 13.5:* Adapted from "Teachers' Reports of How They Perceive and Cope with Problem Students" by Jere Brophy and Mary McCaslin, *The Elementary School Journal,* Volume 93, Number 1, © 1992 by The University of Chicago, pp. 29–30. Reprinted by permission of The University of Chicago Press. **p. 605,** *Map:* Adapted from *History of the World* by Perry, et al. Copyright © 1993 by Houghton Mifflin Company. Reprinted by permission of Houghton Mifflin Company. All rights reserved. **pp. 608–609,** *Graph tests:* Adapted from *Basic Geometry Resource Book* by Jurgensen, et al. Copyright © 1988 by Houghton Mifflin Company. Reprinted by Houghton Mifflin Company. All rights reserved. **p. 615,** *Figure 14.2:* Reprinted, by permission, from *A Question of Thinking: A First Look at Students' Performance on Open-Ended Questions in Mathematics,* © 1989, California Department of Education, Sacramento. **pp. 617–618,** *Business assessment:* "A True Test: Toward More Authentic and Equitable Assessment" by Grant Wiggins, *Phi Delta Kappan,* May 1989, p. 707. Reprinted by permission of Richard M. Esner.

Strategic Solutions Index

Strategic Solutions are specially highlighted strands with extensive practical strategies you can use to solve problems in your own classroom.